An Atlas of
Roman Britain

Barri Jones and David Mattingly

Oxbow Books

Published by
Oxbow Books, Oxford

© Barri Jones and David Mattingly, 1990

First published by Blackwell Publishers 1990
Reprinted by Oxbow Books 2002
Reprinted 2007

ISBN 978-1-84217-067-0   1-84217-067-8

A CIP record for this book is available from the British Library

This book is available direct from

Oxbow Books, Oxford
www.oxbowbooks.com

and

The David Brown Book Company
PO Box 511, Oakville, CT 06779, USA
(Phone: 860-945-9329; Fax: 860-945-9468)

Printed in Great Britain at
the University Press,
Cambridge

Contents

Preface

THE amount of effort that has been expended on the study of Roman Britain in terms of excavation and fieldwork probably makes it the most intensively studied province in the Roman empire. Whilst Romano-British archaeologists may occasionally cast envious glances towards the better-preserved monuments of the Mediterranean, justifiable pride can be drawn from the fact that many of the less-distinguished remains of Britain are better understood than the sites of the core provinces of the Roman world. Nonetheless, such sentiments have not been shared by all; indeed, an eminent Roman historian went so far in a tutorial with the first author of this book as to refer to the archaeology of Roman Britain, as 'two wet bricks in a wet field'. This book is an attempt to offer a corrective to such derogatory views and to present in graphic form the breadth and depth of our knowledge about the British outpost of the Roman empire.

The task of translating this knowledge to map form has no particular claim to novelty. It is an obvious step and we are all too aware of our enormous debt to many other scholars whose work is represented at various levels in the maps that follow. The composite nature of the majority of the maps, drawn from several sources, has rendered it impossible to acknowledge fully every one of those scholars. A list of the more significant acknowledgements is included at the end of the Preface. Nor has it been possible in a book of this sort to provide detailed notes. However, the full bibliography at the end is arranged by chapter division and will assist the interested reader in exploring more deeply the literature to which our maps relate. To all the hundreds of scholars whose works we have consulted and utilized in preparing this book we extend our gratitude; to any whose work we may inadvertently have overlooked we apologize.

The originality of this atlas lies primarily in the gathering together of so much material in one place for the first time. The excellent Ordnance survey map of Roman Britain and the more recently produced sheets of the *Tabula Imperii Romani* for Britain have shown the way here, but one of the problems associated with such maps is that data from a long historical period and of highly varied nature has to be condensed onto a single sheet. The material covered by those maps is necessarily selective, and introduces problems of individual weighting. The presentation of finds evidence on rural settlement, particularly outside the zone of the villa economy, has suffered in this respect. The corpus of maps

and plans in this atlas has been brought together to provide insights into the history, political and settlement geography, culture, society and economy of Britain in the Roman period, in a manner which differs from that of the standard maps and text-books on the subject. Moreover, we have attempted to standardize our presentation to a regular series of scales for ease of comparison. The reader should note that we have adopted a preference for metric measurement throughout. For plans of sites, utilized particularly in the later chapters, we have also tried to impose some degree of uniformity on originals drawn in a wide range of styles and conventions. Unless otherwise indicated north is at the top of each map or plan. Photographs are included throughout to add a further dimension to the visual narrative.

As is so often the case with bright ideas, completion of the project has taken much longer than originally envisaged, but this is, in one sense, yet further testimony to the scope of Romano-British studies. We would emphasize, however, that the final choice of material and the mode of presentation reflects our personal preferences. Whilst we have designed the atlas to present a broad overview of the current state of Romano-British studies, we have occasionally chosen to present innovative and sometimes more speculative ideas reflecting new developments in the subject. The title of the book deliberately does not preclude the possibility that other scholars might have made different choices or laid emphasis in other areas. Nor should we deny that maps can sometimes mislead. It should be borne in mind that many of our maps represent the *current state of knowledge*, not a full and accurate picture of ancient site or artefact distribution. New discoveries will undoubtedly cause revisions and lead to greater comprehension in some cases.

Yet the cartographic approach is in many respects a particularly appropriate way of reviewing archaeological and historical data. The structure of the book is essentially thematic, picking up on major research areas in Romano-British archaeology. The topography of Britain, its climate and natural resources have all shaped the pattern of habitation through the ages and demand consideration in an atlas such as this. Recent work on changing coastal morphology and its interrelationship with settlement location is also reviewed in Chapter 1.

Likewise, much research hs been undertaken on the topographical evidence from ancient sources, reviewed in Chapter 2. In the study of place names, where plausible suggestion notoriously becomes transmuted into received fact, it is important to demonstrate that a significant percentage of locations referred to by some of our sources (for example the *Ravenna Cosmography*) remains unidentified. This chapter is also designed to explore the depth of geographic knowledge about the remote outpost of empire built up by Roman administrators, geographers and travellers, and to assess the contributions of Romans in Britain and of Britons in the Roman empire to the nomenclature of places and landscape features.

The late prehistoric archaeology of Britain has made major advances in recent decades, particularly in our understanding of cross-Channel contacts and trade contacts in the Celtic world. This in turn has added to our characterisation of the emergent state systems of the time, with their incipient urbanization and patterns of coin use (Chapter 3).

Overall, part of the perennial fascination of late Iron Age and Romano-British studies lies in the interplay of difficult and sometimes conflicting archaeological evidence set against a skeleton framework of literary and epigraphic material. The military history, and to a lesser extent the course of civil government of the province, has long been known in outline (Chapters 4 and 5). Yet in both areas, a potential defect in the study has been the search for unitary solutions, specifically the desire to link chronological evidence from one or more sites with some attested historical event and to generalize from that a picture of broader application. The impulse to make such connections between local evidence and historically documented events is all too infrequently resisted. In reality, dating evidence is rarely so precise as to allow us certainty within a few years (or even a decade) for the foundation or abandonment dates of Roman forts or the erection of urban defences to quote but two obvious examples. The date brackets of the distribution maps of forts are deliberately wider in this atlas than has been the fashion in a number of recent studies. In assessing the activity of early Roman governors in Britain we have focused our maps on the general area of their campaigns and have resisted the temptation to ascribe specific fort construction work to these individuals. We have tried to emphasize the ebb-and-flow nature of Roman campaigning and do not endorse the view that these early governors sought to create complex frontiers within lowland Britain.

Although our distribution maps of forts show the broader shifts in garrisoning policy in Britain, they offer less on the nuances of frontier deployment. It is important to remember that not all our sites were occupied simultaneously within the decades covered by our date brackets. However, we believe that attempts to over-refine the phasing of occupation, for instance, of forts in Scotland, represent the greater probability of misleading the reader who is unaware of the detailed numismatic or ceramic evidence. In Chapter 4, therefore, we have attempted to survey the military history of the province, a topic of immense significance in

Britain on account of the disproportionately large garrison maintained there in respect of the size of the territory or its strategic importance. One of the defining characteristics of Roman Britain was its frontier aspect, and the effects of the military presence must have been felt to a varying degree throughout the province.

More large-scale excavations have been carried out in Britain in the last three decades than in the previous century. With the welcome input of archaeological funds in rescue contexts and the growth of a professional archaeological service organized at municipal or county level, more information has been forthcoming than ever before. Inevitably standards have risen to enable us to ask a whole series of more refined questions of our archaeological and historical data. Urban excavations have a special significance in this context and some of the new results are presented in a section on the towns of Roman Britain (Chapter 5).

The latter sections of the book follow varying patterns. Chapter 6, on the economy of Roman Britain, gives greater prominence to that subject than has commonly been the case. It can be argued that it was in part economic motivations that brought Rome to Britain and equally that the developing provinicial economy played its part in keeping the island in the empire for as long a period as it did. A basic division is made here between the early explorative phase, particularly represented by the rapid spread of mining exploitation under military control, and the organic growth of service industries in the civil zone of the province. The distribution maps are balanced here, as in Chapters 5 and 7 by individual plans of important sites. The fact that the prime economic activity in Roman Britain was agriculture receives added emphasis in Chapter 7, where our aim has been to present a wide-ranging picture of the regional variations now evident in the Romano-British countryside. The final selection of plans and maps has been drawn from a truly impressive body of such data, a body that is ever growing thanks to the current boom in air photography. We make no claim therefore for comprehensive coverage of the varied landscapes of Roman Britain, though we have tried to present a representative sample and have included some examples from less well-known regions of the country. Another topic to be covered in detail here is the significance of the Romanized farm or villa, which has been a key focus for excavation work over many decades.

In Chapter 8, covering the evidence for religious worship, the approach has focused on the phenomenon of syncretism in Romano-Celtic provincial religion and the varying degree of penetration of foreign cults and architectural styles. Overall, the evidence is heavily skewed by the far greater abundance of epigraphic material from the northern frontier zone; however, the richness of that data allows us to observe the extreme localization of many of the minor cults of the Hadrian's Wall area.

Our treatment of the final years of Roman Britain represents the result of a conscious decision to limit the time-span under consideration to within the fifth century (Chapter 9). At the same time, the amount of evidence that yields itself to visual presentation is more limited and, as so typical of the period, is sometimes capable of bearing more than one interpretation. As the volume of socio-economic evidence recovered from late Roman phases at towns such as Canterbury, St Albans, Winchester and Wroxeter increases, so are we learning the limited weight that can be borne by generalizations derived from a single structure or suburb of any one of them.

And so the database for the interpretation of the Roman interlude in Britain continues to grow apace, built up brick upon wet brick. We hope that our atlas presents a synthesis of the current state of the subject that will prove a useful tool for students of Roman Britain and of Roman provincial archaeology. The research and writing of this book has been a collaborative effort between the two authors, each contributing something to every chapter. However, the majority of the map research and preparation of roughs was done by the second author who is also mainly responsible for the text of chapters 2, 3 and 4. The first author wrote more of the text for chapters 6, 7 and 8. The writing of chapters 1, 5 and 9 was divided more evenly between us.

Finally, we hope that the atlas can serve as an antidote to the overly compartmentalized view of Roman Britain as a peripheral province of little interest to the history and culture of the Roman empire. The evidence from Roman Britain is detailed, fascinating and, as this atlas shows, plentiful. The effort expended over generations in gathering the minutiae of artefactual and other evidence, which so distinguish scholarship on this province, is most clearly vindicated in a presentation such as this. In the words of St Jerome, small is significant:

non contemnenda ea parva sine quibus magna constare non possunt

Acknowledgements

THIS book could never have been attempted without the major contribution to the mapping of Roman Britain carried out by the Archaeological Division of the Ordnance Survey. Their publications, and most notably the 'Map of Roman Britain', remain the starting point for all serious students. Our debt to numerous other scholars, whether well-known academics, field professionals or enthusiastic amateurs, is clearcut. Many published versions of certain maps now exist, and we have frequently amalgamated and up-dated several sources of information. In the list to be found on p. ix we have acknowledged only the original authorship of maps where the borrowing has been more or less direct, or where we have added little of our own. For any mistakes or omissions in our citations we are profoundly sorry. Every effort has been made to trace all copyright holders of the maps and illustrations that appear in the atlas; should anyone have inadvertently been overlooked we shall be pleased to make proper acknowledgement in future editions.

Our thanks are owed to a number of editorial staff at Basil Blackwell, some of whom have subsequently moved on to other jobs. Their support for the whole venture has been exceptional, despite changes in policy and cost. We are grateful in particular to: John Davey, Janet Godden, Carol Le Duc, and Jeff Borer and Caroline Bundy who oversaw the final stages of production. We thank Oxford Illustrators for drawing the maps; and Barbara Croucher for compiling the index. We would like to acknowledge the special contribution made by Paul Booth, Warwick Archaeological Unit, who read a considerable portion of the atlas in draft and offered many helpful criticisms. Two enthusiastic evening classes in Warwick and Coventry also served as guinea pigs for ideas evolved in the first half of the book.

Particular thanks are also owed to Pat Faulkner and Sylvia Hazlehurst for their typing and improving of the text; to Keith Maude for his assistance with the maps and to Dr J. P. Wild for much discussion and particular help with material for the East Midlands. Professor A. R. Birley, Dr D. K. Breeze, C. M. Daniels, Professor M. Fulford, Dr L. Keppie and Professor M. Todd have all helped in discussion. The underlying contributions of Dr G. Webster, Professor S. S. Frere, Professor J. K. St Joseph, Professor J. Wacher, and the late Professor Sir Ian Richmond will also be apparent.

Jenny Mattingly has been a stern but helpful critic of map roughs and early drafts, and to her patience and support more than anything one half of this book is dedicated. Brigitte Jones has brought her interest in celtica to many aspects of this book, notably the chapter on Romano-Celtic religion. To both our wives we owe a lasting debt of gratitude.

Map Acknowledgements

GENERAL acknowledgements have been made on p. viii. All maps have been drawn by Oxford Illustrators from draft versions compiled by the authors from various sources. Below is a list of detailed acknowledgements for those maps that derive from one or two sources; maps derived from more sources are not credited. The authors would like to acknowledge the contributions made by the sources cited; full references will be found in the Bibliography.

1:3 Hill 1981; 1:4, 1:6, 1:7 Stamp and Beaver 1971; 1:8 Watson and Sissons 1964; 1:13 Cunliffe 1980; 1:14 Jones 1980; 1:15 Simmons 1979, 1980; 1:16 Aston and Barrow 1982, Cunliffe 1966; 1:17 Keillar et al. 1986.

2:3 Dilke 1985; 2:7, 2:13, 2:14, Rivet and Smith 1979; 2:18 Heurgon 1951; 2:19 Rivet 1980; 2:20, Rivet and Smith 1979; 2:21 Rivet 1980.

3:3 Cunliffe 1978, with additions; 3:4 Dunnett 1975; 3:5 Crummy 1977; 3:7–3:11 Cunliffe 1981a; 3:13 Cunliffe 1978; 3:14 Cunliffe 1978, 1984a, Ramm 1978; 3:15 Cunliffe 1984a; 3:16 Cunliffe 1981a; 3:17 Fitzpatrick 1985, Rodwell 1976; 3:18 Lloyd Jones 1984, with additions; 3:19 Breeze 1982a, with additions; 3:20 Breeze 1982a.

4:28 Troussett 1978; 4:30 Maxfield 1980, with additions; 4:33–4:37 Davies 1980, with additions; 4:46 Bennett 1980; 4:60 Breeze and Dobson 1985, with additions; 4:62 Peacock 1977b; 4:63–4:66 Todd 1980.

5:9 J.S. Walker; 5:11 Wacher 1974, with additions; 5:13 Sommer 1984, with additions; 5:14 Frere 1984, Hartley 1983; 5:16 Crummy 1985; 5:17 Hurst 1985; 5:18 Wilson 1984; 5:21 Mackreth 1979; 5:22 Jones and Walker 1983; 5:23 Sedgley 1975, with additions.

6:8 Bristol Mining Club, Jones 1979c; 6:10 Tylecote 1976; 6:11 Shropshire Mining Club, Jones 1979c; 6:12 Cleere 1975; 6:13 M. Fitchett; 6:14 Hall 1982, with additions; 6.15 Fulford 1982; 6:16 Colls et al. 1977; 6:21–6:23 Robertson 1970; 6:24 Swann 1984; 6:25–6:26 Peacock 1982, Swann 1984; 6:27 Wild 1974; 6:28 Swann 1984; 6:29 Greene 1979; 6:30, 6:31 Peacock 1982; 6:33 Hartley and Webster 1973; 6:34 Young 1977a and b; 6:36 McWhirr 1976b, McWhirr and Viner 1978; 6:37 Davey 1976, Williams 1971; 6:38 Pritchard 1986; 6:40 Smith 1969, with additions; 6:41 Smith 1984, with additions; 6:44 Simmons 1980; 6:45 Wild 1982; 6:46 Morris 1979; 6:47 Rees 1979; 6:48–6:49 Jones 1975.

7:1 Fowler 1983, Thomas 1966; 7:2 RCHM; 7:4 Fowler 1983; 7:5 Jones 1979a; 7:6 Rivet 1969, with additions; 7:7 Branigan 1982; 7:8 Jarrett and Wrathmell 1981; 7:9 Collingwood and Richmond 1969; 7:10 Brodribb, Hands and Walker 1968/1978; 7:11 Goodburn 1978; 7:12 RCHM; 7:13 Wild 1974; 7:14 Mackreth 1978; 7:16 Jones 1977; 7:17 Riley 1980a; 7:18 Miles 1984; 7:19 James and Williams 1982; 7:20 Mytum 1982, RCHM 1956/1964; 7:21 Raistrick 1937; 7:23 Higham and Jones 1983; 7:24 Higham and Jones 1975, with additions; 7:25 Jones and Walker 1983; 7:26 Gates 1982.

8:3, 8:5–8:7, 8:18–8:19, Green 1976; 8:20, 8:22–8:25, 8:27 Rodwell 1980; 8:28 Morris 1983, with additions; 8:29–8:31 Thomas 1981; 8:32 Clarke 1979, with additions; 8:33 Green 1974, 1977, 1982; 8:34 Toller 1977, with additions; 8:35 Toller 1977.

9:1 Johnson 1976, with additions; 9:4 Frere 1983; 9:5 Barker 1985; 9:6, 9:8–9:9 Thomas 1981; 9:10–9:11 Johnson 1980.

Photographic Acknowledgements

THE authors are most grateful to the following persons or institutions for permission to reproduce material.

Airviews 1.2, 4.16
Ashmolean Museum, Oxford 3.2, 3.3, 3.4, 4.23, 4.29, 5.3, 5.4, 6.5, 6.6, 6.7, 9.2
Bild-Archiv der Österreichischen Nationalbibliothek, Wien 5.1
Birmingham University Archaeological Unit 8.6
Bodleian Library, Oxford 2.3, 2.4
J. S. Bone 4.3
Cambridge Committee for Aerial Photography 5.6, 5.11
English Heritage 7.3, 8.3, 9.4
Glamorgan/Gwent Archaeological Trust 5.5
Professor D. Harding 5.7
T. James 7.4
Hunterian Museum 4.21

Manchester Museum 3.10
Professor W. H. Manning 4.6
Museum of London 5.12, 5.13, 8.2
Dr. D. N. Riley 4.5, 7.5a
Sheffield University, Department of Archaeology 6.1
Southampton University, Department of Archaeology 9.6
S. Upex 5.2
The Trustees of the British Museum 8.4, 8.8
Vienna Kuntshistorische Museum 2.1
Vindolanda Trust 2.2, 3.14
Dr. J. P. Wild 6.4, 6.10, 8.9, 9.3
Wiltshire County Council 7.2
York Archaeological Trust 5.10

The second author provided plates 3.11 and 5.15. All other photographs derive from the first author.

I
The Physical Context

Any attempt to map out and to understand the pattern of settlement in the British Isles at a particular period must start with a consideration of the physical context. By this we mean not simply the topography and the geology of the landscape, but also the climate and the criteria used for judging land quality. Obviously there are serious pitfalls involved in applying modern data and standards to an assessment of the ancient environment. We cannot be sure exactly how the climate may differ from that in Roman times (probably marginally), nor can we assess fully the significance of the likely changes in the landscape or the technological advances which distinguish modern farming from ancient regimes. In the latter part of this chapter, some attempt is made to examine the question of coastal change (1:12–1:17), but we are ignorant about many other vital problems relating to the landscape of the Roman period, such as historical changes in river courses and their navigability or the extent of forest and woodland cover, to give just two examples. However, the purpose of this chapter is not to give answers, but to raise questions in the reader's mind.

Although they lacked the scientific apparatus of the modern geographer, ancient people were no less aware of the potential and the drawbacks of the British landscape and the British climate. However, their assessments of that knowledge were based on technological and economic criteria which were far removed from those of today. Moreover, regional geographic and climatic conditions vary enormously across Britain and historical geographers must be very wary of making broad generalizations about land quality and land use in a given zone.

Map 1:1 shows a highly simplified view of the solid geology of Britain. To a certain extent, this map suggests that a broad division of Britain can be made between the western and northern region, where the older and harder rocks (including many metamorphic and crystalline formations) are to be found, and the Midlands and southern region, with their sedimentary rock formations. This basic geological contrast has implications for the relief, for natural resources (more minerals and good building stone in the west and north) and for the climate. Nevertheless, it needs stressing immediately that neither of these two supposed zones is a homogenous unit and there are vast regional differences within each. The geological picture is further complicated by drift geology (1:2). In many places, the solid geology provides the

raw material for the overlying soils, but the superimposition of glacial or fluvial drift has buried it deeply in some areas. The corollary is that the creation of these drift deposits has involved the erosion of soils from other areas, particularly mountainous ones. In particular, the great Ice Ages brought fundamental changes to the landscape of both northern and southern Britain through these twin processes of erosion and deposition. The areas of superficial drift geology are significant because it is the character of the drift geology rather than the underlying formations which determines soil type and quality there. In areas of drift geology, soils are derived typically from sands, gravels and boulder clays.

The proposition that Britain is divisible into two broad zones remains highly influential in both physical and historical geography (1:3). The idea of a 'highland/lowland' division was first applied in a systematic way to historical problems by Cyril Fox in 1932 and has been employed widely ever since by historians and archaeologists. On the face of it, the theory is attractive, since the oldest rocks and highest relief lie in the western and northern regions (Cornwall, Wales, northern England and Scotland), giving these areas a distinctive geological history. The lowland zone is for the most part relatively low-lying and contains many of the major river valleys (1:4). This zone today contains a high percentage of the best arable farmland, whilst the highland zone is noted for its upland stock-rearing. However, it is a mistake even today, let alone in relation to ancient farming, to make the generalization that the lowland zone economy is predominantly *agricultural* whilst the highland zone is essentially *pastoral*. Yet precisely this conclusion has been reached by some scholars and, having taken on the status of dogma, has hindered our appreciation of the development of Iron Age and Roman settlement. The generalization is too broad to be valid and takes no account of the great regional variations of landforms, soils and climate. It also promotes the idea that certain parts of the country developed and prospered solely as a result of a form of environmental natural selection and deters analysis of other causal connections.

In fact, the highland/lowland model starts to break down at the simplest level. There are quite extensive areas of low-lying, good quality farmland in the highland zone (in particular, parts of Cornwall, South Wales, the Eden Valley in Cumbria, around the Firth of Forth, eastern Scotland from Strathclyde to Strathmore and on the shores of the Moray

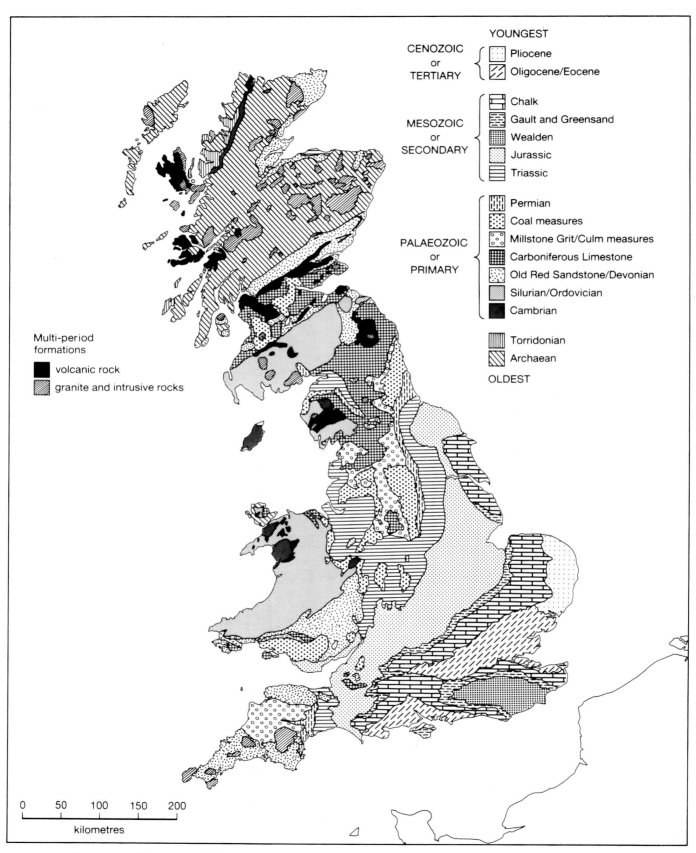

YOUNGEST

CENOZOIC
or
TERTIARY
- Pliocene
- Oligocene/Eocene

MESOZOIC
or
SECONDARY
- Chalk
- Gault and Greensand
- Wealden
- Jurassic
- Triassic

PALAEOZOIC
or
PRIMARY
- Permian
- Coal measures
- Millstone Grit/Culm measures
- Carboniferous Limestone
- Old Red Sandstone/Devonian
- Silurian/Ordovician
- Cambrian

- Torridonian
- Archaean

OLDEST

Multi-period
formations
- volcanic rock
- granite and intrusive rocks

0   50   100   150   200
kilometres

Map 1:1   Solid geology of Britain: simplified

Firth in Scotland), and there is no lack of evidence of ancient cultivation in these zones (see below, 7:3). Conversely, the lowland zone contains some large areas of poor quality uplands (the Wessex plain, parts of the South Downs, and the Weald), whilst other areas such as the Cotswolds and Chilterns are traditionally better suited to pastoral or mixed farming regimes. Neither zone, in fact, is characterized by a uniform landscape or a single farming regime and within each zone the regional variations are all-important.

Another of the more significant geographical features of Britain is its river system (only some of the most important can be shown on 1:4). Many rivers were still navigable in Roman times for a considerable distance inland and were undoubtedly well used for transportation and communication. The main east/west watershed lies towards the west of the island, though in much of central and southern England it lies *outside* the supposed highland zone. The broad valleys of the main rivers to the east of the watershed (notably the Thames, Nene, Trent, Ouse and Tyne) have had a crucial influence not only on communications but also on settlement location. With a few exceptions (notably the Severn/Avon, Dee, Eden and Clyde systems), the rivers to the west tend to be smaller or less penetrative.

Map 1:2 Main drift-covered regions (shaded)

Map 1:3 Highland and lowland zones of Britain

Map 1:4 Main watersheds (thick line); principal rivers of Britain

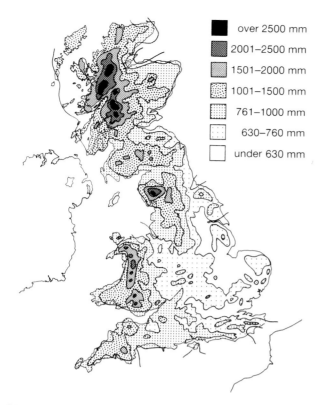

over 2500 mm
2001–2500 mm
1501–2000 mm
1001–1500 mm
761–1000 mm
630–760 mm
under 630 mm

Map 1:5   Average annual rainfall

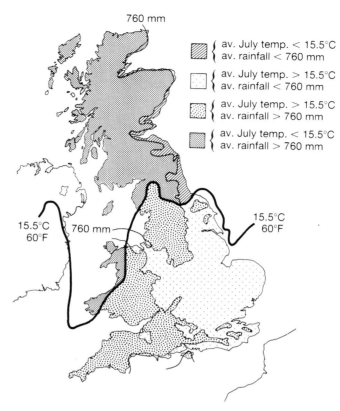

760 mm

{ av. July temp. < 15.5°C
av. rainfall < 760 mm

{ av. July temp. > 15.5°C
av. rainfall < 760 mm

{ av. July temp. > 15.5°C
av. rainfall > 760 mm

{ av. July temp. < 15.5°C
av. rainfall > 760 mm

15.5°C
60°F

760 mm

15.5°C
60°F

Map 1:6   Climatic quadrants in Britain (the 15.5°C isotherm is the supposed northern limit for the economic cultivation of wheat).

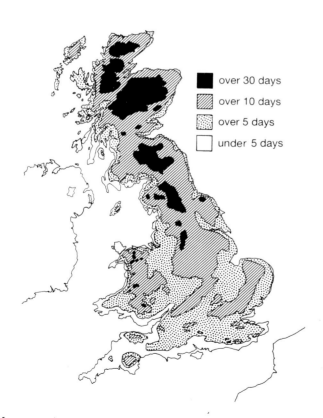

over 30 days
over 10 days
over 5 days
under 5 days

Map 1:7   Average annual number of days with snow lying

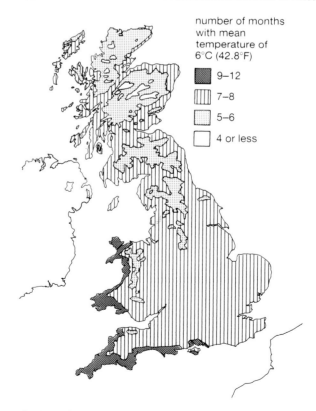

number of months
with mean
temperature of
6°C (42.8°F)

9–12
7–8
5–6
4 or less

Map 1:8   Length of growing season according to temperature

CLIMATE

Rainfall is a key climatic factor and can help determine favoured settlement location, since too much or too little rain on a consistent basis can restrict land use. Average figures (1:5) can be rather misleading because of wide variations from one year to the next, but the map indicates in general terms the areas of potential shortfall or superabundance. Not surprisingly the mountainous or upland regions and the adjacent regions receive the highest rainfall. The fact that a good deal of the weather arrives in Britain from the Atlantic is a further factor which contributes to the higher rainfall over western Britain in general. By contrast, the low-lying parts of eastern England can sometimes be subjected to semi-drought conditions, as in 1976, 1984 and 1989.

Since modern agriculture is reckoned to be more difficult in areas which receive in excess of 760mm of rain per year, it might appear from this map that the traditional view of a highland/lowland division is justified. However, this ignores the effects of floodwater in many of the major river valleys of the lowland zone. In effect, farmers in most areas of Britain have had to cope throughout history with having *too much* water on their land in many years. As a result, attempts to improve drainage, a detailed knowledge of soils and a willingness to diversify production have often characterized British farming.

The way in which temperature and rainfall interact can best be shown by reference to the climatic 'quadrants' of Britain (1:6). Four unequal 'quadrants' are defined by plotting the isohyet line indicating an average annual rainfall of 760mm against the isotherm line indicating an average July temperature of 15.5°C (60°F). The best-suited climatic zone, from an agricultural viewpoint, is that which receives less than 760mm of rain and has average July temperatures of over 15.5°C. This area covers a large part (though not all) of the region defined as the lowland zone (1:3). The worst climatic zone is that which receives over 760mm of rain with an average July temperature of less than 15.5°C and, not surprisingly, this incorporates the *true* highland zone of the Scottish Highland massif and Snowdonia. The remaining two zones are subject to conditions between these two extremes and this hints at the intermediate settlement potential of these areas.

A number of other climatic factors serve to weaken further the case for the traditional definition of the highland/lowland zones. The average number of days with snow lying (1:7) provides a useful gauge of the combined effects of relief and low winter temperatures. Naturally, the Scottish Highlands, North Wales and the Pennines stand out as areas of harsh winter weather, but it is interesting to note the extent to which the Midlands and East Anglia can also be snowbound. By contrast, owing to the favourable climatic influence of the Gulf Stream/North Atlantic Drift, parts of western Britain, Cornwall, South Wales and the south coast of England experience very mild winters.

This mildness of climate in certain far-western parts of England and Wales is also reflected in the length of the growing season (1:8). Once again the true highland massifs are clearly delineated by their shorter cycle, with much of the rest of the country forming a second intermediate category. Devon, Cornwall and parts of southern Wales are clearly compensated to some extent for their high rainfall by milder winters, warm summers and a long growing season.

SOILS AND LAND USE

Although ancient farmers did not have modern soil science to help them spot the better settlement locations, they were well aware of their own capabilities and able to judge the quality of the land. Obviously, light sandy soils of similar fertility to heavy clay ones would be more attractive to farmers operating relatively simple ox- or horse-drawn ploughs. Map 1:9 gives a highly simplified view of regional soil types and it must be stressed that within many of the broad areas defined, there will have been further variation. In general terms one can observe the differences between the soils developed on the old rocks in the west and north and those developed on the limestone and other sedimentary formations of southern Britain. As explained above, there is in addition the impact of drift formations to be considered.

The different categories of soil types represented here are not straightforward indicators of land quality since other factors such as drainage and climate affect that. Nor is this map any substitute for a far more detailed soil map if one wishes to assess the possible relationship between the ancient settlement pattern and soil types at a more regional or local level. The interested reader is referred to the large-scale Soil Survey Maps available from the Ordnance Survey.

Returning to the questions of land quality and land use, it has already been observed that modern value judgements (technical or economic) on what is practical in a given area can be misleading. We have also suggested that the most damaging aspect of the highland/lowland model as applied to ancient Britain is its over-simplified view of farming economies: a pastoral west and north and an agricultural southeast. One means of demonstrating the patent absurdity of this model is to look at the pattern of agricultural and pastoral production (including dairying) in the earlier part of this century (1:10–1:11). In spite of the changed basis of modern agricultural technology, communications and economics, it is abundantly clear that there is no well-defined economic boundary between highland and lowland and that there probably never was. Except in the restricted area of true highland massif, British farming has tended to be based on a mixed economy.

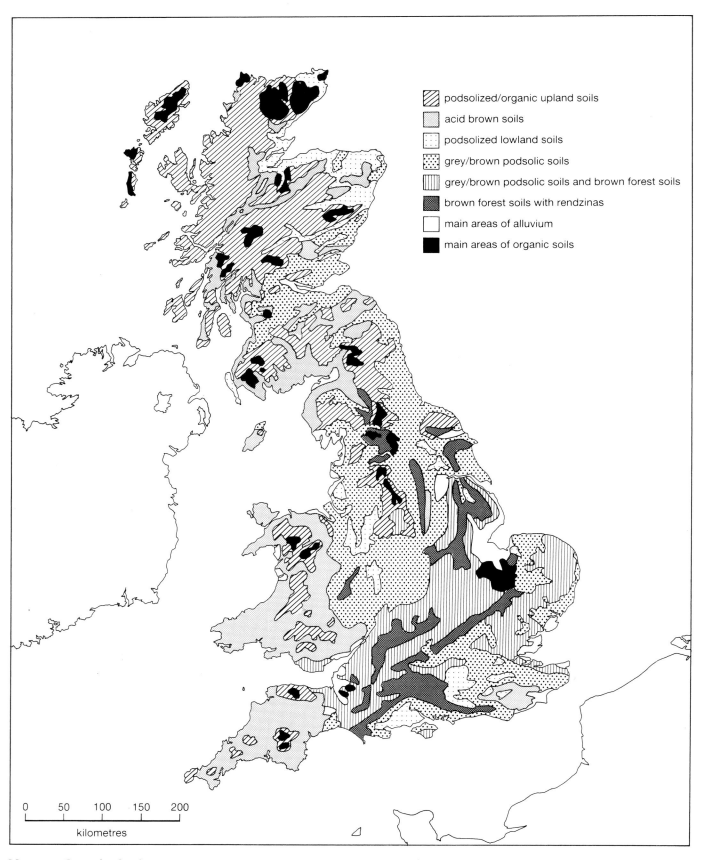

⧄	podsolized/organic upland soils
▨	acid brown soils
⣿	podsolized lowland soils
⣿	grey/brown podsolic soils
▥	grey/brown podsolic soils and brown forest soils
▓	brown forest soils with rendzinas
☐	main areas of alluvium
■	main areas of organic soils

0   50   100   150   200

kilometres

Map 1:9 Generalized soil types in Britain

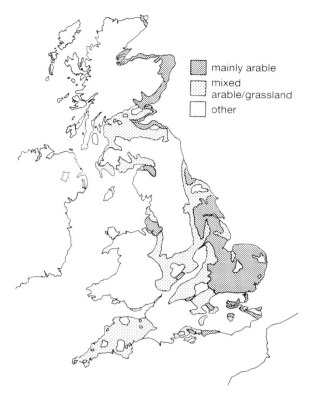

Map 1:10 Chief areas of arable farming in early twentieth-century Britain

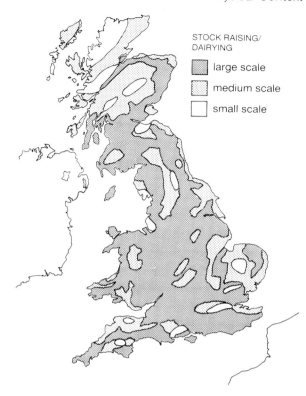

Map 1:11 Cattle and sheep farming in early twentieth-century Britain

In Map 1:10 both the blank areas in the lowland zone and the important evidence for arable cultivation in Cornwall, Wales, Cumbria and Scotland are notable. Cultivation is, and was, practised wherever feasible in the so-called highland zone, whilst stock-rearing is virtually ubiquitous throughout the British Isles. Thus the Roman army on Hadrian's Wall should not have needed to receive *all* its grain from southern Britain, and every town in the south should in theory have been able to meet its own needs in animal products from its surrounding territory.

Other types of land use or exploitation, apart from farming, also operated in Roman Britain. The existence of great forests and woods created a major resource, since timber was used not only as fuel, but was also essential in building and for the production of furniture and a wide range of household objects. Unfortunately, it is not possible to map the extent of the woodland cover in Roman Britain (though attempts have been made in the past). Clearance of woodland was a continuous process from well before the Iron Age until long after the end of Roman Britain, so the picture will in any case have changed through time. Mining (6:1–6:2), quarrying (6:37) and pottery production (6:24) are discussed in later chapters, but clearly the location of the raw materials was a vital factor in each case in dictating settlement and exploitation.

COASTAL CHANGE

In the post-Holocene period after *c*.6,000 BC sea level change associated with shrinking glaciation resulted in appreciable alteration in the coastal morphology of Britain (1:12). In the prehistoric period the coast of Dumfries and Galloway, for instance, was characterized by much larger estuarine indentations, as at Rack's Moss east of Dumfries, where the discovery of a Bronze Age log boat with marine molluscs illustrates the siltation process that had occurred in the transformation of salt-water estuary to fresh-water moss.

Eustatic change (rise or fall) in sea level is further complicated by bradyseism (change in land level) and tidal surges in the North Sea and to a lesser extent in the Solway, Liverpool Bay and the Bristol Channel (where the tidal range is among the highest in the world). The effects of these processes have particular relevance to some coastal sites in the Roman period and several substantial morphological changes, like those of the south-eastern coastline, helped shape historical events in the invasion phase.

The latter point is well illustrated by the way in which the Kentish coast appears to have developed around the Isle of Thanet and in the Romney Marsh area (1:13). For reasons that are not clear, the first invasion of Julius Caesar suffered initially from poor anchorage facilities probably located in

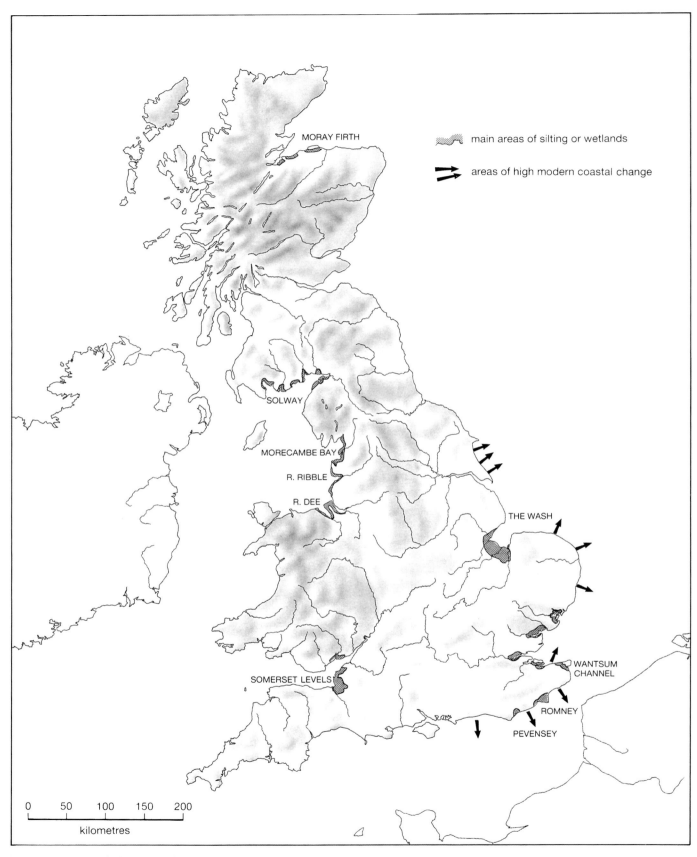

MORAY FIRTH

main areas of silting or wetlands

areas of high modern coastal change

SOLWAY

MORECAMBE BAY

R. RIBBLE

R. DEE

THE WASH

WANTSUM
CHANNEL

SOMERSET LEVELS

ROMNEY

PEVENSEY

0   50   100   150   200

kilometres

Map 1:12   Coastal change (i) all Britain

Plate 1:1   Speed's Map (1610) of south Lancashire and the Wirral shows the extensive lagoon formations where Blackpool and Southport now stand, as well as Martin Mere (arrowed) which still exists, but in shrunken form.

the Deal area. Although Caesar's second campaign apparently saw the use of an improved location, the naturally protected harbourage of Richborough was not used until the Claudian invasion of AD 43. This took advantage of Thanet being at the time a separate island, as indeed it probably remained until the fifteenth century. The invasion beachhead selected by Aulus Plautius for the main thrust of Roman military operations was a detached hill flanking the western side of the Wantsum channel opposite Ebbsfleet, the point where an Anglo-Saxon raiding party landed in AD 449 (see 9:9). The full story of the evolution of *Rutupiae*, as Richborough was called in the Roman period, is not easy to reconstruct thanks to subsequent very substantial morphological change. In the Roman period Richborough was separated from the southern shore by a narrow strip of marsh and could be seen as a small island inside the eastern entrance to the Wantsum. It appears that the Wantsum lay in an intermediate state between sea channel and marsh and that it was partly sheltered by the formation of the Stonar Bank which also appears to have come into existence about this time. Although the Stonar Bank ultimately caused the siltation of the Wantsum, initially it may have served as a breakwater protecting Richborough harbour from the worst effects of storms. It also appears that there were at least two passages through the Stonar Bank and that the inside channel in the Roman period would probably still have been scoured by the tide and thus kept clear of silt. Its navigability throughout the Roman period is not in doubt

and *Rutupiae* still acted in the fourth century as one of the main gateways to and from Britain. The strategic importance of the Wantsum channel is shown by the establishment of two Saxon Shore forts, one at Reculver at the northern end of the channel and the other at Richborough proper.

When we turn to Romney Marsh it is another Saxon Shore fort, namely that at Lympne, that gives us the initial clue to reconstructing the landscape. The Saxon Shore fort at Lympne stands on a scarp edge overlooking the extensive levels that now make up Romney Marsh and run south-eastwards towards Dungeness Point. Recent study has established that the morphology was very different in the Roman period. A glance at a modern map will show that a series of streams, notably the Brede, the Tillingham and the Rother, flow west–east towards the western side of what is now Romney Marsh. The visitor to Bodiam Castle, for instance, will readily appreciate that the channel of the Rother was once navigable well inland, a fact established for the Roman period by the numerous iron smelting sites located on or near its banks (6:12). The so-called Isle of Oxney was originally an area of creeks and inlets at a point where at least three river systems eventually combined to form a tidal bay which extended east-north-east towards Hythe. This in turn explains the position of the Saxon Shore fort. It controlled a small harbour created by a southward spur at Lympne, at the entrance to this strategic estuary – before the shingle bar running north-east from Dymchurch blocked marine access to what is now the central area of the marsh.

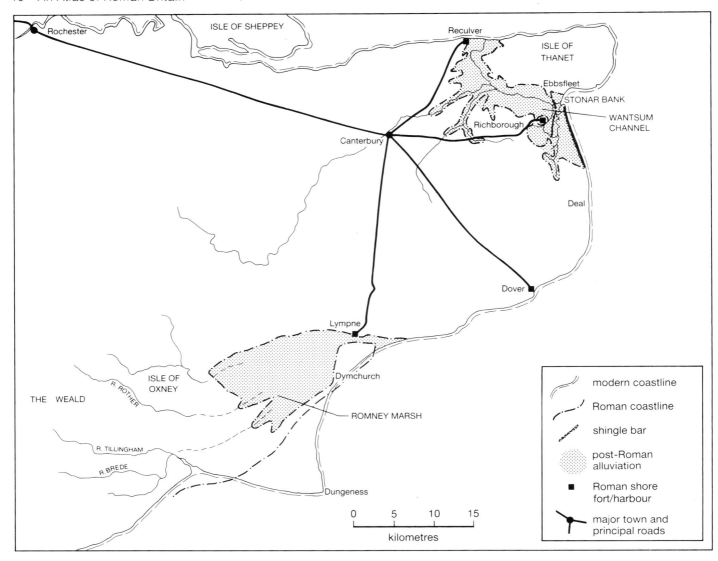

Map 1:13   Coastal change (ii) the Wantsum channel and Romney Marsh

The area of Liverpool Bay has seen much geomorphological change, obvious enough in the case of Morecambe Bay, less so elsewhere (1:12). The mouth of the Ribble, for instance, has been substantially altered by early-modern attempts to deepen its channel. In antiquity this estuary was probably enlarged by the River Douglas entering a much bigger lagoon (now marked by the shrunken Martin Mere) formed behind the coastal dunes bordering the foreshore between Formby and Southport. The Mersey is a self-scouring estuary and was certainly used in the Roman period (a batch of stamped lead ingots was found off Runcorn, see Map 6:10), but the legionary fortress at Chester shows that the Dee on the other side of the Wirral peninsula was the more important river at that time. It remained so until disastrous attempts to deepen the channel by Dutch

engineers in the eighteenth century, as shown by a succession of marine charts (1:14).

The subsequent rapid siltation that choked the Dee estuary also changed the coastal morphology of the north Wirral. West–east longshore drift is a constant factor and it is clear that it played a part in the formation of a considerable island off the Wirral. In the channel to the lee of this formation, between Hilbre and Dove Point, at the tip of the Wirral, there previously existed an anchorage known as Meols. There are hints that the harbourage was already serving as an entrepôt in the late Iron Age; use is well attested in the Roman and Medieval periods. Amongst the many random Roman finds recovered from the foreshore there are many items of metalwork, notably lead. This makes it a possibility that Meols acted as the main port for the export of lead

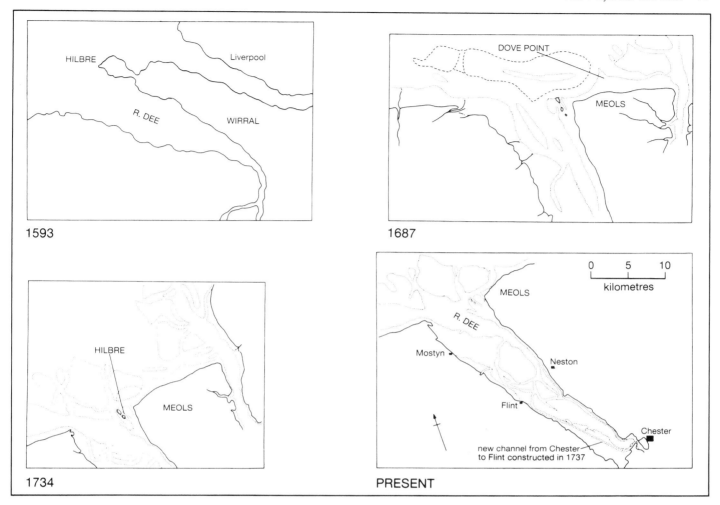

Map 1:14 Coastal change (iii) The Dee Estuary

Plate 1:2 Coastal change on the Wirral: Hilbre Island

objects from the extensive lead workings on Halkyn Mountain (6:7) on the opposite side of the estuary.

The area of the Wash on the east coast is an obvious example of coastal change on a large scale (1:15). The present coastal morphology and the layout of the fens that surround the Wash is largely the result of modern systems of drainage and sea defence. Recent work, often aided by the discovery of archaeological evidence during modern re-cutting of drainage dykes, has shown that the extent of the Wash was far greater in antiquity. It seems that the western littoral stretched from Chapel Hill, east of Sleaford, towards Bourne. This western border has been established by the find spots of Iron Age and much larger amounts of Romano-British material. The marginally greater elevation of this area distinguishes it from the principal area of peat fen in the present Wash basin. Within the basin, however, there are a number of relatively elevated areas which were tidal islands even in antiquity. Iron Age material is rare in these

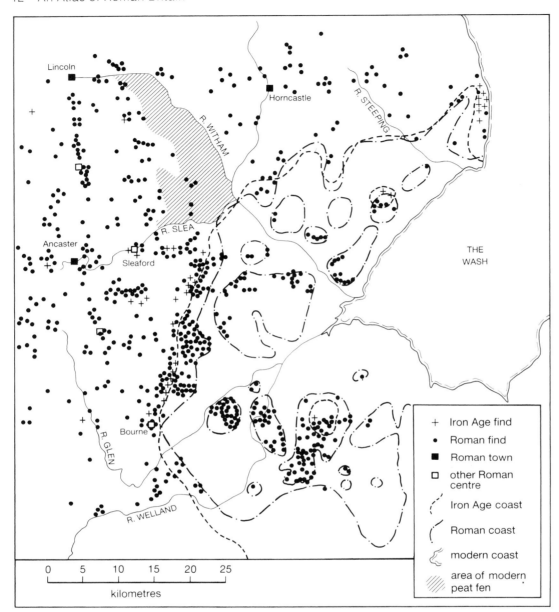

Map 1:15 Coastal change (iv) the Wash area in Iron Age and Roman times

Legend:
+ Iron Age find
• Roman find
■ Roman town
□ other Roman centre
Iron Age coast
Roman coast
modern coast
area of modern peat fen

Map labels: Lincoln, Horncastle, R. WITHAM, R. STEEPING, THE WASH, R. SLEA, Ancaster, Sleaford, R. GLEN, Bourne, R. WELLAND

Scale: 0 5 10 15 20 25 kilometres

relatively higher areas in contrast with the plentiful Roman finds which, to some extent, serve to define the edges of the ancient island formations such as those to the south-west of Boston. Fieldwork, notably that reported by Simmons, continues to produce fresh evidence, and progress has been made concerning the ancient navigability of rivers in the area and the function of the Car Dyke (no longer to be interpreted as a navigable canal). The River Witham undoubtedly served the fortress and colony at Lincoln and beyond, but the navigability of the River Bain as far north as Horncastle has been doubted. As in all the areas under discussion, much detailed work remains to be done.

The Somerset Levels are famous archaeologically for the evidence that they have yielded of prehistoric timber track-ways in the area between the Mendip and the Polden Hills (1:16). The trackways are in reality one fascinating part of human adjustment to the overall processes of morphological change that have affected the area in the prehistoric, Roman and Medieval periods. At the time of the maximum extent of marine transgression eastwards into the area, the Mendip Hills, for instance, projected well out to sea with their west-ernmost point being formed by the detached island of Brean Down, a feature that now marks the present coastline. Two thousand years ago, however, Brent Knoll was an island in the middle of the marine transgression and the area where Weston-super-Mare now stands lay under water. The

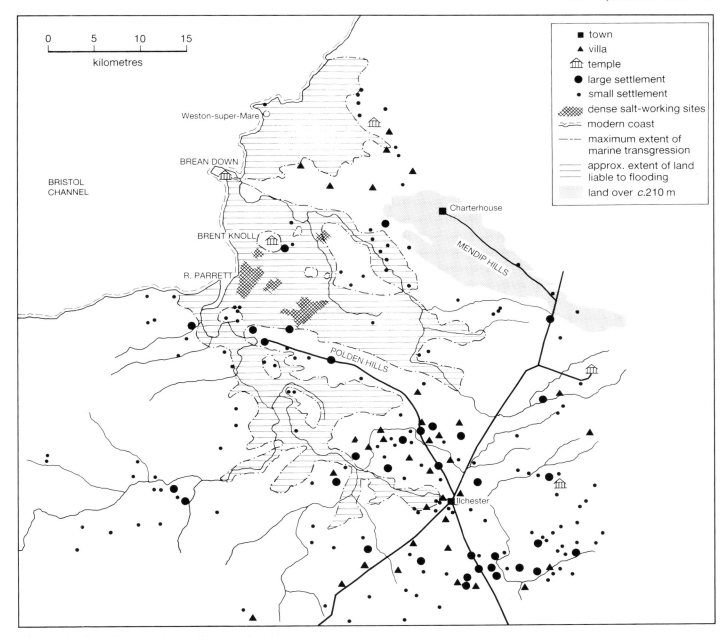

Map 1:16   Coastal change (v) the Somerset Levels

southern side of the Mendip Hills was flanked by the estuary of the River Axe and near Bridgwater the River Parrett formed a major estuary running along the south side of the Polden Hills. The maximum extent of marine transgression had been modified to some extent by the Roman period. Small Romano-British settlements are known to have existed on the Levels some 8–10km north-east of Weston-super-Mare. The locations of harbour sites in this period are much disputed, but some at least of the Charterhouse metal products may have been exported from a possible harbour at

Uphill near Brean Down (see 6:5). Recent fieldwork on the north side of the Polden Hills has located briquetage associated with salt making and pottery along the former line of the River Brue and in places within a few kilometres of the present sea coast. The picture is one of great geomorphological complexity and much more work is required to obtain a fuller understanding of both the prehistoric and Roman exploitation of the Levels.

The Moray Firth in north-eastern Scotland stretches in an arc from the River Deveron to the Ness at one end of the

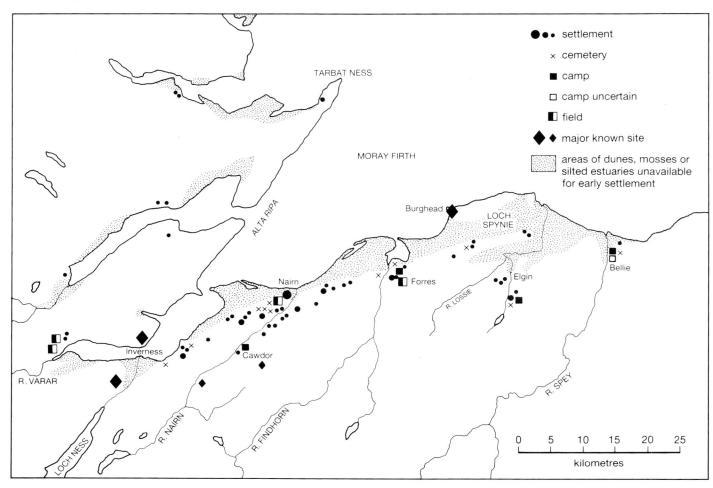

settlement ●●•

× **cemetery**

■ **camp**

□ **camp uncertain**

◧ **field**

◆◆ **major known site**

areas of dunes, mosses or silted estuaries unavailable for early settlement

TARBAT NESS

MORAY FIRTH

ALTA RIPA

Burghead

LOCH SPYNIE

Nairn

Forres

Elgin

R. LOSSIE

Bellie

Inverness

Cawdor

R. VARAR

R. SPEY

LOCH NESS

R. NAIRN

R. FINDHORN

0   5   10   15   20   25

kilometres

Map 1:17   Coastal change (vi) the Moray Firth

Plate 1:3   The coast east of Burghead, which is extending northwards, has left a belt of reclaimed land to the south.

Great Glen (1:17). The Laigh of Moray comprises the area of low-lying fertile land where some of the decisive battles of Scottish history have occurred. Across the Laigh the drainage is substantially north-eastwards in direction. The principal rivers are the turbulent, fast-flowing Spey, the smaller Lossie, the fast-flowing Findhorn and the Nairn. All these streams rise in the Monadhliath mountains and are liable to flash floods, a characteristic that explains the substantial changes in the coastal morphology at the mouths of the Spey, Lossie and Findhorn. Longshore drift from east to west has also pushed the mouths of the Spey and Findhorn westwards and the long sandy spits built up in this way were eventually perforated by the rivers as they cut new channels to the sea. About 2,000 years ago sea level was possibly about the same as today, but there existed a sea channel running from the Burghead area to Lossiemouth. The harbour area of Burghead was once part of an island now connected by a ten-metre storm beach to the mainland mass. Likewise to the east, the contraction of Loch Spynie is traceable in historical times from the period when Duffus

was a flourishing port. The accompanying diagram (1:17) shows how we can reconstruct coastal geomorphology as it may have been in the Roman period. The stippled areas indicate land that was either under water or at least seasonal marsh.

The reconstruction of these morphological changes is fundamental to any discussion of the Roman invasion of north-east Scotland. Armies invading Moray from the south were constrained by the geography to enter from the east and proceed west along the coastal plain as both Edward I and 'Butcher Billy', Duke of Cumberland, did in 1306 and 1746 respectively. However, once the Spey had been crossed any advancing army had to take account of the different morphology of the time. The modern trunk road now runs through areas that were impassable one or two millennia ago, notably around Findhorn Bay and below the Croy ridge on the eastern approaches to Inverness. These geographical factors are relevant to any discussion of possible locations of the battle of Mons Graupius (see 4:14).

2
Britain and the Roman Geographers

THE ROMANS' WORLD

There can be no doubt that the Greeks and Romans were very interested in defining the shape and extent of the world around them. The information they sought, however, and the methods they used sometimes differed considerably from the modern conception of physical or human geography. There are over 100 works by ancient writers which refer to Britain (many collected in Rivet and Smith, 1979, the definitive work on the subject matter of this chapter). Yet because most of these were mere passing references, often only giving the name of the island, the sum of geographical knowledge which these sources have communicated to us is disappointingly small. Moreover, virtually nothing has survived of ancient cartography (with the notable exception of the *Tabula Peutingeriana* referred to below). We are left with a very incomplete understanding of how much the Romans knew, or considered worth knowing, about Britain.

As early as the fourth century BC Alexandrian geographers had argued that the world was spherical and had succeeded in computing the circumference of the globe with considerable accuracy (though their Roman successors chose to accept one of the least accurate estimates with unfortunate consequences). The most detailed knowledge related, naturally, to the Mediterranean basin, whilst travellers' reports built up a vague picture of what lay beyond (2:1). The size of Africa was grossly underestimated and India and Sri Lanka (Ceylon) were the easternmost points of Asia depicted. The overall size of Europe, Asia and Africa filled only a

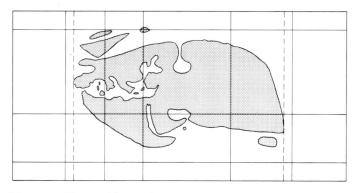

Map 2:1   The world according to Eratosthenes *c*.200 BC

fraction of Eratosthenes' globe – the rest, he reasoned, was taken up with desolate ocean. Part of the mystery and fascination of Britain was that it lay beyond continental Europe, an island outpost of the habitable world. The size and shape of Britain were imprecisely known and the island was generally represented by the Greeks as an obtuse-angled triangle of exaggerated size (see 2:3).

To the average Roman, the invasions of Britain by Julius Caesar and Claudius were spectacular feats which had overcome not simply military opposition, but also Roman suspicion and fear of the Western Ocean. Once occupied permanently, however, Britain lost ground in the public imagination, whilst still suffering the inconvenience of being virtually cut off from the Continent for half the year because of the perils of winter navigation. Its distance from the political and economic centre of the Empire was to disqualify it from playing a truly leading role in the affairs of the Roman world. In comparison with the Mediterranean heartlands therefore, the development of the British province was relatively retarded and limited, though precisely because of its geographical position and late incorporation into the Empire the level of achievement is commendable.

Even after Caesar's invasions, detailed geographical knowledge of Britain was in short supply with most writers reproducing the Greek 'triangular' Britain with revised measurements (2:3) and paraphrasing Caesar's comments on the character of the people. Nor did the Claudian invasion of AD 43 transform the state of knowledge at all quickly. Even Tacitus, our best source of information on first-century events, was confused by the geography of the island or just uninterested in it – though he could have had access to official sources. Detailed information was certainly collected in the invasion period by the army and the fleet, and maps were constructed from it. This information is largely lost to us today, though some of it may have been available (either directly or indirectly) to the best of the Roman geographers, Ptolemy of Alexandria.

PTOLEMY'S GEOGRAPHY

Claudius Ptolemaeus compiled his *Geography* in Greek towards the middle of the second century AD. By that time, the known world had grown somewhat in size and complexity, whilst Britain itself had shrunk to more modest

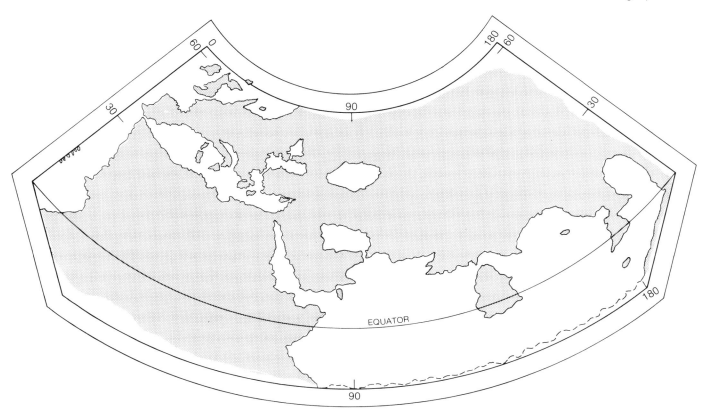

Map 2:2   The world according to Claudius Ptolemaeus (Ptolemy) *c.*AD 150

proportions (2:2). Yet the geographical position of Britain was the same as before, though it was now an outpost of the Empire as well as of Europe. The text of the *Geography* comprises a gigantic gazetteer of peoples and places throughout the Roman Empire and beyond. Ptolemy attempted to give precision to his data by including latitude and longitude co-ordinates for many locations, thus allowing maps to be drawn up from his text (2:2, 2:4). However, the earliest surviving copies of his manuscript (twelfth century and later) do not contain copies of the original maps, so it is uncertain whether the *Geography* was accompanied by such maps initially. Nevertheless, it is clear that Ptolemy must have drawn maps as an aid to the work of compilation and the modern reconstructions are probably not too far removed from what Ptolemy himself had in front of him. The strengths and weaknesses of his work can be judged by comparing Map 2:2 with a modern world atlas.

For Britain, Ptolemy gives a large number of topographic and place names, as well as the names of the principal tribes (2:4). The work is invaluable, but not without major problems – the most obvious being the apparent rotation of Scotland through 90° so that its main axis runs west–east instead of south–north. Ptolemy never visited Britain and so he was entirely dependent on the quality of other people's

work for his basic data. As regards his methodology, it is important to note that his use of latitude and longitude co-ordinates was not as scientifically rigorous as it looks at first sight. It is unlikely that the astronomical data necessary for calculating both latitude and longitude existed for more than a small percentage of the approximate 8,000 locations he named in the Roman world. The majority of sites would have been located on his maps by direct measurement on a bearing from a place whose location had been fixed. For example, many places in southern Britain may have been plotted in relation to their distance and direction from London, and their co-ordinates then simply read off the grid on Ptolemy's map. Any error in either the bearing or the distance of a place from his 'fixed points' would have had serious consequences for Ptolemy's map. This seems to have been the case with St Albans (Roman *Verulamium*, marked as Vrolanium on Map 2:4), which was placed on the same latitude as Leicester (*Ratae*), and with Silchester (*Calleva*), which was placed north of both Cirencester (*Corinium*) and London (*Londinium*) (compare 2:4, 2:5).

Given the date of compilation (*c.*AD 150), there are some surprising omissions from the map, notably Hadrian's Wall, the Antonine Wall, the legionary fortress at Caerleon (confused with the early fortress for the same legion at Exeter –

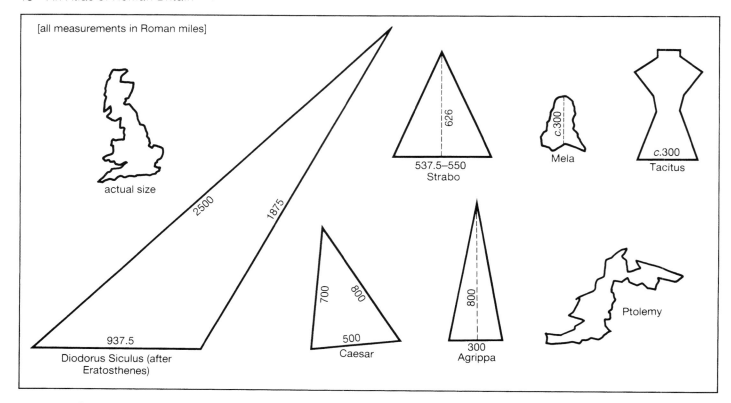

[all measurements in Roman miles]

actual size

2500

1875

937.5

Diodorus Siculus (after
Eratosthenes)

626

537.5–550
Strabo

700   800

500
Caesar

800

300
Agrippa

c.300
Mela

c.300
Tacitus

Ptolemy

Map 2:3   The size and shape of Britain as indicated by various ancient authors

both sites being called *Isca*) and the towns of Gloucester, Dorchester and Caerwent. Ptolemy did have some information dating to the AD 120s or later since he sited the VI legion at York and the XX at Chester, but it is clear that the majority of his data came from much earlier sources, a lot of it relating to the conquest period (AD 43–83). Military archives and military mapping probably lay behind much of his knowledge – though most of the information may have come to him second- or third-hand.

Ptolemy referred to all the places named in his work as *poleis* (singular *polis*), which is the Greek for 'towns', but which he clearly used in the wider sense of 'places with a name'. Ptolemy himself may not have known, or cared overmuch, whether he was including towns, Roman forts or native sites. He simply used a selection of names from whatever sources were available to him to fill up his own maps. Therefore, there is no guarantee that he always selected the most important sites for inclusion or that those chosen were all of one type.

The information for southern Britain (2:5) was derived from several sources (probably communicated to Ptolemy through the lost work of another geographer Marinus of Tyre, with minor additions). These sources were no doubt primarily military, the names of rivers, islands and coastal features reflecting the activity of the fleet, inland locations the work of the army. There are indications that Ptolemy

had access to some information about the subsequent civil development of the province (compare the tribal disposition on Map 2:4 with that shown on Maps 3:2 and 5:11), but the missing town names show that he was not essentially concerned with depicting the second-century administrative organization. The vast majority of names on his map relate to sites which were military bases or native centres (or both) during the conquest period and as such might be expected to have figured in military sources. The names listed by Ptolemy can represent only a fraction of the sites involved in the pacification process (cf. 4:23, 4:31) and the final selection may have been influenced by his recognition of some names from later sources.

Rivet and Smith have recently proposed identifications for three minor sites which found their way onto the map: *Iscalis* (?Charterhouse), *Luentinum* (?Dolaucothi) and *Salinae* (?Droitwich). The first two were mining sites, the last a salt extraction centre, and all operated under military supervision at some point during the first century (see below, 6:2, 6:3, 6:43). A number of other locations in south-western and northern England were plainly Roman forts and fortresses and the unlocated sites in these areas are also likely to have been so. The cumulative picture is that Ptolemy's geographical sources for Britain were military in origin, although he did some revision and updating.

For northern Britain, the situation is at once clearer and

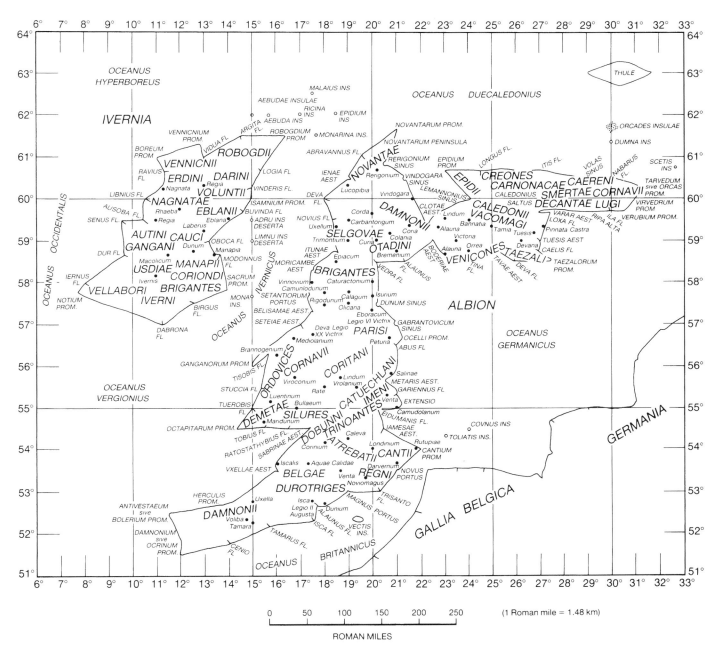

Map 2:4   Britain and Ireland according to Ptolemy

more problematical. The ultimate source for Ptolemy (and Marinus) was a military map relating to the Flavian conquest and brief occupation of the region north of the Tyne–Solway line. Quite a number of place names were listed in association with tribal names (2:4), but the majority are unlocatable on present evidence (2:6). Once again, though, we may infer that the vast majority were Roman forts rather than temporary camps or native settlements but, in spite of increasingly ingenious suggestions, the identification problems posed by the incorrect orientation of Scotland are far

from being resolved. One problem is that there are far more known Flavian forts than places named by Ptolemy and, as already argued, the basis for his selection may have been fairly random. However, on the assumption that Ptolemy was more likely to include sites which lay on the main Roman roads – since these were more likely to have been recorded with the 'accurate' bearing and distance measurements he required – it is unlikely that many of the so-called glen-blocking forts of the Highland line were included. On the other hand, Inchtuthil, the legionary fortress, *ought* to

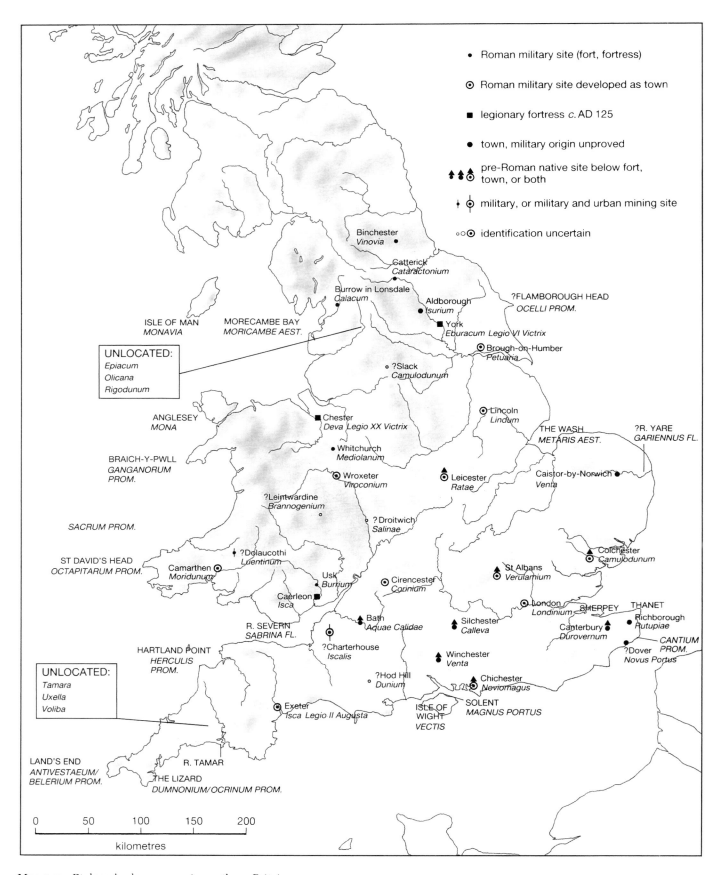

Map 2:5 Ptolemy's place names in southern Britain

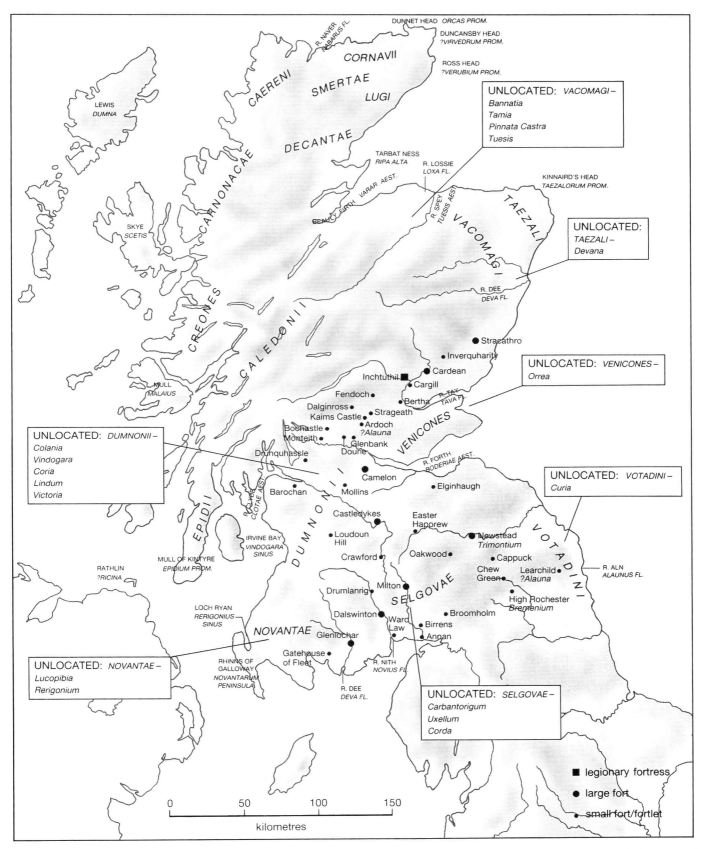

Map 2:6 Ptolemy and Scotland: general locations of named sites in the first century AD, in relation to approximate tribal zones and Roman military deployment

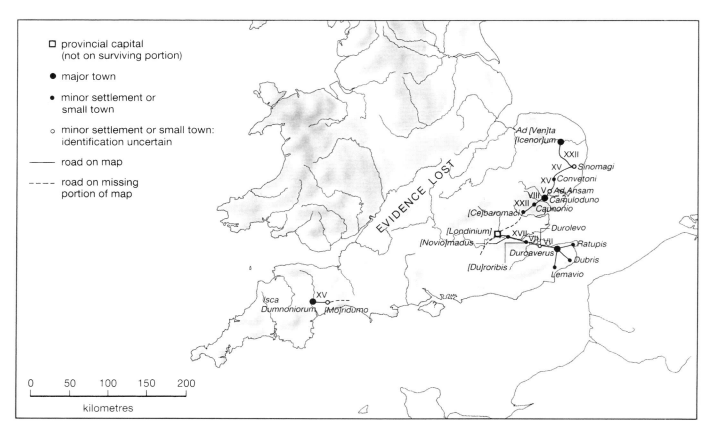

Map 2:7 The *Tabula Peutingeriana* on a modern map

Plate 2:1 Segment 1 of the *Tabula Peutingeriana*, showing part of Britain at extreme left

have been included, and Rivet and Smith's suggestion that it was *Victoria* deserves serious consideration.

Another interesting point concerns the territory of the Vacomagi tribe, which extended into the region on the southern shores of the Moray Firth. A number of sites assigned to their territory appear to lie well beyond the known disposition of Roman forts in Strathmore. *Pinnata Castra* cannot have been an advanced temporary camp in Agricola's final season (as has sometimes been argued) for the simple reason that astronomical observations were made there one Midsummer's Day, whilst Agricola's army cannot have been in the Moray region until near the end of the summer. The positioning of the site by Ptolemy on the Moray Firth beyond the River Spey (2:4) is a strong argument against identifying the name with Inchtuthil, as is still sometimes proposed. Similarly, the name *Tuesis* should indicate a fort somewhere on the Spey, in an area where, until recently, there were believed to be no such forts. Recent discoveries suggest that Roman military installations of some sort may have been occupied for a short while in the area and that Ptolemy's map was more accurate here than people have been prepared to credit.

THE ITINERARIES

Ptolemy's *Geography* (with or without accompanying maps) was designed to define the shape of the world in which he lived. It was not intended for practical use by travellers or officials. In contrast, though, there were other types of maps and written geographical sources which were specifically utilitarian; the most significant of these were the itineraries. They covered the main routes of the Empire and showed in map or tabular form the main places along the roads and the distances between them.

The *Tabula Peutingeriana*

The *Tabula* is a thirteenth-century copy of a Roman road map and depicts the main highways of the Empire and the Persian lands to the east. It was designed to be read not as a topographical map but as a route planner and in consequence it completely distorts the geography of the Roman world, condensing it onto a strip 6.82m long, but only 0.34m wide. Unfortunately, only a small portion of the British section of the original map survived when the Medieval copy was made. This fragment deals in the main with the south-eastern corner of England, showing the three main channel ports of *Ratupis* (Richborough), *Dubris* (Dover) and *Lemavio* (Lympne) and the road leading towards London and from there into East Anglia (cf. Pl. 2:1 and Map 2:7). The island in the channel is perhaps Wight and a small portion of the road from *Isca Dumnoniorum* (Exeter) towards London is also shown – demonstrating the geographical distortion of the map. Not only did the map serve to inform the traveller

of the distances between places but, through different symbols, an indication of the size and likely facilities of the locations could be given. The place name forms and the mileages from this surviving fragment can be compared with those from the other main surviving itinerary source, the *Antonine Itinerary*.

The *Antonine Itinerary*

The *Antonine Itinerary* survived not as a map, but as a manuscript describing 225 of the major roads of the Empire and listing the places and distances along them. There are quite a number of divergences from the roads on the Peutinger map and the material has the appearance of having been assembled in a haphazard way, perhaps reflecting additions to an original document prepared in relation to Caracalla's planned journey from Rome to Alexandria in AD 214–15. The British section is of great importance because it describes fifteen routes and records over 100 different place names. Although not all the names and mileages were transmitted correctly when copies of the original were made in the Middle Ages, it has proved an invaluable source for the location and naming of Roman sites along the roads of England and Wales (2:8). Maps 2:9–2:12 and Tables 2:1– 2:4 illustrate the courses of the individual routes. The place name forms used in the tables are exactly as given in the *Itinerary*; those on Map 2:8 reflect current thought on the correct, nominative forms of these names (after Rivet and Smith, 1979). The wide differences in place name forms revealed here demonstrate both copyists' errors and variance in ancient usage.

The official nature of the document is demonstrated by the manner in which the routes are described. Over half the routes (eight out of fifteen) start at, finish at, or pass through London; three routes start or finish at the Channel ports, three at the northern frontier. Quite a number of routes pass via the legionary fortresses at York (four), Chester (two) and Caerleon (three). Route I runs from Hadrian's Wall to London and Richborough via *both* York and Chester – hardly the most direct line but a route that Roman governors or paymasters were likely to take on a periodic tour of the northern garrison. A number of routes pass through exclusively civil centres (VI – London, St Albans, Leicester, Lincoln; VII – Chichester, Winchester, Silchester, London; IX – Caistor-by-Norwich, Colchester, London; XV – Silchester, Winchester, Dorchester, Exeter). Indeed all the civil administrative centres are named in at least one of the routes (though Cirencester (*Corinium*) has to be restored in a corrupt section of route XIII). However, a number of direct routes between major towns are entirely omitted (notably Fosse Way between Leicester and Exeter via Cirencester, and Stane Street between London and Chichester). This again hints at the use of itineraries for official perambulations in which several centres might be visited in a given order.

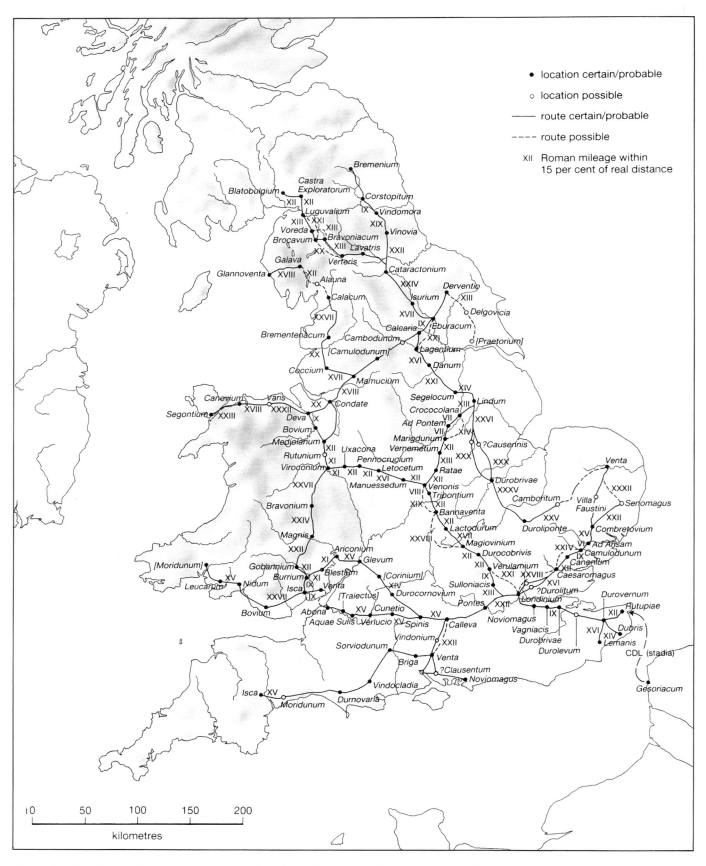

Map 2:8 The *Antonine Itinerary* in Britain. Only mileage distances within 15 per cent of the correct total are shown. CDL stadia (450 stades) records the length of the crossing from Boulogne (*Gesoriacum*) to Richborough (*Rutupiae*).

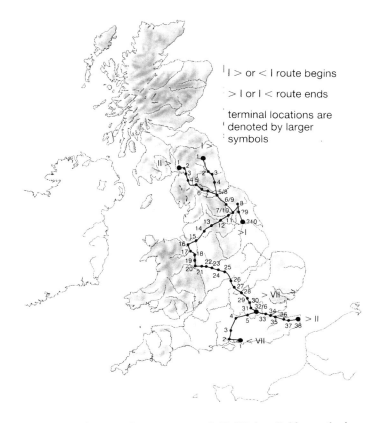

Map 2:9   *Antonine Itinerary* routes I, II, VII (see Table 2:1 for key to numbers)

Table 2.1   Routes I, II and VII from the *Antonine Itinerary* (the forms of names are as given in the *Itinerary*)

Place	Distance	
	in Roman miles	real distance

Route I

Bremenio (High Rochester) to:

		in Roman miles	real distance
1	*Corstopitum* (Corbridge)	20	25
2	*Vindomora* (Ebchester)	9	10
3	*Vinovia* (Binchester)	19	20
4	*Cataractoni* (Catterick)	22	22
5	*Isurium* (Aldborough)	24	25
6	*Eburacum* (York)	17	17
7	*Derventione* (Malton)	7	20
8	*Delgovicia* (?Wetwang/Millington)	13	13
9	Praetorio (Brough-on-Humber)	25	22

Total mileage given at head of list 156 m.p.; total stages 156 m.p.; real total 174 m.p.

Route II

Blatobulgio (Birrens) to:

1	*Castra Exploratorum* (Netherby)	12	14
2	*Luguvallo* (Carlisle)	12	11
3	*Voreda* (Old Penrith)	13	14
4	*Brovonacis* (Kirkby Thore)	13	14
5	*Verteris* (Brough)	13	13
6	*Lavatris* (Bowes)	14	14
7	*Cataractone* (Catterick)	16	21
8	*Isuriam* (Aldborough)	24	25
9	*Eburacum* (York)	17	17
10	*Calcaria* (Tadcaster)	9	10
11	*Camboduno* (?Leeds)	20	14
[12	*Camuloduno* (Slack)	–	20*]
13	*Mamucio* (Manchester)	18	23
14	*Condate* (Northwich)	18	20
15	*Deva leg XX Vici* (Chester)	20	20
16	*Bovio* (?Tilston)	10	11
17	*Medialano* (Whitchurch)	20	11
18	*Rutunio* (?Harcourt Mill)	12	12
19	*Urioconio* (Wroxeter)	11	11
20	*Uxacona* (Red Hill)	11	11
21	*Pennocrucio* (Water Eaton)	12	12
22	*Etoceto* (Wall)	12	14
23	*Manduesedo* (Mancetter)	16	16
24	*Venonis* (High Cross)	12	11
25	*Bannaventa* (Whilton Lodge)	17	19
26	*Lactodoro* (Towester)	12	12
27	*Magiovinto* (Dropshort)	17	16
28	*Durocobrivis* (Dunstable)	12	12
29	Verolamio (St Albans)	12	13
30	*Sulloniacis* (Brockley Hill)	9	9
31	*Londinio* (London)	12	13
32	*Noviomago* (Crayford)	10	13
33	*Vagniacis* (Springhead)	19	8
34	*Durobrovis* (Rochester)	9	9
35	*Durolevo* (?nr Sittingbourne)	13	– ⎫
36	*Durorverno* (Canterbury)	12	– ⎬27
37	*Ad portum Ritupis* (Richborough)	12	13 ⎭

Total mileage given at head of list 481 m.p.; total stages 502 m.p.; real total 523 m.p.

Route VII

Regno (Chichester) to:

1	*Clausentum* (?Bitterne/Wickham)	20	30/20
2	*Venta Belgarum* (Winchester)	10	10/15
3	*Galleva Atrebatum* (Silchester)	22	25
4	*Pontibus* (Staines)	22	27
5	*Londinio* (London)	22	21

Total mileage given at head of list 96 m.p.; total stages 96 m.p.; real total 113/108 m.p.

* hypothetical restoration of a suspected lacuna

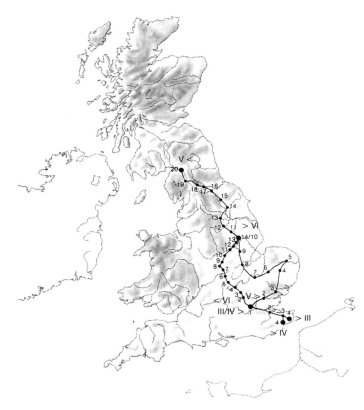

Map 2:10   *Antonine Itinerary* routes III, IV, V, VI (see Table 2:2 for key to numbers)

Table 2.2   Routes III, IV, V and VI from the *Antonine Itinerary* (the forms of names are as given in the *Itinerary*)

Place	Distance	
	in Roman miles	real distance
Route III		
Londinio (London) to:		
1 *Durobrius* (Rochester)	27	30
2 *Durarveno* (Canterbury)	25	27
3 *Ad portum Dubris* (Dover)	14	16

Total mileage given at head of list 66 m.p.; total stages 66 m.p.; real total 73 m.p.

Route IV

Londinio (London) to:		
Durobrivis (Rochester)	27	30
Durarvenno (Canterbury)	25	27
Ad portum Lemanis (Lympne)	16	16

Total mileage given at head of list 68 m.p.; total stages 68 m.p.; real total 73 m.p.

Route V

Londinio (London) to:		
1 *Caesaromago* (Chelmsford)	28	30
2 *Colonia* (Colchester)	24	24
3 *Villa Faustini* (?Scole/Stoke Ash)	35	41/36
4 *Icinos* (Caistor by Norwich	18	18/23
5 *Camborico* (?Lackford)	35	37
6 *Duroliponte* (Cambridge)	25	25
7 *Durobrivas* (Water Newton)	35	36
8 *Causennis* (?Saltersford/Sapperton)	30	30
9 *Lindo* (Lincoln)	26	26
10 *Segeloci* (Littleborough)	14	15
11 *Dano* (Doncaster)	21	23
12 *Legeolio* (Castleford)	16	18
13 *Eburaco* (York)	21	23
14 *Isubrigantum* (Aldborough)	17	17
15 *Cataractoni* (Catterick)	24	25
16 *Levatris* (Bowes)	18	21
17 *Verteris* (Brough)	14	14
18 *Brocavo* (Brougham)	20	20
19 *Luguvalio* (Carlisle)	21	21

Total mileage given at head of list 442 m.p.; total stages 442 m.p.; real total 463 m.p.

Route VI

Londinio (London) to:		
1 *Verolami* (St Albans)	21	22
2 *Durocobrius* (Dunstable)	12	13
3 *Magiovinio* (Dropshort)	12	12
4 *Lactodoro* (Towcester)	16	16
5 *Isannavantia* (Whilton Lodge)	12	12
6 *Tripontio* (Cave's Inn)	12	11
7 *Venonis* (High Cross)	8	8
8 *Ratas* (Leicester)	12	12
9 *Verometo* (Willoughby)	13	14
10 *Margiduno* (Castle Hill)	12	12
11 *Ad Pontem* (East Stoke)	7	7
12 *Crococalana* (Brough)	7	8
13 *Lindo* (Lincoln)	12	13

Total mileage given at head of list 156 m.p.; total stages 156 m.p.; real total 160 m.p.

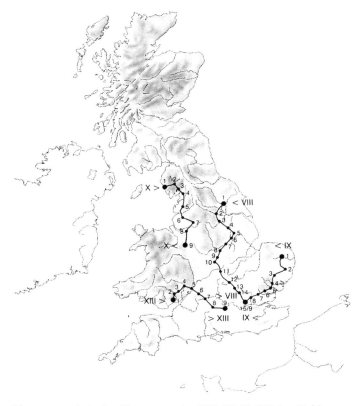

Map 2:11 *Antonine Itinerary* routes VIII, IX, X, XIII (see Table 2:3 for key to numbers)

Table 2.3 Routes VIII, IX, X and XIII from the *Antonine Itinerary* (the forms of names are as given in the *Itinerary*)

Place	Distance in Roman miles	real distance
Route VIII		
Eburaco (York) to:		
1 *Lagecio* (Castleford)	21	23
2 *Dano* (Doncaster)	16	18
3 *Angeloco* (Littleborough)	21	23
4 *Lindo* (Lincoln)	14	14
5 *Crococalano* (Brough)	14	13
6 *Margiduno* (Castle Hill)	14	15
7 *Vernemeto* (Willoughby)	12	12
8 *Ratis* (Leicester)	12	14
9 *Vennonis* (High Cross)	12	12
10 *Bannavanto* (Whilton Lodge)	19	19
11 *Magiovinio* (Dropshort)	28	28
12 *Durocobrivis* (Dunstable)	12	12
13 *Verolamo* (St Albans)	12	13
14 *Londinio* (London)	21	22

Total mileage given at head of list 227 m.p.; total stages 228 m.p.; real total 238 m.p.

Route IX

Venta Icinorum (Caistor by Norwich) to:		
1 *Sitomago* (?nr Yoxford)	32	32
2 *Conbretovio* (Coddenham)	22	23
3 *Ad Ansam* (Higham)	15	15
4 *Camoloduno* (Colchester)	6	7
5 *Canonio* (Kelvedon)	9	10
6 *Cesaromago* (Chelmsford)	12	13
7 *Durolito* (?Chigwell)	16	16
8 *Ludinio* (London)	15	16

Total mileage given at head of list 128 m.p.; total stages 127 m.p.; real total 132 m.p.

Route X

Clanoventa (Ravenglass) to:		
1 *Galava* (Ambleside)	18	20
2 *Alone* (?Watercrook)	12	13
3 *Galacum* (?Burrow in Lonsdale)	19	13
4 *Bremetonnaci* (Ribchester)	27	30
5 *Coccio* (Wigan)	20	22
6 *Mamcunio* (Manchester)	17	18
7 *Condate* (Northwich)	18	20
8 *Mediolano* (Whitchurch)	19	24

Total mileage given at head of list 150 m.p.; total stages 150 m.p.; real total 160 m.p.

Route XIII

Isca (Caerleon) to:		
1 *Burrio* (Usk)	9	8
2 *Blestio* (Monmouth)	11	13
3 *Ariconio* (Weston-under-Penyard)	11	12
4 *Clevo* (Gloucester)	15	15
[5 *Corinio* (Cirencester)	—	18[1]]
6 *Durocornovio* (Wanborough)	14	16
7 *Spinis* (Woodspeen)	15	20
8 *Calleva* (Silchester)	15	16

Total mileage given at head of list 109 m.p.; total stages 90 m.p.; real total 118 m.p.

[1] hypothetical restoration of a suspected lacuna

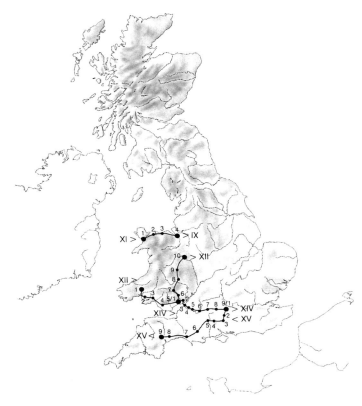

Map 2:12 *Antonine Itinerary* routes XI, XII, XIV, XV (see Table 2:4 for key to numbers)

Table 2.4 Routes XI, XII, XIV and XV from the *Antonine Itinerary* (the forms of names are as given in the *Itinerary*)

Place	Distance	
	in Roman miles	real distance
Route XI		
Segontio (Caernarvon) to:		
1 *Conovio* (Caerhun)	23	24
2 *Varis* (St Asaph)	18	18
3 *Deva* (Chester)	32	34

Total mileage given at head of list 74 m.p.; total stages 73 m.p.; real total 76 m.p.

Route XII

Muridono (Carmarthen) to:

1	*Leucaro* (Loughor)	15	19
2	*Nido* (Neath)	15	13
3	*Bomio* (?Cowbridge)	15	27
4	*Iscae leg II Augusta* (Caerleon)	27	27
5	*Burrio* (Usk)	9	8
6	*Gobannio* (Abergavenny)	12	11
7	*Magnis* (Kenchester)	22	23
8	*Bravonio* (Leintwardine)	24	23
9	*Viriconio* (Wroxeter)	27	27

Total mileage given at head of list 186 m.p.; total stages 166 m.p.; real total 178 m.p.

Route XIV

Isca (Caerleon) to:

1	*Venta Silurum* (Caerwent)	9	9
2	*Abone* (Sea Mills)	14	?
3	*Traiectus* (?)	8	?
4	*Aquis Sulis* (Bath)	6	?
5	*Verlucione* (Sandy Lane)	15	15
6	*Cunetione* (Mildenhall)	20	17
7	*Spinis* (Woodspeen)	15	15
8	*Calleva* (Silchester)	15	16

Total mileage given at head of list 103 m.p.; total stages 102 m.p.; real total ? m.p. There is a probable lacuna in the text between 1 and 2, with 3 perhaps also a confusion.

Route XV

Calleva (Silchester) to:

1	*Vindomi* (Wheatsheaf Inn, North Waltham)	15	12
2	*Venta Velgarum* (Winchester)	21	12
3	*Brige* (Ashley)	11	6
4	*Sorbiodoni* (Old Sarum)	8	18
5	*Vindocladia* (Badbury)	12	23
6	*Durnovaria* (Dorchester)	8	20
7	*Moriduno* (?Sidford)	36	42
8	*Isca Dumnoniorum* (Exeter)	15	15

Total mileage given at head of list 136 m.p.; total stages 126 m.p.; real total 148 m.p. This route also appears by error as an intrusion in the listing of Route XII with the same mileage figures but with the following variants in spelling: 2 *Venta Belgarum*; 4 *Sorvioduni*; 5 *Vindogladia*; 7 *Muriduno*; 8 *Sca Dumnoniorum*.

Plate 2:2   Wooden writing tablet from *Vindolanda* with the top line reading *Londini[um]* (London)

The variations in mileage figures can be explained in part as errors introduced into the document when it was copied in Roman or Medieval times. Some of the minor differences may be on account of distances being measured not from the centre of a major town, but from points on its boundary. In a few cases, where the discrepancy in the mileage figure is large and not easily explicable, it may yet prove that modern site identifications are mistaken.

The *Ravenna Cosmography*

The *Ravenna Cosmography* is another source which is loosely in the itinerary tradition. Compiled by an anonymous cleric at Ravenna *c.*AD 700, the document is little more than a vast list of place names (over 5,000 from all over the Empire). The information was organized crudely by area, with a multitude of careless copying errors. The particular interest of the *Cosmography* is that its compiler clearly had access to a wide range of official maps and sources (presumably the remnant of the imperial archives which had been transferred to Ravenna at the time of the barbarian invasions). For the British section, it is likely that the cosmographer was using at least two maps. Following Rivet and Smith's analysis (1979, pp. 185–215) it is evident that the main map for southern Britain was of similar type to the Peutinger map (though perhaps more detailed and including river names).

The lettering must have been densely packed on this map – adding enormously to the cosmographer's usual quota of copying errors. North of Hadrian's Wall, a different source was used, derived ultimately from the Flavian map known to Ptolemy, but with additions to it including the Antonine Wall. A third map source, also military and early in date, may have been used to add extra detail to the list of names for south-west Britain.

In total, the *Cosmography* lists nearly 300 names in Britain, but its value as a source is seriously undermined by several factors:

1 it contains a great number of copying errors – which distort many place name forms and make *all* uncorroborated spellings suspect;

2 the compiler failed to distinguish the types of feature to which the place names referred, and forts, towns, road stations, native settlements, rivers, islands and tribal names are often included in the same part of the list;

3 though he may have had a road map for Britain, the compiler chose to read names off the map in a random order within a given area, rather than in a logical sequence along a road.

It is, therefore, extremely difficult to identify places named in this source with certainty, unless the name is also known from other sources.

ORKNEY
ISLANDS

?CAERENI (2)
?SMERTAE
R. LOSSIE
R. FARRAR
•Bellie
DECANTAE
?VAGOMAGI
SKYE
?Kintore
?PICTI
?CALEDONES
CANNA
?CREONES
?Cardean
LOCH LINNHE
?Inchtuthil
?MULL
?VENICONES
R. TAY
?Ardoch
?Arthur's O'on
R. FORTH
?Drumquhassie
?Camelon
Carriden
?Barochan
?Castledykes
?VOTADINI
Newstead
R. ALNE (2)
?Easter Happrew
R. COQUET (2)
?EPIDII
DUMNONII
SELGOVAE
High Rochester
?Risingham
?Lochmaben
Bewcastle
R. TYNE
?Ward Law
H Cb Ch Ha Be W
R. WEAR
?IBERNIA
?Glenlochar
Cas Ca
?Stranraer
BS
Bi G V
Cor
Chester-le-Street
R. NITH (2)
Bo
C
Lanchester
?Beckfoot
Old Penrith
Maryport
Kirkby Thore
Binchester
?Rhinns of
Galloway
R. DERWENT
Papcastle
?Moresby
Brough
Bowes
Hardknott
Ambleside
Catterick
Ravenglass
?Watercrook
ISLE OF
MAN
?Burrow in
Lonsdale
?Aldborough
York
?Wetwang
Ribchester
?Tadcaster
Brough-on-Humber
?Leeds
Castleford
R. OUSE/HUMBER
Slack
Manchester
Melandra
Northwich
Brough
Lincoln
ANGLESEY
Buxton
?Horncastle
Caernarvon
Caerhun
Chester
Middlewich
Whitchurch
Carsington
Littlechester
Willoughby
Wroxeter
Wall
Leicester
Water Newton
Caistor-by-Norwich
Leintwardine
Droitwich
Godmanchester
Llanio
?Worcester
?Alcester
Cambridge
?Y Gaer
Kenchester
Towcester
?Llandovery
Gloucester (3)
?Dunstable
Colchester
Abergavenny
?Lydney
St Albans
Chelmsford
Caerleon
Cirencester
Caerwent
R. LOUGHOR
London (2)
R. THAMES
ISLE OF THANET
R. USK (2)
?Sea Mills
Mildenhall
Rochester
Richborough
R. EWENNY
?Bath
Silchester
Canterbury
?R. SEVERN (2)
R. AVON (2)
?East Anton
Dover
?Old Sarum
Winchester
Lympne
Ilchester
Porchester
Chichester
Pevensey
R. TAW
Badbury
?North Tawton
Exeter
Dorchester
ISLE OF
WIGHT
?R. ADUR
Sidford (?4)
R. MEON
?R. ARUN
Land's End (?2)
R. TAMAR
R. DART
R. ERME (2)

KEY TO HADRIAN'S WALL FORTS
from east to west

W   Wallsend
Be   Benwell
R   Rudchester
Ha   Halton
Cor Corbridge
Ch   Chesters
Cb   Carrawburgh
H   Housesteads
V   *Vindolanda* (Chesterholm)
G   Great Chesters
Ca   Carvoran
Bi   Birdoswald
Cas Castlesteads (2)
S   Stanwix
C   Carlisle
BS   Burgh-by-Sands
Bo   Bowness (3)

0   50   100   150   200
kilometres

Map 2:13   Certain and probable identifications of places listed in the *Ravenna Cosmography* (numbers in brackets indicate sites referenced more than once by the cosmographer, question marks indicate less certain identification).

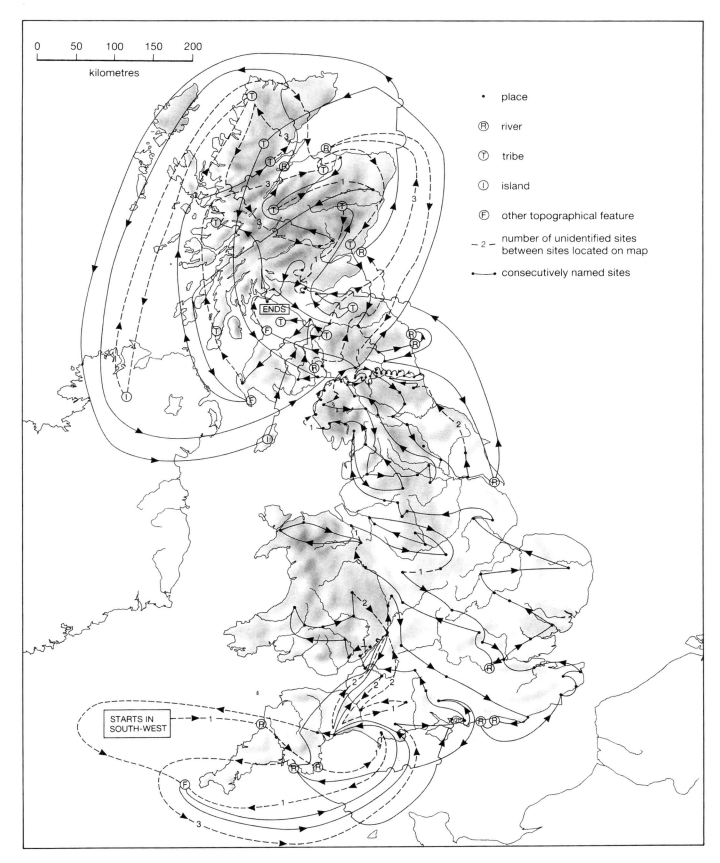

Map 2:14 Order of citation of sites listed in the *Ravenna Cosmography*

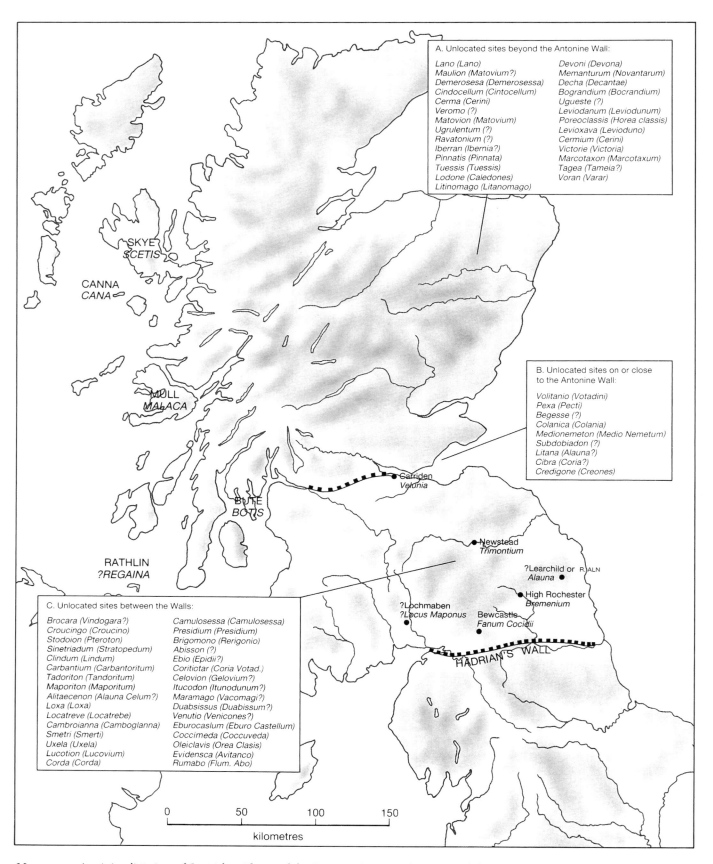

A. Unlocated sites beyond the Antonine Wall:

Lano (Lano)
Maulion (Matovium?)
Demerosesa (Demerosessa)
Cindocellum (Cintocellum)
Cerma (Cerini)
Veromo (?)
Matovion (Matovium)
Ugrulentum (?)
Ravatonium (?)
Iberran (Ibernia?)
Pinnatis (Pinnata)
Tuessis (Tuessis)
Lodone (Caledones)
Litinomago (Litanomago)

Devoni (Devona)
Memanturum (Novantarum)
Decha (Decantae)
Bograndium (Bocrandium)
Ugueste (?)
Leviodanum (Leviodunum)
Poreoclassis (Horea classis)
Levioxava (Levioduno)
Cermium (Cerini)
Victorie (Victoria)
Marcotaxon (Marcotaxum)
Tagea (Tameia?)
Voran (Varar)

B. Unlocated sites on or close to the Antonine Wall:

Volitanio (Votadini)
Pexa (Pecti)
Begesse (?)
Colanica (Colania)
Medionemeton (Medio Nemetum)
Subdobiadon (?)
Litana (Alauna?)
Cibra (Coria?)
Credigone (Creones)

SKYE
SCETIS

CANNA
CANA

MULL
MALACA

BUTE
BOTIS

RATHLIN
?REGAINA

Carriden
Velunia

Newstead
Trimontium

?Learchild or R. ALN
Alauna

?Lochmaben
?Locus Maponus

Bewcastle
Fanum Cocidii

High Rochester
Bremenium

HADRIAN'S WALL

C. Unlocated sites between the Walls:

Brocara (Vindogara?)
Croucingo (Croucino)
Stodoion (Pteroton)
Sinetriadum (Stratopedum)
Clindum (Lindum)
Carbantium (Carbantoritum)
Tadoriton (Tandoritum)
Maporiton (Maporitum)
Alitaecenon (Alauna Celum?)
Loxa (Loxa)
Locatreve (Locatrebe)
Cambroianna (Camboglanna)
Smetri (Smerti)
Uxela (Uxela)
Lucotion (Lucovium)
Corda (Corda)

Camulosessa (Camulosessa)
Presidium (Presidium)
Brigomono (Rerigonio)
Abisson (?)
Ebio (Epidii?)
Coritiotar (Coria Votad.)
Celovion (Gelovium?)
Itucodon (Itunodunum?)
Maramago (Vacomagi?)
Duabsissus (Duabissum?)
Venutio (Venicones?)
Eburocaslum (Eburo Castellum)
Coccimeda (Coccuveda)
Oleiclavis (Orea Clasis)
Evidensca (Avitanco)
Rumabo (Flum. Abo)

0   50   100   150

kilometres

Map 2:15 A minimalist view of Scottish evidence of the *Ravenna Cosmography*: many of the place name forms are corrupt (Rivet and Smith's suggested emendations are given in brackets).

The analysis of Rivet and Smith has marked a major advance in knowledge with many new identifications proposed (2:13). However, their approach is not without potential pitfalls. They suggested that the compiler made a number of accidental repetitions of place names by not realizing that he had returned to the same point on his map. For instance, the names *Glebon colonia*, *Clavinio* and *Coloneas* may all be references to *Glevum Colonia* (Gloucester). Yet this form of analysis is less compelling in the case of the four proposed references to *Moridunum* (?Sidford) – why should not at least one of these references have been to *Moridunum* (Carmarthen)?

Moreover, when the order of citation (as identified by Rivet and Smith) is plotted on a map, an interesting pattern emerges (2:14). Granted that the cosmographer was appallingly careless as a copyist, it is apparent that, where a reasonable degree of certainty exists about the identification of the locations he named, there was an element of coherence in his approach. Thus for Wales and most of England, he copied names from his source map by making a series of zig-zag traverses which rarely followed Roman road lines for long, but which also rarely crossed over each other. We can be reasonably happy about most identifications here since the *Antonine Itinerary* covers the same area. When we come to look at the pattern for south-west England and for Scotland it is obvious that something is badly awry. Even if the cosmographer was using different map sources for these regions, it would be unusual if his geographical selection of names from the maps became so random. At root, the problem lies in our inability to locate place names in these areas with confidence. The textual emendations and identifications proposed by Rivet and Smith cannot all be correct when they so patently fail to make any sense of the order of citation. Equally, it is worth observing that though their emendations of many place name forms in Scotland to match names given by Ptolemy may well be correct, the implication of Map 2:14 is that many of their proposed locations are wrong.

A minimalist view of Roman Scotland from the evidence of the *Ravenna Cosmography* is shown in Map 2:15. The compiler's own geographic divisions are restored and, even if we can propose few certain or probable identifications, the general location of sites implied here may be of some help in dealing with the evidence of Ptolemy's *Geography*. Future epigraphic discoveries from the Antonine Wall or lowland Scotland could yet restore a (limited) measure of confidence in the *Cosmography* as a source.

The *Notitia Dignitatum*

Another source of Romano-British place names is the *Notitia Dignitatum*, a late Roman collection of administrative information which includes lists of civil and military officials and of military units and their forts. All the surviving manuscripts derive from a common eleventh-century copy of the original (the *Codex Spirensis* – now itself lost), which was accompanied by a series of illustrations. These illustrations consisted in the main of official insignia relevant to the offices described in the text and were almost certainly copied from the late Roman originals. Some of the illustrations relate to Britain and appear to show a bird's-eye view of the island (Pls 2:3, 2:4). In reality, the presentation is purely conventional and the illustrations were not intended to be maps. However, the place name information is valuable for comparison with the text. Plate 2:2 shows the insignia of the *Vicarius* of Britain and the five provinces of the diocese (here represented as walled towns). The date of the division of Britain is uncertain, as is the location and even the existence of *Valentia* (see 5:7). Plate 2:3 shows the forts under the command of the Count of the Saxon Shore, but here again the disposition of the names on the 'island' is conventional rather than geographical.

The *Notitia* provides a good deal of information about the Roman civil bureaucracy in Britain (see Chapter 5), but few place names are mentioned in this sphere (we are not even informed of the names of the provincial capitals). However, London is referred to as *Augusta*, a late Roman ?honorary title granted to the town which was the administrative centre of the 'diocese' as well as a provincial capital (2:16). An imperial weaving works (*gynaeceum*) is mentioned at a place called *Venta*, but this could be one of three locations – *Venta Belgarum* (Winchester), *Venta Icenorum* (Caistor St Edmund) or *Venta Silurum* (Caerwent). The first two are considered the most likely options (compare 6:46).

The military sections of the document give far more place names and a large number of sites can be identified with confidence (2:16). Military units were listed in several sectors according to their overall commanding officer and, to some extent, in relation to area. For instance, the Count of the Saxon Shore had command of nine units in nine named forts. However, in the geographical region controlled by this command ten late Roman forts are known, of which Walton Castle is generally considered to be the one not named in the surviving text. Hassall (1977) has suggested that the Roman name for Walton may have been dropped from the list by accident, presumably during the late Roman period since there are only nine forts on the painted insignia (Pl. 2:3). The order of citation in this list may lend some support to this idea, for although the list does not run in a coherent geographical order, it would appear that the Saxon Shore forts were paired with their nearest neighbours (2:17 and Table 2:5). Walton Castle should have paired Bradwell at the head of the list.

The list of troops under the command of the *Dux Britanniarum* poses several problems since a number of places remain unidentified (2:16 and Table 2:6) and, conversely, a number of sites known to have been occupied in the late

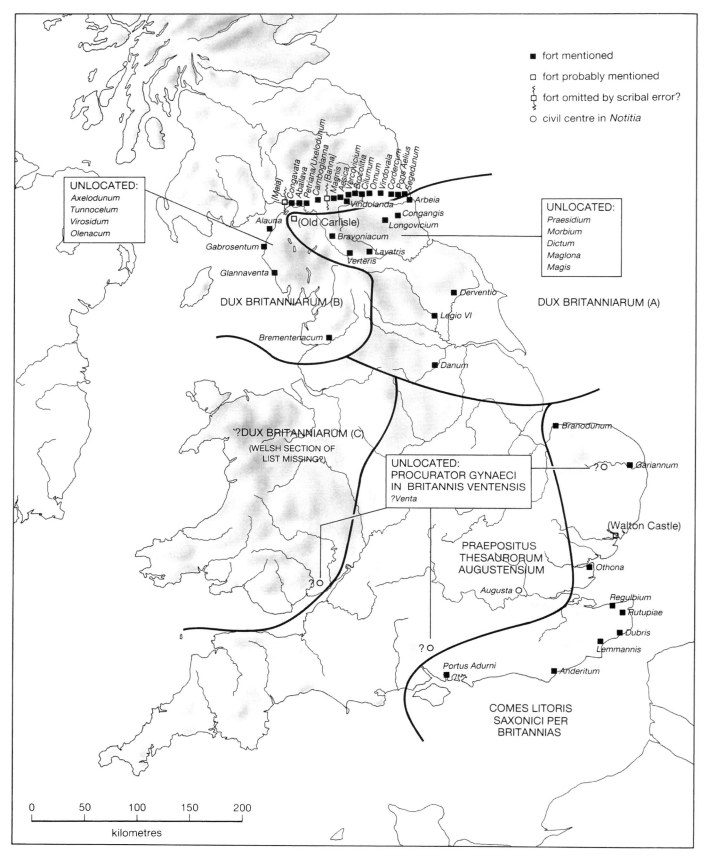

Map 2:16 Britain in the *Notitia Dignitatum*: places which can be identified

The following labels appear within the map:

- fort mentioned
- fort probably mentioned
- fort omitted by scribal error?
- civil centre in *Notitia*

UNLOCATED:
Axelodunum
Tunnocelum
Virosidum
Olenacum

UNLOCATED:
Praesidium
Morbium
Dictum
Maglona
Magis

(Maia)
Congavata
Aballava
Petriana/Uxelodunum
Camboglanna
[Banna]
Magnis
Aesica
Vercovicium
Brocolitia
Cilurnum
Onnum
Vindovala
Cordercm
Pqos Aelius
Segedunum
Vindolanda
Arbeia
Alauna
(Old Carlisle)
Congangis
Longovicium
Bravoniacum
Gabrosentum
Lavatris
Verteris
Glannaventa
Derventio

DUX BRITANNIARUM (B)

DUX BRITANNIARUM (A)

Legio VI

Bremetenacum

Danum

?DUX BRITANNIARUM (C)
(WELSH SECTION OF LIST MISSING?)

Branodunum

? O

Gariannum

UNLOCATED:
PROCURATOR GYNAECI IN BRITANNIS VENTENSIS
?Venta

(Walton Castle)

PRAEPOSITUS THESAURORUM AUGUSTENSIUM

Othona

Augusta O

Regulbium

Rutupiae

Dubris

Lemmannis

? O

Portus Adurni

Anderitum

COMES LITORIS SAXONICI PER BRITANNIAS

| 0 | 50 | 100 | 150 | 200 |

kilometres

Plate 2:3 Insignia of the *Comes Litoris Saxonici per Britanniam* from the *Notitia Dignitatum*, Ms. Canon. Misc. 378, folio 153[v]

Plate 2:4 Insignia of the *Vicarius Britanniarum* from the *Notitia Dignitatum*, Ms. Canon. Misc. 378, folio 150[v]

fourth century do not appear on it (cf. 4:70). This is most obvious for Wales, where an entire section of the list was either mislaid or deliberately dropped from the records.

Table 2.5 Places named in the list of the *Comes Litoris Saxonici*

	Site	
Number in list	Ancient name	Modern name
0	?	Walton Castle
1	*Othona*	Bradwell
2	*Dubris*	Dover
3	*Lemmannis*	Lympne
4	*Branodunum*	Brancaster
5	*Gariannum*	Burgh Castle
6	*Regulbium*	Reculver
7	*Rutupiae*	Richborough
8	*Anderitum*	Pevensey
9	*Portus Adurni*	Portchester

Once again the order of citation can help us to localize the sites which are not firmly identified (2:17 and Table 2:6). The first section (A) commences with York, base of the VI legion, and proceeds via Doncaster (unless there was another site called *Danum*) to South Shields on the Tyne. The three unlocated names in this early sector should, therefore, be located either in East Yorkshire or in the North-East. The next few names run in sequence, south from Chester-le-Street and then north-west up the Stainmore Pass to Kirkby Thore. Either *Maglone* or *Magis* could be Old Carlisle whose Roman name apparently began *Mag* (...). The former is perhaps more likely, leaving *Magis* to be assignable to a site between Old Carlisle and the next fort listed, Lanchester. The list then returns south to finish at Malton, near its starting point. Section A of the list, then, would appear to include many of the forts in the hinterland of Hadrian's Wall, along the major roads leading to the frontier and also some eastern coastal positions (South Shields, and so on).

The second section (B) is described in the document as a listing of the forts along the line of the wall (*per lineam valli*).

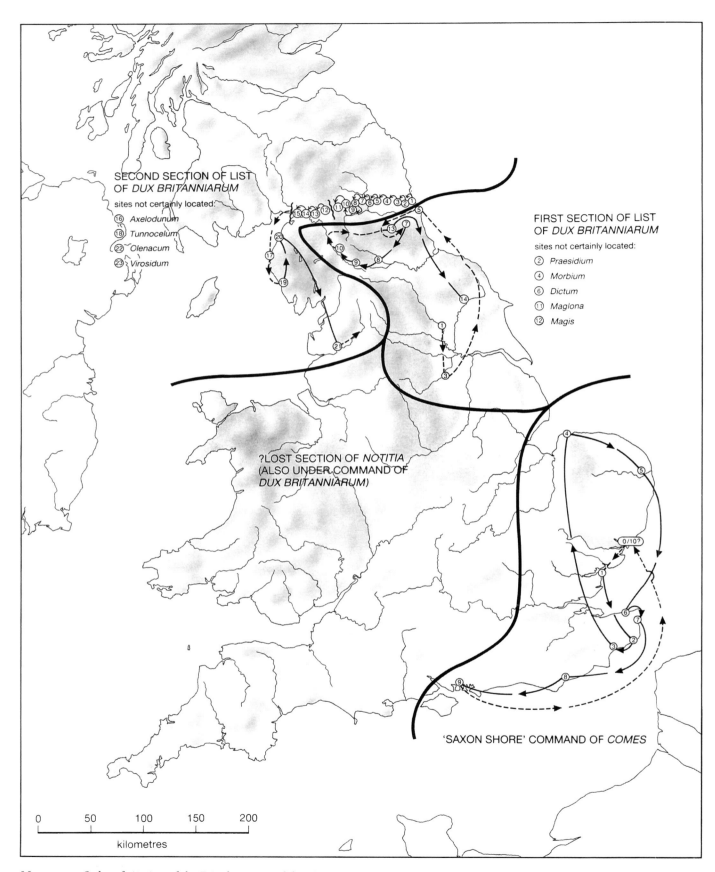

0   50   100   150   200

kilometres

Map 2:17   Order of citation of the British section of the *Notitia Dignitatum*

Table 2.6 Places named in the list of the *Dux Britanniarum* (Latin names 'corrected' according to Rivet and Smith)

Number in list	Site	
	Ancient name	Modern name
Section A		
1	*Legio VI*	York
2	*Praesidium*	?
3	*Danum*	Doncaster
4	*Morbium*	?
5	*Arbeia*	South Shields
6	*Dictum*	?
7	*Concangis*	Chester-le-Street
8	*Lavatris*	Bowes
9	*Verteris*	Brough
10	*Bravoniacum*	Kirkby Thore
11	*Maglona*	Old Carlisle or ?
12	*Magis*	? or Old Carlisle
13	*Longovicium*	Lanchester
14	*Derventio*	Malton
Section B	*Item per lineam valli*	
1	*Segedunum*	Wallsend
2	*Pons Aelius*	Newcastle
3	*Condercum*	Benwell
4	*Vindovala*	Rudchester
5	*Onnum*	Halton Chesters
6	*Cilurnum*	Chesters
7	*Brocolitia*	Carrawburgh
8	*Vercovicium*	Housesteads
9	*Vindolanda*	Chesterholm
10	*Aesica*	Great Chesters
11	*Magnis*	Carvoran
[—	*Banna*	Birdoswald]
12	*Camboglanna*	Castlesteads
13	*[Uxelodunum] Petriana*	Stanwix
14	*Aballava*	Burgh-by-Sands
15	*Congavata*	Drumburgh
[—	*Maia*	Bowness]
16	*Axeloduno*	?
17	*Gabrosentum*	(Moresby)
18	*Tunnocellum*	(?)
19	*Glannaventa*	(Ravenglass)
20	*Alauna*	Maryport
21	*Brementenacum*	Ribchester
22	*Olenacum*	(?)
23	*Virosido*	(?)

Section C [Lost or omitted entirely]

This is generally accurate for the first fifteen names, which are listed from east to west starting at Wallsend. The only anomalies are that Chesterholm (*Vindolanda*) is included, although it lies to the south of the wall, and that Birdoswald (*Banna*) and Bowness (*Mais*) are omitted from the list. These omissions can be explained as copying errors; it is inconceivable that these sites were not named. Stanwix is also described in the *Notitia* as *Petriana*, though it is now thought that this was a 'ghost' name, derived from that of the garrison unit (the *Ala Petriana*), and that its real name was *Uxelodunum*.

The rest of the names in Section B relate either to coastal forts or to inland sites in Lancashire and the Pennines, but the lack of certainly identified sites makes the identification of any coherence in the order of citation very problematical. *Axelodunum* and *Tunnocelum* probably lie on or close to the Cumbrian coast (though Rivet and Smith (1979) suggest that *Axelodumum* is a corrupt repetition of *Uxelodunum*, which had somehow replaced *Maia* in the entry for Bowness). *Olenacum* and *Virosidium* should lie in northern Lancashire or the extreme west of Yorkshire (Rivet and Smith suggest Elslack and Brough-by-Bainbridge).

Some of the problems alluded to above in relation to the listing of the Hadrian's Wall forts have been elucidated by reference to two Roman souvenirs from the Wall, the Rudge Cup and the Amiens *Patera* (2:18). These enamelled bronze vessels were evidently parts of drinking sets, decorated with representations of the Wall and the names of forts along it, and presumably manufactured by the army in northern Britain. Both the surviving examples named the westernmost forts of the Wall from west to east, with the Amiens *Patera* naming one more than the Rudge Cup (Table 2:7). As a result, Birdoswald and Bowness can be restored to the *Notitia* list and the name for Stanwix can be seen to have been *Uxelodunum*.

ROMANO-BRITISH PLACE NAMES

One of the most striking features of Romano-British place names is that the vast majority were entirely Celtic or British in origin (albeit with some Latinization of endings – see Rivet and Smith, 1979; Rivet, 1980). In fact, only about 50 of the known place names were wholly or partly Latin (2:19). Some of the hybrid or compound names simply involved a descriptive tag being attached to a British name (as, for example, *Portus Dubris* – the port of *Dubris*; *Aquae Sulis* – the springs of *Sulis* or *Camulodunum Colonia* – the colony of *Camulodunum*). Clearly in most of these cases it was probably the British element that was used as the abbreviated form in local parlance.

Amongst the purely Latin names, many were descriptive, such as those relating to bridges (*Pontibus, Ad Pontem, Pons Aelii, Tripontium*), or to salt production (*Salinae*), or to some prominent geographical feature. In the last category were *Trimontium*, the triple peak of the Eildon Hills, *Spinis*, meaning 'thorn bushes' and *Concavata*, describing the curving shoreline of Burgh Marsh and the Solway coast. Some of the military names were equally descriptive of function (*Horrea Classis*, 'granary of the fleet', or *Castra Exploratorum*, 'fort of the scouts').

This pattern of nomenclature reveals something very important about the character of the Roman occupation of

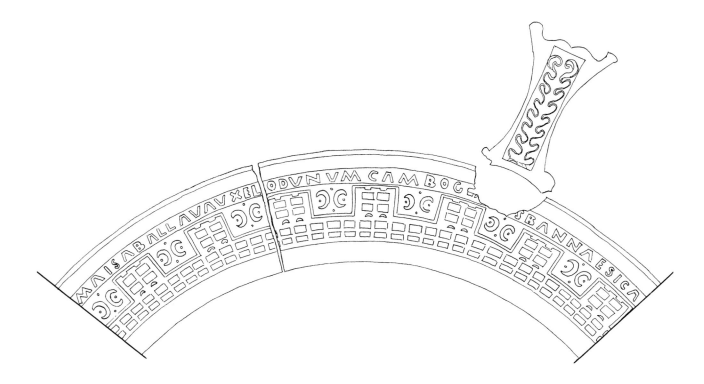

Map 2:18   A section of the *Amiens patera* containing the names of stations along the Wall

Table 2.7   Place names on Hadrian's Wall from various sources (the forms preferred by Rivet and Smith are given in brackets where they differ from the *Notitia Dignitatum* versions; the names for Birdoswald and Bowness were accidentally dropped from the *Notitia* list, but can be restored from the other sources)

Modern name	Notitia Dignitatum	Ravenna Cosmography	Rudge Cup	Amiens Patera	Other
South Shields[1]	Arbeia	—	—	—	—
Wallsend	Segeduno (Segedunum)	Serduno	—	—	—
Newcastle	Ponte Aeli (Pons Aelii/Aelius)	—	—	—	—
Benwell	Conderco (Condercum)	Condecor	—	—	—
Rudchester	Vindobala	Vindovala	—	—	—
Halton Chesters	Hunno (Onnum)	Onno	—	—	—
Chesters	Cilurno (Cilurnum)	Celuno	—	—	—
Carrawburgh	Procolitia (Brocolitia)	Brocoliti	—	—	—
Housesteads	Borcovicio (Vercovicium)	Velurtion	—	—	Ver(...)
Chesterholm[1]	Vindolanda	Vindolande	—	—	Vindolanda
Great Chesters	Aesica	Esica	—	Esica	—
Carvoran	Magnis	Magnis	—	—	Magn(c)es
Birdoswald	(Banna)	Banna	Banna	Banna	Banna
Castlesteads	Amboglanna (Camboglanna)	Gabaglanda/ Cambroianna	Camboglans	Cambog(lani)s	—
Stanwix	Petrianis (Uxelodunum)	Uxelludano	Uxelodum	Uxelodunum	—
Burgh-by-Sands	Aballaba (Aballava)	Avalana	Aballava	Aballava	Aballava
Drumburgh	Congavata (Concavata)	—	—	—	—
Bowness	(Maia/Maium)	Maia/Maio	Mais	Mais	—

[1]   slightly removed from line of Wall

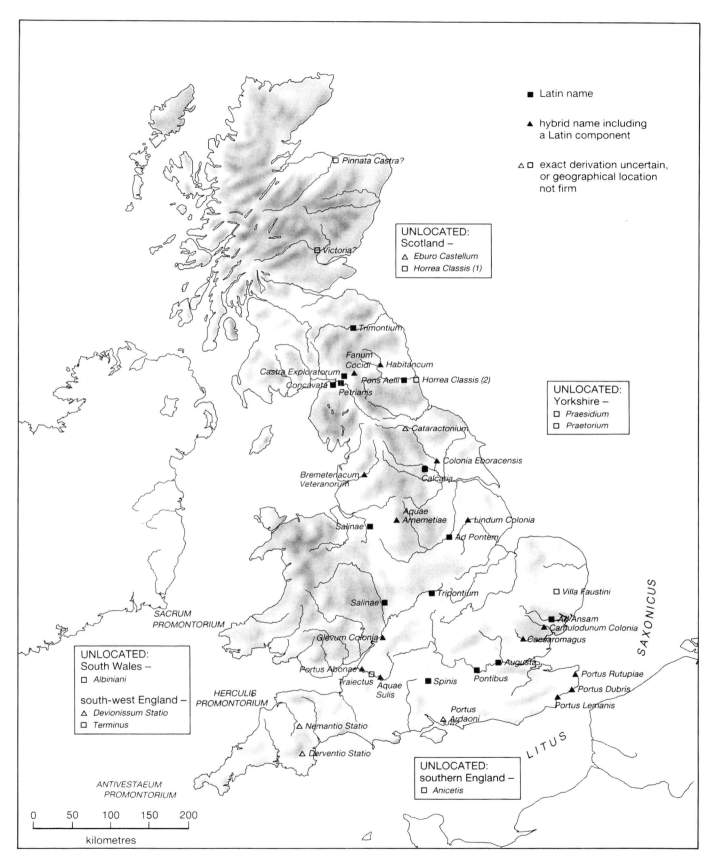

■ Latin name

▲ hybrid name including a Latin component

△ □ exact derivation uncertain, or geographical location not firm

□ Pinnata Castra?

□ Victoria?

UNLOCATED:
Scotland –
△ Eburo Castellum
□ Horrea Classis (1)

■ Trimontium

Fanum Cocidi ▲ Habitancum

Castra Exploratorum ■
Concavata ■■
Petrianis

Pons Aelii ■ □ Horrea Classis (2)

UNLOCATED:
Yorkshire –
□ Praesidium
□ Praetorium

△ Cataractonium

▲ Colonia Eboracensis

Bremetenacum ▲
Veteranorum

■ Calcaria

▲ Aquae
Arnemetiae

▲ Lindum Colonia

Salinae ■

■ Ad Pontem

■ Tripontium

□ Villa Faustini

Salinae ■

▲ Ad Ansam
▲ Camulodunum Colonia
▲ Caesaromagus

SACRUM
PROMONTORIUM

Glevum Colonia ▲

■ Augusta

▲ Portus Rutupiae

UNLOCATED:
South Wales –
□ Albiniani

Portus Abonae ▲
Traiectus □▲
Aquae
Sulis

■ Spinis

■ Pontibus

▲ Portus Dubris

▲ Portus Lemanis

south-west England –
△ Devionissum Statio
□ Terminus

HERCULIS
PROMONTORIUM

Portus
△ Ardaoni

LITUS

SAXONICUS

△ Nemantio Statio

△ Derventio Statio

ANTIVESTAEUM
PROMONTORIUM

UNLOCATED:
southern England –
□ Anicetis

0   50   100   150   200

kilometres

Map 2:19   Latin and hybrid place names

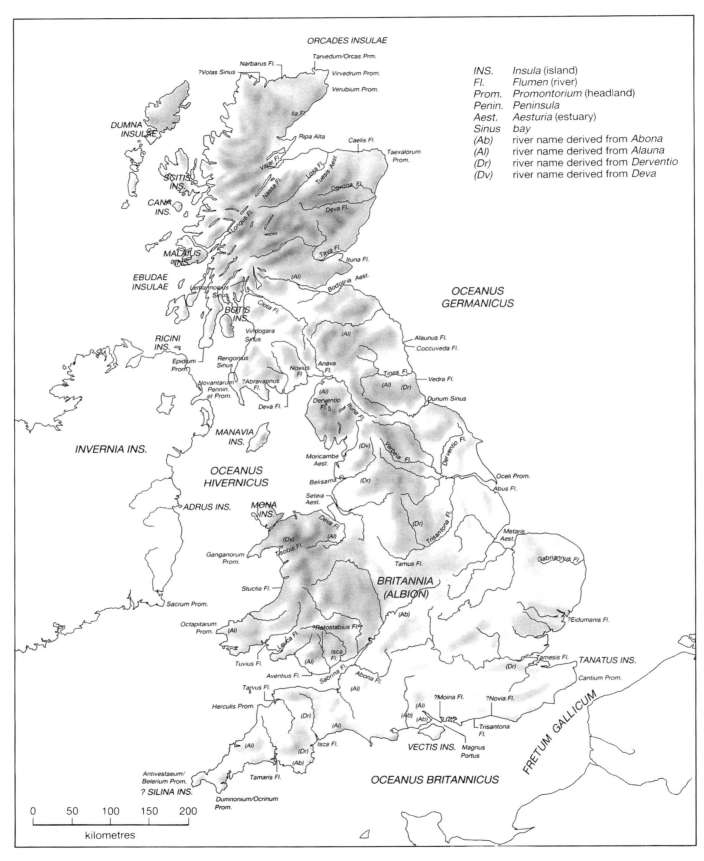

Map 2:20   Names of rivers and natural features

Britain. Plainly, the conquest did not involve the supplanting of the native Britons by hordes of Roman colonists, nor the imposition from above of a new system of place names. Latin became the language of bureaucracy, but the Celtic/British dialects remained as strong as before. Symptomatic of this is the fact that even most Roman forts were known by British rather than Latin names.

A similar picture emerges from a study of the names for rivers, islands and other coastal features (2:20). Once again most Latin usage was purely technical, providing the word for 'river', 'estuary', 'bay', 'island', 'peninsula' or 'promontory'. Only in rare cases were features such as promontories given totally Latin place names (*Herculis, Sacrum, Octapitarum*, for example), but these instances reflect the usage of sailors and navigators rather than that of the local populace. In some cases two names are known for the same feature, such as the pair of names for Land's End: *Antivestaeum* (Graeco-Roman) and *Belerium* (British).

The ascendancy of British names over Latin ones is demonstrated by the derivation of modern river names. Particularly in the north and west of the country, these often relate to pre-Roman British forms. The survival of so many Celtic names through the Roman, Saxon and more recent periods indicates the extreme conservatism of names for natural features.

Another interesting aspect of place name studies involves examining groups of names with a common stem (2:21). Names containing *Duro-/-durum* and *Dunum/-dunum* indicate fortified sites, with the former, in general, used for low-lying forts or fortified towns and the latter for hillforts. As

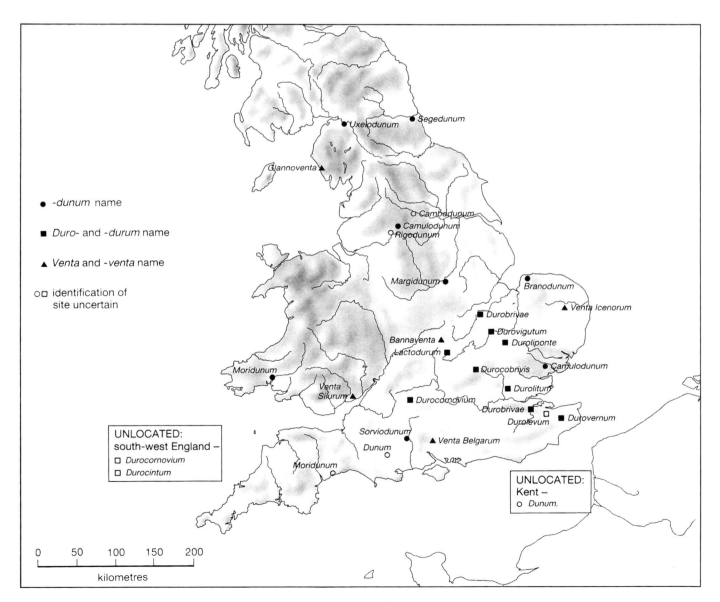

Map 2:21   Place names incorporating the elements *Durum*, *Dunum* and *Venta*

Rivet (1980) has pointed out, these Celtic names sometimes related to pre-Roman Iron Age fortifications (*Sorviodunum* (Old Sarum), *Camulodunum* (Colchester) and *Dunum* (?Hod Hill)). In some other cases, though, the evidence for a pre-Roman fortification is lacking and the name would appear to have been coined in relation to Roman military sites (for example, *Durobrivae* (Water Newton), 'the fort by the bridge', and *Branodunum*, the Saxon Shore fort at Brancaster which was not built before the third century AD). Here again we have spectacular evidence of the adoption of British place names in preference to Latin ones, even for newly founded or military sites.

The term *Venta* (or *-venta*) is presumed to denote a market centre of some sort, though its actual derivation is controversial; it was probably a Celtic rather than a Latin term. It is interesting that three of the tribal capitals established or recognized by Rome should have been called *Venta*, being distinguished only by the tribal prefix (*Venta Belgarum* (Winchester), *Venta Icenorum* (Caistor St Edmund), *Venta Silurum* (Caerwent)). Assuming that the sense was 'market field' or 'market centre', the name must indicate one of the vital functions of these towns, namely the regulation and development of regional economic activity. Two examples of compound names ending in *-venta* should indicate other market centres, though presumably at a lower level in a hierarchical organization of markets. *Bannaventa* was a 'small town' at Whilton Lodge on Watling Street, whilst *Glannoventa* was a Roman fort and associated *vicus* or civilian settlement on the Cumbrian coast at Ravenglass.

Rivet and Smith's exemplary study (1979) of the derivation of Romano-British place names will remain the standard work of reference on this subject for many years to come. Their recognition of the overwhelming bias towards native British place names reinforces the impression given at the start of this chapter, namely that the geographical remoteness of Britain and its unique character distinguished it from other areas of the Roman Empire.

3
Britain before the Conquest

TRIBAL SOCIETY

Written sources for Iron Age Britain are very meagre and usually uninformative, and much more emphasis has to be placed on archaeological evidence in general, and artefact evidence in particular, when attempting to reconstruct the tribal societies which existed then. Naturally this allows for many differences in interpretation between modern scholars*. Even Julius Caesar's account of his campaigns in Britain in 55 and 54 BC provides only tantalizing and perhaps misleading glimpses of the social and geographical organization of his opponents. Caesar had little interest in, or knowledge of, the long-drawn-out development of late Iron Age society and his personal experience of Britain was limited to the south-east of the country (cf. 3:1, 4:1, 4:2). Although traders from the Continent had been reaching a wide area of southern Britain for many years (3:15–3:17), much of Britain was still entirely unknown (*terra incognita*).

When Caesar wrote of there being two principal zones in Britain (a 'civilized', agricultural, maritime part and a more barbaric, pastoral, interior region) he was not describing the effects of a highland/lowland division, as has sometimes been argued. The *maritima pars* was Kent and the *interior pars* was the area immediately north of the Thames. Moreover, his conceptual framework of 'barbarian' peoples being less civilized the further away they were from the coast, or from Rome, is a recurrent and conventional theme in Roman literature. In fact Caesar's account of the British response to the crisis which his invasion posed reveals the falsity of his over-generalized model. Cassivellaunos, who was chosen as the war leader of the temporary and uneasy alliance of normally antipathetic tribes, was tribal chief of a powerful people north of the Thames. This would seem to contradict the assertion that these people were less developed than those of *Cantium* (Kent). Political authority in the latter area was rather fragmented in normal conditions, since four kings are mentioned as ruling in *Cantium*. The six other tribal names referred to by Caesar presumably related to tribal groups north of the Thames. These included the Cassi (perhaps Cassivellaunos' own tribe), the Trinovantes of Essex and the Cenimagi (perhaps the Iceni known later in Norfolk).

* Changing trends in Iron Age studies are reflected by the very different preoccupations of four major conferences which have taken place during the last 30 years: Frere, 1960; Hill and Jesson, 1971; Cunliffe and Rowley, 1976; Cunliffe and Miles, 1984.

Although Caesar saw similarities between these tribes and those of northern France, there were clearly some unique British traits, such as the use of woad and the continued employment of the chariot in warfare.

Overall, the picture derived from Caesar is very different from that revealed by later sources dealing with tribal society in the first century AD (3:2). The major change, of course, was that the Claudian invasion in AD 43 and its aftermath extended Roman knowledge of the British tribes to include the whole island. Yet even in the south-east, major changes had occurred in the century which separated the two invasions. Many of the small tribes named by Caesar had been absorbed or perhaps wiped out in the recurrent warfare between the British tribes. Tribal leadership had become more consolidated, with many groups ruled by kings. The increased political authority of late Iron Age rulers is also reflected in the large tribal groupings or confederations which came into being, though each no doubt comprised numerous sub-tribes.

The most potent military force still lay north of the Thames and in the first half of the first century AD consisted of a fusion of the Catuvellaunian and Trinovantian tribes under a sole authority. The attempts by Catuvellaunian/Trinovantian kings and princes to extend their power and influence over their neighbours was a major destabilizing factor in tribal politics and provided the Roman pretext for the Claudian invasion. In particular, the Cantiaci were perhaps subject to their suzerainty in the first century AD and other neighbours were periodically under threat.

The chief opponent of the Catuvellauni/Trinovantes was the Atrebatic confederation (centred on Surrey, Sussex and Hampshire). The Atrebates were also ruled by kings, as were the Iceni of Norfolk and perhaps the Dobunni of Gloucestershire and Warwickshire (though the latter were evidently split into two factions under separate rulers). The political structure of the Corieltauvi (this name is now preferred to the form Coritani) of Leicestershire and Lincolnshire is less certain since their coins appear to name pairs of rulers. It has even been suggested that some form of magisterial government operated. Little is known of the political organization of the Durotriges of Dorset, though the number of occupied hillforts implies a continued, strong, sub-tribal organization within a confederation. Similar comments might apply to the confederations of the south-west (Dumnonii) and of Wales (Cornovii, Demetae, Ordovices and the

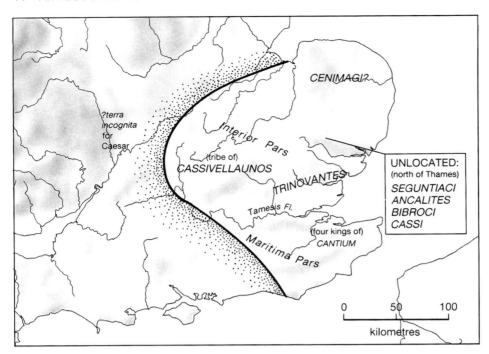

Map 3:1　The tribal situation in Britain as revealed by Caesar

Silures). The Deceangli were possibly one of the sub-tribes of the Ordovices.

Northern England was covered by the great, but rather loose, confederation of the Brigantes. In the early years after the conquest Brigantia was ruled by a queen, but the existence of disparate elements and many sub-tribes brought challenges to her authority. Two sub-tribes are known for certain – the Parisi of south-east Yorkshire and the Carvetii of Cumbria, although the latter were not recognized as a separate semi-autonomous body (*civitas*) until the third century AD.

The tribes of Scotland fell into three broad groups. Firstly, there were the tribes of the Scottish Lowlands, the Votadini, the Selgovae, the Novantae and probably the Dumnonii (whose territory spanned the Forth–Clyde isthmus). The second and third groups were the tribes to the north of the isthmus. The latter two were probably considered as Caledonii by the Romans, but can be divided into two broad groupings. The first of these, being the most important from a Roman military point of view, were the tribes of Moray, Aberdeenshire and Strathmore, the Vacomagi, the Boresti, the Taexali and the Venicones. The remaining group of tribes of the remote highlands and the northern and western seaboard were less intimately known, most information deriving from the fact-finding activities of the Roman fleet.

Had a Roman ever written a detailed account of the tribal geography of Britain in the first century AD it would probably have included the standard comments about declining levels of civilization as one progressed westwards or northwards in the island. The judgement is of course a subjective one

since 'civilization' was what Rome knew or recognized as such. The differences between the south-east and the north and west were not determined by the differences in environment along the lines of a highland/lowland division as discussed in Chapter 1. South-east Britain had become 'civilized' because of its proximity to the Continent, where there were radical developments taking place in the late Iron Age. The tribes of the north and west lagged behind because they were further away from the Continent.

Traditionally, Iron Age studies in Britain have postulated a series of invasions or migrations from the Continent in order to account for significant developments in Britain and as a means of explaining similarities in material culture between the two regions. These ideas are currently being re-evaluated, with mass migration now considered unlikely. Smaller-scale infiltration by a Gallic elite (and their absorption into the British tribal leadership) or trade contacts are possible alternative explanations for the similarities between the regions. The reality may have lain between the extremes of mass movement of people and simple movement of goods. The essential point to arise out of the reappraisal, though, is that the 'Belgic' culture of the southern British tribes was by no means uniform, nor was it identical with that of northern Gaul. Contact between the regions led to development in southern Britain which was imitative of Continental Iron Age civilization. This included urbanization, the use of coinage, and certain forms of tribal organization. However, the effects were uneven and the purely British element of many tribes remained paramount. The area covered by the Cantiaci, Atrebates, Catuvellauni and Trinovantes was the

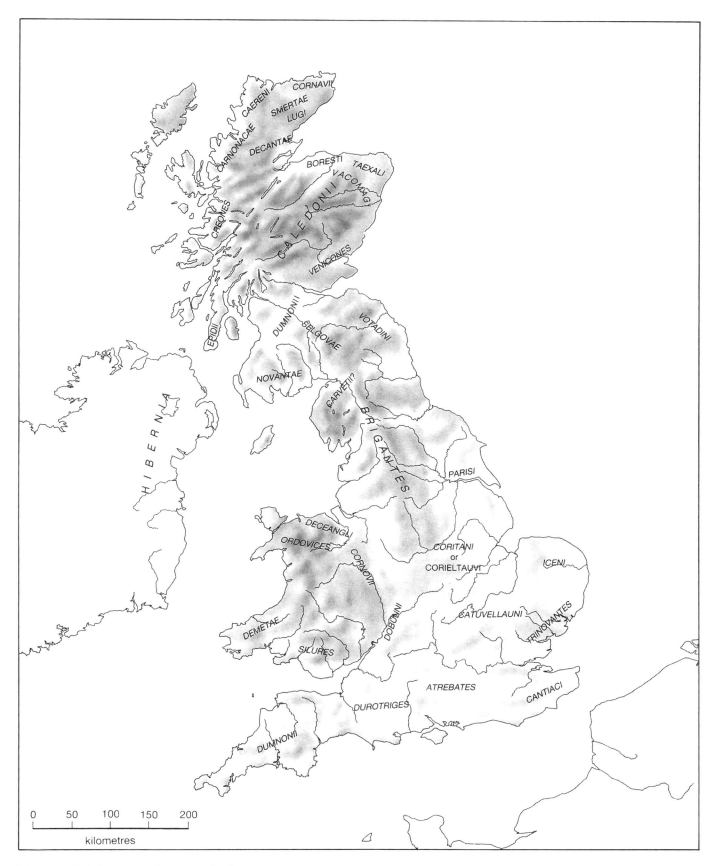

CORNAVII
CAERENI
SMERTAE
LUGI
CARNONACAE
DECANTAE
CREONES
BORESTI
TAEXALI
VACOMAG
C A L E D O N I I
VENICONES
EPIDII
DUMNONII
SELGOVAE
VOTADINI
NOVANTAE
CARVETII?
B R I G A N T E S
PARISI
H I B E R N I A
DECEANGLI
ORDOVICES
CORNOVII
CORITANI
or
CORIELTAUVI
ICENI
DEMETAE
SILURES
DOBUNNI
CATUVELLAUNI
TRINOVANTES
ATREBATES
CANTIACI
DUROTRIGES
DUMNONII

0   50   100   150   200
kilometres

Map 3:2   Tribal society in Britain in the first century AD

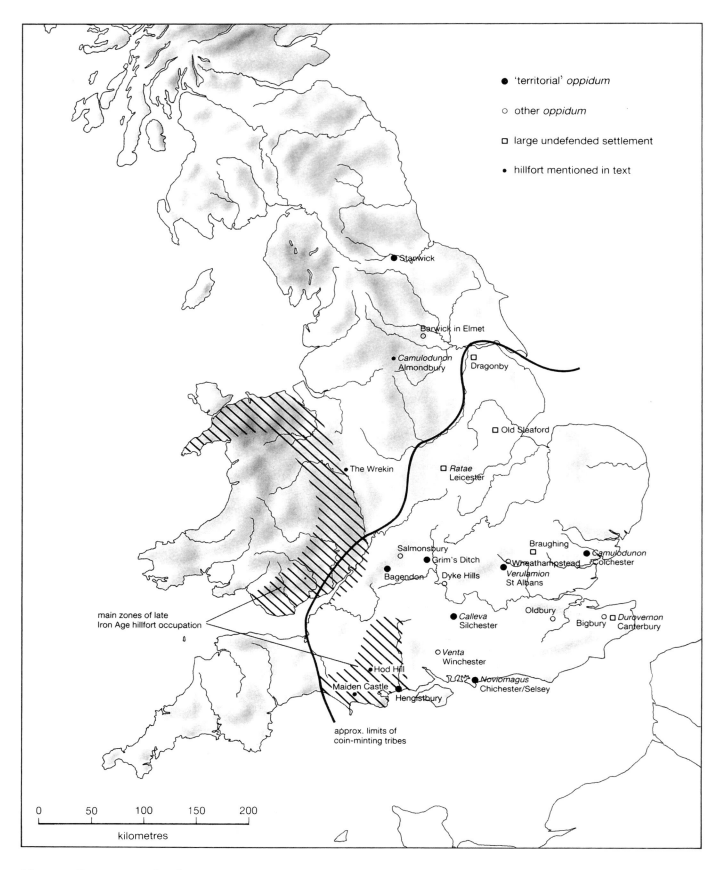

Map 3:3 Progress towards urbanization in late Iron Age Britain: the exact dating of some sites remains uncertain.

most affected by Continental ideas and objects, with the Durotriges, Dobunni, Corieltauvi and Iceni forming a secondary zone of lesser influence. To the north and west of those tribes, the diffusion of the radical, late Iron Age Continental developments was very limited. Yet the tribal society of this zone should not be regarded as inherently inferior. The 'progress' which can be detected in the culture of the south-eastern tribes may have had its drawbacks for the population. We can only speculate, but there may have been violent seizures of power and increased demands by a central authority on peasant producers.

URBANIZATION

Through a combination of warfare and leadership by ambitious elites or individuals, tribal society came to rest on larger and larger units. The political, military and economic organization of such confederations posed considerable problems for the old forms of social management. In areas of the country where there had once been hundreds of minor hillforts, there was a tendency for occupation to concentrate in a handful of large hillforts, some of which were newly constructed. Excavations at a number of hillforts have indicated that their internal planning and apparent functions were becoming more complex. Trade, industry, the use of coinage, and centralized granaries existed at many late hillforts, which also maintained their more obvious connections with military, political and religious affairs. All of this is evidence of what might be described as proto-urbanization (3:3). In at least two cases (Maiden Castle and

The Wrekin), hillforts were to be replaced under Roman rule by tribal towns situated close by.

The processes of urbanization are even more dramatically apparent in areas where hillfort occupation had declined virtually to the point of non-existence by the end of the first century BC. In these areas new types of tribal centre appeared, notably on low-lying sites. Some settlements were open, others defended (the latter being normally referred to as *oppida*). Some of the *oppida* enclosed vast areas of ground within massive systems of dykes and are sometimes referred to as 'territorial' *oppida*. A particularly notable example is *Camulodunon* (Colchester), capital of the Trinovantes and later of their federation with the Catuvellauni (3:4–3:5). It is instructive to compare the large size of the Colchester *oppidum* with both the well-known but far smaller Iron Age hillforts of Maiden Castle and Hod Hill and the size of the Roman town (*colonia*) later established on a small part of the site (3:4).

Although Iron Age finds occur sporadically across most of the 32.5sq km (12.5sq miles) enclosed, it is clear that the vast area of the Colchester *oppidum* was by no means densely built-up. There were a few centres of greater settlement concentration, notably at Sheepen and Gosbecks (around which the dyke systems made a noticeable deviation), whilst Lexden seems to have been a major cemetery area. At Sheepen, excavations have uncovered a 'village' of circular huts, in association with evidence of industrial activity, mint debris and exotic imports from the Roman world. At Gosbecks (3:5) lay a major religious complex, centring on a sacred enclosure (*temenos*). The site was of such great importance that it was maintained in the Roman period with a substantial temple and a theatre complex. It has been

Plate 3:1 Almondbury near Huddersfield, west Yorkshire, is a major late prehistoric hillfort that was thought to have served as a tribal centre for part of the Brigantian confederacy.

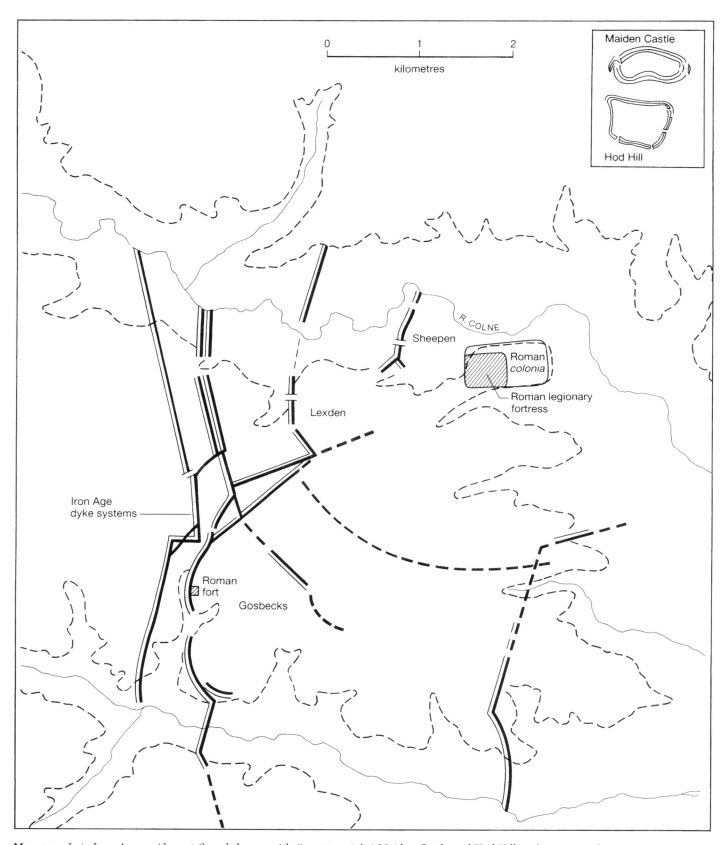

Map 3:4 Late Iron Age *oppidum* at *Camulodunum* with (inset top right) Maiden Castle and Hod Hill at the same scale

Maiden Castle

Hod Hill

kilometres

R. COLNE

Sheepen

Roman *colonia*

Roman legionary fortress

Lexden

Iron Age dyke systems

Roman fort

Gosbecks

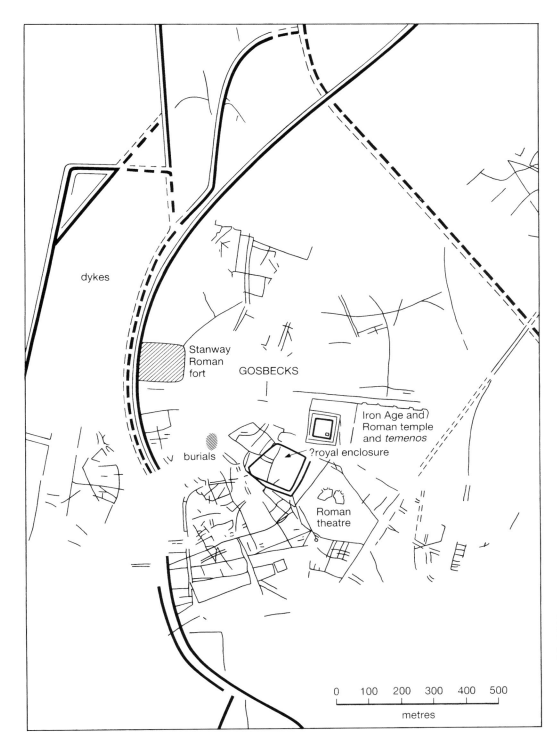

Map 3:5 The Gosbecks area of Iron Age and Roman *Camulodunum* (cf. Map 3:4) showing the Iron Age/Roman temple and possible royal compound. Much of the information is derived from aerial photographs with features of various periods shown superimposed.

suggested that periodic fairs or markets may have been held there in connection with religious festivals and this could well mark the continuation of an Iron Age tradition. Immediately adjacent to the temple compound lay a large well-defended compound which, it has been suggested, might have been the royal seat within the site.

The dispersed settlement and empty spaces within the *oppidum* were unlike later town sites, but the site possessed other characteristics which were certainly 'urban'. That it was the central administrative, religious and military focus of the region cannot be doubted; the evidence of industrial activity, the operation of a mint and markets there, and the existence of trade contacts with the wider world outside Britain are clear indications of the beginnings of urbanization. The development of this type of tribal centre was particularly a feature of the Catuvellauni/Trinovantes alliance and of their rivals, the Atrebates, although the Dobunni and the Brigantes also provide examples of 'territorial' *oppida*. By contrast, the known settlements of the Corieltauvi have revealed little in the way of defences as yet (though the name of Leicester, *Ratae* – meaning 'ramparts' – might have related to unlocated Iron Age defences rather than the Roman fort known to have been established there).

COINAGE

Coinage was another late Iron Age innovation and clearly followed on from Gallic precedents. The earliest Gallic coinage had used a gold stater of Philip of Macedon as the exemplar, and the atrophied horses on many Romano-British coins were the linear descendants of the team which drew the chariot on the reverse of Philip's coin. Initially, coins were imported, but during the first century BC British variants began to be produced by a number of tribes or individuals. Most coins were high value gold or silver issues, indicating that the primary motivation was not to foster a small-change, market economy. Rather, they reflect the increasing complexities of government, social prestige and near-endemic warfare. Coins were needed by the tribal leaders to make certain standard payments – perhaps, for instance, to allies or to mercenaries. They could also have been used to guarantee the purity and weight of tribute and taxation, and for reasons of self-advertisement and prestige.

The distribution of coins of a particular type can indicate the general zone of circulation and in some cases can help us to define tribal limits in rough terms. The use of coins was restricted to south-east Britain (3:3) and thus the evidence applies only to a small number of the British tribes. The distribution of known mint sites gives a far from complete picture (3:6). However, it is worth noting that not all the sites where mint-debris (in the form of moulds for the casting of coin 'blanks') has been found went on to become major Romano-British towns (though this is true of Canterbury, Colchester, Silchester, St Albans and Winchester). We must be careful, then, not to confuse the later, simplified pattern of tribal organization, which was imposed by Rome, with the earlier complexity of late Iron Age political units (see below, 5:12).

One reason why we might expect coins to be produced in a variety of different centres within a single tribal area is connected with the disturbed conditions of the late first century BC. During the last quarter of the century, some individual rulers started putting their names on their coins. This practice, it can be argued, had more to do with competition than stability, and rival dynasts seem to have operated for a while in opposition to each other in some districts. A good example is Dubnovellaunos (perhaps of the Trinovantes), who issued two distinct series of coins, first in Essex and then in Kent, before his period of control was ended (3:7).

The coins of the Atrebatic princes Tincommius and Verica illustrate the vulnerability of territory and kingship at this time. Their father Commius had been a Gallic refugee from Caesar and was the first British ruler to put his name on his coins. Tincommius succeeded to his rule over the Atrebates south of the Thames, but pressure from the Catuvellauni seems to have led to the loss of the northern part of his lands centred on Silchester. He was eventually replaced by his brother Verica, whose coinage shows a more southerly distribution. Verica was in his turn ousted as a result of Catuvellaunian pressure, an event which provoked the Claudian invasion in his support. It is notable that all three of the rulers mentioned up to now were driven out by rivals and ended up as suppliants at the Imperial court in Rome – a clear indication that Rome took a detailed interest in the dynastic rivalries and presumably encouraged them.

As already mentioned, the most aggressive and most successful of the expansionist tribal rulers were those of the Catuvellauni and Trinovantes, particularly once these tribes became federated and acted in concert. The sheer volume of gold and silver coinage assigned to a series of these dynasts (and would-be dynasts) gives an impression of their considerable wealth and influence in the period c.15 BC–AD 43 (3:8). The apogee of Catuvellaunian/Trinovantian power was reached under the rule of King Cunobelinus (3:9). He issued coins in great numbers from both *Camulodunon* and *Verulamion* and their distribution suggests expansion into Kent and to the west towards the territory of the Dobunni (though some would argue that the circulation of the coins could also reflect, for instance, trade or payments to mercenaries from these areas).

The distributions of the later coin issues of the tribes to the north and west of the Catuvellauni and the Trinovantes are no less instructive (3:10, 3:11). The number of hoards of Icenian coins in East Anglia is testimony to the effects of the Boudican revolt as well as to the likely extent of their tribal territory. The coinage of the Dobunni seems surprisingly widespread and indicates that the tribe covered not only Gloucestershire but also the Avon valley in Warwickshire, parts of Hereford and Worcester, western Oxfordshire, western Wiltshire and parts of Somerset. One interesting point to emerge from this coin distribution is that Bath, which was assigned to the Belgae by Ptolemy, plainly lay in Dobunnic territory. A further complication is the fact that at the time of the Claudian invasion, the Dobunni appear to have been divided into two factions. The two other coin-producing tribes were the Durotriges and the Corieltauvi (3:11). The Durotrigian heartlands in Dorset are clearly defined in spite of the wider distribution of individual coins. A distortion in the Corieltauvian distribution is caused by the presence of some hoards found in Brigantian territory – perhaps deposited by refugees fleeing north-west away

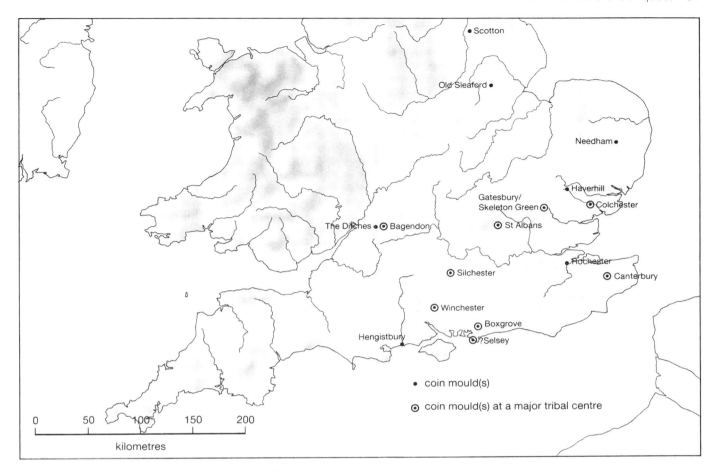

Map 3:6   Iron Age mints and findspots of coin moulds

from the tribal heartlands. An interesting point about these four tribes is that they apparently continued to issue coinage for some years after the Roman conquest.

The cumulative evidence derived from the detailed coin distribution maps is presented on Map 3:12. Tribal boundaries are impossible to pin down exactly on coin evidence alone though on a regional basis more refined analysis of the data is possible. In any case, boundaries will have fluctuated as military fortunes rose and fell. One possible pointer towards a more exact location of a boundary is the White Horse at Uffington on the Ridgeway in south Oxfordshire. The horse has stylistic parallels with the horses on the coins of both the Dobunni and the Atrebates and the hill-carving may have been a visual signal by one tribe or the other that they controlled the Ridgeway and the hillfort of Uffington Castle. The coin evidence supports the view that this was the position of a territorial boundary.

It is apparent that, as Catuvellaunian/Trinovantian power reached its height towards AD 40, the political anarchy which Rome had fostered in Britain for her own interests

was being resolved in favour of the largest grouping. Roman intervention in AD 43 was not entirely based on a hollow pretext; it was also a response to failed diplomacy.

Plate 3:2   Atrebates, gold coin of Verica (Mack 121). He is styled king (*REX*), son of Commius (*COM.F.*). The detail of the horse and rider and the use of Latin lettering mark this out as a late and superior issue of pre-Roman Britain.

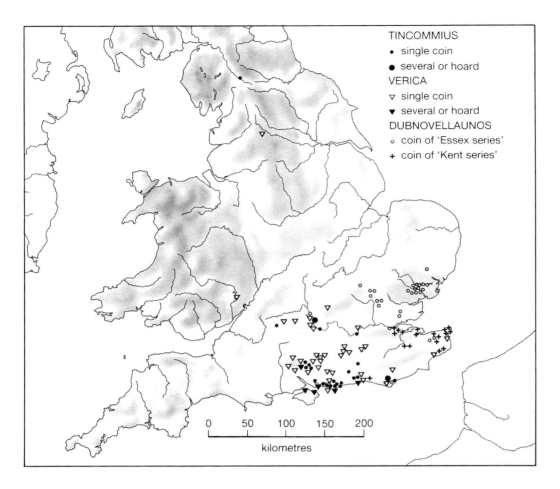

0   50   100   150   200

kilometres

Map 3:7   Distribution of coins of three kings: Tincommius, Verica and Dubnovellaunos

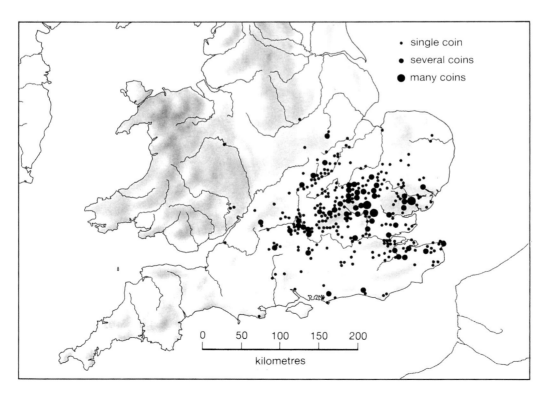

•   single coin
●   several coins
●   many coins

0   50   100   150   200

kilometres

Map 3:8   Generalized distribution of coins of the expansionist Catuvellaunian/Trinovantian rulers: Tasciovarus, Addedomarus, Dubnovellaunos, Cunobelinus and Epaticcus

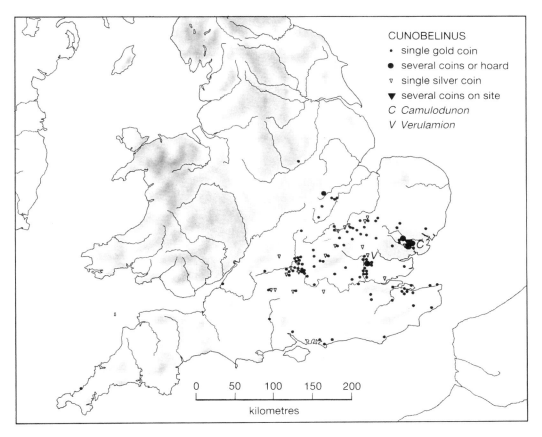

Map 3:9 Distribution of gold and silver coins of King Cunobelinus

CUNOBELINUS
- • single gold coin
- ● several coins or hoard
- ▽ single silver coin
- ▼ several coins on site
- C *Camulodunon*
- V *Verulamion*

Plate 3:3 Atrebates, gold coin of Commius (Mack 92). The designs are highly abstract but recognizable as derivations from a Macedonian coin-type depicting the head of Apollo and a two-horse chariot. These types were widely imitated in Celtic coinage as can be seen in Pls 3:4–3:8.

Plate 3:4 Gold coin of Cunobelinus with the Colchester mint mark *CAMU[LODUNUM]* (Mack 208). Note the ear of barley used as a symbol here.

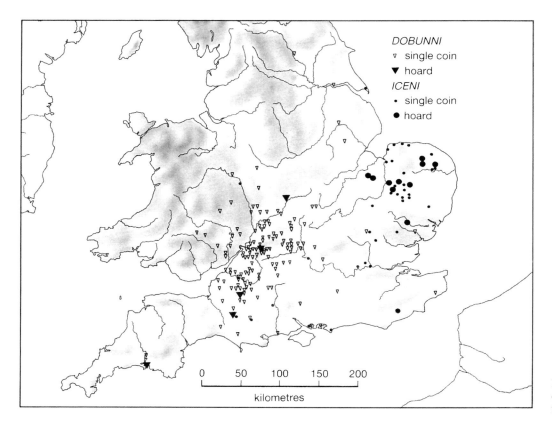

Map 3:10 Distribution of coins of the Dobunni and Iceni tribal group

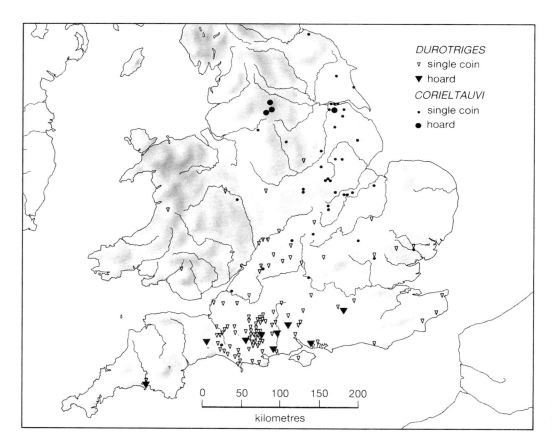

Map 3:11 Distribution of coins of the Durotriges and Corieltauvi tribal groups

Plate 3:5   Dobunni, silver coin (Mack 376)

Plate 3:6   Iceni, silver coin (Mack 413d)

Plate 3:7   Corieltauvi, silver coin (Mack 405a). Note the wild boar-type on the obverse.

Plate 3:8   Corieltauvi, gold coin inscribed *VOLISIOS/[D]UMNOCOVE[RUS]* (Mack 463)

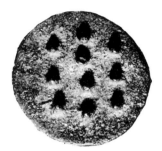

Plate 3:9   Durotriges, cast bronze coin (Mack 345)

Map 3:12   (*below*) Approximate limits of the coin-producing tribal groups in Britain (hatching indicates areas where possession may have switched or been disputed).

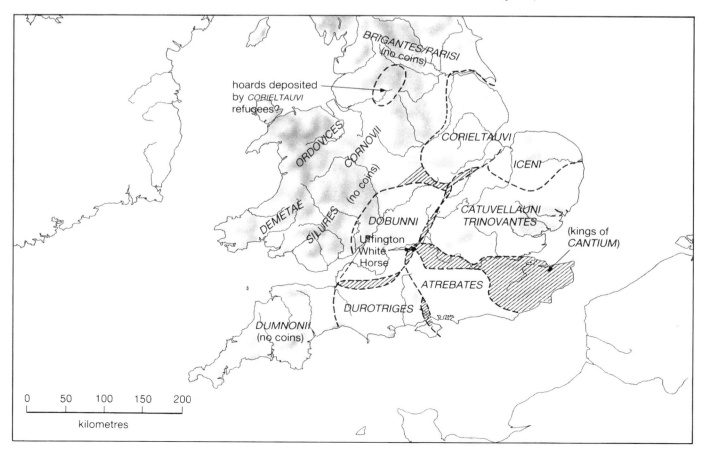

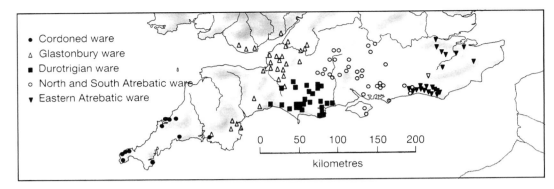

Map 3:13 Late Iron Age pottery styles in southern Britain

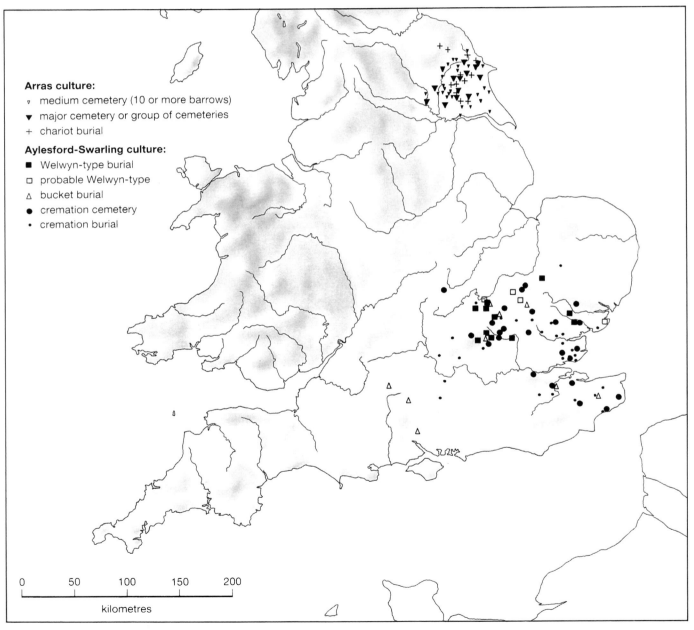

Map 3:14 Two regionalized burial cults: the Arras and Aylesford-Swarling cultures

MATERIAL CULTURE

Apart from coinage, there is a wealth of other evidence for the material culture of the Iron Age people of Britain. Some of it may illustrate the regional differences between the various tribes or sub-tribal groups, whilst in general supporting the broad divisions proposed above (3:13). Regional burial cults can also be informative about tribal limits, as is particularly clear in the case of the Aylesford–Swarling culture of southern Britain (3:14). Finds associated with this cultural division are concentrated in the areas which have been assigned on other grounds to the Trinovantes and Catuvellauni. Similarly the distribution of the Arras culture cemeteries – including some spectacular chariot burials – serves well to demarcate the probable extent of the non-coin-producing Parisi, a part of the Brigantian confederation. Unfortunately the value of this type of information is limited because of a dearth of information on burial practices in many other regions of Iron Age Britain. However, as more information becomes available, it may be possible to identify more inter-tribal distinctions.

TRADE

Trade between Britain and Continental Europe was not something which the Romans needed to initiate when they first came into contact with the island. Trade had been going across the Channel between Gauls and Britons throughout the Iron Age, though with an increasing range and volume of goods as time went on. The bulk of the trade had been with Brittany, Normandy and the Pas de Calais, but there had also been trade with the Mediterranean countries. Exotic imports from the Mediterranean found their way to Britain through the great river valleys of Gaul, notably via the Loire, Seine and later the Rhine – all these goods having come up the Rhône. Some traffic had also followed the Atlantic route up the Spanish coast in search of Cornish tin (3:15).

The Roman conquest of Gaul was to have a significant impact on the pattern of cross-Channel trade. In the early first century BC the main area of trade contact was between Brittany and south-west Britain, with secondary zones developing between northern France and southern and eastern England (3:15). The find spots of Armorican coins in Britain serve to illustrate the point, with major concentrations at the entrepôts of Mount Batten and Hengistbury and the majority of other finds near coastal locations in the south and west of Britain (3:16). Caesar entirely disrupted this trade pattern through his harsh punitive action against the Armorican tribes of north-west France, notably the Veneti, and thereafter trade concentrated on the region between the Seine valley and Calais in France and south-eastern England. By the first century AD, the trade route from the Mediterranean countries to the Roman armies on the Rhine was coming into full operation and goods were arriving at the Channel coast by this and a number of the other, longer-established routes. As a result of the political situation in Britain most of the goods were attracted towards the lands controlled by the Atrebates or Catuvellauni/Trinovantes – whence some were redistributed to the north and west.

The British tribal elites were encouraged to indulge in Roman tastes such as the consumption of Italian wines. Finds of certain types of wine jars (amphorae) are helpful in defining the extent of this trade (3:17). The earliest type (Dressel form IA) is found mainly in the region of Hengistbury Head, the principal Iron Age entrepôt facing Brittany, and relates in the main to the pre-Caesarian trade. The later form (Dressel IB) dates to the late first century BC and early first century AD and its distribution is further confirmation of the dominant role played by the Catuvellauni/Trinovantes federation.

It must be remembered that trade was not all one way. In exchange for its Continental imports, Iron Age Britain exported a wide range of goods including agricultural produce, minerals, slaves, hunting dogs and many other items which leave little trace archaeologically. Knowledge of the trade pattern between Britain and the Continent and some assessment of Britain's potential economic worth were inevitably factors in Rome's evaluation of the merits of reinvasion in the period between Caesar's campaign and the Claudian conquest. Augustus clearly thought that an invasion was not economically viable, but in AD 43 opinion may have valued Britain more highly.

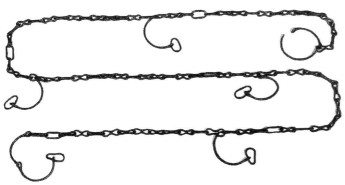

Plate 3:10   Slave chains found at the hillfort of Bigbury, near Canterbury, Kent

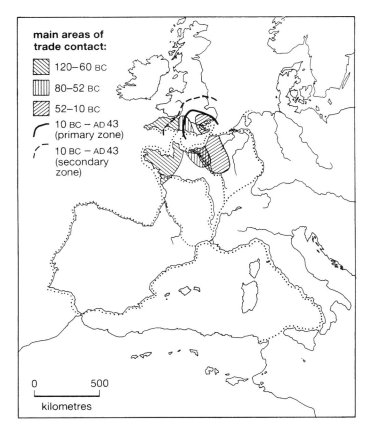

Map 3:15 Trade contact between Britain and the Roman Empire in the period up to AD 43 (dotted lines indicate main sea or river routes).

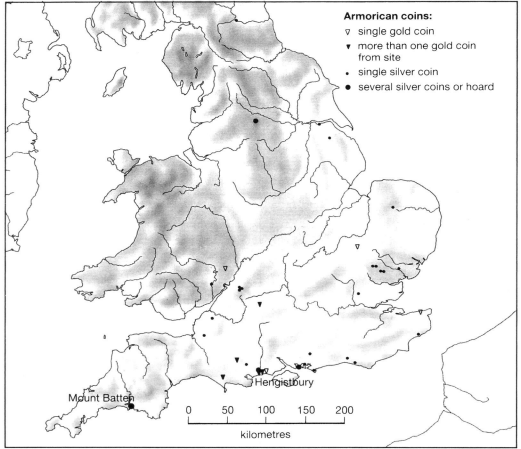

Armorican coins:

∇   single gold coin

▼   more than one gold coin
    from site

·   single silver coin

●   several silver coins or hoard

Hengistbury

Mount Batten

0   50   100   150   200
kilometres

Map 3:16 Distribution of Armorican gold and silver coins in Britain

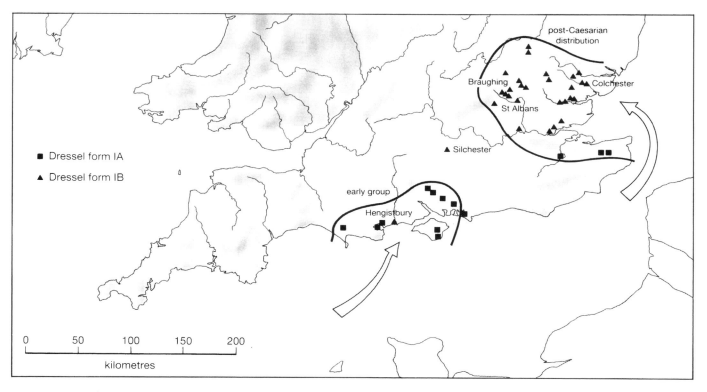

Map 3:17 Distribution of Dressel type amphorae forms 1A and 1B in late Iron Age Britain

IRON AGE SETTLEMENT IN WALES

Although the Iron Age peoples of Wales and Scotland offered the toughest resistance to the Roman conquest and might therefore be expected to feature at length in descriptions of the invasion period, we know far less about their society and culture than about the lowland peoples described above. This is partly a reflection on modern archaeology which has tended to concentrate on the peoples of south-east England. In part, though, it also reflects the problems posed by the limited availability of dating evidence in the fringe areas of Britain (for instance, pottery was unknown in most of Wales in the late Iron Age).

The Welsh landscape is dominated by mountains, great and small, and, not surprisingly, the harshest terrain was sparsely inhabited. Settlement was much denser wherever good farmland existed, particularly in the Welsh Marches (modern Shropshire, and western Hereford and Worcester), in enclaves in the south-east and south-west (Dyfed and the Glamorgan–Gwent plain), and in limited parts of the north-west and north-east (Gwynedd and Clwyd). The settlement pattern was dominated by hillforts right through the century before the Roman conquest and it is thought that the number of hillforts in occupation may have peaked during this period (though it should be noted that many of the sites shown in Map 3:18 have not been dated accurately). The largest hillforts were those built in the Marches, along the

Plate 3:11 (*left*) Wine amphora of Dressel form 1B

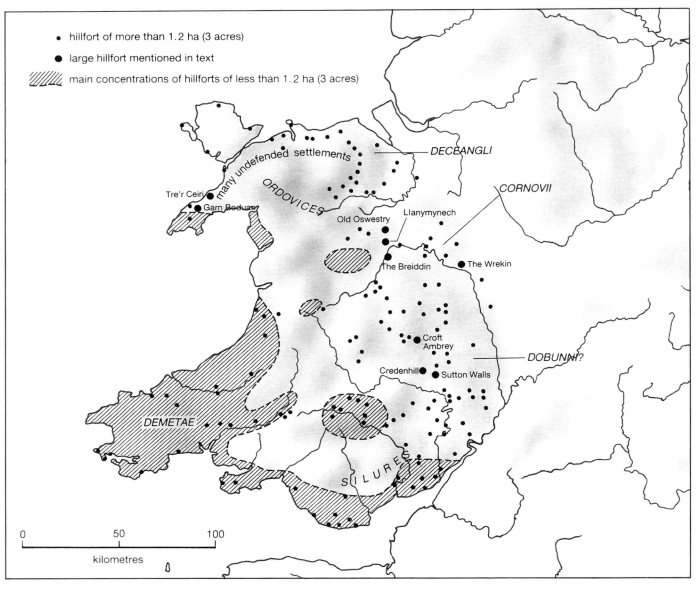

- • hillfort of more than 1.2 ha (3 acres)
- ● large hillfort mentioned in text
- ▨ main concentrations of hillforts of less than 1.2 ha (3 acres)

DECEANGLI

CORNOVII

ORDOVICES

many undefended settlements

Tre'r Ceiri

Garn Boduan

Old Oswestry

Llanymynech

The Breiddin

The Wrekin

Croft Ambrey

DOBUNNI?

Credenhill

Sutton Walls

DEMETAE

SILURES

0   50   100

kilometres

Map 3:18   Distribution of hillforts in Wales

Plate 3:12   Hillfort at Bury Walls, near Clun, Shropshire. Note the multiple defensive circuits.

eastern edge of the Welsh massif, where several exceeded
*c.*8ha (20 acres) in area and that at Llanymynech was a
massive 56ha (140 acres). The location of this site and two
other important sites at Old Oswestry and The Breiddin may
give some clue as to the location of the western boundary
of the Cornovii.

Excavation at some of the hillforts in the Marches (for
example at The Breiddin, Croft Ambrey and Credenhill) has
suggested that these sites were occupied permanently, rather
than used seasonally or in emergencies only. The well preserved, but smaller, site of Tre'r Ceiri in Gwynedd provides
another example of this phenomenon from the territory of
the Ordovices. However, in view of the wide structural
variety in the Welsh hillforts and the absence of investigation
at most sites, caution must be used in making broad conclusions on the basis of the small excavated sample.

There were also large numbers of very small hillforts and
defended homesteads, particularly in the areas occupied by
the Demetae and Silures in southern Wales. The sub-tribes
which made up the Silures may have extended east of the
Wye valley towards the Severn into an area that seems to
have been assigned by Rome at a later date to the Dobunni.
Possible evidence for Roman military operations against a
number of hillforts in the region (notably Sutton Walls, but
see also Map 4:29) would accord better with the inhabitants
of the area being aligned with the Silures rather than with
the Dobunni. Whatever the case, it is likely that Silurian
territory was substantially reduced after their final defeat,
to the advantage of their neighbours who may have been
more co-operative with the Romans.

Apart from the defended sites shown on Map 3:18, quite
a number of undefended settlements are also known. These
are concentrated in the north-western region, where they
were constructed in stone and therefore have survived far
better than similar sites in other regions (for instance, the
Severn Valley) which had a tradition of timber construction.
The Ordovices of north-west Wales were certainly numerous
and many small settlements are known. Some of their more
important hillforts have been excavated (for example, Tre'r
Ceiri and Garn Boduan).

The overall picture provided by archaeology is of a geographical division between east and west and between north
and south, with the settlement pattern in each broad area
reflecting the sub-tribal divisions of the large units identified
in the Roman sources. The density of settlement on the
better quality land also suggests that it was the number of
opponents as well as their guerilla tactics and rough terrain
which made Wales such a difficult conquest for the Romans.
Conversely, the development of agriculture in many regions
(see Map 7:3) and the consequent need to protect and
harvest the crops was a limiting factor on the ability of the
Welsh tribes to withdraw into the mountains at the slow
approach of the Roman army. Rome may have been motiv-
ated primarily by her anxiety to secure the Welsh mineral

resources, but the existence of settled farming communities
on the best land offered the means of breaking down tribal
resistance and of securing the long-term pacification of the
region.

IRON AGE SETTLEMENT IN NORTHERN BRITAIN

The characteristic settlement site of northern Britain in the
late Iron Age was the defended homestead, but there was
immense variety in the design and construction of such sites
(3:19). In the extreme north and west (the so-called Atlantic
province – which was affected only indirectly by the Roman
conquest of the rest of the country) the predominant
forms were the stone-built brochs and duns. Brochs were tall
round towers with walls of great thickness incorporating passages and small chambers, whilst duns were enclosures
which were sometimes built to a similar design though they
were less regular and their walls were far smaller in scale.
Some examples of these sites were also to be found in
Galloway, Strathmore and Strathclyde by the first or second
centuries AD.

It must be stressed that this type of settlement is indicative
of a fragmented society, perhaps based on kin groups, and
from a Roman point of view the more significant areas of
native settlement were those of greatest communal organization – reflected in the construction of larger centres such
as hillforts. As in Wales there are a vast number of small
hillforts spread across the region. The greatest concentration
of sites of 2.5ha (6 acres) and more is, however, to be found
in the eastern part of lowland Scotland between the Tyne
and the Forth. Some of these sites were clearly major tribal
centres. Traprain Law (about 16ha (40 acres) at its greatest
extent) was presumably the main centre for the Votadini,
with Eildon Hill North (also about 16ha (40 acres) and still
containing the visible evidence of nearly 300 huts) serving
the same function for the Selgovae. Following the Roman
conquest in the Flavian period, the large Roman fort of
Newstead was built at the foot of Eildon Hill and a military
watchtower established at the heart of the hillfort – which
was presumably forcibly depopulated at this juncture. By
contrast, Traprain Law continued to be occupied throughout
the Roman period, and has produced extensive evidence of
high status imports from the Roman world, perhaps indicating that the Votadini had a more privileged position as
allies of Rome. These large hillforts were part of a settlement
hierarchy which included many smaller hillforts, palisaded
enclosures, and undefended huts and hut groups (cf. 7:26).
Within the areas assignable to the two tribal confederations
of the Selgovae and the Votadini there were clearly local
variations in settlement type; this no doubt reflected the sub-
tribal divisions.

The western Scottish Lowlands were occupied by the
Novantae of Dumfries and Galloway, with the Dumnonii to

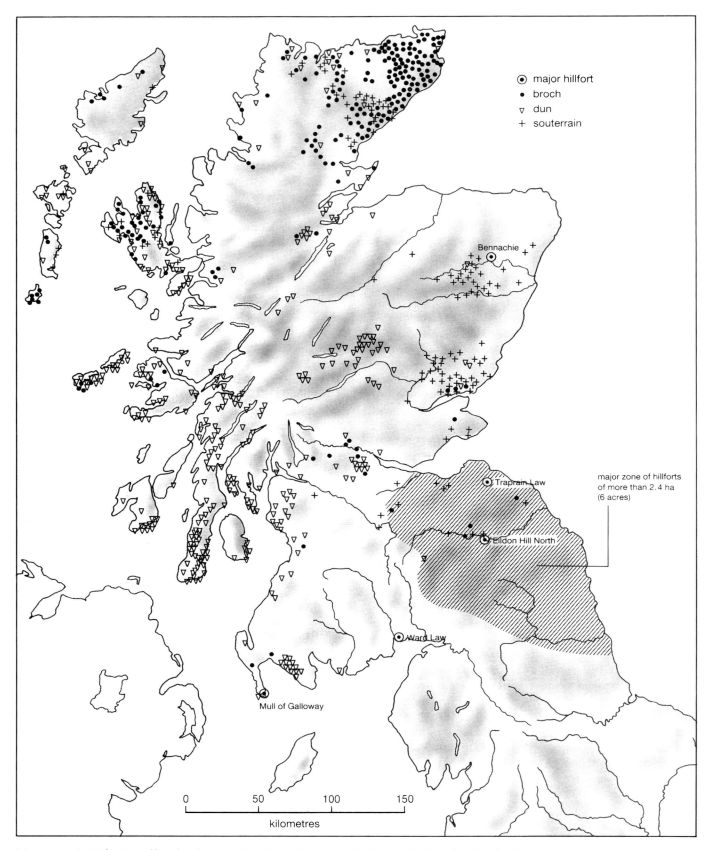

Map 3:19 Distribution of brochs, duns, souterrains and some major hillforts in Iron Age Scotland

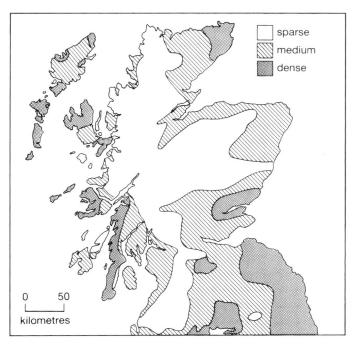

Map 3:20 Generalized density of Iron Age sites in northern Britain

Plate 3:13 Arbory Rings: a prehistoric hilltop settlement with triple ramparts in upper Clydesdale

Plate 3:14 The broch of Gurness, Orkney, and the surrounding settlement were occupied early in the first millennium AD. It has been heavily eroded by the sea.

their north, perhaps extending north of the Forth–Clyde isthmus. Once again, there were many local variations in settlement type (one regional peculiarity was the construction of lake dwellings or crannogs, some of which have yielded imported Roman goods). These local variations must again indicate the federated structure of the tribal groups named by Ptolemy.

North of the Forth–Clyde line in Strathallan/Strathearn and Strathmore on the eastern flank of the Highlands there were fewer major hillforts, but one of the characteristic sites was the small hillfort with timber-laced ramparts. These were often intensely burnt, producing the so-called vitrified defences, the interpretation and dating of which remain problematical. There were also large numbers of apparently undefended hut settlements, sometimes associated with souterrains (underground stone-built tunnels and chambers). The souterrains may well have served mainly as storehouses, but could also have provided refuges for the inhabitants in emergencies.

Apart from in the true highland massif, the Iron Age settlement of Scotland was extensive and occasionally dense (3:20). Recent air photographic work has discovered many new sites on the good agricultural land of Moray, Strathallan/Strathearn and Strathmore. When this information is assimilated the revised picture will more adequately reflect the relative importance of these areas as against the far

north and west, where at present the survival of stone-built sites perhaps distorts their relative social and political significance. It is also clear that estimates of native populations will have to be revised upwards, as will estimates of the extent of agriculture in those areas where conditions were favourable. Nevertheless, because of the limited nature of archaeological evidence, many of the social implications of the information on settlement type and distribution still remain to be resolved.

4
The Conquest and Garrisoning of Britain

JULIUS CAESAR: THE FIRST INVASIONS OF BRITAIN,
55 AND 54 BC

The first Roman invasion of Britain had its origins as much in the political power plays of late Republican Rome as in the sound rationale of military necessity. Julius Caesar had already gone far beyond the notional limits of his military command in Gaul and in 56 BC he was anxious to avoid recall to Rome. His two main rivals in the political infighting of the time, Pompey and Crassus, were both consuls in 55 BC and might have instigated a prosecution against him had he admitted that his conquest of Gaul was complete and returned to Rome.

Caesar's solution was to perceive Britain as a threat to his Gallic conquests and to obtain permission for a campaign against the island. He could argue that Britain was providing a haven for Gallic refugees, that, through established trading links, actual help had been sent from Britain to his enemies and that the British druids posed an insidious threat. Yet beneath the rhetoric one suspects there was a good deal of exaggeration, although recent studies have emphasized the importance of trading relations between south-west Britain and the Veneti of Brittany (3:15, 3:16), whose fleet was defeated by Caesar at a battle in Quiberon Bay.

Preparations for the campaign were minimal. A lieutenant was sent to scout out a landing place and two legions and auxiliaries were gathered in the Somme Valley for embarkation at Ambleteuse and Boulogne (4:1). A number of large Roman army camps are known in the area, notably Liercourt-Erondelle (L on Maps 4:1 and 4:2), Vendeuil Caply and (probably of a later date) Folleville. Finally, Commius of the Gallic Atrebates was sent ahead to try and win over some of the British tribes.

The failure of Commius' diplomatic mission was the first of a series of disasters for Caesar. During the crossing, the cavalry with the convoy became lost and returned to port. The choice of landing place was restricted by the decision of the British tribes to oppose the landing itself and by the inadequate reconnaissance. It is generally agreed that the Romans first sailed beneath the cliffs of Dover before attempting to land on the beaches around Deal. After hard fighting in the shallows and on the foreshore, Caesar secured his beachhead, but was unable to pursue the retreating British for lack of cavalry. Terms were offered to the British, and

tribal leaders started to come in to pay homage and give hostages and assurances regarding their future behaviour.

The equinoctial gales undid all this when they not only prevented a second attempted crossing by the cavalry, but wrecked most of Caesar's ships which had been left rather casually on the open beach. The British tribes immediately returned to the offensive and, without supplies, cavalry or boats, Caesar's position was very grave. In a second battle a foraging party was attacked and Caesar extricated its troops with difficulty. A third battle then took place right in front of the camp as the British tribes tried to exploit their advantage and destroy the invaders. Once again, however, the Roman troops prevailed, but were unable to follow up their victory by pursuing the enemy. Caesar rapidly came to terms with some of the tribes and ignominiously withdrew to Gaul as quickly as he was able.

The first campaign against Britain had been a near-disaster but, ironically, was heralded as a great triumph in Rome. Perhaps Caesar's enemies in Rome hoped that he would repeat his mistakes in his second campaign. A much larger army and fleet were prepared for 54 BC and the landing was made unopposed at the same place as in the previous year (4:2). Caesar marched his five legions 19km inland, where a battle took place at a river (almost certainly the Stour, near Canterbury), and the Roman victory was followed by a siege of a hillfort nearby (possibly Bigbury). Once again, though, the fleet was severely damaged in a storm at a critical juncture and Caesar was obliged to delay the pursuit and set about repairs. When he again marched inland a larger British force led by King Cassivellaunus had assembled. In two days of skirmishing and pitched battle, Caesar broke the British resistance and pursued his opponents to the Thames, where he gained control of a ford (perhaps Brentford or Tilbury?). Once across the Thames, Caesar searched for the tribal centre of Cassivellaunus and was eventually led to it by renegade British kings. Wheathampstead is commonly suggested as the centre which Caesar captured, but whilst its general location satisfies most criteria, alternative sites exist and certainty is impossible.

As in the previous year, Caesar had little opportunity to enjoy his success. Four kings in Kent joined forces in an attack on his beachhead camp and, although it was beaten off, Caesar rapidly concluded terms with Cassivellaunus. The terms of the political settlement must have sounded

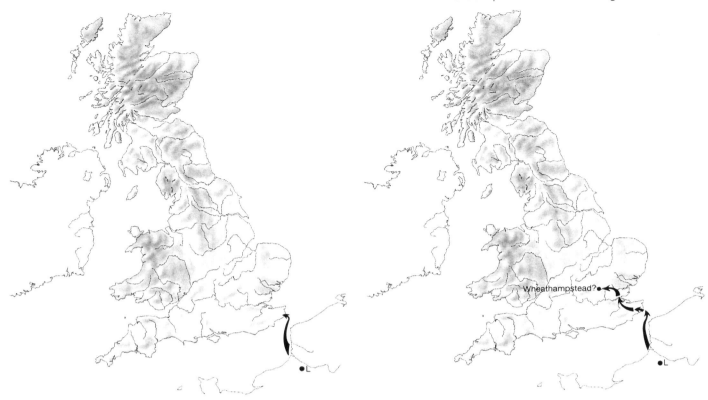

Map 4:1   Caesar and Britain 55 BC (L = Liercourt-Erondelle near Amiens, which is thought to be one of the Caesarian campaign bases)

Map 4:2   Caesar and Britain 54 BC

impressive in Rome, with hostages, tribute and obedience promised by the British rulers. Some scholars have argued that the payment of tribute continued until the reign of Augustus, but in reality, Caesar's two campaigns had resulted in hard-won but empty victories. The outbreak of the Gallic revolt the following year and Caesar's growing confrontation with Pompey diverted attention elsewhere.

CLAUDIUS, AD 43

Although the reinvasion of Britain seems to have been considered several times between 54 BC and AD 43, notably by Augustus and Gaius ('Caligula'), the only actual contacts were diplomatic or mercantile. When Gaius was assassinated i᠃ AD 41, Claudius was dragged from his academic obscurity to fulfil the need for a dynast of the Julio-Claudian family. His position was initially insecure and his most obvious failing was his lack of military prestige. As a keen historian, Claudius astutely foresaw the propaganda value of an invasion of Britain, which would enable him to emulate one of the most famous exploits of Julius Caesar. It is also arguable that there were genuine political or military justifications for the campaign; the ever-increasing band of British émigré princes at Rome may have been exerting its

influence, and the growing power of King Cunobelinus of the Catuvellauni/Trinovantes federation and his family was a destabilizing force in Britain. Nevertheless, the elaborate preparations for the involvement in the campaign of both Claudius himself and elephants hint strongly at the underlying propaganda value of the exercise.

It is uncertain whether conquest was envisaged from the start. The original intention may have been to reinstate pro-Roman client kings and to end the hegemony of Cunobelinus. Nevertheless, material spoils of victory were also expected in the form of slaves, gold and silver (Tacitus, *Agricola* 12).

Four legions were assembled under the overall command of Aulus Plautius, the former governor of Pannonia. With auxiliaries, the total force probably amounted to *c*.40,000 men, but having assembled at Boulogne they refused to embark, perhaps having read between the lines of Caesar's account. Eventually the mutinous atmosphere was dispelled and the fleet crossed in three divisions (Dio 60.19.4). It is not certain whether the landing was at three separate locations, but there was no opposition at first (4:3). It is likely that the whole army disembarked at beachheads in Kent; the idea that one division landed near Chichester, to win over pro-Roman elements there, has little to commend it since the II legion (later to be active in the south and

Map 4:3   Claudian invasion AD 43

south-west) was present at the battle on the Medway. Richborough was certainly one of the beachheads, though the Claudian camp known there is too small to have been used by the whole expeditionary force, even allowing for erosion. After a brief delay, Plautius made contact with the British contingents, defeated them, and advanced to a river (to be identified as the Medway). Here a major battle was fought for two days before British resistance crumbled and the Romans pursued them to the Thames, where another battle took place. At this point it was necessary to send a message to Claudius for him to come and deliver the *coup de grâce*. It is evident that the campaign was not over *before* he arrived with his elephants, in spite of the disparaging accounts of some Roman writers (for example Josephus and Suetonius). Claudius led the army forward to the capture of Colchester and received the surrender of other British tribes through force or diplomacy (Dio 60.21.2–5).

THE CONQUEST PERIOD AD 43–60

The scale of the initial victory seems to have made Claudius decide to create a British province, and although the territory overrun in the first campaign was probably small, there is no reason to doubt that the instructions left to Plautius ordered the complete conquest of the island. In the course of the next four years, the legions were employed in the pacification not only of south-east Britain, but of areas of the south-west and the Midlands as well (4:4). The future emperor Vespasian commanded the II Augusta legion in the south-western sector, conquering two major tribes and capturing 20 *oppida* (Suetonius, *Vespasian* 4). The navy must have played an important role in the campaigning and early supply bases are known at Richborough (R on Map 4:4), Fingringhoe Wick (F), Fishbourne (Fish) and Hamworthy (H).

Some tribes were granted client status in exchange for accepting Roman suzerainty (the Atrebates, the Iceni and the Brigantes were probably the earliest). By the end of Plautius' governorship the main resistance to Rome had been forced back into the mountains and valleys of Wales. There is no evidence that Plautius had been instructed to delimit the expansion of the province by creating a frontier and it is notable that his successor launched a series of attacks into Wales as soon as he had completed the initial work of pacification in 'lowland' Britain. The persistent belief that there was a 'Fosse Way frontier' at this stage is more fully discussed below, but there is nothing in the record of the campaigning which suggests that the Romans intended to call a halt to their expansion inside 'lowland' Britain. After all, the main non-ferrous mineral resources of the island lay in the 'highland' zone (6:1).

Ostorius Scapula took over as governor in AD 47 (4:5). He arrived late in the summer to find British forces in the field but he was able to disperse them with a detachment of auxiliaries (arrow 1). Then, in preparation for campaigns against the tribes in Wales (now led by Caratacus, a son of Cunobelinus), he disarmed some of the peoples previously subdued. This was standard Roman practice as regards conquered people, but it provoked a brief revolt from the nominally autonomous Iceni (arrow 2).

Scapula was then (AD 48?) able to launch a campaign against the Decangi or Deceangli in North Wales. According to Tacitus he was close to the Irish Sea when a rising among the client Brigantes caused him to abandon his original plan. It is likely that he penetrated into the Cheshire plain before returning southward (arrow 3). In *c.*AD 49, the XX legion, which had been left at Colchester (C), was moved up to the Welsh front, probably being stationed partly at Kingsholm, Gloucester (K). In a series of major campaigns in South and Central Wales (arrows 4 and 5), Scapula now brought Caratacus to battle and defeated him.

One particular problem that has prompted much debate centres on locating the so-called last stand of the mixed tribal forces led by Caratacus – who had strategically chosen to move the scene of his activities from the territory of the Silures to that of the Ordovices. Folk memory or antiquarianism has given the name Caer Caradog (Caratacus' fort) to three hillforts, one dominating the Church Stretton gap, another south of Clun and the third in Clwyd. Although

Plate 4:1   Roman gold coin showing the arch erected in Rome to celebrate the Claudian conquest of Britain (the legend reads *DE BRITANN.*) (*RIC 8*).

Plate 4:2   Silver coin of *CARA[TACUS]*, the leader of the British resistance to Rome AD 43–9

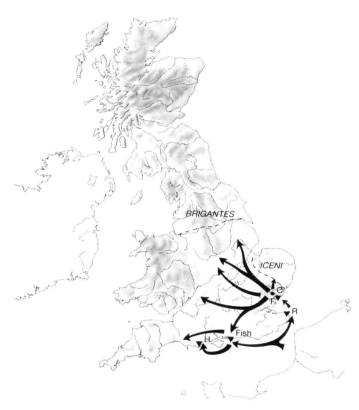

Map 4:4   Governorship of Aulus Plautius AD 43–7 (arrows indicate possible lines of advance).

Map 4:5   Governorship of Ostorius Scapula AD 47–52

the second is relatively close to known Roman marching camps around Leintwardine, none have produced any evidence of investment. Moreover, all lack the nearby major river required by the Tacitean narrative and are in any case far too small to have required the combined attention of a Roman force that probably numbered nearly two legions plus auxiliaries. A more likely possibility is offered by the massive limestone spur of Llanymynech which dominates the western edge of the north Shropshire plain (3:18). It was protected by the marshy confluence of the rivers Tanat, Vyrnwy and Severn and ringed on three sides by cliffs that were adapted as part of the defences of a strongpoint embracing the quite abnormal size of 56 ha (140 acres), sufficient to have housed a mixed army of resistance drawn from all the dissidents of southern Britain. Evidence of a Roman campaign base has now emerged at the western foot of the massif close to a newly discovered Julio-Claudian fort at Llansantffraid to make Llanymynech a strong candidate for identification as Caratacus' chosen position. Its natural strength, however, was not sufficient to prevent a British defeat, although Caratacus escaped to the north in a misplaced reliance on Brigantian protection.

The fugitive Briton was betrayed by Cartimandua, queen of the Brigantes, and taken to Rome for the triumphal procession of Claudius. Scapula's garrisons in South Wales, however, came under pressure and Roman construction and foraging parties suffered a number of defeats as the Silures rebelled against Roman occupation. In AD 52 Scapula died, worn out according to Tacitus, and before the new governor arrived a legionary detachment suffered another defeat.

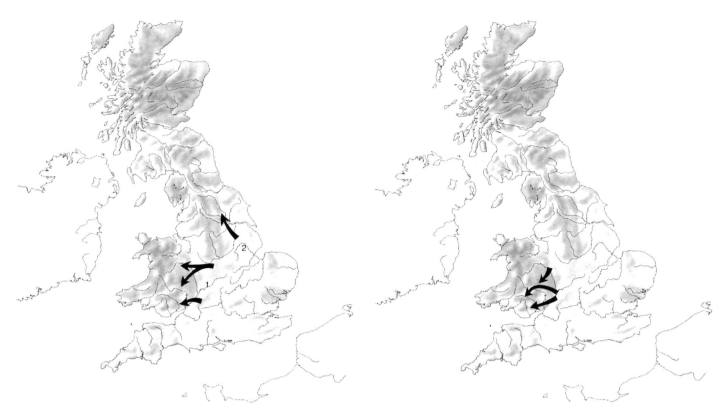

Map 4:6   Governorship of Didius Gallus AD 52–7

Map 4:7   Governorship of Quintus Veranius AD 57

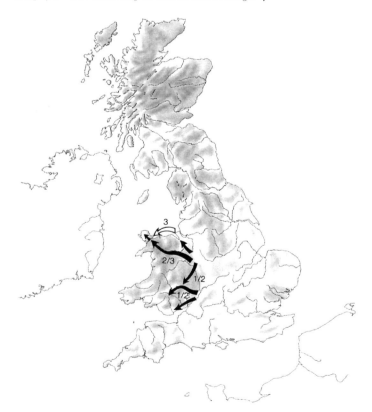

Map 4:8   Governorship of Suetonius Paullinus (i) the Silures and Ordovices AD 58–60

The new governor, Didius Gallus, at least resolved the immediate crisis (4:6, arrow 1), but does not appear to have re-launched the offensive. This may have been largely due to a serious problem with the Brigantes. The client queen, Cartimandua, fell into dispute with her husband Venutius and Roman troops were twice sent to her aid in order to preserve the pro-Roman character of her regime (4:6, arrow 2). Tacitus complains that, for the rest of his governorship, Didius was inactive, merely founding a few forts. The reasons may have had less to do with the governor's personal failings than with directions from above. Claudius was murdered in AD 54 and Nero and his advisors seem to have prevaricated about whether to commit the ultimate insult to his memory and abandon the British province. At the very least a temporary moratorium seems to have been placed on further expansion.

A change in Imperial policy was heralded by the appointment of Quintus Veranius as governor in AD 57, after he had actively canvassed for the office in Rome. He had a good military reputation and was swiftly in action against the Silures (4:7). It is difficult to assess his success since he died in the same year, but he is alleged to have claimed in his will that he could have conquered the rest of Britain within three years.

The appointment of Suetonius Paullinus as the next governor was clearly intended to continue the expansion, as he was a veteran general experienced in mountain warfare. After two successful campaigns (presumably in both South and North Wales, Map 4:8), he launched a third season with an amphibious attack on the island of Anglesey (*Mona*) probably using the large base at Rhyn Park near Chirk as the springboard for campaign into Snowdonia (4:9). The Boudican revolt broke out at the moment of a victory which might otherwise have marked the complete subjugation of Wales.

The Boudican revolt, AD 60–61 (4:9)

The revolt led by Boudica (Boadicea is a Victorian corruption of the name) is comparatively well known to us thanks to the accounts of Tacitus (*Annals* 14. 29–39; *Agricola* 5. 15–16) and Dio (62. 1–12). Nevertheless, there is still disagreement about many important details such as the exact date and length of the revolt and the site of the final battle.

The events leading to the revolt centred initially on the death of Prasutagus, the king of the Iceni and a loyal client. On his death it was decided to annex the kingdom into the Roman province – a process badly mismanaged by the Imperial procurator, Decianus Catus. Boudica, the widow, and her two daughters and other members of the Icenian elite were subjected to humiliating and vicious treatment. The resentment which had been raised in Icenian territory might have been contained but for two other factors. Firstly, the bulk of the provincial army was at that moment engaged on the invasion of Anglesey (*Mona*) and the absence of both the army and the provincial governor offered a unique opportunity for a quick strike. Secondly, the southern neighbours of the Iceni, the Trinovantes, were also in a state of great disaffection. It is clear that the Roman colony at Colchester (*Camulodunum*) lay at the heart of their grievances. The creation of the colony in AD 49 involved large-scale and continuing confiscation of tribal lands. Our sources also indicate that the Trinovantian elite had been obliged to take out loans and to invest in the development of the temple of the Imperial cult at Colchester. The recall of the loans exacerbated their financial difficulties and resentments, and when the revolt broke out the Trinovantes immediately joined it. The hated colony was the first major target for the rebels.

The veterans settled at Colchester appealed to Decianus Catus for military help, but, according to Tacitus, he sent only 200 men to supplement a small garrison on the spot (perhaps from the fort at Stanway by the Gosbecks religious site). The colony was without defences and the settlers were forced to concentrate within the precincts of the temple of Claudius. An attempt to relieve the town by the nearest detachment of the IX legion, led by its legate Q. Petillius Cerialis, was ambushed with the loss of his entire infantry force. As 2,000 soldiers were later drafted from Germany to bring the legion back to strength, it is apparent that no more than half the IX was engaged on that day. Cerialis was

lucky to escape with his cavalry back to his fortress (almost certainly to be identified with the vexillation fortress at Longthorpe). Colchester then fell amid bloody massacre and the appalled Decianus Catus fled to the Continent.

News of the revolt had reached Suetonius Paullinus just after he had captured Anglesey and installed a garrison. He seems to have set off from North Wales immediately with his cavalry forces, ordering the bulk of the infantry to follow as quickly as possible. During his ride (roughly following the line of Watling Street) he must have been informed of the fall of Colchester since he went directly to London. If he had hoped to find the bulk of the troops from south-east England congregated there he was disappointed. The defence of London against the rebel hordes was impossible without an army and he was forced to withdraw his few troops, presumably back north-eastwards towards his advancing army. Those civilians who remained in London were butchered and a similar fate was soon afterwards visited on St Albans (*Verulamium*). Although the revolt had now spread widely in lowland Britain, south of the Thames the client kingdom of Cogidubnus, centred on Chichester, seems to have remained loyal to Rome.

Boudica now seems to have led her forces against the governor in an attempt to force the issue before he could regroup all his legions or receive reinforcement from Europe. The forces available to Suetonius Paullinus at the decisive battle were indeed meagre, comprising the entire XIV Gemina legion, part of the XX Valeria and some of their associated auxiliary units; a total of perhaps 10,000 men. A vexillation of the IX Hispana had been almost wiped out and the rest of that legion was probably based in key strategic positions in the north Midlands and Lincolnshire, where they may have been left deliberately in a successful attempt to deter the client Brigantes from joining the rebellion. The II Augusta legion still had its main bases in the south-west at this date (notably Lake Farm near Wimborne and Exeter). But in view of the large-scale campaigning in North Wales at this time by the XIV and XX legions it is probable that at least one vexillation had been posted in a position to guard South Wales, perhaps at Kingsholm, or as an *ad hoc* temporary replacement for the XX at Usk. The logistical problems of mustering troops split between several bases seems to be the best explanation of the behaviour of a camp prefect of the II, Poenius Postumus, who failed to respond to an order to march out and unite his troops with the governor's army. Similar appeals for help would have been sent to all the vexillations of the II legion, but from Devon and Dorset they could have marched as a united body and, in view of the distance, might have arrived too late to participate in the battle. Only an isolated detachment in South Wales was in a position to rendezvous rapidly with the rest of the army, at a mustering point on Watling Street (Wroxeter or Mancetter perhaps). Poenius committed suicide precisely because his action had prevented his troops from taking part

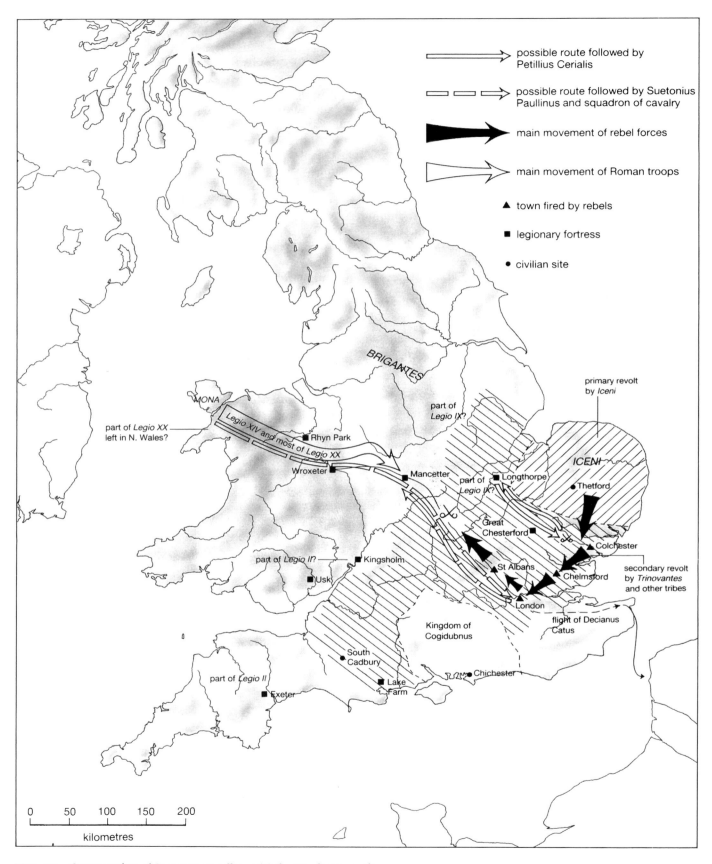

Map 4:9   Governorship of Suetonius Paullinus (ii) the Boudican revolt

in the great victory. Finally, the missing element of the XX legion can be explained as troops who had to be left in the newly conquered area of North Wales in order to prevent an instantaneous rising there as the army turned to face the main rebellion.

The exact location of the battle which decided the fate of Britain is unknown (and from Tacitus' account it is probably unlocatable). Most scholars would now place it somewhere between Mancetter and St Albans, though not necessarily exactly on the line of Watling Street. The hard-fought battle ended as a conclusive Roman victory, but even though Boudica perished soon afterwards (perhaps by poison) the revolt continued. Now the threat had passed, Suetonius Paullinus set about exacting reprisals and in doing so he discouraged the rebels from surrendering themselves to his mercy. There is archaeological evidence from a number of sites which is suggestive of Roman 'repacification measures': South Cadbury hillfort was evidently subjected to a violent siege which is thought to date to the AD 60s rather than the 40s; recent excavations of an Icenian triple-ditched settlement at Thetford have produced evidence of systematic destruction at about this date. There is also evidence of new military dispositions, and additional vexillation fortresses such as that at Great Chesterford were probably constructed to facilitate the work of repacification.

As the guerilla warfare dragged on Suetonius fell into tactical disagreements with the new procurator Gaius Julius Alpinus Classicianus. The rebellion was not finally terminated until after the appointment of a more conciliatory governor, P. Petronius Turpilianus, in AD 61. The casualty figures of 150,000 (70,000 loyal Britons and Romans, 80,000 rebels) are certainly exaggerated, but there is no doubt that the revolt was a disaster (*clades*) for the young Roman administration. The work of pacification, education and acculturation had to begin again.

AD 61–77

In the aftermath of the revolt it is no real surprise to find that successive governors were not credited with military achievements. The main emphasis was bound to be on the reconsolidation and the regarrisoning of parts of south-eastern England and, in any case, it is unlikely that the emperor would have sanctioned action on a broader front with the memory of the near-disaster still fresh. It is likely that in criticizing the lack of military activity of Petronius Turpilianus (AD 61–3) and M. Trebellius Maximus (AD 63–9), Tacitus was (unfairly) ignoring, deliberately or otherwise, the fact that they had simply obeyed orders. One corollary of the lack of campaigns in the AD 60s which is rarely considered is that these two governors were probably great fort builders and many 'Neronian' sites should relate to this phase. It is interesting that in AD 68 the army mutinied because of the lack of campaigning (however this is to be interpreted). Another factor in the decision to suspend the final conquest of Britain was undoubtedly Nero's policy in the East, where problems with Parthia came to a head in the AD 60s. In fact, Nero withdrew the Legio XIV Gemina and eight Batavian cohorts from Britain *c.*AD 66 in preparation for a campaign to the Caucasus. Without Imperial commitment and depleted of troops, there was little chance of military advance in Britain.

Everything changed with the suicide of Nero in AD 68 and the civil war which followed. Galba, Otho and Vitellius came and went before Vespasian ended the political anarchy. In Britain, Trebellius Maximus had been replaced by Vettius Bolanus on the orders of Vitellius and remained in office for a brief period under Vespasian (Map 4:10). There was a major emergency in Brigantia when Cartimandua lost her throne to Venutius and, although Bolanus led an army to rescue her, he was unable to prevent the anti-Roman Venutius from consolidating his position. The brief return of the XIV legion in AD 69, before redeparting for the Rhine, did not resolve the manpower crisis facing the governor and the political uncertainty militated against a governor acting too independently at this time.

The Brigantian problem was left unresolved, therefore, until Vespasian emerged as the assured emperor and his first choice of governor, Petillius Cerialis, arrived in Britain (4:11). A new forward policy had been decided on, presumably partly because of Vespasian's earlier links with the

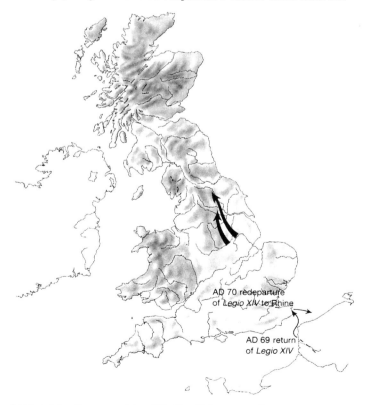

Map 4:10 Governorship of Vettius Bolanus AD 69–71

Map 4:11   Governorship of Petillius Cerialis AD 71–73/4

Map 4:12   Governorship of Julius Frontinus AD 73/4–76/7

province. With an additional legion, the II Adiutrix, the army was brought back to strength and within 15 years the long-delayed conquest of much of Britain was completed.

Petillius Cerialis, with Agricola as legate of the XX legion, concentrated on the subjugation of the Brigantian kingdom, probably operating initially out of bases in the north Midlands into south and east Yorkshire. It has been suggested plausibly that Cerialis may have crossed the Stainmore Pass and advanced as far as Carlisle in the north-west.

The next governor, Julius Frontinus (AD 73/74–76), turned attention back to Wales (4:12) and, in a series of campaigns, he substantially completed the conquest of Wales. This was no mean achievement, as previous experience of the Welsh tribes had shown, but sadly Tacitus denies us the detail, presumably in order to make Agricola appear all the more outstanding amongst his peers.

By c.AD 77 then, the conquest had proceeded a considerable way, with most, if not all, of England and Wales under Roman control. At least one client kingdom, that of Cogidubnus, was probably still in existence, but a number of other tribal areas were already in the process of passing out of military control and being organized as self-governing *civitates*.

A crucial aspect of the conquest period campaigning was the relationship between the emperor and his governor. In Table 4:1 the chronology of the conquest is outlined with

an attempt to trace Imperial policy towards Britain. It was this which dictated the pace and scale of military operations. It is apparent that judgements derived from Tacitus about the military abilities of various governors are inappropriate since they were constrained in their actions by the emperor of the day. Under Claudius, under Nero for a brief period (AD 57–60) and, at first, under the Flavians, an expansionist policy was energetically pursued. The death of Claudius, the Boudican revolt, Rome's preoccupation with Parthia on the Eastern frontier, the civil war and later Domitian's German and Danubian wars were all events which affected Rome's military objectives in Britain. The idea of total conquest of the island was never shelved for long enough in this early period to have become a totally discredited policy. Under the Flavian emperors, in the governorship of Agricola, it briefly became a reality.

Agricola

Cn. Julius Agricola enjoyed two pieces of good fortune in the AD 70s. His career culminated with the prestigious posting to Britain where the Flavians were anxious to continue their expansionist policies. This allowed Agricola almost unrivalled opportunities for conducting offensive campaigns. His second piece of good fortune was in marrying his daughter to the future historian Tacitus, whose biography of

Table 4.1 Governors, emperors and policy in the conquest of Britain

	Emperor	Governor	Events	Policy
AD 43	Claudius	Aulus Plautius	Expansionist warfare: conquest of SW Britain and Midlands. Some tribes accept Roman hegemony and become clients. Resistance concentrated in Wales.	Military glory and booty. Creation of province. Conquest of whole island envisaged. Mineral exploitation in Mendips.
AD 47		P. Ostorius Scapula	Continued expansionist warfare: first attempt to pacify and garrison lands of some of Welsh tribes. Fierce resistance in last years of governorship undid the major effects of the earlier victories in Wales.	No evidence that policy aiming for anything less than total conquest, though this increasingly seen to be a long-term undertaking. But momentum kept up as 'pet' project of Claudius.
AD 52		A. Didius Gallus	New governor faced with minor crises in Welsh Marches and Brigantia	Policy direction perhaps less strong in Claudius' last years, but overall aim remained the same.
AD 54	Nero		Later inactivity – end of first period of concerted campaigning.	After death of Claudius, it is likely that the youthful Nero and his advisers considered abandoning Britain as the ultimate insult to Claudius' memory. This may account for the lack of campaigning whilst policy was reconsidered in Rome.
AD 57 AD 58		Q. Veranius C. Suetonius Paullinus	Resumption of campaigning v tribes of S Wales. Death of Veranius followed by rapid appointment of another experienced general. Concerted campaigning v N and S Welsh tribes.	Forward policy finally decided on. Conquest of Wales pursued earnestly until hiatus of AD 60–1, which necessitated a return to the earlier concern with SE England.
AD 60			Boudican revolt.	
AD 61		P. Petronius Turpilianus	Repacification of SE England necessary. No major campaigns – concentration on fort building (?) and police work.	Cautious policy now advocated though unlikely that abandonment of Britain seriously considered given loss of life in 60–1.
AD 63		M. Trebellius Maximus	No major campaigns. Army restless because of this and governor unpopular.	Main military theatre now in East v Parthia. Britain no longer given priority and some troops removed. But total conquest idea not dropped, merely shelved.
AD 68	Nero dies		Civil war starts in Empire.	Hiatus in policy direction continues until AD 70. Lack of decisive action by the governor shows his dependence on firm guidance from Rome.
AD 69	Galba, Otho, Vitellius, Vespasian	M. Vettius Bolanus	Crisis in Brigantia and some Roman intervention, but position not satisfactorily resolved. Army again mutinous.	
AD 71		Q. Petillius Cerialis	Major campaigns v Brigantes.	Forward policy decided on in Rome – the unresolved problem with the Brigantes provided the first target.
AD 73/ 74		Sex. Julius Frontinus	Major campaigns v Welsh tribes and subjugation of Wales. Fort building in central Wales by AD 75.	Policy continued in Wales with great success. Annexation and garrisoning of area.
AD 77		Cn. Julius Agricola[1]	Completion of pacification of Welsh tribes and Brigantes. Invasion of Scotland.	Further campaigns sanctioned, rapidly going beyond territory of tribes previously encountered. Total conquest of island now in sight.

[1] For a detailed analysis of Agricola's governorship see Table 4.2

Table 4.2   Imperial policy and the campaigns of Agricola (Figures in brackets or followed by question marks are not precisely dated)

	Emperor	Acclamations Vesp.	Titus	Dom.	Events A	Events B	Policy
AD 76	Vespasian	XVIII	XII	—			
AD 77		XVIII	XII	—	Agricola's first campaigns in N Wales		Continuation of Vespasian's forward policy v Ordovician resistance.
AD 78		XIX	XIII	—	Second campaign: v N England and lowland Scotland	Agricola's first campaign: in N Wales	Completion of Welsh conquest allows final conquest of Britain to be undertaken.
		XX(?)	XIV(?)	—			
AD 79	Vespasian dies (June)	XX(?)	XIV(?)	—	Third campaign: as far as Tay.	Second campaign: v N England and lowland Scotland.	Advance into Scotland sanctioned by Vespasian before death.
	Titus	—	XV	—			
AD 80		—	XVI(?)	—	Fourth season: consolidation on Forth–Clyde line.	Third campaign: as far as Tay.	Titus considers change of policy – creation of frontier within Britain.
AD 81	Titus dies (Sept.)	—	XVI(?)	—	Fifth campaign: SW Scotland now overrun for first time in rear of the frontier.	Fourth season: consolidation on Forth–Clyde line.	Consistent with policy of previous season – lands S of the Forth–Clyde to be pacified and garrisoned.
	Domitian	—	XVII	—			
		—	—	(I)			
AD 82		—	—	(II)	Sixth campaign: advance up Strathmore beyond Tay.	Fifth campaign: SW Scotland now overrun for first time in rear of frontier	Domitian reverses policy of Titus and allows Agricola to advance N – ignoring Agricola's suggestion that Ireland worth invading at this point.
		—	—	(III)?			
AD 83		—	—	(III)	Seventh campaign: culminates in B of Mons Graupius.	Sixth campaign: advance up Strathmore beyond Tay.	Agricola allowed one last season to 'complete' conquest of Britain.
		—	—	(IV)			
		—	—	(V)			
AD 84		—	—	V?	Agricola recalled	Seventh campaign: culminates in B of Mons Graupius. Agricola recalled.	Agricola recalled and the consolidation of his conquest left to his unknown successor.
		—	—	VI			
		—	—	VII			

his father-in-law was to establish for all time Agricola's posthumous reputation as a great general.

But, impressively as Agricola's achievements read in Tacitus, we would do well to remember that his campaigns were ultimately controlled by others. It is a complete fallacy to imagine that the Flavian emperors did not keep a very tight rein on events in Britain and that Agricola was allowed to act largely independently of his political masters.

A critical approach to Tacitus' account has also suggested that the conventional chronology may be wrong. A. R. Birley's analysis (1981, 73–81) brings the first year of Agricola's governorship back to AD 77, the year of his consulship. The attraction of the earlier dating is that the major policy changes in these years can be better explained in terms of changes of emperor, as first Vespasian, then Titus, died. In Table 4:2 the early chronology is represented in the column Events A and the interpretation of policy goes with this. Events B shows the conventional chronology for comparison. The taking of acclamations as *imperator* by the emperors after military victories won in their name, is also indicated, though Britain was not the only important military sphere at this time. The taking of IMP XV (that is, acclamation as

imperator for a fifteenth time) by Titus in AD 79 is important because we know that it related to events in Britain (Dio 66.20.3). It might be thought more likely to have related to the events of Agricola's third campaign than to his second (about which Tacitus is rather vague).

For a variety of reasons then, the early chronology is to be preferred. Agricola was sent to Britain straight from his consulship as a trusted servant of the Flavian regime and with unprecedented military experience in the province. His instructions were clearly to continue the policy of concerted military action with a view to the final conquest of the entire island (4:13). He arrived late in the season to find a revolt under way in the newly subdued Ordovician territory. This proved to be only a minor diversion and he quickly ended resistance there and on Anglesey.

The following season Agricola returned to his allotted task, the final conquest of northern England and Scotland. The location of his second campaign, perhaps more in the nature of reconnaissance in force, is disputed. Although the area of Liverpool Bay might well fit the context, many scholars have suggested the Lake District, others lowland Scotland. Preparations for the advance into Scotland no

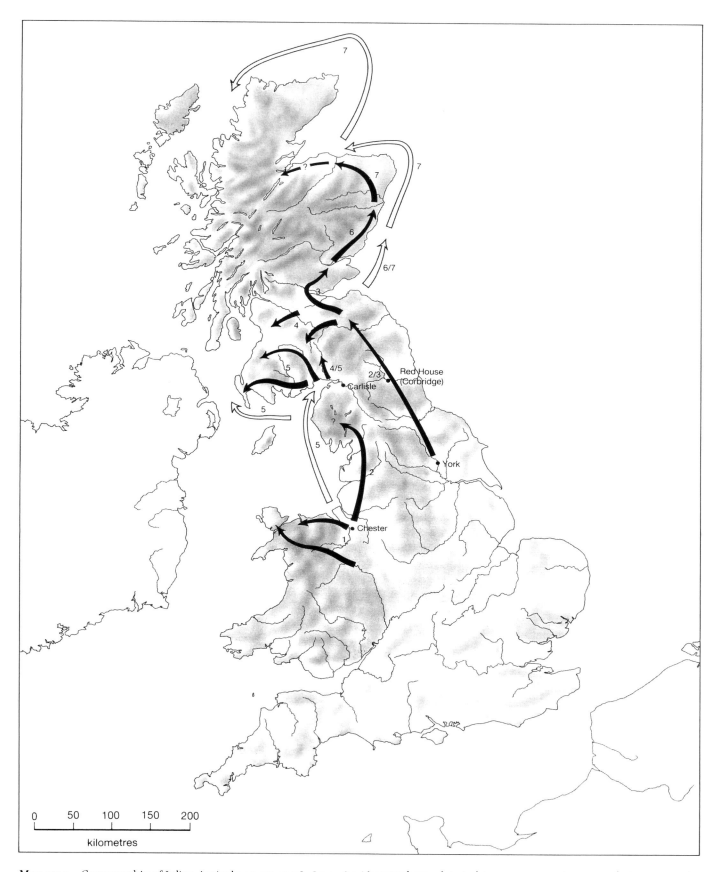

Map 4:13 Governorship of Julius Agricola AD 77 or 78–83 or 84 (the numbers relate to his seven successive campaigning seasons).

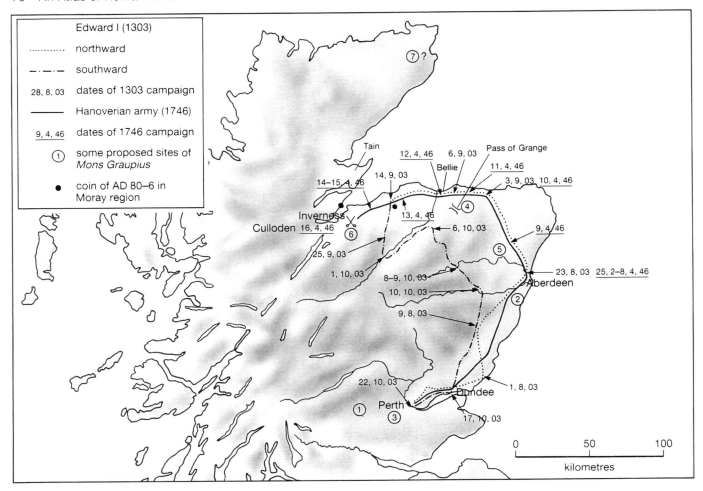

Map 4:14 Mons Graupius, the lost battle: 1 Dalginross, 2 Raedykes, 3 Dunning, 4 Pass of Grange/Knock Hill/Bin of Cullen, 5 Durno, 6 Culloden/Inverness region?, 7 Sutherland/Caithness region

doubt included construction of the important base at Red House, Corbridge. At any rate, with Agricola's third season we are back on surer ground. Tacitus describes a great leap forward to the Tay, presumably indicating the defeat or acquiescence of the main tribes of the eastern and central Lowlands (the Selgovae and Votadini) and preliminary probings beyond the Forth. It is likely that at this stage the campaigning was concentrated up the eastern corridors.

Under the early chronology Vespasian died after the start of this campaign and the change of emperor resulted in a change of strategy the following season. Although Tacitus hedges on this issue, it is clear that the decision to halt the advance on the Forth–Clyde line was Titus' (and the reversal of this policy was made by the despised Domitian – no wonder it was all too much for Tacitus). Two seasons of fort building and minor campaigning to the south and south-west were ordered. The initial construction of the bases at Dalswinton and Glenlochar presumably belong to these years.

The fifth campaign started with an amphibious landing and probably took in Dumfries and Galloway. It culminated with Agricola and his army looking out at the Irish coast (there is no evidence to locate these events further north-west in Kintyre). In his report to Titus it is likely that Agricola now proposed an invasion of Ireland as a logical next step, given the moratorium on further northward campaigns. But events had overtaken the governor. Titus was dead and Domitian ordered a renewed offensive against the Caledonian tribes.

Agricola's closest ties had been with Vespasian and Titus, and given Domitian's nature it is not surprising that Agricola should have been removed from office as soon as he appeared to have won a conclusive victory.

This victory was the culmination of two seasons' activity along Strathmore, with significant naval backup once again as demonstrated by the discovery of sites at Dun and Forres on the edge of Montrose and Findhorn Bays respectively.

One particular problem that has dominated the discussion

of the northward penetration during the Flavian campaigns is the search for the battleground of Mons Graupius (4:14). Attempts to locate the scene of the battle have ranged from as far south as Strathearn (1, 3 on Map 4:14) to as far north as Caithness and Sutherland (7). Appreciation of the possibilities has been enhanced by the additional information now available from aerial photographs, notably those taken by Professor J. K. St Joseph (see site 5, 4:14). His favoured location for the battle lies on the slopes below Mither Tap O'Bennachie, the site of a hillfort some 40km (25 miles) north-west of Aberdeen, where the ground drops away towards the site of the 59ha (144 acre) marching camp known as Durno (5). Unfortunately, the Tacitean description of the battle is insufficiently precise to support this particular identification beyond doubt, or indeed any of the other sites that have been suggested. In particular the description of the extensive use of chariots in front of the Caledonian forces does not accord well with the presence of a river between Durno and Bennachie. Likewise, much modern opinion doubts whether Agricola disposed of an army of a size capable of filling 59 ha (144 acres) under canvas.

Other sites have of course, been proposed, notably Raedykes (2), south of Stonehaven, and latterly also Sillyearn Hill near the Pass of Grange (4), beyond Durno. At the moment the line of known marching camps can be taken only as far as Bellie (Fochabers), but it is clear that the underlying strategy of the campaign lay in the Caledonian defence of the high-quality agricultural land of the Laigh of Moray. In this respect there are a number of other potential battle sites which should be brought into the reckoning, such as the hill behind Forres where the nearby presence of the Pictish Sueno Stone plainly indicates the location of a later major combat. Indeed, it is possible that other sites even further to the west such as the great hillfort on the Ord overlooking the Beauly Firth should perhaps be considered.

The underlying strategic reason for this lies in the possibly analogous evidence from two other campaigns in Scotland of which the better known is the Hanoverian destruction of the Stewart army at Culloden. The stages of the advance will be found marked on Map 4:14, as is the much more relevant progress of Edward I in his ferocious attack on Moray in 1303. The king's perception of a satisfactory conquest involved his presence in Moray for several weeks while armed troops roved as far north as Tain on the Dornoch Firth. The dates of the concluding phases of his campaign recall Tacitus' observation that summer was 'already over' when Agricola brought the Caledones to battle. Intriguingly, once Moray was conquered it was possible to choose much more expeditious return routes to the south and it is known that Edward led an army of over 20,000 men southwards directly over the Grampians through the area of Braemar and hence back to Strathmore. From this it will be apparent that the canvass on which the hunt for Mons Graupius is

based perhaps needs to be extended in a variety of directions.

In the aftermath of the great battle the Romans occupied and garrisoned the agricultural lands of the eastern corridor, presumably aiming to control the tribes of the Highlands and islands through political means (deterrence, treaties, hostages). Tacitus could fairly claim that the conquest of Britain was complete (*Agricola* 10; *Histories* 1.2.1). As Breeze and others have pointed out, however, Agricola was given little time to consolidate his victory. His recall would have followed quickly on the news reaching Rome at the end of AD 83, and by late spring 84 he was probably on his way back to Rome and enforced early retirement, albeit after an exceptionally long governorship.

TEMPORARY CAMPS

Archaeological evidence relating to Roman campaigns during the conquest period comes in several forms, but perhaps the most important type of site in this connection is the temporary camp. In the main these were camps built by the Roman army on the march at each overnight stopping point. The defences were not as formidable as those of permanent forts, but the area enclosed within them was often very large, reflecting the size of battlegroup formations on the march. Because of the necessity to construct such camps before nightfall, the Roman army on campaign tended not to move with great rapidity, but slow, careful progress may have been an effective weapon against enemy morale. One famous Roman general pronounced that Roman victories were often won with the entrenching tool rather than with conventional arms!

In theory, each Roman campaign in Britain should have left its trace in the form of marching camps and, because a military unit on campaign was likely to build camps day by day to suit its own requirements, we should also expect in optimum circumstances to be able to detect regular series of camps of a standard size. The hope exists that if we can identify the route taken by a particular unit on the march, we may also be able to place that series of camps in a specific historical context.

In reality, however, the evidence is not so straightforward. Camp defences were slight features when constructed and are easily destroyed in agricultural or urban contexts (their brief occupation rarely resulted in the sort of rubbish accumulation which would alert archaeologists to their existence). Some camps have survived as earthworks on high ground, but the vast majority have been discovered in recent times by air photography. Here much depends on chance factors such as agricultural rotation or the persistence of air photographers. The number of camps known in Britain far exceeds the total for the rest of the Roman world, but it is still only a very partial picture of the original evidence (4:15). Another problem with assigning camps to

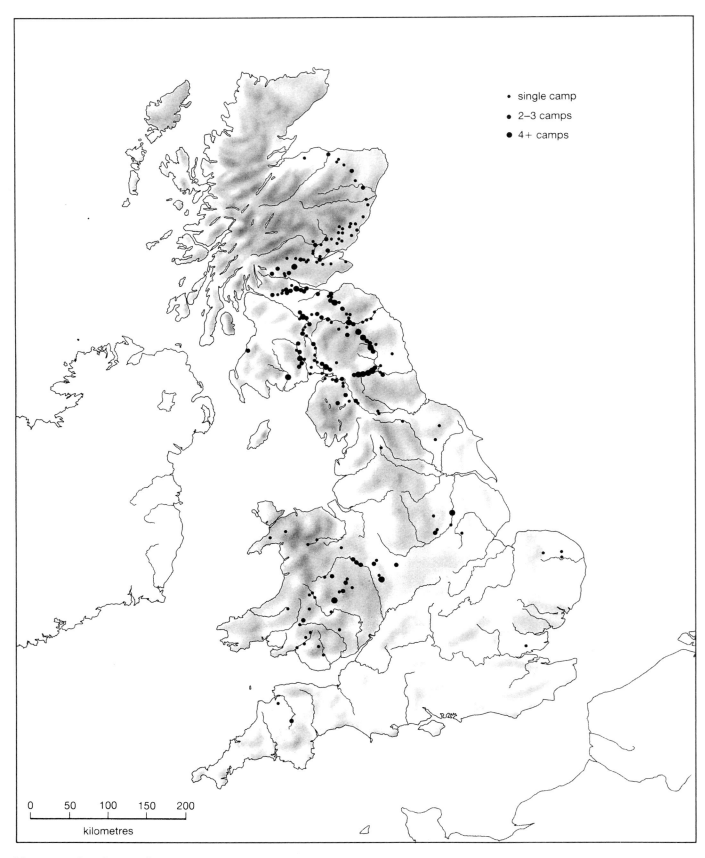

Map 4:15 Distribution of Roman temporary camps in Britain

single camp

2–3 camps

4+ camps

0   50   100   150   200

kilometres

particular invasions is that very often successive campaigns followed the same general route which was in any case dictated by topographical considerations. Excavation has generally been limited and few artefacts have been recovered. Even when pottery has been found it is rarely possible to assign groups of camps to a particular governor. The overall distribution of camps is biased towards the north and west, with few discoveries in the south-east, south-west and Midlands – although we know that a good deal of campaigning took place in these areas early in the conquest period. The bias reflects the greater military problems faced by Rome in Wales and especially in northern Britain. In addition to Agricola's campaigns, we know that there were major armies operating in Scotland under Antoninus Pius (AD 139–41), Ulpius Marcellus (c.AD 180), Septimius Severus and his son Caracalla (c.AD 209–12) and Constantius Chlorus (AD 306) and there may have been many other campaigns for which no written evidence has survived (cf. 4:49, 4:57–59, 4:69).

Attempts have been made by some scholars to identify series of camps in terms of their size and to correlate them with specific campaigns. Both processes are fraught with difficulties. In Maps 4:16– 4:22 the camps of Wales and the Marches and those of northern Britain have been batched in size categories, which have been determined for each area by plotting all known sizes (many of which are in any case approximate) on histograms and assuming that the peaks mark 'standard' sizes. Further discoveries and more precise data on the size of known camps will no doubt refine the picture (the maps include discoveries which were published up to 1988). It should be stressed that the 'standard' sizes are not envisaged as exclusive groups since each category will contain a range of sites spread slightly over and under the 'average' area. In some cases, therefore, two camps placed in two different groups could be quite close in area and have related to the same campaign. This needs to be borne in mind when using the maps.

The range of size groups for Wales differs from that for northern Britain, but this probably reflects differences in battlegroup composition and date. Almost all the Welsh camps should relate to the initial conquest period (AD 43–77). It is not possible, given the incompleteness of the evidence, to assign camps to historical events. However, many of the known camps lie in the Marches and on the routes into central Wales, perhaps reflecting a Roman strategy of driving a wedge between their two main opponents, the Ordovices in the north and the Silures in the south (4:16– 4:17 and Table 4:3). Large semi-permanent or permanent fortresses on Watling Street (Mancetter, Wall, Kinvaston, Leighton, and Wroxeter) or at the lower Severn crossing (Kingsholm, Gloucester) would have served as mustering points, supply bases and operational headquarters for the campaigning. More advanced bases with internal buildings are known at Clyro and Usk, while to the north Rhyn Park

was a base for campaigns against North Wales. Occupation and abandonment at such bases indicates the ebb and flow of the Roman conquest.

The two largest temporary camps were c.25ha (63 acres) in size (4:16, nos. 1 and 2), but their discovery need not imply the existence of a regular series of such camps. It is possible that they also functioned as advance mustering bases, their size perhaps indicating the brief reunion of all the available troops. The implication would seem to be that normally the army operated in two or more separate columns. The most coherent group of camps is a series of sites of about 16ha (40 acres) extending from Watling Street into Ordovician territory (4:16, nos. 5–9) and camps of 12ha (30 acres) and smaller were commonest. More examples of the various sizes of camp are needed before it will be possible to make better sense of the distribution.

The overall picture for northern Britain is rather different. In the first place many more camps are known and some are far larger than those located in Wales. The main axes for the invasion of northern Britain are clearly delineated (4:15), with four lines of advance into lowland Scotland leading to a major concentration north of the Forth–Clyde isthmus following Strathallan and Strathmore up the east side of the highland massif. Yet it must be stressed that this is a fragmentary picture of the total potential evidence for repeated Roman campaigns from the AD 70s to the fourth century and it is unwise to attempt to be too categorical about the historical context of particular camps or series of camps.

Camps are not only classifiable in terms of size. Some of the northern camps had a distinctive and unique form of gate, the so-called Stracathro-type, a form first clearly identified by General Roy at Dalginross as long ago as 1793. This would appear to have been a short-lived Flavian innovation perhaps associated with just one of the British legions at the time of Agricola's northern campaigns. The distribution and size range of known camps with this form of gate is perhaps surprising and well illustrates the weaknesses of the evidence (4:18). The largest such camps were about 25ha (63 acres) in size which, as already noted, is the same as the largest known camps in Wales. Some of the smaller camps may have functioned not as marching camps, but as construction camps for associated forts nearby. Ythan Wells and Auch-inhove in Buchan, however, were certainly part of a campaign series whose other members remain unlocated. Constructional detail and chronological evidence is lacking for most of the other camps and only occasionally, where camps were superimposed as at Ardoch, can one establish even a relative sequence between different groups.

The largest camps (those of c.40ha (100 acres) and more) (4:19) appear to fall into several groups. The dating of these camps is very problematical and it has been claimed that some of them relate to the campaigns of Agricola. The case rests largely on an abraded sherd of Samian pottery, perhaps

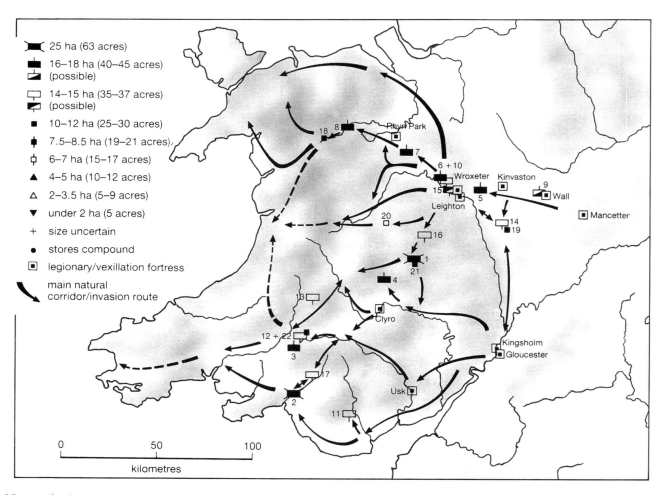

Map 4:16   Temporary camps in Wales I

Table 4.3   Temporary camps in Wales

1 Brampton Bryan	16 Stretford Bridge	31 Derwydd-Bach	46 Craven Arms
2 Blaen-cwm-bach	17 Coelbren (Camnant)	32 Melin Court (Carn Caca)	47 Water Eaton I
3 Arosfa Gareg	18 Llanfor	33 Brompton II	48 Upper Affcot
4 Walton IV	19 Greensforge I	34 Glanmiheli	49 Forden Gaer
5 Burlington I	20 Brompton I	35 Pen-y-Gwrhyd	50 Greensforge IV
6 Uffington I	21 Walford	36 Water Eaton II	51 Red Hill
7 Whittington	22 Y Pigwn II	37 Walton I	52 Brandon camp
8 Penrhos	23 Wroxeter II (Attingham)	38 Burlington II	53 Llanfor
9 Wall I	24 Ystradfellte	39 Wall II	54 Wall III
10 Uffington II	25 Bromfield	40 Leighton	55 Stretton Bridge II
11 Pen-y-Coedcae	26 Greensforge II	41 Walton II	56 Brompton III
12 Y Pigwn I	27 St Harmon (Cwm-is-y-rhiw)	42 Walton III	57 Greensforge V
13 Beulah	28 Esgairperfedd	43 Dolau Gaer	58 Llansantffraid
14 Swindon	29 Twyn-y-Bridallt	44 Greensforge III	59 Abertanat
15 Wroxeter I	30 Clyro	45 Buckton	

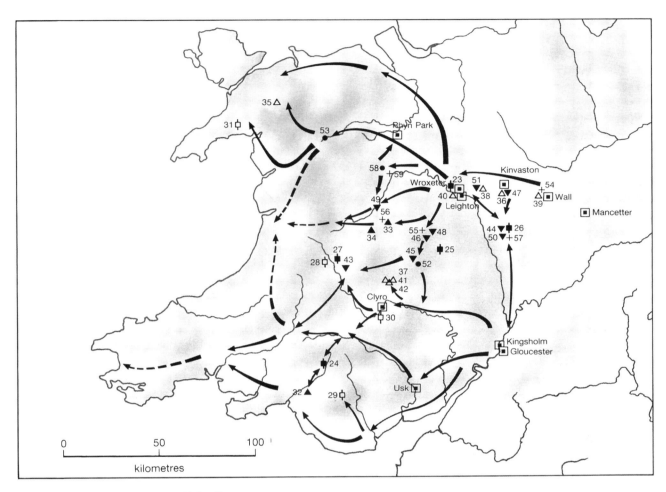

Map 4:17   Temporary camps in Wales II

Plate 4:3   An aerial view of the Roman fort (left) and camp (right) at Stracathro in Strathmore. The camp displays evidence of gateways of a type associated with the early Flavian campaigns in Scotland.

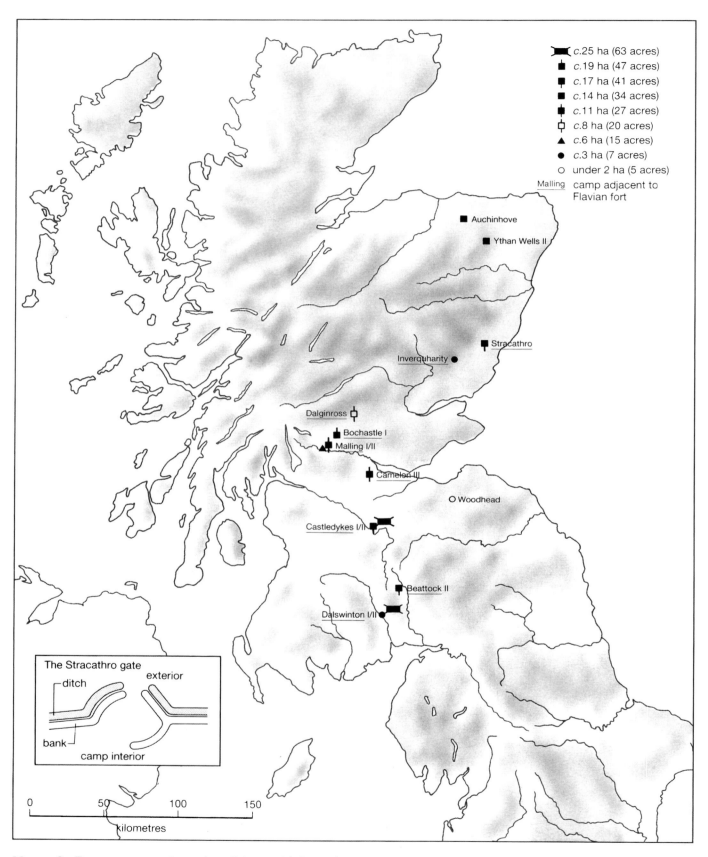

Map 4:18 Temporary camps in northern Britain: with Stracathro gateways

Legend (top right):

c.25 ha (63 acres)
c.19 ha (47 acres)
c.17 ha (41 acres)
c.14 ha (34 acres)
c.11 ha (27 acres)
c.8 ha (20 acres)
c.6 ha (15 acres)
c.3 ha (7 acres)
under 2 ha (5 acres)

Malling camp adjacent to Flavian fort

Map labels:
Auchinhove
Ythan Wells II
Stracathro
Inverquharity
Dalginross
Bochastle I
Malling I/II
Camelon III
Woodhead
Castledykes I/II
Beattock II
Dalswinton I/II

The Stracathro gate
ditch
exterior
bank
camp interior

0   50   100   150
kilometres

of first-century date, from the ditch of the 47ha (115 acre) camp at Abernethy, and St Joseph's view that the exceptionally large camp at Durno was Agricola's camp before the battle of Mons Graupius. As we have seen, the equation between Durno and Agricola cannot be proven, and there are other reasons for considering that the camps of more than 40ha (100 acres) were of second-century or later date. Firstly, we have noted that the largest camps which certainly date to the first century were 25ha (63 acres) in area. This may be our best indication of the size of Agricola's army, since with Wales and northern England only recently conquered, and certainly not fully pacified, it is unlikely that he had a larger army available for his Scottish campaigns. As in Wales, therefore, the first-century camps in Scotland may have included a handful of 25ha (63 acres) examples and large numbers of camps of 16ha (40 acres) and less. The camps of more than 40ha (100 acres) imply a far greater size of army in the field, something which was more feasible in the Antonine and Severan periods when the political stability of Roman Britain freed more of the garrison for campaigning. The very largest camps, of about 67ha (165 acres), may relate to the great Imperial expedition led by Septimius Severus and his son Caracalla, who came to Britain accompanied by substantial reinforcements for the normal British army. Some of the other camps north of the

Forth–Clyde line may represent the further progress of these campaigns, though we cannot rule out other possibilities such as a campaign by Constantius Chlorus in AD 306 (4:69). Full publication of the air photographic evidence is badly needed.

The camps occupying between 17 and 26ha (40 and 63 acres) must have covered several periods of activity (4:20). At least two camps of 25ha (63 acres) were Flavian, but the majority (with a different form of gate) were probably of later date and have often been linked to the Severan campaigns, though once again other possibilities cannot be ruled out. One important piece of evidence is the fact that the 25ha (63 acre) camp at Ardoch was post-dated by a 52ha (130 acre) camp there – though perhaps with little time in between. One possibility which suggests itself, though without any supporting evidence, is that an army which constructed camps of about 52ha (130 acres) when operating in one season might have built two sets of 25ha (63 acres) camps if operating in two columns in another campaign. Elements of other series of camps are evident in lowland Scotland and some are believed to represent the Antonine reconquest of that zone in AD 139–41. It must be appreciated, though, that to be effective the Antonine campaigns must have penetrated well to the north of the Forth–Clyde isthmus and further camps must be sought there.

Plate 4:4 A marching camp at Annan, Dumfries, probably associated with Flavian campaigns into Galloway

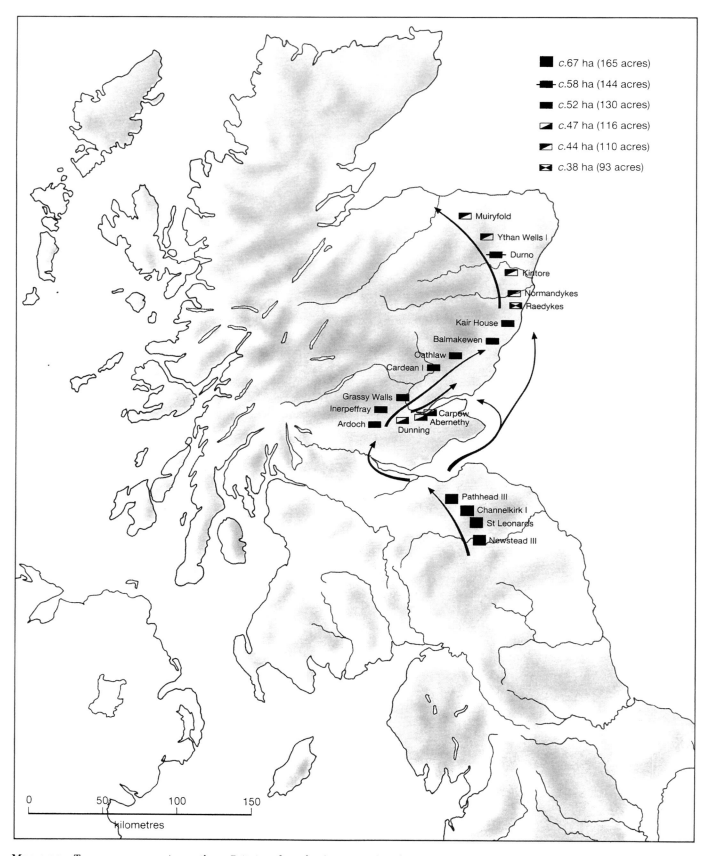

Map 4:19   Temporary camps in northern Britain: of *c.*40ha (100 acres) and more

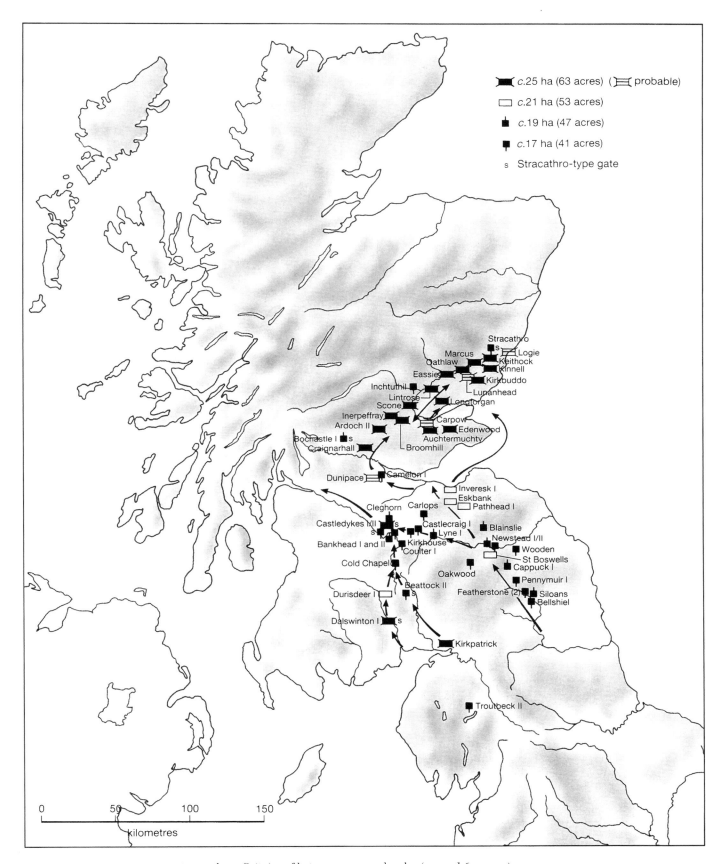

Map 4:20   Temporary camps in northern Britain: of between *c.*17 and 25ha (40 and 63 acres)

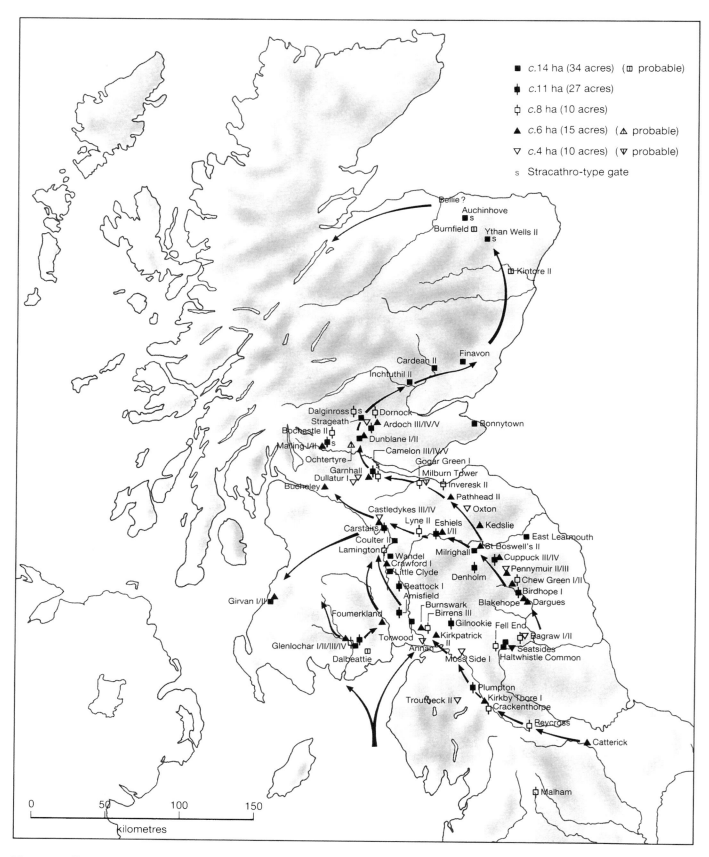

Map 4:21 Temporary camps in northern Britain: of between 4ha and 14ha (10 and 34 acres)

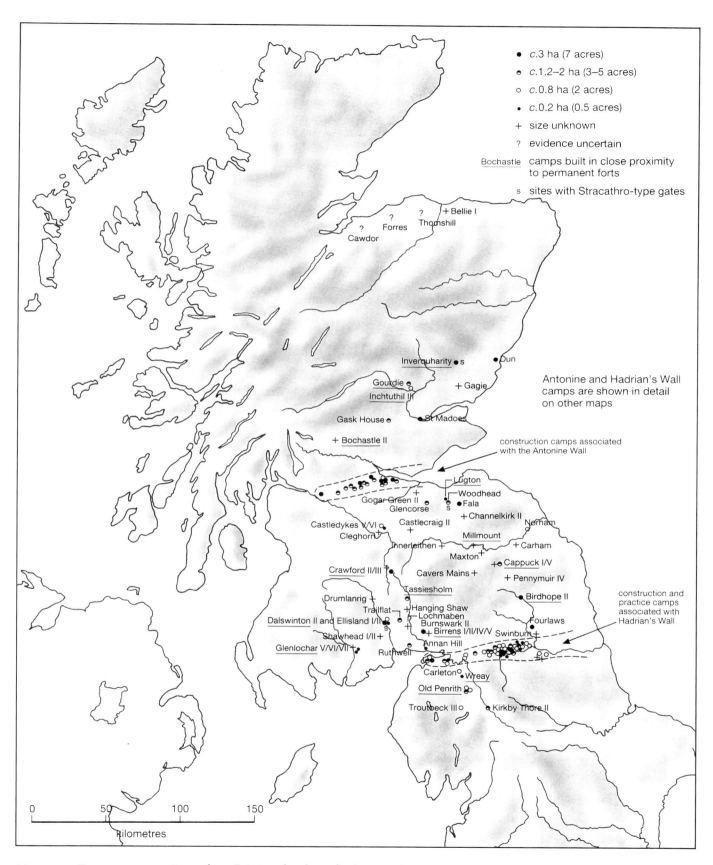

Legend (top right):

- • *c*.3 ha (7 acres)
- ◔ *c*.1.2–2 ha (3–5 acres)
- ○ *c*.0.8 ha (2 acres)
- • *c*.0.2 ha (0.5 acres)
- + size unknown
- ? evidence uncertain
- Bochastle camps built in close proximity to permanent forts
- s sites with Stracathro-type gates

Map labels:

Bellie I
? Forres ? Thornshill
? Cawdor

Inverquharity s • Dun

Gourdie + Gagie
Inchtuthil II

Gask House ○ • St Madoes

+ Bochastle II

Antonine and Hadrian's Wall camps are shown in detail on other maps

construction camps associated with the Antonine Wall

Lugton
Woodhead
Gogar Green II s • Fala
Glencorse + Channelkirk II
Castlecraig II Norham
Castledykes V/VI ○ Millmount
Cleghorn + Carham
Innerleithen + Maxton
Crawford II/III Cavers Mains + Cappuck I/V
Tassiesholm + Pennymuir IV
Drumlanrig + Birdhope II
Trailflat Hanging Shaw
Dalswinton II and Ellisland I/II s Lochmaben Fourlaws
Shawhead I/II + Burnswark II Swinburn
Glenlochar V/VI/VII Birrens I/II/IV/V
Annan Hill
Ruthwell
Carleton ○ Wreay
Old Penrith
Troutbeck III ○ • Kirkby Thore II

construction and practice camps associated with Hadrian's Wall

Scale:
0   50   100   150
Kilometres

Map 4:22 Temporary camps in northern Britain: of under *c*.4ha (10 acres)

Camps of 14ha (34 acres) and less (4:21, 4:22) were fairly common and related to a number of different activities. Those between 4 and 14ha (10 and 34 acres) in size were perhaps most likely to have been constructed as marching camps. For example, the Stracathro-type camps and those of about 14ha (34 acres) in north-east Scotland are often interpreted as evidence for the northward penetration of Agricola's last campaigns. Many camps of 4ha (10 acres) and under may have served as construction camps for neighbouring forts and other fortifications. Alternatively some may have played a minor role in the campaigning (as, for instance, the coastal camp at Dun or the bridgehead at St Madoes opposite Carpow).

The mention of construction camps introduces the question of the transition from conquest to military occupation. When campaigning was intended to be followed by the garrisoning of an area, the final pattern of deployment emerged only after the major field victory had been gained. Although some forts and fortresses might be built in support of the army on campaign, the major work of consolidation and fort building was the sequel to the actual conquest, not a feature of it.

THE MILITARY GARRISON

The early deployment

Whilst Rome's campaigning tactics were relatively slow to change, her defensive strategy in relation to conquered terri-

tory was much more fluid than is sometimes appreciated. It has been commonplace to assume that the same criteria were used to determine military deployment in the early conquest period as were deemed appropriate later. For instance, it has been argued by some people that south-eastern Britain *must* have been covered with a network of forts in the years immediately after the invasion in AD 43 and that a temporary 'frontier' was created along the line of the Fosse Way road between the Trent and the Severn. This theory has, however, become increasingly at variance with the archaeological evidence which now suggests a radically different pattern of deployment (4:23 and Table 4:4). There are actually very few early forts in the south-east and some of these may relate to the post-Boudican repacification rather than to the initial occupation. In any case there are severe problems in dating the occupation of forts of Julio-Claudian date accurately. The chronology is dependent on artefacts which often have a date range spanning several years or even decades, which militates against attempts to associate the construction of forts with the careers of particular governors. An additional common failing of many discussions of the evidence is that the most active generals are assumed also to have been the most conscientious fort builders. This may be true up to a point, but the work of consolidation would have taken place over a period of several years after a victory had been won. Governors such as Didius Gallus, Petronius Turpilianus and Trebellius Maximus who were all criticized by Tacitus for

Table 4.4   Pre-Flavian forts and fortresses in Britain

1 Alcester	25 Hindwell Farm (?)	49 Okehampton	73 Aberffraw (?)
2 Ancaster (?)	26 Hod Hill	50 Osmanthorpe	74 Abergavenny (?)
3 Baylam House	27 Ixworth	51 Redhill	75 Arnold (?)
4 Broxtowe	28 Kelvedon	52 Rhyn Park	76 Clun (?)
5 Caersws I	29 Kingsholm	53 Richborough	77 Chester (?)
6 Cardiff	30 Kinvaston	54 Rossington	78 Ham Hill (?)
7 Charterhouse	31 Kirmington (?)	55 St Albans	79 Llandovery (?)
8 Chelmsford	32 Lake Farm	56 Shapwick	80 Nettleton (?)
9 Chesterfield	33 Leicester	57 Staines (?)	81 Pen-y-Gaer (?)
10 Chichester	34 Leighton	58 Stanway	82 Trent Vale (?)
11 Cirencester	35 Brandon Hill (Leintwardine)	59 Stretford Bridge	83 Silchester (?)
12 Clifford	36 Jay Lane (Leintwardine)	60 Stretton Grandison	84 Fingringhoe Wick
13 Clyro	37 Lincoln	61 Stretton Mill	85 Fishbourne
14 Colchester	38. Littlechester (Strutts Park)	62 Templeborough	86 Hamworthy
15 Droitwich	39 Llanfor (?)	63 Thorpe-by-Newark/East Stoke	87 Richborough
16 Dropshort Farm	40 Longthorpe	64 Tiverton	88 Sea Mills
17 Exeter	41 Lunt I	65 Usk	89 Bury Barton
18 Gloucester	42 Lunt II	66 Waddon Hill	90 Cullompton
19 Godmanchester	43 Mancetter	67 Wall	91 Grove Park, Budbrook
20 Great Casterton	44 Marton	68 Water Newton	92 Killerton
21 Great Chesterton I	45 Metchley	69 Whitchurch	93 Orchard Hill Farm
22 Great Chesterton II	46 Nanstallon	70 Wiveliscombe	94 Dorchester
23 Greensforge	47 Newton-on-Trent	71 Wroxeter I	95 Abertanat
24 Hembury hillfort	48 North Tawton	72 Wroxeter II	96 Llansantffraid

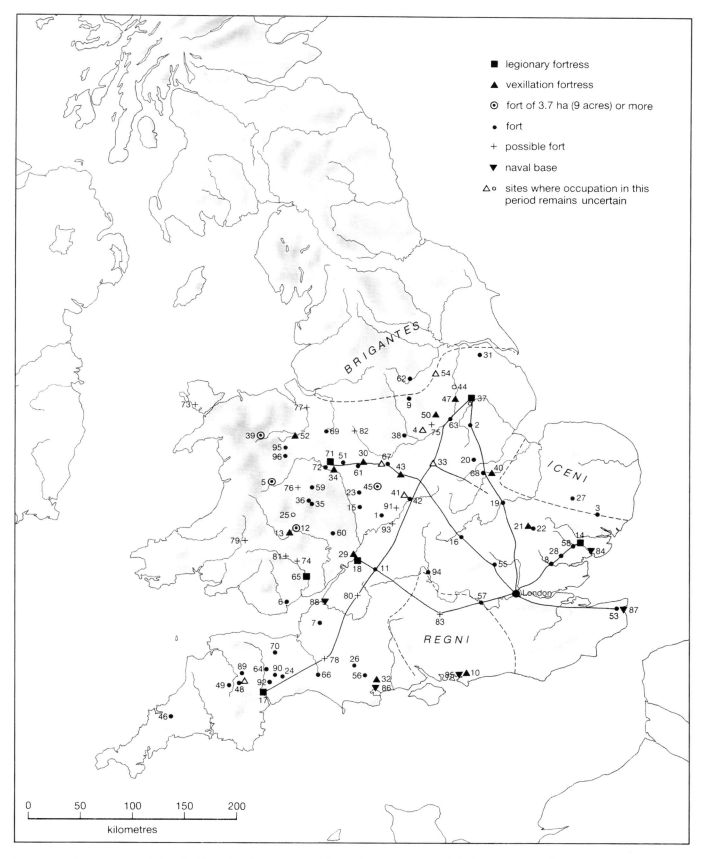

Map 4:23   Military sites of Claudio-Neronian date AD 43–68 (not all sites were occupied at the same time).

lack of military success may in fact have been responsible for the construction of far more forts than their more famous predecessors, and the same applies to Agricola's anonymous successor.

The idea that the army was deployed evenly across conquered territory is plainly a misconception. Some important native centres and river crossings in the south-east were garrisoned, but the map suggests that the vast majority of the troops were kept in front-line positions. The point is exemplified by the distribution of the class of sites conventionally called 'vexillation' fortresses (the term is misleading, but is retained here for convenience). These were large sites of about 8–12ha (20–30 acres) – about half the size of a full-scale legionary fortress. Although the exact dates of almost all these sites remain uncertain, the forts were a particular feature of the fluid military situation of AD 43–77 (4:24). The growing number of such sites, in addition to the number of full legionary fortresses of early date, is a clear indication that Rome's strategy in the early years envisaged conquest of the south-west, west and north of

Britain, rather than a blanket defence and detailed policing of the area initially overrun. The vexillation fortresses may well have been designed to accommodate both auxiliary and legionary troops in mixed battlegroup formations and these sites presumably had an intimate connection with active campaigning or intimidation of the tribes outside the garrisoned area. Some of these fortresses will have served as advanced summer headquarters, others as winter quarters. The close association of some of the sites with naval bases or pre-Roman tribal centres is hardly surprising, but it is worth noting also that several appear to have been installed on or close to the edge of tribal territories, allowing rapid forward deployment against hostile or untrustworthy tribes, whilst at the same time discouraging alliances against Rome. Above all, it must be appreciated that the construction of legionary and vexillation fortresses in the first 30 years of Roman rule represented a versatile and fluid response to the problem of extending the initial conquest of the south-east to the rest of the island. The deployment was designed for expansionism, not defence.

Plate 4:5 The double ditches of the vexillation fortress at Rossington Bridge, south Yorkshire

Plate 4:6 Traces of a timber granary of the fortress at Usk during excavation

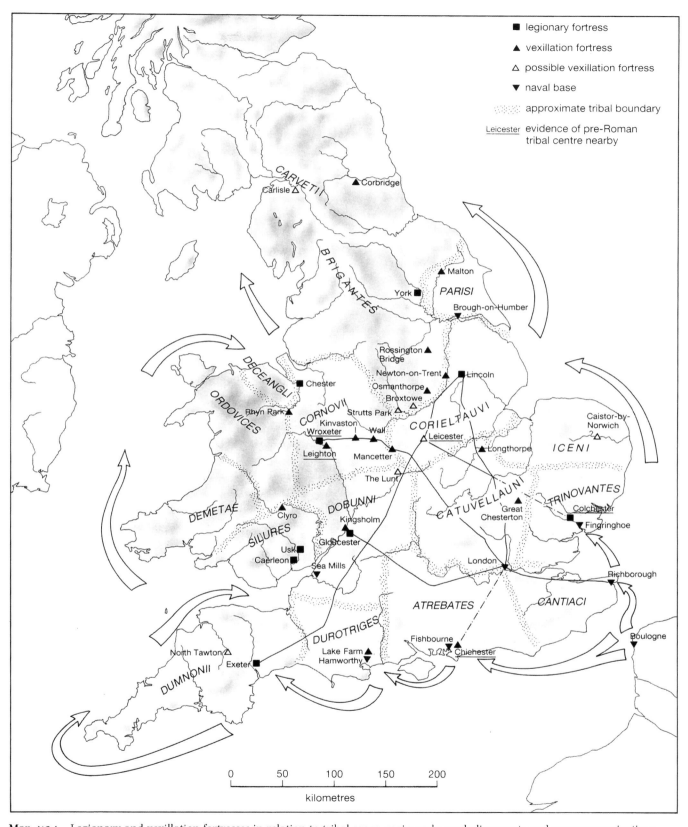

Map 4:24 Legionary and vexillation fortresses in relation to tribal areas, main early road alignments and sea communications

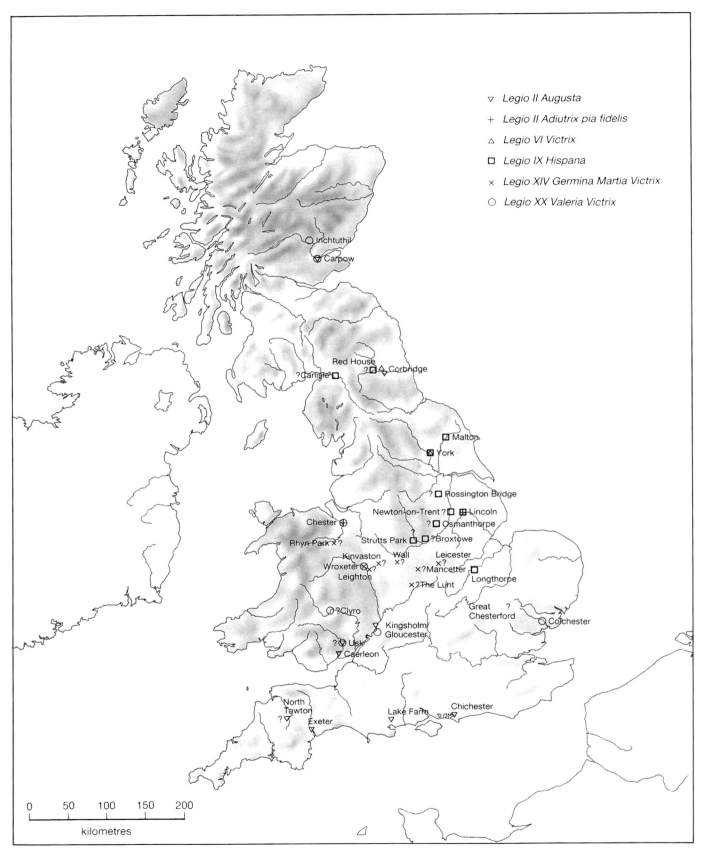

Map 4:25 Probable and possible attributions of legionary fortresses and vexillation fortresses by legion

Legend:

▽ *Legio II Augusta*

+ *Legio II Adiutrix pia fidelis*

△ *Legio VI Victrix*

□ *Legio IX Hispana*

× *Legio XIV Germina Martia Victrix*

○ *Legio XX Valeria Victrix*

Map labels:

Inchtuthil
Carpow
Red House
?Carlisle
? Corbridge
Malton
York
?Rossington Bridge
Newton-on-Trent ? Lincoln
Chester
? Osmanthorpe
Rhyn Park ×?
Strutts Park ?Broxtowe
Kinvaston
Wroxeter ×?
Leighton
Wall ×?
Leicester ×?
?Mancetter
Longthorpe
×?The Lunt
?Clyro
Great Chesterford ?
Kingsholm Gloucester
Colchester
?Usk
Caerleon
North Tawton ?
Exeter
Lake Farm
Chichester

0 50 100 150 200
kilometres

It is uncertain in many cases which garrisons were assigned to the various fortresses (4:25). For much of the conquest period there were four legions in Britain, but from the early second century there were only three, with their permanent fortresses becoming fixed at Caerleon, Chester and York. The contrast with the multiplicity of legionary and vexillation fortresses of first-century date is striking. In spite of the uncertainty about the actual garrison of many sites, possible attributions to particular legions can be made. Some vexillation fortresses may have been garrisoned entirely by auxiliary troops, but they would still have fallen within the orbit of the nearest legion. The regional basis of the operations of the various legions in the early years of the conquest is hinted at. For instance, the II Augusta may have been stationed in the south-west and, later, in South Wales, and the IX Hispana was probably located in the east

Midlands and northern England. The movement of some legions out of Britain or to new fortresses led to the succession of one legion by another at Chester, Lincoln, Wroxeter and York.

The idea that the Fosse Way was an early frontier cannot be reconciled with the view presented here that the Julio-Claudian deployment was essentially expansionist. The theory rests on the misconception that the Romans wished initially to limit their conquest to the lowland zone (4:26). The evidence to support the assumption that the road was garrisoned by forts at regular intervals along its length has not, however, been forthcoming. Many of the positively identified military sites seem to have been constructed later than the presumed date of the Fosse 'frontier'. Some of the forts on the Fosse, such as Cirencester, were related to military routes heading into enemy territory. Furthermore,

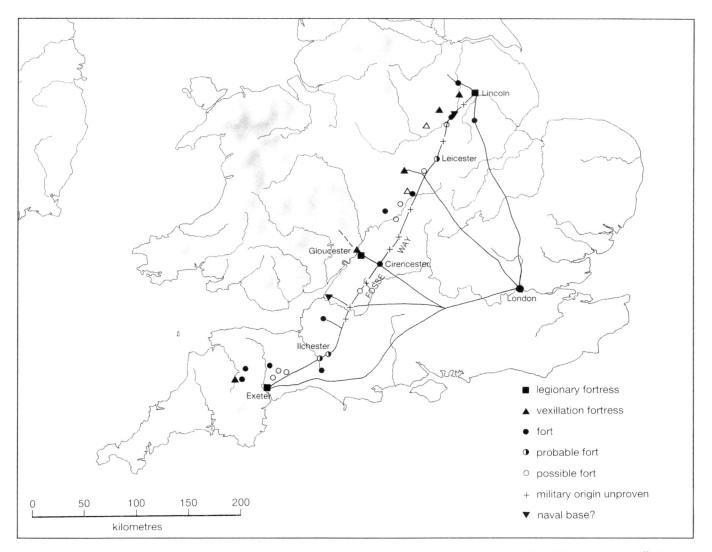

Map 4:26 Fosse Way: a 'frontier' misconceived. Early Roman military sites, within 15 Roman miles of the Fosse (not all sites were occupied at the same time).

the discovery of many early forts and fortresses north and west of the Fosse Way, in comparison with the few to the south and east, is a further argument against the belief that it was ever the front line. Its geographical position is also inappropriate for a frontier since it bisects the territory of several major tribes (Corieltauvi, Dobunni and Durotriges). Also, one may question the rationale of the supposed halt on the 'Trent–Severn' line; granted that south-east Britain contained the most 'civilized' tribes and a good proportion of the well-developed agricultural land, the west also had vital attractions – notably its wealth of mineral resources (see Map 6:1). For this reason alone it is unlikely that the Romans would have considered limiting their conquest to lowland Britain in the early years of their occupation. The twin processes of conquest and pacification, however, took time to accomplish and the total conquest of the island was

evidently planned to advance by stages. As we have seen, the early years saw a fluid deployment of troops, with the majority maintained in large bases when not engaged in active campaigning.

The Fosse Way was certainly a strategic road, even if it was not a frontier. Rather than being a front line, we should perhaps envisage its function as a rearward communication route, uniting the battlegroups formed around the II Augusta legion in the south-west, the XX Valeria in South Wales, the XIV Gemina in mid-Wales and the IX Hispana in the north-east Midlands.

There are further interesting aspects of the layout of the Fosse Way. The Fosse is one of several early military roads in Britain which exhibit regularity of alignment (4:27). The line of the road itself does deviate somewhat because of the topography, but the straight base alignment for the survey

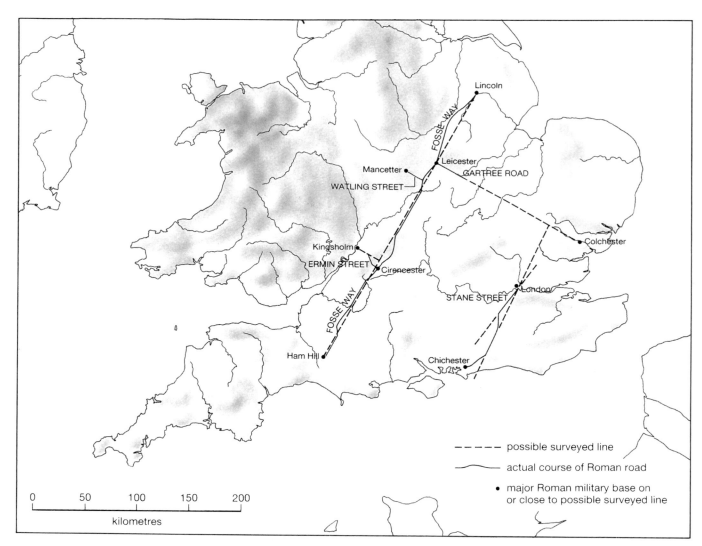

Map 4:27   Early Roman roads and possible surveyed alignments in Roman Britain

would appear to unite Leicester, Lincoln and Ham Hill (with the last two places perhaps being the original *termini* of the survey). At Leicester there is another road on a perpendicular alignment, preserved for some distance as the Gartree Road, which if projected would terminate at Colchester. Furthermore, Mancetter on Watling Street and Kingsholm on Ermin Street are located on sections of Roman road which run at right angles to this proposed Fosse survey baseline. Stane Street between London and Chichester has two very straight sections, one of which is very close to being parallel to the Fosse. The coincidence of these straight alignments with the location of a number of early military bases is striking, particularly with regard to Mancetter and Kingsholm. It is surely a possibility that the Fosse Way road was constructed following a major long-distance survey by the Roman army and that this survey may have been part of a wider scheme of territorial delimitation. The Peddar's way in East Anglia has also been cited in this context. That the army was capable of accurate, long-distance survey cannot be doubted as many examples of schemes based on a square or rectangular grid (centuriation) are known in other parts of the Empire. The purpose of the scheme identified here was clearly not full centuriation, but nevertheless the establishment of a number of perpendicular baselines across the area of Britain which was first incorporated into the Empire could have facilitated calculations of the area of tribal territories and of tribute levels, as well as being useful in the compilation of military maps. For the present this hypothesis remains unsubstantiated, but an interesting parallel to this type of survey can be cited. Around AD 30 a baseline of about 200km was laid out across part of Roman Africa, from close to the legionary fortress at Ammaedara to the Lesser Syrtic Gulf (4:28). This baseline passes right through the site of Sufetula, a town which may well have originated as a military station used at the time of the survey. At the southern end of the baseline, a partial framework for a rectilinear grid was established by boundary markers at certain cardinal spots. Unlike other centuriation schemes in Africa, the land was never subdivided in greater detail and the overall purpose seems to have been the delimitation of tribal land in a region which had recently been absorbed into the Empire (Trousset, 1978).

In the earlier section on campaigning we might reasonably have included a map showing evidence of Roman siege activity or of destruction deposits of appropriate date at Iron Age tribal centres, but the acts of conquest and destruction were only the initial stages in a long-term process of interaction between Roman and native. Recent research suggests that Roman military occupation of British hillforts and lowlying *oppida* was far commoner than was once thought (4:29). In many cases, military occupation may have been fairly brief, but the importance of such sites should not be underestimated. The direct supervision of defeated or reconciled tribes in the early phases of the conquest was of

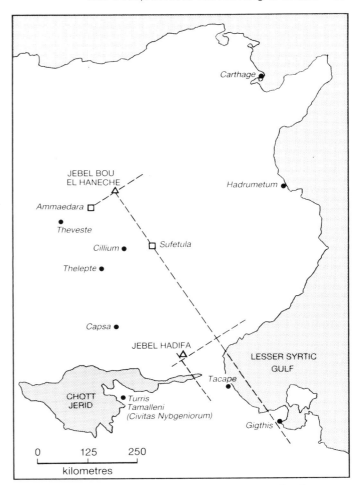

Map 4:28   Long-range surveyed alignments in North Africa

far greater significance than the policing of, for instance, roads and bridges. From the Iron Age centres, the Romans were able to carry out the disarmament of the local population, the organization of supplies, and tribute assessment – perhaps making use of the existing political and socio-economic structures. The installation of Roman forts or barracks within native defensive sites had the added value of preventing any rapid British reuse of these fortifications as centres of resistance.

The south-west of Britain was conquered and pacified in the pre-Flavian period (4:30). This is an area where many recent discoveries have greatly expanded our perception of Roman military activity, particularly in Devon. Few marching camps are known as yet, save those around North Tawton, but campaigning was co-ordinated from the legionary fortress at Exeter and the possible vexillation fortresses at Lake Farm and, perhaps, North Tawton. Roman military occupation is attested at several hillforts, notably Hod Hill, Ham Hill and Hembury. Many new fort sites, such as Okehampton, have been located in Devon; the fort at Nanstallon

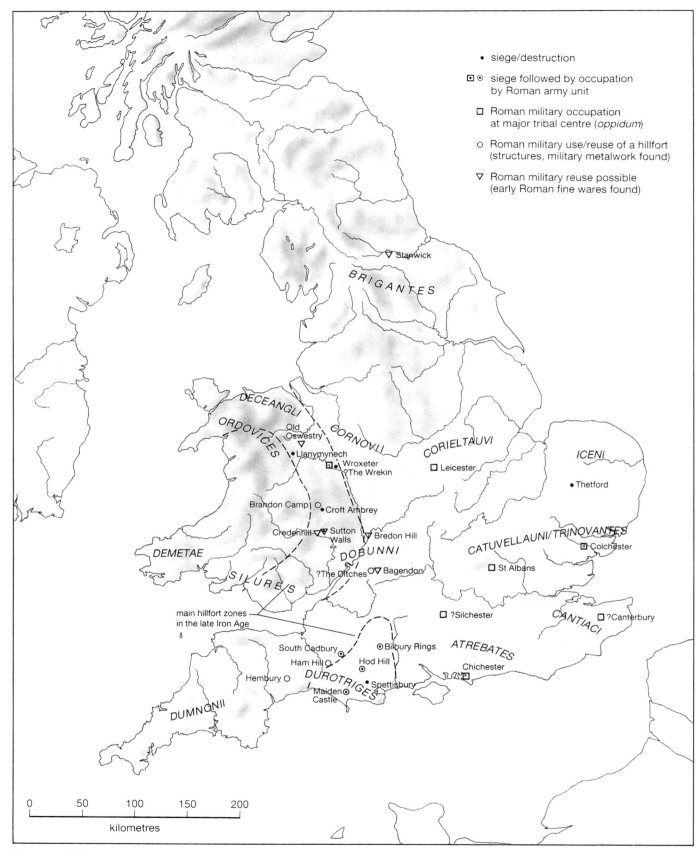

Map 4:29   The Roman army and native sites during the Conquest period: destruction, reoccupation and supervision

in Cornwall cannot have stood alone, so further discoveries are to be expected there. Once it had been conquered, the garrisoning of the region was of relatively short duration. Dating evidence is lacking from many sites, but it is likely that all but a handful were abandoned by the AD 70s. The conquest of Wales and Scotland required changes in the overall deployment of the garrison and troops were withdrawn from areas such as the south-west which had already been pacified.

The pattern of garrisoning that emerged in the Flavian period (c.AD 70–96) (4:31 and Table 4:5) was very different from that of the Julio-Claudian period. The conquest of Wales and Scotland by c.AD 83 marked the end of the earlier expansionist deployment. The vexillation fortresses had served their purpose and were progressively abandoned. Thereafter, the legions were moved less frequently and, although some spare fortresses were kept for a while on a care and maintenance basis, by the end of the first century there were only three fortresses for the three remaining legions, at Caerleon, Chester and York. By contrast, the deployment of auxiliary units in small forts was much more experimental, and some forts cannot have been held for long

before they were abandoned. It was still not the practice, though, to brigade each and every individual unit in its own fort, and many forts (particularly those of 3.6ha (9 acres) and more in size) were no doubt designed to accommodate two or more units. The main emphasis of the deployment was on the policing of Wales and northern Britain and by AD 100 the few remaining sites on or close to the Fosse Way had long been abandoned.

During the reigns of Trajan and Hadrian in the early second century AD the pattern of deployment was gradually changed again (4:32 and Table 4:6). Virtually all sites in the Midlands and Welsh Marches were abandoned by the end of the first century and the Welsh garrison was thinned out steadily thereafter (see 4:33–4:38). From c.AD 86 or 87, the Romans had been obliged to withdraw troops from Britain on a scale which necessitated the abandonment of the idea of total occupation of northern Britain. In stages, the Roman army pulled back from Scotland, and by the early second century a frontier for the province was coalescing on the Tyne–Solway line – a policy which culminated in the construction of Hadrian's Wall. In support of this frontier there was a concentration of small forts in northern England,

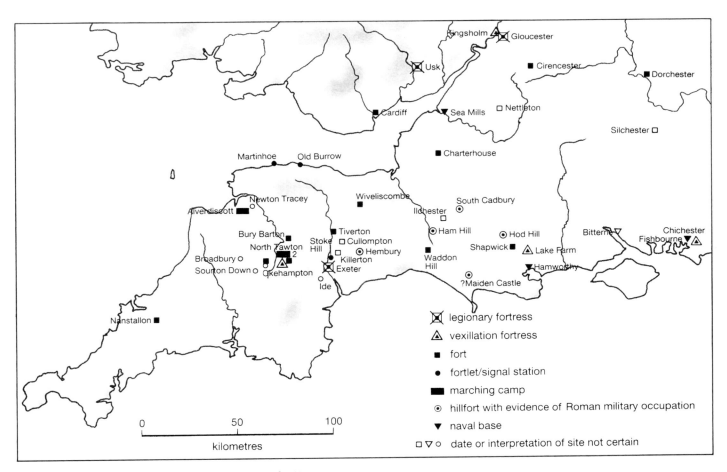

Map 4:30   Pre-Flavian military activity in the South-West

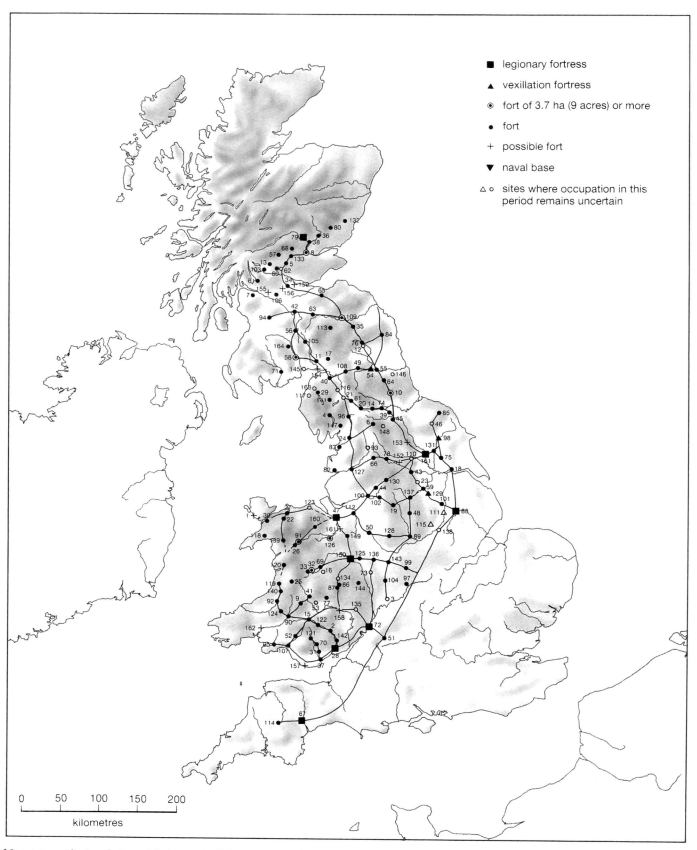

Map 4:3 1　Flavian forts and fortresses in Britain AD 70–96 (not all sites were occupied at the same time).

Table 4.5   Military sites of Flavian date

1 Aberffraw (?)	43 Castleford	85 Lease Rigg	127 Ribchester
2 Abergavenny	44 Castleshaw	86 Jay Lane (Leintwardine)	128 Rocester
3 Alcester (?)	45 Catterick	87 Buckton (Leintwardine)	129 Rossington
4 Ambleside	46 Cawthorn	88 Lincoln	130 Slack
5 Ardoch	47 Chester	89 Littlechester	131 Stamford Bridge
6 Brough-by-Bainbridge	48 Chesterfield	90 Llandovery	132 Stracathro
7 Barochan Hill	49 Vindolanda (Chesterholm)	91 Llanfor (?)	133 Strageath
8 Bertha	50 Chesterton	92 Llanio	134 Stretford Bridge
9 Beulah (Caerau)	51 Cirencester	93 Long Preston	135 Stretton Grandison
10 Binchester	52 Coelbren	94 Loudoun Hill	136 Stretton Mill
11 Birrens	53 Colwyn (?)	95 Loughor	137 Templeborough
12 Blakehope (?)	54 Corbridge (Red House)	96 Low Borrowbridge	138 Thorpe-by-Newark
13 Bochastle	55 Corbridge	97 Lunt	139 Tomen-y-Mur
14 Bowes	56 Crawford	98 Malton	140 Trawscoed
15 Brecon Gaer (Y Gaer)	57 Dalginross	99 Mancetter	141 Troutbeck
16 Brompton	58 Dalswinton	100 Manchester	142 Usk
17 Broomholm	59 Doncaster	101 Marton	143 Wall
18 Brough-on-Humber	60 Doune	102 Melandra	144 Wall Town
19 Brough-on-Noe	61 Drumquhassle	103 Menteith	145 Ward Law (?)
20 Brough-under-Stainmore	62 Dunblane (?)	104 Metchley	146 Washing Well/Whickham
21 Brougham (?)	63 Easter Happrew	105 Milton	147 Watercrook
22 Bryn-y-Gefeiliau	64 Ebchester	106 Mollins	148 Wensley
23 Burghwallis	65 Elginhaugh	107 Neath	149 Whitchurch
24 Burrow in Lonsdale	66 Elslack	108 Nether Denton	150 Wroxeter
25 Cae-Gaer	67 Exeter	109 Newstead	151 York
26 Caer Gai	68 Fendoch	110 Newton Kyme	152 Adel (?)
27 Caerhun	69 Forden Gaer	111 Newton (?)	153 Aldborough (?)
28 Caerleon	70 Gelligaer	112 Northwich	154 Annan (?)
29 Caermote	71 Glenlochar	113 Oakwood	155 Cadder (?)
30 Caernarvon	72 Gloucester	114 Okehampton	156 Castlecary (?)
31 Caerphilly	73 Greensforge	115 Osmanthorpe (?)	157 Cowbridge (?)
32 Caersws I (?)	74 Greta Bridge	116 Old Penrith	158 Kenchester (?)
33 Caersws II	75 Hayton	117 Papcastle (?)	159 Mumrills (?)
34 Camelon	76 High Rochester	118 Pen Llystyn	160 Ruthin
35 Cappuck	77 Hindwell Farm	119 Pen Llwyn	161 Tilston (?)
36 Cardean	78 Ilkley	120 Pennal	162 Carmarthen (?)
37 Cardiff	79 Inchtuthil	121 Pen-y-Darren	163 Blennerhasset
38 Cargill	80 Inverquharity	122 Pen-y-Gaer	164 Drumlanrig
39 Carkin Moor	81 Kirkby Thore	123 Prestatyn	
40 Carlisle	82 Kirkham	124 Pumsaint (Dolaucothi)	
41 Castell Collen	83 Lancaster	125 Redhill	
42 Castledykes	84 Learchild	126 Rhyn Park II (?)	

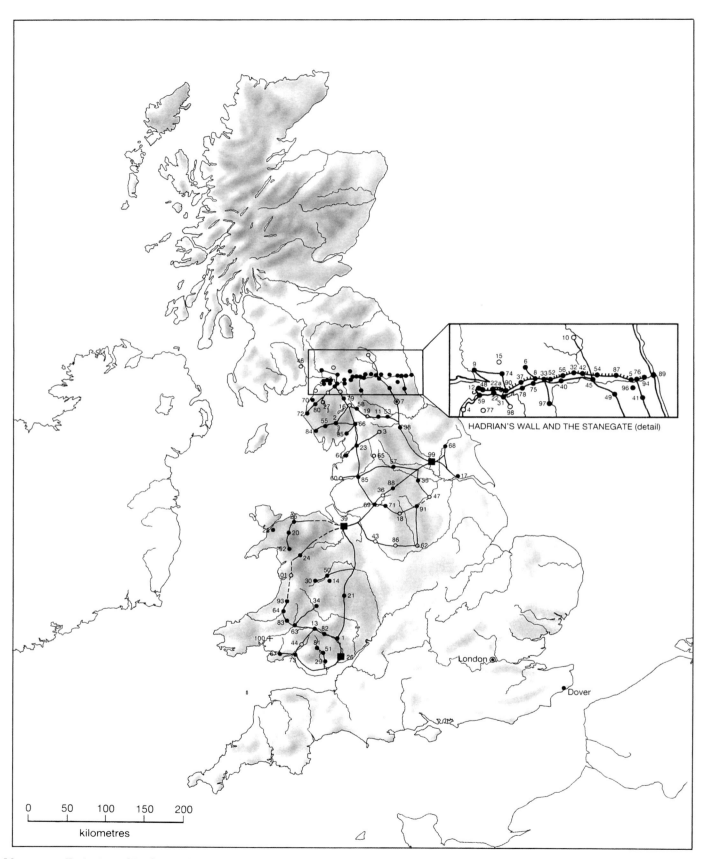

HADRIAN'S WALL AND THE STANEGATE (detail)

Map 4:32 Trajanic and Hadrianic forts and fortresses AD 100–38 (not all sites were occupied at the same time). For key see Map 4:31.

Table 4.6   Military sites of Trajanic or Hadrianic date (AD 100–38)

1 Abergavenny	26 Caerleon	52 Great Chesters	78 Old Church Brampton
2 Ambleside	27 Caermote (?)	53 Greta Bridge	79 Old Penrith
3 Brough-by-Bainbridge (?)	28 Caernarvon	54 Halton Chesters	80 Papcastle
4 Beckfoot	29 Caerphilly	55 Hardknott	81 Pen-y-Darren
5 Benwell	30 Caersws II	56 Housesteads	82 Pen-y-Gaer
6 Bewcastle	31 Carlisle	57 Ilkley	83 Pumsaint
7 Binchester	32 Carrawburgh	58 Kirkby Thore	84 Ravenglass
8 Birdoswald	33 Carvoran	59 Kirkbride	85 Ribchester
9 Birrens	34 Castell Collen	60 Kirkham	86 Rocester (?)
10 Blakehope	35 Castleford	61 Lancaster	87 Rudchester
11 Bowes	36 Castleshaw (?)	62 Littlechester (?)	88 Slack
12 Bowness	37 Castlesteads	63 Llandovery	89 South Shields
13 Brecon Gaer (Y Gaer)	38 Catterick	64 Llanio	90 Stanwix
14 Brompton	39 Chester	65 Long Preston	91 Templeborough
15 Broomholm (?)	40 Vindolanda (Chesterholm)	66 Low Borrowbridge	92 Tomen-y-Mur
16 Brougham (?)	41 Chester-le-Street	67 Loughor	93 Trawscoed
17 Brough-on-Humber	42 Chesters	68 Malton	94 Wallsend
18 Brough-on-Noe (?)	43 Chesterton (?)	69 Manchester	95 Watercrook
19 Brough-under-Stainmore (?)	44 Coelbren (?)	70 Maryport	96 Whickham
20 Bryn-y-Gefeiliau	45 Corbridge	71 Melandra	97 Whitley
21 Buckton	46 Dalswinton (?)	72 Moresby	98 Wreay
22 Burgh-by-Sands I	47 Doncaster (?)	73 Neath	99 York
22a Burgh-by-Sands II	48 Drumburgh	74 Netherby	100 Carmarthen (?)
23 Burrow in Lonsdale	49 Ebchester	75 Nether Denton	101 Pennal (?)
24 Caer Gai	50 Forden Gaer	76 Newcastle (?)	
25 Caerhun	51 Gelligaer	77 Old Carlisle	

Plate 4:7   An aerial view of Hardknott fort showing the consolidated remains of the fort defences (note the distinctive playing card shape), the headquarters building (centre) and a double granary (lower centre)

Plate 4:8 A general view of the main east gate at Rhyn Park after excavation. The supports for the timber box rampart can be seen in the foreground to the main defensive ditch (which lies in deep shadow). The gate lies beyond.

whilst the legions at Caerleon and Chester and the remaining auxiliary units in Wales secured peace there. For the rest of the country, the only troops available were the body which the Roman governor in London had at his immediate disposal, housed in a large fort on the outskirts of the provincial capital, and the men of the British fleet, whose main base was at Dover. At its peak the British garrison probably numbered over 60,000 men or about 10 per cent of the Empire's standing army, a staggering total for such a small and isolated province.

The changing pattern of deployment in Wales and the Marches is reviewed in Maps 4:33–4:38. We may note, in particular, the switch from an offensive deployment in the pre-Flavian period to the blanket policing garrison which was imposed *after* the conquest of Wales was completed in the mid-70s AD. The success of the policy of pacification is demonstrated by the scale of reduction in the size of the garrison which was achieved by the mid-second century (4:37) and by the extent of urban development (4:38).

The Flavian deployment in Scotland fell into two broad phases (4:39, 4:40) and demonstrates how close Rome came to accomplishing total conquest. After Agricola's final victory in AD 83, his successor had the opportunity of establishing Roman control over the entire highland zone. The decision to place the garrison in forts along the edge of the highland line in Strathallan and Strathmore, rather than in the glens, has sometimes been viewed as a sign of lesser ambition. It can be argued, however, that the concentration of forts in Strathmore made better sense in terms of army communications and supply. In particular the siting of the legionary fortress at Inchtuthil at the end of the Dunkeld Gorge, and the location of the other so-called glen-blocking forts (Drumquhassle, Menteith, Bochastle, Dalginross, Fendoch and Inverquharity) was an offensive rather than defensive deployment. From these sites the glens could be patrolled, access from the Highlands into Strathmore controlled and remote tribes supervised. This interpretation is supported by recent work in the Moray region, which suggests that the conventional view that Stracathro was the most northerly fort may not be correct. It is not certain whether this policy was fully realized before the Romans were obliged to rethink their deployment. In the second phase some forts were abandoned, probably because the cumulative effect of troop withdrawals from Britain in the 80s meant that there were not enough units available to continue the ambitious northern plans. The Scottish forts that appear to have been held the longest are shown on Map 4:40. It is interesting that the most northerly of the forts which remained in occupation were of large size (3ha (7 acres) and more).

In between these two broad phases, an attempt may have been made to establish a 'frontier' north of the Forth–Clyde line, enclosing a salient of good agricultural land between the Forth and the Tay (4:41). The evidence for the Gask 'frontier' comprises a series of forts and watchtowers along a road, an arrangement which physically resembles the Domitianic frontier in the Taunus Mountains in Germany. This dating of the Gask frontier has been supported by minimal artefactual evidence from the watchtowers. Whatever the precise date, the occupation of the towers seems to have been very short-lived, though there is no evidence that the abandonment was due to native hostility rather than to an organized withdrawal.

Plate 4:9 Reverse of gold *aureus* (in near-mint condition) of Vespasian, AD 75, located in primary levels at Caersws, mid-central Wales, and dating the foundation of the fort to that year

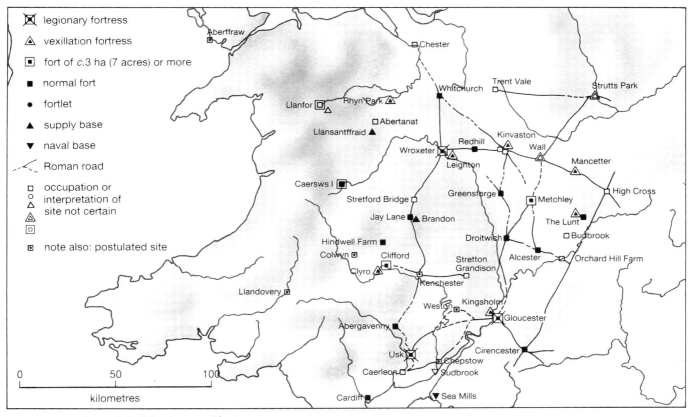

Map 4:33 Wales and the Marches: pre-Flavian

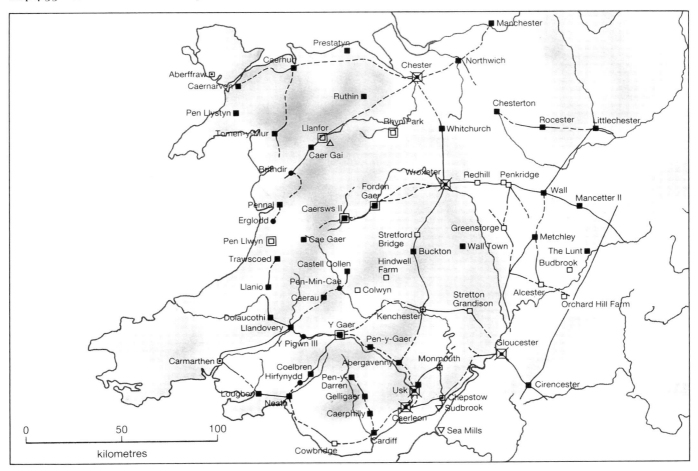

Map 4:34 Wales and the Marches: early Flavian *c.*AD 74–80

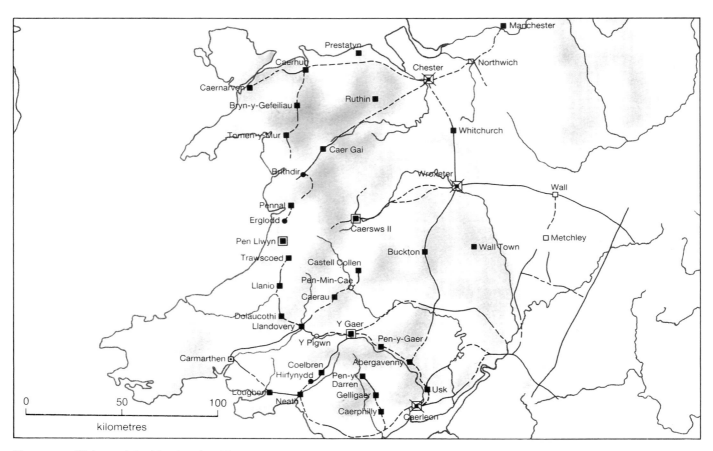

Map 4:35 Wales and the Marches: late Flavian *c.*AD 90–100

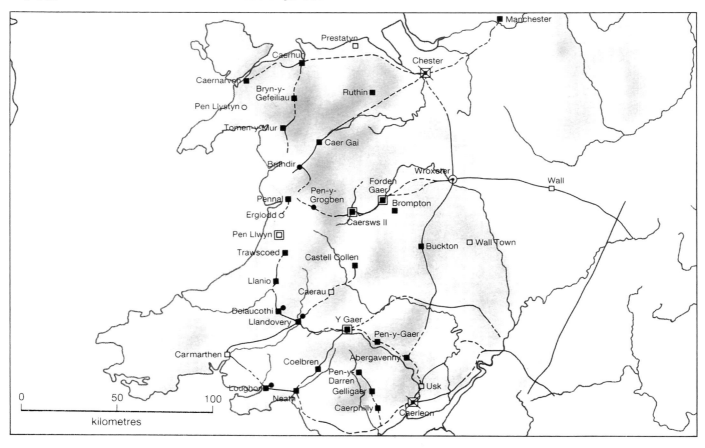

Map 4:36 Wales and the Marches: Trajanic–early Hadrianic *c.*AD 100–25

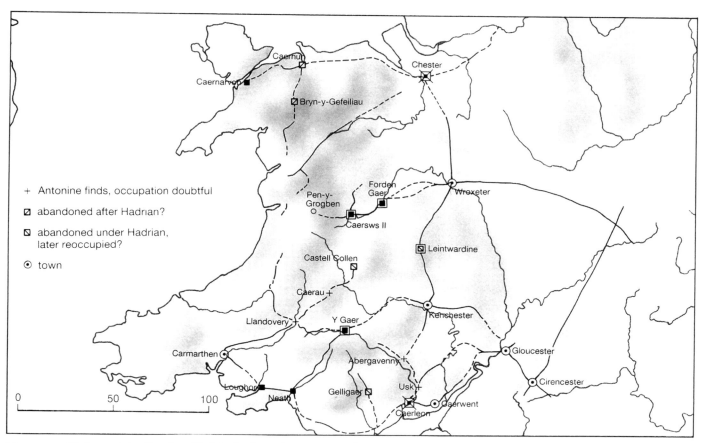

Map 4:37   Wales and the Marches: Hadrianic–Antonine *c.*AD 125–65

+ Antonine finds, occupation doubtful

▨ abandoned after Hadrian?

◨ abandoned under Hadrian,
later reoccupied?

⊙ town

Caerhun
Caernarvon
Bryn-y-Gefeiliau
Chester
Forden Gaer
Pen-y-Grogben
Wroxeter
Caersws II
Leintwardine
Castell Collen
Caerau
Kenchester
Llandovery
Y Gaer
Carmarthen
Gloucester
Abergavenny
Cirencester
Loughor
Neath
Gelligaer
Usk
Caerwent
Caerleon

0   50   100

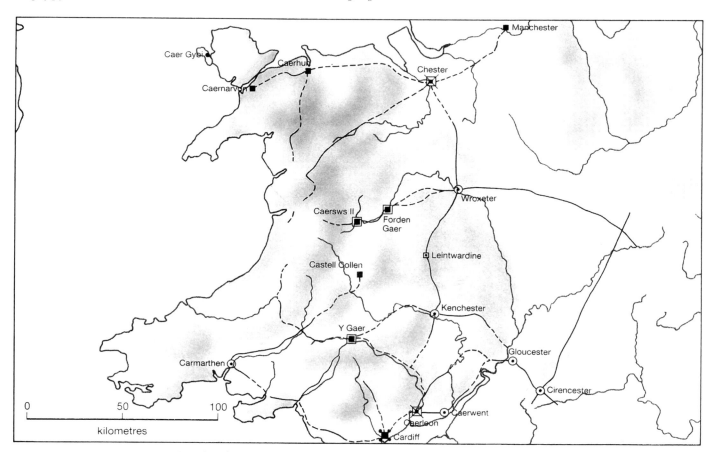

Map 4:38   Wales and the Marches: fourth century AD

Manchester
Caer Gybi
Caerhun
Chester
Caernarvon
Wroxeter
Caersws II
Forden Gaer
Leintwardine
Castell Collen
Kenchester
Y Gaer
Gloucester
Carmarthen
Cirencester
Caerwent
Caerleon
Cardiff

0   50   100

kilometres

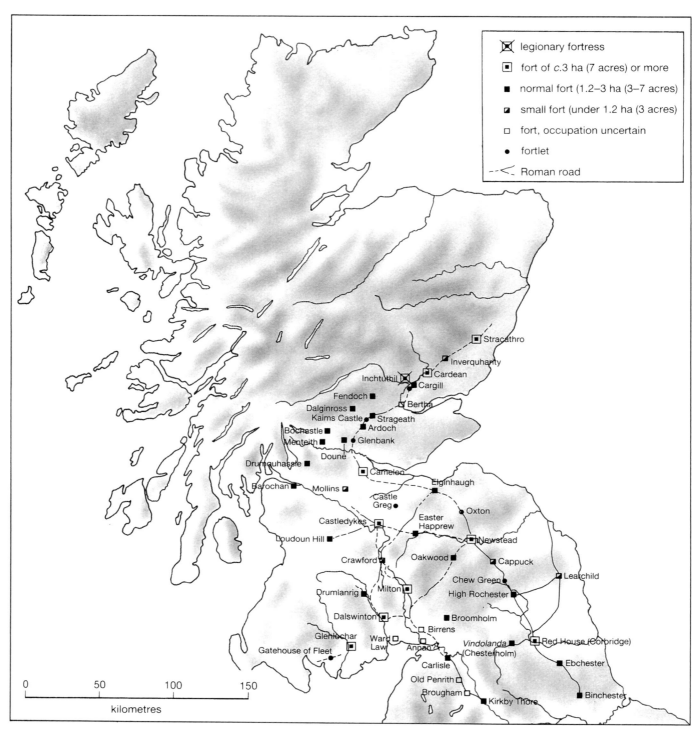

Map 4:39 Early Flavian sites in Scotland c. AD 80–90

Legend:

- ⊠ legionary fortress
- ▣ fort of c.3 ha (7 acres) or more
- ■ normal fort (1.2–3 ha (3–7 acres)
- ◪ small fort (under 1.2 ha (3 acres)
- □ fort, occupation uncertain
- ● fortlet
- –·–< Roman road

Stracathro
Inverquharity
Cardean
Inchtuthil
Cargill
Bertha
Fendoch
Dalginross
Kaims Castle
Strageath
Ardoch
Bochastle
Menteith
Glenbank
Doune
Drumquhassle
Camelon
Barochan
Mollins
Elginhaugh
Castle Greg
Oxton
Easter Happrew
Castledykes
Newstead
Loudoun Hill
Crawford
Oakwood
Cappuck
Leatchild
Chew Green
Drumlanrig
Milton
High Rochester
Dalswinton
Broomholm
Glenlochar
Ward Law
Birrens
Vindolanda (Chesterholm)
Red House (Corbridge)
Gatehouse of Fleet
Annan
Ebchester
Carlisle
Old Penrith
Brougham
Kirkby Thore
Binchester

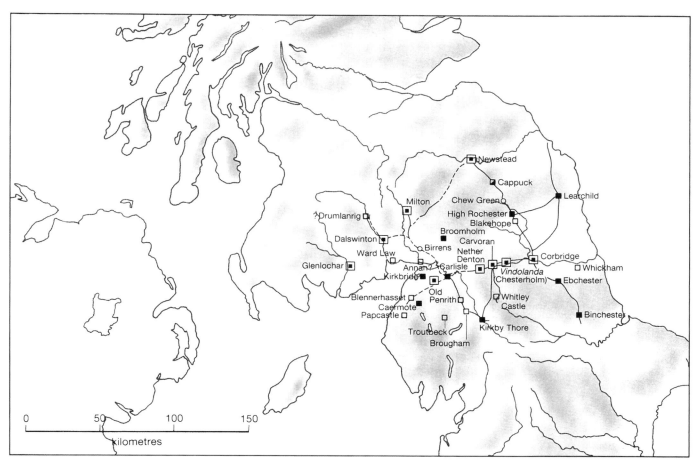

Map 4:40   Later Flavian sites in Scotland *c.*AD 90–105 (key as for Map 4:39)

Plate 4:10   The well-preserved defensive earthworks of a Flavian signal station near the fort of Fendoch, overlooking the mouth of the Sma Glen, Tayside

Plate 4:11 Westmuir signal station at the eastern end of the Gask Ridge has been completely levelled by ploughing. It is now recognizable as a circular crop mark showing briefly in the growing barley (compare Pl. 4:10).

Map 4:41 The Gask 'frontier' watchtowers: 1 Ardoch, 2 Shielhill south, 3 Shielhill north. 4 Westerton, 5 Parkneuk, 6 Raith, 7 Ardunie, 8 Roundlaw, 9 Kirkhill, 10 Muir O'Fauld, 11 Gask House, 12 Witch Knowe, 13 Moss Side, 14 Thorny Hill, 15 Westmuir, 16 Peel, 17 West Mains, Hunting Tower, 18 Greenloaning

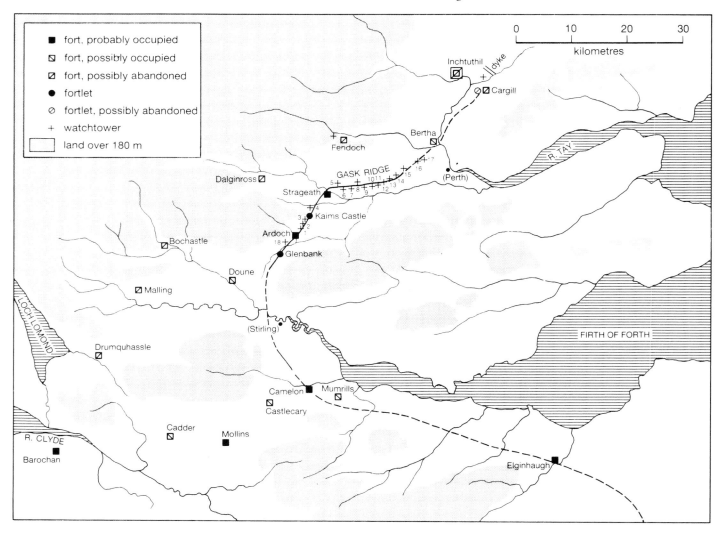

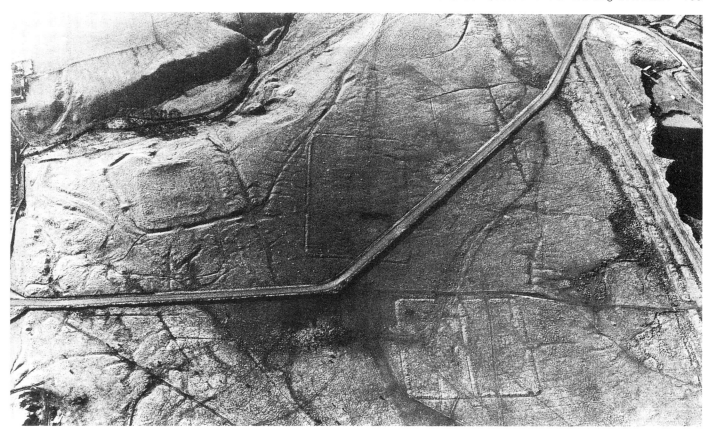

Hadrian's Wall

The construction of Hadrian's Wall across the Tyne–Solway isthmus in the AD 120s–30s was not entirely a novel strategy: it was the culmination of a policy which had begun (if the dating of the Gask frontier is correct) with the decision to withdraw from total occupation of the island. The choice of the Tyne–Solway line for the frontier rather than the shorter Forth–Clyde isthmus was dictated presumably by the continued need to garrison Wales and the Pennines in some depth at this stage. There were simply not enough auxiliary units available to fill the forts of lowland Scotland as well. The first forts on the Tyne–Solway line were Flavian foundations. During the reign of Trajan (and early in that of Hadrian) further sites were added along a strategic road (known by its Medieval name as the Stanegate) built at right angles to the main routes northwards (4:42). In its most developed form around AD 120 the Stanegate 'frontier' consisted of a slightly irregular system of forts, fortlets and watchtowers linked by a road. Experiments with running ditches may have been made in the low-lying terrain at the western end between Burgh-by-Sands and Kirkbride.

The transformation of the Stanegate system into the Hadrianic frontier was a natural strategic progression, but was structurally complex (4:43). There were several changes in

Plate 4:12 (*above*) Marching camps alongside the Stanegate on Haltwhistle Common. The smaller rectangular enclosure to the left is a fortlet relating to the Stangate 'frontier'. The straight lines up the right side are traces of the Hadrianic *vallum*.

plan from the original scheme, which was apparently for a wall to be built to the north of the Stanegate forts. The initial plan was to retain the forts, but when work on the wall had already advanced some way they were replaced by a chain of forts attached to the wall itself. These new forts were then cordoned off from the south by the construction of an earthwork known as the *vallum*, which created a militarized strip immediately behind the wall. Along the wall there was a regular system of 80 mile-fortlets (milecastles) at intervals of one Roman mile, each separated by two towers (or turrets) at one-third of a mile intervals. A similar system of fortlets and towers was also constructed beyond the western end of the wall down the Cumbrian coast. It is now apparent that for part of this sector at least, the idea of a linear cordon was continued by small connecting ditches or palisades between these installations. Although the wall followed a convenient geographical line, it did not respect pre-existing tribal territories and at its western end it would appear that the territory of a Brigantian sub-tribe, the Carvetii, was bisected. In consequence a series of outpost forts was constructed (presumably close to the limits of Carvetian territory) in order to guarantee the security and viability of the land for its inhabitants and perhaps also to maintain diplomatic pressure on tribes dwelling beyond. At a later date, outpost forts were also occupied to the north of the eastern end of the wall.

The physical task of constructing the wall and its attendant works was immensely complicated and, in spite of much archaeological investigation, many questions still remain to be answered (4:44). For instance, even the year in which work commenced is disputed, though the general view is that it coincided with Hadrian's visit to Britain in AD 122. Some work on the wall forts was still continuing in the 130s, shortly before Hadrian's death, which gives some idea of the scale of the task which faced the three British legions (II Augusta, VI Victrix and XX Valeria Victrix) and their auxiliary units. The auxiliaries may have been used mainly for the construction of the *vallum* and the wall ditch. Finds of inscriptions and the identification of certain constructional

Plate 4:13   The line of the later stone wall here diverged northwards (to the left of the turf wall, centre) when this sector of Hadrian's Wall west of Birdoswald fort was replaced in more durable materials. The *vallum* runs parallel on the right-hand side.

features which were characteristic of the different legions allow some estimate to be made of the division of work on the wall and its forts.

Changes of plan were reflected in changes in the structure, though the initial plan was for a 'broad' stone wall of c.10 Roman feet from the Tyne at Newcastle to the Irthing, and a turf wall from the Irthing to the Solway at Bowness. The construction of the 'broad' wall or its foundations had proceeded some way when the gauge was narrowed to c.6–8 Roman feet in order to accelerate the work. This was probably a result of the decision to move the forts onto the wall. The wall was also extended in this 'narrow' gauge east of Newcastle to Wallsend. The reason for the construction of the western sector of the wall in turf may have been because of a 'red rock' fault just west of the River Irthing. Although the red sandstone of northern Cumbria was still satisfactory for wall building, the lack of limestone for lime mortar was, at the time, seen as an obstacle. Even before the end of Hadrian's reign, however, a short section of the turf wall had been replaced in stone at the 'narrow' gauge. The rest was replaced in stone some time later, either at the time of the withdrawal from the frontier in Scotland in the 160s or under the Severans in the early third century, and was built to an 'intermediate' gauge of c.9 Roman feet. Many of the stone quarries used by the Romans are known (especially in the central section) and some still have Roman graffiti and inscriptions preserved on their faces.

As already mentioned, the principle of a linear cordon was continued beyond the end of the wall proper down the Cumbrian coast, at least as far as Silloth (4:45). Even in recent years the Solway has been forded on foot by people setting out from Silloth, and small boats could easily and swiftly have crossed from the present Scottish shore to points still further south. Exactly how far south the small delimiting ditches and palisades were carried beyond Silloth is uncertain at present.

The distribution of temporary camps close to the wall may hold some clues about the process of construction, since some of these camps (which are generally of small size) may have housed working parties (4:46, cf. 4:53). On the other hand, quite a number of the smallest camps have similarities with another type of camp altogether – those built as practice works by the army on manoeuvres. The distribution of practice works in Britain (4:47) reflects the location of the major troop concentrations. We may suspect that the discrete groups in Yorkshire and North and South Wales reflect the peacetime summer manoeuvres of the individual legions with their attached auxiliary regiments. Given the importance of the northern frontier, we might expect further manoeuvres to have taken place there periodically – perhaps involving detachments from all three legions and numerous auxiliaries. The deterrent value of both displays of force and of engineering ability was well known to the Romans and it is conceivable that the practice siege works at Burnswark and Woden Law were constructed by an army on 'peaceful' manoeuvres north of the frontier (and not whilst the Antonine Wall was in use). At any rate, we are justified in believing that *some* of the smallest temporary camps close to Hadrian's Wall were likewise constructed as practice works in peacetime.

The most famous group of practice camps, that on Llandrindod Common in Wales, shows clearly the purpose of the exercise (4:48). The camps were all of miniature size in order to give the troops practice at the most difficult elements, the gates and corners. This activity demonstrates that, even with the construction of a permanent frontier, the Roman army maintained its preparedness for efficient campaigning. The potential for renewed expansion was not surrendered and shortly after Hadrian's death the Roman army once again invaded Scotland.

Plate 4:14 (*left*) Hadrian's Wall approaching Limestone Corner, where the hardness of the rock prevented the complete cutting of the ditch. Note the irregular mounds of spoil to the right-hand side of the ditch line.

Plate 4:15 (*below*) Milecastle 37: a well-preserved mile-fortlet on the central section of Hadrian's Wall

Plate 4:16 Roman fort at Chesters, Hadrian's Wall

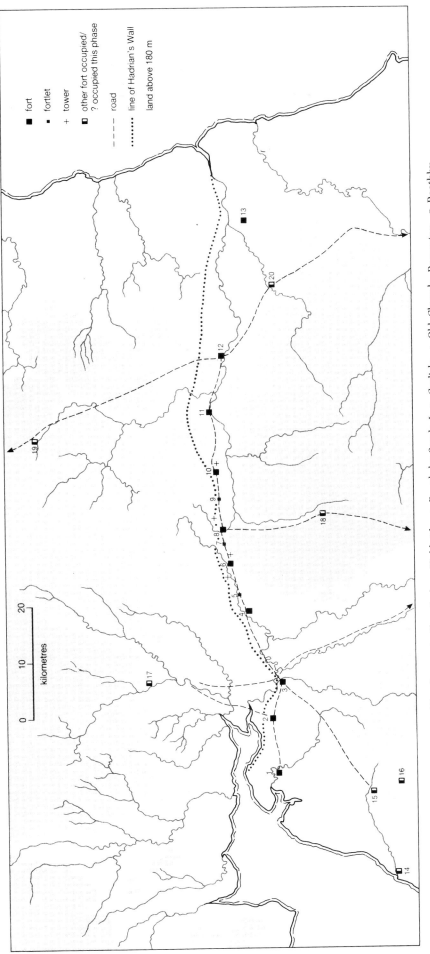

Map 4:42 The Stanegate 'frontier': 1 Kirkbride, 2 Burgh-by-Sands 1, 3 Carlisle, 4 Old Church, Brampton, 5 Boothby, 6 Nether Denton, 7 Throp, 8 Carvoran, 9 Haltwhistle Burn, 10 *Vindolanda*, 11 Newbrough–Fourstones?, 12 Corbridge, 13 Whickham, 14 Maryport, 15 Blennerhasset, 16 Caermote, 17 Broomholm, 18 Whitley Castle, 19 High Rochester, 20 Ebchester (not all sites were certainly occupied at the same time).

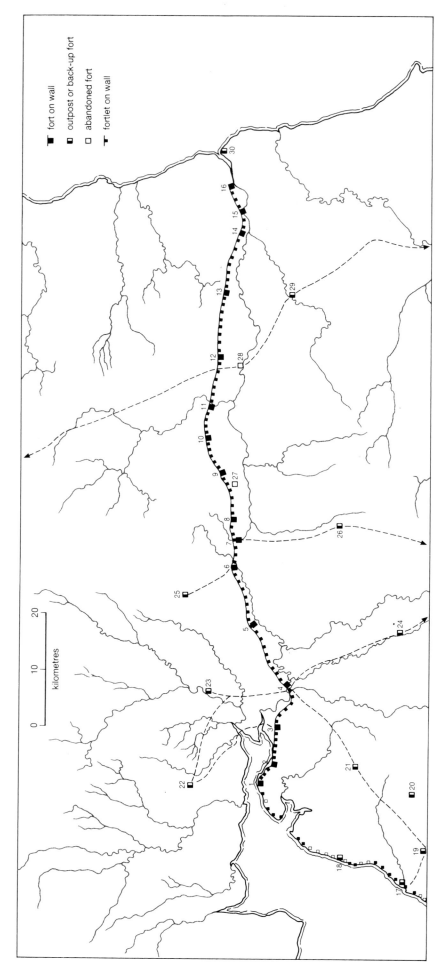

Map 4:43 Hadrian's Wall: 1 Bowness (*Maia*), 2 Drumburgh (*Congavata*), 3 Burgh-by-Sands (*Aballava*), 4 Stanwix (*Uxelodunum*), 5 Castlesteads (*Camboglanna*), 6 Birdoswald (*Banna*), 7 Carvoran (*Magnis*), 8 Great Chesters (*Aesica*), 9 Housesteads (*Vercovicium*), 10 Carrawburgh (*Brocolitia*), 11 Chesters (*Cilurnum*), 12 Halton Chesters (*Onnum*), 13 Rudchester (*Vindovala*), 14 Benwell (*Condercum*), 15 Newcastle (*Pons Aelius*), 16 Wallsend (*Segedunum*), 17 Maryport (*Alauna*), 18 Beckfoot, 19 Ebchester (*Vindomora*), 20 Caermote, 21 Old Carlisle, 22 Birrens (*Blatobulgium*), 23 Netherby (*Castra Exploratorum*), 24 Old Penrith (*Voreda*), 25 Bewcastle (*Fanum Cocidii*), 26 Whitley Castle, 27 Chesterholm (*Vindolanda*), 28 Corbridge (*Corstopitum*), 29 Ebchester (*Vindomora*), 30 South Shields (*Arbeia*)

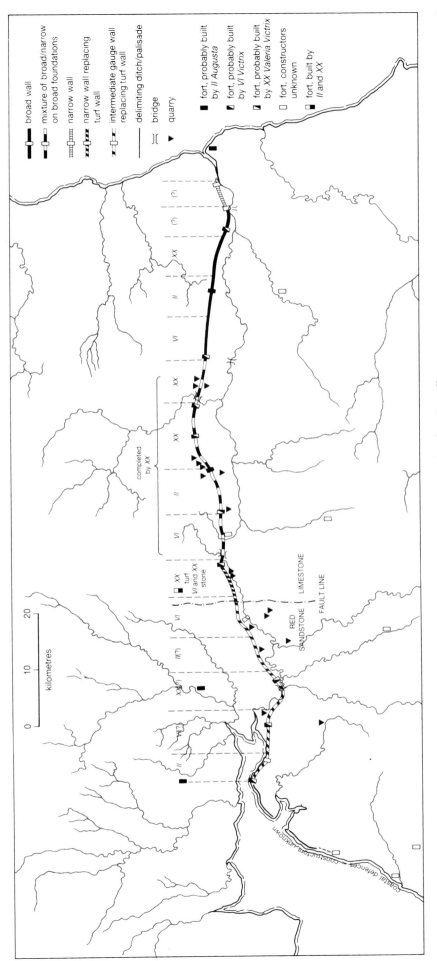

Map 4:44 The construction of Hadrian's Wall

Legend:

- broad wall
- mixture of broad/narrow on broad foundations
- narrow wall
- narrow wall replacing turf wall
- intermediate gauge wall replacing turf wall
- delimiting ditch/palisade
- bridge
- quarry
- fort, probably built by *II Augusta*
- fort, probably built by *VI Victrix*
- fort, probably built by *XX Valeria Victrix*
- fort, constructors unknown
- fort, built by *II* and *XX*

kilometres

0 — 10 — 20

completed by XX

XX turf
VI and XX stone

RED SANDSTONE — LIMESTONE
FAULT LINE

coastal defences — constructors unknown

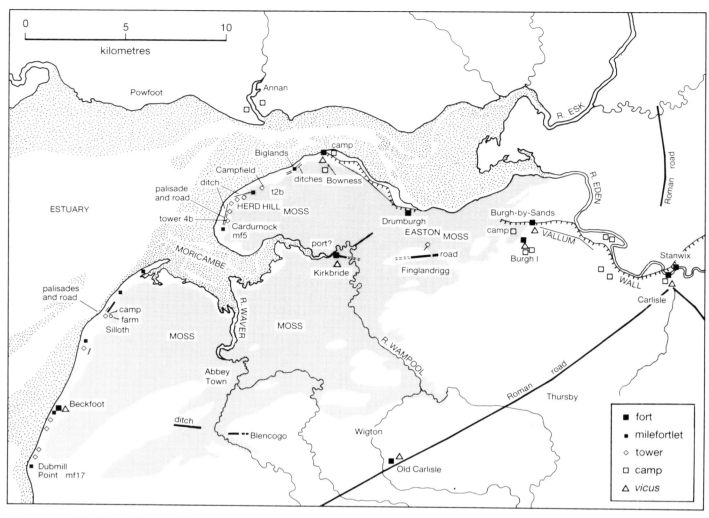

Map 4:45 The Solway frontier defences

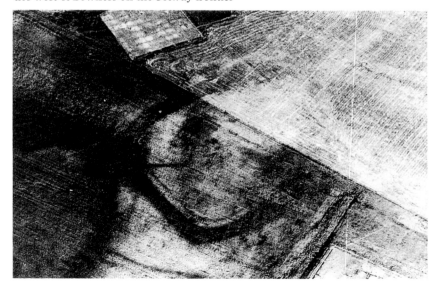

Plate 4:17 (*left*) Stake holes of the coastal palisade at Silloth on the Cumbrian coast

Plate 4:18 (*below*) Crop mark of Milefortlet 5 (Cardurnock), which lies west of Bowness on the Solway frontier

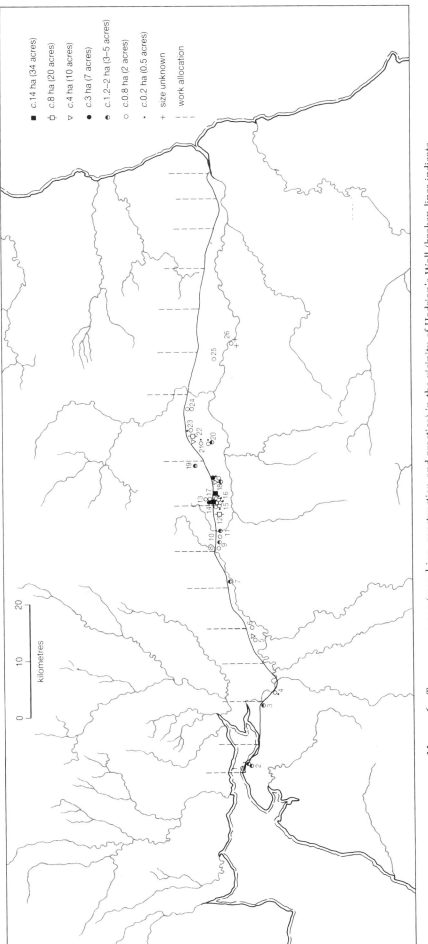

Map 4:46 Temporary camps (marching, construction and practice) in the vicinity of Hadrian's Wall (broken lines indicate possible legionary work stints): 1 Grey Haven's. 2 Brackenrigg. 3 Wormanby. 4 Nowtler Hill I/II. 5 Moss Side I/II. 6 Watch Cross. 7 Abbey Park Wood. 8 Willowford. 9 Crooks. 10 Chapel Rigg. 11 Black Dikes. 12 Peatsteel Crags. 13 Cawfields I–III. 14 Haltwhistle Common I. 15 Haltwhistle Common II–VII. 16 Haltwhistle Burn I–IV. 17 Milestone House. 18 Seatsides I–V. 19 Greenlee Lough. 20 Grinsdale School I–III. 21 Lady Shield I/II. 22 Bagraw I/II. 23 Brown Moor I/II. 24 Walwick I/II. 25 Bishop Rigg. 26 Farnley II

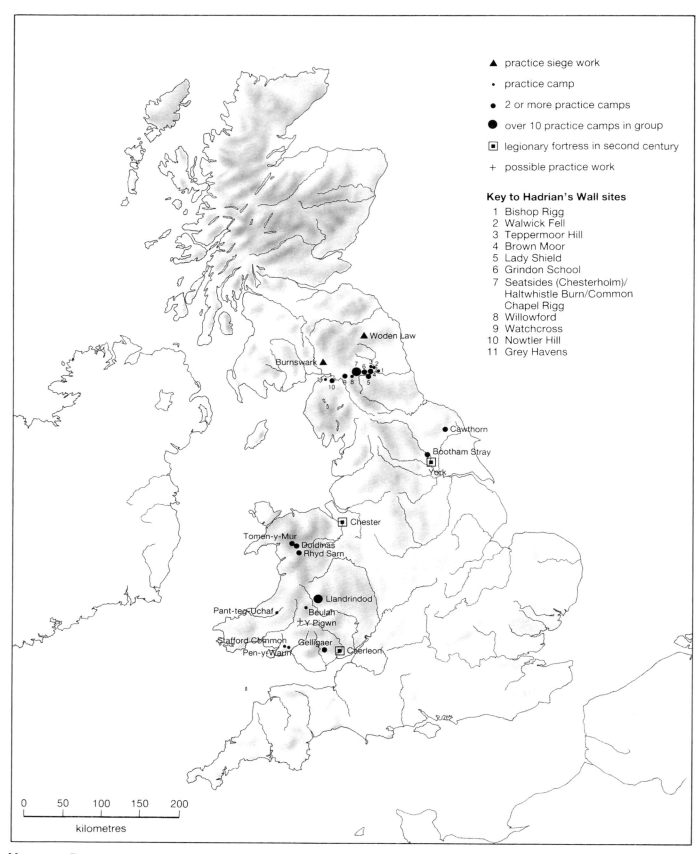

▲ practice siege work

• practice camp

● 2 or more practice camps

⬤ over 10 practice camps in group

▣ legionary fortress in second century

+ possible practice work

Key to Hadrian's Wall sites
1 Bishop Rigg
2 Walwick Fell
3 Teppermoor Hill
4 Brown Moor
5 Lady Shield
6 Grindon School
7 Seatsides (Chesterholm)/
  Haltwhistle Burn/Common
  Chapel Rigg
8 Willowford
9 Watchcross
10 Nowtler Hill
11 Grey Havens

Woden Law

Burnswark ▲

7 6 3 2
Bishop Rigg
4
11 9 8 5
10

Cawthorn

Bootham Stray

York

Chester

Tomen-y-Mur
Doldinas
Rhyd Sarn

Llandrindod

Pant-teg-Uchaf
Beulah
+ Y Pigwn

Stafford Common
Gelligaer
Pen-yr-Waun
Caerleon

0   50   100 150 200

kilometres

Map 4:47 Practice camps and related works in Britain

Plate XII.

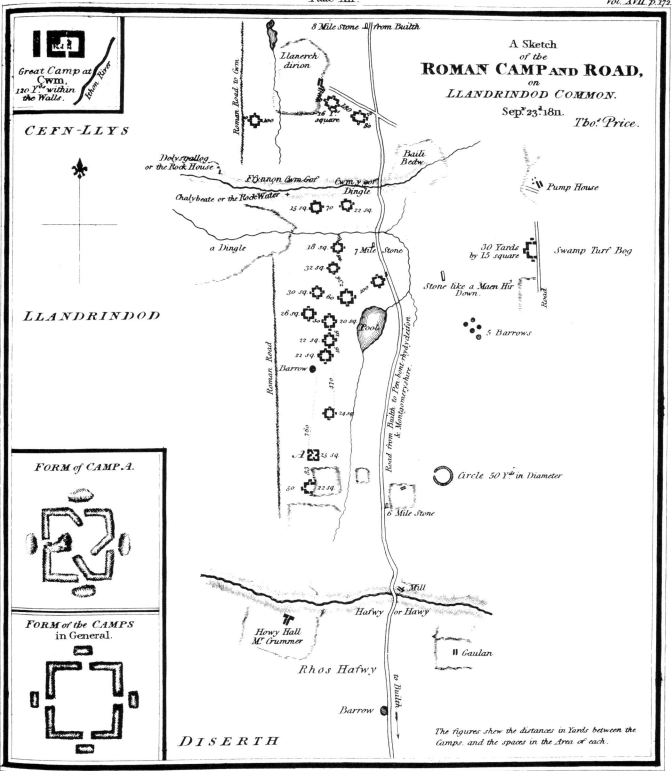

CEFN-LLYS

Great Camp at Cwm, 120 Yds within the Walls.

A Sketch of the
ROMAN CAMP AND ROAD,
on
LLANDRINDOD COMMON.
Sep.r 23.d 1811.
Tho.s Price.

8 Mile Stone from Builth

Llanerch dirion

Roman Road to Cwm

16 square

Dolyspallog or the Rock House

Baili Bedw

Ffynnon Cwm Gof
Cwm y gof Dingle

Pump House

Chalybeate or the Rock Water

15 sq. 70 22 sq.

a Dingle

18 sq.
7 Mile Stone

32 sq.

Swamp Turf Bog

30 Yards by 15 square

30 sq. 60 100

Stone like a Maen Hir Down.

LLANDRINDOD

26 sq. 50 20 sq.

Pool

5 Barrows

Roman Road

22 sq.

22 sq.

Barrow

410

24 sq.

Road from Builth to Pen-bont-rhydvaddion & Montgomeryshire.

Circle 50 Y.ds in Diameter

760

A 25 sq.

83

50 22 sq.

6 Mile Stone

FORM of CAMP A.

Mill

Hafwy or Hawy

FORM of the CAMPS in General.

Howy Hall Mr Crummer

Gaulan

Rhos Hafwy

to Builth

Barrow

DISERTH

The figures shew the distances in Yards between the Camps, and the spaces in the Area of each.

J.s Basire sculp.

Map 4:48   Llandrindod Common: practice camps (*Archaeologia* 17, 1813)

Plate 4:19 The siege camp (right) below the hillfort at Burnswark, Dumfries. It is believed that the siege camp was a practice earthwork.

The Antonine Wall

The renewed campaigning north of Hadrian's Wall in the years AD 139–41 may have been undertaken more to provide Antoninus Pius with a modicum of military glory than to resolve a serious problem (4:49). In fact, Rome's relationship with some of the tribes of lowland Scotland, notably the Votadini (6:21–6:23) may have been good enough to encourage the belief at Rome that part of Scotland could be reincorporated within the Empire. The objectives of the campaigns remain unknown but, since the Antonine reoccupation extended to the Tay, it is apparent that the army must have operated well north of the Forth–Clyde isthmus. In fact, the most serious fighting may have been with the tribes lying beyond the isthmus, since it was they who would have posed the greatest threat to the new frontier arrangements.

The construction of a new frontier wall across the Forth–Clyde isthmus followed the successful completion of the campaigning. The Antonine Wall differs from Hadrian's Wall in certain respects, though not as much as was once believed. The new frontier was constructed as a turf wall and, until recently, it was thought that there was no pro-vision of mile-fortlets or turrets between the forts – which are known at intervals of about 2 Roman miles, as against about 6 miles on Hadrian's Wall. It is now known that, as originally planned (4:50), the Antonine Wall bore much more resemblance to its predecessor and that the apparent differences were in part the result of changes in plan during construction work. Firstly, it is now thought on constructional evidence that in the original scheme only six forts were intended to be built on the wall, with an average interval of about 6 Roman miles. Secondly, it is also generally now accepted that a regular system of about 40 mile-fortlets was built although, to date, only nine examples have been identified conclusively. No towers have yet been found, but it would not occasion surprise if a regular system were eventually discovered at one-third (or half?) mile intervals between the mile-fortlets.

Whilst the wall was being constructed, the original plan was modified and additional small forts were built onto it (4:51). As on Hadrian's Wall, there is also evidence of outpost forts, and of forts and fortlets providing flanking cover along the Clydeside coast to the west of the end of the wall.

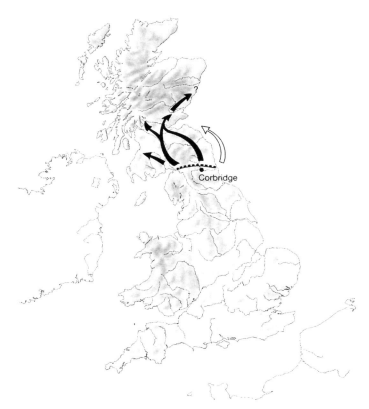

Map 4:49 Reoccupation of Lowland Scotland: possible campaigning AD 139–41

Plate 4:20 The Antonine Wall (running diagonally across the photograph) and the earthworks of Rough Castle fort and annexe

Another feature of the recent reappraisals of the Antonine Wall has been the increasingly refined understanding of the division of the construction work between the three British legions (4:52). Some of the legionary labour allocations are known exactly from Roman commemorative inscriptions which were erected at either end. The evidence is fairly complete for the western end of the wall, but the allocations suggested are much more hypothetical for the eastern sector. Various schemes have been outlined and the divisions proposed here differ slightly from the solutions favoured by other recent discussions. The westernmost sector of the wall was measured in Roman feet and the three legions each built short lengths. When due allowance is made for the lengths of wall built to form the front of forts and fortlets before the construction of the main curtain, it is apparent that the total original length of the sector was $4\frac{2}{3}$ Roman miles. This is the same distance as that recorded on a commemorative slab from the easternmost sector. Other distances recorded on distance slabs are $3\frac{2}{3}$ and 3 Roman miles, and our reconstruction is based on the assumption that the building work was divided evenly between the legions. There could have been, therefore, three sectors of $4\frac{2}{3}$ Roman miles, three of $3\frac{2}{3}$ miles and three of 3 miles. The remaining distance was perhaps divided into three sectors of 2 miles. The subdivision of the western sector between all three legions may indicate that the legion originally assigned to it had been diverted for a while to other activities, perhaps the building of the extra forts added to the wall during construction.

Apart from the evidence of inscriptions defining the termini of labour divisions, there are other possible indications of where the different legions were employed. As on Hadrian's Wall, it appears that each legion may have constructed a recognizably distinct type of mile-fortlet within its sectors. Thus, on the evidence available to date, it looks as if the XX legion built mile-fortlets with short north-south axes, whilst the II and VI legions built 'long axis' fortlets. Variations in the width of the ditch, of the cobble base of the turf wall, or of the material of the turf wall itself, have been observed periodically and they may reflect the work of different groups. Finally, the division of the wall building into blocks of whole miles or multiples of a third of a mile, suggests that the allocation may have been made on the basis of measurement between mile-fortlets or even turrets.

A degree of support for the hypothetical labour division proposed here comes from the known distribution of temporary camps close to the wall. Groups of camps seem to have occurred close to the ends of work sectors (4:53). Moving from west to east we can see that there is a good correlation at Summerston (No. 1), Bar Hill (5 and 6), Dullatur (7 and 8), Castlecary (9 and 11), Seabegs (12 and 13), Camelon (14–16), Inveravon (18–22) and Bridgeness (23 and 24). Only further discoveries of camps, fortlets and inscriptions can help to confirm or contradict this suggested pattern of the division of labour.

The building of the wall was accompanied by the reoccupation of lowland Scotland and the construction of a considerable number of forts and fortlets, particularly along the main roads north (4:54). A line of outpost forts up Strathallan and Strathearn to the Tay brought a useful

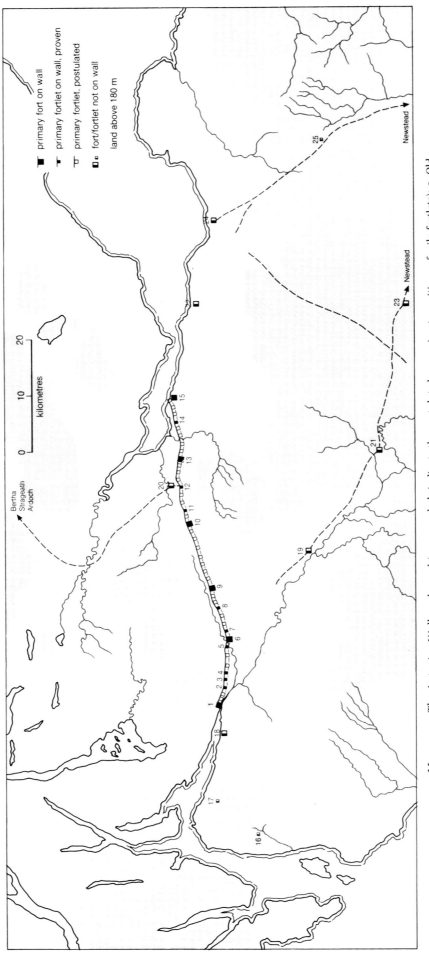

Map 4:50 The Antonine Wall as planned (open symbols indicate the postulated approximate positions of mile-fortlets): 1 Old Kilpatrick, 2 Duntocher, 3 Cleddans, 4 Castlehill, 5 Summerston, 6 Balmuildy, 7 Wilderness Plantation, 8 Glasgow Bridge, 9 Auchendavy, 10 Castlecary, 11 Seabegs Wood, 12 Watling Lodge, 13 Mumrills, 14 Kinneil, 15 Carriden, 16 Outerwards, 17 Lurg Moor, 18 Bishopton, 19 Bothwellhaugh, 20 Camelon, 21 Castledykes, 22 Cramond, 23 Lyne, 24 Inveresk, 25 Oxton

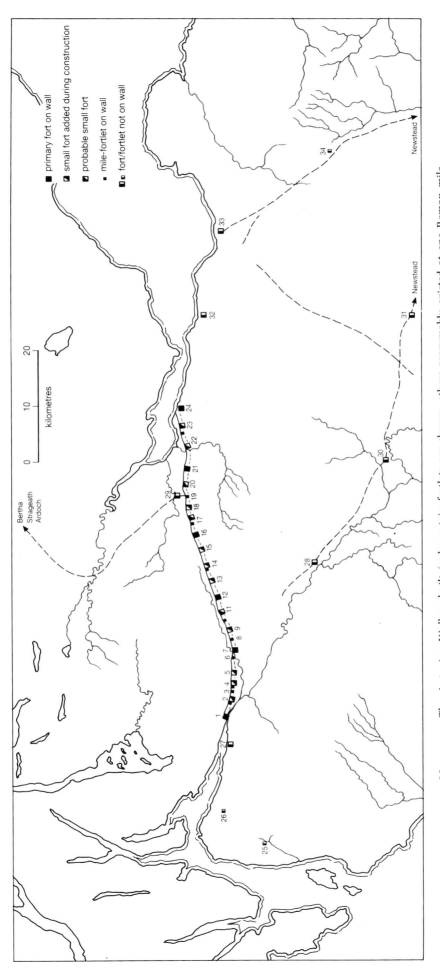

Map 4:51 The Antonine Wall as built (only certain fortlets are shown, others presumably existed at one Roman mile intervals): 1 Old Kilpatrick, 2 Duntocher fort and fortlet, 3 Cleddans, 4 Castlehill fort and fortlet, 5 Bearsden, 6 Summerston, 7 Balmuildy, 8 Wilderness Plantation, 9 Cadder, 10 Glasgow Bridge, 11 Kirkintilloch, 12 Auchendavy, 13 Bar Hill, 14 Croy Hill fort and fortlet, 15 Westerwood, 16 Castlecary, 17 Seabegs fort and Seabegs Wood fortlet, 18 Rough Castle, 19 Watling Lodge, 20 Falkirk, 21 Mumrills, 22 Inveravon, 23 Kinneil fort and fortlet, 24 Carriden, 25 Outerwards, 26 Lurg Moor, 27 Bishopton, 28 Bothwellhaugh, 29 Camelon, 30 Castledykes, 31 Lyne, 32 Cramond, 33 Inveresk, 34 Oxton

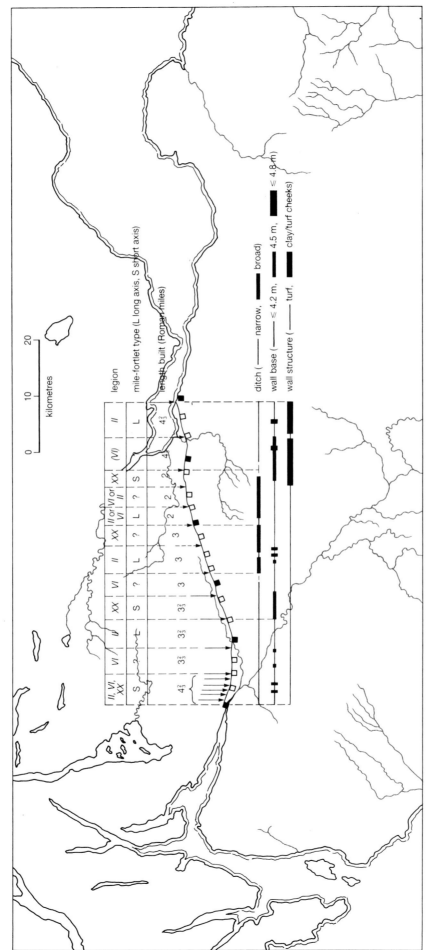

Map 4:52 Construction of the Antonine Wall: possible workshifts and attributions to legions

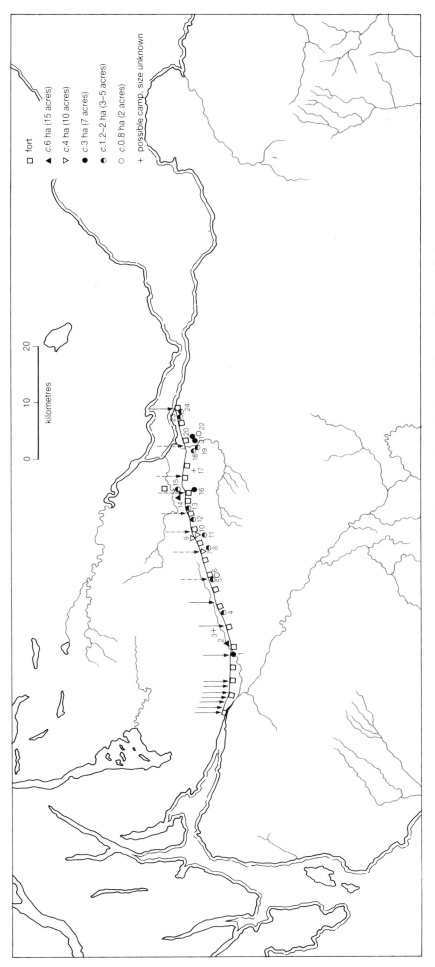

Map 4:53 Construction camps on the Antonine Wall (solid arrows indicate findspots of distance slabs, and broken arrows hypothetical work stints): 1 Summerston, 2 Buchley, 3 Broken Tower, 4 Easter Calder (Adamslee), 5 Twechar, 6 Bar Hill, 7/8 Dullatur I/II, 9/10 Garnhall I/II, 11 Tollpark, 12 Dalnair, 13 Milnquarter, 14 Wester Carmuirs, 15 Easter Carmuirs, 16 Tamfourhill, 17 Langton, 18 Little Kerse, 19 Polmontill, 20–22 Inveravon I–III, 23 Kinglass, 24 Muirhouses

Plate 4:21   Distance slab erected by the XX legion from Hutcheson Hill towards the west end of the Antonine Wall. It records the construction of the three-mile section by the detachment.

Plate 4:22   Kaims Castle fortlet under snow cover. This fortlet was part of the system of outposts to the north of the Antonine Wall and lay midway between the forts of Ardoch and Strageath.

salient of good agricultural land under Roman control, the forts no doubt also serving as bases for the diplomatic control of the tribes living beyond. This first period of occupation ended fairly abruptly around AD 155, perhaps, it has been argued, because of military problems to the south rather than to the north. The Antonine Wall was methodically abandoned, as shown by the careful burial of the distance slabs, and preparations were made to recommission Hadrian's Wall. Within a year or so, however, the situation was stabilized and the Romans returned north for a second, and probably short, reoccupation of the Antonine Wall and lowland Scotland (4:55, 4:56). This second phase came to an end, according to the currently predominating view, around AD 163 (though some scholars would still like to place it somewhat later). The final abandonment seems to have been accomplished in an orderly fashion and was presumably a strategic withdrawal to the Hadrianic frontier rather than the result of pressure from the northern tribes. The chronological arguments in the debate are complex and there is no space for full discussion here.

There was, however, renewed warfare with the northern tribes before the end of the second century. Our sources mention an enemy invasion crossing a wall (this could mean either wall) before Ulpius Marcellus, the Roman commander, drove them back and engaged in punitive action – probably well into Scotland (4:57). The detail surrounding the incident is obscure, but the problems returned by the end of the century and eventually brought the Emperor Septimius Severus to Britain with his two sons, Caracalla and Geta. The campaigns of c.208 or 209 and 210 were organized on a grand scale, with York serving as the military headquarters and advanced supply bases being established at Corbridge and at South Shields, where the interior of the fort was filled with granaries (4:58, 4:59). The Roman sources were scathing about the results of these campaigns, but it is clear that Severus penetrated far to the north. Some of the series of larger marching camps in Scotland are assumed to relate to this period (see above, 4:19, 4:20). The main thrust of the first invasion was no doubt along the traditional eastern route into Strathmore, though there are indications in the sources (which imply a visit to Burgh-by-Sands where a Moorish garrison was stationed) that Severus may have returned to York via south-west Scotland and the western end of Hadrian's Wall. The second campaign was led by Caracalla and may have penetrated further north, though whether he reached Moray is uncertain. The construction of a vexillation fortress at Carpow on the Tay and signs of occupation at the forts of Newstead and Cramond suggest that a major victory had been won and reoccupation of Scotland south of the Tay was being contemplated. There is little evidence from the Antonine Wall, but it is not impossible that some of the forts would also have been reoccupied had not events intervened. The death of Severus in February AD 211 at York and Caracalla's abrupt return to Rome (where he promptly eliminated his brother and co-ruler, Geta) resulted in a withdrawal to Hadrian's Wall once again. For the rest of the Roman period, the northern frontier was based on the Tyne–Solway line, though outpost forts maintained diplomatic contact with lowland Scotland.

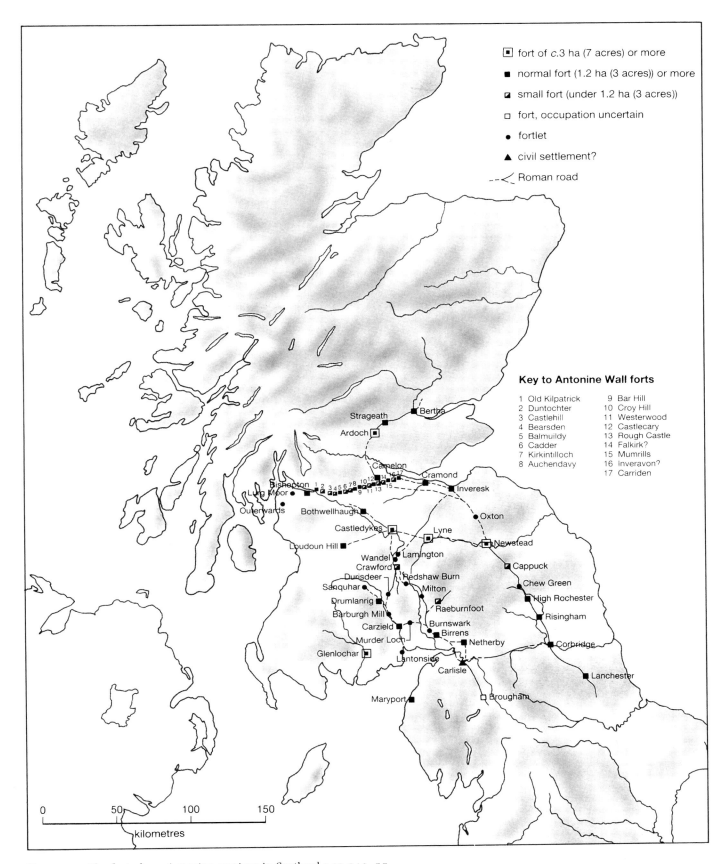

Key to Antonine Wall forts

1	Old Kilpatrick	9	Bar Hill
2	Duntochter	10	Croy Hill
3	Castlehill	11	Westerwood
4	Bearsden	12	Castlecary
5	Balmuildy	13	Rough Castle
6	Cadder	14	Falkirk?
7	Kirkintilloch	15	Mumrills
8	Auchendavy	16	Inveravon?
		17	Carriden

Legend:
- ▣ fort of *c*.3 ha (7 acres) or more
- ■ normal fort (1.2 ha (3 acres)) or more
- ◪ small fort (under 1.2 ha (3 acres))
- □ fort, occupation uncertain
- ● fortlet
- ▲ civil settlement?
- ⌁ Roman road

Map 4:54   The first-phase Antonine garrison in Scotland *c.*AD 142–55

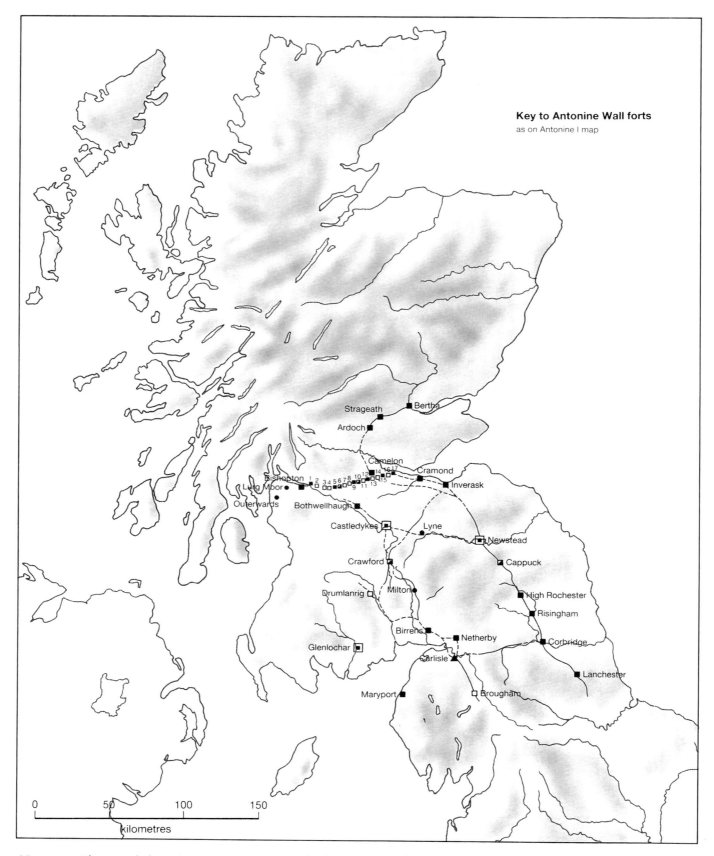

Key to Antonine Wall forts
as on Antonine I map

Bertha

Strageath

Ardoch

Camelon

Cramond

Bishopton

Inverask

Long Moor

Outerwards

Bothwellhaugh

Castledykes

Lyne

Newstead

Crawford

Cappuck

Drumlanrig

Milton

High Rochester

Risingham

Birrens

Netherby

Corbridge

Glenlochar

Carlisle

Lanchester

Maryport

Brougham

0   50   100   150

kilometres

Map 4:55 The second-phase Antonine garrison in Scotland *c.*AD 158–63 (key as for Map 4:54)

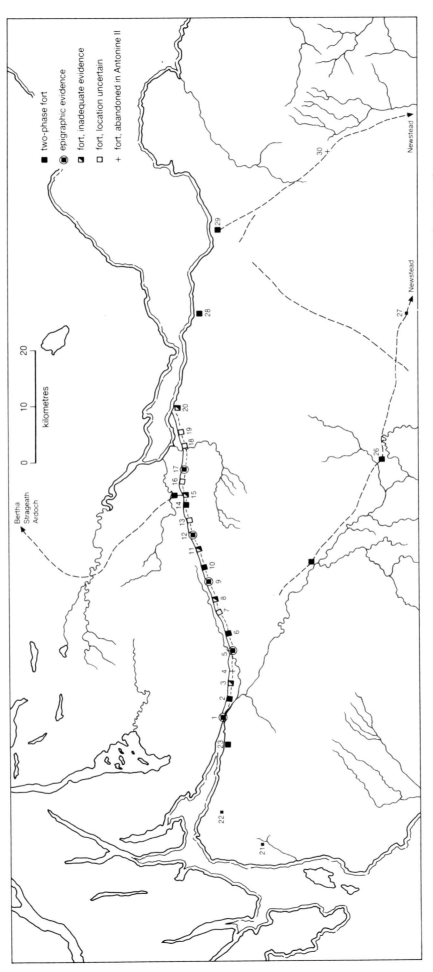

Map 4:56 The Antonine Wall in the second Antonine phase: 1 Old Kilpatrick, 2 Duntocher, 3 Castlehill, 4 Bearsden, 5 Balmuildy, 6 Cadder, 7 Kirkintilloch, 8 Auchendavy, 9 Bar Hill, 10 Croy Hill, 11 Westerwood, 12 Castlecary, 13 Seabegs, 14 Rough Castle, 15 Watling Lodge, 16 Falkirk, 17 Mumrills, 18 Inveravon, 19 Kinneil, 20 Carriden, 21 Outerwards, 22 Lung Moor, 23 Bishopton, 24 Bothwellhaugh, 25 Camelon, 26 Castledykes, 27 Lyne, 28 Cramond, 29 Inveresk, 30 Oxton

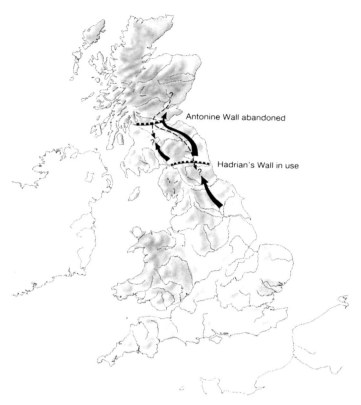

Map 4:57 Possible location of the campaigning of Ulpius Marcellus in northern Britain *c.*AD 180

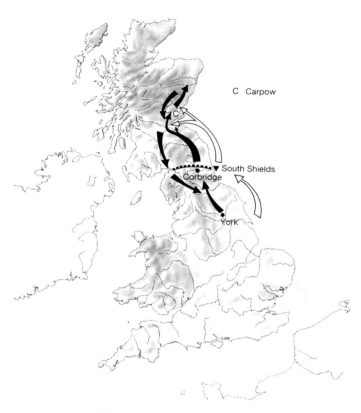

Map 4:58 Possible location of the first campaign of Septimius Severus AD 208–9

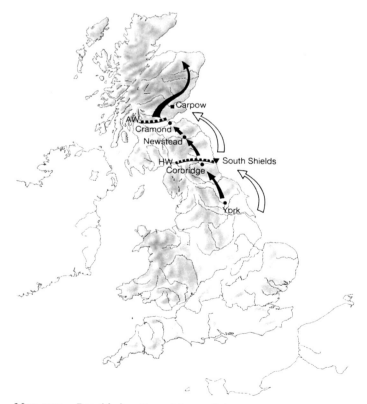

Map 4:59 Possible location of Caracalla's campaign AD 210

Plate 4:23 Silver coin of Septimius Severus celebrating his victory in Britain (*VICTORIA BRIT.*) early in the third century (*RIC* 332)

The late Roman deployment

After the Severan campaigns, the northern frontier remained relatively peaceful throughout the third century (4:60 and Table 4:7). The distribution of troops in Britain still reflected the traditional concern for the security of limited areas in Wales and much of northern England. There were few new forts, but some old forts were reoccupied as the century progressed. A new development was the progressive construction of coastal defences in south-eastern Britain (see further 4:63–4:67).

The shift in the established deployment reflected changing threats during the third century and into the fourth (4:61). Roman diplomacy had always operated in advance of the frontiers of the Empire, binding tribes to Rome and promoting disunity amongst potential enemies. Loyal allies were rewarded, often financially. For a number of reasons the credibility and effectiveness of Roman deterrent diplomacy became reduced in the late Roman Empire, and the advantage of such treaty relationships started to pass to the barbarian tribes who tended to join larger (and more hostile) confederations and extort larger subsidies. Although the northern frontier was fairly quiet during the third century, that peace may have been bought at a high price. Not everyone today accepts Richmond's view that sites such as *Locus Maponus* (near Annan and just to the north of Hadrian's Wall) were the venues for diplomatic meetings between Rome and her northern neighbours, but his belief that close contact was maintained is surely well founded and well shown in other provinces by epigraphic evidence. The changing political structure of extramural native populations and the diminishing effectiveness of Roman diplomacy is demonstrated by the fact that the old tribal names were submerged increasingly in larger confederated units. As early as the Severan campaigns, the tribes of central and highland Scotland were combined into two broad groups, the Maeatae and the Caledones. Later, a new name with wide connotations emerged and in late sources the word 'Pict' was virtually synonymous with the entire spectrum of tribes north of Hadrian's Wall. The increased ability of the northern peoples to operate in concert with each other improved their bargaining power and would have made any Roman treaty relations based on subsidy payments ever more expensive.

Another factor lay in a parallel development in the organization of the tribes of the Scotti in Ireland. The potential danger posed by both Scotti and Picti was increased by the fact that they developed the capacity for seaborne raids on Britain, thus outflanking Hadrian's Wall. Nevertheless the substantial treasure hoards of late Roman metalwork from Traprain Law in Scotland, and Coleraine and Balline in northern Ireland, need not represent plunder, but could have been won from the Roman authorities in return for guarantees of peaceful behaviour.

The most severe new problem, however, may have been Saxon and Frankish raids on the south-east coastline of Britain. The policy of coastal defence which developed has sometimes been explained more in terms of internal political crises than in relation to external barbarian threats, but this is hardly an adequate argument since much of the system was already in place before, for instance, Carausius led his breakaway movement (see below). The reality of the raids (or, at least, the perception of a threat) need not be doubted. It came to a head in AD 367 when the great 'barbarian conspiracy' needed the military intervention of Count Theodosius to stabilize the situation caused by concerted land and seaborne attacks from north, east and west, i.e. from Scotland, Ireland and the Continent.

A Roman fleet had been based in the Channel ports from the second century at the latest. The main port base of the *Classis Britannica* lay at Dover, though it can be suggested on the basis of the distribution of stamped tiles and bricks that a number of other forts may have been associated with the unit (4:62). Boulogne was the principal harbour and fort on the Gallic coast. The activities of the fleet, however, were not limited to patrolling the seas or transporting personnel across the Channel, as the association of brick and tile made by the fleet with iron-working sites in the Weald demonstrates (6:12).

From the early third century, though, the first elements of a new system of fortifications started to appear on the east coast (4:63–4:66). Although the exact dates of construction of the so-called Saxon Shore forts are uncertain, the development of the system was spread over at least a century and a half. Many of the new forts were notable for the increased size of their defences, with huge external bastion towers and other features designed to make them more difficult to storm than old-style forts. Most of the major harbours and river mouths of the east and south-east coasts were protected in this manner. There was a similar series of sites in Gaul, extending along the coast of Brittany as far as Brest.

Coastal defences were not limited to East Anglia and the English Channel (4:67). The fact that raiders were feared elsewhere is illustrated by the construction of other installations, particularly a series of fortlets on the North Yorkshire coast and larger forts at Cardiff Castle (and perhaps Pembroke) in South Wales, Caer Gybi (Holyhead) and Hen Waliau (Caernarvon) in North Wales, and Lancaster and Ravenglass further north. By the fourth century many towns in Britain, both large and small, were also equipped with walls, particularly those close to the sea and navigable rivers. The chronological and morphological sequence involved differs markedly from similar developments on the Continent, but the temptation to ascribe urban wall building to a few attested political crises must be handled with care (see below, Map 5:14). The archaeological dating evidence, often consisting largely of residual pottery recovered from earthen banks, is difficult to assess. In any case large-scale civil

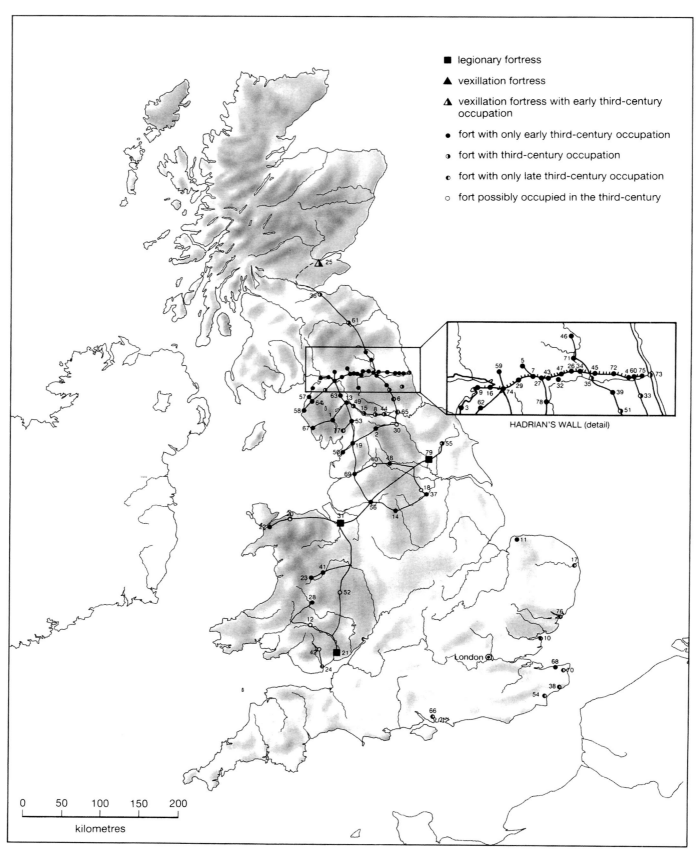

Legend:

■ legionary fortress

▲ vexillation fortress

△ vexillation fortress with early third-century occupation

● fort with only early third-century occupation

◐ fort with third-century occupation

◑ fort with only late third-century occupation

○ fort possibly occupied in the third-century

HADRIAN'S WALL (detail)

London

Map 4:60 Military sites occupied in the third century (not all sites were occupied at the same time and accurate dating of phases impossible at many sites).

Table 4.7 Military sites occupied during the third century

1 Ambleside	21 Caerleon	41 Forden Gaer	61 Newstead
2 Brough-by-Bainbridge	22 Caernarvon	42 Gelligaer (?)	62 Old Carlisle
3 Beckfoot	23 Caersws II	43 Great Chesters	63 Old Penrith
4 Benwell	24 Cardiff	44 Greta Bridge	64 Papcastle
5 Bewcastle	25 Carpow	45 Halton Chesters	65 Piercebridge
6 Binchester	26 Carrawburgh	46 High Rochester	66 Portchester
7 Birdoswald	27 Carvoran	47 Housesteads	67 Ravenglass
8 Bowes	28 Castell Collen	48 Ilkley	68 Reculver
9 Bowness	29 Castlesteads	49 Kirkby Thore	69 Ribchester
10 Bradwell	30 Catterick	50 Lancaster	70 Richborough
11 Brancaster	31 Chester	51 Lanchester	71 Risingham
12 Brecon Gaer (?)	32 Chesterholm	52 Leintwardine (?)	72 Rudchester
13 Brougham	33 Chester-le-Street	53 Low Burrowbridge	73 South Shields
14 Brough-on-Noe	34 Chesters	54 Lympne	74 Stanwix
15 Brough-under-Stainmore	35 Corbridge	55 Malton	75 Wallsend
16 Burgh-by-Sands	36 Cramond	56 Manchester	76 Walton Castle
17 Burgh Castle	37 Doncaster	57 Maryport	77 Watercrook
18 Burghwallis (?)	38 Dover	58 Moresby	78 Whitley
19 Burrow in Lonsdale	39 Ebchester	59 Netherby	79 York
20 Caerhun (?)	40 Elslack (?)	60 Newcastle	

Plate 4:24 Housesteads fort from the north-east showing the late Roman 'chalet style' barracks in the foreground reflecting the changed conditions of army life in the later Empire

Plate 4:25 Third-century rebuilding inscription from the baths at Lancaster

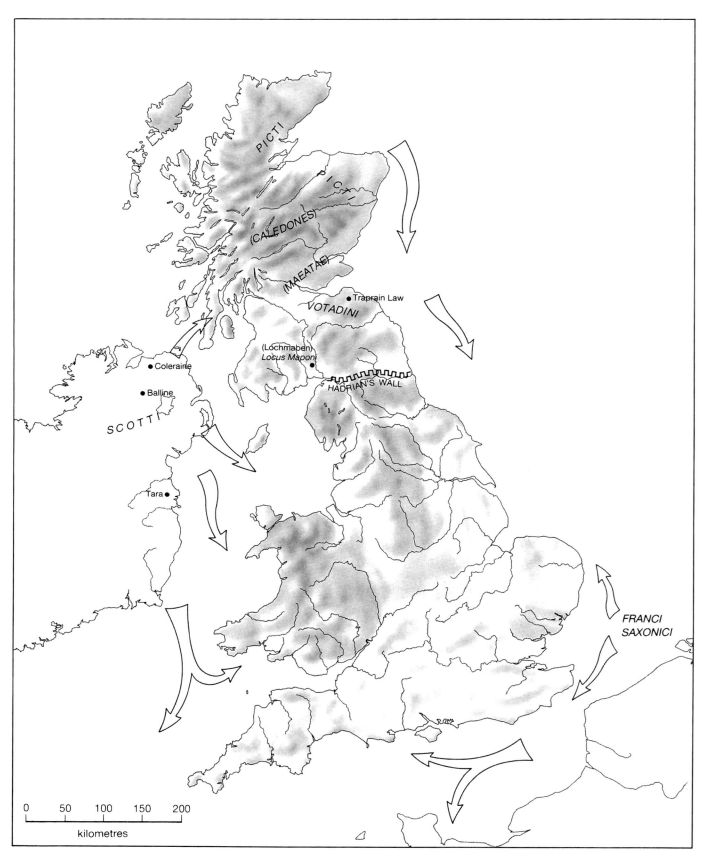

Map 4:6I   Changing threats in the late Roman period

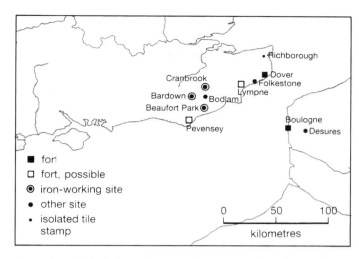

Map 4:62   Distribution of stamped bricks and tiles of the *Classis Britannica*

Plate 4:26 (*right*)   Rampart walk on the north-west of the late Roman coastal defences at Caer Gybi, Holyhead

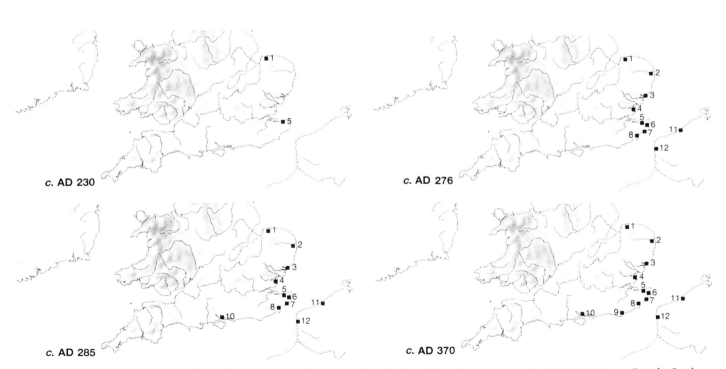

Maps 4:63–4:66   Development of the Saxon Shore defences in the third and fourth centuries AD: 1 Brancaster, 2 Burgh Castle, 3 Walton Castle, 4 Bradwell, 5 Reculver, 6 Richborough, 7 Dover, 8 Lympne, 9 Pevensey, 10 Portchester, 11 Oudenberg, 12 Boulogne

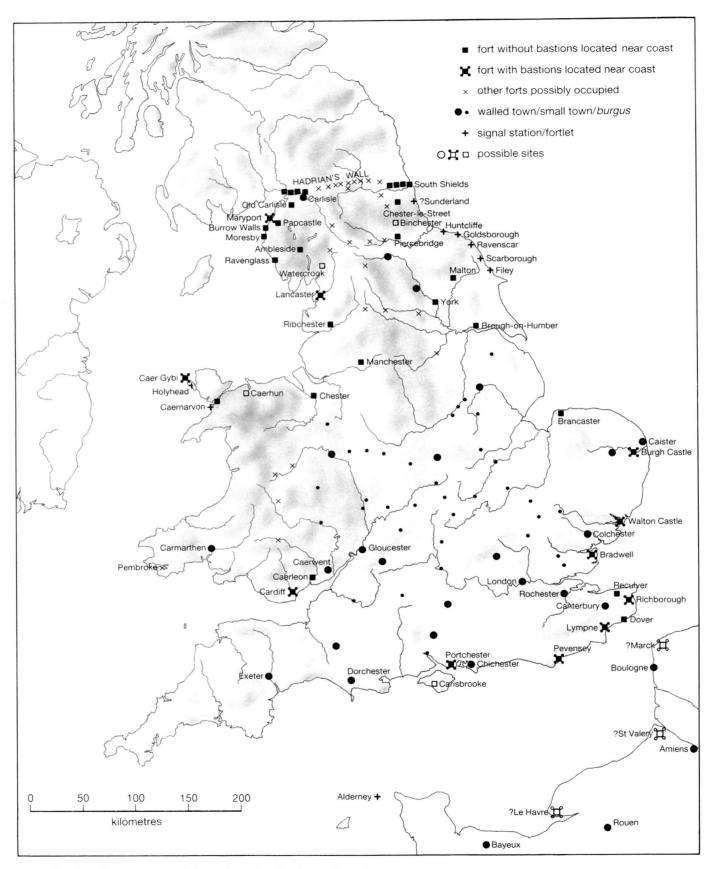

Map 4:67 Late Roman coastal defences including the Saxon Shore forts

Plate 4:27   The Roman signal station (arrowed) on the cliff edge in the grounds of Scarborough Castle. This formed part of the North Sea coastal defensive system in the fourth century AD.

Plate 4:28   The north-eastern corner bastion of the late coastal fort known as the Wery Wall at Lancaster (see also Pl. 9:1). The concrete and stone masonry on the solid bastion has been incorporated in the foundations of an eighteenth-century wall running across the picture.

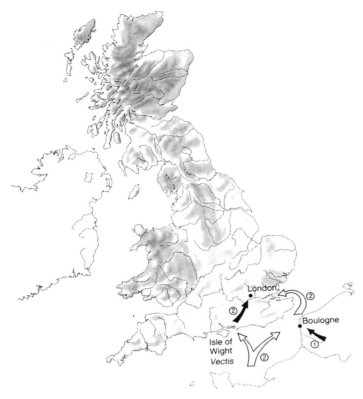

Map 4:68 Campaigns of Constantius (i) against Carausius AD 293 and Allectus AD 296

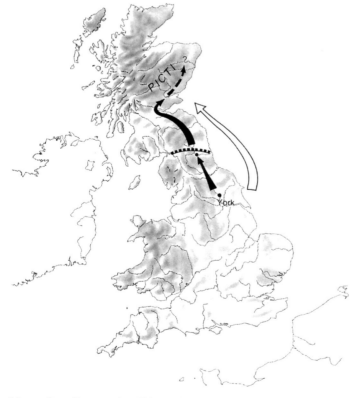

Map 4:69 Constantius Chlorus (ii) in Britain AD 306

engineering, such as the construction of town defences, required the emperor's permission, and those of early date may also have symbolized a developing civic pride in the province. In part at least, though, the defence of many settlements, particularly the small towns (such as Water Newton and Kenchester, Map 5:21; Pl. 5:6), must indicate a sense of insecurity.

The classic example of the sort of political crisis alluded to above was the breakaway 'empire' of Carausius (4:68). Carausius had been in command of the Channel fleet before setting himself up in AD 286 or 287 as a rival to the legitimate emperors (see further Map 5:6). He resisted an initial attempt by Maximian to oust him, but after Constantius Chlorus recaptured Boulogne and whatever territory Carausius had controlled in northern Gaul by AD 293, the renegade was assassinated and replaced by his right-hand man, Allectus. When Constantius launched a seaborne campaign against Britain in AD 296, Allectus was no match for him and the brief offensive culminated with the successful recapture of London before it could be sacked by the defeated army. This kind of incident demonstrates that town walls might, on occasion, have been built in anticipation of a Roman rather than a barbarian attack.

Constantius returned to Britain in AD 306 for a major campaign against the Picts (4:69). How far north he advanced is unknown, but it is by no means impossible that

Map 4:70 (*opposite*) Britain in the *Notitia Dignitatum* (solid symbols indicate sites mentioned in the *Notitia* whose location is fairly certain; open symbols indicate sites with fourth-century occupation, but not mentioned in *Notitia*, or whose Roman place names are uncertain). The suggestion that the list of *Dux* was in three sections (differentiated by different conventional symbols) is our interpretation; not a feature of the original document. Compare also with Maps 2:16–2:17.

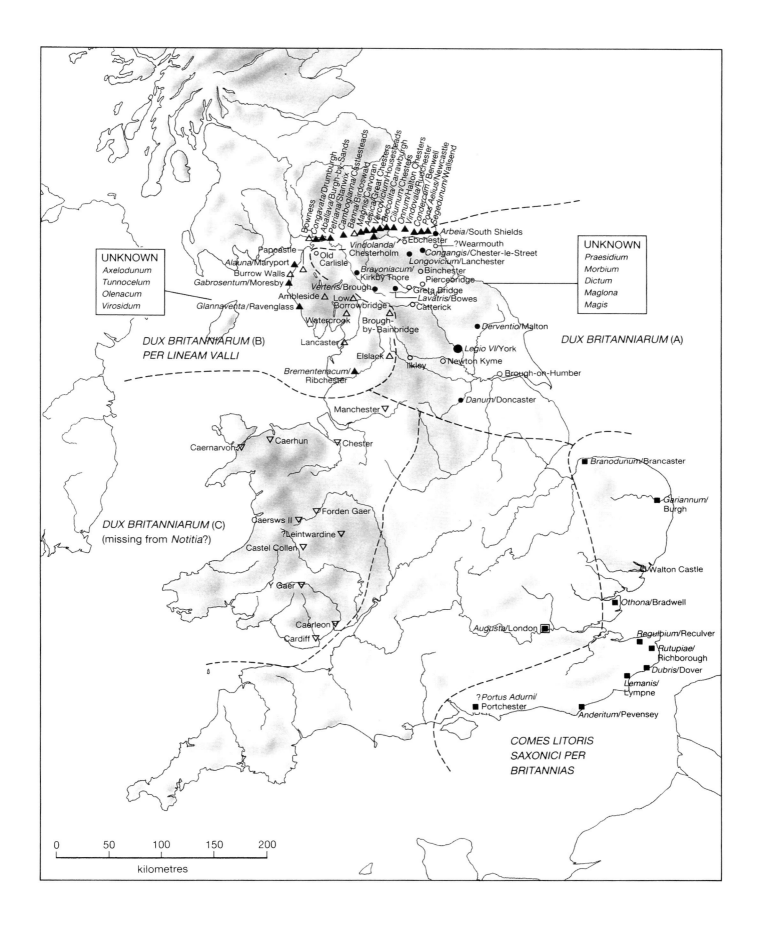

Bowness
Congavata/Drumburgh
Aballava/Burgh-by-Sands
Petriana/Stanwix
Camboglanna/Castlesteads
Banna/Birdoswald
Magnis/Carvoran
Aesica/Great Chesters
Vercovicium/Housesteads
Brocolitia/Carrawburgh
Cilurnum/Chesters
Onnum/Halton Chesters
Vindovala/Rudchester
Condercum/Benwell
Pons Aelius/Newcastle
Segedunum/Wallsend

Arbeia/South Shields
?Wearmouth
Ebchester

UNKNOWN
Praesidium
Morbium
Dictum
Maglona
Magis

UNKNOWN
Axelodunum
Tunnocelum
Olenacum
Virosidum

Papcastle
Alauna/Maryport
Burrow Walls
Gabrosentum/Moresby
Old Carlisle
Vindolanda/Chesterholm
Congangis/Chester-le-Street
Longovicium/Lanchester
Bravoniacum/Kirkby Thore
Binchester
Verteris/Brough
Piercebridge
Ambleside
Low Borrowbridge
Greta Bridge
Lavatris/Bowes
Glannaventa/Ravenglass
Catterick
Watercrook
Brough-by-Bainbridge
Derventio/Malton

DUX BRITANNIARUM (B)
PER LINEAM VALLI

Lancaster
Legio VI/York
Elslack
Newton Kyme
Ilkley
Brough-on-Humber
Brementenacum/Ribchester
Danum/Doncaster
Manchester

DUX BRITANNIARUM (A)

Caernarvon
Caerhun
Chester

Branodunum/Brancaster

Gariannum/Burgh

DUX BRITANNIARUM (C)
(missing from *Notitia*?)

Forden Gaer
Caersws II
?Leintwardine
Castel Collen
Gaer
Caerleon
Cardiff

Walton Castle

Othona/Bradwell

Augusta/London
Regulbium/Reculver
Rutupiae/Richborough
Dubris/Dover
Lemanis/Lympne
?*Portus Adurni*/Portchester
Anderitum/Pevensey

COMES LITORIS
SAXONICI PER
BRITANNIAS

0   50   100   150   200
kilometres

some of the large marching camps in Strathmore (4:19) were built then rather than in the Severan campaigns. Constantius further emulated Septimius Severus by dying at York on his return from the north!

Our sources mention further military activity in Britain later in the fourth century, notably by Constans in AD 343, Lupicinius in AD 360, Count Theodosius in AD 367–9 (following the 'barbarian conspiracy') and, perhaps, by Stilicho in AD 398. The geographical indications are too imprecise to allow useful guesses as to the location of the campaigning.

The final aspect to consider in this chapter is the late Roman pattern of deployment, as known to us from archaeological evidence and from the *Notitia Dignitatum* (4:70; cf. above 2:16, 2:17). According to the *Notitia*, Britain was provided with nine units (six cavalry and three infantry) of the *comitatenses* – the crack troops of the late Empire. The whereabouts of these units is unknown, though they may have been held as a mobile reserve in southern Britain close to the headquarters of a senior military commander, the *comes Britanniarum*. Alternatively, the *comes* and the field army recorded in the *Notitia* may not have been permanently stationed in Britain at all, the entry being a record of an expeditionary force sent to the island on a specific mission. Subordinate to the *comes* in either case would have been

two other commanders, the *comes litoris Saxonici per Britannias* and *dux Britanniarum*, whose troops were, by and large, the downgraded remnants of the old legions and auxiliary units (now generally referred to as *limitanei* and no longer considered as high quality troops). Although the disposition of sites named in the *Notitia* and other sites which have revealed some evidence of fourth-century occupation suggests the continued maintenance of a large garrison, two points need to be considered. Firstly, not all sites were occupied contemporaneously and the total number of sites which were in garrison probably diminished towards the end of the period. Secondly, excavation at several forts has shown that the number of troops in occupation in the fourth-century barrack blocks was a fraction of the number housed in the second century. So, although the garrison of late Roman Britain may appear at first glance to have been comparable in numbers with the earlier deployments, it was in reality much reduced both in size and efficiency. If the military situation in late fourth-century Britain was not as desperate as that in Continental Europe, this was not a sign of the strength of the northern frontier or of the high morale of the garrison. The military problems faced in Britain were simply much smaller in scale than the catastrophes being suffered elsewhere.

5
The Development of the Provinces

FORMATION AND ADMINISTRATION

As noted in the previous chapter, there is no clear evidence that Rome ever intended to limit her conquest to the south-eastern 'civilized' region of Britain. Soon after the invasion of AD 43 the army was active in extending Roman territory towards the west and south-west, while use was made of client rulers to control some of the subjected or acquiescent territory (5:1). Cogidubnus was appointed king over the old Atrebatic territory – he was presumably an Atrebatic 'prince' or a renegade British leader who had thrown in his lot with the Romans at an early stage – and he seems to have continued to rule until the AD 70s at least. The Iceni of Norfolk were apparently another tribal group who collaborated with the Romans in AD 43. In spite of a minor revolt against Roman interference in AD 47, the client kingdom was allowed to continue to issue coins under its ruler Prasutagus (who may have replaced an earlier ruler after the revolt). The mismanagement of the absorption of the Icenian kingdom into the province in AD 60 led to the Boudican revolt (4:9). The third great client tribe was the Brigantes of northern England, ruled at this date by a queen, Cartimandua. From an early date, some Roman troops were even based in Brigantian territory for the twin purposes of deterrence and assistance.

It is also possible that two other tribes, the Corieltauvi and the Dobunni, were granted client status (and continued to issue coins) for a few years after the conquest. By AD 50, however, it is likely that they had been absorbed into the zone controlled directly by the military. These uses of client kingdoms and client tribes are well attested elsewhere in the Empire at this time (5:2). By contrast, the tribes of the south-west, who had offered concerted resistance, were treated initially with harshness, if the war cemetery at Maiden Castle is a typical indication (cf. 4:29).

To the rear of the active military zone, and sandwiched between client tribes, the initial 'civil province' was of small size indeed – comprising, in effect, Kent and the territory of the defeated federation of Trinovantes and Catuvellauni. The development of the old tribal centres of St Albans, Colchester and Canterbury as towns is described in more detail below. Colchester may have been intended to be the provincial capital initially, but the mercantile centre which developed around the Thames bridge at London was in a more advantageous position geographically and was the logical choice as a long-term capital (5:19, 5:20).

Although the Roman Empire had ceased to expand to any great extent after the death of Augustus in AD 14, the conquest of Britain was not the only acquisition in the AD 40s. In AD 39, Gaius (Caligula) had the client king of Mauretania assassinated and the annexation of his lands was still meeting stiff resistance when Claudius came to the throne. In the first few years of his reign, therefore, Claudius was able to claim substantial territorial gains in Africa as well as in Britain (5:2). These expansionist adventures were only possible, however, because a policy of diplomacy and deterrence was followed in other frontier regions, notably on the Rhine and in the East where the major concentrations of legions were based. In the East this was achieved partly through the continued employment of client kings. On the

Map 5:1 Roman Britain c. AD 50

approx. territorial limits of province and client rulers

main axis of continued territorial expansion

● provincial capital

· *colonia*/other town

Cartimandua
BRIGANTES
CORIELTAUVI
Prasutagus
ICENI
DOBUNNI
St Albans
Colchester
London
Cogidubnus
DUROTRIGES
ATREBATES
Canterbury

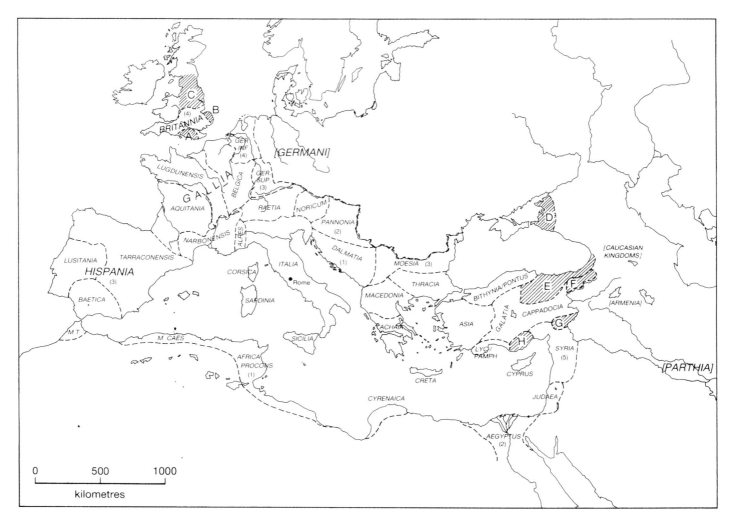

Map 5:2   Britain and the Roman Empire in the reign of Claudius (mid-first century AD) (numbers in brackets indicate the number of legions stationed in the province; hatching indicates client kingdoms): Ger.Inf. = *Germania Inferior*, Ger.Super. = *Germania Superior*, Lyc. and Pamph. = *Lycia* and *Pamphylia*, M.Caes. = *Mauretania Caesariensis*, M.T. = *Mauretania Tingitana*, A = Kingdom of Cogidubnus, B = Iceni, C = Brigantes, D = Bosporus, E = Pontus, F = Lesser Armenia, G/H = Commagene

German frontier treaties were made with the client tribes beyond the Rhine and Danube. At this date there were no well-delineated frontiers and, in theory, renewed expansion was possible in all sectors. In practice, Imperial ambition was limited by Rome's perception of the inherent dangers of overstretching her military resources and engaging in conflicts in too many theatres simultaneously. The early phases in the conquest of Britain and its development as a province were thus bound up with the wider situation of the Empire as a whole and the most rapid advances corresponded with periods of comparative tranquillity in other

frontier lands. Similarly, it has been noted already that the withdrawal from the far north of Britain coincided with a series of major Roman defeats in the Danube region during the reign of Domitian.

The position in AD 150 (5:3) was very different to that of a century earlier. The occupation of the Antonine Wall marked a partial return towards the ideal of total conquest and it is apparent that though the wall may have functioned as a customs frontier, the true territorial limits of *Britannia* lay some way to the north (the approximate extent indicated by the outpost forts occupied at this date). Tribes well beyond

Plate 5:1 Septimius Severus, Julia Domna, Caracalla and Geta's head (defaced in antiquity) on a painted plaque

Map 5:3 Roman Province of Britatin *c.*AD 150

Map 5:4 Provinces of Britain *c.*AD 216

even this limit would have been controlled by diplomatic links and considered as such to be part of Rome's *imperium*.

By the mid-second century, London was the unquestioned provincial capital and base for both the governor and the procurator (for the administrative hierarchy, see Table 5:1). There were three towns with the rank of *coloniae*, all founded for legionary veterans, and about fifteen towns recognized as centres of indigenous local government (*civitas* capitals). Some of these British towns may have attained the intermediate honorific rank of *municipium*, though the evidence is ambiguous. The legions had long since ceased to require more than three permanent bases and the fortresses at Caerleon, Chester and York had been rebuilt largely in stone.

Up to the end of the second century Britain was governed as a single province by a high ranking and trusted senator. The size of the army which was permanently based there (about 10 per cent of the total standing army) made the governorship of Britain one of the top military appointments in the gift of the emperor. The military strength of the British governor was revealed during the civil war of AD 193–7, when Clodius Albinus came extremely close to defeating his ultimately successful rival for the Imperial purple, Septimius Severus. A contemporary source, Herodian, suggests that it was as a result of this that Britain was divided into two unequal portions some time between AD 197 and 216 (5:4). It is believed that the legions of Caerleon and Chester and

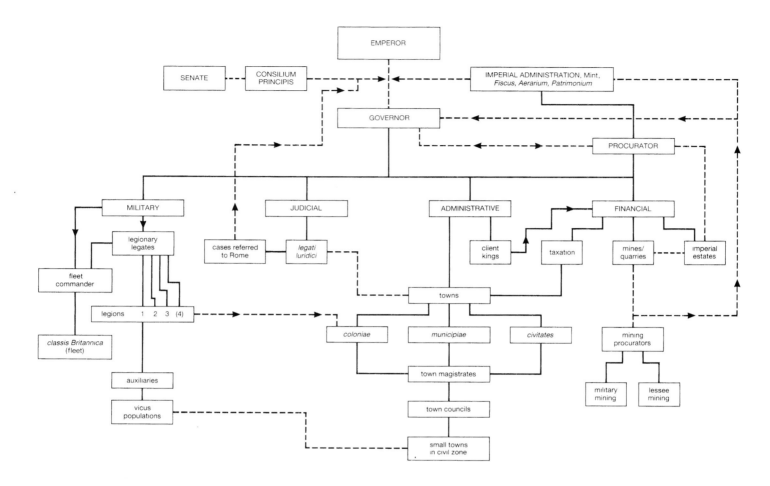

Table 5.1 Bureaucracy in first-century Roman Britain

The invading army of 40,000 men was followed by a small number of administrators. The bureaucracy of the first century remained essentially simple. At its centre sat the governor of Britain, who enjoyed the rank of Imperial Legate and held pro-praetorian power. The governor was an ex-consul of considerable experience, holding office normally for three to five years, and being responsible directly to the emperor. He was likely to be a military commander of proven ability, if opportunity or need arose, operating in concert with one or more of his legionary legates in the field. He also had wide-ranging judicial powers and responsibilities. Only those who held Roman citizenship enjoyed a measure of protection from his arbitrary power and could have their cases referred to Rome for judgement. As the number of provincial citizens increased, so too must have the administrative burden involved. Moreover, in a province such as Britain the situation was complicated by the way in which Celtic codes of law would still have operated alongside the Roman system, particularly in the countryside.

Problems must have centred on questions of land ownership and taxation. It was in this sphere that a separate independent official, the provincial *procurator*, operated largely on behalf of the emperor's financial interests (i.e. those of the Imperial *fiscus*). The story of the Boudican revolt shows that there could be marked differences of approach between governor and Imperial procurator, reflecting not only conflicting characters, but also different constraints, objectives and responsibilities. The

procurator was also responsible for wider financial interests in the province, including the regulation of mines (and other Imperial monopolies) and Imperial estates. Little is understood of the mechanism of tax collection on objects of trade passing into the province where payment, (*portorium*, possibly as high as 25 per cent), was due. However, we know that prior to the actual invasion of Britain, Augustus had levied such a tax on British goods crossing the Channel to the Continent. Such a system would also have operated across the linear barriers of northern Britain once they had been established.

As well as his other duties the governor also supervised the administration of the local government through the medium of town magistrates and town councils in the *coloniae* and tribal cantons. The delegation of much routine administration to local elite groups was a vital component of Roman provincial government and allowed the official bureaucracy to be kept to a minimum, whilst encouraging the elites to identify more closely with the Empire and participate in its running. The demilitarization of increasing parts of southern Britain following the Flavian campaigns in the west and north must have greatly increased the judicial burden. Part of the administrative response at the time can be seen in the arrival of Iavolenus Priscus and Salvius Liberalis, two distinguished jurists who were the first of a series of *legati iuridici* (or legal experts) sent to the province from the AD 70s onwards.

the colonies of Colchester and Gloucester were included in *Britannia Superior*, governed from London by a legate of consular rank. The northern province of *Britannia Inferior* was administered by a praetorian legate, a senator of the rank below consul. It included the legion at York and the colony at Lincoln, with the provincial capital at the former location. The exact line of the territorial division is not known, but common sense would suggest that it observed the existing *civitates* boundaries, with the Cornovii in *Superior* and the Corieltauvi (and perhaps the Iceni?) in *Inferior*. The exact date and context of the subdivision is disputed, though Severus would have clearly had some justification for taking the decision after Albinus' near success. He carried out a similar measure in Syria, where he defeated yet another rival claimant to the Imperial throne, and one of our sources states that the British partition was carried out in the aftermath of Albinus' defeat. Unfortunately, the rest of our evidence, both literary and epigraphic, does not fit in with this simple solution and various convoluted arguments have been advanced to explain the mismatch. Following Birley (1981) the best course may be to assume that Herodian was mistaken. The creation of the two provinces may not have occurred until after Severus' Scottish campaigns, perhaps in the sole reign of Severus' son, Caracalla (*c.*AD 216). It has been suggested that the army in Britain may have reacted unfavourably to the news of Caracalla's assassination of his brother Geta, and that this may have persuaded Caracalla to follow his father's precedent of subdividing provinces. He was certainly responsible for new dispositions in Pannonia at about this time. The nature of the Severan dynasty's own elevation through military strength held important lessons for emperors and would-be emperors alike. The subdivision of some of the largest remaining military governorships is an indication of the increased insecurity which the Severi had brought to the throne by the manner of their initial seizure of power (5:5). In Britain, in spite of the partitioning of the territory, the senior governor seems to have retained some rights to interfere or to act in the junior province.

Another aspect of Severan policy towards Britain, which is illuminated by reference to wider events, is the reinvasion of Scotland and short-lived advance of the frontier. On a number of inscriptions around the Empire, Severus is hailed as *propagator imperii* – 'extender of Empire' and it is clear that in Africa, Britain and the East he made strenuous efforts to merit the praise.

In actuality, the Severan reorganization of the military provinces, aimed at prohibiting any governor from having direct command of more than two legions, did not prevent the repeated collapse of ordered government. The frequent civil wars of the middle years of the third century were part cause, part effect, of a series of military problems on many frontiers (5:6). The mid-third century was unprecedented for the scale of the disasters which threatened the Empire.

Plate 5:2 Ermine Street approaching the river Nene and *Durobrivae* (Water Newton) from the north. The Roman road is revealed by crop marks in the foreground; beyond *Durobrivae* (the irregular polygon arrowed in the middle distance) it is overlain by modern road.

Roman defeats by Persia in the East led indirectly to the creation of a breakaway Palmyrene Empire (AD 259–71). A similar situation pertained in the extreme north-west of the Empire following a series of barbarian raids across the Rhine and Danube, some penetrating deep into the Empire – the Iuthungi, for instance, reached Italy in AD 271. At the height of the troubles there were often several rival contenders for the Imperial throne, and life expectancy was short for both those emperors recognized in Rome and those only acknowledged by their armies. Yet, amidst the turmoil, a measure of stability was attained in the western provinces by the formation of another breakaway empire based on the provinces of Gaul, Germany, Britain and Spain. The so-called

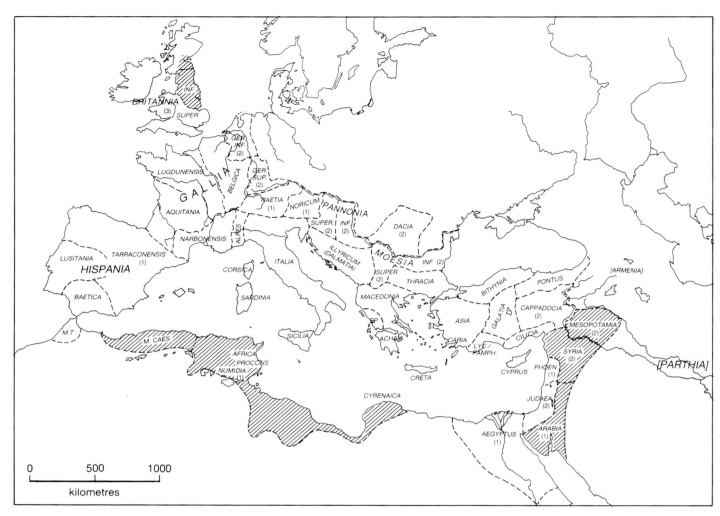

Map 5:5   Britain and the Roman Empire in the Severan era (early third century AD) (numbers in brackets indicate the number of legions stationed in the province; hatching indicates provinces where military advances were made under Severans): Inf. = *Inferior*, Sup. = *Superior*, Ep. = *Epirus*, Ger. = *Germania*, Lyc. and Pamph. = *Lycia and Pamphylia*, M.Caes. = *Mauretania Caesariensis*, M.T. = *Mauretania Tingitana*, Phoen. = *Phoenicia*

Gallic Empire was modelled exactly on the 'legitimate' Empire and functioned for over a decade.

By AD 284 the Empire had been reunited under the authority of a sole ruler, Diocletian, but his position was at first no more secure than that of many of his ill-fated predecessors. Events in Britain were soon to demonstrate that the danger from pretenders was not yet over. Diocletian had appointed one of his leading generals, Maximian, as his Caesar and designated successor and instructed him to operate in the western provinces, where he was to guard against any renewed challenge to the fragile stability. Maximian's appointment of a man called M. Carausius to an important military command in the English Channel was to prove an expensive mistake. When Maximian tried to have Carausius executed for alleged malpractices, the latter revolted. With a powerful fleet and army and a secure power base in Britain, he succeeded in embarrassing the legitimate emperors for seven years. At the height of his power, Carausius apparently controlled not only Britain, but also an extensive area of northern France (5:6). One result of the revolt of Carausius was that Maximian was elevated to co-Augustus with Diocletian. Carausius' insolence in claiming on his coins to be a brother emperor with Diocletian and Maximian led to Diocletian extending his political reforms in AD 293 to inaugurate the system we know as the Tetrarchy. The two Augusti now each appointed another man to be Caesar in their respective halves of the Empire, thus removing the possibility of Carausius being recognized as their colleague.

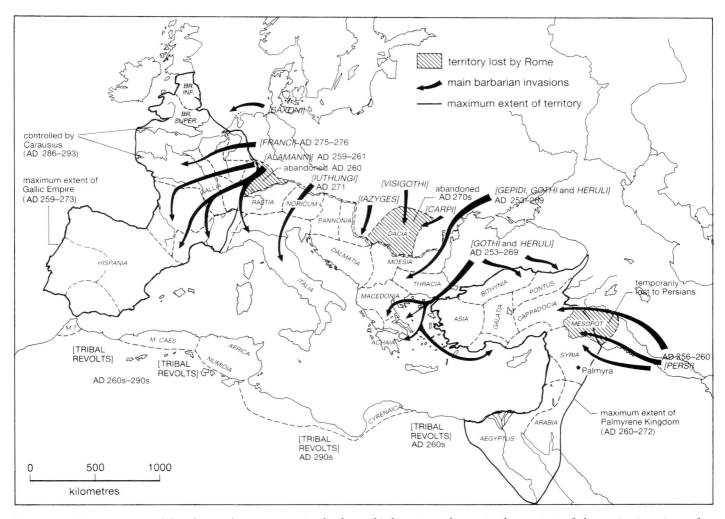

Map 5:6 Britain as part of 'break-away' movements in the later third century shown in the context of the major invasions of this period

Plate 5:3 Coin of Carausius, showing him in the company of Maximian and Diocletian (*CARAUSIUS ET FRATRES SUI*)

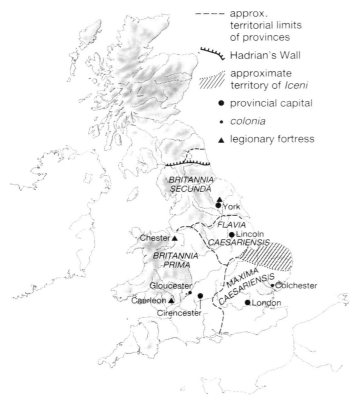

- - - - approx. territorial limits of provinces

Hadrian's Wall

approximate territory of *Iceni*

● provincial capital

· *colonia*

▲ legionary fortress

Map 5:7   Provinces of Britain *c.*AD 312

Plate 5:4   Bronze coin of Maximian, minted in London (*LON* included as mint mark on reverse) (*RIC* 1b)

Flavius Constantius Chlorus, the Caesar in the West, was given the task of dealing with Carausius, and after two campaigns (4:68) Britain was reunited with the Empire.

The administration of the British provinces had not necessarily suffered unduly during these periods of isolation from Rome. However, soon after the reincorporation of the provinces into the Empire, major reforms were carried through. These included a further subdivision, and,

although the exact date of this is uncertain, the new arrangement was certainly in place by AD 312 (5:7). The names of the four provinces which were created are known, but their identification remains somewhat speculative. *Maxima Caesariensis* had the highest ranking governor, a *consularis*, and presumably was centred on London. *Britannia Prima* probably comprised the rest of the old province of *Superior*, with its capital at Cirencester. *Britannia Inferior* seems to have been subdivided into *Britannia Secunda* (capital perhaps at York) and *Flavia Caesariensis* (capital perhaps at Lincoln) – though other combinations are possible in the absence of firm evidence. *Flavia* and *Maxima Caesariensis* were named, no doubt, in honour of Flavius Constantius Chlorus and Maximian. The territory of the Iceni should belong to one or other of these two provinces, but to which is uncertain. Once again it seems reasonable to assume that the new provincial boundaries will have followed those of earlier tribal *civitates*.

The process of further subdivision of the structures of provincial administration involved the increase of officials and a greatly enlarged bureaucracy, not simply in Britain but on an Empire-wide basis (5:8). This trend was amplified by further reforms later in the fourth century. Although many of the first-century provinces had been fragmented into several new-style provinces, each with its own administrative hierarchy, regional groupings of these provinces (*dioceses*) were established under the overall authority of high ranking civil governors (*vicarii*). Increasingly, military command was separated from civil administration and the junior civil governors of the late Empire (*praesides*) rarely had command of troops. At the same time the old policy of placing most troops in the frontier provinces was to some extent superseded by the creation of large mobile field armies assigned on a regional basis (see Table 5:2).

There is some evidence (from the *Notitia* – see Pls 2:3, 2:4 – and from Polemius Silva) that Britain was yet further subdivided during the course of the fourth century, with the creation of a fifth province called *Valentia*. Ammianus Marcellinus connected the name with the victory won in Britain by Count Theodosius in AD 367–8 on behalf of the emperor Valens. Ammianus, however, stated that an existing province had been renamed rather than a new one created, suggesting either that there were never more than four provinces, one having been renamed in *c.*368, or that the fifth province had been created prior to 368 under a different, unknown, title. Not surprisingly there has been a great deal of speculation on the location (or the very existence) of *Valentia*, but the evidence does not permit a satisfactory explanation and no map showing the five provinces has been attempted here. At various times it has been argued that *Valentia* was located in northern England, beyond Hadrian's Wall, in Wales or around London itself. Without epigraphic evidence the problem cannot be resolved, but a northern location is probably the most logical assumption.

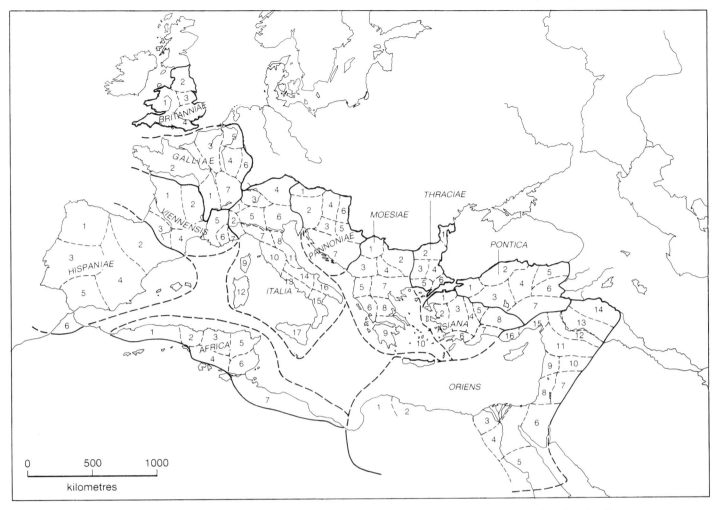

Map 5:8   Britain and the Roman Empire after the Diocletian reforms (early fourth century AD). Provinces listed under Diocese groupings:

Britanniae
1 Britannia Prima
2 Britannia Secunda
3 Flavia Caesariensis
4 Maxima Caesariensis

Galliae
1 Lugdunensis Prima
2 Lugdunensis Secunda
3 Belgica Secunda
4 Belgica Prima
5 Germania Secunda
6 Germania Prima
7 Sequania

Viennensis
1 Aquitanica Secunda
2 Aquitanica Prima
3 Novem Populi
4 Narbonensis Prima

5 Viennensis
6 Narbonensis Secunda
7 Alpes Maritimae

Hispania
1 Gallaecia
2 Tarraconensis
3 Lusitania
4 Carthaginiensis
5 Baetica
6 Mauretania Tingitana

Africa
1 Mauretania Caesariensis
2 Mauretania Sitifiensis
3 Numidia Cirtensis
4 Numidia Militaris
5 Proconsularis
6 Byzacena
7 Tripolitania

Italia
1 Alpes Graine
2 Alpes Cottiae
3 Raetia Prima
4 Raetia Secunda
5 Aemilia
6 Venetia and Histria
7 Liguria
8 Flaminia
9 Corsica
10 Tuscia and Umbria
11 Picenum
12 Sardinia
13 Campania
14 Samnium
15 Lucania and Bruttii
16 Apulia and Calabria
17 Sicilia

Pannoniae
1 Noricum Ripense
2 Noricum Mediterraneum

3 Savia
4 Pannonia Prima
5 Pannonia Secunda
6 Valeria
7 Dalmatia

Moesiae
1 Moesia Prima
2 Dacia
3 Praevalitana
4 Dardania
5 Epirus Nova
6 Epirus Vetus
7 Macedonia
8 Thessalia
9 Achaia
10 Insulae

Thraciae
1 Scythia
2 Moesia Secunda
3 Thracia

4 Haemimontus
5 Rhodope
6 Europa

Asiana
1 Hellespontus
2 Asia
3 Lydia
4 Phrygia Prima
5 Phrygia Secunda
6 Caria
7 Lycia and Pamphylia
8 Pisidia

Pontica
1 Bithynia
2 Paphlagonia
3 Galatia
4 Diospontus
5 Pontus Polemoniacus
6 Armenia Minor
7 Cappadocia

Oriens
1 Libya Superior
2 Libya Inferior
3 Aegyptus Iovia
4 Aegyptus Herculia
5 Thebais
6 Arabia Secunda
7 Arabia Prima
8 Palestina
9 Phoenicia
10 Augusta Libanensis
11 Syria Coele
12 Augusta Euphratensis
13 Osrhoene
14 Mesopotamia
15 Cicilia
16 Isauria

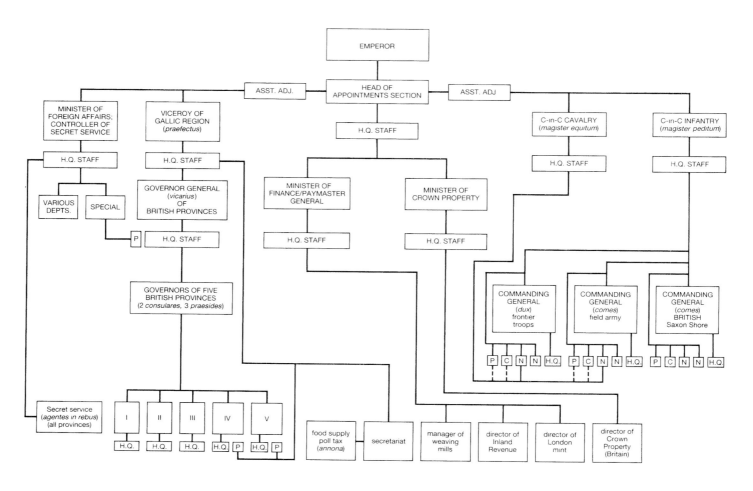

Table 5.2   Bureaucracy in late Roman Britain

The protracted development of the British provinces meant that by the fourth century the governing bureaucracy had substantially evolved from its predecessors. Possibly as many as a thousand lesser officials were involved in the governance of Britain, and we are fortunate in having the *Notitia Dignitatum* to provide an overall view of the structure of the Imperial civil service and the army command system.

Although of early fifth-century date as it stands, the *Notitia Dignitatum* contains a strand of information relating to Britain in the late fourth century when it was still a Roman province (see further 2:16). By this time, as was to be expected, the Imperial estates had grown enormously in scale, partly by confiscation from supporters of unsuccessful British usurpers such as Clodius Albinus. This section of the administration, the Ministry of Crown Property, was in the hands of the provincial head of the *res privata* or Imperial estates, who was naturally responsible to the Imperial bureaucracy at Rome. More generalized finance lay under the head of the section known as *sacrae largitiones,* the Ministry of Finance. Under this official, technically termed a *comes,* the administration was run by two treasury officials both probably based in London and a third more enigmatic official known as the procurator of the Imperial *gynaeceum,* or weaving mill, at *Venta,* a disputed identification that is discussed elsewhere (see further 2:16; 6:46). Civil administration lay with another set of officials under the jurisdiction of the vicar (*vicarius*) of the British provinces (or *diocese* as it was called). The vicar was technically subordinate to the prefect of the Gallic provinces.

The officials at the bottom of this chain were the individual provincial governors, namely the *consulares* of Maxima Caesariensis and Valentia and the *praesides* of Flavia Caesariensis, Britannia Prima and Britannia Secunda. They also seem to have been responsible for some forms of tax collection. In particular this included the *annona militaris* or the requisitioning of supplies for military consumption based, it appears, on a poll tax of the landowning or land-working population.

On the military side the picture is relatively straightforward. Britain lay under the western Imperial command (represented by the *magister peditum* and the *magister equitum* in Gaul) and was controlled by three senior generals, the *dux Britanniarum* in charge of frontier defence, the *comes Britanniae* in charge of the strategic reserve and the *comes litoris Saxonici,* the count of the Saxon Shore, in control of coastal defence particularly in the south-east. To their staff were attached various other departmental officers responsible for the efficiency of the official postal service (*cursus publicus*); likewise some staff liaised with the prefect of the Gallic provinces, and others (*agentes in rebus*) reported back to the central administration on external political developments.

Perhaps the key change from the early bureaucracy, apart from that of scale, was that very few men in the entire system of late Roman provincial administration had direct access to the emperors, with a complicated hierarchy of posts separating provincial governors from their political masters.

CULTURAL DEVELOPMENT

In the centuries following the conquest most of southern England developed an urban landscape of colonies, municipalities and tribal capitals. A vital component of the settlement heirarchy was the Romanized farm, or villa. Indeed, the presence or absence of villas can be used in one kind of assessment of the cultural frontiers of Roman Britain. Villas are, broadly speaking, limited to an area that corresponds closely to the zone of developed urban settlement. Acculturation was a perceivable process that went hand in hand with provincialization, something that some of the ancient sources recognized. (Tacitus, *Agricola* 21; *Histories* 4.73–4; Dio 56.10.1.) The archaeological evidence from southern Britain shows the overall success of acculturation towards the end of the first century. The area was by this time completely demilitarized and the subsequent development of many towns and villas indicates absorption of Roman civilization in its most obvious form.

It would probably be a mistake to see the process as an ongoing steady phenomenon, a point emphasized only too strongly by the Boudican revolt. Numerous factors can affect the speed and development of an urban system and its rural infrastructure. Some commentators have interpreted urban growth as moving hand in hand with the rise of villas and the fostering of a clear economic infrastructure in the rural hinterland. On the other hand, one might argue that the presence of the army in the southern part of the province initially operated in different ways by encouraging the growth of large civil settlements alongside forts without necessarily hastening rural change. With the northward movement of the army, however, socio-economic change must have accelerated in the urbanized south. The growth of towns probably encouraged the development of a larger 'middle-class' element in the population and slow but gradual change in the countryside. Yet it was not until the third and fourth centuries, in contrast with developments on the Continent, that the villa economy reached its heyday (7:6–7:13 below).

The overall extent of acculturation is documented in Map 5:9 which is derived from the data contained in the standard Ordnance Survey map of Roman Britain. The density of villas and urban settlement has been conveyed graphically, and suggests the varying degrees of Romanization. The map shows that there was a relatively high degree of acculturation as far north as Lincolnshire on the east coast, and yet there was relatively low acculturation in the West Midlands.

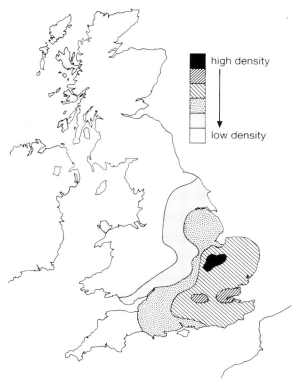

Map 5:9 Boundaries of acculturation as shown by the distribution of towns and villas (this is a computer-generated map).

Plate 5:5 (*right*) Excavation in progress on a courtyard building beside the shore at Cold Knap, Barry, Glamorgan

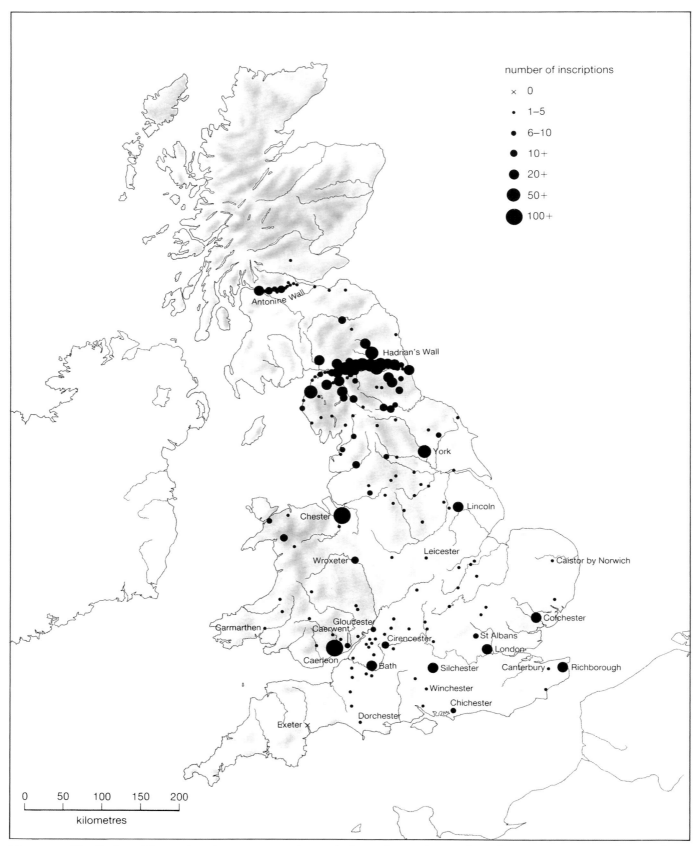

Map 5:10 Distribution of Roman inscriptions on stone (not including milestones) as catalogued in *RIB* I: inscriptions discovered since 1954 are not included, but would not affect the overall pattern greatly; inscriptions/graffiti on everyday objects (*instrumentum domesticum*) are also omitted, since frequently these consist of no more than a name or single word.

Latin inscriptions and language

When the Romans invaded Britain the indigenous population spoke mainly a P Celtic language belonging to the
Brythonic group of Celtic dialects. P Celtic language survives
in part in modern Welsh, Cornish and Breton, Irish and
Scots Gaelic. At the time of the Roman invasion the Brythonic speech was probably roughly the same both on the
Continent and in much of Britain; indeed it offers a major
avenue to understanding the Celtic-based toponomy
through the survival of place names transliterated into Latin
in this country, as well as in Gaul and Germany. A major
problem in assessing the importance of Celtic is that it
did not develop as a written language in Britain, so that
we must rely on unsatisfactory circumstantial arguments.
Nonetheless it seems to have remained predominant
throughout the Roman period.

A relatively small number of Latin speakers were involved
in the conquest. However, Latin enjoyed particular advantages since it was the language of the provincial administration (notably within the army, in local government and
in the law courts). Latin formed the principal tongue of the
major religious cults deriving from the classical pantheon
and must, to some extent, have become the language of
commercial life. Yet for the indigenous Celtic population
linguistic assimilation was probably slow and limited. Auxiliary soldiers, whether Britons conscripted to serve abroad or
foreigners serving in an auxiliary unit in Britain, had to
acquire a working vocabulary in Latin. Above all, the tribal
aristocracy could only improve its status by the acquisition
of Roman citizenship, for which the ability to speak Latin
was essential. The governing classes of the tribal communities thus developed a basic knowledge of Latin and
through it of the Graeco-Roman literary world.

The three colonies founded in the first century, Colchester,
Lincoln and Gloucester, were by definition designed to house
Latin-speaking veterans who would promote an image of
Mediterranean culture. In the tribal areas, although there
is a lack of evidence, the likelihood is that the elite were
bilingual, while the commercial classes in the towns must
have developed a modicum of Latin for everyday needs. In
rural Britain, the pattern may have been more strongly
differentiated. Villa owners are likely to have been Latin
speaking, yet they would have retained sufficient Celtic to
communicate with most of the rural population, amongst
whom the Celtic language probably remained dominant
even in the lowlands.

The distribution of Latin inscriptions reveals two major
concentrations (5:10). The vast majority of the inscriptions
come from military sites, with a lesser number from urban
centres. The lack of a significant number of Latin inscriptions
from villas does not imply that villa dwellers were illiterate,
rather that they did not think it worth erecting such texts
in the strongly Celtic countryside.

In the uplands the Celtic tongue was overwhelmingly
preponderant. The only exceptions would have been in the
areas of acculturation in the immediate hinterland of forts.
There, legionaries and auxiliary soldiers spoke Latin in their
normal working days. The area round the forts and *vici*
along Hadrian's Wall, a thin band stretching from coast to
coast, must have contained a large number of Latin-speaking
people. On a much smaller scale, there must have been a
similar situation on the Antonine Wall in central Scotland.
Yet there are other factors to be taken into account in
interpreting the map. The survival, indeed the very
incidence, of Latin inscriptions is likely to be much greater
in areas where stone is readily available for carving, and will
also reflect the distribution of skilled stone cutters. Naturally
enough the legionary fortresses, forts, military works, colonies and other towns appear strongly represented in any
such distribution map. Yet the numerical totals for many
towns are surprisingly low (in spite of allowances for losses
through redevelopment) and without the army the evidence
for written Latin would be thin indeed.

There remains the problem of estimating the overall proportion of Latin speakers amongst the population, and there
is no clear answer to this question. The failure of Latin to
survive at any significant level beyond the withdrawal of
the Roman administration in the early fifth century supports
the view that Latin had only formed a veneer overlaying a
Celtic linguistic continuum.

URBANIZATION IN ROMAN BRITAIN

The Claudio-Neronian development

The introduction or increased development of urbanization
has long been taken as concomitant with the advent of
classical culture. Most of southern Britain developed an
urban structure based on colonies, tribal capitals and
municipalities. Much of the key to the success of the policy
of deliberate urbanization probably lay in the involvement
in local government of the tribal aristocracies.

A growing body of archaeological evidence now suggests
that the hillforts and *oppida* of the late Iron Age formed the
first towns to be founded in Britain (3:3–3:5). The existence
of such sites as Gosbecks (Colchester) and Prae Wood (St
Albans) materially affected the acceptance of classical
urbanization in the years following the invasion. Given the
current state of knowledge, the origin of British towns is
perhaps better viewed in terms of the social and administrative roles of urban settlement rather than in terms of
the economic stimulus of the Roman military occupation.
The needs of the Roman system of provincial administration
provided the impetus for the further development of a
number of major centres. Local government was delegated
to a large extent to town councils and a hierarchy of urban
centres was brought into existence for this purpose in Britain

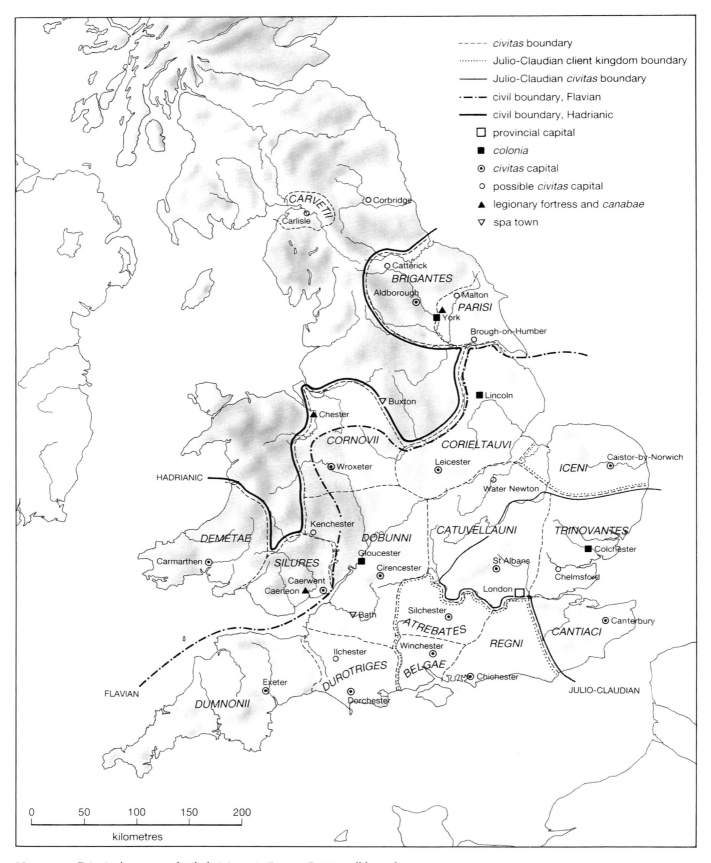

Map 5:11 Principal towns and tribal *civitates* in Roman Britain, all boundaries are approximate.

as elsewhere. The highest ranking towns were colonies of Roman citizens, next were *municipia*, chartered towns of lower status, and finally (for present purposes) there were the *civitas* centres organized around the old tribal divisions (Table 5:1).

Map 5:11 charts the progress towards full urbanism across the southern part of the province. It appears that the colony of Colchester (*Camulodunum*), founded AD 49, was meant to establish a pattern of urbanization that might be followed in the tribal territories. The capitals of the south-eastern tribes, the Catuvellauni, the Trinovantes and the Cantiaci, lay at St Albans (*Verulamium*), Chelmsford (*Caesaromagus*) and Canterbury (*Durovernum Cantiacorum*). At Canterbury the street plan apparently belongs to the 50s or early 60s while extensive excavation at *Verulamium* has revealed Claudian buildings sealed beneath the traces of the destruction occasioned by the Boudican revolt. Like Colchester, Chelmsford and London, *Verulamium* was largely destroyed in the Boudican rebellion, although in this case that refurbishment was not long delayed.

The emergence of London as the provincial capital seems to represent an exceptional case. Tacitus records that by the time of the Boudican revolt its economic potential as an entrepôt had been grasped and within a few years it was to become the provincial capital. Much remains to be established in archaeological terms about the way in which it evolved (5:19, 5:20).

By way of contrast, Chelmsford (*Caesaromagus*) must be judged a failure. With the imposition of the colony close to the original Trinovantian tribal centre at *Camulodunum*, an alternative site for a *civitas* capital had to be found, but the choice of Chelmsford does not appear to have been rewarded by a full rise to prosperous urban status. Chelmsford represents the outstanding failure on the road to early urbanization and was the principal long-term casualty of the Boudican revolt.

Silchester (*Calleva Atrebatum*), Chichester (*Noviomagus Regnensium*) and Winchester (*Venta Belgarum*) probably lay within the client kingdom of Tiberius Claudius Cogidubnus and so the urbanization process may have received special favour. In contrast Caistor-by-Norwich (*Venta Icenorum*) did not develop until long after the deaths of the client king Prasutagus and Boudica, and its small size must reflect the demographic and economic consequences for the Iceni of the revolt of AD 60.

Flavian and Hadrianic development

The clearest statement of official encouragement of urbanization in Britain is Tacitus' description of Agricola's programme of civil works in the late AD 70s (*Agricola* 21). The last quarter of the first century saw both the resumption of large-scale military progress into Wales and the north and a concomitant development of the civilian side of the province.

The major additional tribal groupings assigned the legal status of *civitates peregrinae* included the Dobunni of the Cotswolds and Severn basin, the Dumnonii in the south-west, and the Cornovii and Corieltauvi of the West and East Midlands respectively. The *civitas* capitals of the Regni, the Atrebates and the Belgae (previously within the kingdom of Cogidubnus) were evolving on the same lines. Urban development at Chichester began when a military site, located within the *oppidum* formed by the Chichester dykes, was levelled to form a platform for the initial forum complex. Close by was the temple of Neptune and Minerva, from which a famous inscription citing Cogidubnus himself derives. At Silchester the primary timber basilica and forum belong to the years immediately following AD 78, while formalized urban life began at Winchester around the same time, in close association with a major Iron Age site.

At some other *civitas* capitals urban development depended on the formalization of civilian settlements that had grown up alongside military sites. At Cirencester (*Corinium Dobunnorum*) the abandonment of the fort in the mid-70s saw the emergence of a gridded street plan focused on a forum and basilica. Similar developments can be traced at Exeter (*Isca Dumnoniorum*) and at Wroxeter (*Viroconium Cornoviorum*), where legionary fortresses, rather than auxiliary forts, gave way to cantonal capitals. In c.AD 75 Exeter became the formal capital of the Dumnonii and the former legionary bathhouse was converted into part of the forum complex. Late in the Flavian period Wroxeter saw the development of the gridded civil centre, although the pace of development was slow (see below). Likewise, there was apparent delay in building the forum and basilica at Leicester (*Ratae Corieltauvorum*). The foundation of Dorchester (*Durnovaria*) as the capital of the Durotriges of Dorset was also apparently Flavian in date. The establishment of the colonies at Lincoln and Gloucester (5:17) accentuated the developing urbanization of the demilitarized zone at the end of the first century. In contrast with Colchester the new foundations at Gloucester and Lincoln were set initially within the circuit walls of the earlier legionary fortresses. At Gloucester (5:17) a forum replaced the former headquarters building and the same thing happened at Lincoln.

After the early years of the second century, for which very little precise information is available, Hadrian's visit to Britain in AD 122 may be seen as a watershed in urban development. His personal interest in architecture and civil engineering is well attested and it is only to be expected that the encouragement he gave to building programmes in other provinces should have been extended to Britain. The forum inscription from Wroxeter of AD 129–30 strongly suggests that he encouraged building projects that had been hitherto slow to mature. The construction of Hadrian's Wall also necessitated the demilitarization of increasing parts of the south. In particular the growth of the *civitas* capital of the Silures at Caerwent (*Venta Silurum*) probably belongs to this

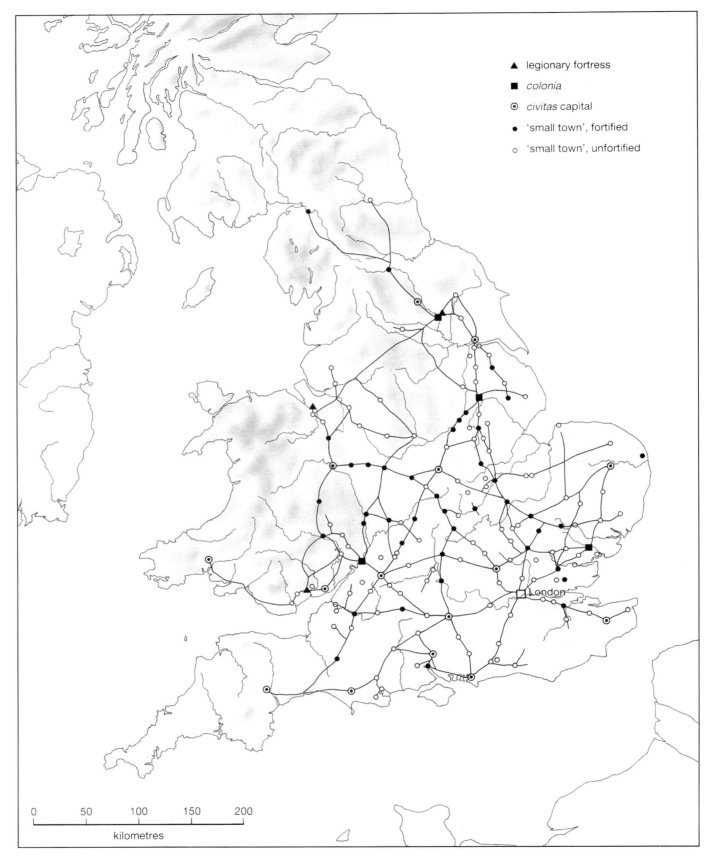

Map 5:12   Distribution of towns and small towns, not including military *vici*

Plate 5:6 The small town of Kenchester is one of the few substantial settlement centres of the Marches. Its size of 9ha (22 acres) is not greatly inferior to that of Caerwent, capital of the Silurian territory to the south. An inscription on a milestone (RIB 2250), however, suggests that in the later third century the town belonged administratively to the *civitas* of the Dobunni. The distance separating Kenchester from the capital of Cirencester and its relatively high development as a small town suggest a role as the western administrative sub-centre for the tribe.

The town sits within a hexagonal wall circuit, presumably of late second-century date or later. As the air photograph shows, the interior contained not a rectilinear street grid but an axial road running east–west across the town with a series of minor streets running off it. The arrangement of buildings in the interior is haphazard and there is no obvious central place. Nonetheless, there are at least two buildings of substantial proportions. On the south side of the main street early excavations located a series of square piers suggesting the presence of a porticoed facade (a feature also attested at Wroxeter). Extra-mural buildings are also known.

period as, apparently, does *Moridunum* centre of the Demetae at Carmarthen in South Wales. Other areas that appear to have been demilitarized were the territory of the Parisi and the adjacent area of the Brigantes, although it remains difficult to interpret the settlement at Brough-on-Humber (*Petuaria Parisiorum*) as a purely civilian town. Perhaps at this time Aldborough (*Isurium Brigantum*) in the Vale of York emerged as the centre of the Brigantes, though the founding date cannot be established precisely.

Small towns

There are a number of minor towns in the civilian province whose status remains uncertain (5:12). Fine examples of small towns, for instance, are shown by Water Newton (*Durobrivae*) (5:21) and Kenchester (Pl. 5:6). It is not possible to assign small towns like these to a particular tribe or tribal sept, as can be done with the major *civitas* capitals. This is in part due to lack of epigraphic evidence and in part to the absence of possible candidates in the tribal names listed in our sources. Nevertheless there are a significant number of these sites, many eventually defended and some of larger size than the smaller *civitas* capitals.

Leaving aside the development of the late colony at York it is apparent that the development of towns across the militarized parts of the province of Britain was incomplete. Effectively, only three northern sites made progress towards full urbanization (5:11). The first and most important of these is arguably Carlisle (*Luguvalium*), the capital of the tribe whose name is probably to be restored as Carvetii. Extensive excavation has also shown the presence of a late town at Catterick (*Cataractonium*). Although the site probably survived into the fifth century, and indeed may appear in the epic poem *Manau Gododdin*, little is known of its status in late Roman Britain. At Corbridge (*Corstopitum*), extensive excavation has allowed us to establish something of the pattern of civilian development that grew up around the sequence of military sites at this important point in the Tyne Valley. The tribal sept of the Textoverdi is known from the central sector of Hadrian's Wall and there is a possibility that Corbridge was designed to act as its focal point.

The development of an extensive town at York was an additional and separate development from the civilian settlement (*canabae*) directly related to the legionary fortress. Although little is known of civilian occupation around the other legionary fortresses at Caerleon and Chester, the spending power of the 5,000 plus legionaries at each location would have encouraged large-scale development there.

Finally, two towns in the special category of religious centres based on spas deserve mention. Buxton and Bath owed their importance not to an administrative or economic role, but to the religious and restorative facilities they provided for pilgrims.

Distribution of military *vici*/towns with military origins

As has been seen, it is no longer possible to ascribe the development of towns simply to the presence and market power of units of the Roman army. This concept is altogether too simplistic. The degree of integration of the army into the local economic structure in the military zone is likely to have varied considerably between areas. In essence it is the presence of the road system which is likely to have increased production, distribution and exchange during the *pax Romana*. Central to any discussion of this kind is the analysis of the civilian settlements or *vici* associated with (and sometimes outliving) Roman forts (5:13).

Cassius Dio (57.18) gave us a picture of the early Romanization patterns in Germany:

> The Romans were holding parts of the country and their soldiers were wintering there and settlements were being founded. The barbarians were adapting themselves to Roman ways, were becoming accustomed to hold markets and were meeting in peaceful assemblages. They had not, however, forgotten their ancestral habits, their native manners, their old life of independence, of the power derived from arms. Hence, so long as they were unlearning these customs gradually and by the way, as one might say, under careful watching, they were not disturbed by the change in the manner of their life, and were becoming different without knowing it.

This is perhaps as good a description as may be obtainable of the peaceful impact of the Roman standing army in the early phases of the conquest. The towns mentioned by Dio would have included the *vici*, and recent studies of *vici* have emphasized that each garrison needed to obtain cereal products from adjacent areas. This line of argument is in turn supported by others minimizing the extent of long-distance transport in view of the costs involved. Thus, for instance, it has been calculated that a garrison of about 500 strong would have required some 160ha (400 acres) of cereal under crop and the effect would, therefore, have been to increase the area of cultivation markedly, at least in the proximity of the fort.

In some cases in southern Britain urban development depended on the formalization of civilian settlements related in a variety of ways to military sites. The colonies of Colchester, Gloucester (5:16, 5:17) and Lincoln and the towns of Wroxeter and Exeter developed from underlying legionary fortresses and their *canabae*. The large-scale presence of civilian settlements around legionary fortresses led at places like *Carnuntum* on the Danube to the formalization of associated civilian settlements as towns with a recognized status. The Severan grant of *colonia* status to the civilian settlement west

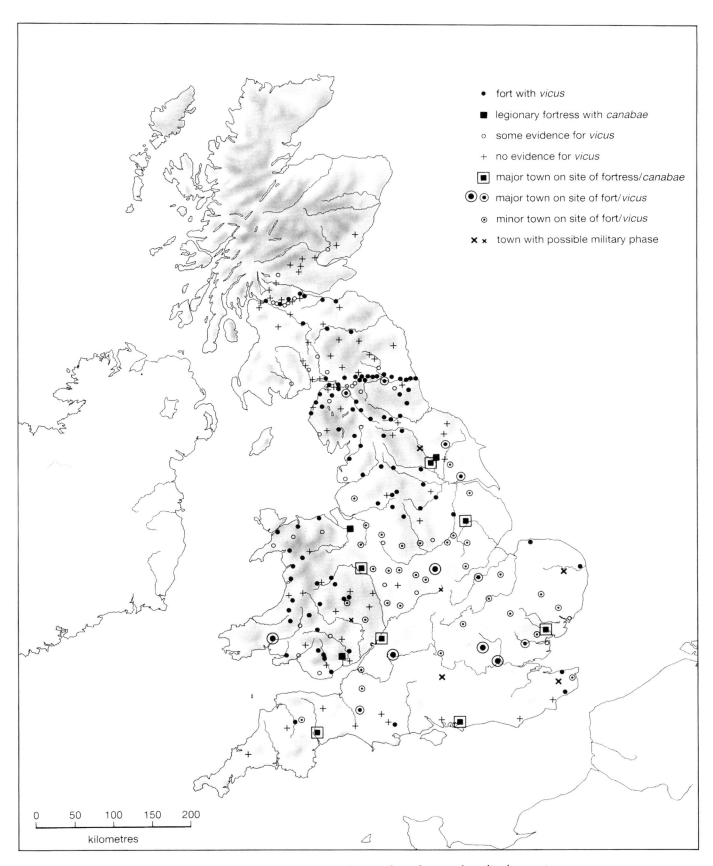

Map 5:13 Distribution of occupied forts, and the contribution of *vici* and *canabae* to urban development

Legend:

- • fort with *vicus*
- ■ legionary fortress with *canabae*
- ○ some evidence for *vicus*
- + no evidence for *vicus*
- ▣ major town on site of fortress/*canabae*
- ⊙ ⊙ major town on site of fort/*vicus*
- ⊙ minor town on site of fort/*vicus*
- ✕ ✕ town with possible military phase

Scale: 0 50 100 150 200 kilometres

Plate 5:7 The civilian settlement at Piercebridge. The broad light stripes indicate the position of roads within the settlement, the thin white lines reveal the plans of the buildings abutting the roads.

Plate 5:8 Vindolanda fort and *vicus* from the north-east

of the Ouse at York can be seen as a belated move in this direction, although not paralleled, it would appear, at Chester. Cantonal capitals such as Cirencester and Carmarthen as well as St Albans and probably Leicester all originated on sites which, like London (5:19, 5:20), saw the presence of a military enclave for a period of time. Yet it is equally apparent that at many locations there was a pre-Roman native presence, whose importance in the subsequent development should not be overlooked (cf. 2:5).

The commonest associated feature of a military fort was a civilian settlement (or *vicus*) alongside. Normally, the *vici* comprised simple buildings with both working and residential accommodation set alongside the main exit roads from each fort. They also had related agricultural or cemetery areas. If the army presence formed the *raison d'être* for the initial settlers, who comprised not only traders but also veteran troops and elements of the indigenous population, there are also good reasons to suggest that some such civilian settlements generated a form of economic independence. At one end of the scale, in northern Britain for instance, it should be remembered that the important sites of Catterick, Carlisle and Corbridge were all of military origin. At Corbridge it is possible to argue that a major unfinished building complex (Site XI) represented an attempt to establish a forum/market area as the heart of the civilian settlement. Such attempts at full urban development were, however, rare within the military zone and *vici* were normally smaller – to judge from the air photographic information available (5:22). Once established, however, such settlements could, it appears, at times generate their own markets, even if the military moved on; this is demonstrable for instance at Caerau (Beulah) in central Wales where the *vicus* outlived the fort by at least a quarter of a century. On Hadrian's Wall the life of the *vicus* at *Vindolanda* was not necessarily controlled by occupation of the adjacent fort, and the *vicus* at Nether Denton on the Stanegate continued in existence long after the replacement of the fort by Birdoswald (which singularly failed to develop an associated civilian settlement). Some remote sites such as Caermote in the Lake District appear never to have developed any civilian adjunct. The explanation is most likely to be the brevity of occupation rather than the hostility of the climate, and this also explains why none of the Flavian forts in Scotland north of the Antonine Wall have yet revealed extensive associated civilian settlement. The future discovery of some traces should not, however, be beyond the bounds of possibility.

As well as being minor market centres and a source of important services for the army, many *vici* may have been involved in actual food production. Furthermore, at a growing number of sites there is evidence of extensive metalworking. Although full urban development of the northern *vici* was rare, it is clear that the population of these agglomerations would not have been negligible and would have played an important role in the economic life of the frontier regions.

Urban defences

The development of urban defences in Roman Britain, and in particular the chronological sequence involved in their structural evolution, has been much debated (5:14). With certain important early exceptions, the great majority of settlements remained open towns until many received earthwork defensive circuits in the second half of the second century. The number of towns involved, ranging from *civitas* capitals to minor road stations, fostered the view that this development formed a concerted programme or at least triggered an immediate chain reaction. Subsequently, many urban defensive circuits were converted from earthworks to stone-faced walls during the third century. This involved cutting back the pre-existing earthen bank to receive a masonry face, a process that was often accompanied by changes in the ditch system and additions to the rear of the rampart core. In a few rare examples, free-standing masonry walls appeared in a fourth century context. A further development was the addition of external towers or bastions to existing walls. This structural innovation, derived from the advances in the use of artillery on military sites, is first attested in Britain at St Albans (*Verulamium*) c.AD 265–70, but for the most part examples belong to the latter part of the fourth century.

There has been a tendency to link the erection of defences with known historical contexts. Thus the episode of Clodius Albinus (AD 193–7) has been seen as the initial stimulus to the creation of defensive circuits, while the visit of Count Theodosius in AD 367 is often suggested as the occasion for the major refurbishing of existing defences. While understandable enough, the attribution of primary developments to specific contexts such as a war or rebellion needs careful handling. Even if the approach were theoretically correct, it is necessary to remember that in the case of Britain our knowledge of crises, particularly in the latter part of the second century, is defective. It had also been recognized that the construction of walls and towers was more often a protracted operation than a quick response to a specific threat of war or rebellion, and there was undoubtedly a longer-term strategic trend in this direction. The evidence and the technicalities of the dating are too detailed to allow discussion here, but social and legal aspects need to be considered alongside the purely historical framework. The construction of a wall circuit required the emperor's specific permission. Equally, the legal status of a settlement and estimates of its future size must have also come into play, though some circuits suggest that the towns involved failed to fulfil their projected spatial development. Likewise there is the question of cost, which, it is generally agreed, fell on the local community in the same way as the construction

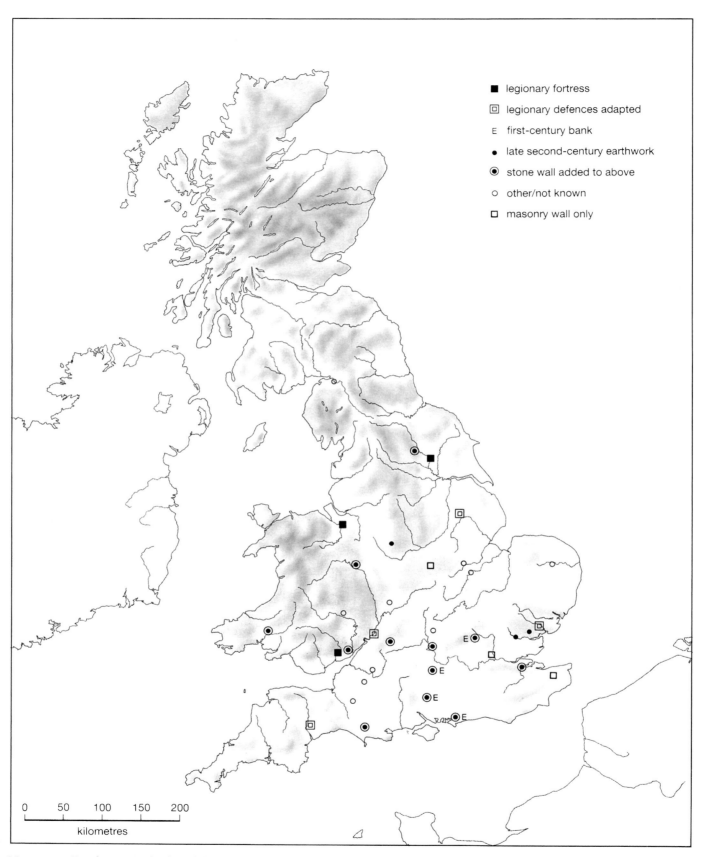

Map 5:14 Development of urban defences at selected sites: the structural sequence is far more complex at a number of places (St Albans, Exeter, Colchester, Chichester) than it is possible to show on this map, there is a considerable date range covered by the examples of masonry walls.

Plate 5:9 The central area of the Corbridge site as seen from the air. The Roman settlement extended well beyond these limits and constituted a small town, albeit one with a military component at various stages. The large rectangular structure to the upper right of the excavated area is the unfinished building XI.

of major public buildings. It is worthwhile looking at wall circuits, in part at least, as reflecting the community's ability to undertake large-scale civil engineering projects. There is much to be said for the idea that in this respect the British provinces were less well endowed than their Continental counterparts, a suggestion that appears to be supported by the larger scale of major public building attested both epigraphically and archaeologically on the Continent.

Civic amenities

The patchwork survival of major public buildings, baths, theatres and amphitheatres is the product of a multiplicity of factors (5:15). Some examples of amphitheatres, such as those at Silchester, Cirencester and Dorchester (where the prehistoric henge known as Maumbury Rings was adapted for Roman use) have survived to the present day. Others, such as that at London, have been discovered by chance in

Plate 5:10 (*right*) Massive Roman sewer at York; it is large enough for a person to walk down.

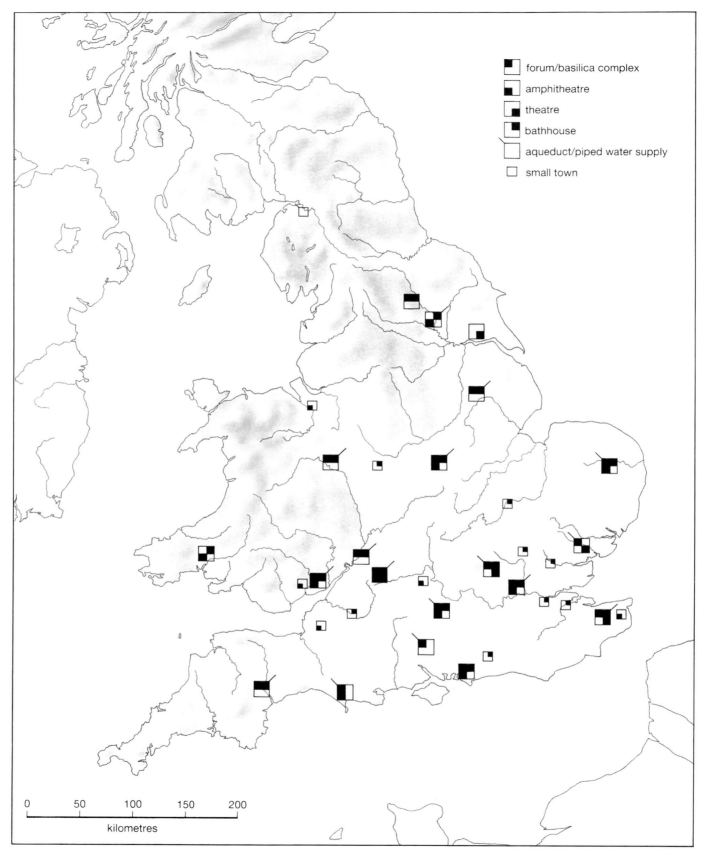

Map 5:15 Civic amenities: derived from archaeological, epigraphic or literary evidence (large symbols = major towns; small symbols = minor towns)

excavation. The legionary amphitheatres at Chester and Caerleon were built roughly on the same scale as the earth-and-timber amphitheatre on the fringes of the mining town of Charterhouse-on-Mendip (6:6). Excavation has also added another example at the *civitas* capital of Carmarthen (*Moridunum Demetarum*), and others may confidently be predicted at major towns such as colonies and *civitas* centres.

While a theatre is attested by an inscription at Brough-on-Humber and one is implied to have existed at Colchester (5:16) by the narrative of the historian Tacitus (*Annals* 14.33), knowledge of most structures of this class results from excavation as, for instance, at St Albans or more recently at Canterbury (appropriately beneath the Marlowe Theatre). The Gosbecks site (3:4) and analogy with Gallo-Belgic sites such as Ribemont-sur-Ancre (Somme) suggest

that more modest examples probably lie undetected at several Romano-British rural sanctuaries.

The distribution of major bath buildings is better understood, with civilian baths (such as the Jewry Wall complex at Leicester) existing in most *civitas* capitals. Their origins differ from centre to centre. At Wroxeter the earliest public baths were unfinished, and perhaps of military origin in any case. The much larger baths opposite the forum were a later development, probably prompted by the Hadrianic programme of urban expansion and renewal. Leicester was another town where the public baths were completed only in the second century.

Although the archaeological picture of urban amenities is limited by the nature of the surviving evidence, it is clear that most of the major towns of Roman Britain did aspire to

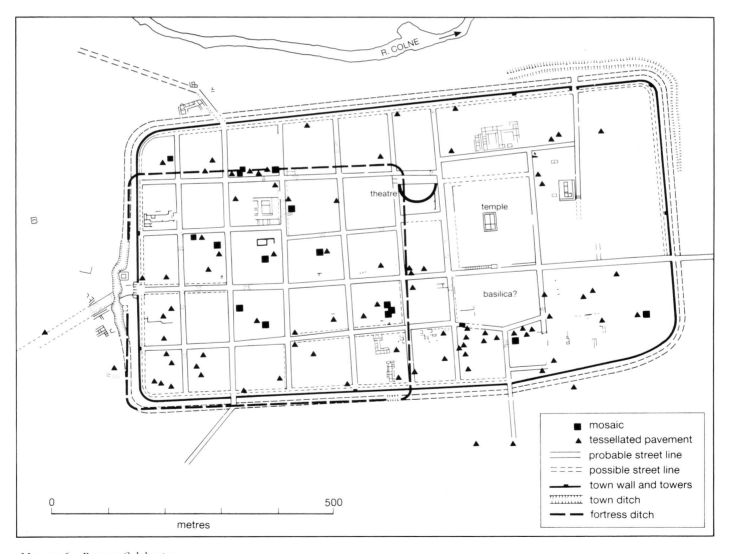

Map 5:16   Roman Colchester

possess the main facilities of Romanized town life. Nevertheless, these amenities were not constructed *in toto* when the towns were founded. Their long-drawn-out development indicates, above all, the financial limitations of the town councils and of the British urban-based aristocracy who would have had to fund the work, whether corporately or as individual acts of generosity.

Case studies

Colchester

A number of case studies have been selected to illustrate the development sequence at some major sites. In this respect Colchester (*Camulodunum Colonia*), apparently established in AD 49, is of particular interest. The early developments have already been described (3:4, 3:5). The overall layout of Colchester still reflects an early Roman road system primarily comprising a sequence of *decumani* (east–west roads) of which the most important runs from the Balkerne Gate eastwards past the site of the temple of the deified Claudius. Minor variations in the road alignment were finally explained by the recognition of the underlying first-century legionary fortress at the western side of the *colonia* enclosure. The south-western and western town wall circuits corresponded with the southern and western sides of an approximately square legionary fortress, the barracks of which have been partly located underlying the remains of Boudican destruction in the area of Lion Walk, in the south-eastern corner of the fortress area. Since this breakthrough in our knowledge, various other elements of the interior have been identified and it is now possible to see the way in which the *colonia* developed beyond the legionary fortress. On the east side, the foundation date for the temple of Claudius remains somewhat problematical, but the presence of the temple explains the variations in the street grid in this area. Very extensive indications of burning in the Boudican revolt have been found over most of the interior and particularly along the southern side of the *colonia*. The presence of a theatre implied by Tacitus has also been corroborated. Pride dictated that the *colonia Camulodunum* should rise again from the ashes of the Boudican disaster and it remained one of the major centres of Roman Britain.

Gloucester

Gloucester has been chosen as an example of a later *colonia* site where the development sequence embodied a transfer of the centre of occupation. It has long been realized that the alignment of the Roman road from Cirencester to Gloucester (Ermin Street) in its descent from Birdlip Hill was not aimed on the presumed centre of the Roman *colonia*. Instead the alignment pointed to the suburb of Kingsholm where excavation has produced the evidence for a major military

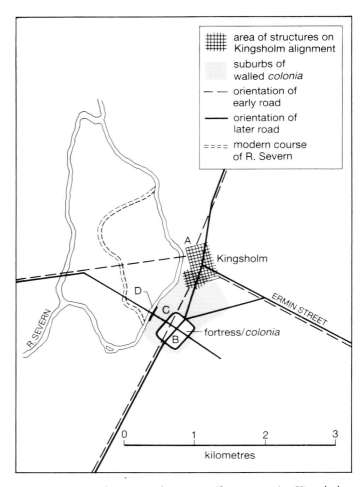

Map 5:17 Development of Roman Gloucester: A = Kingsholm vexillation fortress, B = Gloucester legionary fortress/walled *colonia*, C = main suburbs of Roman town, D = ?Roman quay

establishment alongside the former river edge. The area concerned, where buildings dating from before AD 60 conform to what is termed 'the Kingsholm alignment', covers at least 8 hectares (20 acres) and possibly nearly double that area. From the amount of legionary and auxiliary military equipment found there it is now generally assumed that Kingsholm represents an area where early legionary and possibly auxiliary fortifications were based. The legionary troops concerned probably derived from the XX legion transferred in AD 49 from Colchester. A hint of this appears in the presence of a (now lost) tombstone of a soldier of the XX legion found on the south side of the site.

Epigraphic evidence shows that a colony was created at Gloucester in the final years of the first century AD. The site of the *colonia* was coterminous with the walled area of

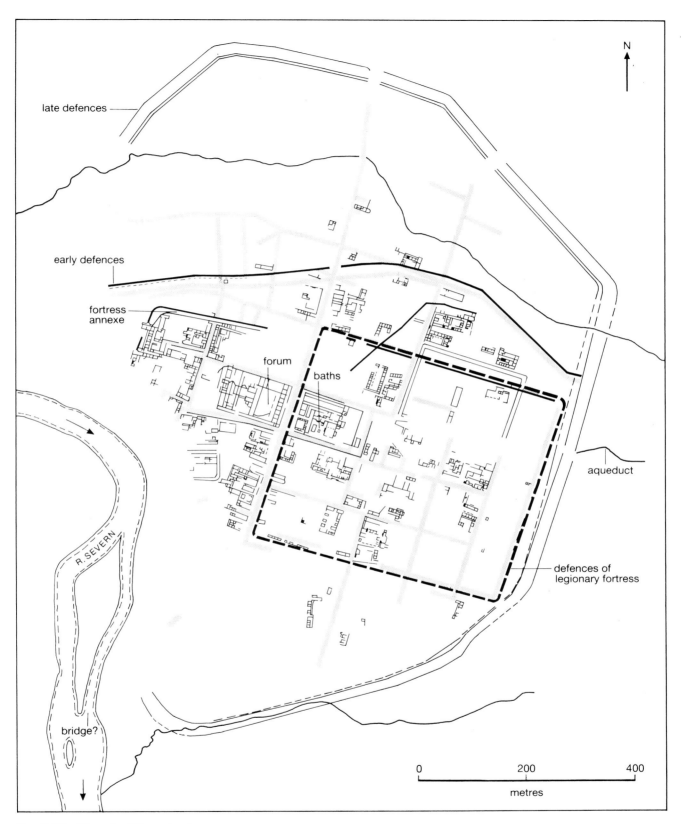

N

late defences

early defences

fortress
annexe

forum

baths

aqueduct

R. SEVERN

bridge?

defences of
legionary fortress

| 0 | | 200 | | 400 |

metres

Map 5:18   Wroxeter (*Viroconium*)

the Medieval city, approaching some 17.5ha (44 acres) in size. Excavations have shown that the earliest phase of occupation was represented by the remains of a legionary fortress. It is thus clear that the origins of the *colonia* actually lay in its direct superimposition on a legionary fortress, which had been developed south of Kingsholm in the early 60s. Excavation has now taken place in several areas in the city, notably in the centre of the town (where part of the forum complex overlying the early legionary headquarters building was found) and on the western side (where there was detailed evidence for the direct conversion of barrack blocks into the first structures of the *colonia* – a feature also now paralleled at Colchester). The first colonists, who were in any case legionary veterans, thus continued to live in the pre-existing legionary barracks, a similar situation to that described by the historian Tacitus writing of sites in Italy in the Julio-Claudian period. Gloucester, however, was the first European site to offer archaeological evidence for this development.

The small size of the wall circuit is misleading as to the town's area: the triangular piece of land between the old Kingsholm fortress and the subsequent *colonia* was also developed as a very extensive suburb, at its maximum extent in the second century.

Wroxeter

The site of Wroxeter (*Viroconium Cornoviorum*) (5:18) was first used by the military shortly after AD 50, when its location on the east bank of the Severn gave it a strategic importance in the conquest of the central Marches. Our knowledge of the legionary fortress here depends partly on air photography which has produced evidence of the northern defences near the north-western corner. In addition there has been detailed excavation of the defences and internal structures along the west side in the area underlying the later baths and market (*macellum*). Webster has shown that there were at least three phases in the timber buildings that occupied the site at this point. These structures were probably barracks and workshops flanking the *via Praetoria*, but precise definition was difficult owing to the restrictions of space.

The relationship of the terminal date of the Wroxeter fortress to the starting date of the legionary fortress at Chester is still debated. Nonetheless, in planning terms the Wroxeter site was left as a *tabula rasa* sealed by a layer of red sand and clay on which it was evidently hoped that a new cantonal capital of the Cornovii would arise. All the available evidence suggests that the process of redevelopment was a slow one.

Although the fortress buildings had been demolished, the alignment of the primary street grid of the city was based in part on the pre-existing road arrangements of the legionary fortress so far as we understand them. This meant that

the core of the city was, like *Colchester*, a reflection of the legionary fortress. Nonetheless the process was a protracted one, the archaeological detail of which is much disputed.

There appear to have been some changes of plan, shown in Atkinson's excavations which uncovered traces of timber houses in the area subsequently used to accommodate the forum. It is debatable whether the bathhouse associated with this forum area represents one of the earliest developments within the urban plan. If this is the case then the primary forum is to be sought elsewhere. An inscription of the Emperor Hadrian dating to AD 128, however, shows that the emperor's presence in the province probably did much to encourage urban regeneration (see 5:11). We may presume that the forum was actually completed after a prolonged period of construction, perhaps spanning as much as 30 years. This development was also accompanied by the construction of a bath block in the opposite *insula*. Presumably also in the second century the city defences began to develop. For this we are partly dependent upon air photographic evidence which suggests that the early defences on the north side of the *civitas* capital ran on the south side of the Bell Brook. These, however, were expanded beyond the stream at a later date to make Wroxeter one of the largest walled cities of Roman Britain. Again it is aerial photography (Pl. 5:11) which enables us to fill much of the interior with the plans of late stone-built buildings principally comprising urban villas. Even though their plans are impressive it is noticeable that appreciable parts of the outer periphery of the city do not appear to have been gridded with streets, and we must therefore presume that the expansion of the wall circuit represents a misjudgement of the eventual size to which the *civitas* capital could in reality aspire. On the other hand, many of the apparently blank spaces within the gridded area must be due to the presence of timber buildings which are not revealed by air photography as are those constructed with stone foundations.

London

Apart from the obvious importance of the Thames estuary as a gateway to south-eastern Britain in the early years of the conquest, the Roman army required in particular a suitable river crossing over the Thames. Much remains to be discovered about the position of the first river crossing, the ancient course of the river bed, and the date of the foundation of the settlement on the north bank of the Thames in the area of the City.

As the first London map (5:19) shows, excavation in Southwark on the south side of the Thames has located two Roman roads converging on a point just upstream of Old London Bridge, the Medieval crossing point. Opposite, on the north bank, a wooden box structure adjoining the later Roman quayside has been interpreted as a bridge/pier support. The evidence for the road on the Southwark side

Plate 5:11 Wroxeter (*Virconium Cornoviorum*) from the air. The modern excavations can be seen in the triangle of land below the crossroads. The 'Old Work', a high-standing wall of the Roman baths complex, casts a shadow across the site of the basilica. Many

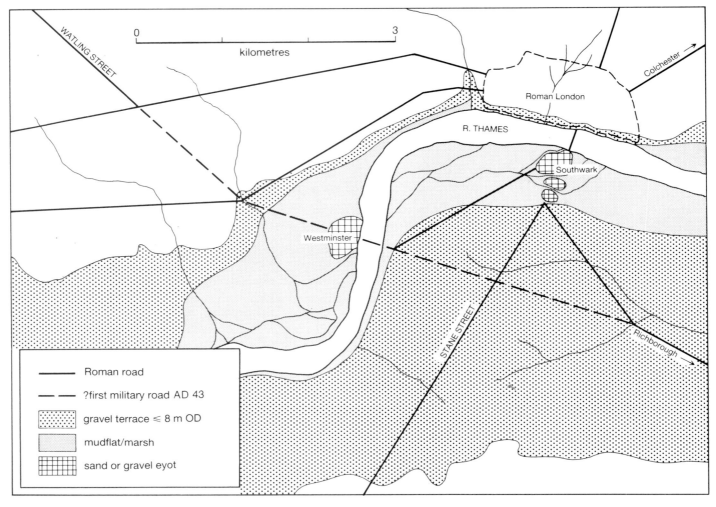

Map 5:19   Roman London I

points to construction round about AD 50, a gap of seven or eight years after the initial conquest. The alignment of the arterial road known as Watling Street (the modern A5, now represented by the Edgware Road) on the north side of the river points to the Westminster area. It has been suggested that the river crossing of the invasion army may have been in that area, and that there was a delay of seven or eight years before the development of the main site on the north side of the Thames. Once founded, however, the latter site had a number of advantages, as it was a relatively flat elevated platform of land divided by the Walbrook but protected by the River Fleet and the marshy ground at the mouth of the Lea Valley. Possibly the site also lay at the tidal head of the Thames at that time, but the evidence is inconclusive. Likewise the evidence of military involvement c.AD 50 is enigmatic, but the layout of the initial street grid may in fact reflect some (currently unknown) military component (5:20).

The settlement grew rapidly until the destruction of the existing buildings in the Boudican revolt. The location of the burnt layer associated with the Boudican destruction is a useful tool in showing that the first settlement was mainly concentrated on the east side of the Walbrook. The town was rapidly rebuilt and its importance was recognized by its becoming the centre of provincial government in Britain. London was, thereafter, the residence of the governor and procurator of Britain. The former probably resided in the major building constructed in the last quarter of the first century AD, near the mouth of the Walbrook. By that time an early elongated forum and basilica had been erected in the Leadenhall area, to be replaced by a far larger rectangular forum complex at the end of the first century.

This massive building project was apparently the occasion for some realignment of the road grid within the area of the settlement. A north–south road ran directly down from the forum to the waterfront installations, where recent exca-

Plate 5:13   London wharf: late second-century timber waterfront

Plate 5:12   Reused stone found in the riverside wall of Roman London. A building dedication stone in the form of an altar records the name of a previously unknown governor who helped restore the temple.

vation has uncovered the remains of the Roman (and early Medieval) quayside. In the north-western part of the city a 5 hectare (13 acre) military fort was built in the second century to act as barracks for troops stationed in the capital. The fort walls were later incorporated in the enclosure of the whole settlement within a circuit wall c.AD 190, the presence of the fort explaining the changes of alignment in the city wall at Cripplegate. The wall extended around three sides of the city from Blackfriars to the Tower of London, a length of over 3 kilometres. It was eventually strengthened by bastions. At least 20 towers were added on the eastern

side of the city wall in the late fourth century, and more await recognition beneath their Medieval adaptations. On the south side it seems that the river was considered an adequate protection until the late third or early fourth century. At that time the eastern and western ends of the land wall were joined together by a new defence that ran along the river front to the rear of the wharves, roughly following the line of Upper and Lower Thames Street. In 1974/5 a massive collapsed section of the wall was uncovered at Blackfriars and was found to contain reused blocks from a demolished monumental arch of late second/third-century date as well as inscriptions of roughly similar date. This evidence suggests that the riverside wall was a hurried response to the development of a threat.

One of the great puzzles about London is that in spite of its long-term importance as a provincial capital (and sometime Imperial mint), the archaeological evidence suggests that for a considerable period of the third century the

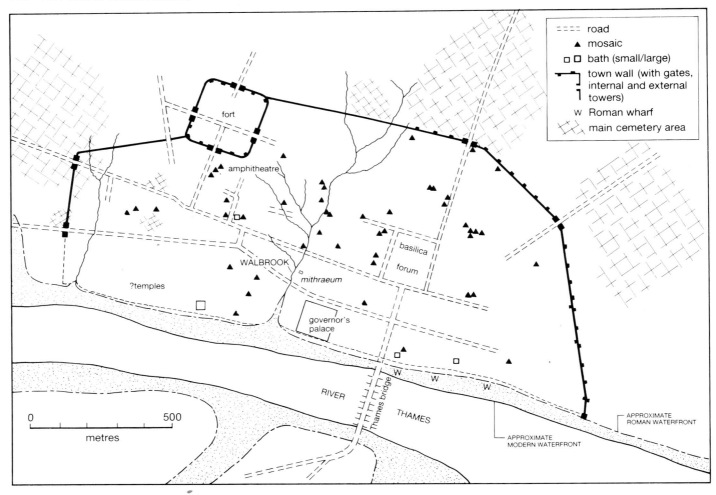

Map 5:20   Roman London II

Water Newton

Urban development on a smaller scale can be illustrated by a number of lesser towns, such as Kenchester in the Hereford Plain (Pl. 5:6) or Water Newton (*Durobrivae*) near Peterborough (5:21). *Durobrivae* may have developed from a civilian settlement (*vicus*) associated with an invasion period fort alongside the line of Ermine Street, the main Roman route towards Lincoln and the North. Our understanding of the town is largely based on aerial photography and this evidence collectively provides the basis for Map 5:21, although the circuit wall is readily appreciated at ground level. The walls show that, at 17 hectares (c.44 acres) in size, the town compares with several *civitas* capitals, but the interior betrays an altogether different style of urban development. Instead of the familiar grid pattern of internal

town was in decline. Only further archaeological work can confirm or modify this impression and suggest explanations.

roads, the air photographic evidence shows the town's origin as a roadside settlement containing only one axial road running south-east to north-west. From it a series of irregular side streets ran into the interior of the town, with further minor streets branching from them. There were substantial unenclosed suburbs extending north of the walled area, though the wall circuit incorporated one area to the south-east, where, to judge from the smaller number of internal streets, development was on a reduced scale.

There can be no doubt as to the exceptional prosperity of the settlement. It lay, of course, in prime agricultural land and was near to extensively worked beds of iron ore (see Map 6:14). It also served as the entrepôt through which many of the products of the Nene Valley ceramics industry must have passed, whether for portation by road or along the inland waterway provided by the Nene on the northern side of the town. From the middle of the second century the manufacture and export of good quality colour-coated pottery (see Map 6:27) must have formed one element of

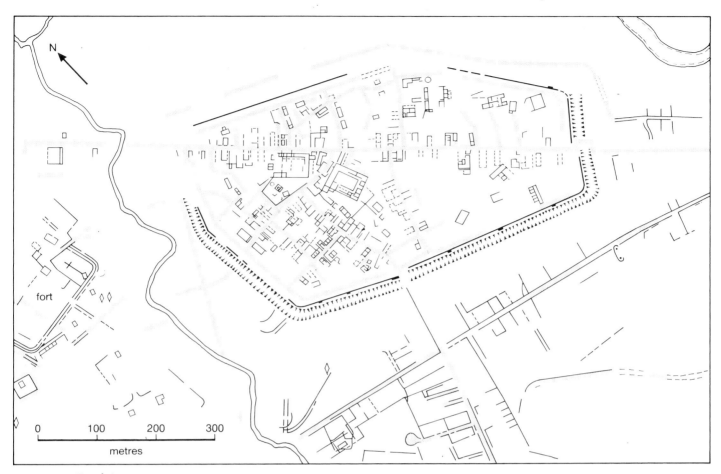

Map 5:2 1 *Durobrivae*

the continuing prosperity of the town. That this may have extended over a considerable time span is hinted at by the most important single find to emerge from the interior, a hoard of silver vessels and other objects of Christian ritual belonging to the first half of the fourth century, and thus of exceptional interest to the study of the development of religious practice at the time (8:29). The recovery of this material through the use of a metal detector had the unfortunate effect of preventing the establishment of a clear context for this, the earliest collection of Christian silverware from any provincial location. It is therefore not possible to relate the discovery to one of the many structures attested by aerial photography in the interior and thus perhaps establish whether it derived from a church or private dwelling.

The majority of the internal structures take the form of strip houses aligned end-on to the axis of Ermine Street. Larger buildings, however, can be seen, notably a major courtyard structure – irregularly aligned, but on a scale to suggest that it may well represent the *mansio* (official inn) to be expected in a town such as this. Another courtyard building to the north may have formed a market. The irregu-

lar compound immediately to the west of the second courtyard building contains the clear traces of several Romano-Celtic temples.

Old Carlisle

The mechanisms whereby *vici* prospered, grew and sometimes outlived their associated fort, or alternatively withered and died, have been much debated. Recent argument has tended to show that the answer to these questions must take into account such factors as the pay level of the relevant army unit (which differed between cavalry and infantry), the degree of acculturation in the local tribe, and the problem of cereal yields, transportation costs and embedded economies. The *vicus* must also be examined in its overall context. In terms of the state of preservation of the Roman landscape pride of place belongs to the extensive remains to be found at Old Carlisle, a fort close to Wigton on the north Cumbrian plain (5:22). The site had long been known, since many of the *vicus* buildings can be seen under low sun conditions by observers on the ground, but the way in which native-style

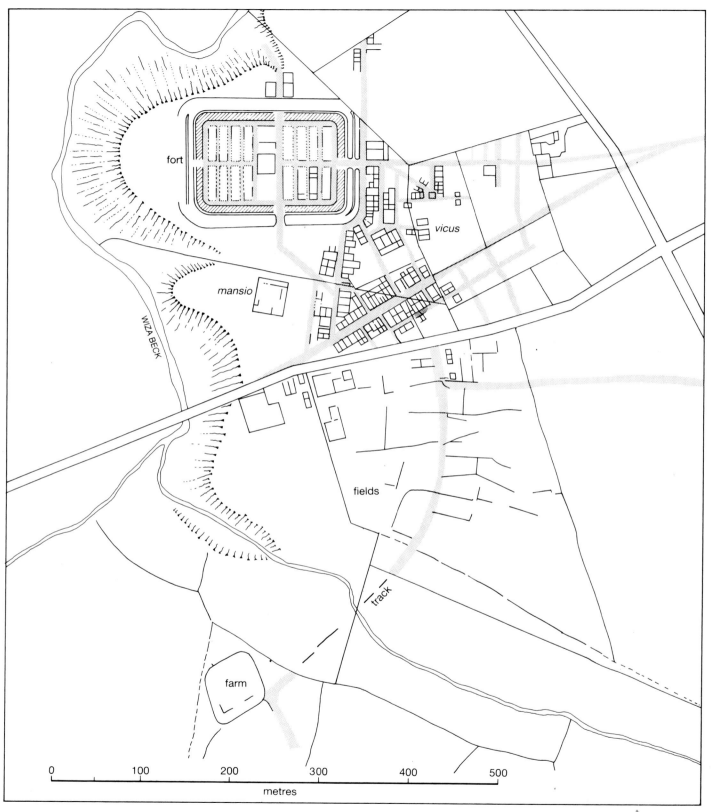

Map 5:22 Old Carlisle, fort, *vicus* and farmstead

Plate 5:14   The fort and civilian settlement at Old Carlisle, Cumbria. The fort platform lies to the right while the low winter light highlights the outlines of civilian buildings flanking the main road from Carlisle.

farms linked into the road system and with the fort itself emerged only through the medium of air photography. The axis of the Roman road from Carlisle to Papcastle formed the principal street of the *vicus*. The individual buildings are plotted in as great a detail as the air photographs allow. It is clear that the major road was linked by a series of minor roads to the eastern gate of the auxiliary fort, from which a northern road is also known to have radiated into one of the few areas where the underlying remains cannot be traced with precision. A large courtyard building close to the south gate represents a structure somewhat different in character from its neighbours and this is provisionally identified as a *mansio*.

On the south side of the settlement a double-ditched trackway leads away from the *vicus* proper in a gradual curve towards the Wiza Beck. As the road bends gently towards the south-west several hectares of field divisions can be observed. The fields, somewhat less than 0.25 hectares in size, convey the impression of a series of small sub-rectangular units, indicating agricultural activity of various kinds close to the fort and *vicus*. The trackway leads directly to a farm in the native style across the Wiza Beck. There is also evidence of another track running south-east from the *vicus*, linking together another series of farms and perhaps ultimately serving the quarry area south of Dalston which supplied Old Carlisle with its building stone.

ROMAN ROADS AND MILESTONES

The construction of substantial metalled roads was just as much a sign of Roman development as were the towns (5:23). The straight alignments of many Roman roads attest to the proficiency of their surveyors; the substantial foundations and surfaces illustrate the large-scale organization and exploitation of labour which was possible under Roman rule. Following the classification implicit in the legal codices there were basically three types of roads:

1   those built by the state,
2   those built by the local government bodies (*coloniae* or *civitates*),
3   those built by smaller communities or individuals for purely local convenience.

Most roads of type 1 were constructed initially for military purposes by the army (perhaps making use of some native forced labour or transport). The arterial routes described in the *Antonine Itinerary* were of this type, as was the Fosse Way. Decent roads allowed for more rapid deployment and communication of army groups and, to some extent, were useful for moving supplies (though use was made of sea or river transport in preference). The fact that many of the early military roads radiate out from London indicates the

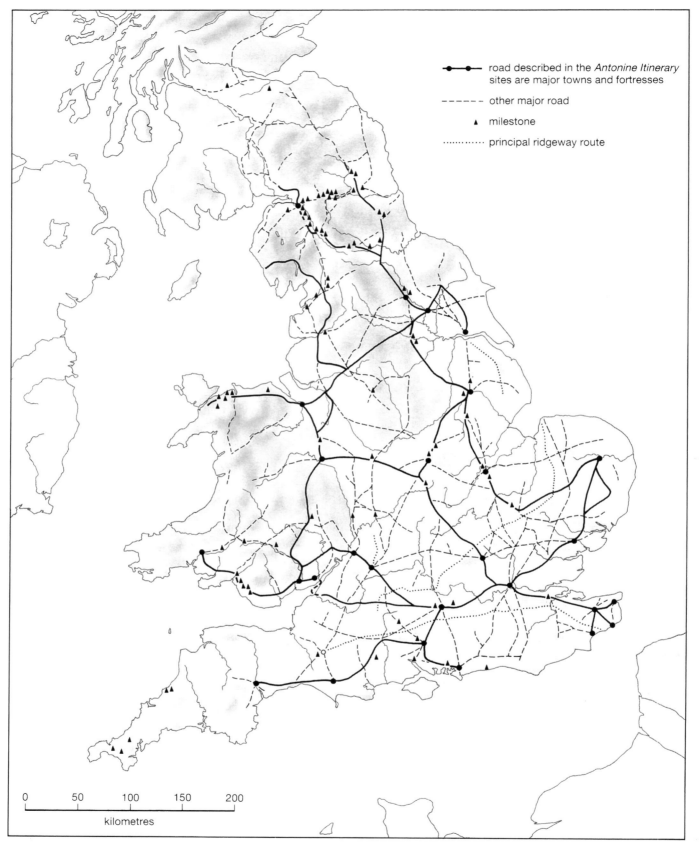

Map 5:23 Main Roman roads and find spots of milestones: more than one specimen was found at some locations.

legend:
— ● — ● — road described in the *Antonine Itinerary* sites are major towns and fortresses

- - - - - other major road

▲ milestone

.... principal ridgeway route

0   50   100   150   200
kilometres

Plate 5:15   Roman road on Wheeldale Moor in north Yorkshire running to the fort of Lease Rigg

Plate 5:16   The Roman West Coast route to the north at Tebay Gorge in Cumbria. The Roman fort at Low Burrow Bridge (arrowed) controls the route which, in contrast with the Medieval road, is now followed by the railway and motorway.

key strategic and administrative roles played by that site in the conquest period and later as the provincial capital. At the other end of the scale, the briefly-used roads associated with the Flavian advance in Scotland are sometimes locatable only by the crop marks of lines of quarry pits adjacent to their poorly preserved causeways.

The second category of road was far less common, since the *civitates* in Britain generally lacked the resources to undertake major programmes of road construction. In any case, they were often burdened with the costs of maintaining the old military routes now in civil use within their territory. Both categories 1 and 2 were normally well-surveyed and well-built, with stone foundations and gravel surfaces. In many cases they have outlasted other signs of Roman civilization, since, until the advent of the motorway network, most of the principal modern trunk roads overlay Roman precursors.

The third category of road is the broadest group and the most problematical. Whereas, 20 years ago, the assumption was that Roman roads could be relocated on maps as long straight alignments, the revolution in aerial photography has shown that many purely local 'roads' or tracks could meander to a considerable extent. Nor should this surprise us unduly, since only a high-level political authority could override existing land-holding arrangements to achieve straight alignments. Many of the minor routes were not metalled and some, at least, marked the continued use of the main prehistoric ridgeways.

It was normal practice for the main roads in a Roman province to be marked by milestones. In Britain, the high premium on building stone, particularly in the south-east, has militated against the widespread survival of Roman milestones. The known distribution does confirm which were the major roads in the province, even if the military distribution is slightly distorted by the number of stones which have been recovered along the Military Way and along the Stanegate behind Hadrian's Wall. The apparent pre-eminence of the York–Carlisle–Scotland and York–Corbridge–Scotland routes over the Chester–Carlisle–Scotland route is probably a reasonable reflection of the pattern of use.

There are some indications from the civil zone that the locations of the quarries from which milestones were cut may, in certain cases, be helpful in assessing the likely extent of civic territories; but more examples of milestones, set up by the *civitates* or *coloniae*, are needed to refine this sort of petrological analysis.

The discovery of five late Roman milestones in Cornwall, where the Roman road network is very imperfectly known, suggests that the level of development achieved there may have been higher than generally believed (cf. Map 5:12). Intensive fieldwork may yet produce the major settlements implied by the construction of roads marked by milestones.

Milestones had an obvious function to play in giving

the distance to or from a major centre and facilitating the calculation (from a listing of the itinerary) of the mileage to the next major or minor town where facilities were available. They were thus of greatest use to official travellers and, perhaps, merchants. For locals travelling a short distance, for instance to a regular market, they were unnecessary landmarks by and large, and they very rarely occur on roads which were not major lines of communication. A secondary function of milestones was connected with Imperial propaganda, since they generally named the ruling emperor. In Britain, comparatively few milestones were erected when the roads were first built, and the majority were raised by short-lived emperors in the third and fourth centuries. During periods of insecurity and civil war it is not surprising that emperors should have tried to ingratiate themselves with provincials by instigating road 'repairs' and ensuring that they were credited for it.

6
The Economy

Roman writers had little or no concept of economic forces as we understand them today. There is only one enumeration of Britain's exports, that of Strabo, writing during the reign of Augustus, which listed wheat, cattle, gold, silver, iron, hides, slaves and hunting dogs and went on to mention as imports bracelets, necklaces, amber and glassware. The perishable nature of many of the items shows how patchy and elusive evidence for the export trade is likely to be. Strabo's list gives first place amongst the exports to corn, but we cannot easily form any estimate of this obviously major factor in the British agricultural economy. Collectively, however, Strabo's mention of gold, silver and iron places minerals in the paramount position amongst British exports. Within a few years of the invasion a number of mines were being exploited in the wake of the invading army. Tacitus stressed that mineral exploitation of Britain was amongst the *pretium victoriae*, or spoils of victory, the expectation of which prompted the actual invasion. State-sponsored mineral extraction, therefore, forms the core of the following discussion.

MINING AND METALLURGY

In the last century BC and the early first century AD Britain was undoubtedly seen by Rome to have a wealth of mineral potential and was later exploited on a substantial scale, with an initial speed and efficiency paralleled by the Augustan exploitation of north-west Spain. The mineral resources of Britain are substantial (6:1), though this is perhaps less appreciated today than at other times, such as the 1790s, when Parys Mountain in Anglesey was the greatest copper mine in the world. The Spanish provinces and Britain were the two major metal producing areas of the western Roman Empire. While considerable iron ore deposits exist in the south-east of Britain and in the East Midlands, the prime metalliferous deposits lie overwhelmingly to the west, in and along the edges of the highland zone, notably the extensive silver-bearing (argentiferous) lead deposits of the Mendips and north-east Wales (6:1, 6:2). The Welsh deposits are varied, including copper and zinc at Parys Mountain, Great Orme and Llanymynech, as well as lead in Dyfed, Glamorgan and Gwent and gold at Dolaucothi (Dyfed). The extensive lead deposits of the Pennine area are generally less argentiferous. Some lead occurs further north at Leadhills but there is no evidence that these deposits were exploited in

antiquity; nor was alluvial gold exploited in Dumfries and Galloway or in the far north at Helmsdale.

Ancient geographic and other sources are intriguing but sparse. Tin is mentioned only in pre-Roman sources, when exploration of the European Atlantic coast is implied by Greek geographers. Caesar believed that Britain exported copper and said that iron occurred, but, according to Cicero, he failed to locate any silver. This is hardly surprising as Caesar's campaigns were limited to the south-east. Strabo noted that Britain exported gold, silver and iron, but the first mentions of lead were left to Tacitus and the Elder Pliny. Pliny records that a production limit had to be set on Britain's easily mined argentiferous lead to prevent it from undercutting existing Spanish operations (*Natural History* 34.17.164).

The archaeological evidence for the exploitation of min-

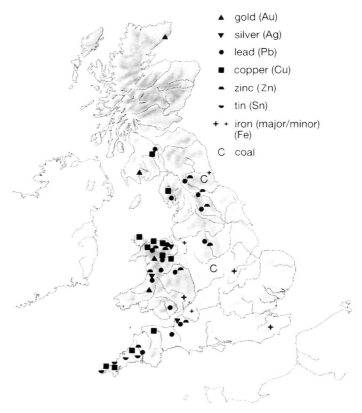

Map 6:1   Mineral resources of Britain

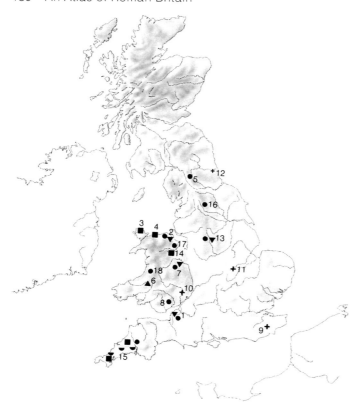

Map 6:2   Roman exploitation of British minerals. Principal sites/areas: I Charterhouse, 2 Halkyn Mt., 3 Parys Mt., 4 Gt Orme, 5 Alston and the Pennines, 6 Dolaucothi, 7 Linley, 8 Draethen, 9 Weald, 10 Forest of Dean, 11 SE Midlands, 12 Co. Durham, 13 Derbyshire, 14 Llanymynech, 15 Cornwall, 16 Yorkshire Dales, 17 Fridd, 18 Plymlimon

erals is problematical (Map 6:2 and Table 6:1). The real problem lies in not being able to estimate, firstly, the scale of extraction of the various minerals (because of reuse of mining locations), and secondly, the degree to which mineral extraction aided the Roman economy and, more particularly, which part of the economy – individuals, companies or the state. Moreover, the crux of the question is whether the extraction of minerals in Roman Britain was economic; that is, did the province make a net gain from the extraction that outweighed the cost of mining? Also, how important were the mineral resources both in intra-provincial terms and compared with other longer-established production areas such as south-west Spain?

There has been much discussion of the role of trade and taxes in the economics of the Roman Empire. Recently there has developed a school of thought which argues that the armies were paid from taxes and that taxes were largely raised in 'peaceful, profitable' provinces. The inhabitants of these provinces then had to earn the silver which they subsequently paid out in taxation through increased trading activity. Thus Hopkins, in particular, argues that taxation

acted as a direct stimulant to trade. Work in the field of Roman mining studies, however, suggests a modification of this approach in one important particular, namely that the potential contribution of bullion to the Imperial revenues needs to be taken into account, whether it came from a core or a frontier province. Mineral rights were vested in the emperor and initially all major mines were controlled through military production, particularly in the case of Britain, where high-quality argentiferous lead made the province important for the extraction of silver. It is arguable that the province of Britain played an important role in the economics of the Empire. At times the production of even a single mine such as Dolaucothi could be of economic significance.

Gold mining at Dolaucothi

The gold mines at Dolaucothi (6:3–6:4) are of unique archaeological interest in the British Isles. The known mining areas demarcate the outcropping of gold-bearing quartz veins. The major axis of their strike is roughly north-east/south-west and there are four major lodes of varying sulphurous and auriferous content, all generally dipping at about 35 degrees to the south-west. They occur on the slopes of Allt Cwmhenog, the main mountain ridge, and Allt Ogofau, its extension to the south-west. The site was probably first exploited in the pre-Roman period but developed enormously in scale after the Roman military conquest of the area *c*.AD 75. In outline the complex comprised three principal features:

1   Two aqueduct systems. The first is the 11km (7 mile) Cothi aqueduct which runs along the northern slope of Allt Cwmhenog and serves a series of reservoirs, tanks and sluices at the head of the mines before turning south to discharge into the valley of the Annell. The second is the 6km (4 mile) Annell aqueduct.
2   Opencast workings and adits along the northern slopes of Allt Cwmhenog, Allt Ogofau and the saddle that separates them. By far the largest of the workings is the main opencast immediately south of Ogofau Lodge. Judging by the survival of conduits and water tanks along the edge of the opencast it appears to have preserved substantially its Roman shape through the periods of modern exploitation. The last of these, in 1937–8, located traces of Roman galleries going down to a depth of 45m below the floor of the opencast. From one of the galleries part of a timber drainage wheel was recovered.
3   Associated features lying in the Cothi valley. They include a fort and substantial settlement beneath Pumsaint village and a bathhouse on the south side of the river.

The hydraulic features offer a way to understand the mining complex. Their antiquity is established by stratified Roman

Table 6.1 Historic mining areas
(Pr = pre-Roman, R = Roman, M = medieval)

No. on map	Area	History	Evidence	Ores
1	Charterhouse-on-Mendip	Pr?, R, M, C19th reworking	Mainly pitting and trenching 6km east to Priddy. Assoc. fort and town	Lead with high silver content
2	Halkyn Mt., Clwyd	Pr?, R, M,C17–C20	a) East. Pitting and trenching across 5km supplying Pentre processing area on Deeside b) West. Adit mining supplying Prestatyn depot. Both areas related to Chester base	Lead Zinc
3	Parys Mt., Anglesey	R, C17–C20	Opencast (with adits?)	Copper
4	Gt. Orme, Llandudno	R, early M? C19th	Adits, trenching	Copper
5	Alston Moor and other Pennine centres	R?. C19th	Trenching; C19th hydraulicing	Lead
6	Dolaucothi (Pumsaint), Dyfed	Pr., R, M?, C19–C20	Adits and opencasts hydraulic methods. Assoc. forts	Gold Cornelian
7	S.W. Shropshire	R, C19th around Shelve	a) Hydraulicing on Linley Hill, b) probable R. extraction around Shelve to supply smelting attested at Brompton fort	Lead
8	Lower Machen, S.W. Gwent	R, later?	Single intact gallery at Draethen. Exploitation related to Caerleon base?	Lead
9	The Weald, Kent, E. Sussex	Pr., R, M	Very extensive dispersed pitting. Major processing centres e.g. Beauport Park, Nr. Hastings	Iron
10	Forest of Dean, Glos.	R, M, Mod.	Extensive dispersed extraction transported especially via Lydney Woolaston	Iron
11	S.E. Midlands	R, M	Pitting, bell-pits, assoc. settlements. Town/villa related	Iron
12	Co. Durham	R, M, Mod.	Some evidence, esp. at Lanchester fort	Iron Coal?
13	Derbyshire	R, M, Ext. Mod.	Mainly pitting S.W. of Matlock around Bonsall and Carsington. Lead strains at Brough-on-Noe	Lead
14	Llanymynech (W. Shrops.)	R, C19th	Intact gallery; other adits around ?opencast	Copper
15	Cornwall, W. Devon	Dispersed tin streaming	Streaming and hydraulicing	Tin
16	Wharfedale (N. Yorks.)	R, M, Mod.	Trenching/pitting	Lead
17	Ffridd (Wrexham)	R, C19th	Unclear but some hydraulic techniques. Related to Chester	Lead
18	Plymlimon	?R, ?M, Mod.	Uncertain; possible evidence at Cwm Ystwyth and Trefeglwys	Lead

material located in a gallery that cut away an outflow channel from the main Cothi aqueduct. The development sequence can be established by studying the overall pattern of the aqueduct system (6:3,6:4). This originated in an aqueduct tapping the marshy ground at the head of the Annell valley 5km due east of the mine. It was associated with the early development of the little-known opencast to the north of the main mine. Indeed, when the major Cothi aqueduct was constructed, tapping a source some 11km to the north of the mine, it had to be carried round the pre-existing opencast on a rock-cut ledge. Ultimately the hushing (sluicing) and washing sequences established on the upper slopes

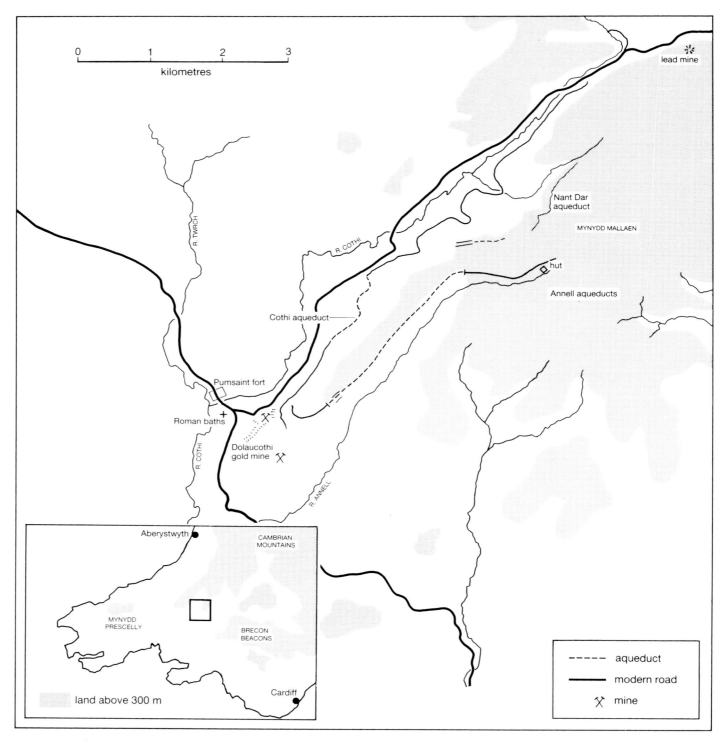

Map 6:3   Dolaucothi: location of gold mine

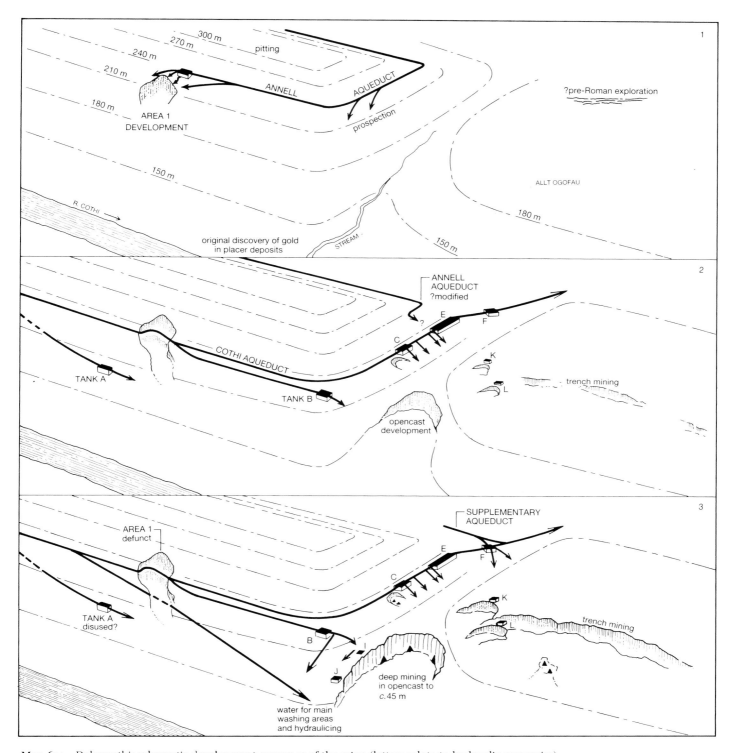

Map 6:4   Dolaucothi: schematic development sequence of the mine (letters relate to hydraulic reservoirs)

above and around the major and minor opencasts were abandoned with the development of the underground phase of the mineral exploitation.

Lead mining

Charterhouse-on-Mendip

The significance of lead mining lies in the fact that in the Roman world silver was produced from argentiferous lead by the process known as cupellation. Silver coinage played a fundamental role in Roman monetary policy; this explains the speed of exploitation of lead deposits in Britain. Dated ingots show that the Mendip mines were producing by AD 49, the Flintshire mines by AD 74, and the Nidderdale mines of Yorkshire by AD 81.

The high silver content of the lead in the Charterhouse-on-Mendip mines was a factor in the exceptionally rapid exploitation on this site. Early working there was certainly under military control, as one might expect. A stamped lead pig of AD 49 countermarked by the II legion has been found at St Valery-sur-Somme in France, while three others in Britain suggest that the export route lay through Southampton Water. The process of de-silvering lead for bullion shows how difficult it is to form any estimate of the economic role played by the new province in the Empire. Ingots stamped with the emperor's name continue until AD 164–9 in the Charterhouse area, but it is clear from countersignature by private companies that lessees were allowed to participate at an early stage. C. Nipius Ascanius, for instance, was a freedman entrepreneur whose countermark

appears on a Mendip ingot of AD 59. The Charterhouse mine was, in fact, only one of many dotted across the 300m levels of the Mendip Hills (6:5). The most accessible ore bodies and, therefore, the earliest to be exploited, conceivably in pre-Roman times, lie south of the Roman fort at Charterhouse (6:6). The veins were worked by a mixture of deep pitting and trench mining and some prominent trenches (6:6) may be original workings. Subsequently, Elizabethan and later exploitation concentrated around the small Roman mining town. The style and geological condition of these workings are quite different from the main workings and comprise shafts up to 61m in depth.

The small fort was no doubt important in supervising the initial Roman production, yet the main Roman occupation was civilian and lies in the area known as Town Field. Air photography shows the existence of an irregular street network curving around the edge of the ridge. The quantity of predominantly late first- and second-century Roman pottery leaves no doubt that a Roman settlement was involved. The extent of the street network also shows that the timber amphitheatre lay on the edge of the mining town. The settlement evolved in response to the lead mining industry. If one thinks in terms of a town from the American West then the analogy would not be too far amiss. While much of the product was exported in the form of bullion, a major ancillary industry of brooch-making developed within the town.

Halkyn Mountain

Halkyn Mountain (6:7) exhibits a complex mineral system containing lead of medium to low argentiferous content together with some zinc and copper. There is evidence for a considerable mining industry in the Roman period, most obviously exemplified by the lead pigs stamped with the tribal name of the Deceangli (Decangi). These pigs must derive from either Halkyn Mountain or the little-known extraction area of Ffridd near Wrexham. The particular interest of the Halkyn Mountain workings is the dispersal of the extraction, primary processing and fine processing areas which make it a classic model of a dispersed industry.

The lead vein system occurs in the carboniferous limestone of the mountain ridge at a height of c.300m. The principal ancient mining trenches occur on the north-west scarp overlooking Flint. A southern suburb of Flint is known as Pentre Ffrwndan – the place of the furnaces – an apt description of the remains of the many smelting and roasting hearths that were found in the seventeenth to nineteenth centuries on the south-east side of the area alongside Nant-y-Flint and Leadbrook. The fine processing was based on the settlement at Pentre proper which appears to have begun life c.AD 90, although earlier military involvement must be suspected. The mining town undoubtedly acted as a port on

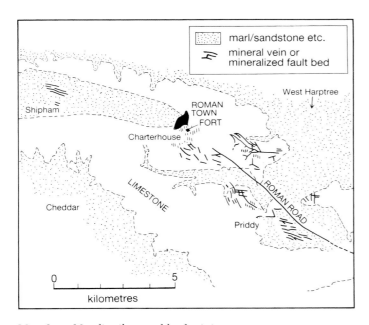

Map 6:5 Mendip silver and lead mining area

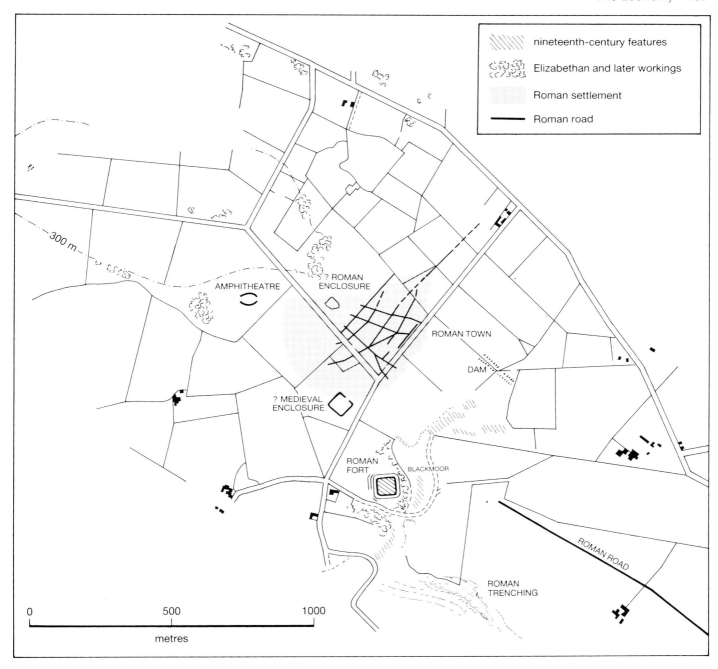

Map 6:6   Charterhouse-on-Mendip: fort and civilian settlement

the estuary of the Dee in contact with the entrepôt of Meols on the tip of the Wirral peninsula (see Map 1:14).

Draethen, Gwent

A gallery mine, perhaps associated with exploitation by lessees, is represented by the lead mine at Draethen (6:8) which was located in the 1960s by the Bristol Mining Club. The system, so far as is known, extends nearly 120m underground. A large entrance chamber is connected by a passage to a gallery in which the remains of a Roman counterfeiting operation were found. The main line of the exploitation continues along Potsherd Passage as far as Comb Rift, where rockfalls prevent further investigation.

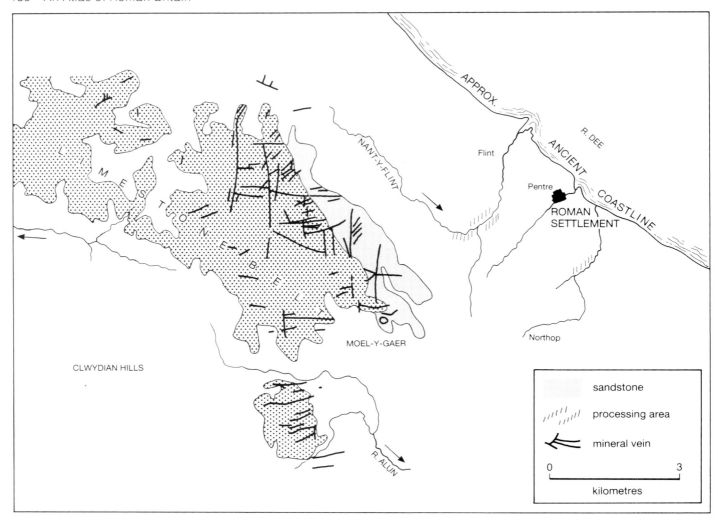

Map 6:7   Halkyn Mountain: lead mining, smelting and settlement

Hydraulicing at Linley, Shropshire

Another of the major fields of Roman metal extraction in Britain appears to have been on the Shropshire/Clwyd border in the Bishops Castle–Montgomery area. A number of inscribed lead ingots of Hadrianic date are known from the parish of Linley, north of Bishops Castle, but no research had been carried out until recently on the sources of metal, the technology used inthe mining, or the character of the associated mining settlements.

Recently, two new factors have been added to the situation. The first was the recognition of the Roman fort nearby at Brompton, where excavation has shown that the site belongs to the late first century/Hadrianic period. Work in the fort and its primary annexe has revealed bowl furnaces which suggest that metal processing was an important, if not prime, function of the site. The second new factor concerns Linley Hall, where the remains of a 'villa' were first exca-

vated in the nineteenth century. As stated above, several lead ingots are known from the vicinity and extensive aerial photographic coverage suggests that the Roman building lay amidst elements of an industrial settlement to the south-east of the hall. Aerial photography also offers a new overall interpretation of the potential mining area by suggesting that extensive areas of the middle and lower slopes of the hillside between Linley and Norbury were worked by hydraulicing, or ground sluicing (6:9). Evidence of this technique can be traced in the fields that have escaped modern ploughing north-west of Glebe Farm in Norbury village and, equally clearly, closer to Linley to the west. The surviving traces take the form of irregularly spaced infilled gulleys running north–south *down* the slope of the hillside, clearly distinguishable from the remains of rig and furrow. The purpose of the sluicing techniques would have been to locate the quartz or quartzite veins that rise to the surface along

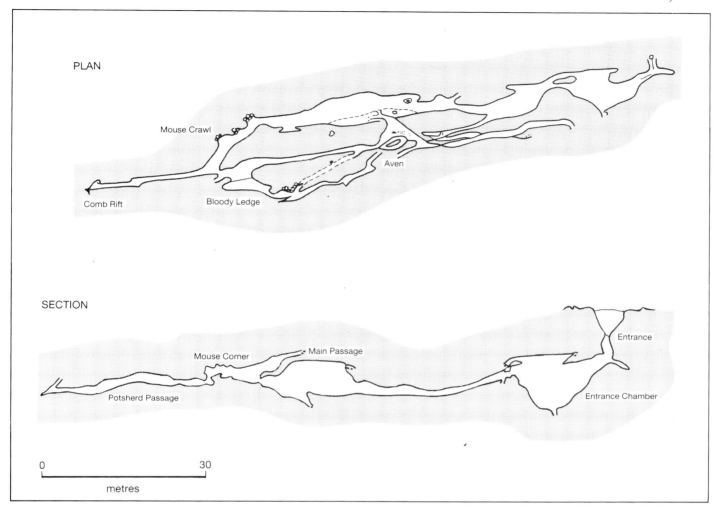

PLAN

Mouse Crawl

Comb Rift   Bloody Ledge   Aven

SECTION

Mouse Corner   Main Passage   Entrance

Potsherd Passage   Entrance Chamber

0   30
              metres

Map 6:8   Draethen, Gwent: lead mining

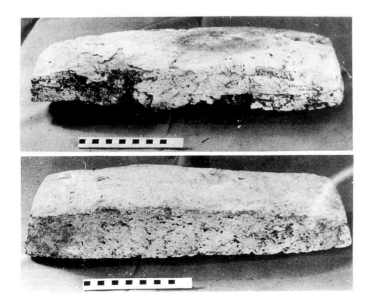

Plate 6:1   Two lead pigs found in a fourth-century Roman rubbish pit at Carsington, Derbyshire

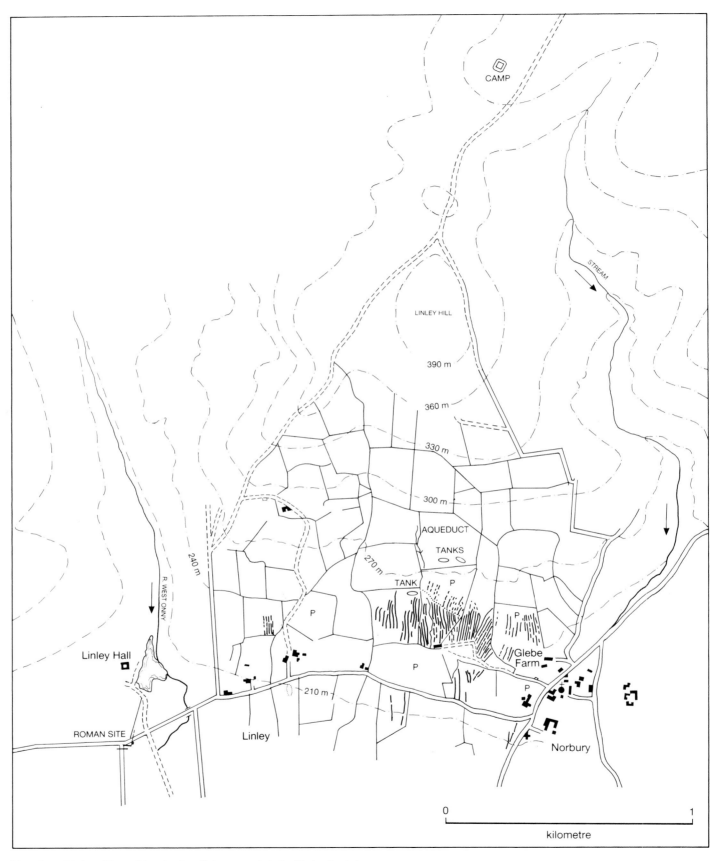

Map 6:9 Linley, Shropshire: hydraulicing associated with lead mining

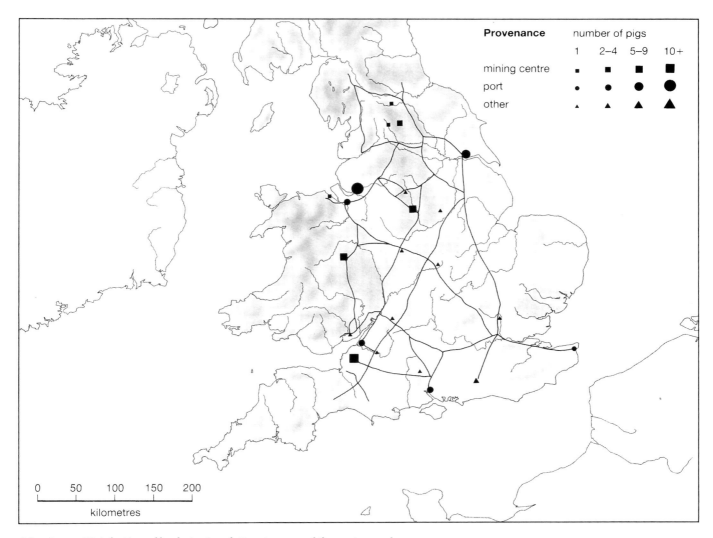

Map 6:10   Distribution of lead pigs in relation to some of the major roads

the sloping shelf and perhaps also partly to ground sluice mineral ores held in the thin topsoil.

Large areas where mineral sediments were ground sluiced have been recognized in north-west Spain. No large reservoirs were used, simply lateral feeder channels running at slight vertical intervals across the hillside. Characteristically, these are relatively smooth and not steeply inclined planes which allow for economical and methodical water utilization.

Silver content and desilverization

Broadly speaking the location of the find spots of lead ingots reaffirms our knowledge of the principal extraction areas (6:10): Derbyshire, the Mendips and the central and northern Marches. Ingots from the Yorkshire Dales are more difficult to assess because their find spots do not relate obvi-

ously to known Roman workings. The find spots also give some hint of the pattern of transportation involved in the metal industry. The three ingots found in the Mersey off Runcorn derived from Halkyn Mountain (6:7). Although some Mendip material might have been shipped from the harbour at Uphill, the majority was probably transported to Southampton Water.

A different point of interest relates to the composition of the ingots. The Mendip deposits were economically very important both because of easy extractability due to vertical vein bedding and because of the relatively high proportion of silver. Silver content in lead can vary considerably and richer veins may well be closer to the surface. An example of this can be seen in the silver content of lead from the Cwmslwyn mine in Dyfed (Table 6:2). There, in AD 1604 the silver was assayed in surface workings at approximately 734 parts per million. By 1710 the assay had dropped to

Table 6.2　Silver lead extraction

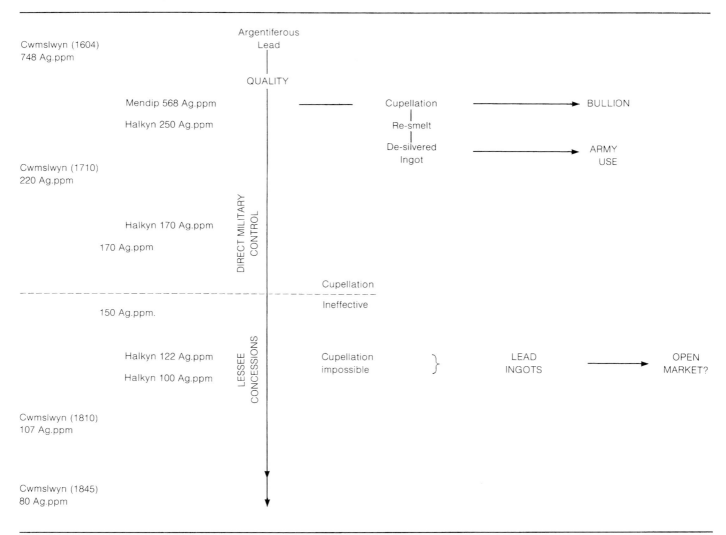

220, by 1811 to between 107 and 122 parts per million, and after 1845 to less than 80 parts per million (ppm). The highest recorded silver content of a Romano-British lead ingot is 560 ppm obtained from one of the lead pigs from Green Ore, Charterhouse (Tylecote No. 67). This particular ingot was awaiting desilverization. Since desilverization becomes worthwhile at around 120 ppm, and more profitable above 170 ppm, the Green Ore example shows the very high silver content available from some parts of Mendip to the first Roman exploiters. The Vespasianic date shows that the mining area was quickly brought into high production, probably largely under military control.

In contrast, many analyses have indicated considerably lower amounts of silver. The mean silver content of Roman pigs derived from Clwyd is 25 ppm. Either the known pigs had already been desilverized or, alternatively, the Clwyd mines had a wide diversity of silver content, often poor.

Tylecote suggests that the former possibility is the more likely as two analyses of galena produced results of 100 parts per million and 170 ppm. A third recent example yielded 122 ppm. Another Vespasianic ingot, from Green Ore (Tylecote No. 64), is entirely devoid of silver and may be regarded as desilverized. So too may be the example from *Clausentum* on Southampton Water with a mere 5 ppm, and others are known from Mendip with 27, 20, 24 and 42 ppm. At a certain stage it would no longer have been profitable for the military to have retained a direct working interest in a particular ore body and at that point it would have been easier for the continued operation of a mining area to be maintained by the introduction of lessees who paid a set rate for the privilege. It is the lessees, therefore, who would have attempted to exploit the lower grade ores in what should normally be seen as the civilian phase in the operation of a mine.

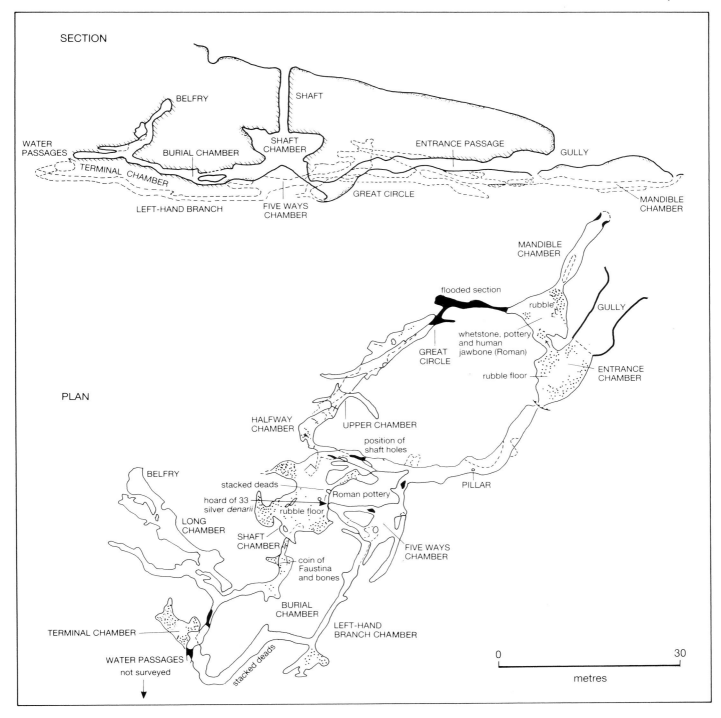

SECTION

BELFRY

SHAFT

WATER
PASSAGES

BURIAL CHAMBER

SHAFT
CHAMBER

ENTRANCE PASSAGE

GULLY

TERMINAL CHAMBER

LEFT-HAND BRANCH

FIVE WAYS
CHAMBER

GREAT CIRCLE

MANDIBLE
CHAMBER

MANDIBLE
CHAMBER

flooded section

rubble

GULLY

whetstone, pottery
and human
jawbone (Roman)

rubble floor

ENTRANCE
CHAMBER

GREAT
CIRCLE

PLAN

HALFWAY
CHAMBER

UPPER CHAMBER

position of
shaft holes

PILLAR

BELFRY

stacked deads

Roman pottery

hoard of 33
silver denarii

rubble floor

LONG
CHAMBER

SHAFT
CHAMBER

FIVE WAYS
CHAMBER

coin of
Faustina
and bones

TERMINAL CHAMBER

BURIAL
CHAMBER

LEFT-HAND
BRANCH CHAMBER

WATER PASSAGES
not surveyed

stacked deads

0   30

metres

Map 6:11   Copper mining: Llanymynech, Shropshire

Copper mining at Llanymynech

Llanymynech Mountain, standing on the edge of the Welsh mountain massif, overlooking the Shropshire plain, is a carboniferous limestone mass containing many malachite deposits. The summit contains widespread vestiges of mineral extraction, including the best-preserved example of a small-scale Roman copper mine in Britain (6:11). The workings are approached down a ramp leading into the main entrance and form an excellent example of a cave-and-gallery mine. Two passages were perhaps prospecting adits, while the main gallery followed the principal lode for a considerable distance. In its final stages the gallery divides repeatedly with ever smaller galleries exploiting the diminishing ore-shoots. Closer to the main working area a vertical shaft was sunk both for ventilation and perhaps for the extraction of ore. The gallery was flanked by two benches and the floor content suggests ore-dressing on the site. In two of the galleries human bones (presumed to have belonged to miners, perhaps of slave status) were found buried along with some coins. This enables us to date the mine to the second century AD.

The main surviving gallery at Llanymynech is only one of several galleries and related mining features to have been discovered on the hill. The evidence is now largely obscured by a golf course and the relatively small scale of the surviving gallery may be very misleading in relation to the overall extent and date range of Roman mining on the hill.

Roman period copper mining is also known to have taken place on a major scale on Parys Mountain (Anglesey) and Great Orme, buit more recent workings there have obliterated most of the evidence.

Iron working

The Weald

The principal southern iron industry lay in the Weald and was based on exploitation of the carbonate ores of the Wadhurst clay in the lower cretaceous Hastings beds (6:12). The hardwoods of the Wealden forest provided an excellent source of fuel. The clays have an average iron ore content of 40 per cent and it is not surprising to find from a reference in Caesar that the industry already existed in the first century BC. The earliest probable sites lay near the coast at Footlands and Crowhurst Park in the Hastings area (Table 6:3).

The organization of the iron extraction is far from clear. Among the larger centres, at Beauport Park the iron production is estimated to have left approximately 50,000 tonnes of slag behind. Operations on this scale must surely imply some kind of central authority, a hypothesis that is strengthened by the discovery of tiles stamped with the monogram of the *Classis Britannica* at Beauport, Bardown and Cranbrook (4:62). Normally only precious metals fell directly under the care of the provincial procurators, but it is clear that the Wealden workings must have stood in some special relationship to the role of the British fleet which is now known to have had forts along this section of the Channel coast.

The Wealden ore exploitation was in the form of small opencast pits. Once extracted the ore was roasted to convert the carbonate to ferrous oxide, which was easier to smelt. At sites such as Broadfields evidence has been recovered both for trench furnaces and for the more common circular type. In these furnaces the oxide was reduced at about 1100°C to obtain iron. Iron ore is not a pure oxide or carbonate but is combined with a great deal of unwanted material which must be 'slagged off'. By far the most common evidence of iron working in the Weald and any other area, therefore, consists of deposits of slag and cinder.

The Wealden industry may be divided into two main

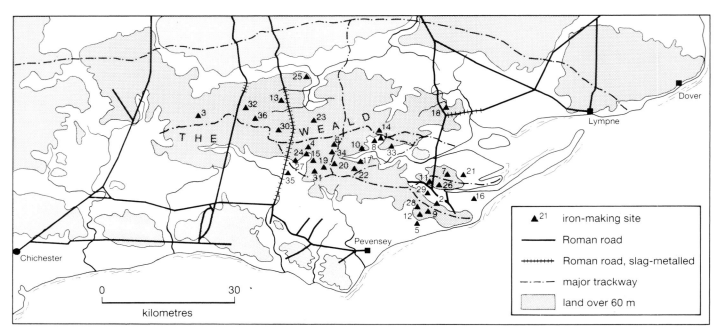

Map 6:12   Iron-making sites in the Weald: for key to numbers see Table 6:3

Table 6.3 Approximate time spans of iron-making sites in the Weald (after Cleere 1975) (solid line indicates certain activity, broken line possible/probable activity)

No. on map 6:123	Date range
	—BC— | ————AD————
	100 | 43 100 200 300 400
1 Bardown	————————————|1
2 Beauport Park	————————————|2
3 Broadfields	– – – – – – – ‑‑3
4 Brook House	– – – – – – – –‑5
5 Bynes Farm	– – – – –‑6
6 Castle Hill	‑‑‑ – – ‑‑‑7
7 Chitcombe	
8 Coalpit Wood	8
9 Crowhurst Park	‑‑‑ ——————— 9
10 Doozes Farm	10
11 Footlands	– – – – – – – – – ‑‑11
12 Forewood	12
13 Great Cansiron	‑‑ |——– – –‑‑13
14 Holbeanwood	————‑14
15 Howbourne Farm	– – – –‑15
16 Icklesham	– – – ‑16
17 Knowle Farm	– – – – –|———17
18 Little Farningham	‑‑‑ – ‑|——‑18
19 Limney Farm	‑ – – – –‑19
20 Little Inwoods	– – – – – ‑‑20
21 Ludley Farm	– – – – – ‑‑21
22 Magreed Farm	22
23 Minepit Wood	– – – – ‑23
24 Morphews	24
25 Oakenden	– – – – – ‑25
26 Oaklands Park	‑ |– – – – ‑‑?26
27 Oldlands	– – – – – – – – – – – ‑‑27
28 Pepperingeye	28
29 Petley Wood	‑ ——— ‑‑‑ -29
30 Pippingford	‑ — ‑‑30
31 Pounsley	– – – – ‑31
32 Ridge Hill	‑‑‑ — |— – – – – ‑32
33 Shoyswell	33
34 Streele Farm	34
35 Strickedridge	– – – ‑35
36 Walesbeech	‑|———‑‑36

areas, an eastern coastal region, and a western region related to two of the major Roman roads of Sussex. The coastal group of sites included Beauport Park, Oaklands Park, Chitcombe, Crowhurst Park, Footlands and Icklesham, some of which were undoubtedly in operation by the end of the first century. Trackways leading to the valleys of the Brede and Rother, suggest that iron was transported by ship away from the area. Markets on the Thames estuary and along the south coast may have been served in this way, but much of the product could have been shipped across to the Continent. In view of the evidence for the involvement of the British fleet, export to the Continent is perhaps to be seen as a major outlet.

Table 6:3 shows that iron production was taking place by the end of the first century at many of the coastal sites and at a few places in the High Weald. By the middle of the second century the scale of operations had increased but at the beginning of the third century changes become detectable. The major workings at Bardown and Crowhurst Park appear to have been run down while satellite sites developed around them. In the mid-third century mining seems to have ceased altogether in the Bardown/Holbeanwood complex and in the Battle area around Beauport Park. Therefore, the major production period for this industry, one of the largest operations of its kind in the Roman Empire, probably had a life span of approximately two centuries or a little more.

The Forest of Dean

The Forest of Dean was also an area of iron extraction on a major scale (6:13; Table 6:4). Although ringed by a series of towns, such as Monmouth, Chepstow, Weston-under-Penyard and Gloucester, there appear to be few major settlements in the area itself. A number of supposed 'villas' may have played an important role in the extraction: Woolaston, like Park Farm, Lydney, offered harbourage facilities and its abnormally large baths are suggestive of a bigger enterprise than normal for a villa. The Woolaston complex seems to date from the second quarter of the second century. The largest of the known workings are clustered round the town of Weston-under-Penyard (*Ariconium*), where an area of 80ha (200 acres) was covered by Roman slag heaps. The iron working appears to have begun towards the end of the first century and grown increasingly in importance towards the end of the Romano-British period.

Recent work has shown that greater emphasis needs to be placed on the study of the use of water transport in the Dean industry. Major processing sites are now attested along the northern edge of the Severn and up the Wye (at Lydney Park, Woolaston, Boughspring, Sedbury, Huntsham, Lancaut and Hadnock Court). These riverine sites, rather than those based on the road system, seem to hold the key to the processing and distribution pattern. In this respect *Ariconium* may have functioned as an administrative centre for the northern sites, whilst being connected by a route across the forest to Woolaston and the Severn. Products, whether finished or in the form of worked blooms, could have been transported up the Severn to Gloucester and beyond into the West Midlands. Downstream, material could have been shipped along the coast to South Wales or across the Severn and up the valley of the Bristol Avon to parts of the south.

The south-east Midlands

Iron mining along the Jurassic ridge is well attested, principally in Northamptonshire. Iron ore can be found in considerable quantities in north Oxfordshire, Northamptonshire and north Lincolnshire, but the ores are carbonates with

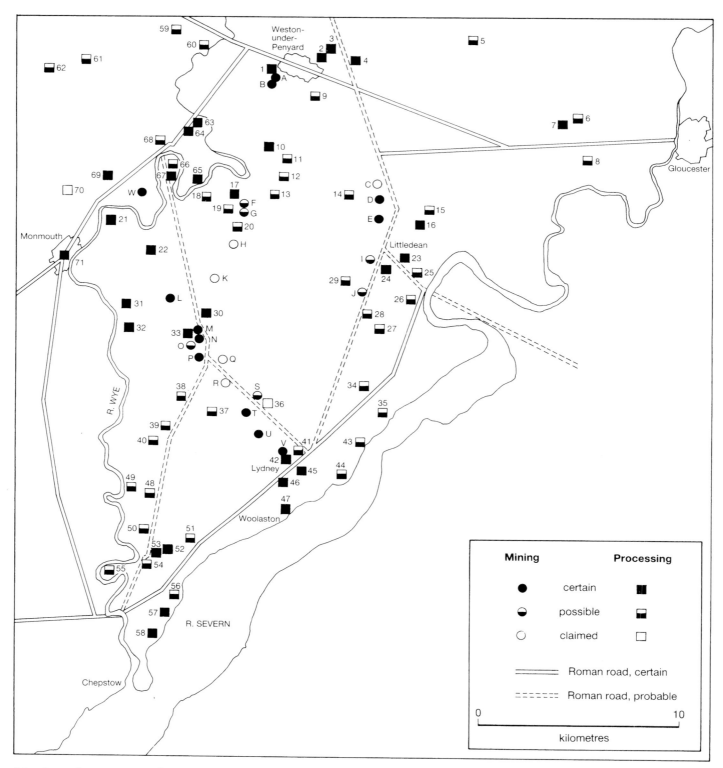

Map 6:13 Iron mining in the Forest of Dean

Table 6.4 Iron working sites in the Forest of Dean

Mining sites

A Penyard Park
B Penyard Park East (by Frogmore)
C Hazel Hill
D Edge Hills
E Collafield
F Hangerberry Wood
G Hangerberry Enclosure
H Edge End
I Abbotswood
J Ruspidge
K Mile End
L Scowles Farm
M Perrygrove Farm
N Lambsquay
O Stock Wood
P Orepool/Deanpool Farm
Q Ellwood Enclosure
R Noxon Park
S Bream
T The Scowles (Devils Chapel) Bream
U Curves Hill
V Camp Hill, Lydney Park
W Great Doward

Processing sites

1 Cinder Hill, West-u-Penyard
2 Bury Hill
3 Bromsash
4 Eccleswall
   (all above around Ariconium)
5 Stallion Hill

6 Rundleshill
7 Beech Wood
8 Churcham
9 Pontshill
10 Old Wood, Marstow
11 Ruardean
12 Smithers Cross
13 The Pludds
14 Nailbridge
15 Plaxley (Westbury Brook)
16 Popes Hill
17 Hangerberry
18 Upper Tump (English Bicknor)
19 Eastbach
20 Worral Hill
21 Hadnock Court
22 Staunton
23 Dean Hall (Dean Hill)
24 Maidenham (Dean Hill)
25 Vostells Brook
26 Bullo Pill
27 Forge Grove, Two Bridges
28 Lower Soudley
29 Ruspidge
30 High Nash, Coleford
31 Furnace Grove, Upper Redbrook
32 Forge Wood, Lower Redbrook
33 Clearwell Farm
34 Hayes Wood
35 Purton
36 Bream
37 Bearse Common
38 Orles Wood

39 St Briavels Common
40 Coldharbour
41 Lydney village
42 Lydney Park
43 Warren Grove
44 Naas Court
45 Park Farm villa
46 Tump Farm, Aylburton
47 Chesters villa, Woolaston
48 Modesgate
49 Madgett Hall, Brockweir
50 East Vaga settlement
51 Stroat
52 Boughspring villa
53 Boughspring
54 Wallhope Farm
55 Liveoaks Troughs, Lancaut
56 Pill House, Tidenham cliffs
57 Sedbury Park
58 Sedbury Park
59 Peterstow
60 Weirend
61 Three Ashes
62 Velindra
63 Cruse
64 Goodrich
65 Coppet Hill
66 Huntsham villa
67 Huntsham hill
68 Old Forge (Marstow)
69 Whitchurch
70 Buckholt
71 Monmouth

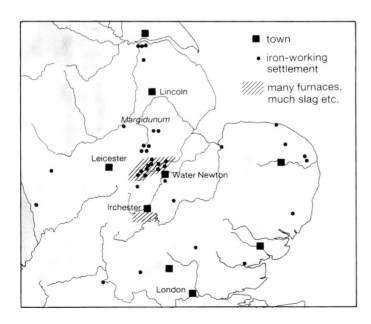

Map 6:14 Iron working in the East Midlands

a relatively low iron content. The principal areas of iron extraction lay around Water Newton and near Irchester. Although many of the sites have been destroyed by modern opencast mining, the geographical extent of the iron working is not in doubt (6:14). At some sites it can be demonstrated that the activity had a pre-Roman origin, while in the second century there occurred a major intensification. Although iron production continued into the third and fourth centuries, it is best interpreted as a domestic operation serving local settlements. There is, therefore, nothing to suggest a scale of activity comparable to that in either the eastern section of the Wealden iron industry or in the Forest of Dean. On the other hand, Water Newton emerges as the obvious centre for iron working, just as it was the centre for pottery production on a very substantial scale (see Map 5:21).

Metalworking and industry

At many of the major mining sites there is evidence of artefact production as well as smelting. Whilst some metal-

Map 6:15   Distribution of pewter moulds in Britain

working was also done in the major towns, it is a misconception to envisage that most traded metal artefacts
would have been made alongside the markets. The location
of brooch or metal tableware manufacture for instance, was
mainly determined by the availability of the raw materials
or by access to wider markets. The point is well illustrated
by the known distribution of pewter moulds (6:15), since
only two of the sites where they have been found are major
towns (Gloucester and Silchester), and the others are divided
between small towns, villas and other rural settlements.
Pewter is made from lead and tin. That the location of five
out of the eight sites occurs near the Mendips, the source of
lead, as against only one in Cornwall, the source of tin, is
significant. It shows that production of the finished artefacts
was geared to the markets of the Bath/Gloucester region
and beyond.

THE GROWTH OF TRADE

Olive oil and Julio-Claudian military supply

The impact of the military market on certain trade patterns
is well illustrated by the information derived from a number
of important shipwrecks. Of particular significance is the
wreck known as Port-Vendres II, which sank in the AD 40s
carrying a mixed cargo of tin ingots, olive oil, wine, fish

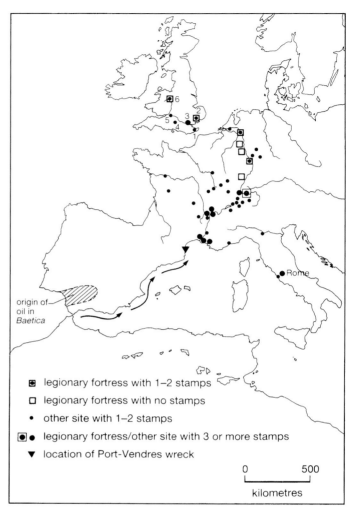

Map 6:16   Julio-Claudian trade routes to Gaul and Britain as
suggested by the distribution of stamped olive oil amphorae of
Baetican origin known from the Port Vendres II wreck

products and fine pottery. The olive oil amphorae were the
standard Baetican type (Dressel form 20) from south-west
Spain, and many examples were found with stamps on the
handles. The overall distribution of amphorae with the same
stamps as those known from the wreck should give us some
idea of the ultimate destination of at least that part of the
cargo (6:16). The stamps are represented at Rome but the
vast majority have been found along the riverine trade
routes of Gaul (cf. 3:15). The conclusion that the Rhône
Valley was of primary importance is unavoidable and it is
likely that olive oil was ultimately reaching the German and
British military garrisons via the Rhône/Rhine axis, rather
than direct from Baetica up the Atlantic coast. Furthermore,
this does not seem to represent direct purchase by the north

Plate 6:2 Handle of an olive oil amphora of Dressel 20 type found during excavation at Northwich (Cheshire). The stamp indicates that the amphora was produced at a kiln in the lower Guadalqivir Valley in Andalusia, southern Spain.

Trade in later years

Once the province was established, developing communities demanded consumer goods on a par with those available in other provinces in the Empire (6:18). Fine pottery with a glossy red exterior known as Samian ware was imported in great quantities from first southern and then central Gaul, along with other pottery from elsewhere in Gaul and the Rhineland. Fine glass was imported from Italy, from the Rhineland and, exceptionally, from the eastern Mediterranean, particularly the Levant and Alexandria. In greater quantity came wine, exported in amphorae from Italy and Spain and apparently also in wooden barrels from Gaul. Spain supplied much of the olive oil for cooking and lamp fuel, again in amphorae – likewise the spicy fish sauce or *garum*. To a lesser extent amphorae containing wine or oil were imported from other parts of the Mediterranean. Additionally, amber was imported from the Baltic area and specialized enamel brooches were brought from lower Germany. Italy was the source of bronze tableware and

European garrisons from Baetica itself, since large numbers of the amphorae got no further than the Rhône. The initiative of individual traders, importing oil to key centres such as Lyons on the Rhône for onward sale to the lucrative military market, may be suspected. This appears to be confirmed by the evidence that the Port-Vendres wreck was carrying goods for no less than eleven different merchants, rather than a bulk holding in one individual's name. Nonetheless, even if the olive oil was not itself ordered direct by the garrisons, it is possible that the trade was subsidized by movement of metals along this route from Spain to the mint at Rome and the army on the Rhine.

With the exception of Silchester, the olive oil was only reaching sites in Britain of a proven military character. This suggests that, for the AD 40s and 50s at least, military supply via the Rhône and Rhine was normal and that the small-scale supply of luxuries like olive oil to native sites, which had developed during the late Iron Age, was disrupted to some extent.

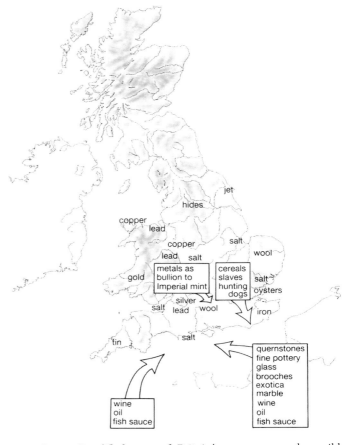

Map 6:17 Simplified map of Britain's resources and possible pattern of import/export in the early Roman period

Plate 6:3 An example of Samian ware imported from central Gaul

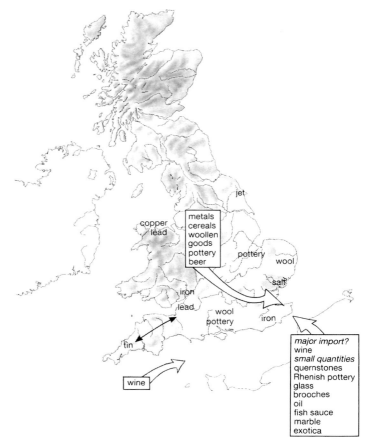

Map 6:18 Simplified map of Britain's resources and the possible pattern of import/export in the late Roman period

lamps, while Germany exported millstones or 'querns'. Marble is also known to have been imported from a wide variety of sources in the Mediterranean (6:38), but in small quantity.

During this early period it is difficult to estimate how much Britain continued to export the corn, hunting dogs and slaves specified by Strabo, but it is certain that bullion was exported to the Imperial mint at Lyons. Likewise, iron from the Wealden deposits was exported to the nearer parts of the Continent.

As the province developed in the later centuries, inevitably it became more self-sufficient in items such as pottery and tableware. The section on the ceramic industry (6:24–6:34) explains the changes in market patterns which are traceable within the province. The import of olive oil and wine, however, obviously continued. Amongst the new industries which appear to have developed at this time on an altogether larger scale should be included the North Yorkshire jet industry, which began exporting to the Continent (6:18). In times of emergency it is clear that a surplus of corn could also be exported to supply the Rhineland garrisons and other areas.

Yet fundamental problems remain. It is comparatively easy to demonstrate the import or export of certain durable items, but altogether more difficult to attempt to quantify the scale of transport. For many perishable commodities we cannot even attest to their distribution pattern, let alone measure their economic importance. Nor is it readily possible to separate evidence relating to redistributive 'trade' connected with officially supervised military supply, from 'free market' activity.

Harbours

With the notable exception of London, comparatively few traces of Roman harbours and quays have been properly examined in Britain. This is in part a reflection on the vulnerability of harbour installations to destruction as a result of coastal or river change, or as a result of continued use of natural harbour sites down to the present day. Yet an island province like Britain must have depended heavily on its sea communications with the Continent and a large number of harbours are known, or can be inferred, to have existed (6:19, cf 2:20). Some of these sites may have been in use already in the late Iron Age and many were no doubt further developed for military purposes during the conquest period. With the civil development in the south and the stabilization of the military garrison positions in the north, some of the many anchorages were developed into more substantial and more important harbours. Pre-eminent amongst them was London, the provincial capital and chief entrepôt.

The cost of transporting goods overland, however, would have outweighed to some extent the risk of navigation in the English Channel, the North Sea and the Irish Sea, and encouraged the wider distribution of goods by sea. Even on rivers which were not accessible to sea-going vessels, boats

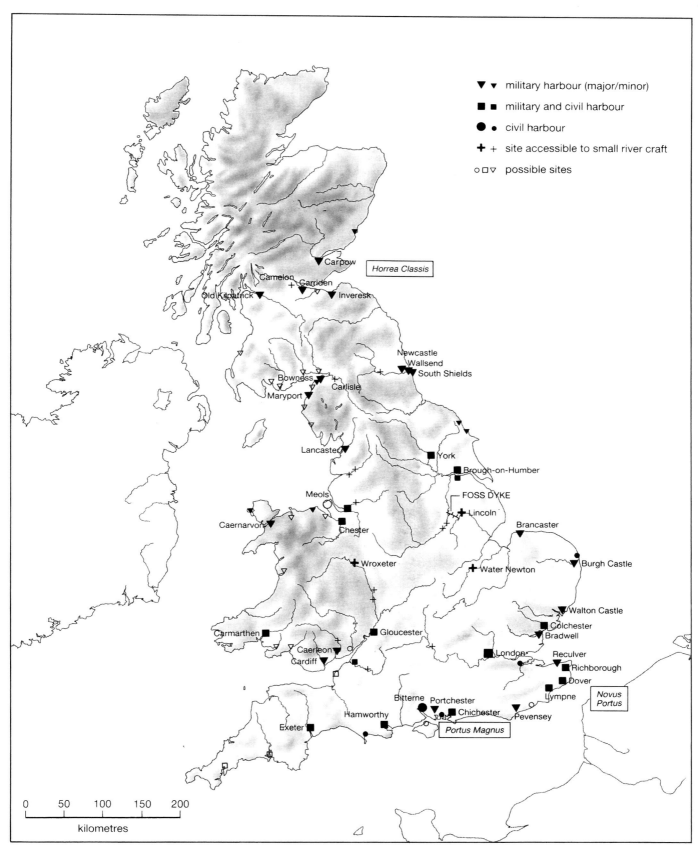

Map 6:19 Distribution of harbours, anchorages and inland ports

of shallower draft could navigate far inland in many cases and some coastal sites may have been used for the tran-shipment of cargoes. At least one Roman canal is known, the Foss Dyke, which connects Lincoln on the River Witham with the River Trent (and from there with the Humber estuary and the North Sea). The much longer Car Dyke of Cambridgeshire and Lincolnshire, which was for many years believed to be another navigation canal, is now thought to have been a discontinuous drainage system (6:44).

In spite of the impressive appearance of the road network (5:23), we need not infer that overland haulage of goods was undertaken readily where a waterborne alternative route existed. Whilst Map 6:20 probably includes the major har-bours, it is undoubtedly far from complete in relation to the overall complexity of the water transport network.

Merchants and traders

The epigraphic evidence for the activities of merchants oper-ating in Britain or between Britain and the Continent is relatively meagre (6:20). However, the indications are that trade was channelled chiefly through Gaul, and through the north-eastern region (*Gallia Belgica*) in particular. Most of the merchants whose place of origin is known for certain were Gallo-Romans, the exception being Barat(h)es of Palmyra, who died at Corbridge and who may have been more of a salesman than a shipper in any case.

The most remarkable groups of inscriptions come from two shrines to the goddess Neihalennia (the 'guardian' or the 'guide' of North Sea shipping) at Colijnsplaat and Domburg near the Rhine mouth on the Dutch coast. Over 150 dedications have been found there, the majority rep-resenting the fulfilment of sailors' and traders' vows after a

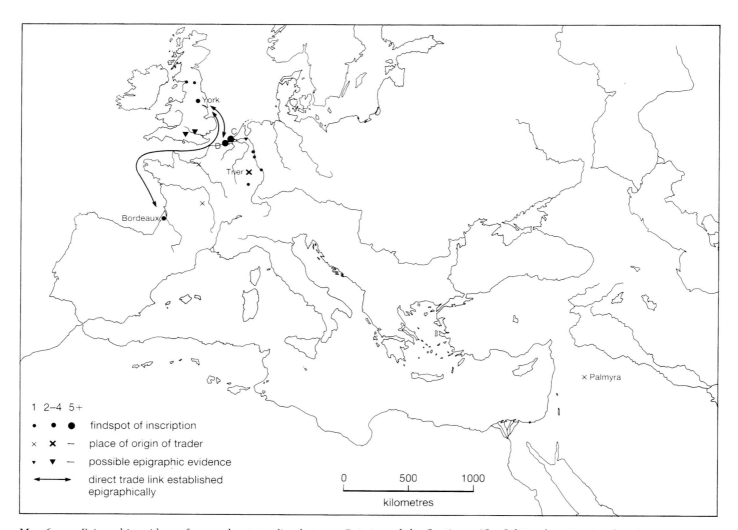

1	2–4	5+	
•	•	●	findspot of inscription
×	✕	—	place of origin of trader
▾	▼	—	possible epigraphic evidence
←	→		direct trade link established epigraphically

0   500   1000
kilometres

Map 6:20   Epigraphic evidence for merchants trading between Britain and the Continent (C = Colijnsplaat, D = Domburg)

safe return from voyages. Whilst much of the traffic may have been following the northern French coast to or from the Rhineland, Britain was also a likely destination for ships departing from here and a number of the inscriptions specify the British connection of their dedicators.

Other inscriptions which mention merchants with specifically British operations are to be found at a number of sites down the Rhine and, in western France, at Bordeaux. One particularly interesting example from Bordeaux is an altar dedicated on his arrival there by M. Aurelius Lunaris, a merchant who held public distinction at both York and Lincoln as a *sevir Augustalis*. He was perhaps trading in wine, with his British distribution centred on the two northern towns. Another trading connection between northern Britain and the Continent is established by an inscription commemorating the construction of an arch and temple in York at the behest of a merchant of Gallic origin called L. Viducius Placidus. The generosity of the donation suggests that the town was the base of his British operation, whilst his Continental connection is attested on an altar from Domburg.

Little trade seems to have been done direct with the Mediterranean, and goods from that region would have tended to arrive in small quantities by way of middlemen in Gaul. Our inscriptions reveal that the items involved in cross-Channel trade included pottery, garments, fish sauces, salt-fish and, probably, wines. All of these products could have originated in the provinces of Britain, Gaul and Germany.

Beyond the frontiers

Distinctive Roman artefacts (notably coins, metalwork, pottery and glass) are found on native sites beyond the northern frontiers. The mechanisms by which these objects arrived there and their distribution in Scotland varied through time. There is evidence from reference to pre-Roman customs that the use of money, particularly in small denominations, was rejected as alien. Of first-century Roman objects located in Scotland (6:21) it would appear that there were a few low-value coins. Yet in essence low-value coinage probably circulated only within the invading army, and the find spots simply reflect random losses rather than the establishment of any market relationship within the indigenous population. Such high-status items as are known include late first-century finds imported into sites in the Lowlands, notably crannogs in Dumfries and Galloway.

The difficulty in interpreting the evidence further lies in the fact that central Scotland formed a frontier zone on two occasions during the second century (6:22). In addition extensive areas of lowland Scotland were under direct military control at a number of periods. The effect is to distort our picture of trade contacts. The central corridor and lowland Scotland in the second century are perhaps best seen as areas into which trade objects, notably coinage, travelled by generally conventional means in a military zone. The occurrence of such items broadly reflects the Roman military presence, particularly on the Antonine Wall in its first phase. The main mechanism for the transfer of coinage and items of material culture must have lain in the presence of *vici*. The growth of a market economy was probably slow and there is no need to conclude that coinage replaced other means of exchange. As the civilian settlements increasingly became centres of production and trade, providing firstly for the garrison, secondly for their own inhabitants and lastly for the population of the hinterland, so low-denomination coinage became of increasing significance.

In the second century, Roman artefacts became much more common on native sites throughout lowland Scotland. Samian pottery in particular is an example of a moderately high-status trade item which reached many sites. Glass and metalwork are found more widely than the former in the first century, occurring particularly on crannog sites. However, the distribution of such finds north of the frontier is limited; while the import of pottery is more general, metalwork and glass wares tend to be found only in the immediate market areas of outpost forts.

The recovery of large amounts of Roman material from Traprain Law, the strongpoint of the Votadini dominating the coastal plain east of Edinburgh, suggests that the tribe was already in some form of client relationship with Rome by the beginning of the second century. The quantity of trade items for both luxury and everyday uses suggests that Traprain Law was in fact the main regional entrepôt for trade with the Roman world. It may have played this role as early as the last quarter of the first century, but its importance was evidently continued into the second century. The widespread evidence for Roman material in the Votadinian territory, in particular in the northern part of the territory, suggests that this tribal area enjoyed considerable prosperity during the second century. If Traprain Law formed the centre of the Votadinian tribal confederacy then it would have been natural that its market hinterland should have received a preferential share of Roman trade items compared with the poorer record from the more remote areas of the tribal territory to the south, although these lie closer to the line of Hadrian's Wall.

Later in the Roman period, when there was no formalized frontier in Scotland, trade is typified by a small but apparently steady flow of items (6:23). These comprised principally coinage, presumably attesting trade within a partly monetarized economy, and higher classes of artefact such as glassware, which can be found as far north as the Orkney Islands. The pattern is therefore reminiscent of that established beyond the Roman frontier in free Germany, Denmark and Scandinavia.

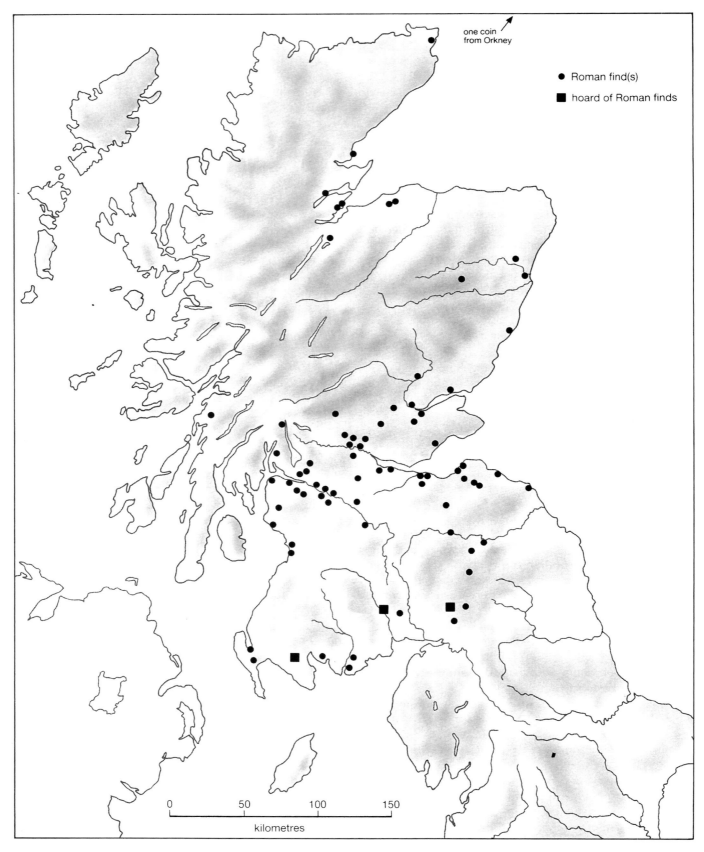

one coin
from Orkney

● Roman find(s)
■ hoard of Roman finds

0   50   100   150
kilometres

Map 6:21 Roman finds from non-Roman sites in Scotland (i) first-century AD material

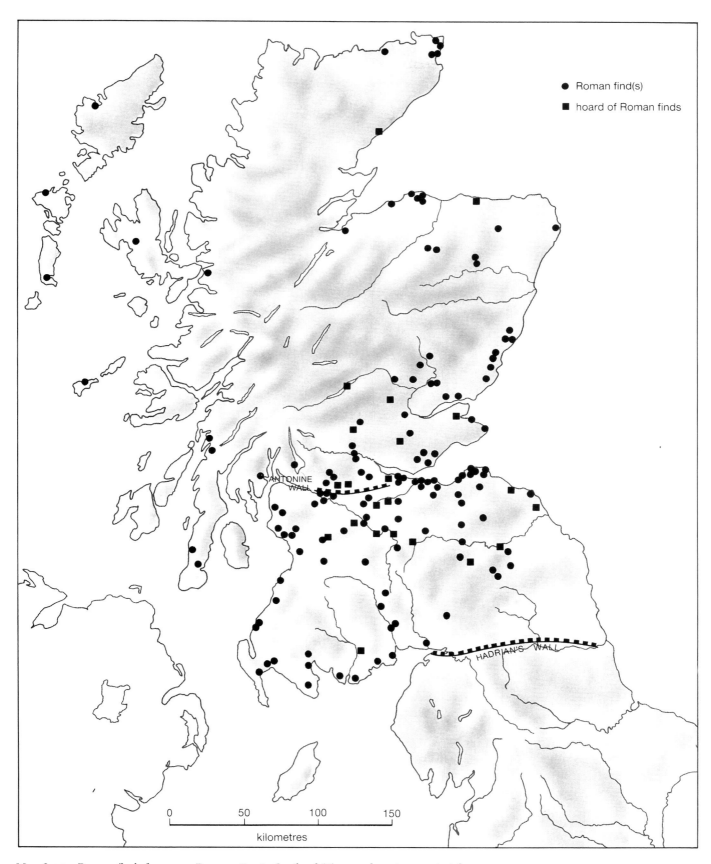

Map 6:22 Roman finds from non-Roman sites in Scotland (ii) second-century material

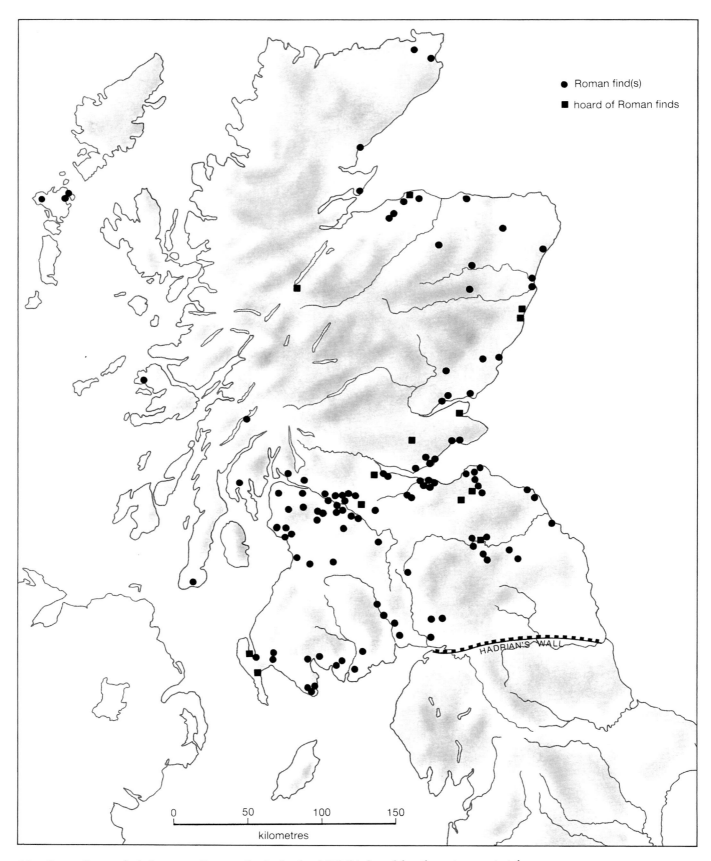

Roman find(s)
hoard of Roman finds

HADRIAN'S WALL

0   50   100   150
kilometres

Map 6:23   Roman finds from non-Roman sites in Scotland (iii) third- and fourth-century material

POTTERY AND OTHER INDUSTRIES

Pottery production sites

The siting of pottery-making centres is conditioned by several factors, notably the existence of the appropriate natural resources – of which clay is the most obvious. Pottery production also requires quantities of sand or some other tempering material to be mixed with the clay. In addition water is an essential requirement both in clay preparation and in the construction of pots. Timber (or some other fuel) is equally necessary for firing. Clay is widely available. It is not surprising, therefore, to find that many kilns were located in river valleys close to other resources (6:24). A further factor which will have affected the location of the major industries was the existence of markets and transport facilities. Apart from the very finest quality products, pottery was not intrinsically valuable and was thus unlikely to be transported far from its place of origin, even where river or sea shipment was easy, unless its distribution was linked to the movement of some more valuable or essential commodity. Whilst the army was known to establish or promote some potteries in the military zone of the province, particularly in the early years of the Roman conquest when civil supplies were less well established, the long-term development favoured potters based in the civil zone (6:25, 6:26). It is also true, however, that the best clays in Britain were to be found south-east of the Jurassic ridge and, in particular, these included the highest quality primary clays needed for the production of the white-fired mixing bowls (*mortaria*) and for other pale fabric wares. Many of the major centres were those where both primary and secondary clays (for coarser wares) were readily available (Colchester, Brockley Hill, the Nene Valley, Mancetter/Hartshill, Oxfordshire and Crambeck).

The presence of a potter's stamp on the rim of a mixing bowl or *mortarium* can be of great value in reconstructing trade patterns and market areas within the province, as shown by the example of the Wilderspool *mortaria* production (6.33). In the initial period after the conquest the military relied to a large extent on imports from the Continent or production by army potters for the supply of bulky items of pottery such as flagons and *mortaria*. The first centres of importance were those near St Albans (*Verulamium*) at Brockley Hill and Radlett. Some of the early potters may have come from the Continent; a certain Q. Valerius Veranius can probably be identified as having moved his workshop from *Bavai* in northern Gaul to a pottery centre somewhere in Kent. Roughly half the products of the

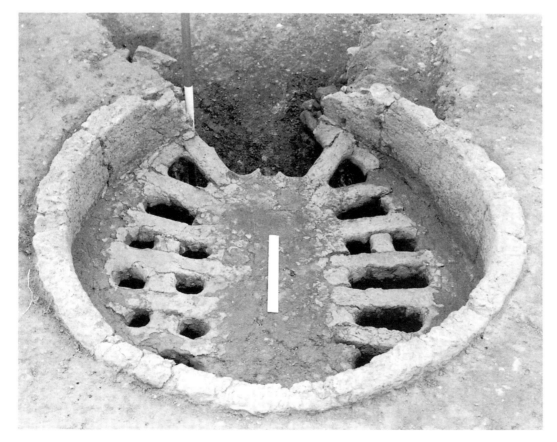

Plate 6:4 Floor of a circular Roman pottery kiln at Stibbington in the Nene Valley

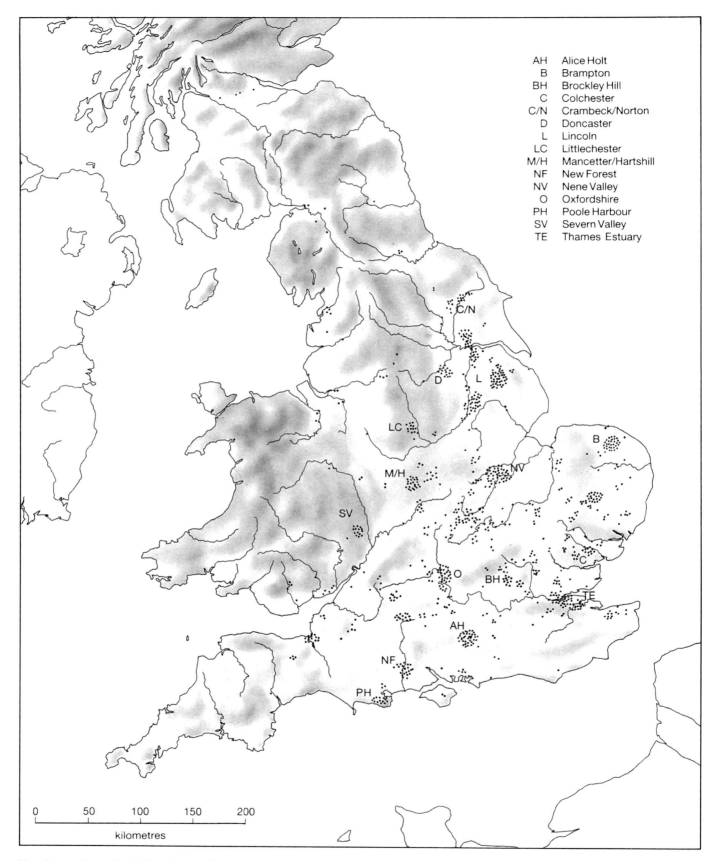

AH   Alice Holt
B   Brampton
BH   Brockley Hill
C   Colchester
C/N   Crambeck/Norton
D   Doncaster
L   Lincoln
LC   Littlechester
M/H   Mancetter/Hartshill
NF   New Forest
NV   Nene Valley
O   Oxfordshire
PH   Poole Harbour
SV   Severn Valley
TE   Thames Estuary

0   50   100   150   200

kilometres

Map 6:24   Generalized distribution of Roman pottery kilns

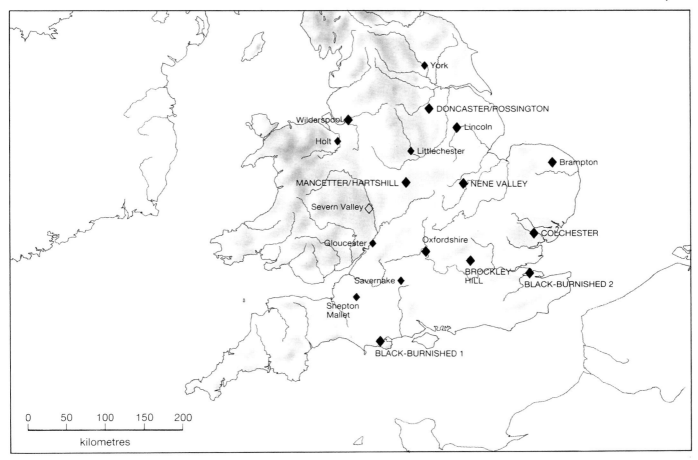

Map 6:25 Main kiln groups in the late first and second centuries

Verulamium area are known to have been distributed in the London and St Albans region, but by the end of the first century perhaps as much as a quarter of the total found its way into the military market on the northern and western limits of the frontier. This is an impressive piece of marketing.

As the frontiers themselves moved forward so it was inevitable that the pattern of pottery production should evolve in response. As a result, the second century saw important changes as the centres of pottery production moved to locations closer to their main institutionalized market, the military one. The stamps of G. Attius Marinus show that he was briefly associated with Radlett (Hertfordshire) as well as Brockley Hill before moving north *c.*AD 100 to the major production centre that was developing in the Mancetter/Hartshill area near Nuneaton. The reasons were, in part, connected with the depletion of fine white-firing clay at the former location and the discovery of large deposits at the latter. It is also probable that the move was designed to exploit the potential of military markets.

The Mancetter/Hartshill kilns were producing *mortaria* in large quantities by AD 125, and these kilns served the army

in the north as late as the fourth century. For the period AD 160–90, for instance, on the evidence of the die-stamps approximately 30 per cent of the *mortaria* from this source were sold to the forts in the Pennine and Hadrian's Wall areas.

During the second century other sources of *mortarium* production came into play, notably in the Nene Valley (6:27). This industry produced a wide range of good quality wares which were also marketed in the northern frontier zone. Colchester *mortaria* were distributed locally in East Anglia and indeed in Kent, but they reached the eastern sectors of the Hadrianic and Antonine walls in greater numbers. It is thought that more pottery from the Mancetter, Nene Valley and Colchester areas was transported northwards to the military commands than was sold in the actual areas of production.

Another factor to note in the distribution maps (6:25, 6:26) is the general shift in the late Roman period away from specific military establishments (Wilderspool, Holt, York, Doncaster), towns and small towns (Colchester, Brockley Hill/St Albans, Gloucester, Nene Valley/Water Newton,

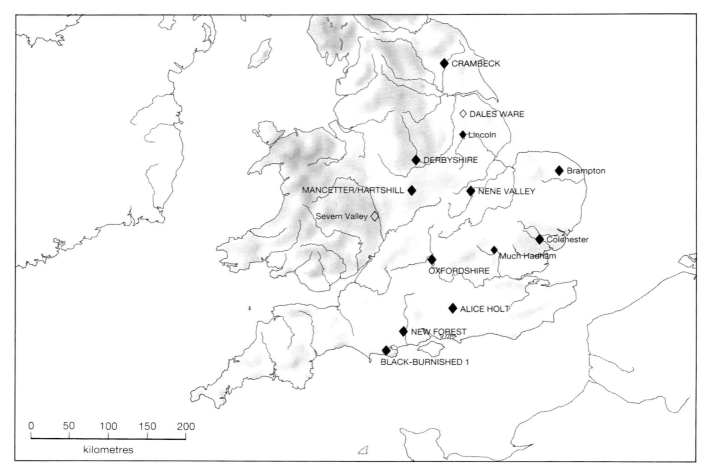

Map 6:26   Main kiln groups in the third and fourth centuries

Mancetter, Littlechester, Lincoln) to extensive rural-based industries such as those in the New Forest, near Alice Holt, in Oxfordshire, in Derbyshire and at Crambeck. There had been some dispersed rural industries earlier, such as the black-burnished ware production near Poole harbour and near the Thames estuary, and some of the Severn Valley ware centres, but, whilst production continued at some major centres such as Colchester, Lincoln, Water Newton and Mancetter, the trend was to move away from the towns. Various explanations can be advanced on a socio-political level, but the simplest explanation may be that, as competition for fuel supplies around many towns increased through the depletion of nearby woodland, it became more economic to exploit fuels and clays beyond their immediate orbit. Yet, since pottery making was a seasonal activity carried out predominantly in the summer months, other explanations which link rural production centres to the organizational and capital base provided by villa estates must also have something to recommend them.

In the late Roman period the most important development in ceramics was the establishment of a pottery industry at Crambeck, near Malton, in North Yorkshire. This production centre was in fact better placed to supply the northern garrison and the York command than any other production centre. Doubtless thanks to this geographical factor the Crambeck industry grew in the last part of the fourth century to the extent that it was able to reduce or even eliminate competitive wares from the Midlands and the south. The Crambeck kilns began life in the first half of the fourth century, but the reorganization of the 360s seems to have given a major stimulus to the development of this production centre. Its cooking pots, bowls, *mortaria* and flagons henceforth supplied most of the needs of the late fourth-century military market. Two other northern production centres should also be recognized, though they never matched the scale of production from Crambeck. Delph ware was produced close to the Humber estuary, while Derbyshire ware was manufactured in kilns at Holbrook and Hazelwood near Sheffield and supplied a relatively wide market straddling the Pennines.

Further south the basic pattern continued with some restriction of the markets served by the various products.

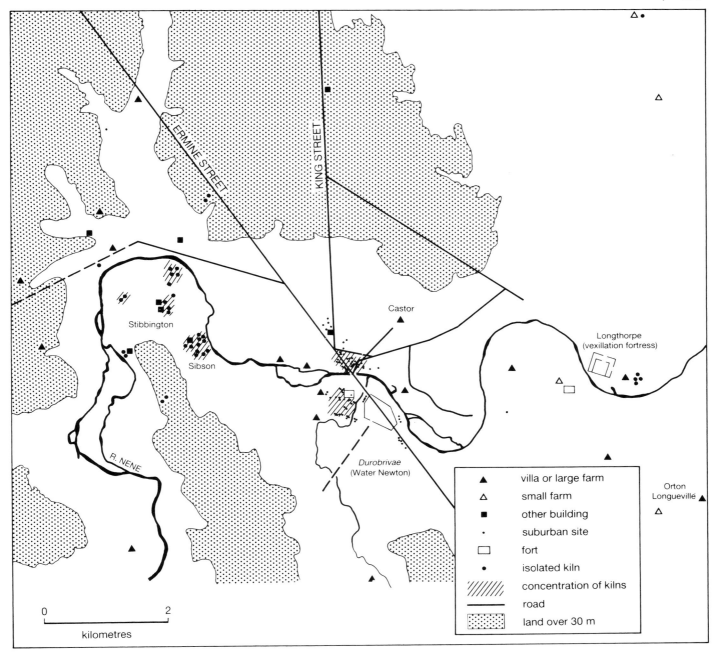

Map 6:27   Nene Valley kilns

The Mancetter/Hartshill kilns, like those of the Nene Valley, continued to have an extensive distribution pattern, while the influence of Oxfordshire wares increased dramatically. The production centres of the New Forest and Alice Holt continued to supply their own hinterlands and the kilns at Much Hadham, Colchester and Brampton catered for the East Anglian market. This general pattern of production and distribution seems to have been maintained to the end of the fourth century.

Kiln distribution in the Nene Valley

Amongst the known potteries of Roman Britain, the Nene Valley industry (6.27) is remarkable because of its growth. Although it was already producing pottery for a localized market in the mid-second century, there occurred a rapid expansion in the distribution of Nene Valley products thereafter, and this type of pottery soon won a large part of the military market in the north and west. This transformation of the fine pottery market was related in some way to the collapse of Samian imports. The position of the industry centring on the town of Water Newton (*Durobrivae*) suggests that the River Nene was a decisive factor in both the production and the transport of the pottery. This water route gave easy access to the east coast and would have been of prime importance in facilitating the northern military contacts.

The pottery consists of colour-coated ware with a wide range of types and decorative motifs, the most common being a running scroll of ivy leaves similar to earlier plain Samian forms. It is sometimes described as 'Castor ware', from the parish in which many of the kilns were found.

New Forest wares

During the latter half of the third century the import of Continental ceramic products to British markets was substantially diminished, with the growth of British potteries producing a complete range of kitchenware, including *mortaria*, finer tableware and drinking vessels. The New Forest kilns were a good example of this development (6:28). Located within 65km of the capitals of Dorchester, Winchester, Chichester and the lesser centre at Ilchester in Somerset, the majority of the pottery produced (comprising a full range of kitchen and table wares) was marketed within the consumer areas formed by the above mentioned towns. The actual kilns lie east of the Hampshire Avon in an area of sand and clay dissected by three tributary streams draining across heathland, which it is presumed was afforested much as it is today. Supplies of clay, sand, wood and water were therefore available to the Romano-British potters, and these factors appear to have controlled the location of the kilns, restricting them to a small area of approximately 14sq km of the forest. Potting may have been conducted on a seasonal basis in the forest, and this may partly account for the clustering of the complexes at Ashley Rails, Crock Hill, Amberwood and Sloden. The most important product in the late third and fourth centuries was fine colour-coated tableware, distributed not only in the main market region, but also across much of southern England, although to a lesser extent. Some of the early styles are copies of Oxfordshire products and likewise some of the later forms and fabrics are very closely related to the products of the Alice Holt/Farnham kilns.

Pottery distribution: some case studies

Lyon ware

Recent studies of Lyon ware, notably by Greene, have considerable significance in relation to the military economic network in the Claudio – Neronian period (6:29). Lyon ware was imported from central Gaul, and some 30 or so examples are known from mid-first century fort sites. Of the other

sites, Bagendon and Salmonsbury represent hillforts of the Dobunni tribe, whose apparently friendly relations with Rome might have led to early imports into their tribal settlements. In contrast, examples have also been found at the Durotrigian hillfort at South Cadbury, a site which was apparently the location of a Roman military detachment in the same period. The remaining sites lie principally on the routes from the Channel ports, notably from Richborough towards London, and do not appear to have military associations. Another group of Lyon ware found its way into this country through the Solent area, perhaps via Hamworthy in Poole harbour. The production of Lyon ware ceased abruptly in AD 69 owing to the difficulties of the civil war and this definite end to the industry makes Lyon ware perhaps the most diagnostically useful of the early imports into Britain. Plotting find spots should give an indication of the extent of the militarized zone up to and including the AD 60s.

Black-burnished ware

Black-burnished ware is one of the commonest forms of pottery to be found in Roman Britain (6:30, 6:31). Its standard range of vessel forms influenced many other pottery industries. Research has shown that there was a widespread development from the localized industry of late Iron Age Dorset into the nationwide industry of the Roman era. An important breakthrough in studying it was the identification of two different varieties, BB1 and BB2. The Dorset Iron Age product and one of its Roman successors, BB1, was black and gritty, while BB2 was wheel-thrown, with a smoother surface. BB2 is normally seen as an imitative development of BB1 at potteries in Essex and Kent in the late first century. The major change came, however, in the first quarter of the second century. Evidently the potters who had previously supplied the local markets of the Durotriges and other parts of the south-west won major supply contracts for the northern army. Black-burnished wares are, therefore, common on Hadrian's Wall and also appear on the Antonine frontier in Scotland. For the best part of a century both varieties of ware were supplied to the northern army, with a drop in the quantities of BB2 in the third century. The supplies of BB1 were evidently supplemented from other potteries, such as that known at Rossington Bridge near Doncaster, and it is probable that several other potteries remain to be found. It was not until the mid-fourth century that the circulation of BB1 diminished in central and South Wales and most of southern England except for East Anglia. The real reasons for the long-distance transport of BB1 and BB2 (and many other categories of low-value pottery) are unknown, but are likely to relate to the pottery travelling 'piggy-back' with some less visible archaeological product such as cereals or salt, and this needs to be kept in mind when considering the precise significance of pottery distributions.

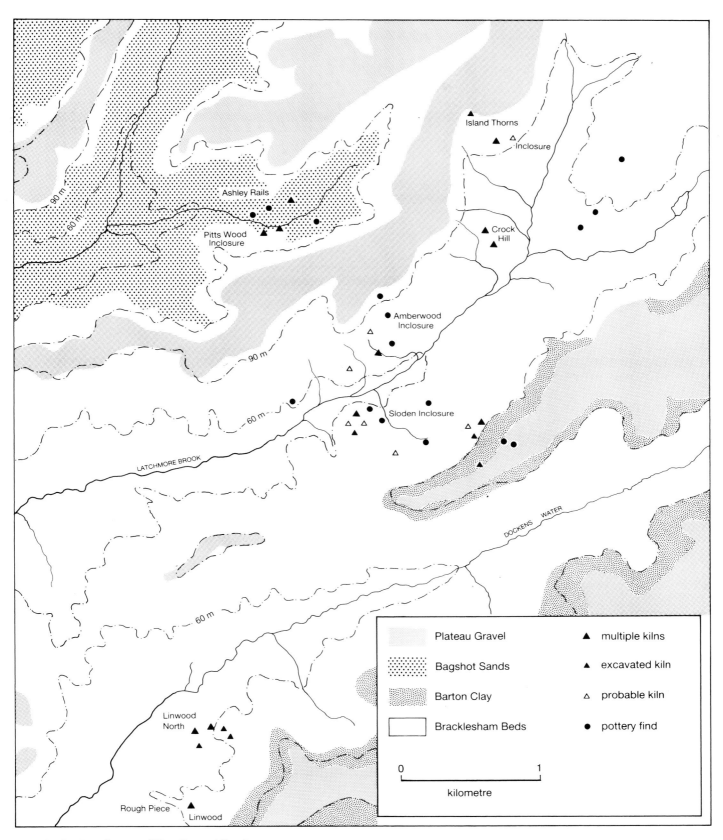

Map 6:28   Distribution of New Forest kiln sites

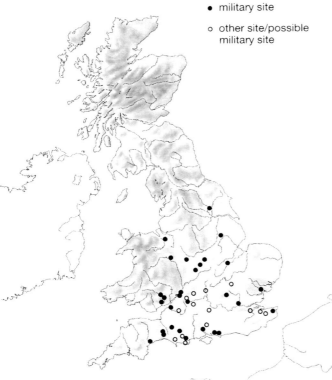

Map 6:29 Distribution of Lyon ware in Britain

Map 6:30 Proposed production centres and generalized distribution of category 1 black-burnished ware

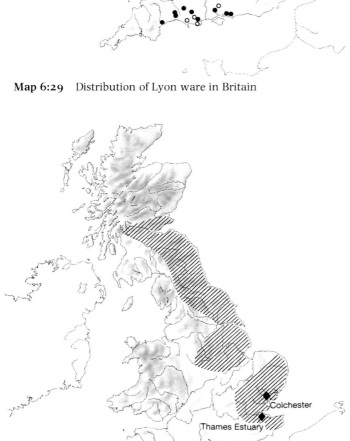

Map 6:31 Proposed production centres and generalized distribution pattern of category 2 black-burnished ware

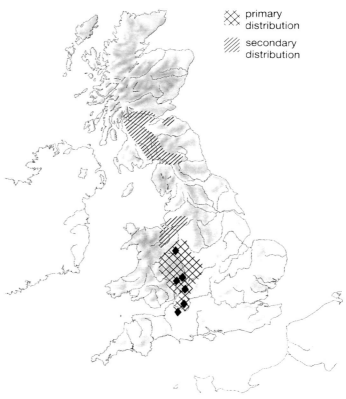

Map 6:32 Possible production sites and generalized distribution of Severn Valley ware

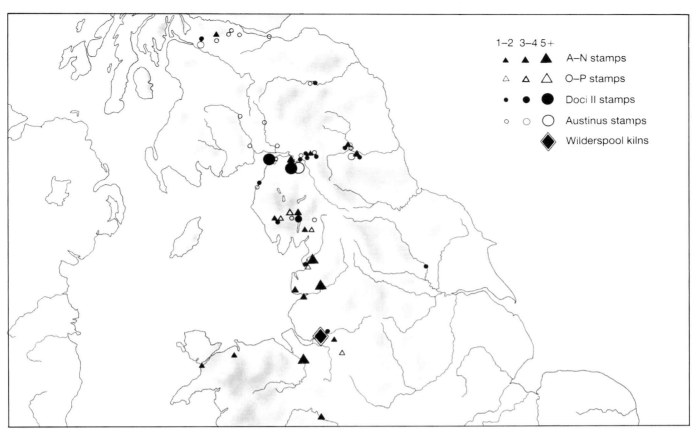

Map 6:33 Distribution of Wilderspool *mortaria* (letters relate to name of potter)

Plate 6:5 Two late-Roman pentice-moulded beakers and a bowl in Oxfordshire ware

Severn Valley ware

Severn Valley ware was manufactured at dispersed production sites and had both a local and a more distant market (6:32). It may have been produced initially to supply the legionary fortresses at Kingsholm/Gloucester and at Wroxeter. The name 'Glevum ware', which is sometimes applied to this variety of pottery, hints at the Gloucester connection, but is too narrow a term for the very dispersed production. The jars, tankards and bowls were normally light buff to orange when fired and were frequently embellished with various burnished areas or lines. The major production centre probably remained in the Gloucester/Cheltenham area, but the pottery is known to have been produced at a number of sites in the Severn Valley and as far to the south as Shepton Mallet. The potteries near Malvern continued in production until the fourth century and the pottery is common at Wroxeter and in the West Midlands/ Welsh Marches area.

Of greater interest perhaps is the spread of Severn Valley ware along the western route to the northern army command, where it is known to have been imported during the primary period along Hadrian's Wall. Here there is an indication of the way in which military markets were secured, as Severn Valley ware appears only in the central and western sectors and not in the east. Like Wilderspool mortaria, it was also exported to the Antonine Wall garrison for a brief period, and some later examples may derive from the Severan campaigns. This marked the end of the largescale dissemination of the ware and in the third and fourth centuries it was to be found in use in its original production area of the lower Severn Valley, while local late variations involving somewhat changed fabrics sprang up in peripheral areas such as the Forest of Dean.

Wilderspool mortaria

In contrast with the very broad market patterns of blackburnished ware, Wilderspool mortaria were distributed from a specialized production centre for a relatively brief period. The topographical advantage of Wilderspool on the River Mersey lay in its nodal position in relation to the transport systems. The development of service industries in the Cheshire plain is discussed elsewhere (6:42) and we are concerned here (6:33) only with the apparently numerous kilns that produced mortaria, flagons and rough-cast beakers during the first half of the second century. Because of its close proximity to the military zone, two-thirds of the Wilderspool-stamped mortaria were marketed to the northern forts. At least fourteen (and probably eighteen) named potters produced stamped mortaria at Wilderspool in a pink to orange-brown fabric, sometimes with a red-brown slip coating the flange. The potters' names are attested in Romano-Celtic forms such as Brico, Decanio, Nanieco,

together with purely Latin names like Ovidus or Ovidius. The distribution of their bowls shows a market that is clearly limited to the western side of the country. Apart from a few examples found along the North Wales coast, the distribution of the material beyond the immediate locality lies almost entirely to the north in Lancashire and Cumbria, and in particular on the western and central parts of Hadrian's Wall. In this area, for instance, roughly half the mortaria known from excavations at Ribchester, Lancaster, Ambleside and Hardknott derive from the Wilderspool potters. One particular potter known as Doccius, who is thought to belong to the Wilderspool group, has products attested at Birdoswald, Carlisle, Chester, Corbridge, Stanwix, Newstead and Maryport. On the Antonine Wall the stamps of Austinus predominate but the work of Doccius is attested at Balmuildy.

Oxfordshire ware

Amongst the indigenous regional potteries, which included the Colchester, Nene Valley and New Forest industries, possibly the largest was the industry based in Oxfordshire. From the first to the fourth century Oxfordshire potters produced a variety of red-coated wares, some very comparable with the plainer Samian forms (6:34). The industry appears to have expanded in the first three-quarters of the second century and suffered something of a recession in the third century before dominating a large area of the south Midlands throughout the fourth century. The most common product was a form of mortarium, but there was also substantial development in the production of colour-coated wares which after c.AD 300 increased considerably in their range until the decline of the industry. The colour-coated bowls, fine tableware and mortaria became the most important items within the overall production pattern and prompted an expansion of the market towards the south-west and into the south Midlands and East Anglia.

Glass production

It is probably true to say that no really elaborate glassware was manufactured in Britain. This is far from saying that the study of glassware in Britain is not of considerable interest. Fine glassware vessels were imported to Britain from different sources according to period. The eastern Mediterranean was the prime source of glassware for the classical world, and bowls, dishes and flagons were imported from there in the first and second centuries. The artistic standards were at times exceptionally high, particularly in the Levant. With the development of the Empire, however, it is clear that a number of glassmakers also moved into Italy, Gaul and the German frontier area. Thus much of the tableware supplied to the Roman army in Britain reached this country from Italy or southern Gaul, while jugs and bottles were

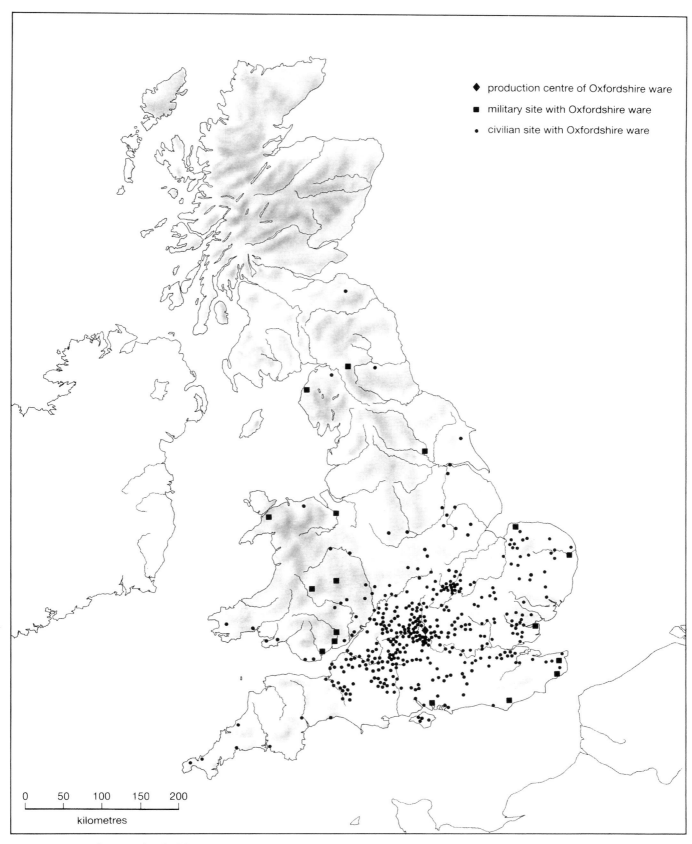

♦ production centre of Oxfordshire ware

■ military site with Oxfordshire ware

• civilian site with Oxfordshire ware

0   50   100   150   200

kilometres

Map 6:34   Distribution of Oxfordshire ware in the fourth century AD

produced in the Rhineland or nothern Gaul. In the late Roman period, the products of the Rhineland predominated, some of the imports being of very high quality.

Indigenous glass production consequently seems to have been relatively modest in both scale and technical achievement (6.35). Glass factories are little known, but examples are thought to have existed on the south side of the forum at London and Caistor-by-Norwich (*Venta Icenorum*). The relatively small number of furnaces, annealing ovens and working hearths at the latter site showed that the scale of production within the two conjoined buildings was not large and this was probably the pattern to be found in most of the urban centres in Britain. The glass-making activity at Wilderspool (a site further discussed in 6:33 and 6:42) comprised at least five glass furnaces and probably one annealing oven. There is nothing to indicate that the technical and artistic standards were more than modest, with the production of vessels centring perhaps on square bottles, the predominant form from the late first century onwards. Window glass was also made, in this case by casting molten glass in a flat tray of wood or stone which made the pane flat and dull on the underside and glossy on the upperside.

Plate 6:6   The base of an hexagonal glass bottle with the abbreviated name of the manufacturer in raised lettering

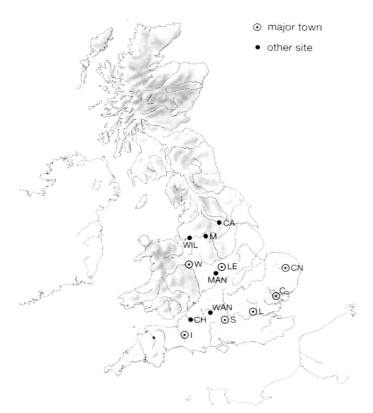

Map 6:35   Glass production sites: C = Colchester, CA = Castleford, CH = Combe Hay, CN = Caistor-by-Norwich, I = Ilchester, L = London, Le = Leicester, M = Melandra, Man = Manchester, S = Silchester, W = Wroxeter, Wan = Wanborough, Wil = Wilderspool

Plate 6:7   A greenish segmental bowl found in 1956 at Wint Hill, Somerset, this fourth-century product came from the production centres at Cologne in the Rhineland. The hunting scene, familiar from many fourth-century mosaics, was engraved in freehand and intended to be viewed through the inside of the bowl.

The distribution of tileries

The production of brick and tile was subject to many of the same requirements and constraints as pottery production (see Map 6:24). Yet there is a basic difference in the history of the two industries in Roman Britain. It has already been noted that the Roman army established and ran several potteries in the conquest period in order to supply some of its basic needs. Tile was also manufactured at a number of these military industrial compounds, notably at Holt (where there was a major legionary works depot), Brampton and York. However, tile and brick manufacture in the military zone of the province seems to have remained an army monopoly, as attested by the impressed stamps. In contrast the army's pottery requirements from the second century onwards were met largely by purchase from civil producers (perhaps via middlemen). The tile kilns in Wales and northern Britain were thus almost all of a military nature (6:36).

In the rest of Britain the pattern was somewhat similar to pottery production; in fact quite a number of tile kilns occur on known pottery-producing sites. Some of the sites with a single kiln or relatively small-scale production were no doubt operating to serve the needs of individual villa estates. By contrast, though, the largest and most industrialized production was centred on the major towns. The scale of usage of brick and tile products in the towns was enormous, particularly in the south-east of the province where good building stone was scarcer (cf. 6:37). Even in the Cotswolds, with its abundant supply of building and roofing stone, brick and tile were produced on a large scale at or close to the major centres of Gloucester (where a municipal tilery is known) and Cirencester (at Minety).

There is, then, a double distinction to be drawn from the distribution of tile kilns; firstly, between military and civil production, and secondly, between small-scale rural production and large-scale manufacture connected with the major towns. The tileries supplying the towns may, in some cases, have developed from estate enterprises, as is well attested in Italy in the first century, through the happy accident of their location in close proximity to an urban centre. Alternatively they may have been specially created by wealthy individuals or by the municipal authorities.

Stone quarrying

Quarrying, like mining, may have been developed and controlled in part as an Imperial monopoly. The Emperor Tiberius had accelerated the process of centralized control in Italy, and by the end of the first century AD most major mining and quarrying operations were under Imperial control. In looking for instances of procuratorial control in Britain, one possible site exists at Coombe Down, Bath. A freedman, an assistant to the procurator, is known from there and a large number of lead seals have been found.

Although some other aspect of an Imperial estate may be in question, the broad distribution of Bath stone certainly points to a centralized industry and the use of lead seals attached to blocks and columns is paralleled at Rome. In less specific cases one may argue from probability alone that, for example, the Greensand quarries at Maidstone and the chief sources of Kentish ragstone may also have been under Imperial control.

Many of the town sites in Britain must have had organized municipal quarrying. It has been suggested that the elaborate levelling arrangements of the southern approach to Wroxeter could be associated with large-scale stone haulage from a municipal quarry to the south. While this is plausible enough, at Cirencester and Aldborough the evidence is more positive. Large quarries existed immediately outside these towns which, from their position, must surely have been under the direct administration of local officials.

It will be apparent from Map 6:37 that the largest supplies of good building stone lay on the Jurassic ridge and to its north and west. The south-east of the country and East Anglia are comparatively poorly served and utilized a number of diverse sources. The incidence of flint and chalk construction was a particularly notable feature of these regions. Although comparatively few Roman quarries have been examined in detail in this country, the stone types found in excavation work reflect the natural diversity of stone sources across the country. As one might expect, the variations in resources led to radically different styles of construction in different areas.

Building stone in Roman London

As the capital of the province, London is of particular interest for the use of building materials both from this country and abroad (6:38). The public buildings in London and the more substantial private houses were built in Kentish ragstone with bonding courses of bricks. In places concrete was made by mixing lime mortar with ragstone rubble. A barge containing the remains of its cargo of ragstone was located near Blackfriars Bridge in 1962. A worn coin of AD 88–9, tucked in the mast-step as a good-luck charm, shows that the vessel was launched some time in the late first or early second century, whilst third-century pottery found with the vessel suggests a century of sailing life. The town circuit wall (5:20) was constructed in Kentish ragstone with an ashlar face and a rubble and concrete core. The bastions that were later added to the circuit were based on chalk rubble. This material, like the ragstone and much smaller quantities of both Kentish shale and lias from the south-west was probably brought in by ships as ballast.

Recent research has indicated the sources from which London drew the far smaller quantities of higher quality ornamental stonework which were required. In addition to the British lias and shales already mentioned, Purbeck

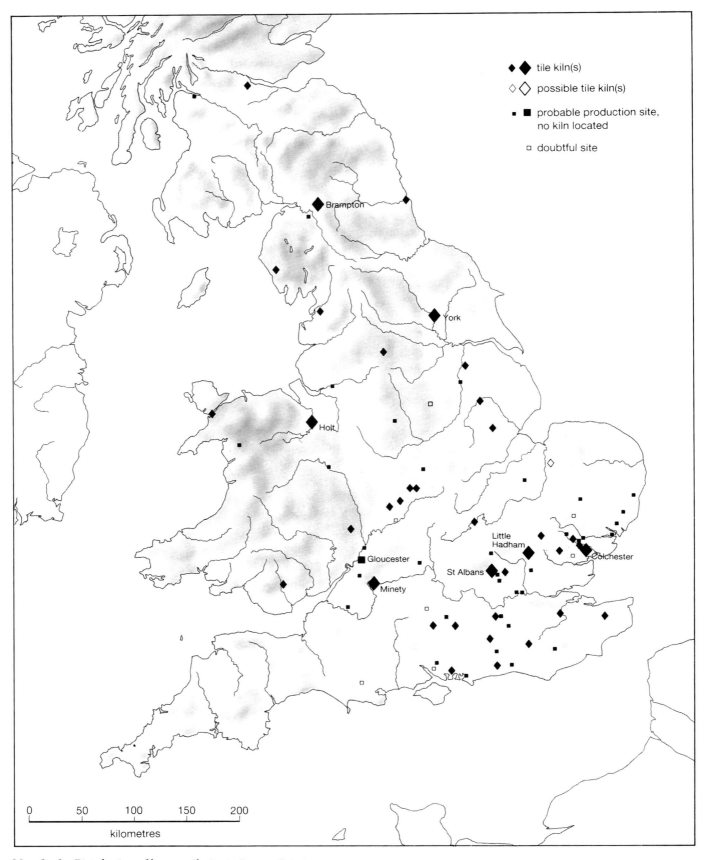

Map 6:36   Distribution of known tileries in Roman Britain

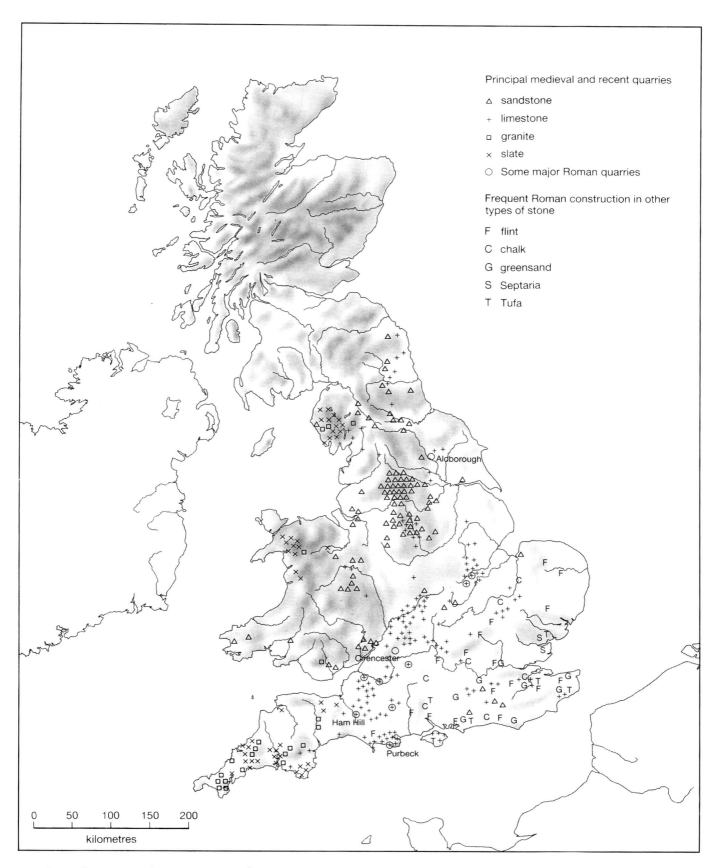

Map 6:37   Quarrying in Britain: Roman and more recent activity

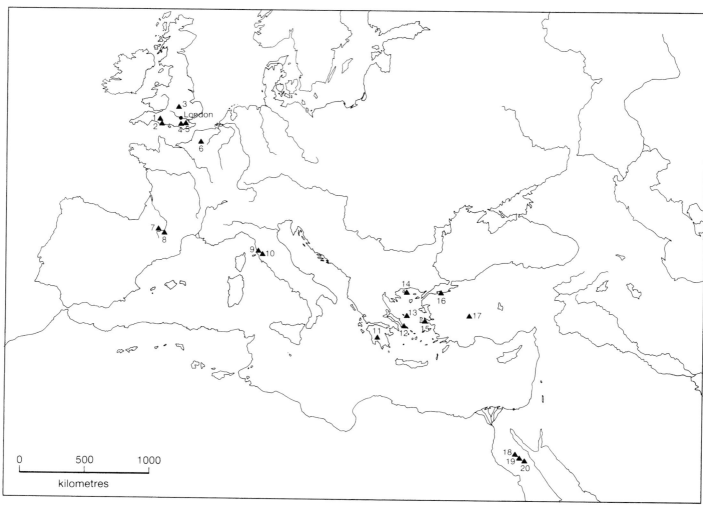

Map 6:38   Sources of ornamental building stone for Roman London: 1 = White Lias, 2 = Purbeck marble, 3 = Alwalton marble, 4 = Chalk, 5 = Grey Wealden shale, 6 = Black marble, 7 = Black and white Aquitanic marble, 8 = Campan Vert, 9 = Carrara, 10 = Bardiglio, 11 = Green Porphyry, 12 = Cipollino, 13 = Semesanto, 14 = Thasos, 15 = Portasanta, 16 = Proconnesus, 17 = Pavonazzetto, 18 = Red Porphyry, 19 = Diorite, 20 = Gabbro/Dolerite

marble from the Dorset coast was used from as early as the AD 70s. It continued to be used throughout the Roman period, but from the last quarter of the first century onwards a small but growing amount of imported marble is also attested. Although these imports include marble from Aquitaine and the famous deposits around Carrara, they derive mainly from the Aegean and Egypt. The Aegean stone includes green porphyry from the Peloponnese, as well as examples from the major quarries of *Proconnesus* and *Carystus*, the source of the white and green banded marble known as *cipollino*. Apart from some Phrygian marble, the rest of the material was drawn from the eastern desert of Egypt and included red porphyry and diorite. In sum, it is significant that the eastern Mediterranean rather than the much more accessible areas of southern Gaul and Italy was the major

source of foreign stone, perhaps reflecting the commercial influence exercised by Imperial-controlled quarries. The market did not decline significantly until the fourth century, although the bulk of the imported material recovered from excavations in London belongs to the two earlier centuries. It must be stressed, however, that the overall quantities of these luxury materials reaching London was small in comparison with the amounts which were traded within the Mediterranean itself.

Mosaics

We possess little direct evidence of the organization of the mosaic industry in Britain, but a certain amount can be inferred from the distribution of known mosaic pavements

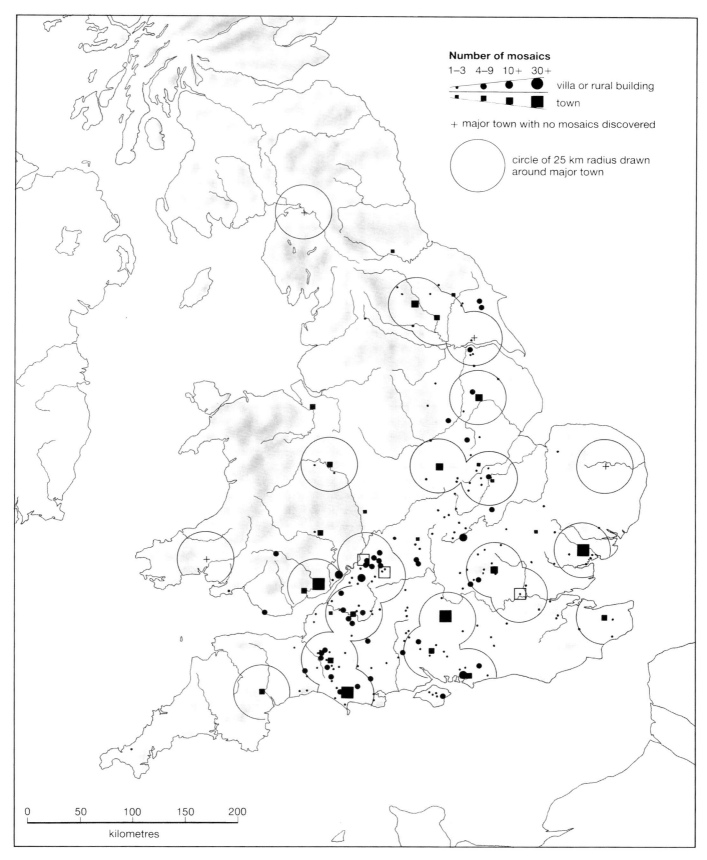

Number of mosaics

1–3 4–9 10+ 30+

● villa or rural building

■ town

+ major town with no mosaics discovered

circle of 25 km radius drawn around major town

0   50   100   150   200

kilometres

Map 6:39   Distribution of mosaics

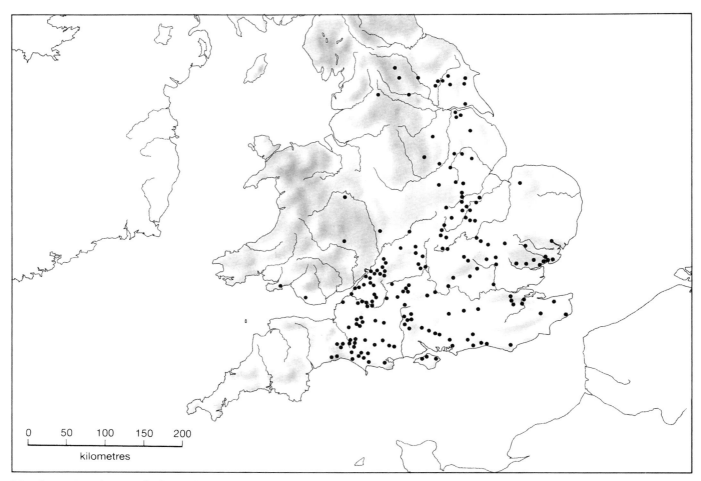

Map 6:40   Distribution of villas with mosaic pavements

and from stylistic affinities between some of them. The mosaic floor, involving a picture or pattern made up from tiny cubes of different coloured stone, was one of the most durable status symbols of the ancient world and hundreds of examples have survived to be recorded in Britain alone (6:39). As a functional floor, in a cold and damp province such as Britain, the mosaic pavement must have had many practical drawbacks, and the widespread distribution is a testimony to the wealth, snobbishness and taste for conspicuous consumption of the provincial elite. There can be no doubt that a small but significant industry was built up to satisfy the aspirations to grandeur among the richer Romano-Britons. Although many mosaics have been found in Roman villas in the countryside (6:40), the cumulative evidence (6:39) would suggest that the mosaicists were based in the major towns rather than being itinerant craftsmen. The largest concentrations of mosaics have been located in towns (notably London, Colchester, Silchester, Dorchester, Cirencester and Caerwent) and the vast majority of all known mosaics fall within the close orbit of a major

town. Quite a number of the mosaics which lie outside the 25km radius circles drawn on Map 6:39 were installed in villas close to small towns or to major Roman roads. We shall see below that some of the major fourth-century schools of mosaicists operated over a very wide area of the country. The point here is not to imply that the distance of 25km had any special significance to the mosaic schools, but to demonstrate that the mosaic industry was based primarily on urban workshops and that most villas were within fairly easy reach of an urban centre.

The chronological implications of the distribution are far harder to bring out. The number of exactly datable mosaics is small and, although our knowledge of fourth-century mosaics from villas is fairly refined, information on earlier mosaics and urban examples (which have tended to survive in far more fragmentary condition) is relatively poor. In broad terms, however, there are relatively few first-century mosaics. There was a steady growth of the industry during the second century, an almost total hiatus in the third, and then a massive resurgence in the fourth. The reasons for the

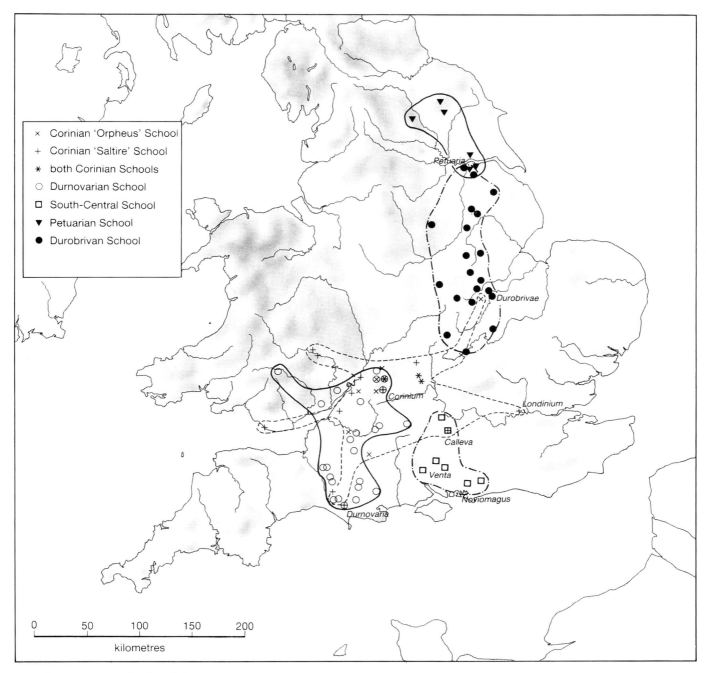

Map 6:41 Mosaic schools in Britain

paucity of third-century mosaics are imperfectly understood at present but it is not inconceivable that the decline was connected with the disappearance of the early schools (for whatever reasons) rather than with a shortage of wealth amongst the British elite. The dramatic revival of mosaic production thereafter may have received some impetus from the arrival of Continental artisans, who may have founded new schools at the start of the fourth century.

The fourth-century schools have been recognized by detailed study of recurrent motifs or combinations of motifs in the design of the pavements (6:41). The analysis becomes ever more refined, notably through the work of Smith (1984), who now recognizes six main schools, including two separate schools based in Cirencester (*Corinium*). One may presume that other minor workshops will be identified as a result of further research. The periods of operation of the different schools are to some degree uncertain. According to Smith (1984) the following approximate date-spans may be assigned:

The Central Southern School (perhaps based on Chichester/Silchester/Winchester)	c.300–25
Corinian 'Orpheus' School (Cirencester)	c.300–20
Corinian 'Saltire' School (Cirencester)	c.320–40/50
Durnovarian School (Dorchester)	c.340/50–70+
Petuarian School (?Brough-on-Humber)	c.340–50
Durobrivian School (Water Newton)	c.350/65–70/80

A particularly interesting aspect of the distribution of the work of these major schools is the distance at which they operated from their apparent main centre. Extensive pre-fabrication of design panels in the workshop, well attested elsewhere in the Roman Empire, was one production practice which facilitated this. Yet it also reflects the way in which wealthy Romano-Britons were prepared to shop outside the orbit of their own *civitas* for certain high-status and high-cost products.

One final comment concerns the areas with minimal evidence for mosaics (6:39). There is an understandable lack of examples in the military zone and in areas with low levels of urban or villa estate development. In this context the absence of mosaics from virtually all of East Anglia is an interesting reminder of the retarded development of the Icenian elite as the long-term legacy of the Boudican revolt. Their territory contains some of the best agricultural land in Britain and the failure to convert that potential into the conventional displays of wealth and status implies some form of discriminatory control by the provincial administration. The existence of really large Imperial estates on confiscated land may be suspected here.

Industry in the Cheshire plain

The Cheshire plain offers good evidence for the development of industries in a regional context (6:42). The production of salt and brine gave the area a particular significance, as it did in the Medieval and early modern period. Salt making is attested archaeologically at Whitchurch, Middlewich (perhaps the most important of the sites in this context), Nantwich and Northwich. At the last site there is evidence for an auxiliary fort closely associated with industrial activity. The Romano-Celtic name Veluvius was found impressed on the side of a lead brine-boiling pan from Northwich, and examples of the elongated hearths on which pans were heated have been recognized at both Whitchurch and, in a better state of preservation, at Middlewich. Iron-smithing is also known from Northwich (where much of the area on the south side of the fort was devoted to this activity), Wilderspool and in particular Manchester, where over 30 hearths have been identified. The date range of these hearths is the second and third centuries. At an earlier period many of these sites had their own potteries. This is known to have been the case at Manchester around the end of the first century and at Northwich at a slightly later period. Many of the products involved are closely comparable with material from the legionary works depot at Holt, south of Chester, and the style of the pots seems to have derived from these military antecedents. At Wilderspool the pottery industry developed on a major scale (6:33), specializing in the production of *mortaria*. Wilderspool is remarkable for the range of industrial activity attested and in addition to pottery and iron-making there is evidence for bronze-working and glass-making. Undoubtedly Wilderspool also developed because of its position on the Mersey. The lead pigs from Halkyn Mountain (6:7) found in the river bed off Runcorn were presumably destined for secondary processing at Wilderspool or Manchester.

Salt production

Salt had a far greater importance in the ancient world than it has today. Before the advent of refrigeration or modern additives, salt was the chief method of preserving food. This was especially the case in the north-western provinces of the Empire, where the alternative of sun drying was less practicable than in the Mediterranean. Salt was used chiefly to preserve meat and fish products during the winter months, when herds and flocks were reduced in size because of the problems of feeding them, and when sea-fishing was curtailed because of the weather conditions. The growth of large urban populations in the Roman period further increased the significance of salt, since the majority of town dwellers were dependent for their subsistence on food produced by others. As a consequence, salt production was frequently subject to Imperial monopoly or control.

The evidence for salt production in Britain is of several types (6:43). The Iron Age tradition is exemplified by the small-scale coastal operations, which were particularly intensive in marshy locations, such as the Wash (6:44) and the Somerset Levels. There is a great deal of information from the Essex coast, but this perhaps reflects both the good preservation of the production sites and the relatively intensive study of sites in that region, rather than an ancient primacy in salt production. The coastal production sites were characterized by hearths on which clay containers of brine were subjected to heating and evaporation in order to

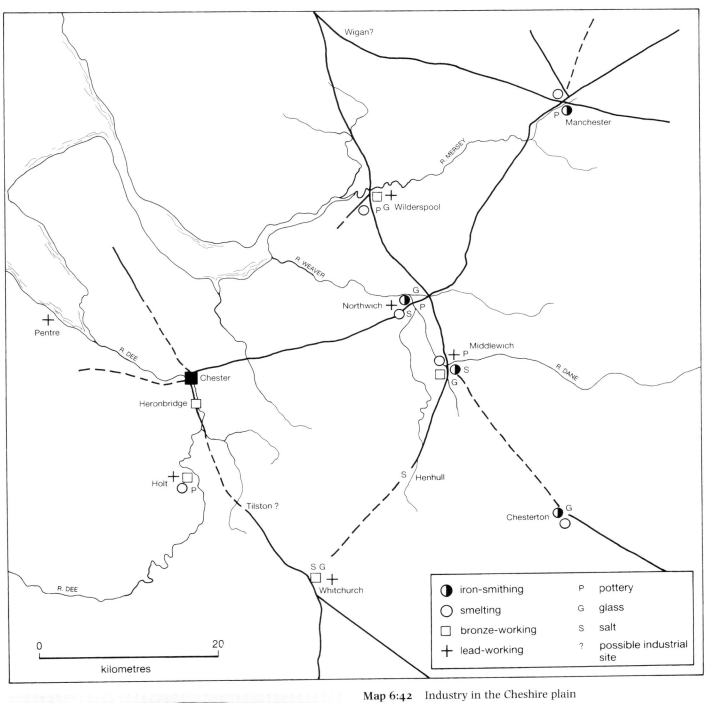

Map 6:42 Industry in the Cheshire plain

Plate 6:8 Retrograde stamp of *VELUVI* (*VELUVIUS*) on a brine boiling pan from Northwich, Cheshire

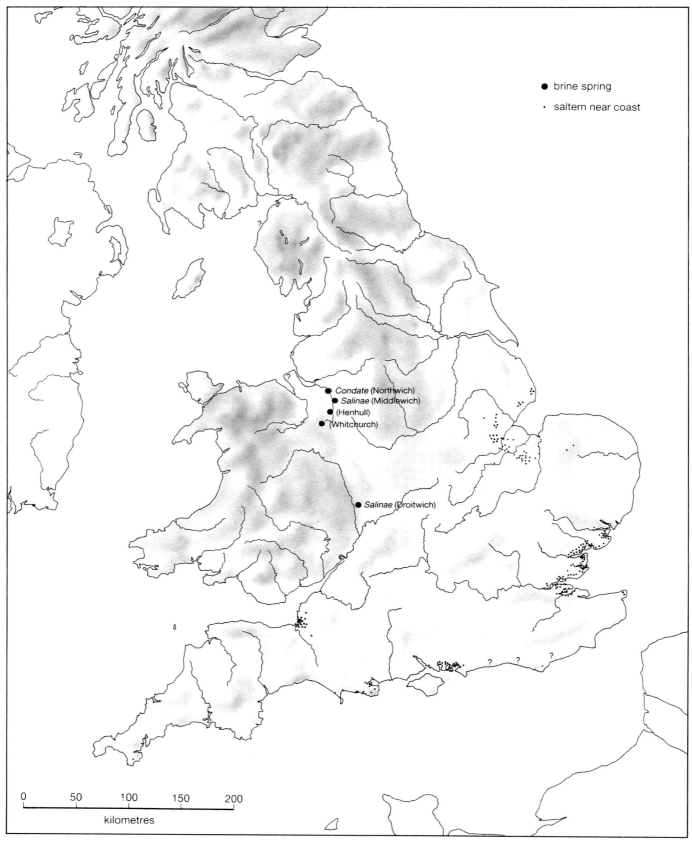

Legend:
● brine spring
· saltern near coast

Condate (Northwich)
Salinae (Middlewich)
(Henhull)
(Whitchurch)

Salinae (Droitwich)

0   50   100   150   200
kilometres

Map 6:43   Salt production

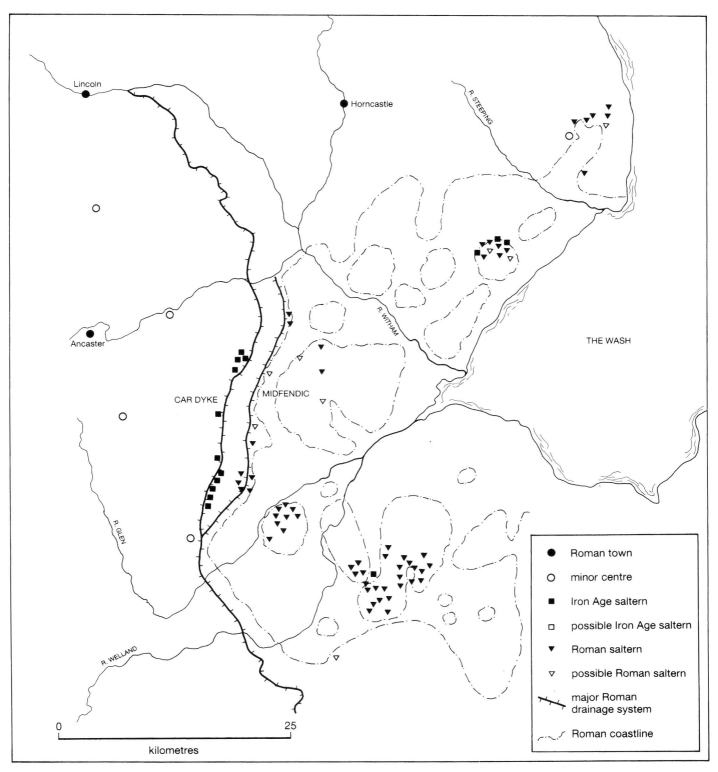

Map 6:44   Iron Age and Roman salt production sites around the Wash

produce small cakes of crystalline salt. Typically these sites appear as mounds of fire-reddened debris and 'Red Hills' is the common name assigned to them. The identification of the fired-clay hearth furniture and receptacles (briquetage) which are found at the sites and their easily recognizable appearance has led to the increasing discovery of such sites around the coast of Britain and at some inland locations. The activity was no doubt very much a cottage industry in the Iron Age, but the cumulative evidence hints at production well above the subsistence needs of the immediate hinterland in many cases.

For Essex, at least, some major changes are evident in the organization of the industry in the early Roman period. Many salterns around Colchester were abandoned and the centres of the early Roman production were located further north or south. Changes are also discernible in the production technology and both these factors point to direct Roman control or supervision of the industry in the initial years of the conquest period.

The Wash industry has been selected for more detailed comment (6:44) because it illustrates another element of locational change. The Iron Age salterns lay close to the presumed Iron Age coastline (near the line of the Roman Car Dyke, cf. Map 1:15). The Car Dyke is now no longer believed to have been a Roman navigation canal. In fact it seems to have operated in conjunction with the so-called Midfendic as a drainage scheme for this part of the fen. The result of this Roman scheme was the advance of Romano-British farming and salt-making activity out into the old marshlands. Some of the islands of higher ground within the Wash estuary area were also used more intensively as salt production sites. Yet again, the scale of the engineering scheme for the dykes and the consequent relocation of the salterns implies a high level of Roman interest in, and supervision of, the production of salt.

A second category of salt-producing sites needs to be mentioned. This is the inland brine spring, the most notable examples of which were at Droitwich and Middlewich, although there were a number of other sites in Cheshire (6:42). Presumably some of these sites had already been developing in Iron Age times. Indeed distribution of Iron Age salt containers from Droitwich reveals the economic organization of the industry at that stage. In the early years of the Roman occupation there were forts at Droitwich and Northwich and, once again, the implication is that the production of salt was initially taken into state control. Discoveries of large lead brine pans and other technical innovations at some of these sites demonstrate that production was organized on a huge scale. It is significant that both Droitwich and Middlewich seem to have been named *Salinae* after the Roman term for salt.

The evidence for the production of salt in Roman Britain as a whole is impressive, though of uneven quality. Much more work is needed to refine the dating of the main phases of activity in many regions and to assess the extent to which the Iron Age industry was affected by the conquest. The distribution of salt poses altogether more complex problems, since it is either invisible or disguised archaeologically. Trade in pottery has been described above, and it has been suggested that the transhipment of pots (and particularly coarse wares) was economic only if riding 'piggy-back' on the movement of some essential commodity. Salt was such a commodity, and it may well be no coincidence that some of the major pottery production centres grew up close to the areas of intensive salt production. The Nene Valley potteries, the Colchester industry, the production of black-burnished ware 2 near the Thames estuary, the production of black-burnished ware 1 around Poole harbour and the Severn Valley kilns near Droitwich could all have developed in part in relation to the salt trade. Some widely distributed wares may even have served as salt containers in transport.

FARMING

Distribution of woolcombs in Roman Britain

In the Medieval period Britain was rightly famous for its wool production and there is evidence to suggest that this picture may be projected backwards in time into the Roman period. Not only was there an item of heavy weather clothing, the *byrrus Britannicus*, a kind of hooded duffle coat, specifically associated with Britain, but also in the late Roman period an Imperial official was put in charge of a state weaving mill at *Venta* (2:16). There are numerous problems of interpretation that surround this issue. A *gynaeceum* or weaving mill might in reality comprise a dispersed cottage industry with a small administrative headquarters. The procurator of the woollen mill and his staff certainly needed administrative offices and stores for warehousing both the clipped wool and finished textiles. The problem lies in identifying *Venta*. Leaving aside *Venta Silurum* (Caerwent), the two more obvious candidates are either *Venta Belgarum* (Winchester) or *Venta Icenorum* (Caistor-by-Norwich), both of which are in areas noted for their wool production. The distribution of woolcombs simply strengthens the arguments for the choice lying between these two areas (6:45). Woolcombs have in fact been found predominantly in the Wessex chalklands or in the Breckland. It is in these two areas, therefore, that we should see the greatest exploitation of sheep pasture and the most organized wool production in the British province.

Distribution of corn-drying ovens

The distribution of the structures usually interpreted as corn-drying ovens offers another approach to understanding the Romano-British agricultural economy (6:46). The structures are simple in themselves: hot air from the fire in the

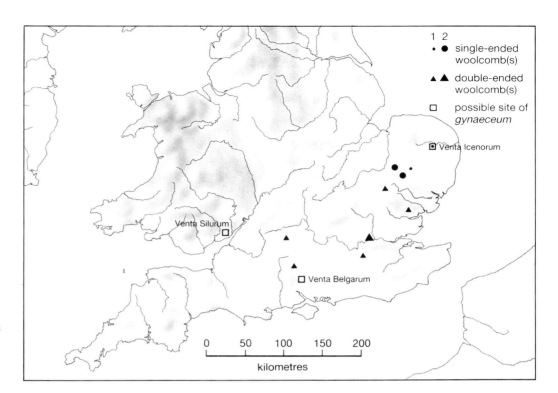

Map 6:45 Distribution of iron woolcombs in Britain in relation to possible sites of the Roman government weaving centre (*gynaeceum*)

Legend within map:

1 2
• ● single-ended woolcomb(s)
▲ ▲ double-ended woolcomb(s)
□ possible site of *gynaeceum*

Venta Icenorum
Venta Silurum
Venta Belgarum

0   50   100   150   200
kilometres

Plate 6:9 A presumed corn-drying oven, Carmarthen (*Moridunum Demetarum*)

Map 6:46 Distribution of corn-drying ovens

stoke hole passed along the central flue or flues before rising through a vertical flue to a chimney or vent. The heated floor created in the interior of the normally square or sub-rectangular structure was thus suitable for the charring or drying of grain, a process that seems, where sufficiently detailed evidence is available, to have been carried out under cover. Altogether approximately 130 such drying ovens have been located in Roman Britain. The great majority of ovens are to be found on chalk or limestone terrain and it may be possible to interpret these areas as centres for the production of winter cereal, especially spelt wheat. The possible developmental relationship between grain storage pits and corn driers remains a matter for debate. Although it has been claimed, probably on insufficient evidence, that corn driers date back to the late Iron Age, they only appear to become a common feature of parts of the countryside in the third and fourth centuries AD.

The arguments regarding the use of these structures are not wholly settled. It has been suggested that they could serve as pottery drying areas or as hop kilns in the production of beer, but the two most likely uses comprise the drying of wet grain or the essential charring of spelt wheat prior to threshing. The development of this class of farmyard structure in the latter half of the Romano-British period has also led to the argument that there occurred a climatic deterioration at this stage involving either the onset of a wetter climate or the increasing 'continentalization' of the seasonal pattern with more severe winters and warmer summers. This conclusion must be regarded with caution at present and it may be safer to assume that the rise of the corn drier related to the increased production of spelt wheat. In any case it seems certain that the areas where the corn driers are most frequently found are different to the areas largely dominated by sheep ranching in the later Roman period. Sites like Little Sombourne (Hampshire), which have been examined with a full range of palaeoenvironmental techniques, show that the late Iron Age bias towards cereal production remained and was reinforced in the Roman period.

Agricultural implements

The distribution of agricultural equipment represented on Map 6:47 primarily comprises the evidence for ploughs. Ancient methods of arable cultivation have been much debated, but the paucity of surviving material reduces the firmness of any general conclusions that can be reached. It is now known that scratch ploughing, followed by ploughing with the ard, has a long development in the prehistoric period, and remains of prehistoric ards have been found at both Lochmaben and Milton Loch in Scotland. Ards of late Iron Age type have recently been discovered at Walesland in Dyfed, where the site is thought to date to the first century BC, and at Odell near Bedford, where the ard probably belongs

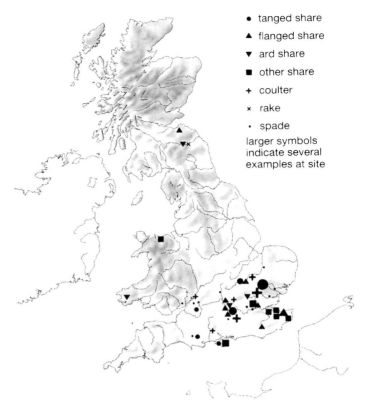

Map 6:47   Agricultural tools/equipment

to the middle of the first century AD. That the ard could survive into the Roman period essentially in its late Iron Age form is shown by recent discovery from Abingdon, Oxfordshire, where the implement is firmly dated to the third century AD. Even though the last hints at a strong Iron Age–Roman continuum, there was considerable development of the iron ploughshare, although much of the evidence is now regarded as late within the Romano-British period. Pointed and broad-edged shares of the short variety are known from Crawford, Caburn, Bigbury, Wallingford and from two northern contexts at Eckford and Traprain Law in Scotland. Three of the longer, flanged shares are known from the hillfort of Bigbury, near Canterbury, and three from the London area. The heavier, tanged shares are best known from the example recovered from the Box villa near Bath and have also been found at Hansbury near Northampton and Woodcote in Cranbourn Chase. Five examples with coulters to cut the ground in advance of the share proper are known from Great Chesterford and two have been found at Silchester.

The resulting pattern is unremarkable, concentrated as it is in south-eastern Britain, and is broadly comparable to the pattern of drying ovens already discussed. The occurrence of the majority of the less familiar share types in the London and Kent areas perhaps suggests that they were more open to innovative ideas derived from the Continent.

Plate 6:10 Iron implements from the Nene Valley

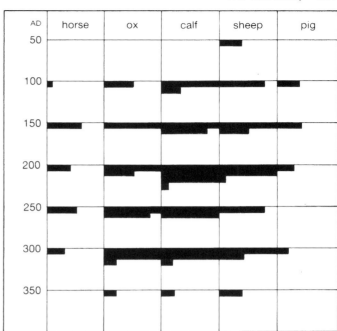

Map 6:48 Distribution of animal bones at Whitchurch (*Mediolanum*) against a chronological basis (each square represents a one-hundred animal unit)

Chronological representation of animal species in the Midlands

Palaeoenvironmental evidence in the form of animal bones can be of great importance in assessing the pattern of agricultural intensification in differing regions. When set against a chronological framework provided by excavation such material can point to changes in stock-raising, and two examples from the Midlands are used to illustrate this point (6:48, 6:49). At Whitchurch (*Mediolanum*) in the centre of the Shropshire/Cheshire plain, adult cattle always formed an important part of the food economy, but during the third and fourth centuries the number of bones shows a gradual increase, indicating that the good quality grazing in the area was increasingly exploited. During this period there was also a marked increase in the number of both sheep and calf bones. Assuming that lambing occurred from February onwards it appears that the majority of sheep were slaughtered at the onset of winter, that is at 9 to 12 months, while others were killed off at $1\frac{1}{2}$ to 2 years of age. The rise in the number of calf bones during the last two centuries of the

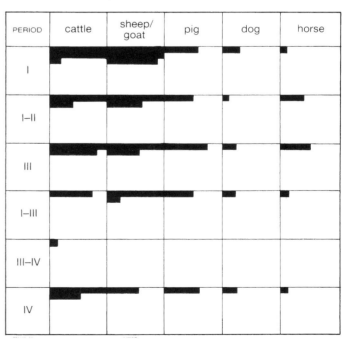

Map 6:49 Distribution of animal bones at Castle Hill (*Margidunum*) against a chronological basis (each square represents a one-hundred animal unit)

Roman period parallels the rise in the total number of animals but is much more dramatic. Calves were often slaughtered at around the age of 2 months at this time, presumably to meet the demands of meat consumption. Alternatively, they were killed off as young adults around 2 years of age. Throughout the Roman period pigs seem to have been the least important part of the farming stock. The virtual absence of red deer bones combined with the development of cattle raising suggests that woodland clearance in this naturally afforested area must have been extensive. Whether the development of meat production was a response to local or broader needs is arguable because, with the ready availability of brine for curing purposes, Cheshire would have been ideally suited to meet the requirement of military bulk meat contracts.

As a cross-check on developments in the East Midlands we might examine the material from excavations at Castle Hill (*Margidunum*) in Nottinghamshire. Although the stratigraphic contexts are not so tightly established, a number of points can be made. The animals were kept by a population largely dependent on arable production. Sheep and goats formed the bulk of the livestock in the first century on a site which had developed from a military base into a civilian settlement. Most of the sheep and goats were killed for meat at an age of 1 to $2\frac{1}{2}$ years. In the later periods the sheep and goats appear to have died at a greater age, thus suggesting that meat production became secondary to wool and milk production. In the period AD 250–*c.*AD 400 the decline in sheep and goats was compensated for by a notable increase in cattle raising. None of the animals there died at a very early age; some were killed off at about $3\frac{1}{2}$ years, clearly for meat consumption, but the majority lived to over 5 years and were probably kept for breeding or as draught animals. Pigs seem to have been kept as domestic animals, being slaughtered at the end of their main growth period, that is at about 3 years of age. This is the most economic time for slaughter. The complete absence of red deer again attests major clearance of forest cover in what was, like Cheshire, a naturally wooded area.

In this way we can see that the analysis of the faunal remains from two comparable sites can go some way to answering the underlying questions relating to the development of the Romano-British countryside. When perishables from arable production are involved, however, problems are greater. At *Margidunum*, as was stated above, the early stages in the agricultural life of the settlement were probably related largely to arable farming. *Margidunum* is one of the very few sites from the Roman period with positive information about crops. There, spelt and emmer predominated over barley in the first century AD, but this position was reversed by the third and fourth centuries. Oats formed a considerable proportion of the cereal crops at *Margidunum* throughout the fourth century, but elsewhere, earlier in the Imperial period, it appears to have been grown with rather mixed results. As palaeobotanical research on Romano-British sites increases, the analyses will no doubt become considerably more refined. Current indications are that the economic conditions of Roman Britain were immensely more complex and variable than has hitherto been appreciated.

7
The Countryside

In recent years our appreciation of the late Iron Age and Romano-British countryside has developed very substantially. To the long established study of often well-preserved field monuments in the chalklands of southern Britain has been added the major, if at times random contribution of extensive air photographic survey elsewhere. This has changed our understanding of a variety of zones including the gravel valleys of the East Midlands and elsewhere, the magnesium limestone belt further north and the Pennine uplands. It is now possible to proceed beyond generalizations centred on the introduction of the Roman villa system to a series of regional pictures which are the product of recent archaeological discoveries, whether from excavation, field survey or aerial photography. This chapter begins with examples of our changing appreciation of the rural archaeology of the late Iron Age, analyses certain aspects of the villa system and finally presents a selection of farms or farming landscapes on a regional basis.

Sidbury

As a starting point for this survey of ancient land-use we may turn to the chalklands of Wessex, where there is abundant material, often surviving as visible fieldworks. Pollen samples show that the climatic deterioration of the early first millenium BC gave way to warmer, drier conditions by about 400 BC. There seems to have been a tendency to favour sheep ranching rather than cattle in the husbandry systems of the time, although increased reliance on sheep farming also relates to other factors on the downlands. In a classic early investigation of Iron Age farming, Bersu's excavation of Little Woodbury in Wiltshire produced data which showed the existence of mixed farming with a substantial concentration on grain production. The inappropriate and facile dichotomy between an arable-based 'Little Woodbury' economy in the 'lowland zone' and a pastoral-based, so-called 'Stanwick' economy in the 'highland zone' has already been mentioned (1:3, 1:4). In fact the settlement record in Wessex is complex and, in particular, hillforts and their associated settlements vary substantially in their organization.

Much new material regarding the ancient environment has come to light in recent years. It shows that in the late prehistoric period the principal crops normally comprised spring-sown barley and autumn-sown spelt wheat, with emmer wheat and perhaps other cereals playing a lesser part. Evidence also suggests that rotation cropping was practised with both cattle and sheep providing manure. On the downland sites, as opposed to the clay loams, barley perhaps predominated. The fields represented on the map of Sidbury and its environs for instance (7:1) were probably ploughed with ards made of wood tipped with iron which were pulled by a team of oxen. The faunal evidence in these chalklands suggests a bias towards mature cattle and sheep production and there is growing evidence from sites such as Old Down Farm (Hampshire) to suggest that animals were slaughtered on a scale too great for local consumption. In this context it is interesting to examine the late Iron Age/Romano-British remains at areas like Sidbury with the satellite sites of Chisenbury Warren and Figheldean Down where there is clear evidence for both major ditch or dyke systems and also for 'Celtic' field boundaries. This particular example, which has parallels at Cawley, Danebury and Whitsbury, also in Hampshire, shows the way in which a hilltop nucleus continued into the Romano-British period as the focal point of the linear ditch systems that had developed around a hillfort in the prehistoric period. The layout, like that of other sites such as Wallbury (Hampshire), is assumed to show divisions between areas of open pasture and arable fields. That the pattern continued into the Roman period is established by the Roman date for the village at Chisenbury Warren, probably the finest example of its kind preserved on the chalk downlands.

Yeavering Bell

By way of geographical contrast the area of the Cheviots has been selected as an example of a pre-Roman landscape on the edge of the Millfield plain around the hillfort of Yeavering Bell (7:2). The prominent hillfort with its relatively well-preserved interior lies amidst an archaeological landscape, the extent of which is now much better appreciated through the help of field survey and aerial photography. The hillfort is enclosed by a stone circuit wall some 2m thick protecting an internal area of slightly less than 6ha (15 acres). Features within the enclosure principally comprised

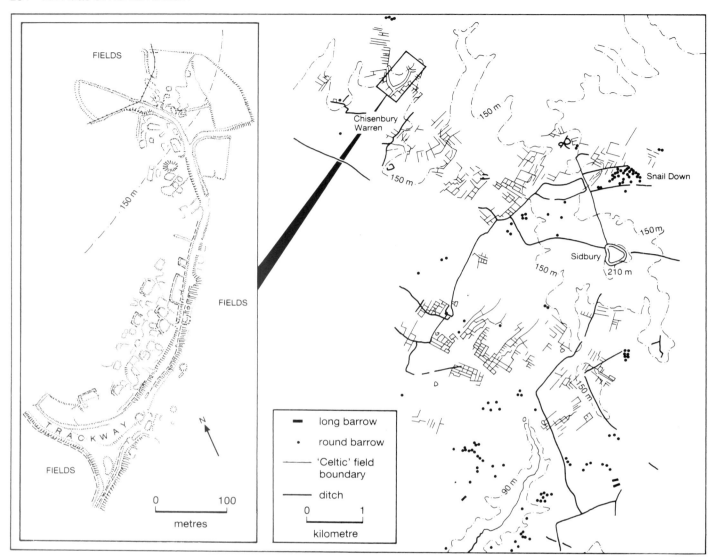

FIELDS

Chisenbury
Warren

150 m

150 m

FIELDS

Snail Down

Sidbury
210 m

90 m

T R A C K W A Y

FIELDS

N

0   100

metres

━━	long barrow
•	round barrow
───	'Celtic' field boundary
───	ditch

0   1

kilometre

Map 7:1   Wessex landscape: Sidbury, Hampshire. Note the presence of Celtic field systems and dykes radiating from the hillfort. The village of Chisenbury Warren is shown at enlarged scale on the left.

hut circles, probably of late prehistoric date. To both east and west additional banks and ditches created annexes. The interior of the fort also contains traces of a cairn which appears to date from earlier in the prehistoric period.

Additional survey has set the fort within a palimpsest of associated landscapes. Two well-preserved settlements with associated field systems are of particular interest. One, on the eastern side, represents an agricultural settlement that may have related to the Northumbrian royal palace at Yeavering, a post-Roman site which lies just off the northern edge of the accompanying plan. As this settlement is probably later than the late prehistoric centre, the other settlement is likely to be contemporary. It comprises a series of field and hut terraces following the contours on the south side of the hill. Their position below a gateway in the rampart strongly suggests that they may be broadly contemporary with a phase in the development of the hillfort. The slopes below the hillfort are also the sites of other settlements and field systems suggesting the former existence of farming units enjoying, to judge from their morphological development, a long period of occupation. In short, despite the relative lack of excavation, the variations in settlement morphology suggest that the area around the hillfort was occupied by a largely farming community from the Bronze Age (or possibly from the Neolithic) through to the Medieval period.

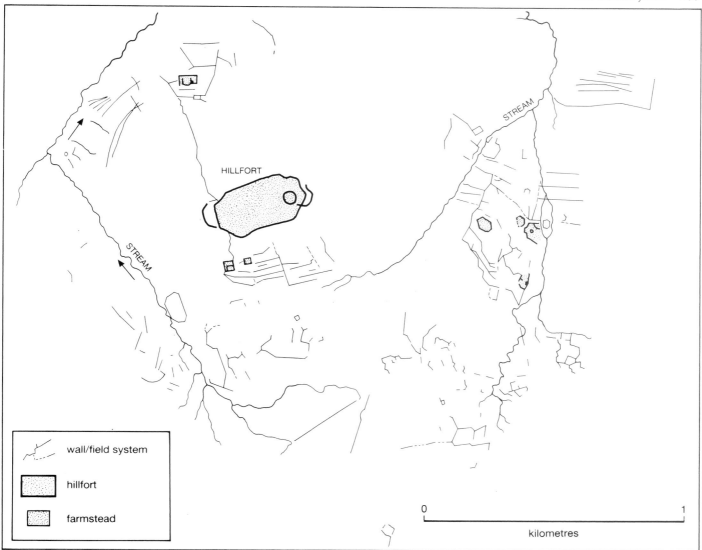

HILLFORT

STREAM

STREAM

wall/field system

hillfort

farmstead

0   1

kilometres

Map 7:2   Cheviot landscape: Yeavering Bell

'Celtic fields' and Celtic agriculture

One of the more obvious manifestations of late Iron Age agriculture comprises the extensive remains of so-called Celtic fields which are to be found in many areas of Britain. Field divisions as such are now known to have a long pedigree going back in the case of Dartmoor and its reaves (field systems) to the second millenium BC. The term 'Celtic fields', however, has a long history of semantic and archaeological misuse. The ethnic ascription was originally intended to draw a distinction between Saxon and earlier agricultural systems, although there were also overtones of an innovation by Iron Age immigrants to Britain. However this may be, 'Celtic fields has become the term regularly applied to later prehistoric and Romano-British field systems in Britain, particularly on the chalk downs of Wessex and Sussex, where they can often be observed in low light conditions or after ploughing. The term has remained in general use despite the recent dating of some systems on Dartmoor to the second millenium BC and despite increasingly sophisticated appreciation of the functional roles involved. As long as the term is not taken to indicate a chronological or indeed typological unity, then it can be accepted as a description of the checker-board land divisions involved.

Earlier attempts to draw a broad dichotomy between what was assumed to be the largely arable 'Little Woodbury' economy of Wessex and the southern downlands, and the

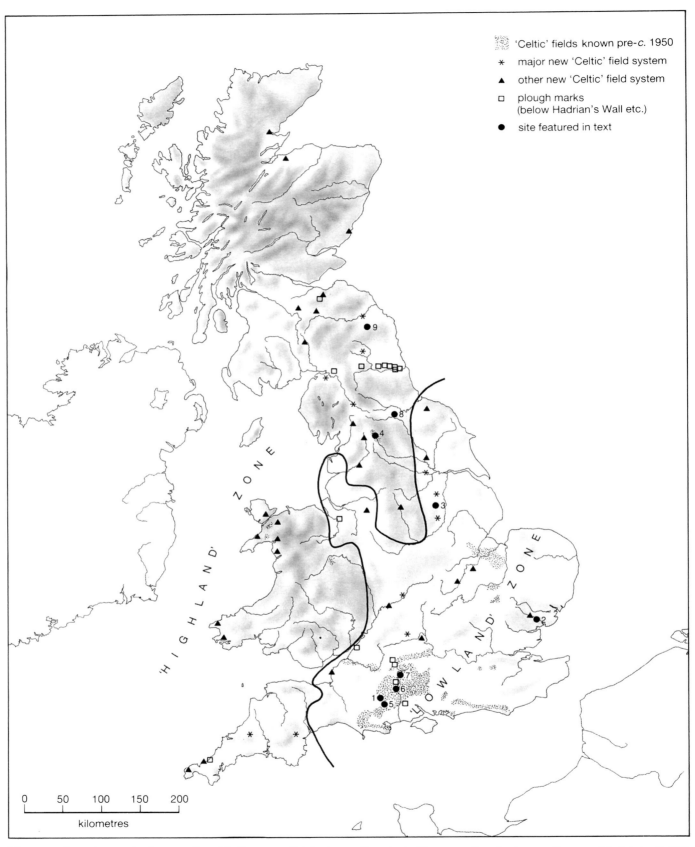

Map 7:3 Iron Age agriculture: 1 Berwick Down, 2 Colchester, 3 Dunston's Clump, 4 Grassington, 5 Gussage All Saints, 6 Little Woodbury, 7 Sidbury, 8 Stanwick, 9 Yeavering Bell

Legend:

'Celtic' fields known pre-*c*. 1950

* major new 'Celtic' field system

▲ other new 'Celtic' field system

□ plough marks (below Hadrian's Wall etc.)

● site featured in text

'HIGHLAND' ZONE

'LOWLAND' ZONE

0 50 100 150 200

kilometres

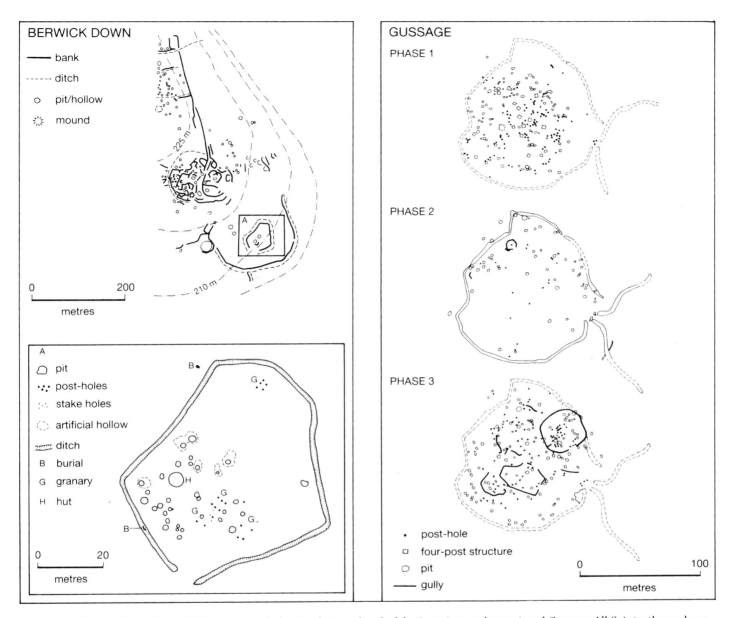

Map 7:4 Wessex Farms: Berwick Down general plan (with inset detail of the Iron Age settlement) and Gussage All Saints, three-phase development

pastoral 'Stanwick' economy of the north and west have to be modified. It is now clear that the difference between north and south was largely one of size and intensity of production, as is shown by the recently recognized extent of Celtic field systems and agricultural activity in the northern uplands. Map 7:3 shows that there is now extensive evidence for prehistoric Iron Age and Roman agriculture in the highland zone.

Iron Age settlements

The two sets of plans shown in Map 7:4 take the analysis down to a more detailed level and are classics of their kind.

The three major phases of the extensive settlement at Berwick Down, Tollard Royal, Wiltshire, were spatially distinct and exhibit morphological differences. The Iron Age settlement took the form of an unenclosed nucleus of round houses and associated features shown at the top of the plan. To the south-east of it lay an enclosed site of the early first century AD comprising a single-phase farmstead of huts and granaries (four and six posters) set within an irregular ditch that left space for a yard on its north-east side. The latest settlement in the sequence occupied the central area where a series of Romano-British buildings largely of rectilinear shape lay alongside a ditched roadway. These remarkable remains offer a rare example of multiple sites displaced hori-

Plate 7:1 Galloberry Rings in North Cornwall is typical of late prehistoric sites in the area

zontally across a distance of *c*.600m, rather than super-imposed over the same nucleus.

The extensively excavated site of Gussage All Saints in Dorset is another important example and has revealed much about the changing trends in the late Iron Age agronomy. Again three main phases were involved, spanning the period *c*.550 BC to AD 50. The earliest enclosure was dominated by the presence of internal granaries (four and six posters) and storage pits. The early phase at Gussage All Saints can therefore be seen as the most detailed example yet available in the Little Woodbury tradition. The later periods uncovered, however, show substantial change in the economic base. The drop in the amount of storage space in the second phase is partly explained by the presence of huts (features strangely missing from the primary phase) and metal-casting on the eastern side of the site. In the third phase the outer ditch was no longer operative and a small oval enclosure set amongst a variety of irregular compounds occupied the northern part of the site. These late developments were associated with moves towards a more mixed economy with some evidence for pastoralism. From these few examples relating to the development of late Iron Age rural settlement and farming it is apparent that the Iron Age people of Britain had already made a great impact on the landscape.

Plate 7:2 Celtic field system at Ablington Down, Figheldean. The ancient field boundaries in the pasture fields are shown up by the low sun but they are only visible as crop marks in the small arable field (top left). They are not visible at all in the larger arable field at the bottom of the photograph because they have been ploughed away.

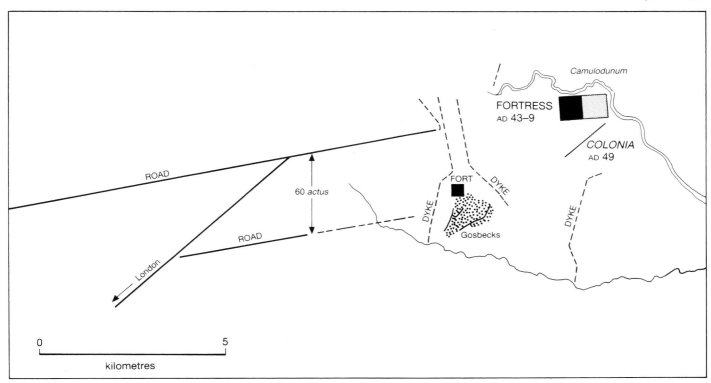

Map 7:5   Colchester and environs: an imposed landscape

Roman land division

The cases so far discussed all relate to the pattern of late Iron Age agriculture and its archaeological manifestations. The possibility of some direct Roman imposition of Mediterranean-style land divisions within the civilian province also needs consideration. Land use is a difficult issue which surfaces infrequently in the literary sources relating to the provinces. Yet one would expect examples of the gridded land allocation known as centuriation to have occurred in the newly formed province, particularly perhaps in connection with the foundation of the colony at Colchester. In this context land use is mentioned by Tacitus, albeit obliquely (*Annals* 12.32), where he states that the Roman colony of *Camulodunum* was founded on expropriated land (*in agros captivos*). Taken at face value, this indicates a takeover of tribal lands and the full implications have perhaps not received the attention they deserve.

Previous (and little-credited) attempts to trace land organization within the Trinovantian territory have centred on the area north of Chelmsford rather than close to the colony proper where the *territorium* might more logically be expected. As already indicated (3:4, 3:5 and 5:16) it is now known that the main tribal centre within the area of Colchester lay not on the Sheepen Dyke but to the south and south-east at Gosbecks. To this one might add the evidence of the Roman road system on the western side of Colchester (7:5). A development sequence seems to be involved. This is most clearly demonstrated by the route taken by the London–Colchester road. Instead of heading directly for Colchester, the road from London joins the Braughing–Colchester road near Stanway, well to the west of the town. An east–west road seems to have originally served the Gosbecks site. Significantly it ran parallel to the Colchester–Braughing alignment and was precisely 60 Roman *actus* away from it. The *actus* was the standard Roman land measure, and 20 *actus* divisions (*c*.710m) normally formed the principal grid lines within a centuriation system. There have also been suggestions of some land division on the eastern side of Gosbecks. In other words there seems to be evidence for substantial pre-Boudican land expropriation and reorganization in the tribal heartland of the Trinovantes. As such it may be seen as a major cause of the Boudican revolt. Comparable instances of land division should have existed close to the later colonies; outside Gloucester, for instance, small land units have been identified by excavation close to the line of Ermin Street, although no larger-scale elements of a centuriation system have been recognized.

VILLAS

Villas form an obvious diagnostic feature of the Roman provincial landscape and have been a long-standing focus for antiquarian and modern archaeological interest. The much-debated word 'villa' is currently used in archaeology as a description bearing a spread of meaning. Latin (and indeed modern Italian) has a number of more specific terms which might well be better applied. The semantic survival of the term *villa* as French *ville*, German *Weiler* and English *village* marks a shift of meaning that may derive from the great size of some villa establishments in Germany and above all in northern Gaul, where aerial photography has revolutionized our knowledge of the size and density of these rural centres.

The pattern of much of the southern Romano-British landscape centres on villa distribution, and Map 7:6 represents a chronological amalgam of many sites which might be termed villas. The overall pattern of distribution, however, may be seen as a concomitant of urban growth (5:11–5:15). Broadly speaking it appears that the development of an economic infrastructure in the countryside was a relatively slow process, and taxation together with the presumed creation of some Imperial estates may actually have militated against dramatic rural change in certain areas. The absence of villas, for instance, in the Weald and Cranborne Chase has been used to suggest that these areas were incorporated within Imperial estates. While neither of these arguments is sustainable to the point of certainty, it may be said that in contrast with the Continent it was not until the third and fourth centuries that the development of the villa economy reached a higher level.

Quite apart from the problems of possible Imperial estates there are examples of areas where rural buildings of the villa pattern were distinctly slow to spread. This is certainly true of the Cornovian area where the north-westernmost example of a villa proper lies at Eaton, near Tarporley, in central Cheshire. On the other hand, there are areas like the Cotswolds and parts of Somerset where the distribution of villas is relatively dense. To the north the distribution is predominantly an eastern one with a number of villas known in the territory of the Parisi. Beyond the Yorkshire Wolds in the north-east the pattern changes again, with sites that might be described as villas known at Castledykes near Ripon, at Holmes House near Piercebridge and at Old Durham, providing the few attested examples beyond the *civitas* of the Parisi.

There is, therefore, an obvious correlation between the distribution of the great majority of villa sites in Britain and the pattern of urbanization within the major areas of acculturation. The development of the rural infrastructure, linked as it was with the trend towards urbanization, must have been a complex sequence controlled by many factors including regional socio-economic considerations which elude archaeological detection.

Villa structures and landscapes

In all too few cases has excavation of a villa extended to an examination of its micro- and macro-environment. Yet fresh approaches such as this have enabled archaeologists to begin to evaluate the villa system in connection with the enormously expanded volume of social and economic data now available from Roman Britain. There remains, however, a tendency to view the villa structure *in parvo*, as an entity in itself. This trend stems from the study of the architectural evolution of the villa-type, with which this section must inevitably begin.

The development sequence from late Iron Age farm to Romanized building is relatively well understood at a number of places allowing, of course, for chronological variations from region to region. The simplest form of villa structure may be termed a cottage house, represented for example by Park Street I (7:7). In this plan, which directly overlaid the circular and sub-rectangular elements of its Belgic predecessor, the basic architectural component was a range of rooms linked by an external verandah which functioned as a corridor. The plan, which in this case belongs to the mid-first century AD, reflects the modest needs (and finance) of a farming family. Room functions and social arrangements are rarely demonstrable because of the general absence of well-defined internal doorways. Nevertheless, in those cases where there was no corridor such links must have been incorporated in the plan. The height of the structure is more debatable and in some cases it appears that the sill walls of the foundation supported a half-timbered superstructure. This class of site is now known in south-east Britain at Lockleys I, Little Milton, Cox Green I, Ditchley I, Hambledon I and Bignor I. The further development of the villa depended on the landowner's financial resources and/or the degree of economic growth in the area concerned. All the sites mentioned above except one became larger, more elaborate villas. Little Milton, however, remained unaltered and the basic class is also attested in the third/fourth century at Iwerne in Dorset. In areas where the process of acculturation was retarded the development of Romanized villas may have progressed no further than the cottage house.

The development of Whitton shows how a site in Glamorgan changed from a ditched enclosure with round timber huts into a Romanized farmstead still set within an enclosure (7:8). The transformation occurred in the second century and the stone-built residential building (centre left facing the entrance) is of the simplest variety. Two sites in Dyfed probably reflect the same kind of social and architectural progress (7:19), while at Penrith in Cumbria

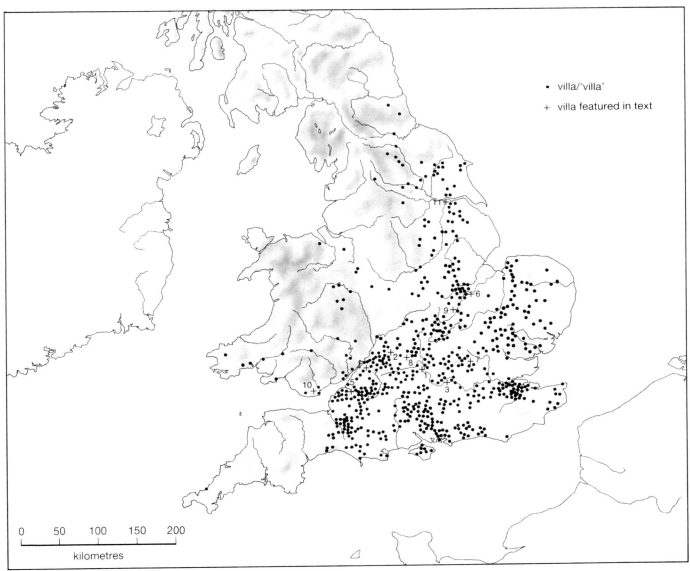

Map 7:6   Overall distribution of villas in Britain. Sites illustrated below: 1 Bury Barton, 2 Clear Cupboard, 3 Cox Green, 4 Frocester, 5 Kingsweston, 6 Orton Hall Farm, 7 Park Street, 8 Shakenoak, 9 Stanwick (Raunds), 10 Whitton, 11 Winterton

the move from round huts to rectangular structures (in this case timber-built) is not attested until the fourth century (7:23).

While the simple cottage houses shown in the previous examples continued in places into the third and fourth centuries, elsewhere the pressure of social developments naturally led to elaboration in the layout of the main building (7:9). The emergence of the winged corridor house represents a social change in that a distinction was made between the various elements of the family and other people through the allocation of public and private space within the building. This was achieved by the provision of a corridor running along the front of the building with projecting,

normally major, rooms at either end. The evolution of this kind of structure represents a development common to many of the northern provinces of the Roman Empire. This kind of architectural elaboration came increasingly into play during the second century and is well shown at Ditchley and Park Street. It is the more elaborate forms such as Kingsweston, Cox Green, Frocester Court and Clear Cupboard that are more typical of the group as a whole.

In reality, however, it is wrong to separate the villa, large or small, early or late, from its surrounding structures. The Roman villa at Shakenoak (7:10) lies in a shallow valley drained by a small tributary of the River Thames in the parish of North Leigh, Oxfordshire. The main building was

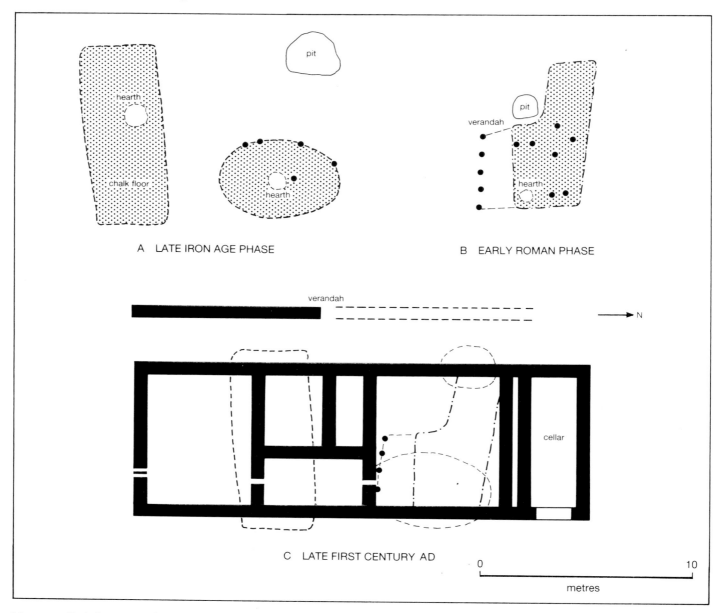

A   LATE IRON AGE PHASE

B   EARLY ROMAN PHASE

verandah

N

cellar

C   LATE FIRST CENTURY AD

0   10

metres

Map 7:7   Park Street, Hertfordshire: the late Belgic phases in relation to the late first-century villa

a residential block built at the northern end of the complex at the end of the first century and occupied until *c.*AD 250. The earliest structure on the site had been a circular timber hut. This was succeeded by a simple masonry building (B) which was enlarged by a corridor in the first half of the second century. It developed into a more substantial winged corridor structure with a hypocaust on its western side. The middle of the third century saw the demolition of two-thirds of this building, leaving in use only the four rooms at the western end and a small part of the northern corridor. A fishpond separated the residence from the large agricultural buildings to the south-west which had a more prolonged

life. They were first erected early in the second century, were twice rebuilt with increasing complexity and reached their largest size in the middle of the fourth century, remaining in use into the early years of the fifth. In the Saxon period the site was used as a cemetery. Building A sat in its own walled enclosure which overlay a ditch from one of the primary periods of the site. The principal feature of the associated courtyard was a timber-lined pit, and much of the courtyard surface was cobbled. In essence this kind of plan represents the penultimate stage in the development of major villas comprising buildings set around a courtyard, such as the example from Winterton below.

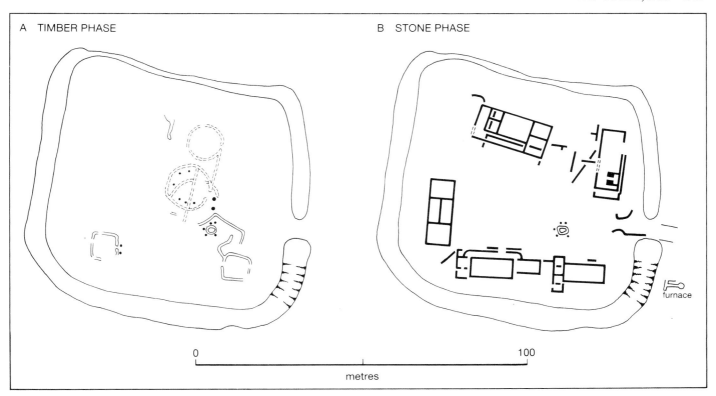

A TIMBER PHASE

B STONE PHASE

furnace

0

100

metres

Map 7:8   Whitton: the two-phase development sequence

Excavations by Stead and then by Goodburn at Winterton on the edge of the Lincolnshire Wolds collectively provide perhaps the best model of a working Roman farm in Britain (7:11). The earliest buildings excavated on the site (E and J) were both circular and belong to the earlier years of the second century AD. In plan they resemble the traditional round huts of the Iron Age. The third circular building (H), added after AD 180, may have served as a cart shed. Around AD 180 the site was cleared and redeveloped to an entirely new tripartite plan. The winged corridor house (G) was the principal, if relatively modest structure and stood at the western end of the farmyard area. Ancillary buildings flanked the other sides of the tripartite plan. Initially, the southern range comprised a small barn (A) which was enlarged into an aisled barn (B) in the second quarter of the third century. It included accommodation for both humans and animals. A further range of rooms (C) extended as far east as the boundary wall of the farmyard. Between the main building and the northern range there lay a small L-shaped bathhouse (F). The main aisled barn (D), like barn (B), contained domestic accommodation partly heated by a hypocaust system, but combined this domestic role with agricultural activities indicated by a number of furnaces. Other aisled barns, (K) and (L), lay south of and behind the north-western corner of the farm. In the mid-fourth century the principal house saw the addition of an elaborate dining

room or *triclinium* and was remodelled to face away from the farmyard. In this late phase the two main aisled barns, (B) and (D), continued to provide the accommodation for the working farmhands, while many of the smaller ancillary buildings were razed.

A villa plan, such as that at Winterton, laid out around three sides of a farmyard, is often referred to as belonging to a tripartite category. It may be more helpful, however, to use the terms applied to the triple division of buildings as suggested in the layout recommended by Columella (*On Agriculture* 1.6). In this, the main residential building is referred to as the *villa urbana*, clearly to be compared with town houses. The large aisled barn (D) is in fact a *villa rustica*, probably incorporating the living quarters of the bailiff or *rusticus*. The smaller barn with its great emphasis on storage facilities should technically be termed the *villa fructuaria*, the villa building designed to store agricultural produce (*fructus*). These functional, rather than architectural, terms should perhaps be preferred to generalized descriptions of such buildings as aisled barns.

All the examples of villas dealt with so far were first and foremost working farms in spite of the addition of mosaics and hypocausts to the main residence in many cases. Most Romano-British villas were not on a really palatial scale (Fishbourne being a particularly notable exception). The examples illustrated here suggest that the roots of villa

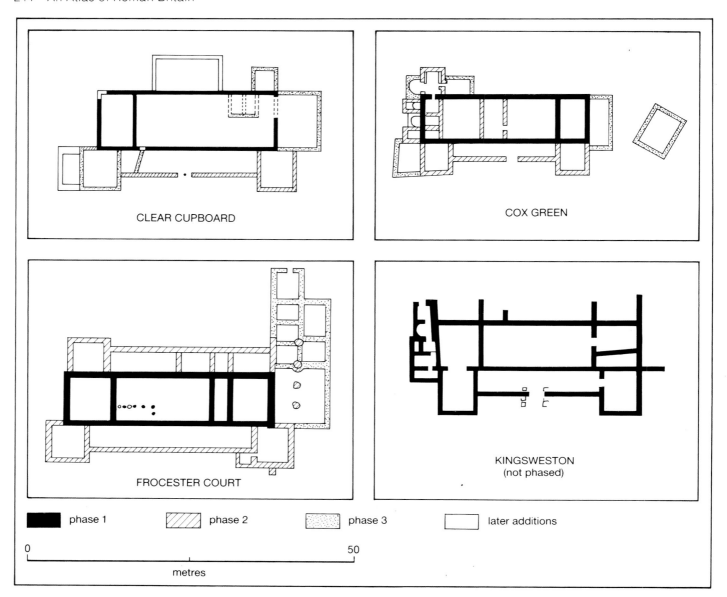

Map 7:9   Villa plans: main buildings

development lay to a large extent in pre-existing Iron Age farming communities, rather than in 'colonial' settlement of foreigners. The growth of modest Romanized farms (and even largish villas such as Winterton) would appear to reflect the success of the native elite. The social and economic orientations of villas become even clearer when their local context is more fully examined. A major archaeological objective in recent years has been the recovery of more reliable and detailed information regarding the surroundings of villa buildings. In this way it is hoped to build up a picture of at least the infield pattern around the site nucleus. At such places as the Ditchley and Frilford villas in Oxfordshire it has proved possible to attempt an estimate of the land-

holdings involved. Likewise, at Godmanchester, near Cambridge, a long-term programme of excavation has defined part of the small field system related to the main villa.

Evidence on an altogether different scale is promised through new initiatives, notably the comprehensive area stripping of the Stanwick villa (not to be confused with the Iron Age centre in Yorkshire) being done by the Central Excavation Unit as part of the Raunds project (7:12). This is the most extensive excavation ever carried out on a villa site in this country. The project is part of a detailed exploration of the historic landscape of the middle Nene Valley around the village of Raunds, near Wellingborough, Northamptonshire. The Roman villa will be destroyed by quar-

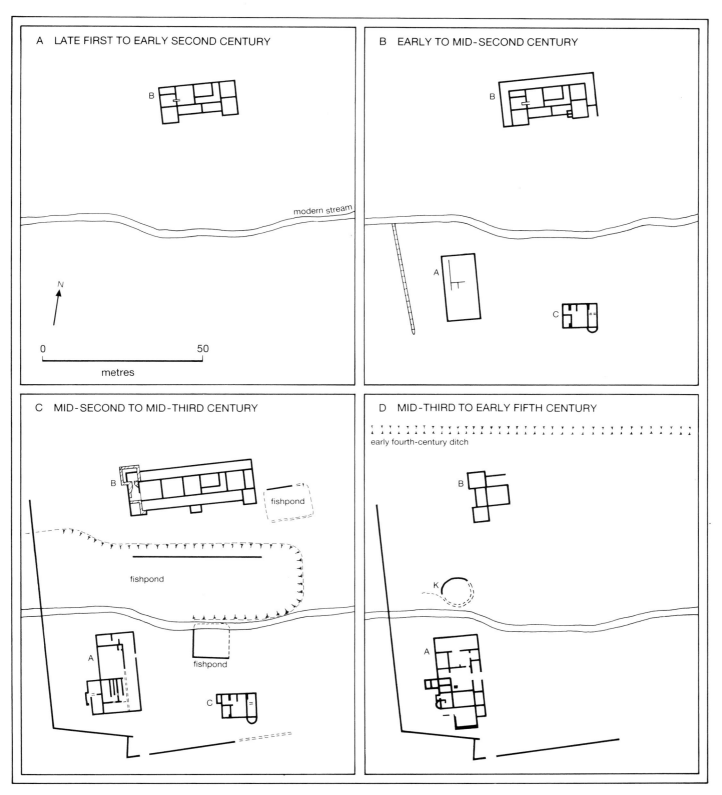

Map 7:10 Development of the Shakenoak villa, Oxfordshire (the letters designate the excavated buildings with the residential block north of the modern stream and agricultural buildings to the south).

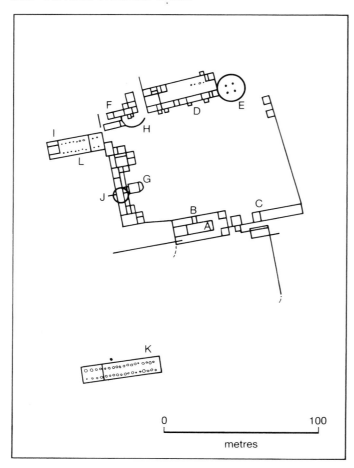

0   100

metres

Map 7:11 Winterton: a tripartite layout

excavation has already shown that the Stanwick site does not consist simply of a series of dependent houses around the villa nucleus. It also includes a number of separate substantial farm buildings laid out along trackways leading north-eastwards from the main site. Eventually, the survey and excavation will fill in the pattern of the development of a late Iron Age and Roman farming community which will give us a more detailed picture than ever before of the agricultural economy of the gravel valleys in which Stanwick is set. Likewise, an important aspect of the project centres on the later Roman period and the mechanics of the decay of the agricultural pattern and the movement of the settlement centre to one or other of the nearby Saxon sites.

The Stanwick villa lies in the middle Nene Valley. The lower part of this important river system has been chosen to illustrate the distribution pattern of villas in a broader context (7:13). The Nene formed an important commercial waterway in the Roman period (see 6:27) and it is not surprising to find one of the densest agglomerations of villa sites along its length. The sites tend to lie on the first terrace (close to the 30m contour) where many examples have been discovered through aerial photography and field survey. Concentrations of sites can be recognized both around the small settlement at Ashton and also, most obviously, around the major commercial centre at *Durobrivae* (5:21). The villa distribution reflects the economic interdependence of the urban nucleus with the lesser rural components, many of which, like Stibbington, had an industrial as well as agricultural function, extending topographically towards the fen edge east of sites at Longthorpe and the Ortons. It has been suggested that an overall site density of perhaps one substantial settlement every square kilometre is to be expected, rising to a higher figure in especially favoured locations. Domesday records suggest that population levels remained high in the East Midlands and in this context there is an argument for a degree of settlement continuity.

Orton Hall Farm near Peterborough (7:14), extensively examined by the Nene Valley Research Committee, offers an example of some form of continuity of settlement location. The late Roman courtyard buildings appear, broadly speaking, to have functioned into the very late fourth century, if not into the early fifth. Saxon pottery confirmed the presence of later structures, including pits and a possible sunken hut (*Grubenhaus*) on the eastern side of the site. Their location shows that they skirt the perimeter of the courtyard and also respect the latest Roman structures. To generalize, therefore, there is good reason to believe that the elements of the Saxon layout were controlled by upstanding Roman structures or other recognizable features such as ditches. A comparable but only partly excavated site north of Peterborough also suggests a form of continuity into the early Saxon period. Yet the circumstances whereby immigrant groups in the early fifth century could settle around upstanding Roman structures must have been complex.

rying in the next few years. Rescue excavation has shown that the relatively modest villa structures lay amongst a series of irregular sub-rectangular fields which are presumed to belong, at least in part, to an earlier farm presumably in the late Iron Age tradition. The villa structure was examined in 1985–7 together with three groups of buildings which lay some distance to the north. Geophysical survey followed by excavation revealed at least three enclosures linked to a number of trackways that surrounded the villa proper. The enclosures incorporated a number of buildings. In the earliest phase these comprised round huts, structures which were transformed later into rectangular stone buildings built like the farm at Whitton. The most substantial structure yet recovered, again set inside an enclosure, was a large house, probably the *villa rustica* or bailiff's house. This was set within a walled courtyard flanked at the two outer corners by two tower-like rooms. Along the same building axis, but at some distance away, lay a small circular structure containing a miniature bronze axe and part of a votive figurine of Venus. The circular structure is, therefore, best identified as a shrine associated with the farm buildings. The

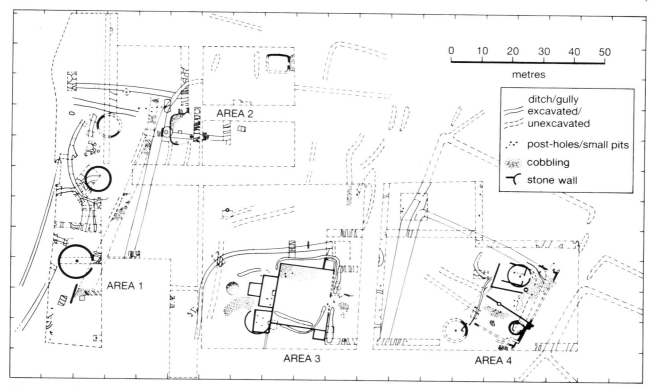

Map 7:12 Stanwick, Northamptonshire: the extensive complex of circular and rectilinear structures to the north of the main building under excavation by the Central Excavation Unit

Plate 7:3 Plough damage to the mosaic at the Stanwick villa, Northamptonshire

Map 7:13   Lower Nene Valley villas in their landscape

Until more sites have been excavated and analysed the question of early Saxon continuity is likely to produce more problems than answers. Nonetheless, there are in places reasonable grounds for suspecting a degree of landscape continuity between the Roman and later periods (7:15), although these tend to be on a much smaller scale than on the Continent. There, the presence of centuriation systems has fossilized land divisions to a greater or lesser extent,

ranging from the massive relict landscapes that dominate much of the Po Valley in Italy to the fragmentary Roman landscape recognizable round Valence in southern France. In Britain landscape history has developed in different ways and, as Orton Hall Farm demonstrates, is not easy to interpret. The landscape around Withington in Gloucestershire has been claimed to represent a land unit originally associated with a late Roman villa which passed as a unit into

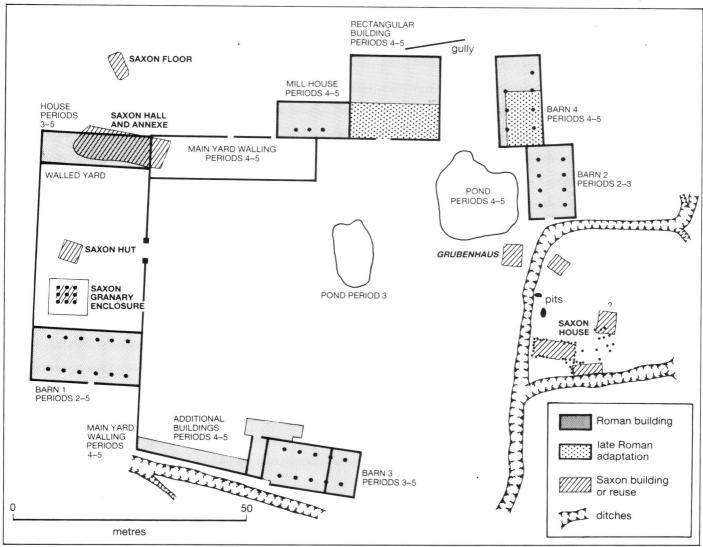

RECTANGULAR
BUILDING
PERIODS 4–5

gully

SAXON FLOOR

MILL HOUSE
PERIODS 4–5

BARN 4
PERIODS 4–5

HOUSE
PERIODS
3–5

**SAXON HALL
AND ANNEXE**

MAIN YARD WALLING
PERIODS 4–5

BARN 2
PERIODS 2–3

WALLED YARD

POND
PERIODS 4–5

SAXON HUT

GRUBENHAUS

**SAXON
GRANARY
ENCLOSURE**

POND PERIOD 3

pits

**SAXON
HOUSE**
?

BARN 1
PERIODS 2–5

MAIN YARD
WALLING
PERIODS
4–5

ADDITIONAL
BUILDINGS
PERIODS 4–5

BARN 3
PERIODS 3–5

0   50

metres

	Roman building
	late Roman adaptation
	Saxon building or reuse
	ditches

Map 7:14   Orton Hall farm near Peterborough

land held by the early church. A clearly nucleated area of a Cotswold valley such as Withington is the kind of topographical unit where a degree of continuity in land area might be expected to survive.

Apart from this, the continued use of Roman roads in much of southern Britain has ensured that they form an enduring landscape feature. There are suspicions of fossilized landscapes around the *coloniae* of Colchester (7:5) and perhaps Gloucester. Furthermore, Roman roads surviving in use formed obvious lines of demarcation and it has been suggested that parish boundaries in part of Somerset, around Ilchester in particular, relate to an axial road alignment. This may reflect late Roman land units based on villa estates and suggest the way in which the parish was formed; but

reasonable presumption is one thing, firm archaeological proof quite another in this difficult area of interpretation.

The impact of the Romano-British period on the British countryside has survived in a variety of ways that are difficult to present cartographically without substantial caveats. The major roads that have remained a feature of the infrastructure of subsequent communications across Britain are not shown here (see further 2:7–2:12, 5:23). What are indicated are areas where substantial areas of relict agricultural units (settlements and fields for the most part) survive as recognizable surface features. These landscapes therefore occur principally in the upland zones of the west, Wales and the Pennines. Additionally some landscapes also survive as surface features on the chalklands of Wessex and

Map 7:15   Possible relict landscapes

the Yorkshire Wolds. Map 7:15 is intended as a general indication only and in some areas proof of the continued Romano-British settlement of a prehistoric landscape requires detailed confirmation; likewise in some areas, such as the Yorkshire Dales, relatively little has been done to establish the chronology of the multi-period layouts involved.

REGIONAL LANDSCAPES

Air photographic reconnaissance has already been referred to in the introductory paragraph of this chapter. Its role can be seminal in changing the archaeological database of relatively unexplored areas, given certain prerequisites such as favourable crop rotation, opportune climatic conditions and suitable subsoils such as the sands and gravels of the river valleys of the East Midlands. At the same time repeated aerial photography over the theoretically less productive zones in exceptional weather conditions, such as the droughts of 1976, 1984 and 1988, can produce an altogether more reliable and balanced view of settlement distribution. The resulting patterns are not to be taken, however, as representing a fairly complete picture of ancient settlement since there are too many uncertainties concerning contemporaneity and overall visibility.

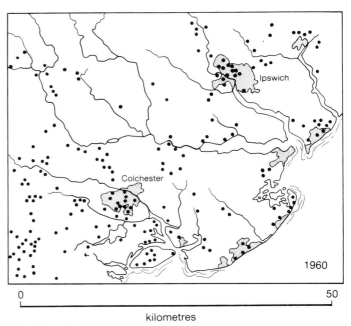

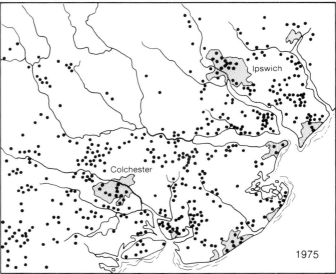

Map 7:16   The contribution of aerial survey: Colchester/Ipswich area

Essex

A good case of knowledge gained from air photography can be shown in the Ipswich/Colchester hinterland (7:16) where by 1960 air photography had established a pattern of settlement that appeared to be based largely on the river valleys, eschewing the raised areas, primarily composed of London clay, between the major estuaries. Later intensive block flying, however, redressed this pattern and showed that the settlement could be seen to extend relatively evenly from the river sands and gravels onto the higher ground of the London clays. This is the kind of developing information that one should expect from repeated air photography in an area, a point made in another way in the Solway area (7:24, 7:25).

East Midlands and South Yorkshire

One of the major contributions of aerial photography has related to the growing understanding of the East Midlands in the late Iron Age and Romano-British periods. Much of the area on either side of the Trent is highly susceptible to aerial reconnaissance and on the Nottingham side, for instance, extensive areas of agricultural settlement have been located. The area near the modern town of Bawtry shown in Map 7:17 is referred to as Dunston's Clump. The features depicted represent the elements that divided up the landscape into what archaeologists term a 'brickwork pattern'. In this case large areas were divided by ditched field boundaries running in roughly parallel east–west lines, with shorter connecting ditches running north–south. This is a tiny fraction of a highly organized agronomy which, on air photographic evidence, extended at least from the Trent northwards up the magnesium limestone belt to the area of Wetherby and beyond. Immediately south of Wetherby at Dalton Parlours a whole farming settlement has been excavated in the midst of a system such as shown here. This established that the chronological sequence involved the transition from an Iron Age farm taking the form of a number of circular huts through to Romanized rectangular buildings including one with a hypocaust. There is some evidence for continuing occupation into the early Saxon period. Dalton is one of the few such sites to have been excavated in full. Sample excavation elsewhere in the brickwork field systems has shown that most of the farms such as Dunston's Clump were occupied in the second and third centuries AD. The development of the farm at Dunston is clear enough and one might expect the majority of the Roman farms located in Nottinghamshire, South Yorkshire and North Yorkshire to follow this chronological sequence.

Thames Valley, Oxfordshire

Aerial photography has also been the key to the increased understanding of gravel areas such as the Welland, Ouse and Thames valleys. In the last in particular major cropmark concentrations have been known since the pioneer photography of Allen in the 1930s. Archaeology has been slow to follow up this work, but there is now emerging a picture of the agricultural organization integrating a hierarchy of different types of settlement. In the Thames Valley the evidence now shows that there were major villages, such as Ashville, where intensive crop production took place in the Iron Age period, alongside pastoral sites generally of a smaller size often situated on the flood plains. Barton Court (Oxfordshire.) was a large site in the late Iron Age (7:18),

arable cultivation having been established as early as the period of grooved-ware, at the same time as on other sites such as Mount Farm, Dorchester-on-Thames, in the same county. Excavation has produced abundant plant remains and the processing debris includes waste material from crops. In contrast the sites that are thought to be more related to pastoralism have tended to produce only weeds and chaff. A priori therefore there is some evidence to suggest that the largest sites such as Barton Court acted as the cereal producers for a rural economy by supplying other, smaller sites. Barton Court with its complex development pattern, now largely understood through excavation by the Oxfordshire Archaeological Unit, is a fine example of a class of site that is becoming increasingly known and understood along the river gravels of south-east Britain. The confluences of the Thames and its tributaries have attracted substantial settlement foci around Lechlade, Stanton Harcourt, Cassington, Oxford and Dorchester.

Barton Court Farm at the confluence of the Ock and the Thames at Abingdon forms part of this pattern. In the second half of the first century AD a trapezoidal enclosure replaced the Iron Age farmstead on the site. The 95m by 52m compound was divided by a central ditch with an offset entrance. The southern half of the enclosure contained an elongated rectangular timber building. Six-post structures flanking the southern entrance are interpreted as grain stores. Subsequent reconstruction across the third and fourth centuries saw the main building remodelled as an elongated farmhouse or cottage villa reminiscent of Whitton (7:8), Cwmbrwyn, Trelissey or indeed Piercebridge. The cottage villa comprised eight rooms with a feature interpreted as a cellar. The main site was set within a ditched enclosure and further surrounded by ditched paddocks covering 1.4ha. In turn within these features lay wells, waterholes, corn-drying ovens and, something first noticed at the Hambledon villa, an area of infant burials. The site continued as a farming centre in part of the Saxon period, but the group of *Grubenhäuser* concerned were located to the south-east and were not directly superimposed on their Roman predecessor (compare with Orton Hall Farm 7:14).

Dyfed, Wales

South-west Wales (Dyfed) abounds with small defended enclosures, most of which apparently began life in the latter half of the Iron Age. A large percentage of these settlements survive as well-preserved earthworks on uplands although a number have also been recovered through air photography on lower-lying ground. To this may be added many promontory forts along the indented coastline near St Davids. Map 7:19 shows those sites where some form of occupation in the Roman period is attested, normally through the presence of pottery, although very few sites have been subjected

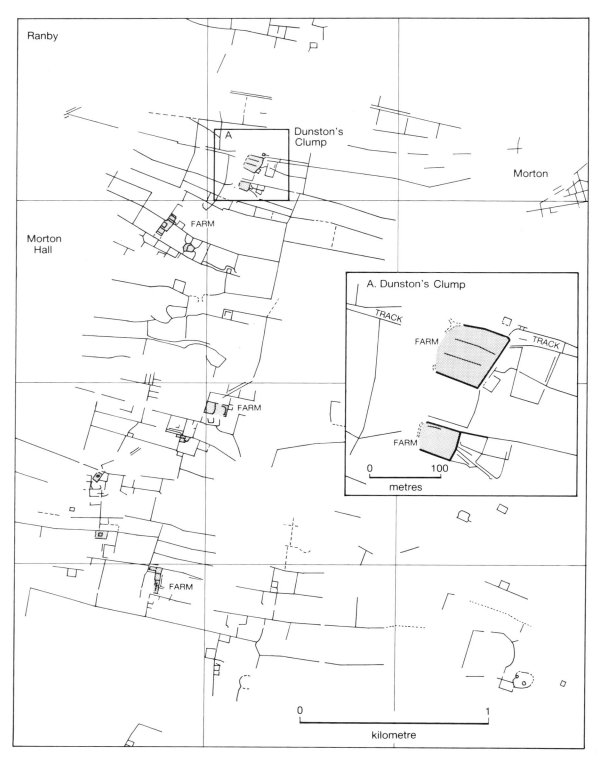

Ranby

A

Dunston's
Clump

Morton

Morton
Hall

FARM

FARM

FARM

A. Dunston's Clump

TRACK

FARM

TRACK

FARM

0   100

metres

0   1

kilometre

Map 7:17   East Midlands: Dunston's Clump, Nottinghamshire

Map 7:18 Thames Valley: Barton Court Farm, Abingdon, Oxfordshire

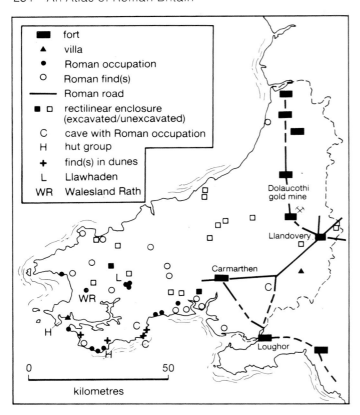

Map 7:19   Dyfed: sites with Romano-British material

Plate 7:4   Greenala Point promontory fort (near Stackpole, Pembrokeshire, viewed from the south-east). This strongly defended promontory consists of a single main defence with an internal entrance on the west. There are additional defences on the north and west, the latter enclosing a small 'annexe' outside the entrance. This monument is typical of the many promontory forts of the area, and would date from the Iron Age, although some earlier occupation, as well as settlement during the Roman period, is highly likely.

to excavation. In reviewing the body of evidence, however, it is essential to look back at the origins of these sites, which seem to belong in several cases to the last two centuries BC.

Much new evidence has been obtained from around Llawhaden, where a number of these small hillforts, comparable with Irish 'raths' and Cornish 'rounds', have been investigated in an intensive landscape study by the Dyfed Archaeological Trust. In this study area, for example, three such sites (Broadway, Pilcornswel and Holgan) were apparently the three early nuclei in a sequence of these miniature hillforts, the life of which continued into the late Iron Age. These extensively defended sites seem to have given way to a series of 'ring' forts in this particular area. The three sites in question, Dan-y-Coed, Woodside and Drim, lay close together, the first two a mere 60m apart – a proximity which perhaps reflects the Celtic and later Welsh custom of partible inheritance whereby land was shared between the sons of the family. The sites had elaborate entrances reminiscent of the arrangement at certain hillforts and the interiors were given over to a mixture of round-houses and granaries. The structural sequences of the interior are complex and involve many rebuildings of both the circular hut arrangements and the sub-rectangular post-hole layouts assumed to have supported granaries.

The plan of Walesland Rath revealed by total stripping confirms the character of the internal arrangement of this class of sites. The centrally placed hut at Woodside perhaps indicates something of the social hierarchy of the inhabitants, whose status was reflected by the well-metalled approach roadway and the associated elaborate banks and ditches. The neighbouring site of Dan-y-Coed did not exhibit the same internal organization and it is arguable that at some stage it may have been a defended food store rather than a formalized habitation. The defences appear to have been a less significant part of the site and the main building comprised a sub-rectangular house and cow-barn. The evidence for occupation in the Roman period depends on a few sherds of pottery. Closer to the *civitas* capital of *Moridunum Demetarum* (Carmarthen) two sites show evidence of a greater degree of Romanization in structural terms. At Trelissy, near Tenby, and Cwmbrwyn further east there is evidence for Roman-style rectangular stone buildings set within the kind of roughly circular enclosures discussed above (7:8).

Although these 'Romanized' sites may come under the rubric of 'villas', they are some way removed from the better appointed dwellings of, for instance, the Cotswolds, a reflection no doubt of the differing regional patterns of rural development.

Snowdonia, Wales

In the area of Snowdonia (7:20) associated with the Ordovices tribe the level of acculturation was marginal. Through

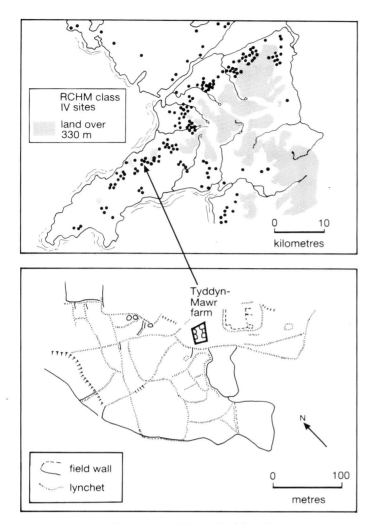

Map 7:20 Snowdonia: upland farms, Tyddyn-Mawr

enclosures, concentric sites with circular huts set inside an outer enclosure and, the main category, enclosed homesteads associated with terraced or lyncheted fields. The enclosed homesteads have been termed Class IV sites. This last category is the one that has exhibited the largest amount of Roman artefactual material and may be compared in essentials with the lynchet(s) raths previously mentioned in Dyfed. The Class IV sites are all associated with terraced fields and are normally to be found at heights up to 240m on the drier soils. The oval enclosed homesteads of this type (Class IVb) tend to lie on average slightly higher than the rest, as do thin-walled oval enclosures (Class IVii). The unenclosed settlements (Classes IIa and IIc) lie on the poorest soils and it is clear that they cannot have supported significant cultivation, owing to both the poor soils and the problems of exposure. On the other hand, the lowland, unenclosed groups and enclosed homesteads took advantage of better land, evidently to support higher quality cultivation and pasture. Estimates of the chronologies involved differ, but most commentators suggest an Iron Age and Roman date for Class II settlements, although Hogg would prefer to see this class predominantly in the Roman period. There are obvious problems in a dating system which is extensively based on morphological parallels with upland settlement elsewhere. Some of the Class IV sites undoubtedly relate to the Roman period at least, but in most cases it is perhaps better to assume initially a broad date range allowing for a complex development (as now attested archaeologically at Tyddyn-Mawr and more particularly Cefn Graeanog following excavation by the Gwynedd Archaeological Trust).

Northern England

In recent years there have been major advances in our knowledge of ancient settlement and agriculture in the north. Part of the potential richness of the area has long been apparent from field systems such as that in the Grassington area of the Yorkshire Dales (7:21). It forms the largest and most coherent field system surviving in the Pennine uplands, although there are many examples of the same kind of feature on a lesser scale. Aerial photography, particularly under snow conditions, has shown a pattern of small, normally sub-rectangular fields, organized between a system of trackways. Little can be said about the agronomy involved, except there must be a presumption of arable as well as pastoral farming. This field system in the upper valley of the River Wharfe, some 21km (13 miles) north-west of Ilkley, extends for over 100ha (250 acres) along one of the limestone benches overlooking the river valley. Dating evidence shows that the fields and farms were cultivated between the second and fourth centuries AD. Some of the pottery recovered from the fields may have been transported there as part of a manuring process in an attempt to improve the poor quality of the soil thinly covering the limestone

its continuing isolation, relative lack of development and the durability of many features in upland agriculture, however, there is plentiful information on the distribution of ancient farms. The marginal environment of Snowdonia is the controlling factor in this area, yet its effects are not necessarily constant. Environmental thresholds can fluctuate to a considerable degree and the success of a farm is limited by the environmental potential of its location. Early frost, a poor growing season, excessive rain at sensitive growing periods taken along with relative poverty of the soils substantially affect agricultural potential. Much archaeological research has been undertaken, notably by the Royal Commission (Wales) and the Ordnance Survey, Archaeology Division. Several hundred farms and their associated field systems have been examined and provisionally classified, principally in terms of their structural morphology. The material comprises isolated huts, unenclosed huts associated with walled

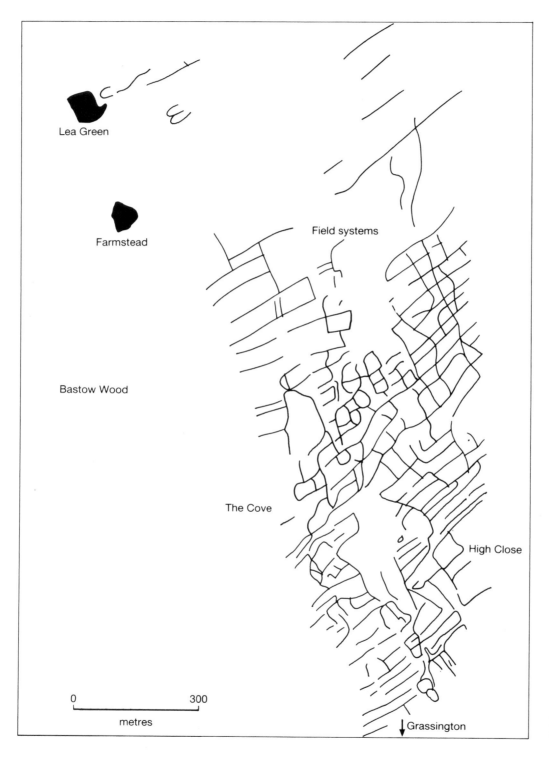

Lea Green

Farmstead

Field systems

Bastow Wood

The Cove

High Close

0   300

metres

↓ Grassington

Map 7:21 Grassington field systems, North Yorkshire

Plate 7:5 a and **b**   Ancient field systems at Grassington, in the Yorkshire Dales. The upper photograph contrasts the remains of small ancient fields (see Map 7:21) picked out by deep shadow with the present stone walls. The lower picture shows the settlement of Lea Green shown on the upper left of the same plan.

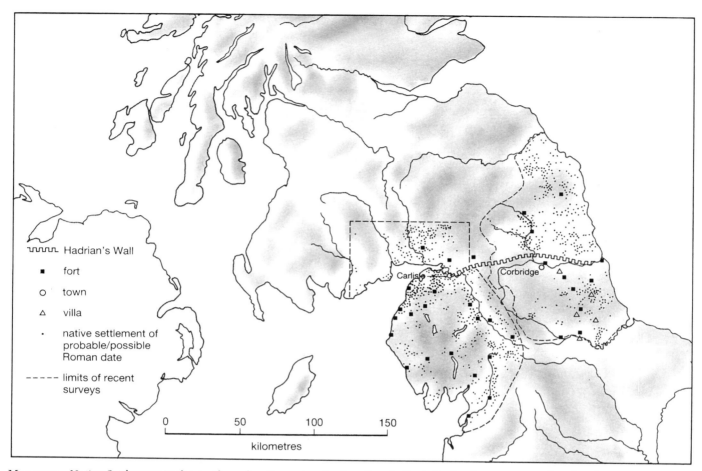

Map 7:22   Native Settlement in the northern frontier region (broken lines indicate limits of zones surveyed in detail).

Plate 7:6   Upland farm at Crosby Ravensworth, Cumbria

bedrock. Whether or not one sees this extensive field system as a response to the market economy established by the Roman army along the northern frontier, there is considerable interest about the fields themselves. They are defined by both lynchets and field banks and average a little over 0.5ha (1.2 acres) in size. The smallest enclosures seem to be associated with farmsteads occupied by small circular huts, with parallels in Cumbria at Ewe Close near Crosby Ravensworth and in many other neighbouring sites.

Recent work has necessitated revision of our view of the overall scale of rural settlement in northern England in the Roman period. Evidence of settlement distribution is now available for practically the entire region (7:22). The development clearly began in the late Iron Age (7:3). Pollen evidence suggests that farming was more advanced in the east by the end of the Iron Age period than in the west. Elements of the Romano-British rural settlement pattern have been known, particularly in Cumbria, since the work of the Royal Commission on the uplands published in 1936. Latterly aerial reconnaissance of the valleys and plain of north Cumbria and renewed work in Northumbria and Lancashire have led to a reassessment of the density of settlement in the area. By the end of the 1970s a much greater database had been acquired. It showed that there were major concentrations of settlements on good farmland as well as on the uplands, where preservation of ruins is better. For instance, the central Eden Valley, a belt of grade II agricultural land, contains not only numerous farmsteads but also three major Roman fort sites. By these means, therefore, it has been possible to rectify the upland bias that has hitherto affected our concept of native settlement distribution in the Roman period. This is particularly the case with the large body of evidence available from the Solway plain, where previously only a handful of sites were known (7:24). These lowlands of northern Cumbria provide an isolated area of good quality agricultural land over-shadowed by the uplands of the lakeland massif, the central Westmorland ridge, the Pennines and the uplands of south-west Scotland. In the plain the greatest concentration of the sites stretches from the area around Wigton into the Irthing Valley and, more extensively, into the twin valleys of the Petteril and the Eden. The richest zone in the latter valley comprises the mixed glacial deposits of the Eamont area

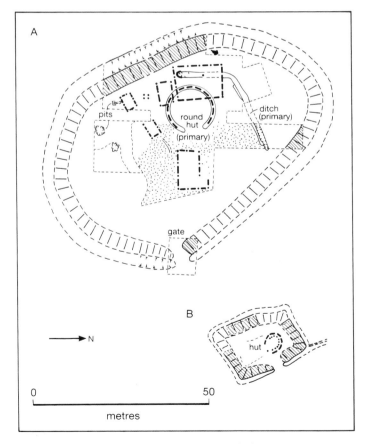

Map 7:23   Cumbria: the Penrith and Silloth farms

making Penrith the centre of one of the few arable areas remaining in north-west England. It clearly fulfilled a comparable function in the Roman period. Overall much still remains to be surveyed in the Pennine area; this base-map demonstrates the lacunae in our present knowledge, whether through lack of resources or other reasons.

With the existence of this new and greatly increased database, excavation of selected sites became a high priority and two contrasting farms were examined recently. The first and larger of these lay close to the Roman road immediately north of Penrith, while the second, Silloth Farm, was a relatively small site in the immediate hinterland of the Solway frontier system. Both sites are examples of the wide native tradition in the northern zone (7:23). The site at Penrith occupied a scooped enclosure some 0.2ha (0.5 acres) in size and involved a sequence from round hut to sub-rectangular buildings set within a circuit rampart and with a problematic early ditch cutting off the north-western sector of the farm. The small Silloth site, some 400m from the Solway frontier defences, belonged to the end of the second century and comprised a small hut dwarfed by a ditch and bank immediately surrounding it. Despite their obvious difference in size the sites are comparable with those raths of the Irish Sea province which have artefactual evidence from this period. Quantitatively, however, the Roman material from Penrith and Silloth is slim, and the absence of coinage both from here and from Cumbrian farm sites in general suggests a non-monetary economy. While the Silloth farm probably relates to the period of the Severan refurbishment of the Solway defences, the Penrith settlement had a far longer life, beginning in the early years of the second century and continuing until at least the fourth. Neither site yielded substantial quantities of bone, but cattle bones predominated. Red deer bones were also found on the Penrith site. Pig bones were noticeably absent and, perhaps surprisingly, only a small number of sheep bones were recognized. The settlements were not isolated but formed part of a landscape involving field systems as well as unenclosed areas of pasture, woodland or waste. There is a strong likelihood of cereal cultivation at Penrith given the relatively high quality of the soils and one may assume that both sites practised a mixed agriculture.

One of the key questions in relation to the frontier zone is what effect the intense military occupation had upon the native population and its settlement patterns (7:24; 7:25). As we have already seen elsewhere, one of the effects was the development of *vici* or civilian settlements outside the forts (5:13). It was once believed that the Solway plain at the western end of Hadrian's wall was thinly occupied save around forts or along the line of the arterial roads. Recently, however, a programme of systematic low-level air photography has produced a substantially different picture. To summarize, by 1982 over 180 sites had been recorded in an area of 700sq km (260sq miles). This may be compared with

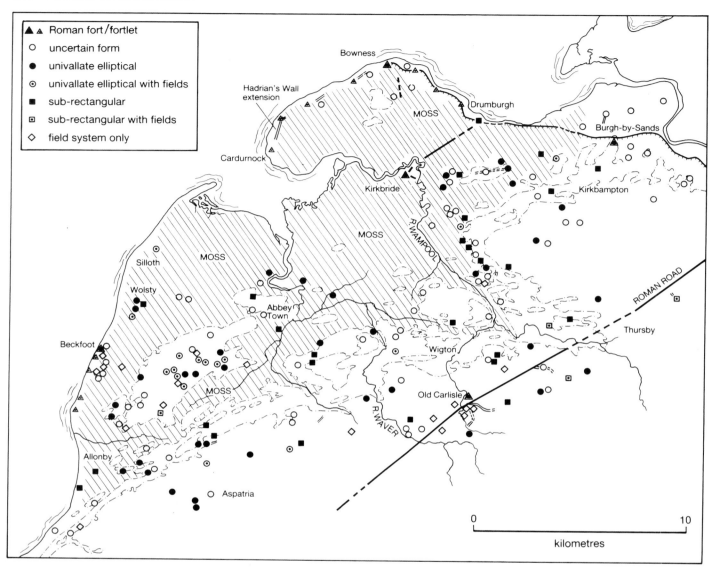

Map 7:24   Solway I: general distribution plan of sites

a similar area on the north side of the Solway where 82 sites were located in a zone comprising 800sq km (300sq miles). It will be clear that the site densities are very different south and north of the Roman frontier, with one site nucleus every 9.7sq km on the north side as opposed to one every 3.77sq km on the south.

As Map 7:25 shows, the native settlements vary between circular and rectangular, are often associated with field systems and are sometimes enclosed by multiple defensive arrangements. Like the differences in density it is believed that these morphological variations also tell their own story in demonstrating contrasts between north and south. North of the Solway, for instance, none of the sites so far recorded from the air has a directly associated field system and very

few of the known sites exhibit the kind of rectangular layout that is often associated with the Romano-British period. As a counterpoint, however, nearly one-fifth of the sites to the north were protected by multiple defensive ditches as opposed to a mere two per cent south of the line of the wall. Even allowing for a broad chronological range the implication is obvious and suggests that the protection afforded by Hadrian's Wall provided more suitable conditions for the development of stable agriculture. One needs to be careful, however, in defining the success of these settlements. Overall it may be claimed that development was restricted to the lower end of the settlement hierarchy. Apart from Carlisle and to some extent the *vici*, for example, there is little or no progress in the area towards fully developed

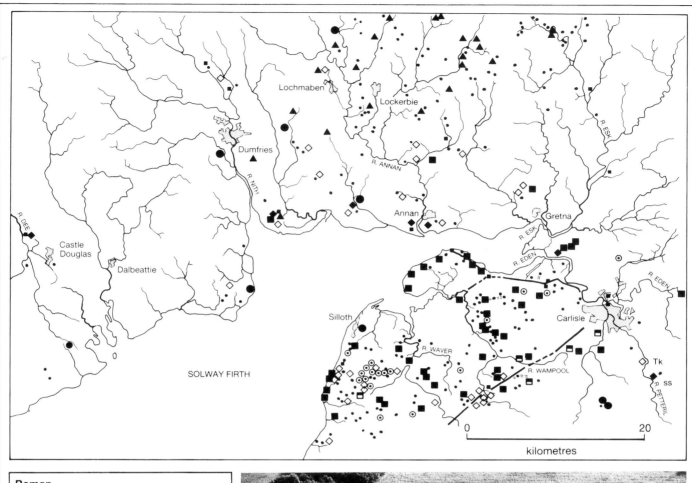

Plate 7:7 Settlements at Sandy Brow, Wigton, one sub-rectangular and the other circular, and the associated field system, typify the components in the distribution map.

Map 7:25 Solway II: site morphology

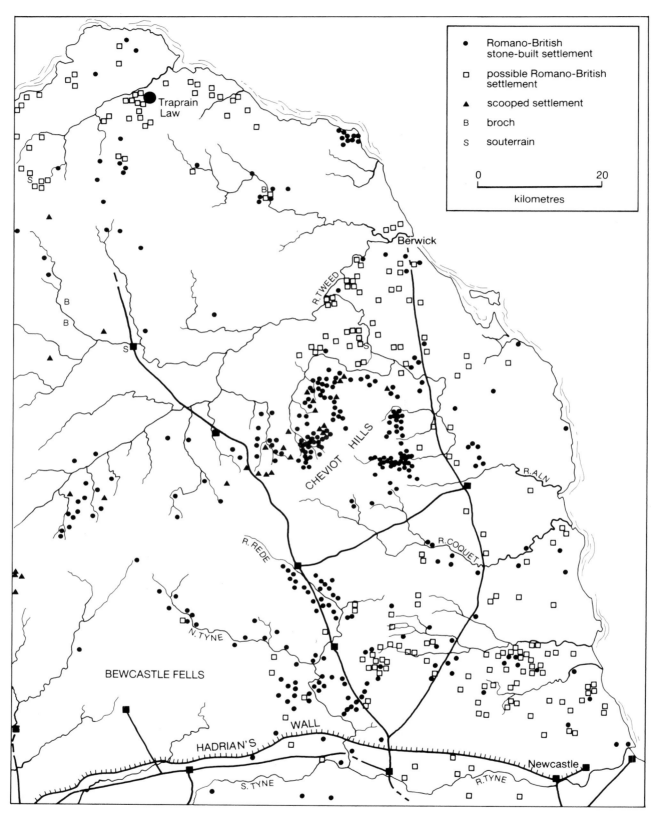

Map 7:26   Settlement in the Cheviots

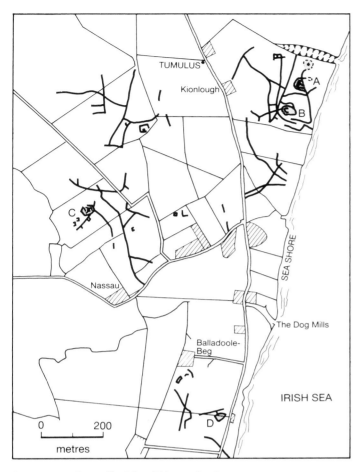

Map 7:27 Dogmills, Isle of Man: a landscape continuum

during the Roman period has received considerable study (7:26). The distribution pattern represents those settlements that have yielded Roman artefacts (as already discussed from another standpoint (6:21–6:23)). The sites represented here exhibit a varied morphology. For two periods in the second century they lay within the Empire when the Antonine Wall was occupied, and during the Scottish campaigns of Severus early in the third century they must have briefly come under Roman control again. It is probably more relevant, however, to see the northward drift of material to the Votadini and their farms as a steady process from an early stage when Rome may have entered into treaty relationships with the tribe. This emerges principally by comparison with the settlements of the Selgovae and Novantae to the west which reveal an altogether smaller order of acculturation. There, the settlement morphology shows little or no direct influence which may be attributed to the Romanization process, as can be seen from the study of the Solway settlements in the previous section.

The Isle of Man

By way of comparison this section includes information drawn from a recent survey in the Isle of Man where air photography has shown the existence of late prehistoric landscapes, largely unrelated to the previously known distribution of finds or standing remains. Map 7:27 is the result of a three-year survey of the sands and gravels of the northern plain which has shown the presence of extensive, and in places cohesive, prehistoric landscapes of which this example, around Dogmills, typifies the whole. We may take the Dogmills archaeological landscape as probably late Bronze Age or Iron Age in date based on a number of substantial site nuclei related to their own field systems. Here, there was no direct Roman involvement whatsoever and we may assume that the rural pattern was eventually replaced by Pagan Norse settlement based on altogether different nuclei which partly survive today as the smaller villages of the northern plain.

urban settlements. This is typical of much of north-west England where the dominant pattern of settlement is restricted to fort, *vicus* and farm, with no development pattern stretching upwards to villas, villages and smaller towns.

North of the frontier line of Hadrian's Wall the distribution of native sites occupied wholly or partly by the Votadini

8
Religion

Religious practice in the northern provinces was largely an intriguing amalgam of cults derived from worship of the classical pantheon, extended to include a state-sponsored worship of the Imperial family, and indigenous Celtic beliefs. It is often assumed that Romanization in religion was actively pursued, and partly achieved through the process of syncretizing an imported classical deity with an indigenous Celtic cult. However, the effect must have been limited in the conservative rural communities. Although elements of classical and Imperial cults were accepted, the rich evidence available for the Celtic cults of the Cotswold–Severn basin, for instance, demonstrates their continuing strength; the inhabitants responded to the stimulus of freshly introduced epigraphy and iconography by adapting such techniques to their previously non-representational religious practice. Thus the Roman iconographic input in some cases rendered elements of the pre-existing Celtic religion archaeologically recognizable. The danger of misjudgement through lack of evidence is apparent enough and should be borne in mind in the following selective analysis of the geographical distribution of religious practice in Britain.

There seems to have been considerable survival of Celtic Iron Age religious traditions and deities in Roman Britain. The evidence is neither very extensive nor uniform in nature, consisting mainly of sculptured portraits and, far more rarely, inscriptions. In broad terms non-representational religious worship, which seems to characterize the pre-Roman period, became anthropomorphic (that is, the gods were given human form). The tradition of worship which centred on the forces of nature remained strong. Three main categories of native deity can be defined. The gods of natural features such as rivers, which in the Iron Age were regarded as dwelling in a particular physical feature, were now worshipped in anthropomorphic form under Roman influence. A representation of the Tyne river god has been discovered at Chesters and the sculptured head of Tamesis (Thames) was found at the London *mithraeum*. Similarly a water nymph, Coventina, personified the deity of the sacred well at Carrawburgh. Secondly, there were the more Romanized cults where deities frequently appeared in amalgamated form (syncretized) with a Roman god or goddess. A Celtic deity thus in some cases assumed additional attributes. In Cumbria the native god Cocidius was combined with Mars, taking on warlike attributes; in Northumberland, combined with Silvanus, he appeared in a gentler, more rustic guise.

Thirdly, there were deities that were actually imported. These somewhat Romanized Celtic deities are paralleled on the Continent. The Matres seem to belong to this category and they, like some of the other cults, may have been imported by soldiers. An example of this can be seen in the transportation of Apollo Anextlomarus from eastern Gaul to Hadrian's Wall.

The Celtic peoples, one might say, worshipped a *numen* rather than a *deus*. Their religion concerned divine forces with wide and indeterminate powers. Some were located in natural objects like springs or rivers, others were tribal divinities. This form of worship contrasted with the personalized deities of the Graeco-Roman pantheon, each limited to specific powers. The occurrence of crude wooden carvings on the Continent, together with Caesar's references to images of Mercury, indicate that some form of anthropomorphism did exist in late Iron Age Celtic society, but this in itself may be an example of Roman cultural influence proceeding ahead of the actual Roman invasion of these areas. The amount of anthropomorphic worship may always have been limited and in the minority. If the making of religious images had been a common practice in the late Iron Age, it would seem likely that stone and bronze would have been included in the media as well as more perishable materials like wood. Certainly in the highland zone more stone representations would have been expected and there seem to be too few examples of religious imagery to indicate that it was ever necessarily an important feature of cult worship.

Although we have clear iconographic evidence for the importation of classical and Gallic deities and their assimilation with native British gods after the Roman conquest of Britain, there is also the strong probability of much continuity with the non-representational past practice. It is not possible to draw firm conclusions about the relative importance of the two forms of worship.

THE CLASSICAL PANTHEON

The Imperial cult

Under the Roman Empire varying degrees of divinity were ascribed to the living emperor, the Imperial family or his ancestors. In general terms outright personal divinity was accorded to living emperors only in the eastern provinces;

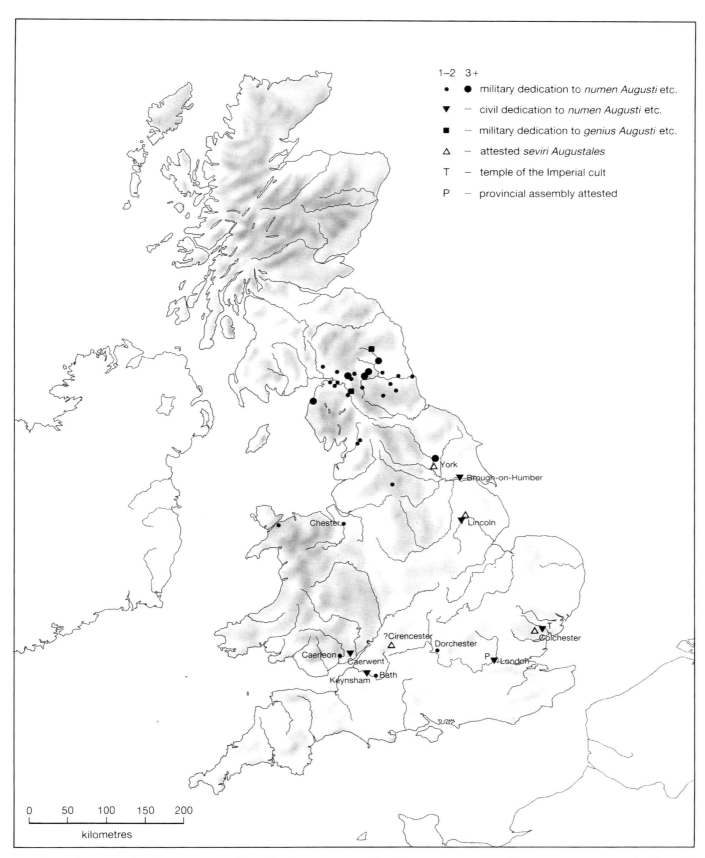

Map 8:1 The Imperial cult in Britain. In this and subsequent maps the dedications are primarily inscriptions on stone listed in *RIB*, with occasional additions of more recent discoveries.

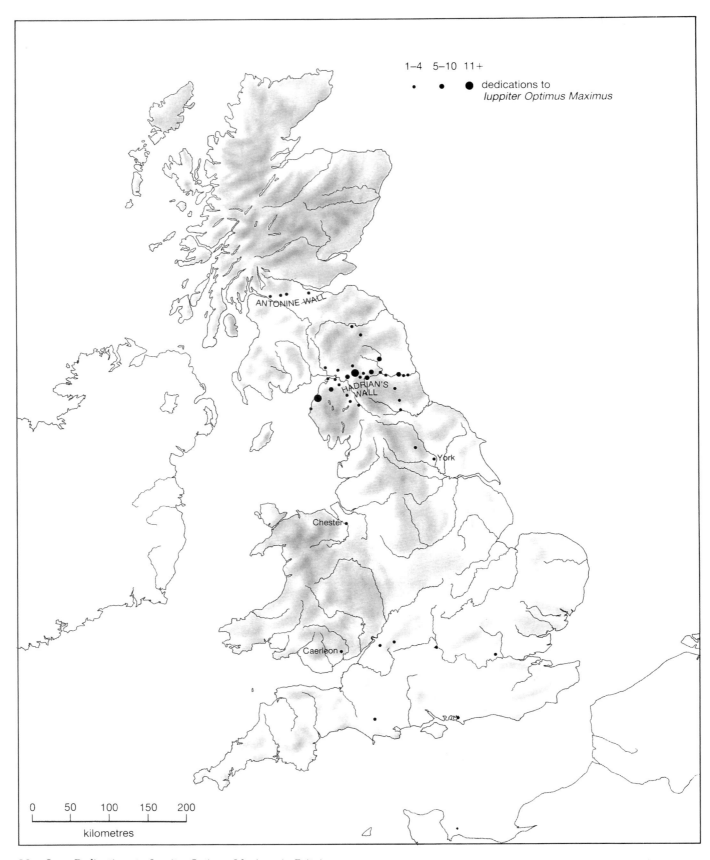

Map 8:2 Dedications to *Iuppiter Optimus Maximus* in Britain

more commonly the cult focused on emperors and members of their families who had been deified after death, or on their health, spirit and safety whilst alive. Britain was an example of a northern province where the attempt to introduce the Imperial cult, centred on the deified Claudius or rather his *numen*, proved premature. It was a major cause of the Boudican revolt. Whereas similar initiatives in other centres such as Lyons had been better received by the provincial populations, the involvement of the local British aristocracy in the role of *seviri* (or priests) caused problems: they were encouraged, if not compelled, to disburse money in the display of politico-religious loyalty. Likewise the temple of the deified Claudius itself served to arouse hostility. In the period of Flavian and later acculturation, however, the Imperial cult spread, as shown by the bronze head of Hadrian from London and the *seviri Augustales* attested at Lincoln and elsewhere (8:1). Predictably, London and Colchester emerge as the main civil centres where the cult is known.

In the military zones the Imperial cult took on a special significance that is well represented in the Hadrian's Wall area. Buildings, or repairs to buildings, were executed in the name of the emperor. More specifically, as we learn from the *Feriale Duranum* from Dura Europos at the other limit of the Empire, the auxiliary garrisons took annual oaths of loyalty to the emperor and the Imperial family. The remarkable series of altars recovered from the area of the parade ground at Maryport on the Cumbrian coast must be interpreted in this context. The fine condition of their surfaces implies that, like the Antonine Wall distance slabs, they were interred as religious objects to avoid damage or destruction. Some of the inscriptions link the cult of the emperor with that of the head of the Capitoline triad, Jupiter, thus strengthening conformity with the classical pantheon.

Jupiter

This deity appears in a number of guises throughout the provinces and, if one is looking for a British characteristic, then it may well be the absence of dedications to Jupiter as part of the Capitoline triad and likewise the paucity of dedications to his consort, Juno, who in Britain is principally attested on gemstones. As the head of the classical pantheon, however, Jupiter was the regular recipient of dedications, in particular from army units using the form *'I.O.M.'* or *'Iuppiter Optimus Maximus'* (Jupiter, best and greatest). The overwhelmingly northern distribution pattern (shown in Map 8:2) is not simply a reflection of the dearth of good carving stone in the south, as discussed above (6:37), but is also a product of northern military concentrations. The southern evidence is very sparse; apart from another military dedication at Caerleon, there is only a handful of civil inscriptions. Dedications to Jupiter Dolichenus (normally termed *Iuppiter Optimus Maximus Dolichenus*) show a similar, almost wholly northern, distribution pattern.

The geographical imbalance is partly explained by the fact that evidence of the Jupiter cult in the civilian areas frequently took other forms than inscriptions (8:3). Jupiter appears in classical form in a number of statues and uninscribed dedications. Of particular note are two possible Jupiter columns (including an example from Cirencester probably associated with the fourth-century pagan revival, see Map 8:31). Numerically greater are the appearances of Jupiter in non-classical form. On present evidence it is not possible to assert that Jupiter was specifically equated with Taranis, the Gaulish sky-god. The ceremonial priestly regalia from Willingham Farm, however, incorporates elements from Celtic mythology including a wheel, the symbol of Taranis. Part of the regalia recovered from the Farley Heath temple depicts another wheel alongside a representation of a Jupiter-Taranis deity.

Mars

The cult of Mars is very widely attested in Britain, though it appears that Celtic deities, syncretized with Mars both in Britain and Gaul, were not simply equated with the deity as the god of war. Although sometimes referred to by a single name, Mars is more frequently attested in complex forms (e.g. Mars Victor or Mars Ultor – the Avenger), but most commonly by syncretism with Celtic deities (e.g. Mars Toutates). These are plotted separately below (8:9, 8:10, 8:17). Map 8:4 shows that the overall distribution pattern of the Mars cult in terms of actual dedications on inscriptions is heavily weighted, as one might expect, to the northern frontier, where he was almost exclusively represented in warrior guise, exemplified by the Corbridge statue. This is not the whole picture, however, because of the variation in the south (8:5), where Mars appears to have had somewhat interchangeable features with Mercury, a conflation more apparent in Gaul. In Britain, Mars appears as a healer. He was Mars Lenus at Chedworth and Caerwent, for instance, and Mars Nodens at the 'healing' centre identified at Lydney. Altogether about twenty syncretized versions of Mars are known in Britain, but it should be noted that the iconographical evidence, however Celticized in style, almost invariably portrays a martial deity. In Britain and Gaul, Mars is also represented by a number of equestrian statues in bronze or stone and, although not a major feature of the Mars cult overall, there are twenty or so examples of clay or bronze figurines and stamped equestrian figures on pottery from such centres as Brigstock and Kelvedon.

Other classical deities

On the Continent, Mercury (*Mercurius*) appears as one of the most ubiquitous cult deities, whether in classical guise or syncretized with the Celtic god Cernunnos. He was associated with a range of other cults such as the Genii Cucullati

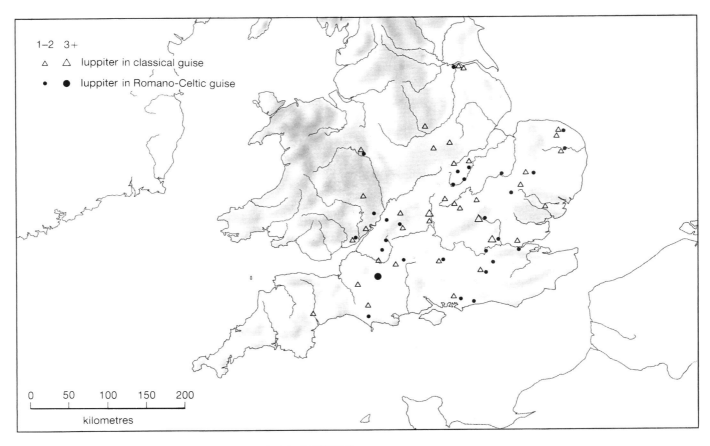

1–2 3+

△ △ Iuppiter in classical guise

• ● Iuppiter in Romano-Celtic guise

0   50   100   150   200
kilometres

Map 8:3 Evidence (mainly non-epigraphic) for the cult of Jupiter in the non-military zone of Roman Britain

Plate 8:1 Altar to I.O.M. (Jupiter best and greatest) from Maryport, Cumbria

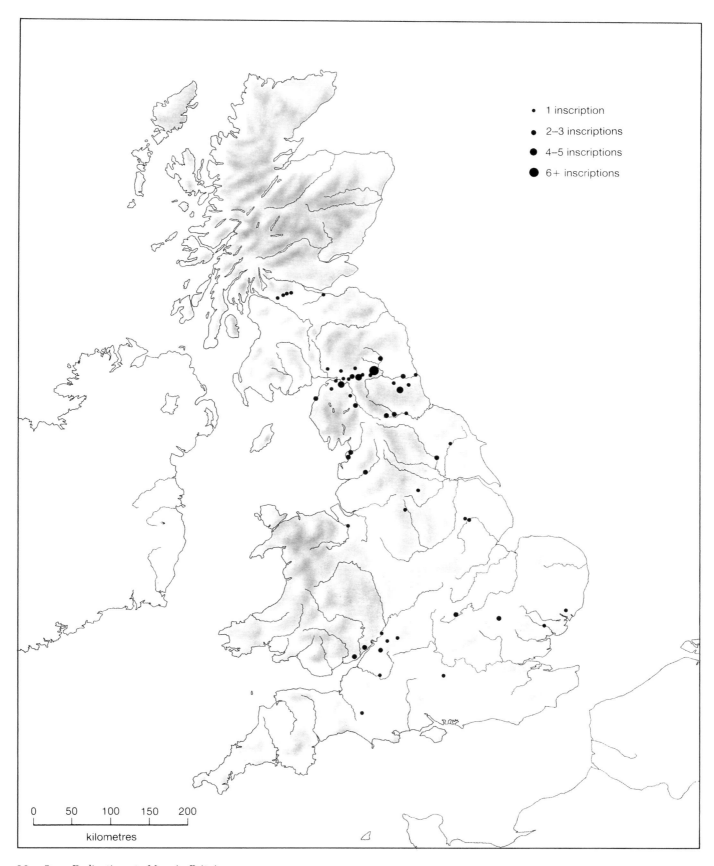

Map 8:4   Dedications to Mars in Britain

1 inscription
2–3 inscriptions
4–5 inscriptions
6+ inscriptions

0   50   100   150   200

kilometres

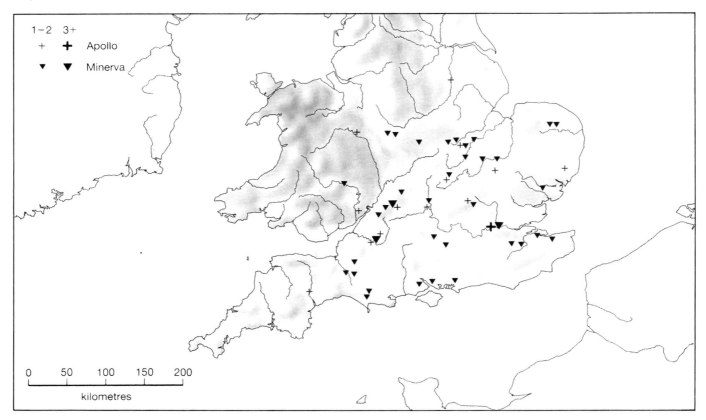

Map 8:5   Evidence (mainly non-epigraphic) for the cult of Mars in the non-military zone of Roman Britain

and the Matres. Although found to a lesser extent in Britain, the cult of Mercury is nonetheless represented by over 50 bronze figurines, 25 reliefs or sculptures and a roughly equal number of examples of his emblem, the cockerel, in bronze or terracotta (8:6). Unfortunately, few of these finds can be attributed to a precise religious context. An exception is the evidence of Mercury in classical guise from the Walbrook *mithraeum* (see Map 8:21), where his role as the conductor of the dead in the Underworld probably explains the presence of the cult. In many examples Mercury appears linked with his consort, the Gallo-Roman Rosmerta who, at least in the south-west, occurs in contexts associated with the Matres and the Genii Cucullati. He appears in only one case with asyncretizing Celtic epithet, namely Mercurius Andescocivoucus, joined with a dedication to the Imperial cult at Colchester, although the dearth of epigraphic evidence from southern Britain as a whole makes it difficult to be certain how significant this is.

The classical hero Hercules was also adapted within the broader framework of Romano-Celtic religion, and in Britain is occasionally conflated with the Celtic Saegon ('all conquering'). It is possible, but not proven, that the figure cut into the Dorset chalk at Cerne Abbas represents an ithyphallic giant depiction of Hercules. Yet he was not simply a god of strength and virility. Like Mercury-Cernunnos he was also a healing deity, sometimes associated with the afterlife, the latter trait exemplified by the inclusion of a terracotta figurine of him in a child's grave at Colchester. Hercules is represented in widely differing ways, ranging from the classical to the heavily Celticized with typically striated hair and a torc around the neck.

Atypically for southern Britain, the cult of Minerva is well attested epigraphically (8:7). In the shrine dedicated by King Cogidubnus at Chichester she was evidently worshipped in a purely classical guise along with Neptune. On the other hand eight inscriptions from the shrine at Bath show an equation between the classical goddess and the Celtic water deity probably known as Sulis, rather than Sul. Votive figurines of the goddess are also known, especially from the urban centres of Colchester and London. In these the classical form is dominant throughout, as reflected by some representations of the goddess in the form of a helmeted bust. She appears to have shed an element of her warlike image in the process of partial Celticization, notably on evidence from the south-west. Her veneration at Bisley in the Cotswolds appears to have been of a partly domestic nature, as

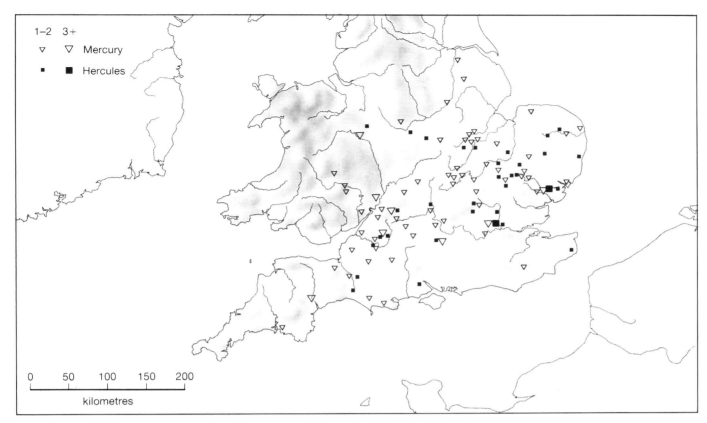

Map 8:6 Evidence (mainly non-epigraphic) for the cults of Mercury and Hercules in the non-military zone of Roman Britain

Plate 8:2 Relief from the monumental arch, London, showing Mercury

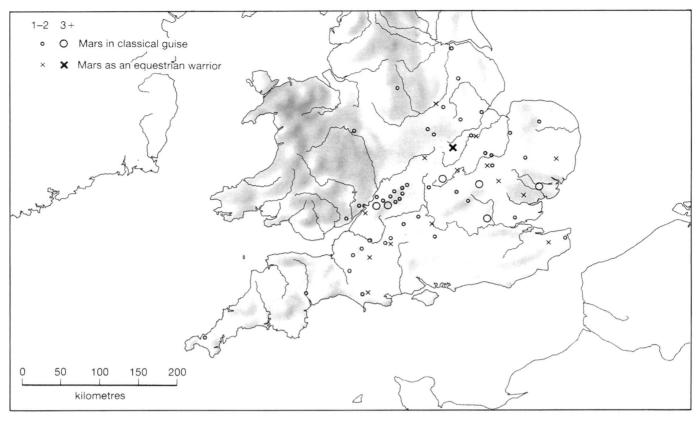

Map 8:7   Evidence (mainly non-epigraphic) for the cults of Apollo and Minerva in the non-military zone of Britain

also suggested by the evidence found in association with the Genii Cucullati at Lower Slaughter in the same area.

The nature of the cult of Apollo in the civilian province (8:7) appears to be relatively uncomplicated by the processes of syncretism so common on the northern frontier. In southern Britain, Apollo is rarely attested with a Celtic epithet, although as in Gaul, where such syncretism is common, there may be a connection with healing cults at shrines. Two of the three stone statues of Apollo derive from the cult centre at Bath and there is a dedication to Apollo from the presumed healing shrine principally devoted to Nodens at Lydney in Gloucestershire. On the other hand as the god of the hunt he is, not surprisingly, associated with Silvanus, god of the woods (see Map 8:11) and Diana the huntress; at the Nettleton temple north-east of Bath the dedication refers to him as Apollo Cunomaglus ('Lord of the Hunting Hounds').

AFRICAN AND EASTERN CULTS

In contrast with the southern distribution patterns which we have been examining, the evidence for African and oriental deities (8:8), excluding Mithraism and Christianity (see Maps 8:21, 8:28), is an object lesson in the influence of the Roman army as a propagator of imported cult worship. As the map shows, the pattern is almost wholly dominated by Hadrian's Wall and its hinterland and so examples from the south of the province attract especial interest. The cults concerned are principally those of the Phrygian mother goddess Cybele and her consort Atys, and the Egyptian deities Isis and Serapis. The cult of Cybele and Atys, initially introduced at the end of the third century BC at Rome, was prevented by its initiation ceremonies, which involved castration, from gaining official recognition until the time of Claudius in the middle of the first century AD. It was brought to Britain by devotees either in or attached to the military or through trade that brought merchants to the province, especially London, where at least nine items attesting the cult are known. Steelyard weights bearing the engraved head of Cybele may directly reflect the presence of merchants who were her cult followers and the presence of a statue certainly implies a shrine in the city, though this was unlikely to have ranked with those in Lyons or Autun in Gaul. The cult is also attested in London by statuettes of Atys and a highly decorated and carefully repaired implement found in the

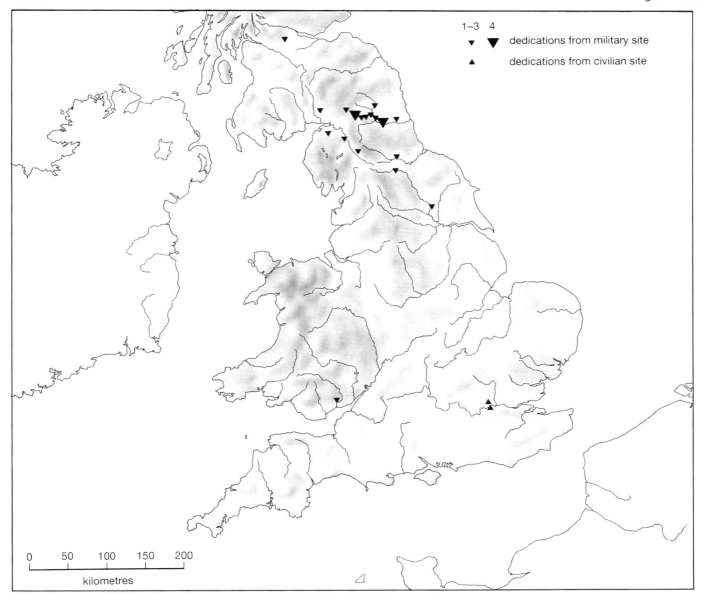

Map 8:8 Dedications to African and oriental deities in Britain, not including Mithras or Christianity

Thames has been claimed as forceps for ritual castration. In the rural south only two other bits of evidence for the cult are known, a probable depiction of Atys in a mosaic from Pitney in Dorset and a statue of Atys from Froxfield near Hungerford, Berkshire. London has also yielded a dedication to Atargatis, the Syrian mother-goddess who may be equated with Cybele.

Apart from some very minor cults, evidence for the worship of Egyptian deities centres on the cults of Isis and Serapis, a Ptolemaic conflation of Osiris and the bull god Apis. Unusually, their cults are southern orientated, with the emphasis predictably on the polyglot commercial centre of London, where in the late first century there was already a temple of Isis, or *Isaeum*, as attested by a graffito on a coarse ware jug. The Walbrook *mithraeum*, however, was also associated with the cult of Serapis and yielded a fine classicized head of Serapis amongst the statuary recovered there. Isis is also known from engraved steelyard weights in the city, while *sistra*, or priest's rattles, have been found as miniatures at Exeter, Dorchester and Canterbury. Silchester has produced a head of Serapis, another example of which was also found in the funerary context of a grave at Highworth in Wiltshire. Further north, Atys is known in a similar context from York (and possibly Chester), while there is also

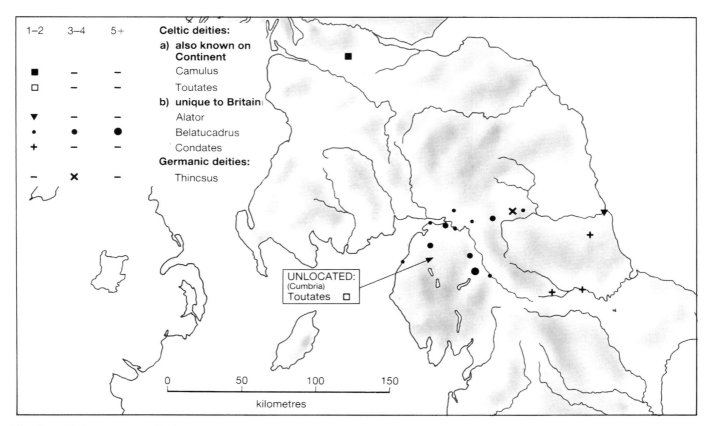

Map 8:9   Dedications to gods identified with Mars in northern Britain (i) Camulus, Toutates, Alator, Belatucadrus, Condates, Thincsus

evidence to imply the former existence of a *Serapaeum* at York.

Other eastern deities include Jupiter Dolichenus, a conflation of the head of the classical pantheon with his equivalent Baal-figure, Doliche of Commagene. Another conflation with Baal, this time from Baalbek (Heliopolis), is Jupiter Heliopolitanus. As with Cybele, cult practice in civilian Britain is limited almost entirely to London, and accordingly the portrait of Dolichenus on a castor ware pot found at Sawtry (Cambridgeshire) acquires greater interest.

The northern frontier, however, provides the richest evidence from the inscriptions that have been recorded there. The spread of the worship of Dolichenus among the soldiery is shown by dedications at Croy on the Antonine Wall as well as at Corbridge and Great Chesters. This seems to have been primarily a third-century phenomenon. The presence of a particular cult may in some cases be explained by the origins of the associated auxiliary unit at a particular period. Thus at Carvoran the attested worship of the Syrian mother-goddess and Jupiter Heliopolitanus is very probably to be explained by the epigraphically proven presence of the cohors I Hamiorum, originally from Syria.

Another cult, that of Sol Invictus (the All-conquering Sun)

gained vogue through Imperial devotees both in the latter part of the second and in the third century, although on a limited scale in Britain.

The evidence for the eastern cult of Mithras is discussed elsewhere.

CELTIC DEITIES

Celtic religion and the northern frontier

The relative wealth of epigraphic evidence from the northern frontier allows us to draw a far more detailed picture of the processes of syncretism and of the often highly localized distribution of certain cults. This is particularly the case in relation to the cult of Mars and those Celtic deities, some paralleled on the Continent, others unique to Britain, that were conflated with him.

Of the Celtic deities known from the Continent one of the most frequent syncretisms was that of Mars Belatucadrus (8:9). Evidence of his worship, in the form of altars, is effectively limited to Cumbria and the central section of Hadrian's Wall with a particular concentration at Brougham in the Eden Valley. There are several variations in the precise spelling of the name, which is normally trans-

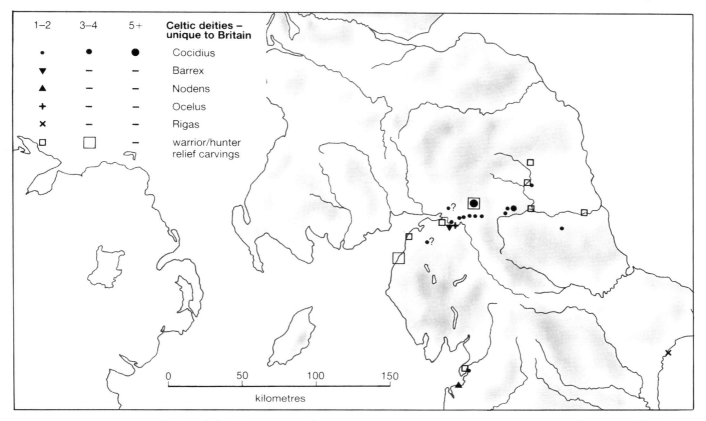

Map 8:10   Dedications to gods identified with Mars in northern Britain (ii) Cocidius, Barrex, Nodens, Ocelus and Rigas; and distribution of warrior/hunter reliefs in northern Britain

lated as 'bright shining one'. Both the relatively small size of the altars and the low rank of the dedicants (an *optio* at Maryport, but an ordinary soldier and a veteran from Kirkbride and Old Carlisle) characterize the cult as one practised by the lower military orders.

A Germanic deity, Mars Thincsus, is known at Housesteads in association with lesser female deities known as the Alaisiagae, while Mars Alator is attested at South Shields and Mars Condates (i.e. the god of the river confluence) is known at Piercebridge, Chester-le-Street and Bowes. Mars Camulus, a deity associated particularly with the Remi in north Gaul, occurs at Bar Hill on the Antonine Wall. Another imported cult, that of Mars Toutates, possibly to be translated as 'ruler of the people', is known from Cumbria and in an inscription from Hertfordshire.

Other Celtic deities who were identified with Mars, all unique to Britain, are shown in Map 8:10. Of these the most interesting is probably Cocidius, who is mainly found without equation with a classical deity, but who is twice linked with Mars and once with Silvanus. The social status of the dedicants was high, including a number of the third-century unit commanders from the fort at Bewcastle, north of Hadrian's Wall. The headquarters building excavated at

the fort yielded two silver plaques dedicated to Cocidius, thus strengthening the argument that has sought to identify Bewcastle as the *Fanum Cocidii* (shrine of Cocidius) mentioned in the *Ravenna Cosmography*. There is, however, an equally dense concentration of dedications to Cocidius a few miles to the south in the Irthing Valley. The puzzlingly large *vicus* known from aerial photography alongside the Stanegate fort at Nether Denton may in fact be a more appropriate site for a religious centre as it is closer to Hadrian's Wall.

A single inscription from Malton attests the cult of Mars Rigas. Mars Nodens, well known from the major cult centre at Lydney, appears in the north only at Cockersand Moss near Lancaster. Mars Ocelus, an epithet of uncertain implication, but evidently related to the Treveran cult of Mars Lenus, is known from Carlisle, as is Mars Barrex.

Another god who was worshipped extensively by soldiers in the northern military zone was Silvanus, the god of hunting and the forest (8:11). His cult was evidently equated with those of Cocidius and Vinotonus. Two examples will suffice. On Scargill Moor, south of Bowes on the Stainmore Pass, a prefect, Lucius Caesius Frontinus, and a centurion, Julius Secundus, set up altars to Vinotonus and Silvanus

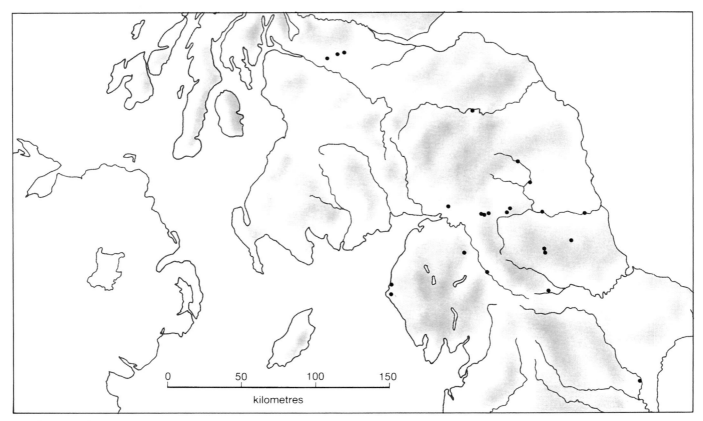

Map 8:11   Dedications to Silvanus in northern Britain

Vinotonus respectively. They were probably prompted to do so by success in the hunt. On Bollihope Common near Weardale, Gaius Tetius Veturius Micianus, prefect of the Sebosian cavalry, recorded the slaying of a fine boar that had previously evaded capture. The language and feelings of the dedicants reflect the spirit of the colonial in a frontier land.

The cult of Veteres – the deity or deities known by such variant spellings as Veteris, Hveteris, Vitires and Vheteris – is attested by 54 inscriptions overwhelmingly located near the centre or towards the eastern end of Hadrian's Wall (8:12). The spelling of the name with an intrusive 'h' has led some to suggest that the cult is Germanic in origin, but the location of the majority of the dedications, which are known at many of the wall forts, especially Carvoran, suggests otherwise. It is more reasonable to treat the name, whether singular or plural, as demonstrating the continued worship of a deity or deities equated with an old god or gods. At Carvoran, where no less than thirteen dedications are known, nine demonstrate the singular form and four the plural. The votaries at Carvoran appear to be mixed in origin and at least one female dedicant is known from Great Chesters. The relatively poor quality of the altars suggests that the cult was one of quite low social status. There is also

some support for the idea that, like Belatucadrus, the deity may be associated with the horned gods of north Britain.

The Latin name for Mainz (*Mogontiacum*) on the Rhine strongly suggests that the cult of Mogons, which is known in a number of variant spellings as well as in the plural, was a Germanic import (8:13). In addition to four certain occurrences, at Netherby, *Vindolanda* (Chesterholm), Risingham and Old Penrith, there is also another probable example from High Rochester. The significance of the cult remains unclear, although in the example from Netherby the cult is linked with that of Vitire (Veteres).

In locational terms the cult of Maponus, whose name is somehow preserved in the Welsh heroic sagas known as the *Mabinogion*, has long attracted especial interest. However widespread his cult may once have been, the available evidence is strictly limited (8:13). Altars from Corbridge and Ribchester show that the Celtic deity, whose name probably signified 'young man', was syncretized with Apollo the harpist. The presence of Diana on the carvings also signifies a relationship with hunting, Apollo's other role. That the cult had a centre north of the Solway appears to be shown by the clear reference to the *locus Maponi*, or shrine of Maponus, listed in the *Ravenna Cosmography* along with other tribal meeting points in lowland Scotland. This may

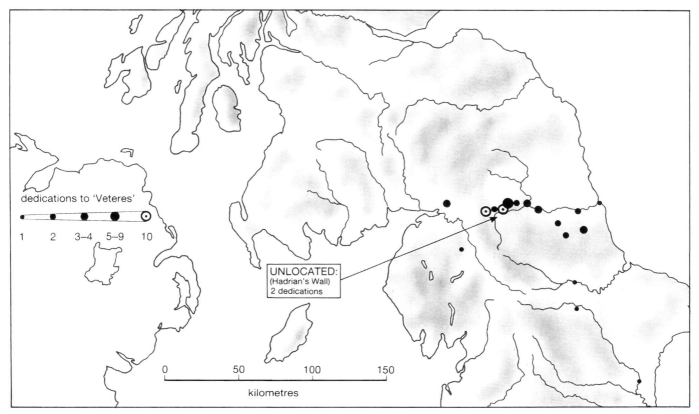

Map 8:12   Dedications to Veteres in northern Britain (a silver plaque relating to the cult has also been found at Thistleton Dyer, Leicestershire.

have been at either Lochmaben north-west of Birrens or Lochmabenstane at Gretna Green, the obvious hosting point on the northern side of the Solway.

Some of the lesser cults are examined in Maps 8:14 and 8:15. Amongst the male figures known only in north Britain was Antenociticus, whose shrine has been uncovered on the south side of the fort at Benwell. Contrebis, of unknown significance, enjoyed a cult in the Lune Valley. A unique dedication to Matunus was made at the eastern outpost fort of High Rochester by the provincial governor, while the unit commander made dedications to Vinotonus on the moor south of the fort at Bowes. Silvanus, equated with Vinotonus in one of the Bowes inscriptions, was syncretized with Cocidius at Housesteads, the only instance of its kind. Vernostonus is attested once at Ebchester; the other examples are also single occurrences and include two examples of syncretism, Hercules Magusanus and Apollo Grannus from the Antonine Wall.

Amongst the female divinities the largest number of dedications derive from Carrawburgh fort in the central section of Hadrian's Wall and relate to Cov(v)entina. Until recently it was generally thought that worship of this deity was strictly localized, but the recent discovery of a similar dedication from Galicia in north-west Spain throws open the question

of whether the cult was imported. At Carrawburgh her cult was specifically associated with a well in which votive offerings were deposited. Altogether fourteen inscriptions are currently known from the site and the cult attracted the support of the third-century garrison commander, as well as that of soldiers from other units. A problematical inscription instigated by the *curia*, or tribal senate, of the Textoverdi, a tribal sept apparently based in the valley of the southern Tyne, celebrates the goddess Saitada, possibly to be associated with grief. At Ilkley the goddess Verbeia personifies the River Wharfe, and several of the other names attested may also represent personifications of places or natural features in the Celtic tradition. Britain as a whole is to be found personified as Britannia in two inscriptions from York and another from the Antonine Wall.

Amongst the Celtic deities found only in Britain the cult of Brigantia and her male consort Bregans has obvious geographical ramifications (8:16). The goddess was evidently the eponymous deity associated with the principal tribe of north Britain and her cult must have been extensive. It is interesting, therefore, that all the dedications known at present cluster close to the northern or southern limits of Brigantian territory. The four northern dedications in the frontier zone were all made by military personnel or officials,

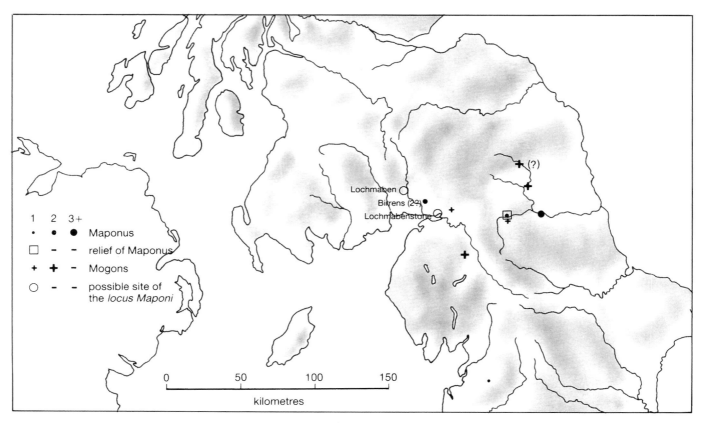

Map 8:13   Dedications to Maponus (identified with Apollo) and Mogons in northern Britain

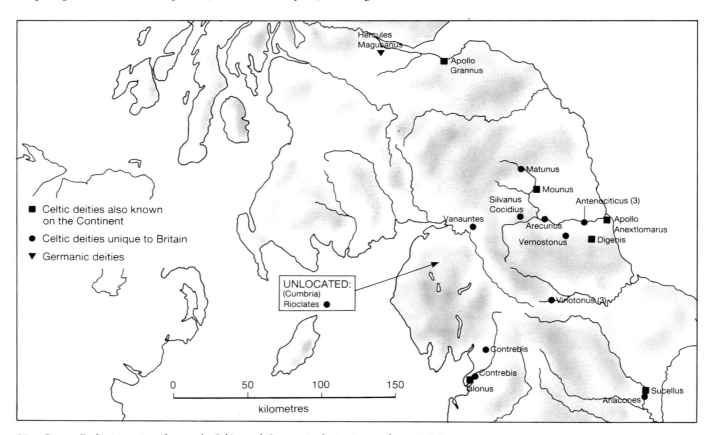

Map 8:14   Dedications to other male Celtic and Germanic deities in northern Britain

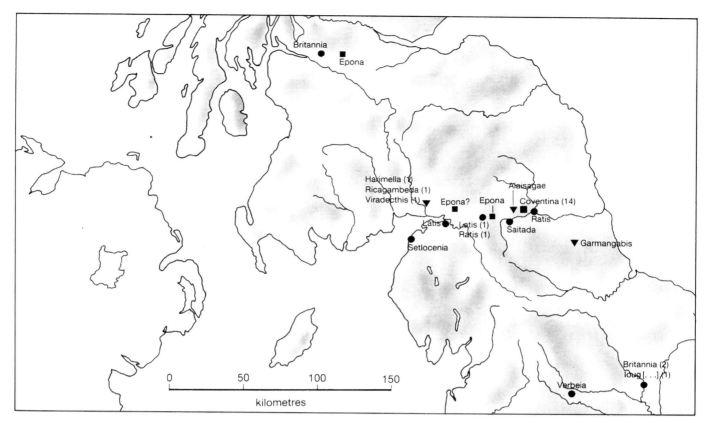

Map 8:15   Dedications to other female Celtic and Germanic deities in northern Britain (key as for Map 8:14)

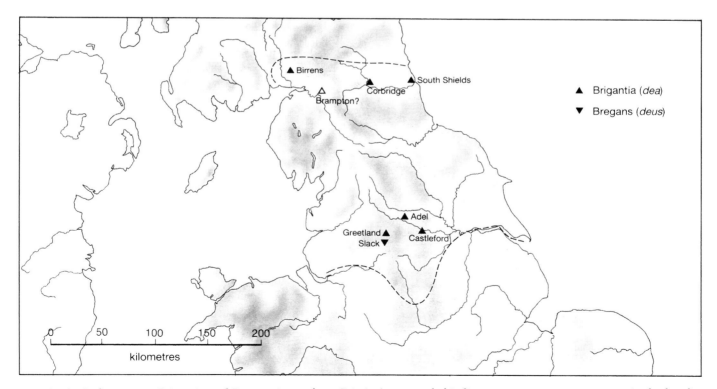

Map 8:16   Dedications to Brigantia and Bregans in northern Britain (open symbol indicates exact provenance uncertain; broken line indicates approximate presumed limits of territory of Brigantia).

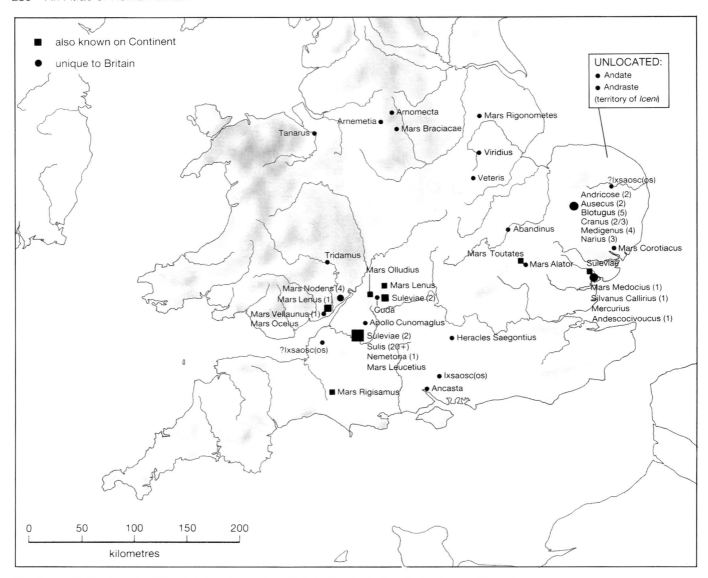

■ also known on Continent

● unique to Britain

UNLOCATED:
● Andate
● Andraste
(territory of *Iceni*)

Arnemetia ● Arnomecta
● Mars Braciacae
● Mars Rigonometes

Tanarus ●
● Viridius
● Veteris

?Ixsaosc(os)

Andricose (2)
Ausecus (2)
Blotugus (5)
Cranus (2/3)
Medigenus (4)
Narius (3)

● Abandinus
● Mars Corotiacus

Tridamus ●
Mars Toutates ■ Mars Alator
Suleviae

Mars Olludius
■ Mars Lenus
Mars Nodens (4) ●
Mars Lenus (1) ■
● Suleviae (2)
Mars Medocius (1)
Silvanus Callirius (1)
Mercurius
Andescociyoucus (1)

Mars Vellaunus (1) ■
Mars Ocelus

Guda
● Apollo Cunomaglus

?Ixsaosc(os) ●
Suleviae (2)
Sulis (20+)
Nemetona (1)
Mars Leucetius
● Heracles Saegontius

Ixsaosc(os) ●

■ Mars Rigisamus
● Ancasta

0   50   100   150   200
kilometres

Map 8:17   Dedications to Celtic divinities in southern Britain (not including dedications to Matres)

one a *procurator Augusti*, one a centurion and the other an architect. The southern group from west Yorkshire (which includes a single dedication to Bregans from Slack) probably belongs to civilian contexts. Corporately the evidence for the cults suggests the extent of the tribal territory, which may be seen to have extended north of the line of Hadrian's Wall.

Celtic deities in the south of Britain

As already emphasized, the civilian province has far less epigraphic evidence available than the frontier zone. Nonetheless the distribution pattern of dedications is of interest

(8:17). Of the deities known in Britain, the Suleviae, deities akin to the Matres and well attested in Germany, are represented in the Cotswolds and at Colchester. Celtic syncretisms with Mars are particularly rich: Mars Medocius at Colchester and Mars Corotiacus at Martlesham (Suffolk). Mars Lenus, a conflation known in the Moselle area, is attested either side of the Severn, whilst Mars Vellaunus and Mars Ocelus are recorded at Caerwent. Further upstream the Romano-British Mars Nodens, a god of healing, was the principal deity worshipped at the cult centre at Lydney. Other known forms are Mars Rigisamus from Dorset, and Mars Toutates and Mars Alator from Barkway (Herts.). The last two are also attested on Hadrian's Wall. Colchester has

Map 8:18 Evidence (mainly non-epigraphic) for the cults of the Genii Cucullati, horned gods (excluding Cernunnos), Epona and Sucellus

Plate 8:3
The Genii Cucullati

produced evidence for conflation of Silvanus with Callirius and of Mercury with the Celtic deity Andescocivoucus.

Little is known of some of the deities recorded in the territory of the Iceni, many being unique to Britain: Andate, Andraste, Ixsaoscos, Andricose, Ausecus, Blotugus, Cranus, Medigenus and Narius. The last six names were added to that of the god Faunus and inscribed on some silver spoons of the Thetford hoard. The uniqueness of the Thetford dedications illustrates well the great limitations of both the surviving evidence and our attempts to understand the underlying rituals.

Relatively few of the surviving names from the south appear to be personifications of places. The most obvious is Arnemetia (Arnomecta) associated with the sacred spring at Buxton. Of the female godesses Nemetona was associated with sacred groves, while the significance of Andrasta from Bitterne (Southampton) is not known.

Epona was another deity with Continental connections. She should correctly be considered Celtic in origin. Being a deity connected with horses, as her name implies, she is sometimes shown on a horse or between two ponies. The transfer of soldiers from the Danube (the area where her cult was most popular) may explain the northern military dedications on both the Antonine and Hadrianic Walls. Yet she was also venerated in the civilian province, as an incised pot from Alcester shows by its graffito dedication. Other evidence of her cult comes from Colchester, Caerwent and South Collingham.

The Genii Cucullati (so-called because they are normally depicted wearing the *cucullus* or hooded cloak) have long attracted attention (8:18). The British evidence portrays them as triple dwarf-gods, in contrast with the larger representations more commonly to be found in Germany. Their cult was associated with prosperity and perhaps fertility, a feature emphasized by their occasional depiction carrying an egg or by their association with the Matres cult (notably in the Cotswolds).

The very limited evidence for the worship of Sucellus also includes examples from the Cotswolds. This Celtic deity is shown on the priest's regalia from the Farley Heath temple as a smith-god wearing a conical hat and with smith's tongs above and below. A raven connotes a link with death. The wheel-god Taranis is also included in the scene.

The stag-horned deity Cernunnos, familiar from Gaul, is scarcely attested in Britain. This may be explained by the spread of the rival north British cult of the horned god, symbolizing strength and virility. With one exception, all the representations, whether on small votive offerings or carved in stone, depict males. The cult appears to have been widely dispersed across southern Britain.

FERTILITY CULTS

The quest for fertility is a commonplace of religion and in civilian Roman Britain the cult of the mother-goddesses or Matres was a popular one, to judge by the number and distribution of relief statues and inscriptions (8:19). Nearly twenty relief statues of the triple mother-goddesses are currently known in the civilian province. The presence of a statue and associated dedications strongly suggests that there may have been cult centres at London and Ancaster. In a number of cases the cult is linked with other deities, notably Jupiter and Mercury. It is also known in the west at Caerwent and Lydney, where in the latter case the cult is associated with a single deity rather than a plurality. Nearly all of the 60 British dedications to the triad of the Matres (known by several different nomenclatures) derive from the military zone. Most of them were found along the line of Hadrian's Wall and in its hinterland, from such sites as Housesteads and Binchester and, interestingly, from the south gate of Milecastle 19. Three have been found on the Antonine Wall.

Plate 8:4   (*right*) Bronze statuette of Venus from Colchester

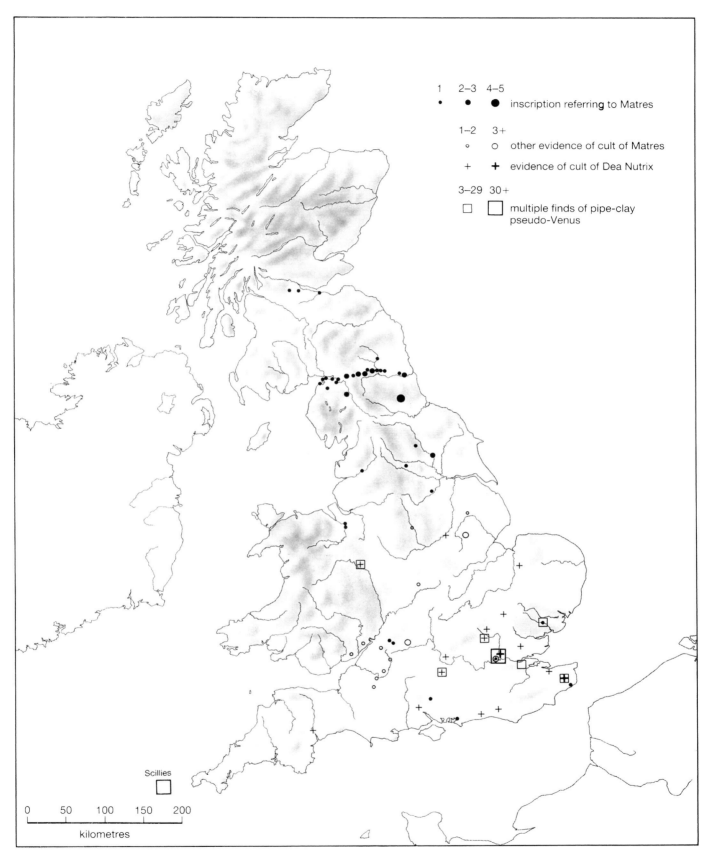

Map 8:19 Dedications to the Matres and other evidence for mother goddess and fertility cults in Britain. The information on the cult of Dea Nutrix and pipe-clay figurines of pseudo-Venus relates only to the non-military zone of Britain.

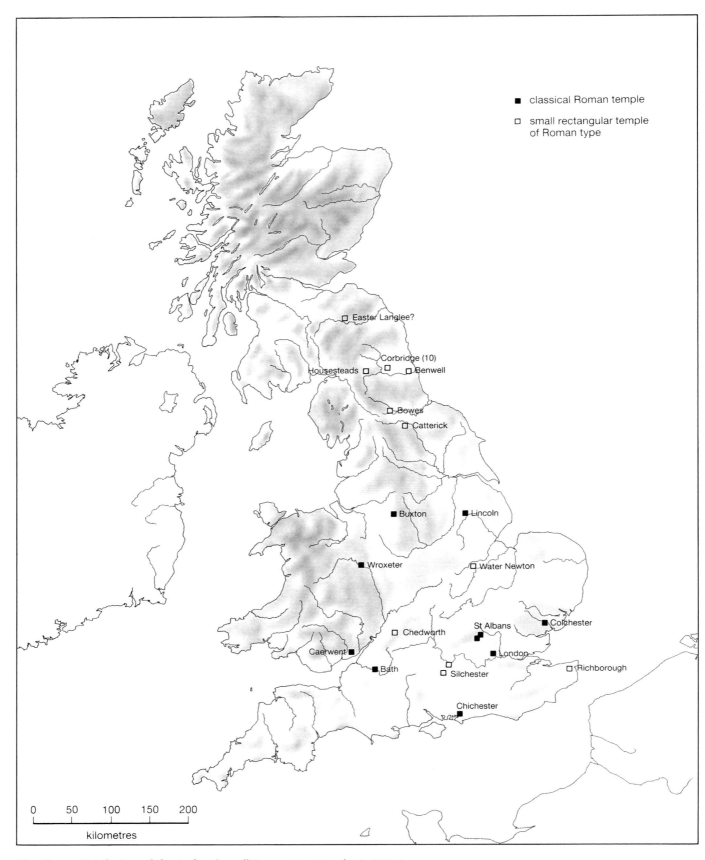

Easter Langlee?

Corbridge (10)
Housesteads □ □ Benwell

□ Bowes

□ Catterick

■ Buxton   ■ Lincoln

■ Wroxeter   □ Water Newton

■ Colchester
□ Chedworth   St Albans
■
Caerwent ■   ■ London

■ Bath   □ Silchester   □ Richborough

Chichester
■

■ classical Roman temple

□ small rectangular temple
of Roman type

0   50   100   150   200

kilometres

Map 8:20 Distribution of classical and small Roman-type temples in Britain

The importance of fertility cults in antiquity means that other dedications of a similar nature are known in Britain. The worship of the three Fates (Paecae) attested at Lincoln probably belongs to this pattern. However, some merging of the classical Fates and the triple mother-goddesses of the Treveri in the Moselle area may be implied. It seems likely that the Suleviae, female deities associated with the cult of Sulis (Minerva) at Bath, fulfilled the same role. Although they are well attested in Gaul, in Britain specific examples are known from only three places, Colchester, Cirencester and Bath (8:17).

Another fertility cult, associated with small clay figurines, is well attested in the civilian province. It is agreed that the figurines represent either Venus, the goddess of fertility (hence their name, pseudo-Venus figurines) or an equivalent goddess, Dea Nutrix. The figurines imitate the classical form of Venus and represent imports from production centres in central Gaul or Cologne in the first two centuries AD. Although some examples, like the majority of their Gallic counterparts, derive from religious sanctuaries such as Springhead and Bath, where the association with water-healing is typical of Continental arrangements, the majority of the British examples probably derive from private shrines (aediculae). Even more specifically related to childbirth is the representation of Dea Nutrix in the form of Juno Lucina, the goddess of childbirth. Her figurines, so far as understood, show the same kind of distribution pattern as those of Venus.

TEMPLES

Despite the fact that temple sites have long attracted the excavator (and latterly the treasure hunter), only recently has appreciation grown of the full range of pre-Roman, Roman, and Romano-Celtic religious foci. In particular much more is now understood of the wide range of pre-Roman shrines and temples, the influence of which formed a continuum in Romano-Celtic cult practice alongside temples derived architecturally from the classical repertoire.

Classical temples

The number of avowedly classical temples is limited (8:20). The earliest and architecturally most distinguished was associated with the Imperial cult of the Divine Claudius at Colchester (5:16) which was comparable with other major provincial cult centres, such as Schonbuhl, Augst. Another major early temple (to Neptune, and presumably of classical form) is epigraphically attested, but not located, at Chichester. At Bath, the temple dedicated to Minerva Medica in her Celticized form of Sulis is mostly classical in form. Lesser examples (and with fewer certain dedications) are also known from Castor (near Water Newton), London, Wroxeter and, somewhat later, at St Albans.

The range is spread by smaller examples at Caerwent, Lincoln and Buxton (like Bath the site of an extraordinary spring, here associated with the goddess Arnemetia). Two small, classical-type temples have been discovered in the military vici at Housesteads and Benwell, and further small rectangular temples of Roman type are known at Corbridge, Catterick and Bowes in the military hinterland.

Mithraea and basilical temples

Of special interest for its wholly non-British origin and military connections is the worship of Mithras and its associated cults. These originated in the Middle East, where Mithras or Mitra was viewed as an agent of the good or light (the sun) in the endless struggle against evil or darkness (the moon). The eastern wars from the first century BC onwards saw the spread of the cult westwards not only into Roman society, but also amongst the legionaries who could readily associate with a cult that was male-only, with ascending grades of rank for a limited number of devotees. The Mithraic congregations normally met in underground, or partly underground, basilical or long rectangular buildings. Preserved examples like S. Maria Prisca or S. Clemente in Rome show that the two side aisles took the form of continuous raised benches to seat the congregation. As Map 8:21, shows a number of such structures in Britain may be positively identified as Mithraic centres, but many basilical temples are of uncertain interpretation and certainty is only possible with associated evidence for the cult (as at the Walbrook mithraeum in London). Fortunately, however, dedications or statues to Mithras and his attendants Cautes (day) and Cautopates (night) also imply the presence of the cult, which was sometimes linked from the later second century with the cult of the sun (Sol Invictus) or other Eastern deities associated with the Mithraic cult such as Arimanius.

The best evidence occurs along Hadrian's Wall at Rudchester, Housesteads and, most informatively, at Carrawburgh – while the cult is implied by inscription or other evidence elsewhere. Another Mithraic temple in a military context is known at Caernarvon.

Romano-Celtic temples

Over fifty temples of the Romano-Celtic variety are currently known from Britain and demonstrate an overwhelmingly southern distribution pattern, in part redressing the northern bias of the epigraphic evidence for religious activity. Conventionally viewed as a fusion of classical and Celtic ideas, it is perhaps better to describe the type as representing a widespread Gallo-British continuum, though increasingly expressed in different building materials and with a Romanized architectural finish. The large number of Gallic shrines (some 180 currently) provides comparisons with the British evidence, the principal difference lying in the greater size range. British religious centres such as those at Gosbecks,

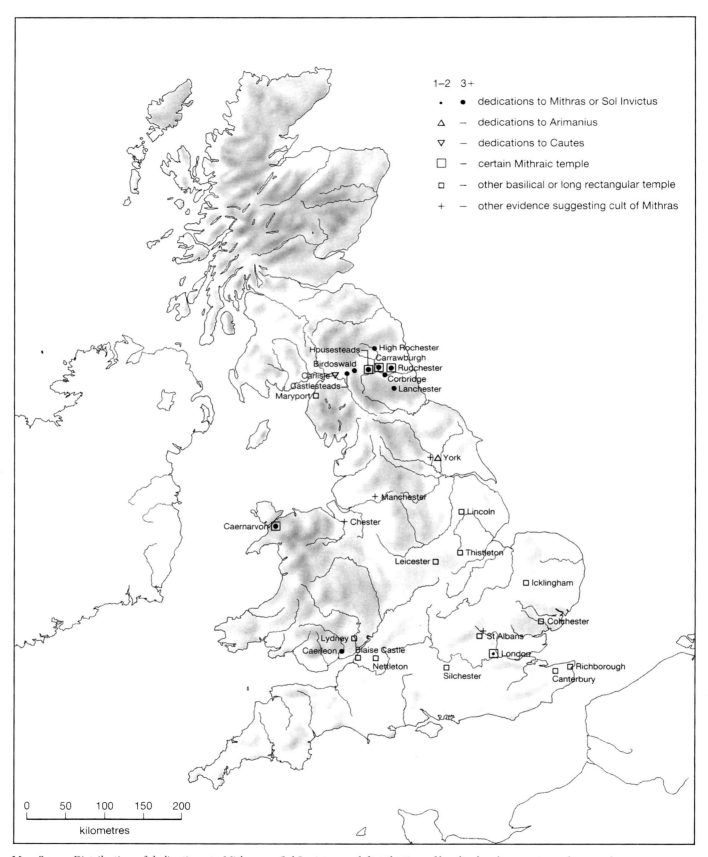

Map 8:21 Distribution of dedications to Mithras or Sol Invictus and distribution of basilical or long rectangular temples

Plate 8:5 a and **b**   An aerial view of the fort at Carrawburgh (with the *mithraeum* arrowed) on the top, and a detailed view of the *mithraeum* at ground level

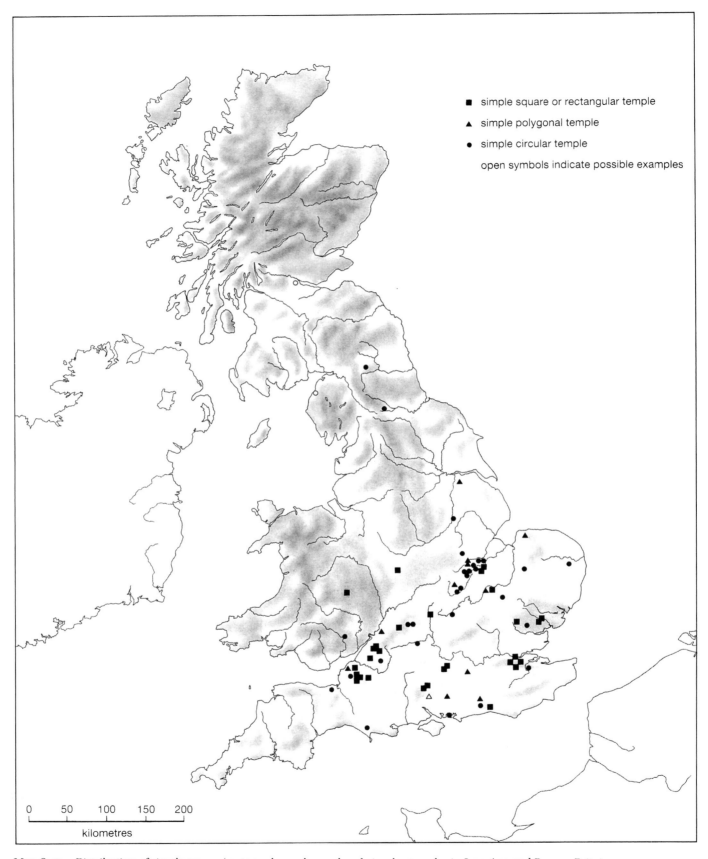

Map 8:22 Distribution of simple square/rectangular, polygonal and circular temples in Iron Age and Roman Britain

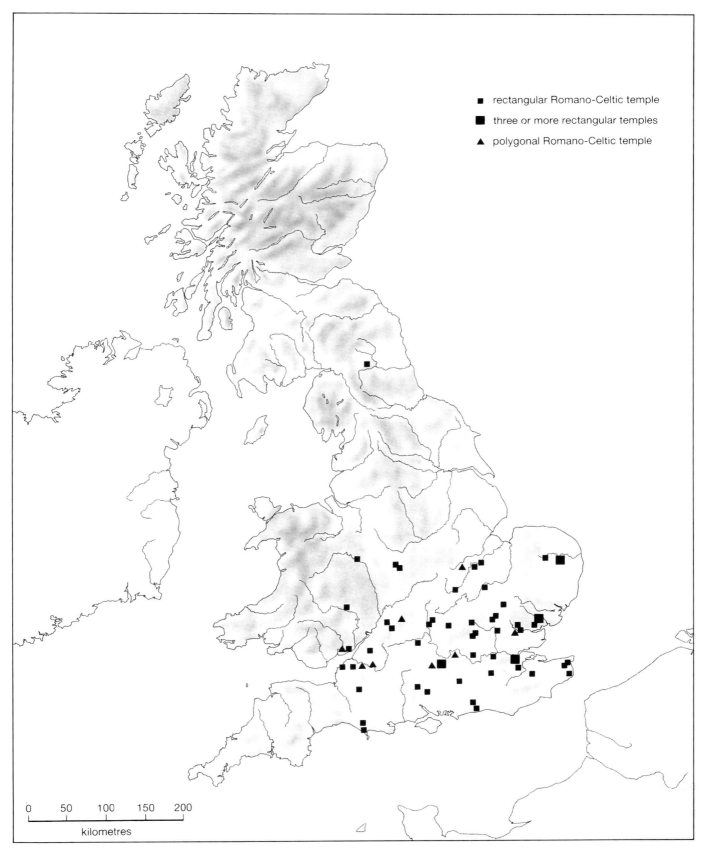

Map 8:23 Distribution of rectangular and polygonal Romano-Celtic temples in Britain

rectangular Romano-Celtic temple

three or more rectangular temples

polygonal Romano-Celtic temple

0   50   100   150   200

kilometres

Springhead, Brigstock and Lydney do not approach the overall size of the complexes at Sanxay or Trier for example.

The temples which provide the central focus of a cult site may be divided broadly into two categories. The simpler form is exemplified by a round, rectangular or polygonal structure (8:22). In the more complex form (8:23) the ground plan comprises concentric rectangular, polygonal or circular walls, the inner *cella*, or shrine, frequently being bounded by a portico of the same shape. It is often assumed that such *cellae*, especially the commonest square ones, were roofed over, but the arguments (largely based on wall-widths) are far from clear-cut, especially in the case of those examples centred around a sacred pool or spring (see 8:26 for the Dean Hall water shrine).

Britain is relatively rich in the simpler variety of shrine, notably in multiple groups such as the complexes at Collyweston and Brigstock (Northamptonshire), Colchester and the major group at the confluence of sacred springs at Springhead (Kent). There are over twenty other sites known, including the celebrated (and totally demolished) Arthur's O'on near the Antonine Wall in central Scotland. In general terms the date range involved spans the second and third centuries with rural sites developing later, although allowance should be made for the fact that much of the evidence derives from early-modern excavations, whereas more refined evidence might be collated today. At Springhead and Colchester the more complex Romano-Celtic form also occurred alongside the simpler forms, and their overall distributions (8:23) are very similar. The most notable example is perhaps to be found at Gosbecks outside Colchester (3:5), where the presence of a nearby theatre meant that the site was probably the focus of political and cultural, as well as religious, assemblies. Certainly the evidence from Wood-eaton (Oxfordshire) suggests the presence of an associated market and fairground. Furthermore, in terms of location it has plausibly been suggested that some other examples, such as Frilford and Nettleton Shrub, may have stood at the boundary between tribal territories.

From *temenos* to temple

Knowledge of the late prehistoric ritual enclosures, or *temenoi*, and the shrines within them has increased only slowly, but is an essential part of any understanding of Romano-Celtic religion. Unfortunately, the largely timber structures and associated votive material from middle and later Iron Age sanctuaries can only be recovered from large-scale modern excavations, although at Uley (8:27), for example, the subsequent Romano-British temple had destroyed much of the earlier evidence. Sacred groves, pools or other features could exist within enclosures large (Slonk Hill, Harlow) or small (Uley, Colchester (Temple 6), Hayling) (8:24). At the centre of the enclosure a variety of ritual structures may be identified. Three-sided enclosures, sometimes associated with

Plate 8:6 The foundation trenches of the Romano-Celtic temple at Coleshill, Warwickshire

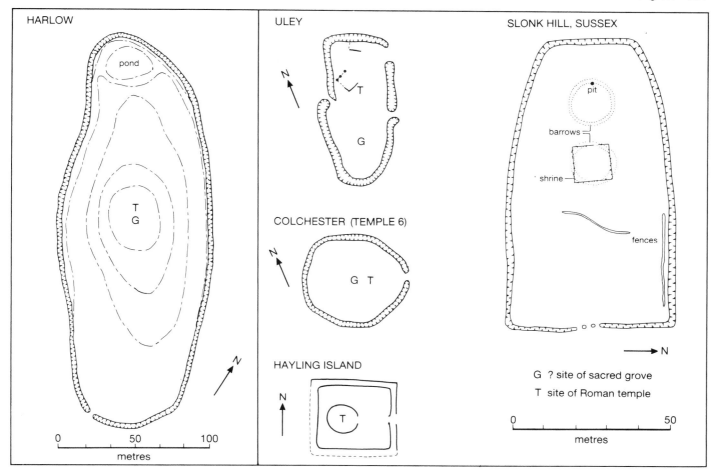

Map 8:24 Celtic *temenoi*

infant burials, appear in religious contexts at Danebury and Uley (see 8:27, structures B and C). South Cadbury has produced a rectangular timber building comprising a shrine and a porch, while square structures with an ambulatory known at Heathrow and Danebury anticipate the form of the stone Romano-Celtic temple. In origin, this last type may have similarities with earlier prehistoric mortuary enclosures, but timber round-houses similar to domestic accommodation may also have served a religious purpose. The timber round-house at Maiden Castle is generally thought to have fulfilled a religious role and this is certainly the case at Hayling Island (8:25), where a round-house containing a ritual pit sat within a rectangular *temenos* in the first half of the first century AD.

The following examples are chosen to illustrate the development of Romano-Celtic shrines, albeit at very different scales. The sites have recently been excavated, each having its own regional relevance.

The pre-Roman phase of the shrine at Hayling Island in Portsmouth harbour took the form of a sub-rectangular enclosure roughly 25m square, bounded by a timber palisade with a single entranceway to the east (8:25). The entranceway led across the interior to a circular structure slightly less than 10m in diameter which contained a central depression, probably a votive pit. The late Iron Age shrine abounded in ritual deposits comprising weapons and various items of cavalry equipment. Yet when the temple was completely reconstructed in *c*.AD 50 the new building was entirely lacking in any weapons deposited as votive objects. This shows, in archaeological terms, the reality behind the imposition of the Roman law against the carrying of arms, the bone of contention with the Iceni in AD 49 (4:5). The scale of reconstruction in the second phase must relate in some way to the ambitious building programme undertaken in the client kingdom of Cogidubnus. The late Iron Age timber structure was replaced in masonry on an altogether enlarged scale. A formal entrance stairway led to an ambulatory approximately 38m square on the outside and some 5.5m wide between the outer and inner walls. Beyond the ambulatory was a court, bounded on all four sides by a

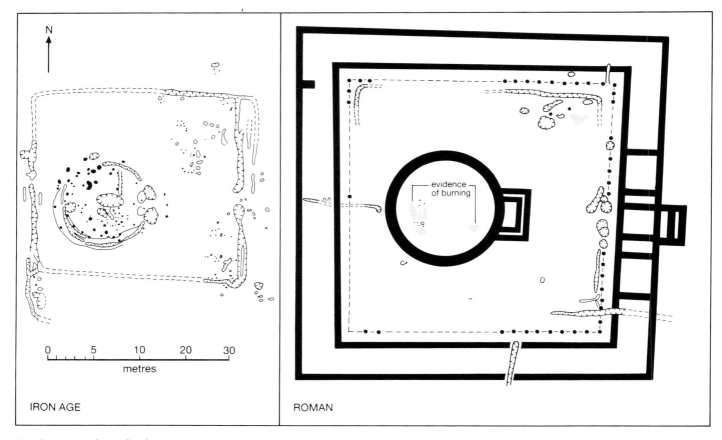

IRON AGE   ROMAN

Map 8:25   Hayling Island

series of post-holes set comparatively close to the inner wall of the ambulatory, presumably forming a roofed, colonnaded portico. The circular central shrine (13.5m diameter) faced the entrance and was also approached by a formal staircase. The Romano-Celtic shrine at Hayling Island may be viewed as a major cult centre with late Iron Age origins and a scale of construction that probably reflects the patronage of the client king Cogidubnus.

On a smaller scale, recent work at Dean Hall, near Newnham-on-Severn in the Forest of Dean, has revealed a two-period water shrine on a hilltop overlooking the River Severn where the tidal bore reaches its most impressive proportions. Two series of post-holes, one roughly rectangular, the other of circular layout occupying an area 8m north-south by 9m east-west, indicate structures set round a small water source at a point where a bed of old red sandstone comes to the surface in compression between two bands of yellow clay (8:26). This represents part of a spring line which still functions today. The roughly circular timber layout around the spring head resembles the inner timber shrine of the structure at Hayling Island in its late Iron Age phase.

The secondary structure was planned on a more substantial scale using timber and wattle and daub along roughly the same plan as the preceding phase. The walls at the western end rested on a masonry plinth preserving the most obvious remains of the building, divisible on the western side into at least two sub-phases and containing niches where cult statues were probably placed. There is a parallel to this plan in the nearby forum temple at Caerwent, but the replacement of the niches and the resulting plan is very reminiscent of the well-known late temple structure at Lydney. The flooring of the main room exhibited two stages, the first showing evidence of a cobble line leading from an entrance on the eastern side towards the spring head, again comparable with the Hayling Island arrangements. The second period saw substantial areas covered by old red sandstone *tesserae* forming a rough pavement leading into the ambulatory that extended round the central shrine. The use of old red sandstone *tesserae* in this manner is paralleled at the nearby Clearwell villa. The spring head went through at least two and probably three phases of development, and in its later form comprised a formalized pool from which a masonry drain ran north-west through the contemporary walls of the ambulatory.

The dating of the initial years of the secondary phase is difficult to establish but, on pottery evidence, may belong to the late second century AD. The Dean Hall temple may,

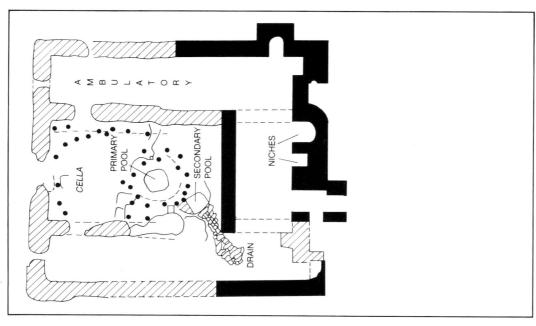

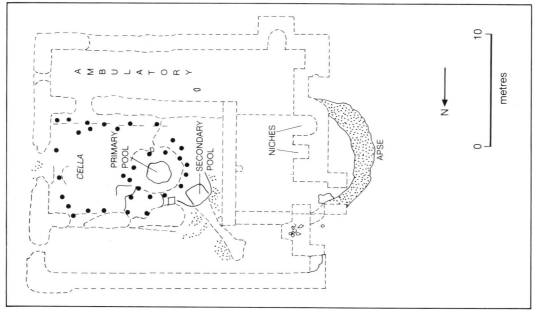

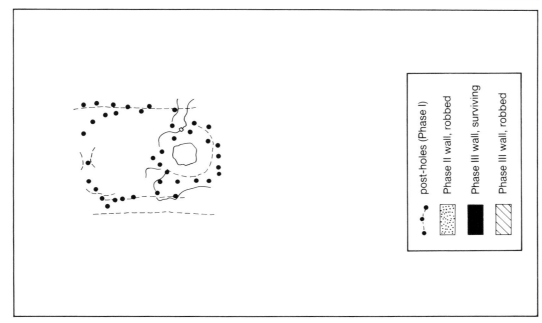

post-holes (Phase I)

Phase II wall, robbed

Phase III wall, surviving

Phase III wall, robbed

Map 8:26 Dean Hall temple

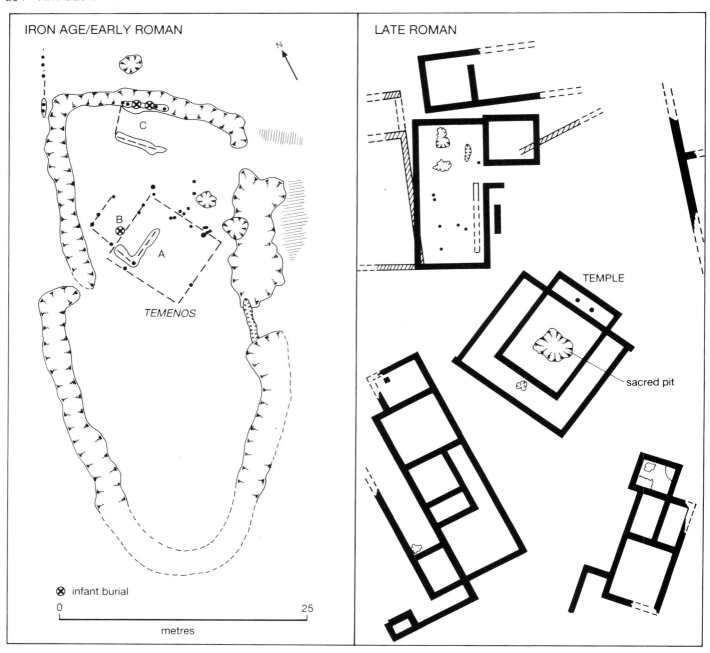

IRON AGE/EARLY ROMAN

C

B

A

TEMENOS

⊗ infant burial

0   25

metres

LATE ROMAN

TEMPLE

sacred pit

Map 8:27   Uley, West Hill

therefore, be interpreted as a two-period water shrine with a long span of occupation extending probably from the late Iron Age to at least the late fourth century. There are several parallels to the site to be found at Uley on the other side of the Severn (see below), and the layout of the spring head arrangement has a close parallel at Hochsheid, near Trier in West Germany. In interpreting the cult overall it is difficult to divorce the site from its position overlooking the great horseshoe bend of the Severn, the optimum position to

observe the run of the famous Severn bore, which must naturally have made a great impression on the Romano-British population, as it still does on us today.

The religious centre on West Hill, Uley, is associated with the defensive circuit at Uley Bury on the western edge of the Cotswold ridge overlooking south-west Gloucestershire and the Severn estuary. Recent excavation has shown the lengthy development of this religious centre from its beginnings as an irregularly ditched oval enclosure measuring c.48m by 25m in the early Iron Age (8:27). By the early first century AD a palisade had effectively replaced the largely silted ditches, save where a detached eastern ditch had been constructed. The ditch contained a central pit with many iron projectiles (cf. the weaponry recovered from the first temple at Hayling Island, 8:25 above). The vestiges of a centrally placed rectangular timber structure (A) survived beneath the later Romano-British temple. Before the latter was constructed in the second quarter of the fourth century, two buildings (B and C) both containing votive objects occupied part of the area. The stone temple comprised a version of the Romano-Celtic layout with a sacred pit set inside a *cella*, which was surrounded on three sides by an ambulatory. Lead curse-tablets (*defixiones*) indicate that the deity worshipped in Romanized form was Mercury. Contemporary with the temple were two ranges of stone buildings; they can be interpreted as dormitories or waiting rooms along the lines identified at the temple sites of Colchester (Temple 6), Thistleton or, across the Severn at Lydney.

The latest recognizable phases of occupation at Uley are of unique interest. The stone temple was thoroughly demolished in the last quarter of the fourth century, an act convincingly interpreted as Christian demolition of a pagan shrine, with the cult statue of Mercury being smashed and incorporated in later foundations. The small stone and timber structures (not shown here) that were subsequently erected on the sacred area are difficult to interpret with any certainty. The presence of an apse with altar base, however, hints at a Christian function. Use into and perhaps across the fifth century and even later is possible, making the late Roman and early post-Roman development of the ritual enclosure at Uley of more than regional significance. The excavation has demonstrated the continuity of worship and religious structures on the hilltop across the best part of a millenium.

CHRISTIANITY AND PAGANISM IN LATE ROMAN BRITAIN

The message of Christianity, if we are to believe a statement of Tertullian, did not effectively reach Britain until the late second century, at which time it was still an outlawed religion. In this case the Manchester Deansgate word-square (a palindrome reading identically along the sides and re-arrangeable into a cruciform PATERNOSTER with repeated pairs of *alpha* and *omega*) may be the earliest datable evidence for the Christian message in Britain. The words were found cut onto the shoulder of an amphora fragment found in rubbish of the *vicus* and dated to the third quarter of the second century AD. Its closely dated context distinguishes it from a similar but less well dated palindrome found scribbled on a wall at Cirencester in 1868. Scholars remain divided

on the question of whether the palindrome had pagan significance also, but the balance of probability is that both examples do indeed reflect Christian activities.

By the early fourth century, Christianity had yielded its three British martyrs, Alban, Aaron and Julius, under the persecutions of the Emperors Decius (AD 250–1) and Valerian (AD 257–9), or during what Gildas calls 'the nine year persecution of the tyrant Diocletian', the end of which was effectively marked by Galerian's grudging Edict of Toleration in AD 311. The truth was that after the Rescript of Gallienus in AD 260, when Christian belief had been officially recognized as a *religio legitima*, its devotees had become too numerous and influential to be eliminated. Soon after the Edict of Toleration, Constantine the Great and his fellow emperor Licinius recognized Christianity as their 'first and principal concern' at Milan in March AD 313. That the Christian Church in Britain was already organized is shown by the presence of bishops from the dioceses of London, York and probably Colchester at the Council of Arles in Provence in the following year. In AD 325 the British bishops in attendance accepted the decrees of the Council of Nicaea (Iznik in northwest Asia Minor).

Yet, if the existence of an early British church is proven, in archaeological terms recognition of specifically Christian practice is not easy to establish (8.28), even in the case of some of the structures identified as churches, notably at Richborough, Canterbury, Lincoln, St Albans, Silchester and Icklingham, the last two examples also having associated baptisteries. Icklingham is notable also for its lead tanks with Christian symbols, normally the Chi-Rho monogram, the first two letters of Christ's name in the Greek spelling. On this evidence a more widely dispersed group of similarly sized but plain lead tanks has also been interpreted as baptismal fonts.

Much of the other evidence for Christianity in Britain is recognizable only by its iconographic context. The famous chapel with the painted walls depicting *orantes*, or worshippers, at Lullingstone, Kent, is a case in point. Four villas in Dorset have yielded Christian iconography, notably the depictions of Christ at Hinton St Mary and the panels of Christian allegory at Frampton, both near Dorchester. The local strength of Christianity is shown by the adoption of Christian motifs by the local Dorchester mosaic school (6:41) and likewise in the presence outside Dorchester of the substantially Christian cemetery at Poundbury (see below 8:33). Other Christian cemeteries have been recognized, notably at Icklingham in Suffolk.

More difficult to assess are the hoards, largely of silver, but with some gold, from a wide variety of places. No certain Christian objects are included in the famous Mildenhall (Suffolk) hoard nor in lesser hoards from Great Harwood (Bucks.), Sutton (Suffolk) and Dorchester (Oxon.), but opinion is divided over their possible Christian implications. In any case the hoards are best viewed as the property of

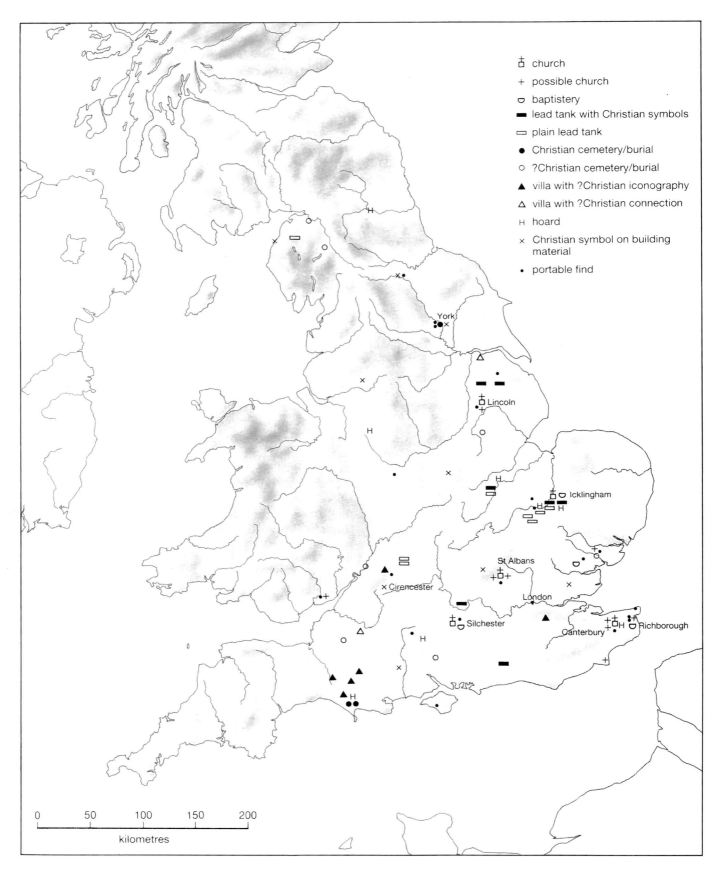

Map 8:28 Archaeological evidence for Christianity in Roman Britain

Legend:

church
+ possible church
baptistery
▬ lead tank with Christian symbols
▭ plain lead tank
● Christian cemetery/burial
○ ?Christian cemetery/burial
▲ villa with ?Christian iconography
△ villa with ?Christian connection
H hoard
✕ Christian symbol on building material
• portable find

York
Lincoln
Icklingham
St Albans
London
Cirencester
Silchester
Canterbury
Richborough

0   50   100   150   200
kilometres

Plate 8:7 The central portion of a word square thought to be a cryptic reference to Christianity, incised on the side of an amphora found in a late second-century pit in the *vicus* of the Roman fort at Manchester

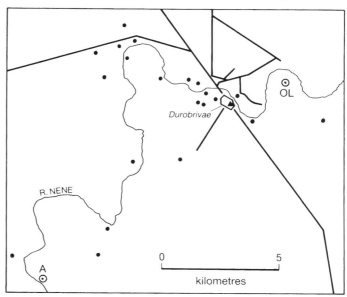

Map 8:29 Late Roman Christianity in the area of *Durobrivae* and the Nene Valley (black circles mark villas or large farms, A = Ashton lead tank, OL = Orton Longueville Christian tag or nail-cleaner)

wealthy Christian households or communities, buried in a period of instability.

Some interesting insights into a Christian community have been gained by the recovery in 1975 of the Water Newton hoard from the south-eastern corner of the major town of *Durobrivae* near Peterborough (8:29; cf. 5:21). Nearby Ashton and Orton Longueville had also previously produced objects with Christian significance. There is no doubt of the hoard's Christian context, although the discovery of the treasure through the use of a metal detector has most regrettably severed it from its archaeological context. Among the 27 objects recovered, 15 bear the stamp of an early form of the Chi-Rho symbol (see Pl. 8:8).

The occurrence of four names, one male (Publianus) and three belonging to women (Iamcilla, Viventia and Innocentia), support the identification of the hoard as the silver plate of a Christian community, probably concealed (we shall never know how) at a time of disturbance or threatened attack. Thus the great dish can be interpreted as being for use in Communion and the jugs and strainer for wine at the Eucharist. The plaques comprising part of the hoard appear, like some of the silverware, to represent craft products accumulated across a span of time and indeed there is evidence of lengthy use on some of the silverware. The combination of stylistic and other arguments suggests a date for the deposition of the hoard probably within the first half of the fourth century. There are no criteria for distinguishing the likeliest of the possible scenarios put forward to explain the circumstances of deposition; the simplest would be that the silver plate belonged to a fourth-century Christian community within the town, and the location of *Durobrivae*

Plate 8:8 A silver bowl from the Water Newton treasure, with the Chi-Rho symbol and an engraving along the rim of the bowl which may be translated as 'O Lord, I Publianus, trusting in you, honour your holy sanctuary'.

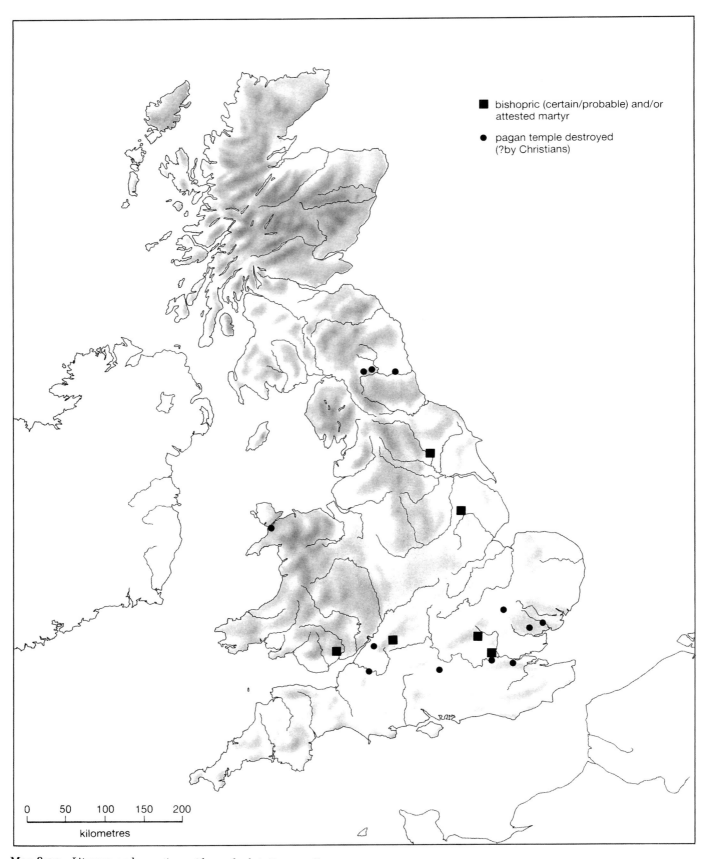

Map 8:30 Literary and negative evidence for late Roman Christianity in Britain

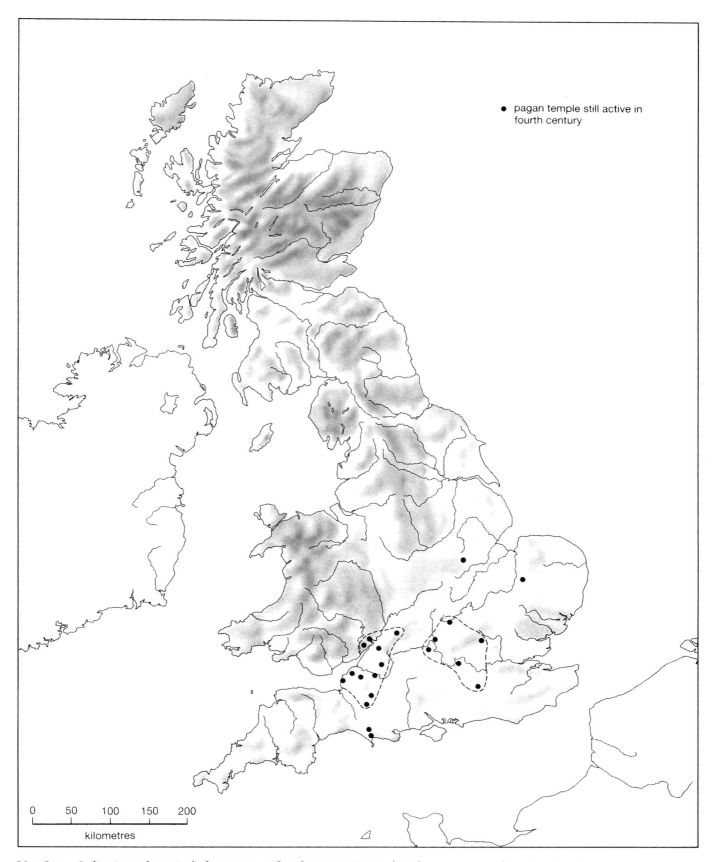

Map 8:31　Indications of a revival of paganism in fourth-century Britain based on votive coin deposits at temples

on the main road to the north raises the question of whether the centre had achieved episcopal status.

To the physical evidence of Christianity, as represented by the archaeology of churches and Christian artefacts as described above, we can add information from literary sources and the negative evidence of those pagan temples which we know were violently destroyed in the fourth century (8:30). The literary evidence concerns on the one hand evidence (or hints) of bishoprics at York, London, Lincoln and perhaps Cirencester and, on the other hand, the martyrs attested at St Albans and Caerleon.

The theory that violent and systematic destruction of pagan shrines was a Christian-inspired act has much to recommend it and, as we saw at Uley, there is the possibility that the destroyed shrines were in some cases superseded by Christian ones.

Whatever the extent of development of Christianity within the province it is clear that fourth-century Britain was not unanimous in its acceptance of Christianity. This was first suggested in relation to the Jupiter column at Cirencester which was restored during the brief reign of Julian the Apostate c.AD 360. The majority of the evidence, however, for the survival of paganism derives from temples that were still active in the fourth century (8:31). The evidence, particularly from the south-west, suggests that there was actually a pagan revival at some time in the fourth century. At Maiden Castle in Dorset the early excavators uncovered the remains of a late fourth-century temple, complete with accommodation for its priest, functioning within the massive ramparts of the famous hillfort. At Uley (8:27) the temple structures reached their most complicated form in the late Roman period and included accommodation for devotees alongside the religious building proper. The evidence from Lydney, however, requires careful consideration because recent research has tended to adjust the late chronology suggested in the original publication of the site. So far as the evidence for paganism extends, however, it is limited to the civilian area with, as already stated, a heavy concentration in the Cotswold–Severn basin.

DEATH AND BURIAL

Despite the occasional eye-catching discovery, funerary archaeology in Britain suffers from a relative paucity of evidence, although cemeteries can be expected wherever settlement existed. Thus it can be presumed that every fortress, fort, city and town had its associated burial area or areas. These are often attested epigraphically without actual burial evidence having been located. Even where cemetery areas have been identified, few have been excavated systematically or on a large scale. Map 8:32 gives some indication of the current poor state of knowledge, by noting simply those sites with 50 or more excavated burials.

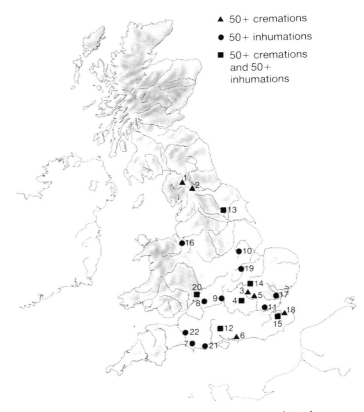

▲ 50+ cremations

● 50+ inhumations

■ 50+ cremations and 50+ inhumations

Map 8:32   Major Roman cemeteries, 50 or more burials, excavated in Britain: 1 Brougham, 2 Brough, 3 Baldock, 4 St Albans, 5 Puckeridge, 6 Chichester, 7 Dorchester/Poundbury, 8 Cirencester, 9 Cassington, 10 Ancaster, 11 Mucking, 12 Winchester, 13 York, 14 Guilden Morden, 15 Ospringe, 16 Chester, 17 Colchester, 18 Canterbury, 19 Ashton, 20 Kingsholm, 21 Ulwell, 22 Ilchester

Of the two burial practices, cremation was far more common than inhumation in the first two centuries AD. If associated grave goods are not present, as on many military sites, cremation cemeteries can be difficult to locate. Grave goods are generally common, however, and often set in boxes made of wood or tiles, as attested at Colchester and Puckeridge. The cremated ashes were placed within a glass or pottery vessel, sometimes a terracotta face-urn, again common around Colchester. The inhumations were generally of later date and, in the poorest circumstances, were simply dug in the ground with the body extended. While sarcophagi (see Maps 8:34, 8:35) were used in richer graves, the commoner burial practices took two forms, best illustrated from the extensive cemeteries known at York, particularly from Trentholme Drive. In one type, cists were sunk into the ground with walls of roughly coursed stones set around the skeleton and a roofing slab or slabs laid on top. Alternatively, two rows of large roofing tiles (*tegulae*) were

Plate 8:9 An inhumation burial from a cemetery at Caistor (Water Newton)

Plate 8:10 Bronze mirror: part of the grave goods from a burial at Whitchurch

leant over the corpse with two terminal tiles at the ends, and a row of *imbrices* forming the top. In neither case apparently was the name of the deceased incorporated in the arrangement.

Other altogether more imposing settings were possible. Burial in round, and to a lesser extent, square barrows was known in prehistory and continued into the early Empire. The cemetery at Lexden outside Colchester comprised royal barrows dating from the immediate pre-conquest period and contained rich grave goods with many Roman imports, including a magnificent medallion portraying the Emperor Augustus. The best-known examples of Roman period barrows are in Belgium, the Moselle valley, and in Britain, where they occur principally in the old tribal territories of the Cantiaci, Catuvellauni and Trinovantes. Groups of six and eight occur at Stevenage and Bartlow in the last two areas, while outlying examples are known at Hovingham (N. Yorkshire), Riseholme (Lincolnshire) and Woodlands (Dorset).

Some barrows were surrounded by precinct walls, and this characteristic reappeared in examples of walled cemeteries. Burial areas of this kind are well attested in Britain and Gaul, although varying from precincts with a single central grave monument to those containing multiple burials. Limited to south-eastern Britain, with the notable exception of the Shorden Brae Mausoleum near Corbridge, such walled cemeteries as Harpenden (Herts.), and Southfleet and Sutton Valence (Kent) reflect the proximity of major roads and prosperous rural settlement.

Walled precincts or funerary gardens have not yet been located in Britain in an urban context, where there were long-standing regulations to be observed: 'No one may bring, burn or bury a corpse within the boundaries of the town, as they shall be defined by the plough. No new crematorium shall be established within half a mile of the town.' Such were Caesar's regulations for the town of Urso. But towns could grow and change, as did London (5:20), after the Boudican sacking. Hence London's first-century burials lie in cemeteries near Newgate, from St Martins Le Grand to Warwick Square, in Bishopsgate and Finsbury, and at the Minories. To the west another area around Fleet Street also began as a cemetery in the mid-first century but was partly overlain by the spread of the walled city across an enlarged area. The pattern of extramural cemeteries continued into the Christian period. Although no early intra-mural churches are yet known in London, extramural examples may be expected where churches known to contain Anglo-Saxon fabric overlie the traces of Roman cemeteries, notably St Bede's, Fleet Street, and St Andrew's, Holborn.

The problem of recovering sufficient evidence from deep urban rescue excavations in London or other built-up areas makes it unlikely that knowledge will progress rapidly and additional importance is therefore attached to early Christian cemetery areas where, for whatever reason, detailed

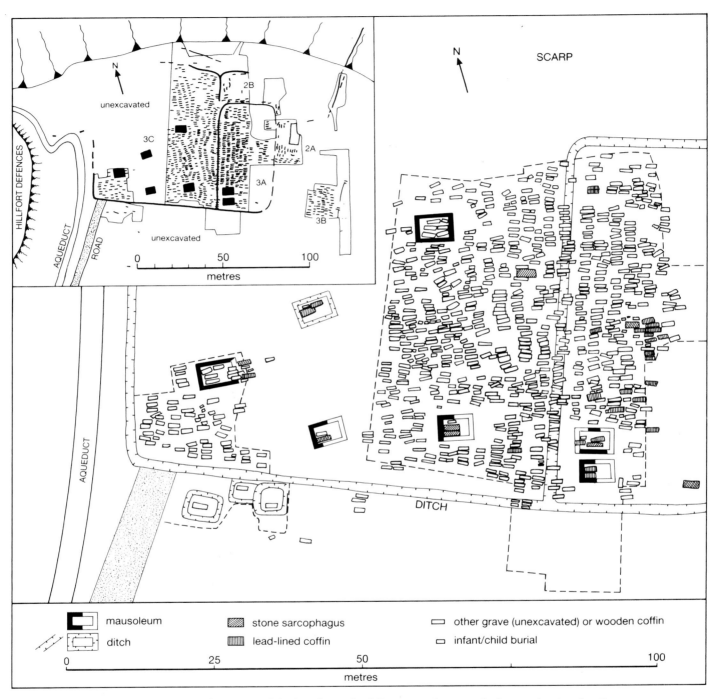

Map 8:33 Poundbury cemetery, Dorchester. Top left plan shows the full excavated extent, the larger plan is a detail.

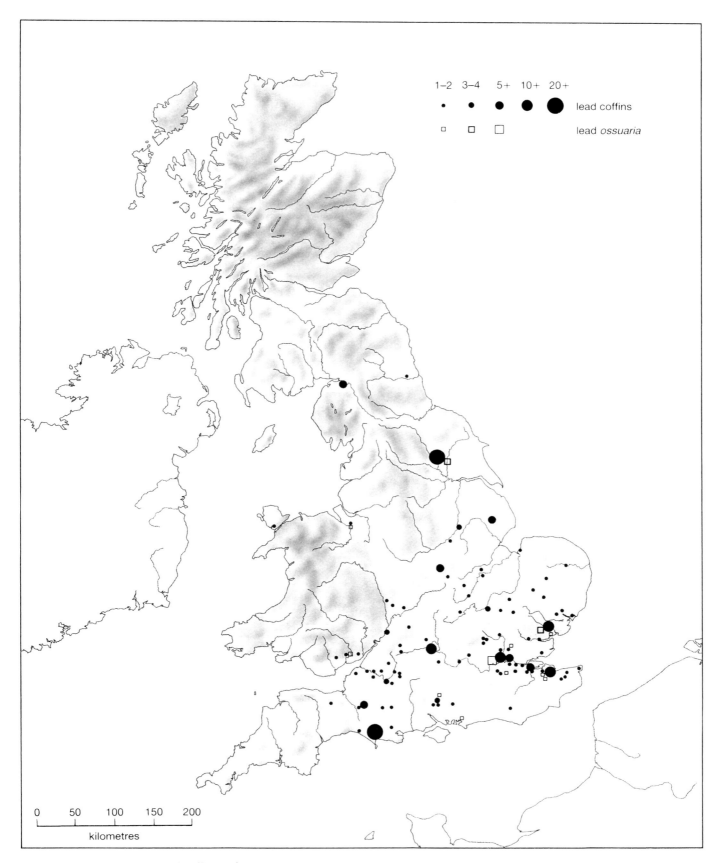

Map 8:34 Distribution of lead coffins and *ossuaria*

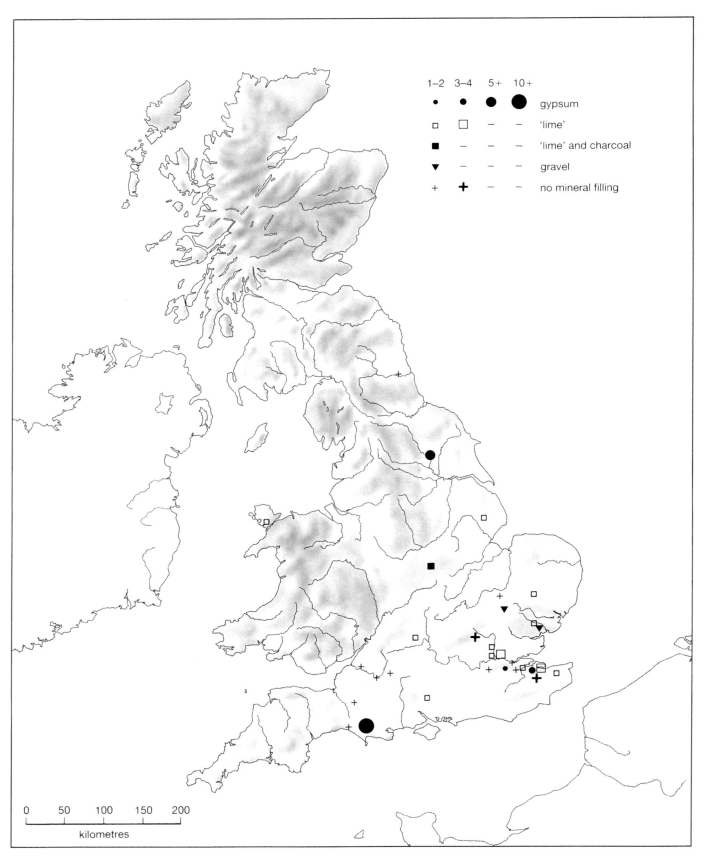

Map 8:35 Distribution of lead coffins with mineral fillings (no information on fillings exists for over two-thirds of all known lead coffins).

evidence is available. Poundbury (8:33) on the western outskirts of Dorchester (Dorset) is a case in point, along with the Lankhills cemetery at Winchester, where there is a high probability of a segregated Christian burial area. At Poundbury, close to the *civitas* capital of *Durnovaria* (Dorchester), long-term excavation has located an extensive extramural cemetery originally containing perhaps 2,500 burials (of which over 1,100 have been excavated), producing strong evidence for fourth-century Christian burial practice. The burial area concerned was about 0.9ha (2.2 acres) in extent, defined by ditches and characterized by clearly ordered east–west burial alignments. Over 75 per cent of the burials were simple inhumations, but 9 per cent (100) were given special treatment. At the top end of the scale were a number of small rectangular mausolea, two of which yielded painted plaster containing scenes depicting men carrying staves. These are best viewed as *memoriae*, or cult shrines, erected alongside or over the graves of noteworthy local Christians. The cemetery also contained examples of burials in stone sarcophagi or elaborate wood coffins (sometimes lined with lead) as well as gypsum burials. In all categories grave goods were absent or very rare. The special graves show a marked tendency to cluster and this may suggest that these were concentrated within clearly demarcated areas of the cemetery or within mausolea. The lines of humbler graves between these special groupings seem to represent orderly infilling of the space available, whilst generally respecting access paths to earlier graves.

While the wealthier Romano-British could have purchased elaborately carved marble sarcophagi, the moderately well-to-do could only have aspired, as we have seen, to burial in plain sarcophagi of stone or coffins of wood lined with lead (8:34). The distribution of lead-lined coffins lies almost entirely in the civilian area of the province, the exceptions being over twenty from York, seven from Carlisle and one from Benwell on Hadrian's Wall.

Mineral fillings, such as lime, charcoal or gravel, were sometimes added to the contents of the coffins (8:35), but the commonest, well attested at York and Poundbury for instance, was gypsum. This had the effect of forming a cast and thereby sometimes preserves fragments of textile wrapping. It has been suggested that the use of mineral fillings in coffins was favoured by Christian communities, though (unfortunately) it does not seem to have been exclusive to them. The practice is likely to have been much more prevalent in the civilian area of the province.

9
Devolution

The year AD 410 is generally held to mark the end of Roman Britain although a case can also be made for AD 409 (see below). The exact date of the Roman renunciation of further central government involvement is in fact much debated as, of course, are its consequences. The decision to relinquish the British provinces was almost certainly not seen as irrevocable at the time, nor was it wholly unexpected. Britain had always retained its own specific character within the Empire and a new phase in its evolution was already well in progress by the early fifth century. In a sense, then, AD 409 or 410 did not mark a sharp divide between on the one hand a system of Roman provinces and on the other hand a series of early Medieval kingdoms. The changeover was more gradual, extending from the late fourth century well into the fifth. This concluding chapter briefly examines some of the difficult and occasionally contradictory evidence relating to this crucial period in British history. Unfortunately, information from both historical and archaeological sources is very sparse and there is virtually no hint as to the personal motivations and attitudes of the British population, the Roman authorities or the Saxon incomers. On current evidence, for instance, we cannot take it for granted that the Romano-British population was committed to preserving all aspects of 'civilized' Roman life or that the Saxon warrior aristocracy was intent on dismantling the urban basis of that lifestyle. Isolated snippets of evidence both for change and for continuity between Roman and sub-Roman Britain can suggest different interpretations of the socio-political context of events. The first section which follows looks at the late Roman administration in Britain, and in particular its military dispositions. The vital question of how far continuity of town life and Christian religious practice were maintained by the relict Romano-British population follows, with the final section assessing the evidence for early Saxon settlement in Britain.

DEFENCE OR DERELICTION?

Earlier chapters have already shown something of the late Roman administration (5:7 and Table 5:2) and military organization (4:63–4:67, 4:70) in Britain. On the face of it the evidence suggests a continuing high level of official concern for the frontier defence of the British provinces. The units and forts noted in the *Notitia Dignitatum* (4:70)

certainly imply an impressive military organization. There was fresh activity in the mid–late fourth century in various coastal sectors, with a number of new fortifications or refurbishments. The Saxon Shore fort at Pevensey is particularly notable, since its irregular oval plan and bastions along the walls and at the gates demonstrate in architectural terms a transitional stage between Roman fort and Medieval castle. Indeed, on the new site at Pevensey, a coin of AD 330–5 sealed under a bastion could provide a relatively secure *terminus post quem* for renewed defensive initiatives, possibly associated with the visit of the Emperor Constans in the winter of AD 342. Hitherto practically no chronological information has been available for the Irish Sea province, where sites are known at Holyhead and Caernarvon. However, the 'coastal fort' known as the Wery Wall at Lancaster can now be closely dated to the AD 330s on the evidence of coins associated with the destruction of an underlying bathhouse and the primary silt of the ditch belonging to the coastal fort. There is supplementary evidence from coin histograms (9:1), for instance from Portchester and Richborough, to support the idea of renewed activity in the 330s. With the exception of Lympne, all the shore forts represented in the histograms seem to have remained in commission into the very early years of the fifth century, as probably did Lancaster. However, this and similar evidence for the forts on Hadrian's Wall, for example, could easily be over-emphasized in assessing the level of military preparedness and efficiency in late Roman Britain.

By the end of the fourth century the nature of the Roman army had changed. Most of the permanent field army, the *comitatenses*, was based in continental Europe, North Africa and the East. Much of the recruitment for these 'elite' units was from barbarian fighting groups, hired *en bloc* to defend the Empire against an equivalent enemy. Britain was no longer a prime military province and its defence rested with lower-grade troops, the *limitanei*. Although the *limitanei* included many of the units known in Britain at earlier periods, as well as some newly created ones, their size, mobility and efficiency was not comparable with the earlier *auxilia*. With no permanent provision, as far as is known, of *comitatenses* it is small wonder that the late fourth century brought military problems for the authorities in Britain. There was trouble with the Picts and Scots in AD 360, with the Picts, Scots, Saxons and Attacotti in 365, and with the same groups plus the Franks in 367 – the latter being a

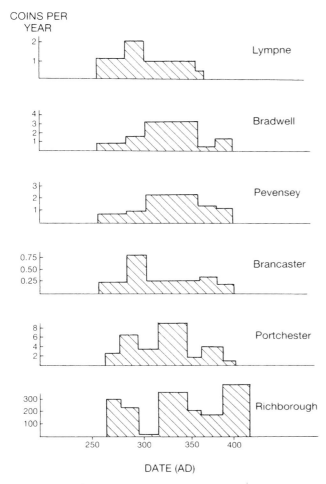

COINS PER YEAR

Lympne

Bradwell

Pevensey

Brancaster

Portchester

Richborough

DATE (AD)

Map 9:1   Coin histograms from a number of the Saxon Shore forts

Plate 9:2   Gold coin (solidus) of Magnus Maximus from London (*RIC* 2b)

Plate 9:1   *Hypocaust* of the bath-house at Lancaster with standing *pilae* floor supports, truncated by the digging of the V-shaped ditch of the Wery Wall 'coastal fort' (see also Pl. 4:28)

synchronized assault known as the 'barbarian conspiracy'. In each case troops had to be drafted in from Gaul to restore the situation. The seemingly impressive garrison list in the *Notitia Dignitatum* and the continuing occupation evidence from many northern military sites, along with impressive defences of the shore forts, should not necessarily deceive us. By this period the defence of Britain was founded on a fragile base and – most significantly – any major military problem was liable to affect the south-eastern civilian zone as well as the military north and west, a development reflected by the late construction of walls around Canterbury. One consequence was that late Roman town councils were much more concerned with the erection and maintenance of town walls than with the provision of public amenities.

The partial recovery of Britain's fortunes after the reconstruction programme of Count Theodosius in the late 360s was interrupted by its involvement in the *coup d'état* of Magnus Maximus in AD 383. He was probably the *dux Britanniarum* at the time that he launched his claim to the Western Empire and, after a successful campaign in Gaul against the Emperor Gratian, he held power until his death at the hands of Theodosius I in AD 388. In the process he almost certainly stripped Britain of all its better calibre troops. There is some evidence that, in order to minimize the effect of this on Britain, Maximus deliberately devolved responsibility for some local policing onto urban-based tribal leaders whose successors formed the major dynasties of the fifth century. The reason for associating Maximus with these moves stems partly from the evidence of the Welsh folk legends known collectively as the *Mabinogion*, one of which, the tale of Macsen Wledig, specifically relates to him and portrays him as the founder of a number of lineages.

The next outbreak of trouble is attested when the Vandal general, Stilicho, the strong man of the Western Empire at the time, apparently directed expeditions involving attacks on the Picts, the Scots and the Saxons in AD 396–8. This naturally implies major difficulties in Britain, but by AD 401 greater pressures on the Continent forced Stilicho to remove troops for the safeguarding of Italy.

The following years mark the withdrawal of Britain from the Roman Empire in both military and political terms. In AD 406–7 three usurpers (Marcus, Gratian and Constantine III) are known in Britain, their rise perhaps a response to local demands for better defence than that provided by the central administration. Paradoxically it was the *success* of Constantine III that perhaps did most to ensure the precipitate demise of the British provinces. He had rapidly crossed to the Continent in pursuit of his claim to the Western Empire and, like Maximus, eventually fell victim to his ambition, being defeated and executed in AD 410 by Honorius. We can only speculate on how far his campaigning deprived Britain of better quality troops or administrators. Once again considerable extra responsibilities may have been placed on town councils. In AD 409 Britain rebelled from Constantine's rule and because of the military anarchy of the time was never reconciled either to him or to the government of Honorius. The reassimilation of areas of the Empire which had been on the losing side of civil wars was always difficult. The late fourth-century experience of Britain clearly stretched the core–periphery relationship to breaking point. Equivalence and compatibility of interests was lost in the sense that the central input of resources no longer matched the needs and expectations of the local ruling aristocracy and there was apparently no great enthusiasm on the British side for reunification after AD 409.

In this context the well-known 'rescript' of Honorius in AD 410, in which he announced the Roman abrogation of responsibility for the area was the *de jure* recognition of a *de facto* situation. It has recently been argued that the 'rescript' in fact related not to Britain but to Bruttium in southern Italy, but even if that were to prove correct, there is no doubt that the changed political realities which the 'rescript' was recognizing could have applied equally well to Britain. The Western Empire was in a state of siege and near collapse (AD 410 was the year of the Gothic sack of Rome after all). In these circumstances the question of whether or not to reoccupy the Atlantic outpost was hardly one to command serious thought. The moment never did come again and after an initial period of parallel existence Britain and Roman Gaul drifted into very different post-Roman histories.

The end of Roman Britain was not accompanied by military disaster in the island itself, nor can we be sure of its immediate effects on administration. The prime change was likely to have been the diversion of state taxation levies to the advantage of the town councils. The use of such monies to hire mercenary troops for the defence of the towns may have been a prime consequence of this, with some precedent perhaps in the events of the rebellions of Magnus Maximus and Constantine III. The presence in the civilian zone of Germanic mercenaries, known on the Continent as *laeti*, may be recognizable through the distribution of certain items of distinctive metalwork (9:2). The arguments centre around a number of late fourth/early fifth century products,

notably belt-buckles, some of Continental production, some of suspected British manufacture in imitative form. The Continental evidence points to the use of these belt fittings as a sign of rank and status, notably amongst military personnel. The evidence from Britain is more problematic since the majority of finds come from known civilian sites (towns and indeed villas) rather than military ones. Whilst some of the metalwork may well relate to soldiers or mercenaries quartered in the civilian zone, the suggestion that the uniform of late Roman civil servants may also have included such dress items has much to recommend it in view of the fact that their service was described by the verb *militare*. The chronological context of the finds extends from the later fourth to well into the fifth century.

Nonetheless, the literary sources on the early sub-Roman period (notably Gildas, Nennius, Bede and the Anglo-Saxon chronicles) certainly support the idea of the use of large numbers of mercenaries by the old *civitates* in the fragmented

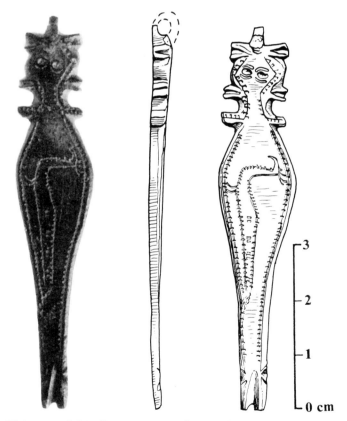

Plate 9:3   A late Roman strap-end (or nail cleaner) from Lynch Farm, Orton Longueville, near Peterborough. The decoration of the border was chip-carved, while the elongated, pear-shaped centre depicts a peacock that might be interpreted as a crypto-Christian symbol.

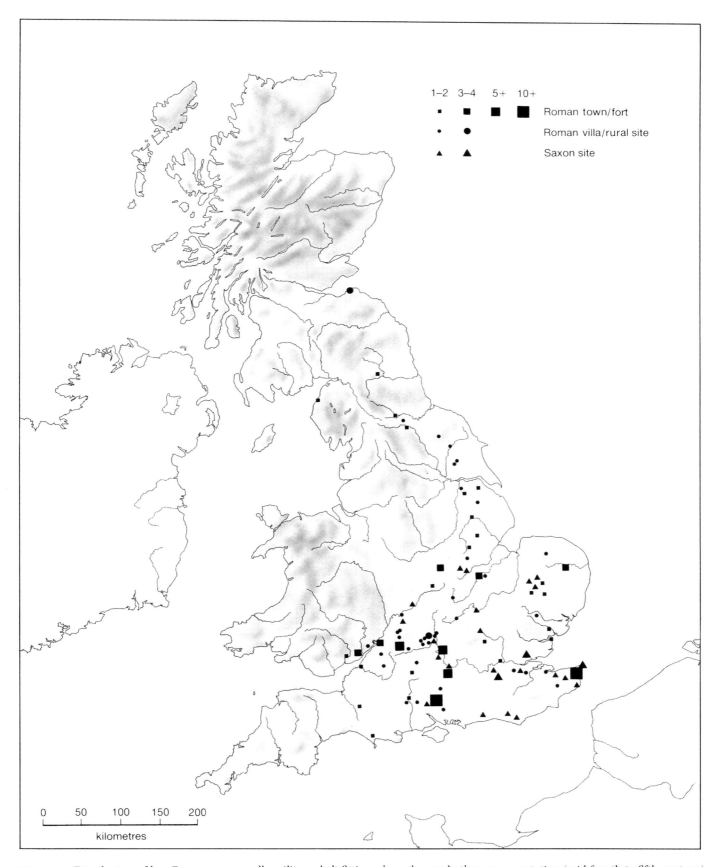

Map 9:2 Distribution of late Roman, supposedly military, belt fittings, brooches and other ornamentation (mid-fourth to fifth century)

political conditions of the fifth century. Since many of those defending the Romanized towns will have been barbarian *foederati*, we cannot resort to generalizations about the immediate sub-Roman political alignments. There need have been no uniformity of purpose amongst the towns to unite them all against a perceived common threat. Old rivalries between neighbouring towns may have easily escalated into more damaging confrontations. By AD 410 these tendencies had probably existed for some time as Romanized town life declined; after AD 410 there was less restraint and in time it seems clear that the towns became the military power bases for individuals risen either from their ruling aristocracies or from the military personnel gathered there.

CONTINUITY AND CHANGE

As already stated, the fusion of random and possibly unreliable historical sources with the archaeological record, where it exists, is nowhere more difficult than during the final phase of Roman Britain. While the documentary evidence and the archaeological evidence may potentially relate to the same period they may convey different and mutually exclusive information, the one historical, the other primarily social or economic. Inevitably most of the very limited evidence from excavation again derives from the urban, rather than rural, context. In archaeological terms most attention has concentrated on the question of continuity (as defined or inferred in a variety of ways) across the fifth century.

There was no identifiable continuity of administration from Roman Britain to Anglo-Saxon England. While in Cornwall and Wales the Celtic language survived and revived, England adopted another tongue. Similarly, although the organized episcopacy survived in modified form, the pattern of rural land ownership apparently changed altogether save possibly in a few areas, notably the area of the Hwicce in the Severn–Cotswold zone. In archaeological terms the problem centres on the absence of artefacts (especially coins) that can be securely dated to the fifth century after the traditional end of Roman Britain in AD 410.

Towns

Yet the picture has changed somewhat, with a welcome growth in urban excavation complementing evidence from other sources such as the presence of a still-functioning public water system at Carlisle attested by St Cuthbert in AD 685. A walled circuit had a defensive potential not lightly to be discarded and literary or archaeological evidence now attests some activity at most of the major Romano-British towns (9:3). More specifically, we now know that at *Verulamium* (which featured in the *Life of St Alban*, whose name was transferred to the later town nearby) a piped water

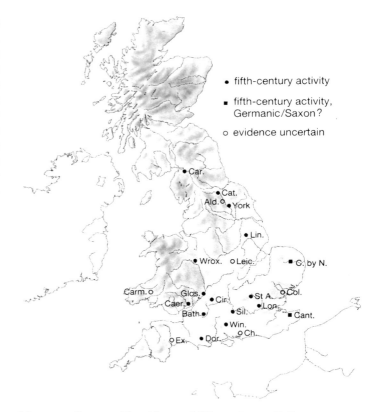

Map 9:3   Towns with evidence of fifth-century activity

supply functioned in the mid-fifth century, implying the continued operation of some civic amenities (9:4). Excavation by Frere has shown that a courtyard house (A) built *c*.AD 370 continued in use long enough to undergo both the insertion and subsequent repair of additional mosaics and tessellated pavements. A corn-dryer was eventually inserted in one room before the building was demolished to make way for a large store-building (C/C perhaps associated with post-holes D), itself demolished and overlaid by a wooden water pipe (F/F). The time lapse involved, albeit from a relatively small context, takes us towards the mid-fifth century and provides the civic setting for the pilgrimage of St Germanus to the shrine of St Alban attested in 429. Recovery of detailed later evidence of this kind from St Albans, it may be noted, is largely dependent on the absence of Medieval disturbance.

At the similarly open site of Wroxeter, fifth-century continuity of a kind is now established (9:5; see also 5:18). This large *civitas* capital was probably in decline and more thinly inhabited by the mid-fourth century, as shown by the abandonment in disrepair of the baths and basilica complex *c*.AD 350. Commercial activity, however, continued long enough for wheel ruts to have been worn into the collapsed columns. In place of upstanding stone buildings there emerged a remarkable collection of (at times elaborate) timber successors elucidated by the long-term programme

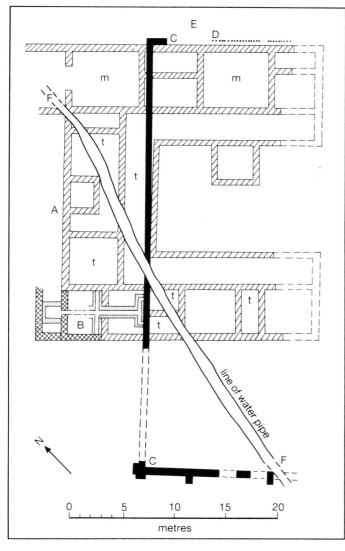

Map 9:4   Fifth-century *Verulamium:* the *Insula* XXVII building

has more of the appearance of a power-base for an individual rather than a town. Indeed the tombstone of an Irish chieftain is now also known, perhaps belonging to the early years of the sixth century.

At Winchester, Lincoln and Canterbury (9:6) there is also relevant evidence. Winchester possibly enjoyed some prosperity in the fourth century (perhaps because of the presence of the Imperial weaving mill, see 6:45), but at Canterbury urban decline apparently began early in the third century and was considerably advanced by AD 270–90 in places. By the fifth century timber buildings were cut into pre-existing street levels or building rubble in both towns. At Canterbury this takes the form of huts with sunken floors yielding a form of Anglo-Frisian pottery of mid-fifth century date from the Marlowe Theatre area. These finds derive effectively only from one suburb of the *civitas* capital and it would be unwise to generalize, particularly because, along with London, Canterbury is likely to exhibit a degree of continuity. Indeed there is conflicting evidence suggesting both continuity and decline within the various quarters, even within the same buildings. At the public baths, for instance, while the main building decayed, the portico was extended over the adjacent street in the early fifth century. By the late fifth century Canterbury was a cultural amalgam; the Adelaide Place family burial included both Anglo-Saxon beads and a coin of Zeno (*c.*AD 475), an item evidently in circulation at the same time as another coin, a clipped Visigothic gold *tremessis* found elsewhere. It was in this setting at the end of the next century that Augustine was to dedicate the intra-mural church of the Holy Saviour generally thought to have been destroyed by the construction of the Norman cathedral.

Christianity and continuity

Canterbury prompts further questions in relation to its early ecclesiastical buildings (9:6). Bede records that Queen Bercta, Bishop Liudhard and retinue used to pray in a church evidently built on the east side of the city in the Roman period. The church of St Martin has generally been thought to fulfil the necessary criteria and its core resembles a square *cella* or mausoleum reminiscent of the primary element contained within the nearby church at Stone-by-Faversham. Recently, however, excavation (which produced a pierced coin of Liudhard) has shown that the structure was domestic rather than funerary in origin. Another candidate has previously been canvassed closer to both the city walls and St Augustine's Priory, namely the primary structure within the church of St Pancras. Whatever the truth, and the churches of St George and St Gabriel (not on the map) deserve consideration; the point to note is that Bede, drawing on information provided by Albinus, Abbot of St Augustine's, attests the existence of a church regarded in the early eighth century as being of late Roman date in origin.

of excavation initiated by Barker. Rows of timber shops and booths have been identified chiefly by their marginally different rubble platforms, some being built as lean-to structures against lengths of surviving stone walls (B, C, D). A major timber building (A) occupied most of the nave of the basilica. Such discoveries, recently paralleled at Canterbury, reflect the increasing sophistication of excavation techniques, and similar structures may be expected to be found at other towns. Some post-holes at Wroxeter were found to contain sherds of Mediterranean amphorae of fifth-century date but, in chronological terms, much remains uncertain. It is important to note above all that the change of use of one of the major public buildings at Wroxeter occurred before, not after, AD 410. Although some of the timber buildings at Wroxeter were on a large scale, this should not obscure the apparent overall decline of the site. It

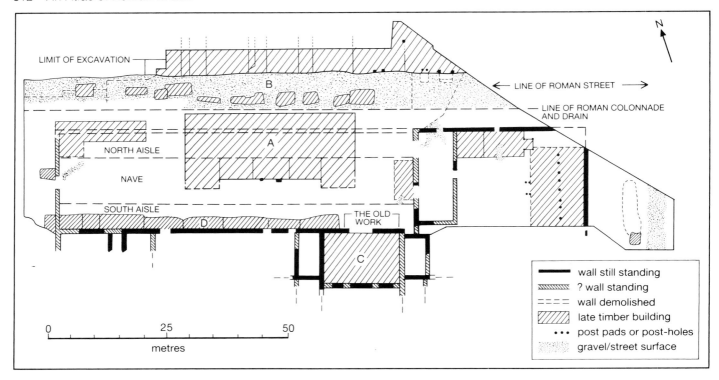

LIMIT OF EXCAVATION

B

NORTH AISLE

A

NAVE

SOUTH AISLE

D

THE OLD
WORK

C

N

←— LINE OF ROMAN STREET —→

— LINE OF ROMAN COLONNADE
   AND DRAIN

▬▬▬	wall still standing
▨▨▨	? wall standing
====	wall demolished
▨▨▨	late timber building
•••	post pads or post-holes
▒▒▒	gravel/street surface

0   25   50

metres

Map 9:5   Fifth-century Wroxeter: the baths basilica site

St Albans offers roughly comparable evidence relating to the British Christian martyr Albanus who died (in common with Julius and Aaron) under the 'nine year persecution by the tyrant Diocletian', according to Gildas. Although a Diocletianic date has been questioned at times, the central issue is not in doubt. The grave of Albanus, whose cult spread to Gaul and Germany, later formed the martyrial shrine, perhaps in the form of a *cella*, visited by St Germanus in AD 429. Whatever the form of the shrine it can safely be presumed to lie not beside the extramural church identified on Verulam Hills Field south-east of *Verulamium*, but amid the early cemetery known to underlie the enclosure of the abbey church, or cathedral, situated across the River Ver on the hill to the north-east and around which the modern town developed.

Given the continuing importance of the Romano-British towns into the fifth century (and in some cases beyond) it is no surprise to find evidence for churches within or close to walled towns (see Maps 8:28, 9:8).

Another facet of the location of early churches is shown in Map 9:7. The defences of long-standing Roman forts in Britain (and particularly in the north where there were few towns) offered obvious advantages for the location of settlement of one kind or another. Although very little is known about this in any detail, it is clear that a number of early churches were established within forts, and more particularly, in some cases within the *principia*, where the

surviving elements of the cross hall would offer much of the requisite plan on which to re-erect a place of worship. Direct continuity is difficult to establish and a much later context of reuse is possible, with the earlier ruins providing a suitable stone quarry. Whilst an early date is unprovable for many of the churches at the sites on the map, the possibility remains that churches (indicative of a wider continuity of settlement) were in some cases deliberately sited inside fortifications in the turbulent years of the early sub-Roman period.

However, the story does not stop here; Bede (*A History of the English Church and People* 1,30) states that Pope Gregory instructed his bishops not to destroy adaptable buildings such as pagan temples but to use them for Christian practice where possible. In this context it should be noted that most of the early churches of the Tyne and Wear area which were not in old forts, namely Hexham, Jarrow, Monkwearmouth, Escomb, Bywell and Ovingham, occur at places where Roman occupation is attested. Much more work needs to be undertaken to examine the way in which early post-Roman structural evidence may occur on such sites, both civilian and military, as currently shown by the recovery of timber buildings adapting a Roman stone granary at Birdoswald.

In its tantalizingly limited way, the self-criticism of St Patrick (see Map 9:9) for his lack of fluency in Latin may be symptomatic of the ideological divisions that arose in the fifth-century Christian Church as a whole (9:8). Little is

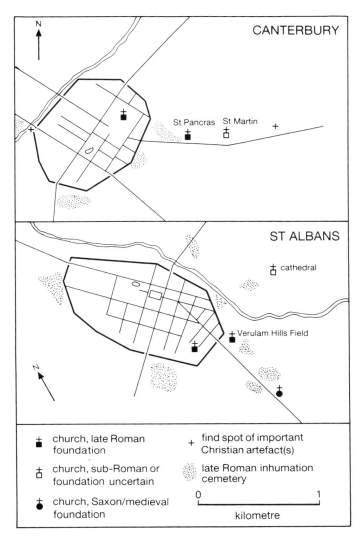

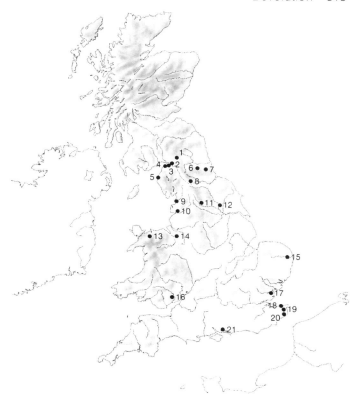

Map 9:7 Distribution of Roman forts with ecclesiastical buildings superimposed: 1 Bewcastle, 2 Stanwix, 3 Burgh-by-Sands, 4 Bownes, 5 Moresby, 6 Ebchester, 7 Chester-le-Street, 8 Bowes, 9 Lancaster, 10 Ribchester, 11 Ilkley, 12 York, 13 Caerhun, 14 Chester, 15 Burgh Castle, 16 Caerleon, 17 Bradwell, 18 Reculver, 19 Richborough, 20 Dover, 21 Portchester

Map 9:6 Churches and cemeteries of late Roman Canterbury and St Albans

known of Christian centres at the time, but the linguistic point is perhaps relevant to the development for which the fifth-century British Church became best known, namely the Pelagian heresy. Pelagius, a British cleric who became sufficiently influential to provoke the doctrinal opposition of St Augustine of Hippo, advocated a far less fatalistic view of the human condition than the Church hierarchy, favouring the belief in self-determinism. It is easy to see this as a reflection of the self-reliance perforce thrust upon a peripheral province in which, it has been argued, a more conservative form of Latin endured. Little or nothing of these intellectual disputes surfaces in the archaeological record. The attested visits to Britain by St Germanus, who campaigned against the Pelagian heresy between AD 422 and AD 432 at the behest of Pope Celestine, may be seen as part

of the ideological dispute. Naturally the south-east is likely to have formed the centre of orthodoxy and this seems implicit in the foundation of the Abbey of St Augustine at Canterbury (9:6) close to the site of a church acknowledged to have its origins in the late Roman period.

Canterbury lay in the area of pagan Saxon control by the late fifth century and for evidence of the survival of Christianity one must take strands of information from the west and north, in what might be termed Celtic Britain. The practice of Christian religion may reasonably be inferred at surviving western *civitas* centres whose name continued in latinized form into this period. It is also likely to have occurred at sites where the 'eccles' place-name element, derived from the Latin *ecclesia*, suggests, but does not prove, the presence of a church or mother church (*matrix ecclesia*). A number of important inscriptions in debased Latin also attest the existence of Christian clergy in Cornwall, parts of Wales and, most remarkably, in Galloway, where such inscriptions have been found at Kirkmadrine and Whithorn. The latter is very important for the existence of the 'White

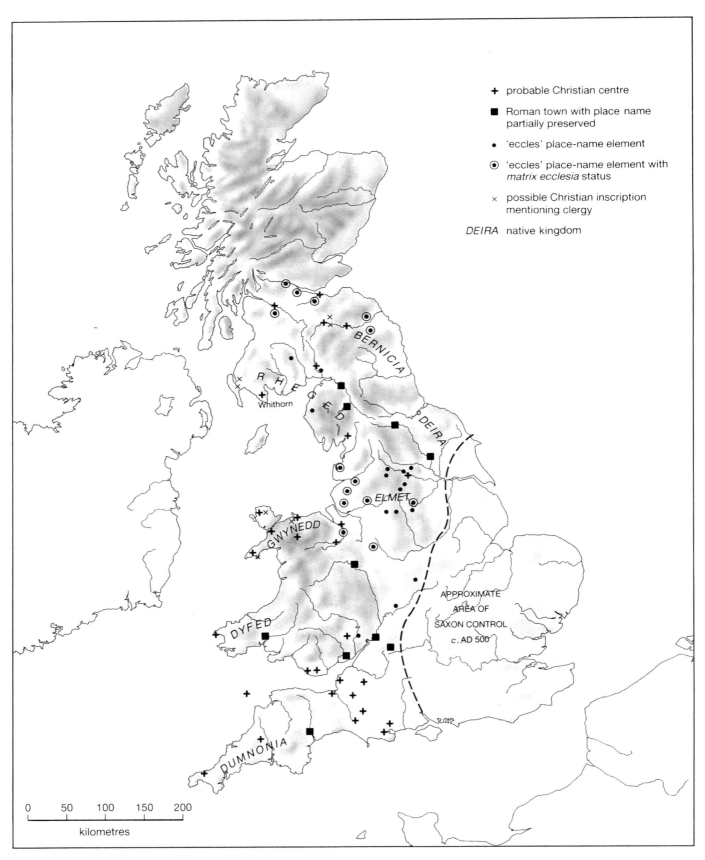

Map 9:8 Survival of Christianity in fifth-century Britain

Legend:

+ probable Christian centre

■ Roman town with place name partially preserved

• 'eccles' place-name element

⊙ 'eccles' place-name element with *matrix ecclesia* status

× possible Christian inscription mentioning clergy

DEIRA native kingdom

Map labels: BERNICIA, DEIRA, RHE...ED, Whithorn, ELMET, GWYNEDD, DYFED, DUMNONIA, APPROXIMATE AREA OF SAXON CONTROL *c.* AD 500

Scale: 0 50 100 150 200 kilometres

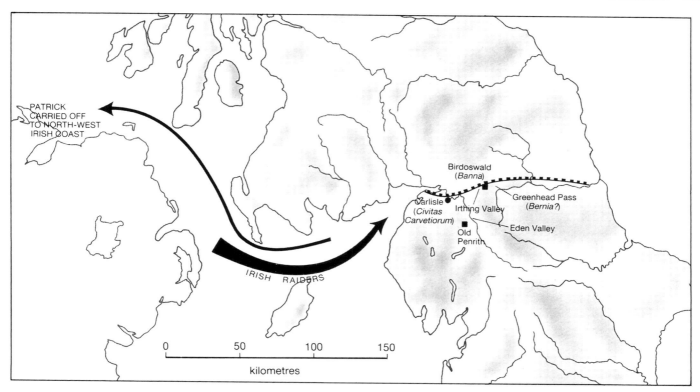

Map 9:9 The World of Patrick

House' (*casa candida*). This was an early church which may also have developed within the monastic tradition. At Ninkirk, 2km east of Penrith, and Ruthwell, 10km west of Annan (Dumfries), religious centres appear to have developed from settlements that were in existence by at least the last quarter of the fourth century. This northern setting is probably the one in which St Patrick grew up (9:9).

A useful glimpse of late Roman Britain is intriguingly contained in the life of St Patrick, the patron saint of Ireland, and depends on his two accepted surviving writings, the

Plate 9:4 Stone granary at Birdoswald which was reused as the foundations of a probable sub-Roman timber structure

Plate 9:5 The church built over the headquarters building of the Roman fort at Burgh-by-Sands, Cumbria. The body of Edward I lay in the church following his death on the nearby Solway crossing.

Letter to the Soldiers of Coroticus and the later *Confessio*. The evidence of these two documents shows that Patrick (or Patricius as he was called) was the son of Calpornius, who had served both as a Christian deacon and a decurion, that is, as a member of the local *civitas* council, implying that the family was one of standing and wealth. The Christian element in the family was further extended back by Patrick's grandfather, Potitus, who had served as a Christian priest. This apparently stable scene was abruptly disrupted when the sixteen-year-old Patrick was captured by Irish/Scottish raiders and taken away from his father's country estate with some of the family servants. For six years he worked as an enslaved farmhand, possibly in the north-west of Ireland. He escaped, probably via southern Ireland, and joined a ship that apparently crossed to Brittany, whence he was able to return eventually to Britain. In Gaul he underwent formal training in a Christian setting, became a deacon probably about the age of 30, and returned to Ireland in the capacity of a bishop or, as he put it, 'a slave for Christ' amongst the people who had earlier enslaved him.

His natural language was late British (i.e. insular Celtic) but he could read Latin and was able to memorize parts of the Latin Bible; yet he confessed that when he spoke or wrote Latin he did so with some difficulty. Despite the enormous literature that has developed around the subject of his life few facts emerge. His father's estate with its servants would have been linked to a town house in the *civitas* capital where his father Calpornius served as decurion. Current scholarly opinion now favours the idea that Patrick was born in the early fifth century and captured in the 430s, returning to Ireland between 450 and 460. Where his family home was located has caused great debate. He quotes the place name of his father's residence, namely '*vicum Bannaven taburniae*', a further source of much scholarly dispute. The usual reconstruction of the place name as '*vicus Banna venta Berniae*' points to a civilian settlement in the Irthing Valley near to *Banna*, i.e. Birdoswald on Hadrian's Wall. *Venta* is simply the additional word meaning market place or local centre. Other candidates are possible, notably the *Bannaventa* near Daventry in Northamptonshire, but the north-western location is favoured here with *Luguvalium*, Roman Carlisle, and the *civitas Carvetiorum* serving as the focus for the administrative activities of his father.

Patrick may be seen as a figure living in the Christian world of fifth-century Celtic Britain. The eastern and south-eastern parts of Britain were, however, subject to the Anglo-Saxon incursions of the time and assessments of their impact raise fundamental questions of interpretation.

THE SAXON INHERITORS

There are several views of the Anglo-Saxon invasions of the last half of the fifth and the sixth centuries. The traditional school of thought views the invasions as a cataclysm that overwhelmed late Roman civilization to such a degree that little mark of it remained upon Anglo-Saxon England. A second perspective, while admitting a degree of survival that the former school of opinion might find hard to accept, nevertheless believes the invasions to be characterized by a large influx of peasant settlers; and a third view interprets the invasion as essentially a resettling of a warrior aristocracy on a native peasantry. It seems clear that Saxons had been present as mercenaries in the early fifth century and if any reliable impression can be drawn from the legend of Vortigern, Hengist and Horsa it is that Saxon mercenaries serving British rulers could have provided the bridgehead for larger-scale invasions.

While no historian would hold the view today that the pre-existing Romano-British population was either wholly annihilated or driven westwards into the mountain retreats of Wales and Cornwall, there is evidence primarily in the form of cemeteries (shown by Maps 9:10 and 9:11) that there was a large migration of Germanic peoples into the eastern half of sub-Roman Britain. There remains the question of the character of that migration, and the degree to which archaeological and other evidence bears out the assumption that Anglo-Saxon people, place names and institutions replaced their late Roman counterparts. In his classic discussion of the problem J. N. L. Myres, while minimizing the significance of racial divisions between Jutes, Angles and Saxons, stated that the invaders of Britain previously populated the territory between the Elbe and the Ems to capacity and that this is demonstrated by the large numbers of cemeteries in that region. In assessing the ramifications of this argument for mass cross-Channel migration it is important to remember that life expectancy was very low. Arguably birth and death rates were so delicately balanced that it might take only a failed harvest to tip the scale in favour of sharp population decline in a given year, particularly with epidemics also taking their toll.

Any explanation must also be bound up in the inability of the Roman Empire to defend its own frontiers and in the bankruptcy of the Western Empire at the end of the fourth century. Roman Imperial policy had long been effectively geared to cautious frontier control, either by stirring up inter-tribal border disputes or by paying subsidies to maintain Roman interests. In the fourth and fifth centuries the Roman central administration became at times incapable of paying for mercenary service. At the same time Germanic society apparently underwent a transformation which, amongst other things, eliminated the old tribal names of the first and second centuries. A unit, independent of the tribe, called a *comitatus* was formed, the purpose of which was to loot wealth wherever it could be found. It was just such a *comitatus* which 'then came in three ships to Britain and ... Ebbsfleet' (*Anglo-Saxon Chronicle* for AD 449, see also Map 1:13). Maps 9:10 and 9:11 attempt to give the fifth-century evidence for the spread of Saxon culture through several

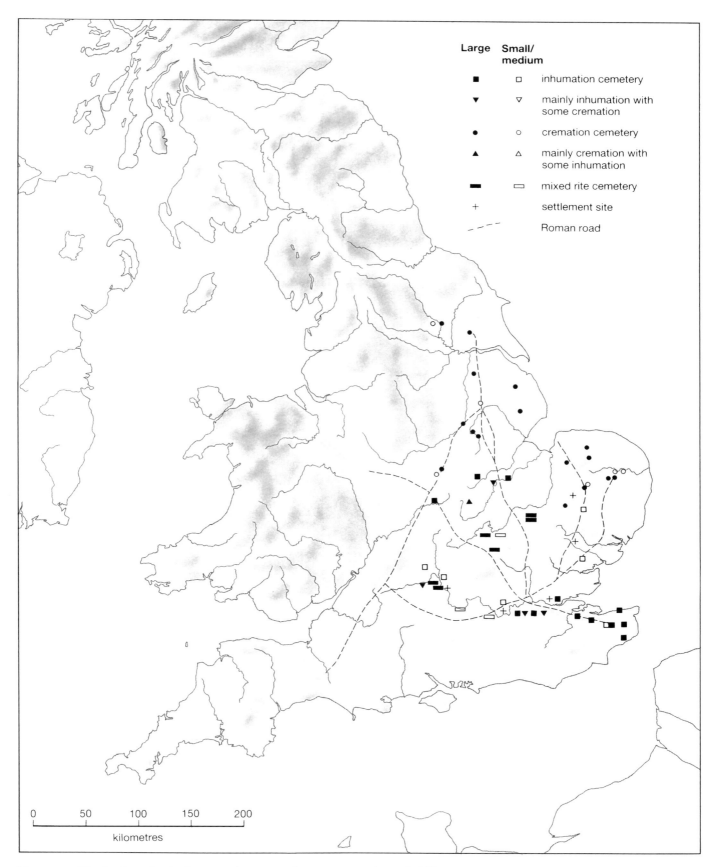

Large Small/medium

■ □ inhumation cemetery

▼ ▽ mainly inhumation with some cremation

● ○ cremation cemetery

▲ △ mainly cremation with some inhumation

▬ ▭ mixed rite cemetery

+ settlement site

--- Roman road

0   50   100   150   200
kilometres

Map 9:10 Distribution of main Saxon settlements and cemeteries in the early fifth-century

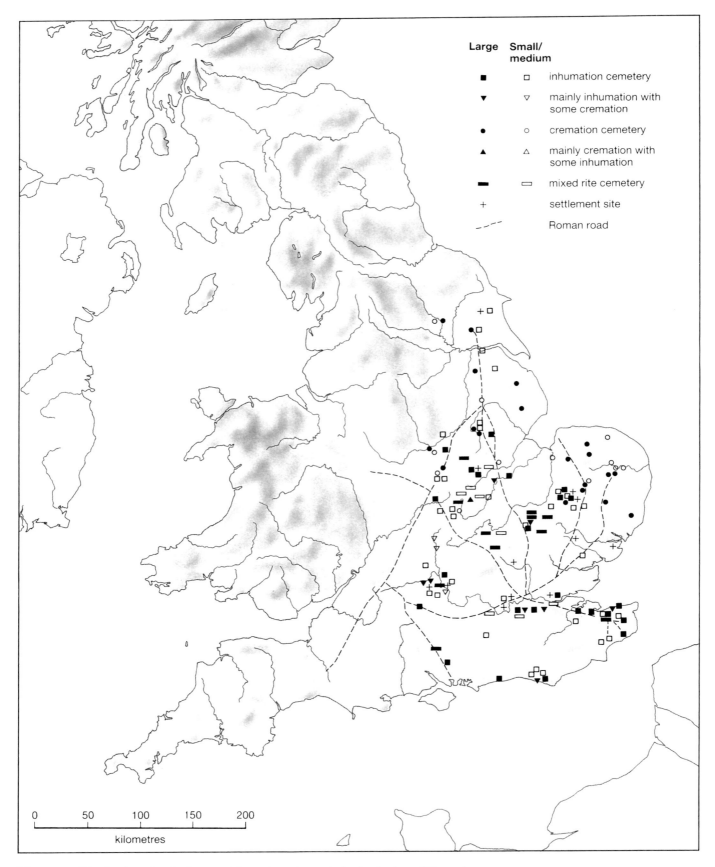

	Large	Small/medium	
	■	□	inhumation cemetery
	▼	▽	mainly inhumation with some cremation
	●	○	cremation cemetery
	▲	△	mainly cremation with some inhumation
	▬	▭	mixed rite cemetery
	+		settlement site
	– – –		Roman road

0   50   100   150   200

kilometres

Map 9:11 Distribution of main Saxon settlements and cemeteries by the later fifth-century

---

Plate 9:6 An aerial photograph of a Saxon village at Chalton Down, with the timber halls showing clearly against the chalk subsoil

.

Danish and Norman invasions of East Anglia has shown that personal names reflected not the racial composition of the area under study, but the fashion of copying the names of the prevalent ruling order. There is little reason to think that this did not happen during the Anglo-Saxon period, so that within a few generations the native population would be masked under post-conquest personal names. On the other hand the royal titles of the Anglo-Saxon kings indicate that they knew something about politics and royal protocol in Roman and sub-Roman times. The word *Britannia* naturally revived as soon as the English had accepted Roman Christianity and, indeed, after the battle of Heavenfield (AD 634) Oswald was ordained as *totius Britanniae imperator*, a singularly Roman-sounding title.

Bibliography

GENERAL READING

BAR: *British Archaeological Reports*, Oxford.

Birley, A. R., 1979: *The People of Roman Britain*. Batsford: London.

Birley, A. R., 1981a: *The Fasti of Roman Britain*. Oxford University Press: Oxford

Blagg, T. F. C. and King, A. C. eds, 1984: *Military and Civilian in Roman Britain. Cultural relationships in a frontier province*. BAR 136: Oxford.

Bonser, W., 1964: *A Romano-British Bibliography*. 2 vols. Oxford University Press: Oxford.

Branigan, K., 1980a: *Rome and the Brigantes: the impact of Rome on Northern England*. Department of Archaeology and Prehistory, Sheffield University: Sheffield.

Branigan, K., 1985: *The Catuvellauni*. Sutton: Gloucester.

Branigan, K. and Fowler, P. F. eds, 1976: *The Roman West Country*. David & Charles: Newton Abbot, Devon.

Breeze, D. J., 1982a: *The Northern Frontiers of Roman Britain*. Batsford: London.

Breeze, D. J. and Dobson, B., 1987: *Hadrian's Wall*, 3rd edn. Penguin: London.

Burnham, B. C. and Johnson, H. B. eds, 1979: *Invasion and Response: the case of Roman Britain*. BAR 73: Oxford.

Butler, R. M. ed., 1971: *Soldier and Civilian in Roman Yorkshire*. Leicester University Press: Leicester.

Casey, P. J. and Reece, R. eds, 1974: *Coins and the Archaeologist*. BAR 4: Oxford.

Casey, P. J. ed., 1979a: *The End of Roman Britain*. BAR 71: Oxford.

CBA: *Council of British Archaeology*. London.

Chapman, J. and Mytum, H. eds, 1983: *Settlement in North Britain 1000 BC–1000 AD*. BAR 118: Oxford.

Collingwood, R. G. and Myres, J. N. L., 1937: *Roman Britain and the English Settlements*, 2nd edn. Oxford University Press: Oxford.

Collingwood, R. G. and Richmond, I. A., 1969: *The Archaeology of Roman Britain*. Methuen: London.

Collingwood, R. G. and Wright, R. P., 1965: See RIB.

Cunliffe, B. W., 1973: *The Regni*. Duckworth: London.

Detsicas, A., 1984: *The Cantiaci*. Sutton: Gloucester.

Dunnett, R., 1975: *The Trinovantes*. Duckworth: London.

Finley, M. I. ed., 1977: *Atlas of Classical Archaeology*. Chatto & Windus: London.

Frere, S. S., 1987: *Britannia: A History of Roman Britain*, 3rd edn. Routledge & Kegan Paul: London.

Frere, S. S. and St Joseph, J. K., 1983: *Roman Britain from the Air*. Cambridge University Press: Cambridge.

Goodburn, R. and Bartholomew, P., 1976: *Aspects of the Notitia Dignitatum*. BAR International Series 15: Oxford.

Hanson, W. S. and Keppie, L. J. F. eds, 1980: *Roman Frontier Studies 1979: Papers presented to the 12th International Congress of Roman Frontier Studies*. BAR International Series 71: Oxford.

Hanson, W. S. and Maxwell, G. S., 1983: *Rome's North West Frontier: the Antonine Wall*. Edinburgh University Press: Edinburgh.

Hartley, B. R. and Fitts, L., 1988: *The Brigantes*. Sutton: Gloucester.

Hartley, B. R. and Wacher, J. S. eds, 1983: *Rome and her Northern Provinces*. Sutton: Gloucester.

Higham, N. J. and Jones, G. D. B., 1984: *The Carvetii*. Sutton: Gloucester.

Hill, D., 1981: *An Atlas of Anglo-Saxon England 700–1066*. Basil Blackwell: Oxford.

Johnson, D. E. ed., 1977a: *The Saxon Shore*. CBA Research Report 18: London.

Johnson, S., 1980: *Later Roman Britain*. Routledge & Kegan Paul: London.

King, A. and Henig, M., 1981: *The Roman West in the Third Century*. BAR International Series 109: Oxford.

Longworth, I. and Cherry, J., 1986: *Archaeology in Britain since 1945: new directions*. British Museum Publications: London.

Maxwell, G. S., 1983a: *The Impact of Aerial Reconnaissance on Archaeology*. CBA Research Report 49: London.

Maxwell, G. S. and Wilson, D. R., 1987: Air reconnaissance in Britain 1977–1984. *Britania* 18:1–48.

McWhirr, A., 1981: *Roman Gloucestershire*. Sutton: Gloucester.

Miles, D. ed., 1982: *The Romano-British Countryside*. BAR 103: Oxford.

Ordnance Survey, 1924: *Map of Roman Britain*. Ordnance Survey Publication.

Ordnance Survey, 1931: *Map of Roman Britain*, 2nd edn. Ordnance Survey Publication.

Ordnance Survey, 1956: *Map of Roman Britain*, 3rd edn. Ordnance Survey Publication: Chessington.

Ordnance Survey, 1978: *Map of Roman Britain*, 4th edn. Ordnance Survey Publication: Southampton.

Potter, T., 1986: A Roman province: Britain AD 43–410. In Longworth and Cherry 1986: 73–118.

RCAHMS: *Royal Commission on the Ancient and Historical Monuments of Scotland*. Many regional volumes published on county basis.

RCHM: *Royal Commission on Historical Monuments of England*. Many regional or county volumes published for England and Wales.

RIB: Collingwood, R. G. and Wright, R. P., 1965: *The Roman Inscriptions of Britain*. Vol. 1: *The Inscriptions on Stone*. Oxford University Press: Oxford.

Richmond, I. A., 1963: *Roman Britain*, 2nd edn. Penguin: London.

Richmond, I. A. ed., 1958a: *Roman and Native in North Britain*. Nelson: Edinburgh and London.

Rivet, A. L. F., 1964: *Town and Country in Roman Britain*, 2nd edn. Hutchinson: London.

Rivet, A. L. F. and Smith, C., 1979: *The Placenames of Roman Britain*. Batsford: London.

Roman Britain in 19XX (various editors), 1921–1969: In *Journal of Roman Studies*, 1969ff in *Britannia*.

Salway, P., 1980: *Roman Britain*. Oxford University Press: Oxford.

St Joseph, J. K., 1951f: Air reconnaissance in Britain. *Journal of Roman Studies* 41 (1951): 52–65; 43 (1953): 81–97; 45 (1955): 82–91; 48 (1958): 86–101; 51 (1961): 119–35; 55 (1965): 74–89; 59 (1969): 104–28; 63 (1973): 214–16; 67 (1977): 125–61.

Tabula Imperii Romani, 1985: *Condate – Glevum – Londinium – Lutetia*. British Academy: London.

Tabula Imperii Romani, 1987: *Britannia septentrionalis*, British Academy: Oxford.

Temporini, H. *et al.*, *ANRW: Aufstieg und Niedergang der Römischen Welt: Geschichte und Kultur Roms in Spiegel der neueren Forschung*. Walter de Gruyter: Berlin and New York.

Thomas, C. ed., 1966: *Rural Settlement in Roman Britain*. CBA Research Report 7: London.

Todd, M., 1973: *The Coritani*. Duckworth: London.

Todd, M., 1980: *Roman Britain (55 BC–AD 400)*. Harvester Press: Brighton.

Todd, M. ed., 1978: *Studies in the Romano-British Villa*. Leicester University Press: Leicester.

Todd, M. ed., 1989: *Research on Roman Britain: 1960–89*. Britannia Monograph 11: London.

Wacher, J., 1978: *Roman Britain*. J. Dent: London.

Wacher, J., 1979: *The Coming of Rome*. Routledge & Kegan Paul: London.

Webster, G, 1975a: *The Cornovii*. Duckworth: London.

Whimster, R. H., 1983: Aerial reconnaissance from Cambridge: a retrospective view 1945–80. In Maxwell 1983: 92–108.

Wilson, D. R., 1975c: *Aerial Reconnaissance for Archaeology*. CBA Research Report 12: London.

CHAPTER 1 · THE PHYSICAL CONTEXT

Anderson, J. G. C. and Owen, T. R., 1968: *The Structure of the British Isles*. Pergamon Press: Oxford and London.

Aston, M. and Burrow, I., 1982: *The Archaeology of Somerset*. Somerset County Council: Bridgwater.

Atlas, 1963: *An Atlas of Britain*. Oxford University Press: Oxford.

Baker, A. R. H. and Harley, J. B. eds, 1973: *Man Made the Land: essays in English historical geography*. David & Charles: Newton Abbot, Devon.

Bilham, B. G., 1938: *The Climate of the British Isles*. Macmillan: London.

Carter, H. *et al.* eds, 1974: *An Advanced Geography of the British Isles*. Hulton Educational: Amersham.

Coppock, J. T., 1964: *An Agricultural Atlas of England and Wales*. Faber: London.

Cunliffe, B. W., 1980: The evolution of Romney Marsh: a preliminary statement. In Thompson 1980: 37–55.

Cunliffe, B. W., 1966: The Somerset Levels in the Roman period. In Thomas 1966: 68–73.

Evans, J. G., Limbrey, S. and Cleere, H. eds, 1975: *The Effect of Man on the Landscape: the highland zone*. CBA Research Report 11: London.

Fowler, P. J., 1978: Lowland landscapes: culture, time and personality. In Limbrey and Evans 1978: 1–12.

Fox, C., 1932: *The Personality of Britain*. University of Wales: Cardiff.

Jones, G. D. B., 1980: Archaeology and coastal change in the North-west. In Thompson 1980: 87–102.

Keillar, I., Daniels, C. M. and Jones, G. D. B., 1986: 'In fines Borestorum' – to the land of the Boresti. *Popular Archaeology* 7.3 (April): 2–16.

Land Utilisation Survey (Stamp, L. D. ed.), 1937/1946: *The Land of Britain*, in 92 parts. Geographical Publications: London.

Leech, R., 1982: The Roman interlude in the south-west: the dynamics of economic and social change in Romano-British south Somerset and north Dorset. In Miles 1982: 209–67.

Limbrey, S. and Evans, J. G. eds, 1978: *The Effect of Man on the Landscape: the lowland zone*. CBA Research Report 21: London.

Manning, W. H., 1975: Economic influences on land use in the military and highland zone during the Roman period. In Evans *et al.* 1975: 112–16.

Piggott, S., 1958: Native economies and the Roman occupation of North Britain. In Richmond 1958a: 1–27.

Simmons, B. B., 1979: The Lincolnshire Car Dyke: navigation or drainage? *Britannia* 10: 183–96.

Simmons, B. B., 1980: Iron Age and Roman coasts around the Wash. In Thompson 1980: 56–73.

Soil Survey of Great Britain, 1948b: *Annual Reports*. HMSO: London.

Stamp, L. D., 1962: *The Land of Britain: its use and misuse*, 3rd edn. Longman: London.

Stamp, L. D. and Beaver, S. H., 1971: *The British Isles: a geographic and economic survey*, 6th edn. Longman: London.

Taylor, J. A. and Yates, R. A., 1967: *British Weather in Maps*, 2nd edn. Macmillan: London.

Thompson, F. H. ed., 1980: *Archaeology and Coastal Change*. Society of Antiquaries: London.

Watson, J. W. and Sissons, J. B., 1964: *The British Isles: a systematic geography*. Nelson: London.

Wood, H. J., 1931: *An Agricultural Atlas of Scotland*. Gill: Edinburgh.

CHAPTER 2 · BRITAIN AND THE ROMAN GEOGRAPHERS

Birch, T. W., 1964: *Maps: topographical and statistical*. Oxford University Press: Oxford.

Black, E. W., 1984: The Antonine Itinerary: aspects of government in Roman Britain. *Oxford Journal of Archaeology* 3.3: 109–21.

Cowen, J. D. and Richmond, I. A., 1935: The Rudge Cup. *Archaeologia Aeliana*[4] 12: 310–42.

Crone, G. R., 1968: *Maps and Their Makers: an introduction to the history of cartography*, 4th edn. Hutchinson: London.

Dilke, O. A. W., 1985: *Greek and Roman Maps*. Thames & Hudson: London.

Dillerman, L., 1978: Observations on Chapter V, 31, Britannia in the Ravenna Cosmography. *Archaeologia* 106: 61–73.

Finley, M. I. ed., 1977: *Atlas of Classical Archaeology*. Chatto & Windus: London.

Goodburn, R. and Bartholomew, P., 1976: *Aspects of the Notitia Dignitatum*. BAR International Series 15: Oxford.

Harley, J. B. and Woodward, D. eds, 1985: *The History of Cartography I*. University of Chicago: Chicago and London.

Hassall, M., 1976: Britain in the Notitia. In Goodburn and Bartholomew 1976: 103–17.

Hassall, M., 1977: The historical background and military units of the Saxon Shore. In Johnston 1977: 7–10.

Heurgon, J., 1951: The Amiens patera. *Journal of Roman Studies* 41: 22–4.

Hind, J. G. F., 1975: The British 'provinces' of Valentia and the Orcades. *Historia* 245: 101–11.

Hind, J. G. F., 1977: The Genounian part of Britain. *Britannia* 8: 229–34.

Hind, J. G. F., 1980: Litus Saxonicum – the meaning of 'Saxon Shore'. In Hanson and Keppie 1980: 317–24.

Jackson, K. H., 1970: Romano-British names in the Antonine Itinerary. *Britannia* 1: 68–82.

Jervis, W. W., 1936: *The World in Maps*. Philip & Son: London.

Johnson, S., 1979: *The Roman Forts of the Saxon Shore*, 2nd edn. Elek: London.

Keillar, I., Daniels, C. M. and Jones, G. D. B., 1986: 'In fines Borestorum' – to the land of the Boresti. *Popular Archaeology* 7.3 (April): 2–16.

Maxwell, G., 1984: New frontiers: the Roman fort at Doune and its possible significance. *Britannia* 15: 217–23.

Miller, K. ed., 1962: *Die Peutingersche Tafel*. Stuttgart.

Ordnance Survey, 1978: *Map of Roman Britain*, 4th edn. Ordnance Survey Publication: Southampton.

Richmond, I. A., 1958c: Ancient geographical sources for Britain north of the Cheviot. In Richmond 1958a: 131–55.

Richmond, I. A. and Crawford, O. G. S., 1949: The British section of the Ravenna Cosmography. *Archaeologia* 93: 1–50.

Rivet, A. L. F., 1970: The British section of the Antonine Itinerary. *Britannia* 1: 34–82.

Rivet, A. L. F., 1974: Some aspects of Ptolemy's Geography of Britain. In R. Chevallier ed., *Littérature Greco-romaine mélanges offerts à R. Dion*. Picard: Paris, 55–79.

Rivet, A. L. F., 1977: Ptolemy's Geography and the Flavian invasion of Scotland. *Studien zu den Militärgrenzen Roms II, Vortrage des 10. Internationalen Limes Kongress*: Budapest, 45–64.

Rivet, A. L. F., 1980: Celtic names and Roman places. *Britannia* 11: 1–20.

Rivet, A. L. F. and Smith, C., 1979: *The Placenames of Roman Britain*. Batsford: London.

Rodwell, W., 1975: Milestones, civic territories and the Antonine Itinerary. *Britannia* 6: 76–108.

Wild, J. P., 1976: The Gynaecea. In Goodburn and Bartholemew 1976: 51–81.

CHAPTER 3 · BRITAIN BEFORE THE CONQUEST

Allen, D. F., 1944: The Belgic dynasties of Britain and their coins. *Archaeologia* 90: 1–46.

Allen, D. F., 1960: The origins of coinage in Britain: a reappraisal. In Frere 1960: 97–308.

Allen, D. F., 1962: Celtic coins. *Ordnance Survey* 1962: 19–32.

Allen, D. F., 1970: The coins of the Iceni. *Britannia* 1: 1–33.

Allen, D. F., 1975: Cunobelin's gold. *Britannia* 6: 1–19.

Allen, D. F. and Haselgrove, C., 1979: The gold coinage of Verica. *Britannia* 10: 1–17.

Blagg, T. F. C. and King, A. C. eds, 1984: *Military and Civilian in Roman Britain. Cultural relationships in a frontier province*. BAR 136: Oxford.

Branigan, K., 1985: *The Catuvellauni*. Sutton: Gloucester.

Breeze, D. J., 1982a: *The Northern Frontiers of Roman Britain*. Batsford: London.

Collis, J., 1971: Markets and money. In Hill and Jesson 1971: 97–103.

Collis, J., 1979: City and state in pre-Roman Britain. In Burnham and Johnson 1979: 231–40.

Crummy, P., 1977: The Roman fortress and the development of the colonia. *Britannia* 8: 65–105.

Cunliffe, B. W., 1973: *The Regni*. Duckworth: London.

Cunliffe, B. W., 1976: The origins of urbanization in Britain. In Cunliffe and Rowley 1976: 135–61.

Cunliffe, B. W., 1978: *Iron Age Communities in Britain*. Routledge & Kegan Paul: London.

Cunliffe, B. W. ed., 1981a: *Coinage and Society in Britain and Gaul: some current problems*. CBA Research Report 38: London.

Cunliffe, B. W., 1981b: Money and society in pre-Roman Britain. In Cunliffe 1981a: 29–39.

Cunliffe, B. W., 1984a: Relations between Britain and Gaul in the first century BC and early first century AD. In Macready and Thompson 1984: 3–23.

Cunliffe, B. W., 1984b: *Danebury: the anatomy of an Iron Age hillfort*. Batsford: London.

Cunliffe, B. W., 1985: Aspects of urbanization in northern Europe. In Grew and Hobley 1985: 1–5.

Cunliffe, B. W. and Miles, D. eds, 1984: *Aspects of the Iron Age in Central Southern Britain*. Monograph 2. Committee for Archaeology, Oxford University Press: Oxford.

Cunliffe, B. W. and Rowley, T. eds, 1976: *Oppida: the beginnings of urbanization in barbarian Europe*. BAR International Series 11: Oxford.

Detsicas, A., 1984: *The Cantiaci*. Sutton: Gloucester.

Dunnett, R., 1975: *The Trinovantes*. Duckworth: London.

Feachem, R. W., 1966: The hillforts of northern Britain. In Rivet 1966a: 59–88.

Fitzpatrick, A., 1985: The distribution of Dressel 1 amphorae in north-west Europe. *Oxford Journal of Archaeology* 4.3: 305–40.

Fitzpatrick, A., 1986: Camulodunum and the early occupation of south-east England. Some reconsiderations. In Planck 1986: 35–41.

Fowler, P. J., 1983: *The Farming of Prehistoric Britain*. Cambridge University Press: Cambridge.

Frere, S. S. ed., 1960: *Problems of the Iron Age in Southern Britain*. Institute of Archaeology: London.

Hanson, W. S. and Maxwell, G. S., 1983: *Rome's North West Frontier: the Antonine Wall*. Edinburgh University Press: Edinburgh.

Harding, D. W., 1974: *The Iron Age in Lowland Britain*. Routledge & Kegan Paul: London.

Harding, D. W. ed., 1982: *Later Prehistoric settlement in south-east Scotland*. University of Edinburgh, Dept of Archaeology Occasional Paper No 8: Edinburgh.

Haselgrove, C., 1984: Romanisation before the conquest: Gaulish precedents and British consequences. In Blagg and King 1984: 5–63.

Higham, N. J. and Jones, G. D. B., 1984: *The Carvetii*. Sutton: Gloucester.

Hill, D. and Jesson, M., 1971: *The Iron Age and its Hill-forts*. University of Southampton: Southampton.

Hogg, A. H. A., 1966: Native settlement in Wales. In Thomas 1966: 28–38.

Jarrett, M. G. and Mann, J. C., 1969: The tribes of Wales. *Welsh Hist. Review* 4: 267–69.

Jobey, G., 1966: Homesteads and settlements of the frontier zone. In Thomas 1966: 1–14.

Jobey, G., 1974: Notes on some population problems in the area between the two Roman walls. *Archaeologia Aeliana*[5] 2: 17–26.

Kent, J. P. C., 1981: The origins of coinage in Britain. In Cunliffe 1981a: 40–42.

Lloyd Jones, M., 1984: *Society and Settlement in Wales and the Marches 500 BC–AD 1100*. BAR 121: Oxford.

Macinnes, L., 1982: Pattern and purpose: the settlement evidence. In Harding 1982: 57–74.

Mack, R. P., 1964: *The Coinage of Ancient Britain*, 2nd edn. Stockwell: London.

Macready, S. and Thompson, F. H. eds, 1984: *Cross-channel Trade between Gaul and Britain in the pre-Roman Iron Age*. Soc. of Antiqs., Occ. Paper 4: London.

Maxwell, G. S., 1980a: The native background of the Roman occupation of Scotland. In Hanson and Keppie 1980: 1–14.

Maxwell, G. S., 1983b: Recent aerial survey in Scotland. In Maxwell 1983a: 27–40.

Ordnance Survey, 1962: *Map of Southern Britain in the Iron Age*. Ordnance Survey Publication.

Peacock, D. P. S., 1971: Roman amphorae in pre-Roman Britain. In Hill and Jesson 1971: 161–88.

Peacock, D. P. S. and Williams, D. F., 1986: *Amphorae and the Roman Economy: an introductory guide*. Longman: London.

Ramm, H., 1978: *The Parisi*. Duckworth: London.

Rivet, A. L. F. ed., 1966a: *The Iron Age in Northern Britain*. Edinburgh University Press: Edinburgh.

Rodwell, W., 1976: Coinage, oppida and the rise of Belgic power in south-east Britain. In Cunliffe and Rowley 1976: 181–366.

Sellwood, L., 1984: Tribal boundaries viewed from the perspective of numismatic evidence. In Cunliffe and Miles 1984: 191–204.

Stanford, S., 1980: *The Archaeology of the Welsh Marches*. Collins: London.

Todd, M., 1973: *The Coritani*. Duckworth: London.

Tomlin, R. S. O., 1983: Non Coritani sed Corieltauvi. *Archaeological Journal* 63.2: 352–55.

Wacher, J. 1979: *The Coming of Rome*. Routledge & Kegan Paul: London.

Webster, G., 1975a: *The Cornovii*. Duckworth: London.

CHAPTER 4 · THE CONQUEST AND GARRISONING OF BRITAIN

Barrett, A. A., 1980: Chronological errors in Dio's account of the Claudian invasion. *Britannia* 11: 31–3.

Bennett, J., 1980: 'Temporary' camps along Hadrian's Wall. In Hanson and Keppie 1980: 151–72.

Birley, A. R., 1973: Petilius Cerialis and the conquest of Brigantia. *Britannia* 4: 179–90.

Birley, A. R., 1976: The date of Mons Graupius. *Liverpool Classical Monthly* 1, 2: 11–14.

Birley, A. R., 1981a: *The Fasti of Roman Britain*. Oxford University Press: Oxford.

Birley, E., 1961: *Research on Hadrian's Wall*. T. Wilson: Kendal.

Birley, E., 1971: The fate of the Ninth Legion. In Butler 1971: 70–80.

Bogaers, J. E., 1979: King Cogidubnus in Chichester: another reading of *RIB 91*. *Britannia* 10: 243–54.

Breeze, D. J., 1975: The abandonment of the Antonine Wall: its date and implications. *Scottish Archaeological Forum* 7: 67–80.

Breeze, D. J., 1979: *Roman Scotland: a guide to the visible remains*. Frank Graham: Newcastle-upon-Tyne.

Breeze, D. J., 1980a: Agricola the builder. *Scottish Archaeological Forum* 12: 14–24.

Breeze, D. J., 1980b: Roman Scotland during the reign of Antoninus Pius. In Hanson and Keppie 1980: 45–60.

Breeze, D. J., 1982a: *The Northern Frontiers of Roman Britain*. Batsford: London.

Breeze, D. J., 1986: The frontier in Britain 1979–1983. In Planck 1986: 21–34.

Breeze, D. J. and Dobson, B., 1976: A view of Roman Scotland in 1975. *Glasgow Archaeological Journal* 4: 124–43.

Breeze, D. J. and Dobson, B., 1987: *Hadrian's Wall*, 3rd. edn. Penguin: London.

Breeze, D. J. and Dobson, B., 1985: Roman military deployment in north England. *Britannia* 16: 1–19.

Bruce, J. C., 1851: *The Roman Wall*. London.

Bruce, J. C., 1978: *Handbook to the Roman Wall*, 13th edn, ed. C. M. Daniels. Frank Graham: Newcastle-upon-Tyne.

Carroll, K. K., 1979: The date of Boudicca's revolt. *Britannia* 10: 197–202.

Casey, P. J., 1977: Carausius and Allectus – rulers in Gaul? *Britannia* 8: 283–301.

Cleere, H., 1977: The Classis Britannica. In Johnston 1977: 16–19.

Collingwood, R. G. and Richmond, I. A., 1969: *The Archaeology of Roman Britain*. Methuen: London.

Crawford, O. G. S., 1949: *The Topography of Roman Scotland North of the Antonine Wall*. Cambridge University Press: Cambridge.

Crummy, P., 1977: Colchester: the Roman fortress and the development of the colonia. *Britannia* 8: 65–105.

Daniels, C. M., 1970: Problems of the Roman northern frontiers. *Scottish Archaeological Forum* 2: 91–101.

Daniels, C. M., 1980: Excavations at Wallsend and the fourth century barracks on Hadrian's Wall. In Hanson and Keppie 1980: 173–93.

Davies, J. L., 1980: Roman military deployment in Wales and the Marches from Claudius to the Antonines. In Hanson and Keppie 1980: 255–77.

Dobson, B., 1979: *The Tenth Pilgrimage of Hadrian's Wall*. T. Wilson: Kendal, Cumbria.

Dobson, B., 1980: Agricola's life and career. *Scottish Archaeological Forum* 12: 1–13.

Dunnett, R., 1975: *The Trinovantes*. Duckworth: London.

Fitzpatrick, A., 1986: Camulodunum and the early occupation of south-east. Some reconsiderations. In Planck 1986: 35–41.

Frere, S. S., 1980a: Review of Ordnance Survey: Map of Roman Britain, 4th edn. *Britannia* 5: 1–129.

Frere, S. S., 1980b: The Flavian frontier in Scotland. *Scottish Archaeological Forum* 12: 89–97.

Frere, S. S., 1986: The use of Iron Age hillforts by the Roman army in Britain. In Planck 1986: 42–6.

Frere, S. S. and St Joseph, J. K., 1974: The Roman fortress at Longthorpe. *Britannia* 5: 1–129.

Gillam, J. P., 1975: Possible changes in plan in the course of construction of the Antonine Wall. *Scottish Archaeological Forum* 7: 51–6.

Gillam, J. P. and Mann, J. C., 1970: The northern British frontier from Antoninus Pius to Caracalla. *Archaeologia Aeliana*⁴ 48: 1–44.

Goodburn, R. and Bartholomew, P., 1976: *Aspects of the Notitia Dignitatum*. BAR International Series 15: Oxford.

Hanson, W. S., 1978b: Roman campaigns north of the Forth–Clyde isthmus: the evidence of the temporary camps. *Proceedings of the Society of Antiquaries of Scotland* 109: 140–50.

Hanson, W. S., 1986: Rome: the Cornovii and the Ordovices. In Planck 1986: 47–52.

Hanson, W. S., 1987: *Agricola and the Conquest of the North*. Batsford: London.

Hanson, W. S. and Keppie, L. J. F. eds, 1980: *Roman Frontier Studies 1979: Papers presented to the 12th International Congress of Roman Frontier Studies*. BAR International Series 71: Oxford.

Hanson, W. S. and Maxwell, G. S., 1983: *Rome's North West Frontier: The Antonine Wall*. Edinburgh University Press: Edinburgh.

Hartley, B. R., 1971: Roman York and the northern military command to the third century AD. In Butler 1971: 55–69.

Hartley, B. R., 1972: The Roman occupation of Scotland: the evidence of the samian ware. *Britannia* 3: 1–55.

Hassall, M., 1976: Britain in the Notitia. In Goodburn and Bartholomew 1976: 103–17.

Hassall, M., 1977: The historical background and military units of the Saxon shore. In Johnston 1977: 7–10.

Hassall, M., 1983: The building of the Antonine Wall. *Britannia* 14: 262–4.

Henderson, A. A. R., 1984: From 83 to 1983: on the trail of Mons Graupius. *Deeside Field Club* 1984: 23–9.

Henderson A. A. R., 1985: Agricola in Caledonia: the sixth and seventh campaigns. *Classical Views* 29 (ns 4): 318–35.

Higham, N. J., 1979: *The Changing Past*. University of Manchester: Manchester.

Higham, N. J. and Jones, G. D. B., 1975: Frontier, forts and farmers. Cumbria aerial survey 1974–75. *Archaeological Journal* 132: 16–53.

Higham, N. J. and Jones, G. D. B., 1984: *The Carvetii*. Sutton: Gloucester.

Holder, P. A., 1982: *The Roman Army in Britain*. Batsford: London.

Jackson, K. H., 1979: Queen Boudicca? *Britannia* 10: 255.

James, S., 1984: Britain and the late Roman army. In Blagg and King 1984: 161–86.

Jarrett, M. G., 1964: Early Roman campaigns in Wales. *Archaeological Journal* 121: 23–39.

Jarrett, M. G. and Mann, J. C., 1970: Britain from Agricola to Gallienus. *Bonner Jahrbuch* 170: 178–210.

Johnson, D. E., 1977: *The Saxon Shore*. CBA Research Report 18: London.

Johnson, S., 1976: *The Roman Forts of the Saxon Shore*. Elek: London.

Johnson, S., 1980: *Later Roman Britain*. Routledge & Kegan Paul: London.

Johnson, S., 1983: *Late Roman Fortifications*. Batsford: London.

Jones, G. D. B., 1976: The western extension of Hadrian's wall: Bowness to Cardurnock. *Britannia* 7: 236–43.

Jones, G. D. B., 1978: *Rhyn Park Roman Fortress*. Border Counties Archaeological Group: Manchester.

Jones, G. D. B., 1979a: Invasion and response in Roman Britain. In Burnham and Johnson 1979: 57–79.

Jones, G. D. B., 1979b: The Western Stanegate and the development of the coastal frontier. In Dobson 1979: 27–9.

Jones, G. D. B., 1982: The Solway frontier: interim report 1976–81. *Britannia* 13: 283–97.

Jones, M. J., 1975: *Roman Fort Defences to AD 117*. BAR 21: Oxford.

Keppie, L. J. F., 1974: The building of the Antonine Wall: archaeological and epigraphic evidence. *Proceedings of the Society of Antiquaries of Scotland* 105: 151–65.

Keppie, L. J. F., 1979: *Roman Distance Slabs from the Antonine Wall: a brief guide*. Hunterian Museum: Glasgow.

Keppie, L. J. F., 1980a: Milefortlets on the Antonine Wall. In Hanson and Keppie 1980: 107–12.

Keppie, L. J. F., 1980b: Mons Graupius: the search for a battlefield. *Scottish Archaeological Forum* 12: 79–88.

Keppie, L. J. F., 1982: The Antonine Wall 1960–1980. *Britannia* 13: 91–111.

Keppie, L. J. F., 1986: *Scotland's Roman Remains*. John Donald: Edinburgh.

Keppie, L. J. F. and Walker, J. J., 1981: Fortlets on the Antonine Wall at Seabegs Wood, Kinneil and Cleddans. *Britannia* 12: 143–62.

Lloyd Jones, M., 1984: *Society and Settlement in Wales and the Marches 500 BC–AD 1100*. BAR 121: Oxford.

Luttwak, E. N., 1976: *The Grand Strategy of the Roman Empire*. Johns Hopkins University Press: Baltimore.

MacDonald, G., 1934: *The Roman Wall in Scotland*, 2nd edn. Oxford University Press: Oxford.

Mann, J. C., 1974: The northern frontier after AD 369. *Glasgow Archaeological Journal* 3: 34–42.

Mann, J. C., 1979: Hadrian's Wall: the last phases. In Casey 1979: 144–51.

Maxfield, V. A., 1980: The Roman military occupation of south-west England: further light and fresh problems. In Hanson and Keppie 1980: 297–309.

Maxwell, G. R., 1980b: Agricola's campaigns: the evidence of the temporary camps. *Scottish Archaeological Forum* 12: 25–54.

Maxwell, G. S., 1986: Sidelight on the Roman military campaigns in North Britain. In Planck 1986: 50–63.

McWhirr, A., 1970: The early military history of the Roman East Midlands. *Transactions of the Leicestershire Archaeological and Historical Society* 45: 1–19.

Miller, M., 1975: Stilicho's Pictish War. *Britannia* 6: 141–5.

Nash-Williams, V. E., 1969: *The Roman Frontier in Wales*, 2nd edn. Jarrett, M. ed. Cardiff University Press: Cardiff.

Ogilvie, R. M. and Richmond, I. A., 1967: *Cornelii Taciti de vita Agricolae*. Oxford University Press: Oxford.

Ordnance Survey, 1969: *The Antonine Wall*. Ordnance Survey Publication: Southampton.

Ordnance Survey, 1972: *Map of Hadrian's Wall*, 2nd edn. Ordnance Survey Publication: Southampton.

Ordnance Survey, 1978: *Map of Roman Britain*, 4th edn. Ordnance Survey Publication: Southampton.

Peacock, D. P. S., 1977b: Bricks and tiles of the Classis Britannica: petrology and origin. *Britannia* 8: 235–48.

Pitts, L. F. and St Joseph, J. K., 1985: *Inchtuthil: the Roman legionary fortress excavations 1952–65*. Sutton: Gloucester.

Planck, D., 1986: *Studien zu den Militärgrenzen Röms, Vorträge des 13 Internationalen Limeskongress, Aalen 1983*. Konrad Theiss Verlag: Stuttgart.

Potter, T. W., 1979: *Romans in North-West England*. T. Wilson: Kendal, Cumbria.

Ramm, H., 1978: *The Parisi*. Duckworth: London.

Reed, N. H., 1971: The fifth year of Agricola's campaigns. *Britannia* 2: 143–8.

Reed, N. H., 1976: The Scottish campaigns of Septimius Severus. *Proceedings of the Society of Antiquaries of Scotland* 107: 92–102.

Richmond, I. A., 1958a: *Roman and Native in North Britin*. Nelson: Edinburgh and London.

Richmond, I. A., 1958b: Roman and native in the fourth century AD and after. In Richmond 1958a: 112–30.

Riley, D. N., 1980b: Two new military sites in mid-Nottinghamshire. *Britannia* 11: 330–5.

Riley, D. N., 1983: Temporary camps at Calverton, Notts. *Britannia* 14: 270–1.

Robertson, A. S., 1974: Roman signal stations on the Gask Ridge. *Transactions and Proceedings of the Perthshire Society of the Natural Sciences. Special Issue*: 14–29.

Robertson, A. S., 1979: *The Antonine Wall*, 3rd edn. Glasgow Archaeological Society: Glasgow.

Roy, W., 1743: *Military Antiquities*. Society of Antiquaries: London.

Shotter, D. C. A., 1976: Coin evidence and the northern frontier in the second century. *Proceedings of the Society of Antiquaries of Scotland* 107: 144–97.

Simpson, G., 1964: *Britons and the Roman Army*. The Gregg Press: London.

St Joseph, J. K., 1951f: Air reconnaissance in Britain. *Journal of Roman Studies* 41 (1951): 52–65; 43 (1953): 81–97; 45 (1955): 82–91; 48 (1958): 86–101; 51 (1961): 119–35; 55 (1965): 74–89; 59 (1969): 104–28; 63 (1973): 214–46; 67 (1977): 125–61.

St Joseph, J. K., 1970: The camps at Ardoch, Stracathro and Ythan Wells: recent excavations. *Britannia* 1: 163–78.

St Joseph, J. K., 1978: The camp at Durno and Mons Graupius. *Britannia* 9: 271–88.

Steer, K. A., 1960: The Antonine Wall 1934–1959. *Journal of Roman Studies* 50: 84–93.

Stevens, C. E., 1966b: *The Building of Hadrian's Wall*. Cumberland and Westmorland Antiquarian and Archaeological Society: Kendal, Cumbria.

Todd, M., 1973: *The Coritani*. Duckworth: London.

Todd, M., 1984: Hembury (Devon): Roman troops in a hillfort. *Antiquity* 58, 224: 171–4.

Todd, M., 1985: Oppida and the Roman army: a review of recent evidence. *Oxford Journal of Archaeology* 4.2: 187–99.

Troussett, P., 1978: Les bornes du Bled Segui: Nouveaux aperçus sur la centuriation du sud Tunisie. *Antiquités Africaines* 12: 125–78.

Webster, G., 1958: The Roman military advance under Ostorius Scapula. *Archaeological Journal* 105: 49–98.

Webster, G., 1970: The military situations in Britain between AD 43 and 71. *Britannia* 1: 179–97.

Webster, G., 1975a: *The Cornovii*. Duckworth: London.

Webster, G., 1978: *Boudica: the British revolt against Rome AD 60*, 2nd edn. Batsford: London.

Webster, G., 1979: *The Roman Imperial Army of the First and Second Centuries AD*, 2nd edn. A & C Black: London.

Webster, G., 1980: *The Roman Invasion of Britain*. Batsford: London.

Webster, G., 1981: *Rome Against Caractacus: The Roman Campaigns in Britain AD 48–58*. Batsford: London.

Welsby, D. A., 1982: *The Roman Military Defence of the British Province in its Later Phases*. BAR 101: Oxford.

Wilson, D. R., 1974: Roman camps in Britain. *Actes du Xᵉ Congrès International d'Etudes sur les frontières romaines*, Bucharest; Cologne: 343–50.

Wilson, D. R., 1975b: Air reconnaissance and Roman military antiquities in Britain. *Scottish Archaeological Forum* 7: 13–30.

CHAPTER 5 · THE DEVELOPMENT OF THE PROVINCES

Barker, P. A., 1985: Aspects of the topography of Wroxeter (Viroconium Cornoviorum). In Grew and Hobley 1985: 109–17.

Barrett, A. A., 1979: The career of Tiberius Claudius Cogidubnus. *Britannia* 10: 227–42.

Birley, A. R., 1979: *The People of Roman Britain*. Batsford: London.

Birley, A. R., 1981a: *The Fasti of Roman Britain*. Oxford University Press: Oxford.

Birley, R. E., 1977: *Vindolanda: a Roman frontier post on Hadrian's Wall*. Thames & Hudson: London.

Blagg, T. F. C. and King, A. C. eds, 1984: *Military and Civilian in Roman Britain. Cultural relationships in a frontier province*. BAR 136: Oxford.

Blockley, R. C., 1980: The date of the 'Barbarian Conspiracy'. *Britannia* 11: 223–5.

Bogaers, J. E., 1979: King Cogidubnus in Chichester: another reading of *RIB* 91. *Britannia* 10: 243–54.

Boon, G. C., 1974: *Silchester: The Roman town of Calleva*. David & Charles: London.

Branigan, K., 1980b: Villas in the north: change in the rural landscape. In Branigan 1980a: 18–27.

Branigan, K., 1985: *The Catuvellauni*. Sutton: Gloucester.

Burnham, B. C., 1986: The origins of Roman-British small towns. *Oxford Journal of Archaeology* 5.2: 185–203.

Casey, P. J., 1977: Carausius and Allectus – rulers in Gaul? *Britannia* 8: 283–301.

Casey, P. J., 1982: Civilians and soldiers – friends, Romans and countrymen? In Clack and Haselgrove 1982: 123–32.

Chevallier, R., 1976: *Roman Roads*. Batsford: London.

Clack, P. A. G. and Haslegrove, S. eds, 1982: *Rural Settlement in the Roman North*. Dept. of Archaeology, Durham University: Durham.

Cleary, S. E., 1987: *Extra-Mural Areas of Romano-British Towns*. BAR 169: Oxford.

Collingwood, R. G. and Myres, J. N. L., 1937: *Roman Britain and the English Settlements*, 2nd edn. Oxford University Press: Oxford.

Collingwood, R. G. and Richmond, I. A., 1969: *The Archaeology of Roman Britain*. Methuen: London.

Cornell, T. and Matthews, J., 1982: *Atlas of the Roman World*. Equinox: Oxford.

Crickmore, J., 1984: *Romano-British Urban Settlement in the West Midlands*. BAR 127: Oxford.

Crummy, P., 1977: Colchester: the Roman fortress and the development of the colonia. *Britannia* 8: 65–105.

Crummy, P., 1982: The origins of some major Romano-British towns. *Britannia* 13: 125–34.

Crummy, P., 1985: Colchester: the mechanics of laying out a town. In Grew and Hobley 1985: 78–85.

Cunliffe, B. W., 1973: *The Regni*. Duckworth: London.

Davies, J. L., 1984: Soldiers, peasants and markets in Wales and the Marches. In Blagg and King 1984: 93–27.

Detsicas, A., 1984: *The Cantiaci*. Sutton: Gloucester.

Dornier, A., 1982: The province of Valentia. *Britannia* 13: 253–60.

Dunnett, R., 1975: *The Trinovantes*. Duckworth: London.

Esmonde Cleary, A. S., 1987: *Extra-Mural Areas of Romano-British Towns*. BAR 169: Oxford.

Frere, S. S., 1972: *Verulamium I*. Society of Antiquaries: London.

Frere, S. S., 1975a: Verulamium and the towns of Britannia. *Aufstieg und Niedergang der Römischen Welt* II, 3: 290–327.

Frere, S. S., 1975b: The origin of small towns. In Rodwell and Rowley 1975: 4–7.

Frere, S. S., 1983: *Verulamium II*. Society of Antiquaries: London.

Frere, S. S., 1984: British urban defences in earthwork. *Britannia* 15: 63–74.

Frere, S. S. and St Joseph, J. K., 1983: *Roman Britain from the Air*. Cambridge University Press: Cambridge.

Fulford, M., 1982: Town and country in Roman Britain – a parasitical relationship? In Miles 1982: 403–19.

Goodburn, R. and Bartholomew, P., 1976: *Aspects of the Notitia Dignitatum*. BAR International Series 15: Oxford.

Grew, F. and Hobley, B. eds, 1985: *Roman Urban Topography in Britain and the Western Empire*. CBA Research Report 59: London.

Hartley, B. R., 1983: The enclosure of Romano-British towns in the second century AD. In Hartley and Wacher 1983: 84–95.

Higham, N. J. and Jones, G. D. B., 1984: *The Carvetii*. Sutton: Gloucester.

Hingley, R., 1982: Recent discoveries of the Roman period at the Noah's Ark Inn, Frilford, South Oxfordshire. *Britannia* 13: 305–9.

Hodder, I. and Hassall, M., 1971: The non-random spacing of Romano-British small towns. *Man* 6: 391–407.

Hodder, I. and Millett, M., 1980: Romano-British villas and towns: a systematic analysis. *World Archaeology* 12: 69–76.

Hurst, H. R., 1985: *Kingsholm*. Gloucester Archaeology Reports 1: Gloucester.

Hurst, H. R., 1986: *Gloucester: the Roman and later defences*. Gloucester Archaeology Reports 2: Gloucester.

Isaac, P., 1976: Coin hoards and history in the West. In Branigan and Fowler 1976: 152–62.

Johnson, D. E., 1979: *An Illustrated History of Roman Roads in Britain*. Spurbooks: Buckinghamshire.

Jones, G. D. B., 1984: 'Becoming different without knowing it' The role and development of *vici*. In Blagg and King 1984: 75–92.

Jones, G. D. B. and Walker, J., 1983: Either side of the Solway: towards a minimalist view of Romano-British agricultural settlements in the north-west. In Chapman and Mytum 1983: 185–204.

MacKreth, D., 1979: Durobrivae. *Durobrivae* 7: 19–21.

Maloney, J. and Hobley, B. eds, 1983: *Roman Urban Defences in the West*. CBA Research Report 51: London.

Margary, I. D., 1965: *Roman Ways in the Weald*. J. Dent: London.

Margary, I. D., 1967: *Roman Roads in Britain*, rev. edn. J. Baker: London.

Marsden, P., 1980: *Roman London*. Thames & Hudson: London.

McWhirr, A., 1981: *Roman Gloucestershire*. Sutton: Gloucester.

Merrifield, R., 1983: *London: City of the Romans*. Batsford: London.

Milne G., 1985: *The Port of Roman London*. Batsford: London.

Morris, R., 1982: *Londinium. London in the Roman Empire*. Weidenfeld & Nicolson: London.

Rivet, A. L. F., 1966b: Summing up: some historical aspects of the civitates of Roman Britain. In Wacher 1966a: 101–13.

Rodwell, W. and Rowley, T. eds, 1975: *The Small Towns of Roman Britain*. BAR 15: Oxford.

Salway, P., 1965: *The Frontier People of Roman Britain*. Cambridge University Press: Cambridge.

Salway, P., 1980: The *vici*: urbanisation in the north. In Branigan 1980: 8–17.

Sedgley, J. P., 1975: *The Roman Milestones of Britain*. BAR 18: Oxford.

Selkirk, R., 1983: *The Piercebridge Formula: a dramatic new view of Roman History*. Patrick Stevens: Cambridge.

Simco, A., 1984: *Survey of Bedfordshire: The Roman Period*. Bedford County Council: Bedford.

Smith, R. F., 1987: *Roadside Settlements in Lowland Roman Britain*. BAR 157: Oxford.

Sommer, C. S., 1984: *The Military Vici in Roman Britain: aspects of their location and layout, administration, function and end*. BAR 129: Oxford.

St Joseph, J. K., 1951f: Air reconnaissance in Britain. *Journal of Roman Studies* 41 (1951): 52–65; 43 (1953): 81–97; 45 (1955): 82–91; 48 (1958): 86–101; 51 (1961): 119–35; 55 (1965): 74–89; 59 (1969): 104–28; 63 (1973): 214–46; 67 (1977): 175–61.

St Joseph, J. K., 1976: The towns of Roman Britain. The contribution of aerial reconnaissance. In Wacher 1966a: 21–30.

The Viatores, 1964: *Roman Roads in the South-east Midlands*. Gollancz: London.

Todd, M., 1970: The small towns of Roman Britain. *Britannia* 1: 114–30.

Todd, M., 1973: *The Coritani*. Duckworth: London.

Todd, M., 1976: The vici of western England. In Branigan and Fowler 1976: 99–119.

Wacher, J. ed., 1966a: *The Civitas Capitals of Roman Britain*. Leicester University Press: Leicester.

Wacher, J. ed., 1966b: Earthwork defences of the second century. In Wacher 1966a: 60–9.

Wacher, J., 1974: *The Towns of Roman Britain*. Batsford: London.

Webster, G., 1966: Fort and town in early Roman Britain. In Wacher 1966a: 31–45.

Webster, G., 1975a: *The Cornovii*. Duckworth: London.

Webster, G., 1975b: Small towns without defences. In Rodwell and Rowley 1975: 53–66.

Webster, G., 1983: The function and organisation of late Roman civil defences in Britain. In Maloney and Hobley 1983: 118–20.

Webster, G., ed., 1988: *Fortress into City: the consolidation of Roman Britain*. Batsford: London.

Wilson, D. R., 1975a: The small towns of Roman Britain from the air. In Rodwell and Rowley 1975: 9–49.

Wilson, D. R., 1984: The plan of Viroconium Cornoviorum. *Antiquity* 58, 223: 117–20.

CHAPTER 6 · THE ECONOMY

Anderson, A. C. and Anderson, A. S., 1981: *Roman pottery research in Britain and North-West Europe: papers presented to Graham Webster.* BAR International Series 123: Oxford.

Barnes, J. W., 1979: The first metal workings and their geological setting. In Crawford 1979: 44–84.

Birley, A. R., 1979: *The People of Roman Britain.* Batsford: London.

Birley, A. R., 1981b: The economic effects of Roman frontier policy. In King and Henig 1981: 39–45.

Blagg, T. F. C., 1977: Schools of stonemasons in Roman Britain. In Munby and Henig 1977: 51–70.

Blagg, T. F. C. and King, A. C. eds, 1984: *Military and Civilian in Roman Britain. Cultural relationships in a frontier province.* BAR · 136: Oxford.

Branigan, K., 1985: *The Catuvellauni.* Sutton: Gloucester.

Breeze, D. J., 1977: The fort at Bearsden and the supply of pottery to the Roman army. In Dore and Greene 1977: 133–46.

Breeze, D. J., 1982b: Demand and supply on the northern frontier. In Clack and Haselgrove 1982: 148–65.

Brisay, K. de and Evans, K. A. eds, 1975: *Salt: the study of an ancient industry.* Colchester Archaeological Group: Colchester.

Brodribb, G., 1987: *Roman Brick and Tile.* Sutton: Gloucester.

Buckland, P. C., Magilton, J. R. and Dolby, M. J., 1980: The Roman pottery industries of south Yorkshire. *Britannia* 11: 145–64.

Carson, R. A. G. and Kraay, C. eds, 1978: *Scripta Nummaria Romana.* Spink: London.

Casey, P. J., 1986: *Understanding Ancient Coins.* Batsford: London.

Cleere, H., 1971: Ironmaking in a Roman furnace. *Britannia* 2: 203–17.

Cleere, H., 1975: The Roman iron industry in the Weald and its connection with the Classis Britannica. *Archaeological Journal* 131: 171–99.

Cleere, H., 1978: Roman harbours in Britain south of Hadrian's Wall. In Taylor and Cleere 1978: 36–40.

Cleere, H., 1982: Industry in the Romano-British countryside. In Miles 1982: 123–35.

Cleere, H. and Crossley, D., 1986: *The Iron Industry of the Weald.* Leicester University Press: Leicester.

Collingwood, R. G. and Myres, J. N. L, 1937: *Roman Britain and the English Settlements,* 2nd edn. Oxford University Press: Oxford.

Colls, D., Etienne, R., Lequement, R., Liou, B., 1977: L'épave Port-Vendres II et le commerce de la Bétiue à l'époque de Claude. *Archaeonautica* I.

Cookson, N. A., 1984: *Romano-British Mosaics: a reassessment and critique of some notable stylistic affinities.* BAR 135: Oxford.

Crawford, H., 1979: *Subterranean Britain: aspects of underground archaeology.* John Baker: London.

Cunliffe, B., 1973: *The Regni.* Duckworth: London.

Darvill, T. and McWhirr, A., 1982: Roman brick production and the environment. In Miles 1982: 137–50.

Davey, N., 1976: *Building Stones of England and Wales.* Bedford Square Press: London.

Davies, O., 1935: *Roman Mines in Europe.* Oxford University Press: Oxford.

Detsicas, A., 1984: *The Cantiaci.* Sutton: Gloucester.

Detsicas, A. ed., 1973: *Current Research in Romano-British Coarse Pottery.* CBA Research Report 10: London.

Dore, J. N. and Greene, K, eds, 1977: *Roman Pottery Studies in Britain and Beyond: papers presented to John Gillam.* BAR International Series 30: Oxford.

Dunnett, R., 1975: *The Trinovantes.* Duckworth: London.

Elkington, H. D. H., 1976: The Mendip lead industry. In Branigan and Fowler 1976: 183–97.

Fowler, P. J. ed., 1975: *Recent Work in Rural Archaeology.* Moonraker: Bradford-on-Avon.

Fulford, M., 1973: The distribution and dating of New Forest pottery. *Britannia* 4: 160–78.

Fulford, M., 1977a: The location of Romano-British pottery kilns: institutional trade and the market. In Dore and Green 1977: 301–16.

Fulford, M., 1977b: Pottery and Britain's foreign trade in the later Roman period. In Peacock 1977a: 35–84.

Fulford, M., 1978: The interpretation of Britain's late Roman trade: the scope of Medieval historical and archaeological analogy. In Taylor and Cleere 1978: 59–69.

Fulford, M., 1982: Town and country in Roman Britain – a parasitical relationship? In Miles 1982: 403–19.

Fulford, M., 1984: Demonstrating Britannia's economic dependence in the first and second centuries. In Blagg and King 1984: 129–42.

Gillam, J. and Greene, K., 1981: Roman pottery and the economy. In Anderson and Anderson 1981: 1–24.

Gillam, J. P., 1973: Sources of pottery on northern military sites. In Detsicas 1973: 55–62.

Gillam, J. P., 1974: The frontier after Hadrian – a history of the problem. *Archaeologia Aeliana*[5] 2: 1–12.

Goodburn, R. and Bartholomew, P., 1976: *Aspects of the Notitia Dignitatum.* BAR International Series 15: Oxford.

Greene, K., 1978: Roman trade between Britain and the Rhine provinces: the evidence of pottery to c. AD 250. In Taylor and Cleere 1978: 52–8.

Greene, K., 1979: *Report on the excavations at Usk 1965–1976: the pre-Flavian fine wares.* University of Wales: Cardiff.

Greene, K., 1986: *The Archaeology of the Roman Economy.* Batsford: London.

Grigson, C. and Clutton-Brock, J. eds, 1984: *Animals and Archaeology. Vol V. Husbandry in Europe.* BAR International Series 227: Oxford.

Hall, D., 1982: The countryside of the south-east Midlands and Cambridgeshire. In Miles 1982: 337–50.

Hanson, W. S., 1978a: The organisation of the Roman military timber supply. *Britannia* 9: 293–305.

Hanson, W. S., 1980a: The first Roman occupation of Scotland. In Hanson and Keppie 1980: 15–44.

Hanson, W. S., 1980b: Agricola on the Forth-Clyde isthmus. *Scottish Archaeological Forum* 12: 55–68.

Hartley, K. F., 1973: The marketing and distribution of mortaria. In Detsicas 1973: 39–51.

Hartley, K. F. and Webster, P. V., 1973: Romano-British pottery kilns near Wilderspool. *Archaeological Journal* 130: 77–103.

Hassall, M., 1978: Britain and the Rhine provinces: epigraphic evidence for Roman trade. In Taylor and Cleere 1978: 41–8.

Hassall, M., 1979: Military tile stamps from Britain. In McWhirr 1979a: 261–6.

Higham, N. J. and Jones, G. D. B., 1984: *The Carvetii*. Sutton: Gloucester.

Hind, J., 1983: Caledonia and its occupation under the Flavians. *Proceedings of the Society of Antiquaries of Scotland* 113: 373–8.

Hodder, I., 1974: Some marketing models for Romano-British pottery. *Britannia* 5: 340–59.

Hopkins, K., 1980: Taxes and trade in the Roman empire (200 BC–AD 200). *Journal of Roman Studies* 70:101–25.

Johnson, D. E., 1977b: The central southern group of Romano-British mosaics. In Munby and Henig 1977: 195–215.

Johnson, S, 1979: *The Roman Forts of the Saxon Shore*, 2nd edn. Elek: London.

Jones, G. D. B., 1975: The North-western interface. In Fowler 1975: 93–106.

Jones, G. D. B., 1979c: The Roman evidence. In Crawford 1979: 85–99.

Jones, G. D. B. and Lewis, P. R., 1971: *The Roman Gold Mines at Dolaucothi: a guide*. Carmarthen County Museum Publication: Carmarthen.

Jones, G. D. B. and Lewis, P. R., 1974: Ancient mining and the environment. In P. Raatz ed. *Rescue Archaeology*. Penguin: London: 130–49.

King, A., 1978: A comparative survey of bone assemblages from Roman sites in Britain. *Bulletin of the Institute of Archaeology London* 15: 207–32.

Lewis, P. R. and Jones, G. D. B., 1969: The Dolaucothi gold mines. I: the surface evidence. *Archaeological Journal* 89: 244–72.

Loughlin, N., 1977: Dales Ware: a contribution to the study of Roman coarse pottery. In Peacock 1977a: 85–146.

Lyne, M. A. B. and Jeffries, R. S., 1979: *The Alice Holt/Farnham Pottery Industry*. CBA Research Report 30: London.

Macready, S. and Thompson, F. H. eds, 1984: *Cross-channel trade between Gaul and Britain in the pre-Roman Iron Age*. Soc. of Antiqs., Occ. Paper 4: London.

Maltby, M., 1981: Iron Age, Romano-Britian and Anglo-Saxon husbandry – a review of the faunal evidence. In Jones and Dimbleby 1981: 155–203.

Maltby, M., 1984: Animal bones and the Romano-British economy. In Grigson and Clutton-Brock 1984: 125–38.

McWhirr, A. ed., 1979a: *Roman Brick and Tile*. BAR International Series 68: Oxford.

McWhirr, A., 1979b: Tile-kilns in Roman Britain. In McWhirr 1979a: 97–189.

McWhirr, A., 1981: *Roman Gloucestershire*. Sutton: Gloucester.

McWhirr, A. and Viner, D., 1978: The production and distribution of tiles in Roman Britain with particular reference to the Cirencester region. *Britannia* 9: 359–77.

Miles, D. ed., 1982: *The Romano-British Countryside*. BAR 103: Oxford.

Milne, G., 1985: *The Port of Roman London*. Batsford: London.

Morris, P., 1979: *Agricultural Buildings in Roman Britain*. BAR 70: Oxford.

Munby, J. and Henig, M. eds, 1977: *Roman Life and Art in Britain*. BAR 41: Oxford.

Neal, D., 1981: *Roman Mosaics in Britain*. Britannia Monograph Series 1: London.

Peacock, D. P. S., 1977a: *Pottery and Early Commerce: char-acterization and trade in Roman and later ceramics*. Academic Press: London and New York.

Peacock, D. P. S., 1978: The Rhine and the problem of Gaulish wine in Roman Britain. In Taylor and Cleere 1978: 49–51.

Peacock, D. P. S., 1982: *Pottery in the Roman World*. Longman: London.

Peacock, D. P. S. and Williams, D. F., 1986: *Amphorae and the Roman Economy: An Introductory Guide*. Longman: London.

Price, J., 1978: Trade in glass. In Taylor and Cleere 1978: 70–8.

Pritchard, F. A., 1986: Ornamental stonework from Roman London. *Britannia* 17: 119–89.

Rainey, A., 1973: *Mosaics in Roman Britain: a gazeteer*. David & Charles: Newton Abbot, Devon.

Reece, R., 1984: Mints, markets and the military. In Blagg and King 1984: 143–60.

Rees, S. E., 1979: *Agricultural Implements in Prehistoric and Roman Britain*. BAR 69: Oxford.

Rivet, A. L. F., 1969a: *The Roman Villa in Britain*. Routledge & Kegan Paul: London.

Rivet, A. L. F., 1975: The rural economy in Roman Britain. *Aufstieg und Niedergang der Römischen Welt* II. 3: 328–63.

Robertson, A. S., 1970: Roman finds from non-Roman sites in Scotland. *Britannia* 1: 198–226.

Robertson, A. S., 1978: The circulation of Roman coins in North Britain: the evidence of hoards and site finds from Scotland. In Carson and Kraay 1978: 156–216.

Rodwell, W., 1979: Iron Age and Roman salt-winning on the Essex coast. In Burnham and Johnston 1979: 133–75.

Simmons, B. B., 1979: The Lincolnshire Car Dyke: navigation or drainage? *Britannia* 10: 183–96.

Simmons, B. B., 1980: Iron Age and Roman coasts around the Wash. In Thompson 1980: 56–73.

Smith, D. J., 1965: Three fourth century schools of mosaics in Roman Britain. In *La Mosaigue Greco-Romaine*. CNRS, Paris: 95–115.

Smith, D. J., 1969: The mosaic pavements. In Rivet 1969: 71–125.

Smith, D. J., 1975: Roman mosaics in Britain before the fourth century. In *La Mosaique Greco-Romaine II*. CNRS, Paris: 269–90.

Smith, D. J., 1976: The mosaics at Winterton. In Stead 1976: 251–72.

Smith, D. J., 1984: Roman mosaics in Britain: a synthesis. In R. Favioli Campanati ed. *III Colloquio Internazionale sul Mosaico Antico*. Ravenna: 357–80.

Stead, I. M., 1976: *Excavations at Winterton Roman Villa and Other Sites in Northern Lincolnshire*. HMSO: London.

Swan, V. G., 1984: *The Pottery Kilns of Roman Britain*. HMSO: London.

Taylor, J. du Plat and Cleere, H. eds, 1978: *Roman Shipping and Trade: Britain and the Rhine provinces*. CBA Research Report 24: London.

Thompson, F. H., 1965: *Roman Cheshire*. Cheshire County Council: Chester.

Thompson, F. H. ed., 1980: *Archaeology and Coastal Change*. Society of Antiquaries: London.

Todd, M., 1973: *The Coritani*. Duckworth: London.

Todd, M. ed., 1978: *Studies in the Romano-British Villa*. Leicester University Press: Leicester.

Tylecote, R. F., 1976: *A History of Metallurgy*. The Metals Society: London.

Webster, G., 1975a: *The Cornovii*. Duckworth: London.

Webster, P. V., 1977: Severn Valley ware on the Antonine frontier. In Dore and Green 1977: 163–76.

Whittick, G. C., 1982: The earliest Roman lead-mining on Mendip and in north Wales: a reappraisal. *Britannia* 13: 113–23.

Wild, J. P., 1970: *Textile Manufacture in the Northern Roman Provinces*. Cambridge University Press: Cambridge.

Wild, J. P., 1976: The Gynaecea. In Goodburn and Bartholemew 1976: 51–81.

Wild, J. P., 1978a: Cross channel trade and the textile industry. In Taylor and Cleere 1978: 79–81.

Wild, J. P., 1982: Wool production in Roman Britain. In Miles 1982: 109–22.

Williams, D. F., 1977: The Romano-British Black-Burnished industry: an essay on characterisation by heavy mineral analysis. In Peacock 1977a: 163–220.

Williams, J. H., 1971: Roman building materials in south-east England. *Britannia* 2: 166–95.

Young, C. J., 1977a: Oxford ware and the Roman army. In Dore and Greene 1977: 289–94.

Young, C. J., 1977b: *The Roman Pottery Industry of the Oxford Region*. BAR 43: Oxford.

CHAPTER 7 · THE COUNTRYSIDE

Applebaum, S., 1972: Roman Britain. In H. P. R. Finberg ed. *The Agrarian History of England and Wales*, I.ii. Cambridge University Press: Cambridge: 1–277.

Blagg, T. F. C. and King, A. C. eds, 1984: *Military and Civilian in Roman Britain. Cultural relationships in a frontier province*. BAR 136: Oxford.

Bowen, H. C. and Fowler, P. J., 1966: Romano-British rural settlements in Dorset and Wiltshire. In Thomas 1966a: 43–67.

Branigan, K., 1976: Villa settlement in the West Country. In Branigan and Fowler 1976: 120–41.

Branigan, K., 1977: *The Roman Villa in South-west England*. Moonraker: Bradford-on-Avon.

Branigan, K., 1980b: Villas in the north: change in the rural landscape. In Branigan 1980a: 18–27.

Branigan, K., 1982: Celtic farm to Roman villa. In Miles 1982: 81–96.

Branigan, K., 1985: *The Catuvellauni*. Sutton: Gloucester.

Brodribb, A. C., Hands, A. R. and Walker, D., 1968/78: *Excavations at Shakenoak Farm near Wilcote, Oxfordshire*. Parts I–IV.

Buckley, D. G. ed., 1980: *Archaeology in Essex to AD 1500*. CBA Research Report 34: London.

Clack, P. A. G. and Haselgrove, S. eds, 1982: *Rural settlement in the Roman North*. Department of Archaeology, Durham University: Durham.

Collingwood, R. G. and Myres, J. N. L., 1937: *Roman Britain and the English Settlements*, 2nd edn. Oxford University Press: Oxford.

Collingwood, R. G. and Richmond, I. A., 1969: *The Archaeology of Roman Britain*. Methuen: London.

Cunliffe, B. W., 1973: *The Regni*. Duckworth: London.

Davies, R. W., 1971: The Roman military diet. *Britannia* 2: 122–42.

Detsicas, A., 1984: *The Cantiaci*. Sutton: Gloucester.

Drewett, P. L. ed., 1978: *Archaeology in Sussex to AD 1500*. CBA Research Report 29: London.

Dunnett, R., 1975: *The Trinovantes*. Duckworth: London.

Evans, J. G., Limbrey, S. and Cleere, H. eds, 1975: *The Effect of Man on the Landscape: the highland zone*. CBA Research Report 11: London.

Feachem, R. W., 1973: Ancient agriculture in the highland of Britain. *Proc. Prehist. Soc.* 39: 332–53.

Fowler, P. J., 1983: *The Farming of Prehistoric Britain*. Cambridge University Press: Cambridge.

Fowler, P. J. ed., 1975: *Recent Work in Rural Archaeology*. Moonraker: Bradford-on-Avon.

Gates, T., 1982: Farming on the frontier: Romano-British fields in Northumberland. In Clack and Haselgrove 1982: 21–42.

Gillam, J. P., 1958: Roman and native: AD 122–97. In Richmond 1958a: 60–90.

Goodburn, R., 1978: Winterton: some problems. In Todd 1978: 93–101.

Green, H. J. M., 1978: A villa estate at Godmanchester. In Todd 1978: 103–16.

Higham, N. J., 1979: *The Changing Past*. University of Manchester: Manchester.

Higham, N. J., 1980: Native settlements west of the Pennines. In Branigan 1980: 41–7.

Higham, N. J., 1982: The Roman impact upon rural settlement in Cumbria. In Clack and Haselgrove 1982: 105–22.

Higham, N. J. and Jones, G. D. B., 1975: Frontier, forts and farmers. Cumbria aerial survey 1974–75. *Archaeological Journal* 132: 16–53.

Higham, N. J. and Jones, G. D. B., 1983: The excavation of two Romano-British farm sites in north Cumbria. *Britannia* 14: 45–72.

Higham, N. J. and Jones, G. D. B., 1984: *The Carvetii*. Sutton: Gloucester.

Hodder, I. and Millett, M., 1980: Romano-British villas and towns: a systematic analysis. *World Archaeology* 12: 69–76.

James, H. and Williams, G., 1982: Rural settlement in Roman Dyfed. In Miles 1982: 289–312.

Jarrett, M. and Wrathmell, S., 1981: *Whitton: an Iron Age and Roman farmstead*. University of Wales: Cardiff.

Jobey, G., 1966: Homesteads and settlements of the frontier zone. In Thomas 1966: 1–14.

Jobey, G., 1974: Notes on some population problems in the area between the two Roman walls. *Archaeologia Aeliana*[5] 2: 17–26.

Jobey, G., 1982: Between Tyne and Forth: some problems. In Clack and Haselgrove 1982: 7–20.

Johnson, N. and Rose, P., 1982: Defended settlements in Cornwall – an illustrated discussion. In Miles 1982: 151–207.

Jones, G. D. B., 1977: The Colchester and Ipswich aerial survey. *Aerial Archaeology* 1: 23–5.

Jones, G. D. B., 1979a: Invasion and response in Roman Britain. In Burnham and Johnson 1979: 57–79.

Jones, G. D. B., 1979b: Aerial photography in the north. In Higham 1979: 75–86.

Jones, G. D. B. and Walker, J., 1983: Either side of Solway: towards a minimalist view of Romano-British agricultural settlement in the north-west. In Chapman and Mytum 1983: 185–204.

Jones, G. R. J., 1972: Post-Roman Wales. In Finberg 1972: 283–382.

Jones, M. K., 1981: The development of crop husbandry. In Jones and Dimbleby 1981: 95–127.

Jones, M. K., 1982: Crop production in Roman Britain. In Miles 1982: 97–107.

Jones, M. K. and Dimbleby, G. eds, 1981: *The Environment of Man: the Iron Age to the Saxon period*. BAR 97: Oxford.

Leach, P. E. ed., 1982: *Archaeology in Kent to AD 1500*. CBA Research Report 48: London.

Leech, R., 1976: Larger agricultural settlements in the West Country. In Branigan and Fowler 1976: 142–61.

Leech, R., 1982: The Roman interlude in the south-west: the dynamics of economic and social change in Romano-British south Somerset and north Dorset. In Miles 1982: 209–67.

Mackreth, D. F., 1978: Orton Hall Farm, Peterborough: a Roman and Saxon settlement. In Todd 1978: 209–29.

Manning, W. H., 1975: Economic influences on land use in the military and highland zone during the Roman period. In Evans *et al.* 1975: 112–16.

Maxwell, G. S., 1983: 'Roman' settlement in Scotland. In Chapman and Mytum 1983: 233–61.

McWhirr, A., 1981: *Roman Gloucestershire*. Sutton: Gloucester.

Miles, D. ed., 1982: *The Romano-British Countryside*. BAR 103: Oxford.

Miles, D. ed., 1984: *Archaeology at Barton Court Farm, Abingdon, Oxon*. CBA Research Report 50: Oxford.

Morris, P., 1979: *Agricultural Buildings in Roman Britain*. BAR 70: Oxford.

Mytum, H. C., 1982: Rural settlement of the Roman period in north and east Wales. In Miles 1982: 313–35.

Percival, J., 1976: *The Roman Villa: an historical introduction*. Batsford: London.

Phillips, C. W. *et al.* ed., 1970: *The Fenland in Roman Times*. Royal Geographical Society Research Series 3: London.

Potter, T. W., 1981: The Roman occupation of the central Fenland. *Britannia* 12: 79–133.

Raistrick, A., 1937: Prehistoric cultivations at Grassington, West Yorks. *York. Arch. Journal* 33: 166–74.

RCHM (Wales). 1956/64: *An Inventory of Ancient Monuments in Caernarvonshire*.

Riley, D. N., 1980a: *Early Landscapes from the Air*. Dept. of Prehist and Arch. University of Sheffield: Sheffield.

Rivet, A. L. F., 1969b: Social and economic aspects. In Rivet 1969a: 173–216.

Rivet, A. L. F., 1975: The rural economy in Roman Britain. *Aufstieg und Niedergang der Römischen Welt* II, 3: 328–63.

Smith, C. A., 1977: Late prehistoric and Romano-British enclosed homesteads in northwest Wales. *Arch. Camb.* 126: 38–52.

Smith, J. T., 1982: Villa plans and social structure in Britain and Gaul. *Caesarodunum* (Tours) 17: 321–6.

Stead, I. M., 1976: *Excavations at Winterton Roman Villa and Other Sites in Northern Lincolnshire*. HMSO: London.

Stevens, C. E., 1966a: The social and economic aspects of rural settlement. In Thomas 1966: 108–28.

Taylor, C., 1975: Roman settlements in the Nene Valley: the impact of recent archaeology. In Fowler 1975: 107–20.

Thomas, C. ed., 1966: *Rural Settlement in Roman Britain*. CBA Research Report 7: London.

Todd, M. ed., 1978: *Studies in the Romano-British Villa*. Leicester University Press: Leicester.

Webster, G., 1969: The future of villa studies. In Rivet 1969a: 217–49.

Wild, J. P., 1974: Settlement in the Lower Nene Valley. *Archaeological Journal* 131: 140–70.

Wild, J. P., 1978b: Villas in the Lower Nene Valley. In Todd 1978: 59–69.

Wilson, D. R., 1974a: Romano-British villas from the air. *Britannia* 5: 251–61.

CHAPTER 8 · RELIGION

Allason-Jones, L. and McKay, B., 1985: *Coventina's Well: a shrine on Hadrian's Wall*. Sutton: Gloucester.

Barley, M. W. C. and Hanson, R. P. C. eds, 1968: *Christianity in Britain 300–700*. Leicester University Press: Leicester.

Birley, A. R., 1979: *The People of Roman Britain*. Batsford: London.

Birley, E., 1986: The deities of Roman Britain. *Aufstieg und Niedergang der Römischen Welt II, Principat* 18.1: 3–112.

Boon, G. C., 1974: *Silchester: The Roman town of Calleva*. David & Charles: London.

Breeze, D. J. and Dobson, B, 1987: *Hadrian's Wall*, 3rd edn. Penguin: London.

Charlton, D. B. and Mitcheson, N. M., 1983: Yardhope: a shrine to Cocidius. *Britannia* 14: 143–53.

Clarke, G., 1979: *The Roman Cemetery at Lankhills*. Oxford University Press: Oxford.

Collingwood, R. G. and Richmond, I. A., 1969: *The Archaeology of Roman Britain*. Methuen: London.

Green, C. J. S., 1974: Interim report on excavations at Poundbury, Dorchester, 1973. *Dorset Natural History and Archaeological Society* 95: 97–100.

Green, C. J. S., 1977: The significance of plaster burials for the recognition of Christian cemeteries. In Reece 1977: 46–52.

Green, C. J. S., 1982: The cemetery of a Romano-British community at Poundbury, Dorchester, Dorset. In Pearce 1982: 61–76.

Green, M. J., 1976: *The Religions of Civilian Roman Britain*. BAR 24: Oxford.

Green, M. J., 1983: *The Gods of Roman Britain*. Shire Archaeology: Princes Risborough.

Green, M. J., 1986: The iconography and archaeology of Romano-British religion. *Aufstieg und Niedergang der Römischen Welt II, Principat* 18.1: 113–62.

Guy C. J., 1981: Roman circular lead tanks in Britain. *Britannia* 12: 271–6.

Harris, E. and Harris, J., 1965: *The Oriental Cults in Roman Britain*. Leiden.

Henig, M., 1984: *The Religion of Roman Britain*. Batsford: London.

Henig, M. and King, A., 1986: *Pagan Gods and Shrines of the Roman Empire*. Oxford University Committee for Archaeology: Oxford.

Lewis, M. T., 1966: *Temples in Roman Britain*. Cambridge University Press: Cambridge.

McWhirr, A., 1981: *Roman Gloucestershire*. Sutton: Gloucester.

McWhirr, A., Viner, D. and Wells, C., 1982: *Romano-British Cemeteries at Cirencester*. Cirencester Excavation Committee, Cirencester Excavations II.

Morris, R., 1983: *The Church in British Archaeology*. CBA Research Report 47: London.

Pearce, S. M. ed., 1982: *The Early Church in Western Britain and Ireland*. BAR 102: Oxford.

Raatz, P. and Watts, L., 1979: The end of Roman temples in the west of Britain. In Casey 1979a: 183–210.

Reece, R. ed., 1977: *Burial in the Roman World*. CBA Research Report 22: London.

Rodwell, W. ed., 1980: *Temples, Churches and Religion in Roman Britain*. BAR 77: Oxford.

Ross, A., 1967: *Pagan Celtic Britain*. Routledge & Kegan Paul: London.

Thomas, C., 1971: *Britain and Ireland in Early Christian Times AD 400–800*. Thames & Hudson: London.

Thomas, C., 1981: *Christianity in Roman Britain to AD 500*. Batsford: London.

Toller, H., 1977: *Roman Lead Coffins and Ossuaria in Britain*. BAR 38: Oxford.

Toynbee, J. M. C., 1982: *Death and Burial in the Roman World*. Thames & Hudson: London.

Webster, G., 1986: *The British Celts and their Gods under Rome*. Batsford: London.

Wenham, L. P., 1968: *The Romano-British Cemetery at Trentholme Drive, York*. HMSO: London.

CHAPTER 9 · DEVOLUTION

Arnold, C. J., 1982: The end of Roman Britain: some discussion. In Miles 1982: 451–9.

Arnold, C. J., 1984: *Roman Britain to Saxon England*. Croom Helm: London.

Barker, P. A., 1979: The latest occupation on the site of the Baths Basilica at Wroxeter. In Casey 1979a: 175–81.

Barker, P. A., 1985: Aspects of the topography of Wroxeter (Viroconium Cornioviorum). In Grew and Hobley 1985: 109–17.

Bartholemew, P., 1982: Fifth century facts. *Britannia* 13: 261–70.

Bohme, H. W., 1986: Das Ende der Romerherrschaft in Britannien und die angelsachsische Besiedlung Englands in 5. Jahrhundert. *H/Jahrbuch des Rom-Ger., Zentralmuseums* 33: 469–574.

Breeze, D. J., 1982a: *The Northern Frontiers of Roman Britain*. Batsford: London.

Brooks, D. A., 1986: A review of the evidence for continuity in British towns in the fifth and sixth centuries. *Oxford Journal of Archaeology* 5.1: 77–102.

Casey, P. J. ed., 1979a: *The End of Roman Britain*. BAR 71: Oxford.

Casey, P. J., 1979b: Magnus Maximus in Britain. In Casey 1979a: 66–79.

Clarke, G., 1979: *The Roman Cemetery at Lankhills*. Oxford University Press: Oxford.

Esmonde Cleary, A. S., 1989: *The Ending of Roman Britain*. Batsford: London.

Frere, S. S., 1966: The end of towns in Roman Britain. In Wacher 1966a: 87–100.

Johnson, S., 1980: *Later Roman Britain*. Routledge & Kegan Paul: London.

Frere, S.., 1983: *Verulamium Excavations II*. Society of Antiquaries: London.

Hawkes, S. C., 1974: Some recent finds of Late Roman Buckles. *Britannia* 5: 386–93.

Hawkes, S. C. and Dunning, G. C., 1981: Soldiers and Settlers in Britain, fourth to fifth century. *Med. Arch.* 5: 1–70.

Johnson, S. 1976: *The Roman forts of the Saxon Shore*. Elek: London.

Kent, J. P. C., 1979: The end of Roman Britain: the literary and numismatic evidence. In Casey 1979a: 15–22.

Mann, J. C., 1974: The northern frontier after AD 369. *Glasgow Archaeological Journal* 3: 34–42.

Mann, J. C., 1979: Hadrian's Wall: the last phases. In Casey 1979: 144–51.

Miller, M., 1975: Stilicho's Pictish war. *Britannia* 6: 141–5.

Miller, M., 1978: The last British entry in the Gallic chronicles. *Britannia* 9: 315–18.

Muhlberger, S., 1983: The Gallic chronicle of 452 and its authority for British events. *Britannia* 14: 23–33.

Reece, R., 1980: Town and country: the end of Roman Britain. *World Archaeology* 12.1: 77–92.

Reece, R., 1983: The end of Roman Britain revisited. *Scottish Archaeological Review* 2.2: 149–53.

Simpson, C. J., 1987: Belt buckles and straptends of the late Roman Empire. *Britannia* 17: 192–223.

Thomas, C., 1971: *Britain and Ireland in Early Christian Times AD 400–800*. Thames & Hudson: London.

Thomas, C., 1979: St Patrick and fifth-century Britain: an historical model explored. In Casey 1979a: 81–101.

Thomas, C., 1981: *Christianity in Roman Britain to AD 500*. Batsford: London.

Thomas, C., 1986: *Celtic Britain*. Thames & Hudson: London.

Thompson, E. A., 1977: Britain AD 406–410. *Britannia* 8: 303–18.

Thompson, E. A., 1979: Gildas and the history of Britain. *Britannia* 10: 203–26.

Thompson, E. A., 1983: Fifth century facts? *Britannia* 14: 272–4.

Thompson, E. A., 1984: *Saint Germanus of Auxerre and the End of Roman Britain*. The Boydell Press: Woodbridge.

Ward, J. H., 1972: Vortigern and the end of Roman Britain. *Britannia* 3: 277–89.

Wood, I., 1987: The fall of the western empire and the end of Roman Britain. *Britannia* 18: 251–63.

Index

Page references to maps and photographs are in bold.